PRENTICE HALL

WORLD STUDIES

AFRICA, ASIA, AND AUSTRALIA

Geography • History • Culture

PEARSON
Prentice
Hall

Boston, Massachusetts
Upper Saddle River, New Jersey

13-digit ISBN 978-0-13-360328-6
10-digit ISBN 0-13-360328-8
2345678910   11 10 09 08

Program Consultants

Heidi Hayes Jacobs

Heidi Hayes Jacobs, Ed.D., has served as an education consultant to more than 1,000 schools across the nation and abroad. Dr. Jacobs serves as an adjunct professor in the Department of Curriculum on Teaching at Teachers College, Columbia University. She has written two best-selling books and numerous articles on curriculum reform. She received an M.A. from the University of Massachusetts, Amherst, and completed her doctoral work at Columbia University's Teachers College in 1981. The core of Dr. Jacobs' experience comes from her years teaching high school, middle school, and elementary school students. As an educational consultant, she works with K–12 schools and districts on curriculum reform and strategic planning.

Michal L. LeVasseur

Michal LeVasseur is the Executive Director of the National Council for Geographic Education. She is an instructor in the College of Education at Jacksonville State University and works with the Alabama Geographic Alliance. Her undergraduate and graduate work were in the fields of anthropology (B.A.), geography (M.A.), and science education (Ph.D.). Dr. LeVasseur's specialization has moved increasingly into the area of geography education. Since 1996 she has served as the Director of the National Geographic Society's Summer Geography Workshops. As an educational consultant, she has worked with the National Geographic Society as well as with schools and organizations to develop programs and curricula for geography.

Senior Reading Consultants

Kate Kinsella

Kate Kinsella, Ed.D., is a faculty member in the Department of Secondary Education at San Francisco State University. A specialist in second language development and content area literacy, she consults nationally on school-wide practices that support adolescent English learners and striving readers to make academic gains. Dr. Kinsella earned her M.A. in TESOL from San Francisco State University, and her Ed.D. in Second Language Acquisition from the University of San Francisco.

Kevin Feldman

Kevin Feldman, Ed.D., is the Director of Reading and Early Intervention with the Sonoma County Office of Education (SCOE) and an independent educational consultant. At the SCOE, he develops, organizes, and monitors programs related to K–12 literacy. Dr. Feldman has an M.A. from the University of California, Riverside in Special Education, Learning Disabilities and Instructional Design. He earned his Ed.D. in Curriculum and Instruction from the University of San Francisco.

Cartography Consultant

DK Andrew Heritage

Andrew Heritage has been publishing atlases and maps for more than 25 years. In 1991, he joined the leading illustrated nonfiction publisher Dorling Kindersley (DK) with the task of building an international atlas list from scratch. The DK atlas list now includes some 10 titles, which are constantly updated and appear in new editions either annually or every other year.

Academic Reviewers

Africa
Barbara B. Brown, Ph.D.
African Studies Center
Boston University
Boston, Massachusetts

Ancient World
Evelyn DeLong Mangie, Ph.D.
Department of History
University of South Florida
Tampa, Florida

Central Asia and the Middle East
Pamela G. Sayre
History Department,
    Social Sciences Division
Henry Ford Community College
Dearborn, Michigan

East Asia
Huping Ling, Ph.D.
History Department
Truman State University
Kirksville, Missouri

Eastern Europe
Robert M. Jenkins, Ph.D.
Center for Slavic, Eurasian and
    East European Studies
University of North Carolina
Chapel Hill, North Carolina

Latin America
Dan La Botz
Professor, History Department
Miami University
Oxford, Ohio

Medieval Times
James M. Murray
History Department
University of Cincinnati
Cincinnati, Ohio

North Africa
Barbara E. Petzen
Center for Middle Eastern Studies
Harvard University
Cambridge, Massachusetts

Religion
Charles H. Lippy, Ph.D.
Department of Philosophy
    and Religion
University of Tennessee
    at Chattanooga
Chattanooga, Tennessee

Russia
Janet Vaillant
Davis Center for Russian
    and Eurasian Studies
Harvard University
Cambridge, Massachusetts

United States and Canada
Victoria Randlett
Geography Department
University of Nevada, Reno
Reno, Nevada

Western Europe
Ruth Mitchell-Pitts
Center for European Studies
University of North Carolina
    at Chapel Hill
Chapel Hill, North Carolina

Reviewers

Sean Brennan
Brecksville-Broadview Heights
    City School District
Broadview Heights, Ohio

Stephen Bullick
Mt. Lebanon School District
Pittsburgh, Pennsylvania

Louis P. De Angelo, Ed.D.
Archdiocese of Philadelphia
Philadelphia, Pennsylvania

Paul Francis Durietz
Social Studies
    Curriculum Coordinator
Woodland District #50
Gurnee, Illinois

Gail Dwyer
Dickerson Middle School,
    Cobb County
Marietta, Georgia

Michal Howden
Social Studies Consultant
Zionsville, Indiana

Rosemary Kalloch
Springfield Public Schools
Springfield, Massachusetts

Deborah J. Miller
Office of Social Studies,
    Detroit Public Schools
Detroit, Michigan

Steven P. Missal
Plainfield Public Schools
Plainfield, New Jersey

Catherine Fish Petersen
Social Studies Consultant
Saint James, Long Island, New York

Joe Wieczorek
Social Studies Consultant
Baltimore, Maryland

North Carolina Program Advisors

The North Carolina program advisors provided ongoing input in the development of World Studies. Their valuable insights ensure that the perspectives of teachers throughout North Carolina are represented within this Social Studies series.

Michael Boyes, M.Ed.
Social Studies Teacher
Marvin Ridge Middle School
Waxhaw, North Carolina

Jason A. Epstein
J.N. Fries Middle School
Concord, North Carolina

Linda Murray
Teacher
C.C. Griffin Middle School
Concord, North Carolina

Paula Davidson
Teacher
Weddington Middle School
Weddington, North Carolina

Angela Green
Teacher
Cramerton Middle School
Cramerton, North Carolina

Bodie Island Lighthouse near Nags Head, Cape Hatteras National Seashore

Africa, Asia, and Australia

Develop Skills

Use these pages to develop your reading, writing, and geography skills.

AFRICA

Build a Regional Background

Learn about the geography, history, and culture of the region.

Focus on Countries

Create an understanding of the region by focusing
on specific countries.

ASIA AND AUSTRALIA

Build a Regional Background

Learn about the geography, history, and culture of the region.

Focus on Countries

Create understanding of the region by focusing on specific countries.

MAP MASTER™

- Learn map skills with the MapMaster Skills Handbook.
- Practice your skills with every map in this book.
- Interact with every map online and on CD-ROM.

DK

Maps and illustrations created by DK help build your understanding of the world. The DK World Desk Reference Online keeps you up to date.

Discovery CHANNEL SCHOOL™ Video/DVD

The World Studies Video Program takes you on field trips to study countries around the world.

Interactive Textbook

The *World Studies* Interactive Textbook online and on CD-ROM uses interactive maps and other activities to help you learn.

COUNTRY DATABANK

Read about all the countries that make up Africa.

COUNTRY DATABANK

Read about Australia and the countries that make up Asia.

COUNTRY PROFILES

Theme-based maps and charts provide a closer look at countries, regions, and provinces of Africa.

COUNTRY PROFILES

Theme-based maps and charts provide a closer look at countries, regions, and provinces of Asia and Australia.

Citizen Heroes

Meet people who have made a difference in their countries.

Links

See the fascinating links between social studies and other disciplines.

Skills for Life

Learn skills that you will use throughout your life.

Target Reading Skills

Chapter-by-chapter reading skills help you read and understand social studies concepts.

Eyewitness Technology

Detailed drawings show how technology shapes places and societies.

Literature

Selections by noted authors bring social studies to life.

Explore the geography, history, and cultures of the countries of Africa.

Explore the geography, history, and cultures of Asia and Australia.

Maps and Charts

MAP MASTER™

MAP MASTER™ Interactive

Go online to find an interactive version of every MapMaster map in this book. Use the Web Code provided to gain direct access to these maps.

How to Use Web Codes:

1. Go to **www.PHSchool.com**.
2. Enter the Web Code.
3. Click Go!

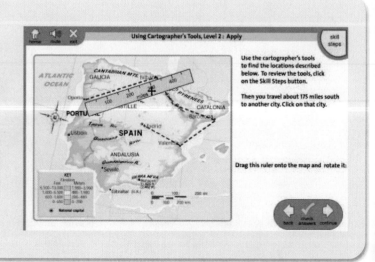

Charts, Graphs, and Tables

Charts, Graphs, and Tables

Student Guide to North Carolina Standard Course of Study and Testing

View from the Blue Ridge Parkway in North Carolina

Understanding the North Carolina Standard Course of Study

The **North Carolina Standard Course of Study for Grade Seven** outlines the knowledge and skills you will need to understand the important issues that affect people and regions around the world. It also provides a framework for building your communication and evaluation skills, which will help you become an informed and active citizen.

The Standard Course of Study for Grade Seven Social Studies is organized into 13 **Competency Goals**. For each Competency Goal, the state gives a list of **Objectives** that explain the details of what you will learn.

This textbook uses a special naming system to identify the Standard Course of Study Competency Goals and Objectives. The examples below will help you to understand these codes.

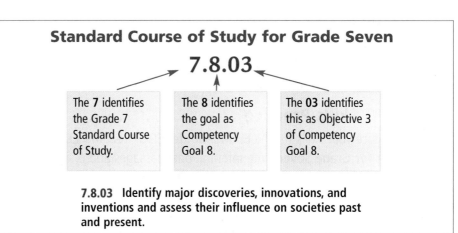

Standard Course of Study for Grade Seven

7.8.03

| The **7** identifies the Grade 7 Standard Course of Study. | The **8** identifies the goal as Competency Goal 8. | The **03** identifies this as Objective 3 of Competency Goal 8. |

7.8.03 Identify major discoveries, innovations, and inventions and assess their influence on societies past and present.

Standard Course of Study: Social Studies Skills

The North Carolina Standard Course of Study also includes a set of Competency Goals and Objectives that focus on social studies skills. These goals apply to all courses in social studies from Kindergarten to Grade 12.

SS.1.02

| The **SS** identifies the subject as social studies. | The **1** identifies the goal as Competency Goal 1. | The **02** identifies this as Objective 2 of Competency Goal 1. |

SS.1.02 Summarize to select main ideas.

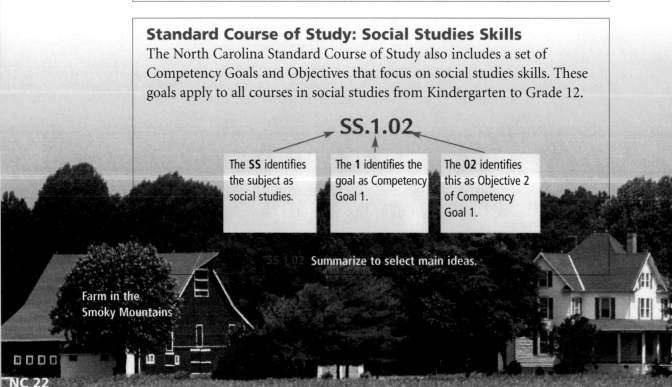

Farm in the Smoky Mountains

Why are the Competency Goals and Objectives important to me?

The **North Carolina Standard Course of Study** provides the information you need to understand important world issues and to develop as a capable, independent citizen.

Grade Seven Competency Goals

Goal 1: The learner will use the five themes of geography and geographic tools to answer geographic questions and analyze geographic concepts.

Objectives:

7.1.01 Create maps, charts, graphs, databases, and models as tools to illustrate information about different people, places and regions in Africa, Asia, and Australia.

7.1.02 Generate, interpret, and manipulate information from tools such as maps, globes, charts, graphs, databases, and models to pose and answer questions about space and place, environment and society, and spatial dynamics and connections.

7.1.03 Use tools such as maps, globes, graphs, charts, databases, models, and artifacts to compare data on different countries of Africa, Asia, and Australia and to identify patterns as well as similarities and differences.

Goal 2: The learner will assess the relationship between physical environment and cultural characteristics of selected societies and regions of Africa, Asia, and Australia.

Objectives:

7.2.01 Identify key physical characteristics such as landforms, water forms, and climate and evaluate their influence on the development of cultures in selected African, Asian and Australian regions.

7.2.02 Describe factors that influence changes in distribution patterns of population, resources, and climate in selected regions of Africa, Asia, and Australia and evaluate their impact on the environment.

7.2.03 Examine factors such as climate change, location of resources, and environmental challenges that influence human migration and assess their significance in the development of selected cultures in Africa, Asia, and Australia.

Link to Real Life

You and your friends want your town to create a skate park. How will your geography knowledge and skills help you research the best location? How can you meet the needs of both those who will use the skate park and those who won't?

Creating a pros and cons chart to compare different locations will help you pick the best one.

▶ To learn more about land use across the globe, turn to page M16 of the MapMaster Skills Handbook.

What You Will Learn

You will study climate, and examine how the environment influences settlement in a region. You will learn how Africa's large rivers provide fertile farmland and electricity. By studying a climate map of Africa, you will discover the different climate regions of this continent. In addition, you will recognize how poor soil and little fresh water have limited the size of the population in the Pacific's low islands. You will also analyze why most people in China settled on the plains and coast.

Grade Seven Competency Goals

Link to Real Life

A new student who has just moved from India to North Carolina has joined your class. Think about what you know about India. What might you want to learn about his daily life in India and the customs of the country? What questions will you ask him? How might learning about his culture help you understand better other people and places?

▶ To learn more about India, turn to page 403.

Goal 3: The learner will analyze the impact of interactions between humans and their physical environments in Africa, Asia, and Australia.

Objectives:

7.3.01 Identify ways in which people of selected areas in Africa, Asia, and Australia have used, altered, and adapted to their environments in order to meet their needs and evaluate the impact of their actions on the development of cultures and regions.

7.3.02 Describe the environmental impact of regional activities such as deforestation, urbanization, and industrialization and evaluate their significance to the global community.

7.3.03 Examine the development and use of tools and technologies and assess their influence on the human ability to use, modify, or adapt to their environment.

7.3.04 Describe how physical processes such as erosion, earthquakes, and volcanoes have resulted in physical patterns on the earth's surface and analyze the effects on human activities.

Goal 4: The learner will identify significant patterns in the movement of people, goods, and ideas over time and place in Africa, Asia, and Australia.

Objectives:

7.4.01 Describe the patterns of and motives for migrations of people and evaluate the impact on the political, economic, and social development of selected societies and regions.

7.4.02 Identify the main commodities of trade over time in selected areas of Africa, Asia, and Australia and evaluate their significance for the economic, political, and social development of cultures and regions.

7.4.03 Examine key ethical ideas and values deriving from religious, artistic, political, economic, and educational traditions, as well as their diffusion over time, and assess their influence on the development of selected societies and regions in Africa, Asia, and Australia.

What You Will Learn

You will study Africa, Asia, and Australia and discover how people have changed because of their environment and how they have used their environment to suit their needs. For example, you will study how farmers plant crops according to the flood cycle of Egypt's Nile River. You also will learn how summer monsoons in Southeast Asia flood streets and cause transportation problems. You will analyze the influence of the environment on the migration of the Bantu people in Africa.

Did you know?

By 1700, North Carolina had about 4,000 freeholders, or people who owned land. Most of them were English. They depended on the help of Native Americans and indentured servants from Europe to raise tobacco, corn, and livestock.

Grade Seven Competency Goals

Goal 5: The learner will evaluate the varied ways people of Africa, Asia, and Australia make decisions about the allocation and use of economic resources.

Objectives:

7.5.01 Describe the relationship between the location of natural resources and economic development and analyze the impact on selected cultures, countries, and regions in Africa, Asia, and Australia.

7.5.02 Examine the different economic systems (traditional, command, and market) developed in selected societies in Africa, Asia, and Australia and assess their effectiveness in meeting basic needs.

7.5.03 Explain how the allocation of scarce resources requires economic systems to make basic decisions regarding the production and distribution of goods and services and evaluate the impact on the standard of living in selected societies and regions of Africa, Asia, and Australia.

7.5.04 Describe the relationship between specialization and interdependence and analyze its influence on the development of regional and global trade patterns.

Goal 6: The learner will recognize the relationship between economic activity and the quality of life in Africa, Asia, and Australia.

Objectives:

7.6.01 Describe different levels of economic development and assess their connections to standard of living indicators such as purchasing power, literacy rate, and life expectancy.

7.6.02 Examine the influence of education and technology on productivity and economic development in selected nations and regions of Africa, Asia, and Australia.

7.6.03 Describe the effects of over-specialization and evaluate their impact on the standard of living.

Link to Real Life

You would like your school store to have a trading section, where students can bring in items to swap for other things they need or want. What types of items do you think students would bring to trade? How might this affect the school store's business?

▶ To learn more about trade, turn to page 329.

North Carolina Standard Course of Study

What You Will Learn

You will learn how people in Africa, Asia, and Australia make decisions about resources to develop their economies. You will study how Japan rebuilt its post-war economy with high-technology industries. You also will learn how petroleum increased the wealth of countries such as Libya and Algeria. You will learn how industries in India, such as the computer software industry, have given the country the second-fastest-growing economy in Asia.

Historical homes in Winston-Salem, North Carolina

Link to Real Life

You want to write an article for your school newspaper about a current event in Africa. How might your knowledge of past events help you to understand a current event? How can you include historical information to improve your article?

▶ To learn more about the influence of Africa's colonial past on its current economy, see page 67.

Grade Seven Competency Goals

Goal 7: The learner will assess the connections between historical events and contemporary issues in Africa, Asia, and Australia.

Objectives:

7.7.01 Identify historical events such as invasions, conquests, and migrations and evaluate their relationship to current issues.

7.7.02 Examine the causes of key historical events in selected areas of Africa, Asia, and Australia and analyze the short- and long-range effects on political, economic, and social institutions.

Goal 8: The learner will assess the influence and contributions of individuals and cultural groups in Africa, Asia, and Australia.

Objectives:

7.8.01 Describe the role of key historical figures and evaluate their impact on past and present societies in Africa, Asia, and Australia.

7.8.02 Describe the role of key groups such as Mongols, Arabs, and Bantu and evaluate their impact on historical and contemporary societies of Africa, Asia, and Australia.

7.8.03 Identify major discoveries, innovations, and inventions and assess their influence on societies past and present.

What You Will Learn

You will study major historical events and people in Africa, Asia, and Australia. You also will learn how European exploration and colonization of Africa changed the continent. You will study how migration brought Chinese knowledge and customs to Korea. You also will analyze how influential leaders, such as China's Mao Zedong, can bring sweeping political and economic changes to their countries.

Grade Seven Competency Goals

Goal 9: The learner will analyze the different forms of government developed in Africa, Asia, and Australia.

Objectives:

7.9.01 Trace the historical development of governments, including traditional, colonial, and national, in selected societies and assess their effects on the respective contemporary political systems.

7.9.02 Describe how different types of governments such as democracies, dictatorships, monarchies, and oligarchies in Africa, Asia, and Australia carry out legislative, executive, and judicial functions and evaluate the effectiveness of each.

7.9.03 Identify the ways in which governments in selected areas of Africa, Asia, and Australia deal with issues of justice and injustice and assess the influence of cultural values on their practices and expectations.

7.9.04 Describe how different governments in Africa, Asia, and Australia select leaders and establish laws in comparison to the United States and analyze the strengths and weaknesses of each.

Goal 10: The learner will compare the rights and civic responsibilities of individuals in political structures in Africa, Asia, and Australia.

Objectives:

7.10.01 Trace the development of relationships between individuals and their governments in selected cultures of Africa, Asia, and Australia and evaluate the changes that have evolved over time.

7.10.02 Identify various sources of citizens' rights and responsibilities, such as constitutions, traditions, and religious law, and analyze how they are incorporated into different government structures.

7.10.03 Describe rights and responsibilities of citizens in selected contemporary societies in Africa, Asia, and Australia, comparing them to each other and to the United States.

7.10.04 Examine the rights, roles, and status of individuals in selected cultures of Africa, Asia, and Australia and assess their importance in relation to the general welfare.

Link to Real Life

Your school's student council is creating a new constitution, or set of rules, for the school. They have asked students for their ideas. How will writing a constitution help your council? What rights and responsibilities should students have? Learning about democracy around the world can give you ideas about how to improve student government.

▶ To learn more about democracy in Africa, turn to page 63.

North Carolina Standard Course of Study

What You Will Learn

You will learn about the different governments and compare the rights of citizens in the regions of Africa, Asia and Australia. You will learn how citizens in Botswana participate in their democratic government by having lively political debates in public areas, or "freedom squares." You will learn why for many centuries Japan's emperors did not have as much power as China's emperors.

Herbert C. Bonner Bridge,
Cape Hatteras, North Carolina

Grade Seven Competency Goals

Link to Real Life

A group of students at your school wants to hold a "Cultural Heritage Day." How does a day that honors various cultures bring people together? What types of activities might take place on "Cultural Heritage Day"?

▶ To learn more about cultural diversity, turn to page 84.

Goal 11: The learner will recognize the common characteristics of different cultures in Africa, Asia, and Australia.

Objectives:

7.11.01 Identify the concepts associated with culture such as language, religion, family, and ethnic identity and analyze how they can link and separate societies.

7.11.02 Examine the basic needs and wants of all human beings and assess the influence of factors such as environment, values, and beliefs in creating different cultural responses.

7.11.03 Compare characteristics of political, economic, religious, and social institutions of selected cultures and evaluate their similarities and differences.

7.11.04 Identify examples of economic, political, and social changes, such as agrarian to industrial economies, monarchical to democratic governments, and the roles of women and minorities, and analyze their impact on culture.

Goal 12: The learner will assess the influence of major religions, ethical beliefs, and values on cultures in Africa, Asia, and Australia.

Objectives:

7.12.01 Examine the major belief systems in selected regions of Africa, Asia, and Australia and analyze their impact on cultural values, practices, and institutions.

7.12.02 Describe the relationship between and cultural values of selected societies of Africa, Asia, and Australia and their art, architecture, music, and literature and assess their significance in contemporary culture.

7.12.03 Identify examples of cultural borrowing, such as language, traditions, and technology, and evaluate their importance in the development of selected societies in Africa, Asia, and Australia.

Goal 13: The learner will describe the historic, economic, and cultural connections among North Carolina, the United States, Africa, Asia, and Australia.

Objectives:

7.13.01 Identify historical movements such as colonization, revolution, emerging democracies, migration, and immigration that link North Carolina and the United States to selected societies of Africa, Asia, and Australia, and evaluate their influence on local, state, regional, national, and international communities.

7.13.02 Describe the diverse cultural connections that have influenced the development of language, art, music, and belief systems in North Carolina and the United States and analyze their role in creating a changing cultural mosaic.

7.13.03 Examine the role and importance of foreign-owned businesses and trade between North Carolina and the nations of Africa, Asia, and Australia and assess the effects on local, state, regional, and national economies and cultures.

What You Will Learn

You will study the many aspects of the cultures of Africa, Asia, and Australia, such as language, religion, family, and ethnic identity. You will learn why Israel has great diversity within its Jewish population. You also will learn why Pakistan was created to settle differences among religious groups. You will study India's caste system and compare it to the social structure of the United States.

Social Studies Skills

Goal 1: The learner will acquire strategies for reading social studies materials and for increasing social studies vocabulary.

Objectives:

SS.1.01 Read for literal meaning.

SS.1.02 Summarize to select main ideas.

SS.1.03 Draw inferences

SS.1.04 Detect cause and effect.

SS.1.05 Recognize bias and propaganda.

SS.1.06 Recognize and use social studies terms in written and oral reports.

SS.1.07 Distinguish fact and fiction.

SS.1.08 Use context clues and appropriate sources such as glossaries, texts, and dictionaries to gain meaning.

Goal 2: The learner will acquire strategies to access a variety of sources and use appropriate research skills to gather, synthesize, and report information using diverse modalities to demonstrate the knowledge acquired.

Objectives:

SS.2.01 Use appropriate sources of information.

SS.2.02 Explore print and non-print materials.

SS.2.03 Utilize different types of technology.

SS.2.04 Utilize community-related resources such as field trips, guest speakers, and interviews.

SS.2.05 Transfer information from one medium to another such as written to visual and statistical to written.

SS.2.06 Create written, oral, musical, visual, and theatrical presentations of social studies information.

Goal 3: The learner will acquire strategies to analyze, interpret, create, and use resources and materials.

Objectives:

SS.3.01 Use map and globe reading skills.

SS.3.02 Interpret graphs and charts.

SS.3.03 Detect bias.

SS.3.04 Interpret social and political messages of cartoons.

SS.3.05 Interpret history through artifacts, arts, and media.

Link to Real Life

This year, you can help decide where your family will go on vacation. What research skills will you use to decide where to go? How will your social studies skills help you find reliable sources, such as Web sites and books, to help you plan your trip?

► To learn more about finding reliable information, turn to the Skills for Life on page 234.

North Carolina Standard Course of Study

What You Will Learn

You will learn skills that will help you read, research, and analyze social studies information. In the Country Profiles throughout the book, you will analyze many different sources of information to learn about specific countries. For example, you will compare a map, graph, and chart to learn about the culture of Vietnam.

Link to Real Life

Some students want your school to sponsor more dances. They created a petition and want you to sign it. Other students are against having more dances at school. These students prefer the dances at the local teen center, where they can meet students from other schools. They feel that if the school has more dances, fewer people will attend dances at the center.

How will you decide whether to sign the petition?

What are the pros and cons of both sides?

▶ To learn more about expressing your opinions in writing, turn to page RW3 in the Reading and Writing Handbook.

Goal 4: The learner will acquire strategies needed for applying decision-making and problem-solving techniques both orally and in writing to historic, contemporary, and controversial world issues.

Objectives:

SS.4.01 Use hypothetical reasoning processes.

SS.4.02 Examine, understand, and evaluate conflicting viewpoints.

SS.4.03 Recognize and analyze values upon which judgments are made.

SS.4.04 Apply conflict resolutions.

SS.4.05 Predict possible outcomes.

SS.4.06 Draw conclusions.

SS.4.07 Offer solutions.

SS.4.08 Develop hypotheses.

Goal 5: The learner will acquire strategies needed for effective incorporation of computer technology in the learning process.

Objectives:

SS.5.01 Use word processing to create, format, and produce classroom assignments/projects.

SS.5.02 Create and modify a database for class assignments.

SS.5.03 Create, modify, and use spreadsheets to examine real-world problems.

SS.5.04 Create nonlinear projects related to the social studies content area via multimedia presentations.

What You Will Learn

You will study how democratic nations offered training, equipment, and money to help solve problems in Kyrgyzstan and Tajikistan. You will learn how Kenyans living in Nairobi support one another. You will also explore the values that kept Japan separated from the outside world for about 200 years.

Did you know?

North Carolina has an unsolved mystery! The English colonists who settled on Roanoke Island in the 1580s disappeared. One possible explanation suggests that most of the colonists traveled by land to the southern shores of Chesapeake Bay, where they were killed by members of the Powhatan tribe.

Prepare for Grade Seven Testing

The **North Carolina End-of-Grade (EOG) Reading Comprehension Test for Grade Seven** uses multiple-choice questions to test how well you understand what you read. You will read nine selections that are both literary and informational and then answer questions related to what you read. Choose the best answer to each question. You will have 115 minutes to complete a total of 56 questions.

The **North Carolina General Writing Assessment for Grade Seven** contains one prompt that asks you to write an argumentative response. You must explain the reasons why your point of view is valid and you must also persuade the reader to take your point of view. Your response should be focused, organized, and grammatically correct.

How will my social studies course help me prepare for the test?

Many of the skills you learn in social studies—reading, analyzing, comparing, and writing— are the same skills that will help you succeed on the North Carolina End-of-Grade (EOG) Reading Comprehension Test and the General Writing Assessment.

The writing activities throughout this textbook will help you prepare for the Writing Assessment. Your textbook provides test-taking tips throughout the text to help you prepare.

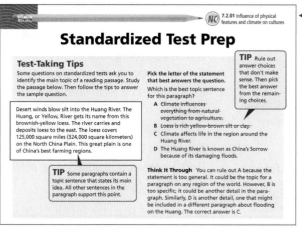

◄ Your textbook provides multiple-choice practice and test-taking tips at the end of each chapter.

Skills Practice

The following pages contain skills practices that will help you prepare for the seventh grade tests. You will read two informational passages on Africa and Asia. Then, you will answer questions related to the reading selections. You will also review a sample student response to an argumentative writing prompt and then practice writing your own essay.

Many European countries wanted access to Africa's resources. This selection describes African peoples' response to colonization. Read the selection and answer the questions that follow.

African Resistance to Colonization

Although Europeans were successful in taking over nearly all of Africa by 1914, they had to fight Africans for control of many places. When Europeans colonized an area, they brought their cultures and customs with them. Often Europeans expected people living in the colony to start doing things the European way. They also took power away from people who lived in the colonies. Africans saw their natural resources stripped away to run factories that were springing up across Europe. People from colonized areas became tired of this treatment and wanted to end European rule. Larger African kingdoms were able to raise large armies to resist occupying forces. However, their musket guns, gained through earlier trade, were no match for new European weapons such as machine guns.

In southern Africa during the 1830s and 1840s, the Zulu, led by their king Dingane, unsuccessfully fought Dutch settlers who attempted to settle the Natal region. As the scramble for Africa progressed, battles with the occupying armies became increasingly bloody. In separate campaigns, or series of military operations in a war, France achieved control of Madagascar and Morocco, and Britain seized the Sudan.

Although European nations competed with one another for African territory, they did not want this competition to lead to war. As a result, the leaders of several European nations met in Berlin, Germany, in 1884 to set rules for colonization. These rules explained which European countries could claim which African lands. The Italians, who claimed Ethiopia during the Berlin Conference, attempted to take control of Ethiopia in the early 1890s. The Ethiopian emperor, Menelik, resisted the Italians. In 1896, the disagreement led to a war in which the Ethiopians defeated the Italian army. After the war, Menelik extended his empire by conquering lands to the south and southwest as far as the ancient kingdom of Kafka near Lake Turkana.

Liberia, located on the west coast of Africa, was recognized as an independent country when the scramble for Africa began. It had been established as a republic in 1847 after having been settled by freed slaves who had left the United States. During the colonial period, Britain and France forced Liberia to give up some of its land. However, it maintained its political independence.

The scramble for Africa caused long-lasting problems. The Europeans had gained power partly by encouraging various African ethnic groups to compete among themselves. They also drew new political boundaries, dividing some ethnic groups and forcing different groups to live together. These boundaries would later cause great conflict in Africa.

European Land Claims in Africa

Country	Land Claims
Britain	Sierra Leone; Nigeria; the Gold Coast (now Ghana); Egypt; Sudan; southern Africa
Belgium	The Congo
France	Algeria; Niger; Chad; Mali; Mauritania; Senegal; Gambia
Italy	Libya and lands along the horn of Africa along Indian Ocean trading routes
Germany	Cameroon; Tanzania; Namibia

1. From the chart, what is the *main* reason Italy wanted colonies in Africa?

   A to bring the Roman Catholic religion to Africans

   B to gain control over trade routes

   C to have a place to send criminals from Italian prisons

   D to learn new methods for growing crops

2. What is the *main* purpose of the passage?

   A to entertain readers with exciting battle stories

   B to inform readers of Africa's peaceful history

   C to persuade readers that Africa should belong to Europe

   D to tell readers that Africans fought to be independent

3. What is the *most likely* reason different ethnic groups in Africa did not get along?

   A They favored different European countries.

   B They had very different cultures and customs.

   C Some wanted to be colonists while others wanted to be independent.

   D Some were very wealthy while others were extremely poor.

4. Why might some think that Menelik's actions did not make sense?

   A He fought to keep Ethiopia independent but later conquered other nations.

   B He agreed to Italian colonization at the Berlin Conference but later resisted it.

   C He led his unwilling people into war with Italy, and many Ethiopians died.

   D He offered Italy the kingdom of Kafka so the Italians would not colonize Ethiopia.

5. Liberia lost land to which two countries?

   A Britain and Belgium

   B France and Belgium

   C Britain and France

   D France and Italy

6. What detail proves that the Zulu were determined to resist European rule?

   A France gained control of Madagascar and Morocco.

   B Great Britain seized the Sudan.

   C The Zulu unsuccessfully fought Dutch settlers in the Natal region.

   D Battles with occupying armies became increasingly bloody.

Emperor Asoka

This selection describes how he changed from a warrior to a religious leader. Read the selection and answer the questions that follow.

Asoka's Leadership

Around 321 B.C., a leader named Chandragupta Maurya conquered many kingdoms in northern India. By the time of his death, the Maurya Empire covered much of the Indian subcontinent.

Chandragupta passed the leadership of the Maurya Empire on to his son. When his son died, Chandragupta's grandson, Asoka, gained power. Asoka, whose name means "without sorrow," further expanded Chandragupta's empire. By the end of his lengthy rule in 232 B.C., Asoka had built the greatest empire India had ever seen.

For more than 35 years, Asoka ruled an empire that included much of the Indian subcontinent. During the first years of his rule, Asoka was as warlike as his grandfather had been. He conquered new territories and added them to his empire.

Early in his rule, Asoka led his army south into the state of Kalinga. In about 261 B.C., he won a bloody battle in which thousands of people were injured or died. The great slaughter at Kalinga was a turning point in Asoka's life. He was filled with sorrow over the bloodshed. He gave up war and violence. He freed his prisoners and restored their land. Later he chose to convert, or change his beliefs, to Buddhism. Asoka also spread the message of Buddhism to the people of his empire.

Asoka practiced and preached the teachings of the Buddha. He did not allow the use of animals for sacrifices. He gave up hunting, the traditional sport of Indian kings.

Asoka thought of his people as his children and was concerned about their welfare. He asked government officials to treat common people with kindness. He had hospitals built throughout his kingdom—for both people and animals! He even had wells dug every mile beside the roads so that travelers would not go thirsty.

Asoka was also concerned with his people's moral and spiritual life. To carry the Buddha's message throughout his vast empire, Asoka issued writings of moral advice. Some writings urged people to honor their parents. Others asked people not to kill animals. Still others encouraged people to behave with truthfulness and tolerance, or freedom from prejudice. Asoka also issued laws requiring that people be treated humanely. Throughout his empire, his advice and laws were carved on stone pillars about 40 feet (12 meters) high. One pillar bore these words:

"Both this world and the other are hard to reach, except by great love of the law, great self-examination, great obedience, great respect, great energy."

Asoka practiced religious tolerance toward all religions and gave them financial support. Because of his tolerance and support of the Hindus, many of the Buddha's teachings became part of Hinduism during Asoka's rule. Buddhism grew under Asoka. He sent missionaries far and wide to spread its message.

1. **What is the *main* purpose of this passage?**

   A to describe how one man led India

   B to teach readers about the Buddhist religion

   C to persuade readers to be non-violent

   D to explain why India has tall stone pillars

2. **What is *one* way in which Asoka differed from other Indian rulers?**

   A He was elected by the people to his position as emperor.

   B He was warlike and led his army in bloody battles.

   C He did not hunt animals.

   D He did not issue laws.

3. **Which describes what Asoka would *most likely* do if he lived today?**

   A He would make plans to conquer neighboring Pakistan.

   B He would establish Buddhism as India's only religion.

   C He would pass laws to punish crimes with the death penalty.

   D He would call for world peace in a United Nations speech.

4. **What is the *most likely* reason Asoka converted to Buddhism?**

   A He no longer believed in war and violence.

   B His grandfather had been Buddhist.

   C He disagreed with the teachings of Hinduism.

   D He wanted his people to practice a religion.

5. **What *most likely* explains Asoka's violent behavior in his early life?**

   A He needed to protect India from invaders.

   B His people staged many rebellions.

   C His grandfather had been warlike.

   D He wanted to earn the title "emperor."

6. **How were Indian rulers selected in the time of Asoka?**

   A They inherited their positions.

   B The wealthy landowners selected the rulers.

   C Buddhist priests selected the ruler.

   D The people voted for their rulers.

Writing Assessment Practice

Social studies can help you practice your writing skills for success on the **North Carolina General Writing Assessment for Grade Seven.** This test asks you to respond to an argumentative writing prompt. The prompt asks you either to solve a problem or to state your opinion on a given topic.

North Carolina uses two rubrics, or scoring guides, to evaluate your responses. The content rubric is used to judge the organization of your ideas. The conventions rubric is used to assess your sentence structure, grammar, and spelling. Turn to pages NC 38 and NC 39 to view these rubrics.

The following pages show you how to approach an argumentative writing prompt, provide a sample of a student response, and show you how to evaluate it. Page RW3 of the Reading and Writing Handbook provides more tips for writing argumentative responses.

General Writing Assessment Prompt for Grade Seven

Sample Prompt   A local newspaper's essay contest challenges students to think about one world problem and offer a solution. You have decided to write about the problem of food and water shortages in Africa.
Write an essay that describes the reasons for the shortage problems and how these problems can be solved.

As you write your essay, remember to

- Focus on the topic of the essay. Be sure you clearly understand which position you want to take.

- Choose words that are well suited to the purpose, audience, and content of your essay.

- Organize your essay so that your ideas flow logically from beginning to end.

- Include details that clearly support the position you take.

- Edit your essay for standard grammar and language usage.

Sample Student Response

In many countries of Africa, people face the problems of too little water and food. These problems can be solved with the help of people from throughout the world.

Teacher's Comment: This is a strong opening paragraph. The topic sentence states the essay's main idea.

People and governments of other countries could give money, equipment, and training so that Africans could irrigate their crops. Irrigation pipes would carry water from nearby lakes and rivers. This would help farmers produce crops.

Teacher's Comment: A transition word, such as *First*, placed at the beginning of the first sentence would tie this paragraph to the one before it. Irrigation is a good example of a solution.

Also, world organizations, such as the Peace Corps, could help people dig wells so that villages with little or poor water could get enough good water for their citizens.

Scientists from around the world can also help fix Africa's food and water problems. They have invented new kinds of seeds that produce larger and more nutritious crops.

Teacher's Comment: The second sentence supports the first sentence but needs support, such as an example of a crop grown from these new seeds.

Countries with tons of food that's more than enough for their own people could send food to Africa. Many countries are already doing this. Some have groups, such as the American Red Cross, that deliver food in emergencies.

Teacher's Comment: *Tons of food* is an informal expression. Essays require formal language. A more formal expression might be *a great deal of food.*

Although these problems are serious they can be solved with the help of caring people and governments in the world.

Teacher's Comment: Your conclusion successfully summarizes the main idea.

Score	Notes
3	**Content Score** Clear, focused point made about a single topic. Sufficient and relevant details though one lacked supporting information. Generally appropriate language. Transition sentences and words used in most cases. Sentence flow generally smooth.
2	**Conventions Score** Thorough control of sentence formation. Few errors, if any, are present in grammar, spelling, and punctuation. While some informal language interfered with style, it did not interfere with meaning.

Now You Try!

Use the prompt below to practice writing your own argumentative response. The content and conventions rubrics will help you evaluate your work.

General Writing Assessment Prompt for Grade Seven

> You and your family members recycle newspapers, cardboard boxes, glass bottles, soda cans, and other containers at home. You have noticed that your school does not recycle in the classrooms or in the cafeteria.
>
> How would you get your school to start a recycling program? Explain to your principal what the benefits of a recycling program would be and how the school could organize such an effort.

As you write your essay, remember to

- Focus on the topic of the essay. Be sure you clearly understand which position you want to take.

- Choose words that are well suited to the purpose, audience, and content of your essay.

- Organize your essay so that your ideas flow logically from beginning to end.

- Include details that clearly support the position you take.

- Edit your essay for standard grammar and language usage.

North Carolina Conventions Rubric

Points	Descriptions
2	**Exhibits reasonable control of grammatical conventions appropriate to the writing task** • Exhibits reasonable control of sentence formation • Exhibits reasonable control of standard usage including agreement, tense, and case • Exhibits reasonable control of mechanics including use of capitalization, punctuation, and spelling
1	**Exhibits minimal control of grammatical conventions appropriate to the writing task** • Exhibits minimal control of sentence formation • Exhibits minimal control of standard usage including agreement, tense, and case • Exhibits minimal control of mechanics including use of capitalization, punctuation, and spelling.
0	**Lacks control of grammatical conventions appropriate to the writing task** • Lacks control of sentence formation • Lacks control of standard usage including agreement, tense, and case • Lacks control of mechanics including use of capitalization, punctuation, and spelling

North Carolina Content Rubric

Points	Descriptions
4	• Topics/subject is clear, though it may not be explicitly stated • Maintains focus on topic/subject throughout the response • Organizational structure establishes relationships between and among ideas and/or events • Consists of a logical progression of ideas and/or events and is unified and complete • Support and elaboration are related to and supportive of the topic/subject • Consists of specific, developed details • Exhibits skillful use of vocabulary that is precise and purposeful • Demonstrates skillful use of sentence fluency
3	• Topic/subject is generally clear, though it may or may not be explicitly stated • May exhibit minor lapses in focus on topic/subject • Organizational structure establishes relationships between and among ideas and/or events, although minor lapses may be present • Consists of a logical progression of ideas and/or events and is reasonably complete, although minor lapses may be present • Support and elaboration may have minor weaknesses in relatedness to and support of the topic/subject • Consists of some specific details • Exhibits reasonable use of vocabulary that is precise and purposeful • Demonstrates reasonable use of sentence fluency
2	• Topic/subject may be vague • May lose or may exhibit lapses in focus on topic/subject • Organizational structure may establish little relationship between and among ideas and/or events • May have major lapses in the logical progression of ideas and/or events and is minimally complete • Support and elaboration may have major weaknesses in relatedness to and support of the topic/subject • Consists of general and/or undeveloped details, which may be presented in a list-like fashion • Exhibits minimal use of vocabulary that is precise and purposeful • Demonstrates minimal use of sentence fluency
1	• Topic/subject is unclear or confusing • May fail to establish focus on topic/subject • Organizational structure may not establish connection between and among ideas and/or events • May consist of ideas and/or events that are presented in a random fashion and is incomplete or confusing • Support and elaboration attempts to support the topic/subject but may be unrelated or confusing • Consists of sparse details • Lacks use of vocabulary that is precise and purposeful • May not demonstrate sentence fluency
NS	• This code may be used for compositions that are entirely illegible or otherwise unscorable: blank responses, responses written in a foreign language, restatements of the prompts, and responses that are off-topic or incoherent.

Reading Informational Texts

Reading a magazine, an Internet page, or a textbook is not the same as reading a novel. The purpose of reading nonfiction texts is to acquire new information. On page M18 you'll read about some ↻ **Target Reading Skills** that you'll have a chance to practice as you read this textbook. Here we'll focus on a few skills that will help you read nonfiction with a more critical eye.

Analyze the Author's Purpose

Different types of materials are written with different purposes in mind. For example, a textbook is written to teach students information about a subject. The purpose of a technical manual is to teach someone how to use something, such as a computer. A newspaper editorial might be written to persuade the reader to accept a particular point of view. A writer's purpose influences how the material is presented. Sometimes an author states his or her purpose directly. More often, the purpose is only suggested, and you must use clues to identify the author's purpose.

Distinguish Between Facts and Opinions

It's important when reading informational texts to read actively and to distinguish between fact and opinion. A fact can be proven or disproven. An opinion cannot—it is someone's personal viewpoint or evaluation.

For example, the editorial pages in a newspaper offer opinions on topics that are currently in the news. You need to read newspaper editorials with an eye for bias and faulty logic. For example, the newspaper editorial at the right shows factual statements in blue and opinion statements in red. The underlined words are examples of highly charged words. They reveal bias on the part of the writer.

More than 5,000 people voted last week in favor of building a new shopping center, but the opposition won out. The margin of victory is irrelevant. Those radical voters who opposed the center are obviously self-serving elitists who do not care about anyone but themselves.

This month's unemployment figure for our area is 10 percent, which represents an increase of about 5 percent over the figure for this time last year. These figures mean unemployment is getting worse. But the people who voted against the mall probably do not care about creating new jobs.

Identify Evidence

Before you accept an author's conclusion, you need to make sure that the author has based the conclusion on enough evidence and on the right kind of evidence. An author may present a series of facts to support a claim, but the facts may not tell the whole story. For example, what evidence does the author of the newspaper editorial on the previous page provide to support his claim that the new shopping center would create more jobs? Is it possible that the shopping center might have put many small local businesses out of business, thus increasing unemployment rather than decreasing it?

Evaluate Credibility

Whenever you read informational texts, you need to assess the credibility of the author. This is especially true of sites you may visit on the Internet. All Internet sources are not equally reliable. Here are some questions to ask yourself when evaluating the credibility of a Web site.

- ☐ Is the Web site created by a respected organization, a discussion group, or an individual?
- ☐ Does the Web site creator include his or her name as well as credentials and the sources he or she used to write the material?
- ☐ Is the information on the site balanced or biased?
- ☐ Can you verify the information using two other sources?
- ☐ Is there a date telling when the Web site was created or last updated?

Writing for Social Studies

Writing is one of the most powerful communication tools you will ever use. You will use it to share your thoughts and ideas with others. Research shows that writing about what you read actually helps you learn new information and ideas. A systematic approach to writing—including prewriting, drafting, revising, and proofing—can help you write better, whether you're writing an essay or a research report.

Narrative Essays

Writing that tells a story about a personal experience

1 Select and Narrow Your Topic

A narrative is a story. In social studies, it might be a narrative essay about how an event affected you or your family.

2 Gather Details

Brainstorm a list of details you'd like to include in your narrative.

3 Write a First Draft

Start by writing a simple opening sentence that conveys the main idea of your essay. Continue by writing a colorful story that has interesting details. Write a conclusion that sums up the significance of the event or situation described in your essay.

4 Revise and Proofread

Check to make sure you have not begun too many sentences with the word *I*. Replace general words with more colorful ones.

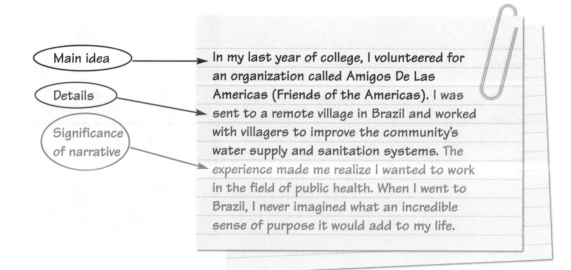

Main idea

Details

Significance of narrative

In my last year of college, I volunteered for an organization called Amigos De Las Americas (Friends of the Americas). I was sent to a remote village in Brazil and worked with villagers to improve the community's water supply and sanitation systems. The experience made me realize I wanted to work in the field of public health. When I went to Brazil, I never imagined what an incredible sense of purpose it would add to my life.

Persuasive Essays

Writing that supports an opinion or position

① Select and Narrow Your Topic

Choose a topic that provokes an argument and has at least two sides. Choose a side. Decide which argument will appeal most to your audience and persuade them to understand your point of view.

② Gather Evidence

Create a chart that states your position at the top and then lists the pros and cons for your position below, in two columns. Predict and address the strongest arguments against your stand.

③ Write a First Draft

Write a strong thesis statement that clearly states your position. Continue by presenting the strongest arguments in favor of your position and acknowledging and refuting opposing arguments.

④ Revise and Proofread

Check to make sure you have made a logical argument and that you have not oversimplified the argument.

Main Idea

Supporting (pro) argument

Opposing (con) argument

Transition words

It is vital to vote in elections. When people vote, they tell public officials how to run the government. Not every proposal is carried out; however, politicians do their best to listen to what the majority of people want. Therefore, every vote is important.

Expository Essays

Writing that explains a process, compares and contrasts, explains causes and effects, or explores solutions to a problem

1 Identify and Narrow Your Topic

Expository writing is writing that explains something in detail. It might explain the similarities and differences between two or more subjects (compare and contrast). It might explain how one event causes another (cause and effect). Or it might explain a problem and describe a solution.

Cause 1	Cause 2	Cause 3
Most people in the Mexican countryside work on farms.	The population in Mexico is growing at one of the highest rates in the world.	There is not enough farm work for so many people.

Effect
As a result, many rural families are moving from the countryside to live in Mexico City.

2 Gather Evidence

Create a graphic organizer that identifies details to include in your essay.

3 Write Your First Draft

Write a topic sentence and then organize the essay around your similarities and differences, causes and effects, or problem and solutions. Be sure to include convincing details, facts, and examples.

4 Revise and Proofread

Research Papers

Writing that presents research about a topic

1 Narrow Your Topic

Choose a topic you're interested in and make sure that it is not too broad. For example, instead of writing a report on Panama, write about the construction of the Panama Canal.

2 Acquire Information

Locate several sources of information about the topic from the library or the Internet. For each resource, create a source index card like the one at the right. Then take notes using an index card for each detail or subtopic. On the card, note which source the information was taken from. Use quotation marks when you copy the exact words from a source.

Source #1
McCullough, David. *The Path Between the Seas: The Creation of the Panama Canal, 1870-1914.* N.Y., Simon and Schuster, 1977.

3 Make an Outline

Use an outline to decide how to organize your report. Sort your index cards into the same order.

Outline
I. Introduction
II. Why the canal was built
III. How the canal was built
   A. Physical challenges
   B. Medical challenges
IV. Conclusion

Introduction

Building the Panama Canal

Ever since Christopher Columbus first explored the Isthmus of Panama, the Spanish had been looking for a water route through it. They wanted to be able to sail west from Spain to Asia without sailing around South America. However, it was not until 1914 that the dream became a reality.

Conclusion

It took eight years and more than 70,000 workers to build the Panama Canal. It remains one of the greatest engineering feats of modern times.

④ Write a First Draft

Write an introduction, a body, and a conclusion. Leave plenty of space between lines so you can go back and add details that you may have left out.

⑤ Revise and Proofread

Be sure to include transition words between sentences and paragraphs. Here are some examples:

To show a contrast—*however, although, despite.*

To point out a reason—*since, because, if.*

To signal a conclusion—*therefore, consequently, so, then.*

Evaluating Your Writing

Use this table to help you evaluate your writing.

	Excellent	Good	Acceptable	Unacceptable
Purpose	Achieves purpose—to inform, persuade, or provide historical interpretation—very well	Informs, persuades, or provides historical interpretation reasonably well	Reader cannot easily tell if the purpose is to inform, persuade, or provide historical interpretation	Purpose is not clear
Organization	Develops ideas in a very clear and logical way	Presents ideas in a reasonably well-organized way	Reader has difficulty following the organization	Lacks organization
Elaboration	Explains all ideas with facts and details	Explains most ideas with facts and details	Includes some supporting facts and details	Lacks supporting details
Use of Language	Uses excellent vocabulary and sentence structure with no errors in spelling, grammar, or punctuation	Uses good vocabulary and sentence structure with very few errors in spelling, grammar, or punctuation	Includes some errors in grammar, punctuation, and spelling	Includes many errors in grammar, punctuation, and spelling

CONTENTS

Go Online PHSchool.com Use Web Code lcp-0000 for all of the maps in this handbook.

Five Themes of Geography

Studying the geography of the entire world is a huge task. You can make that task easier by using the five themes of geography: location, regions, place, movement, and human-environment interaction. The themes are tools you can use to organize information and to answer the where, why, and how of geography.

▲ **Location**
This museum in England has a line running through it. The line marks its location at 0° longitude.

LOCATION

1 Location answers the question, "Where is it?" You can think of the location of a continent or a country as its address. You might give an absolute location such as 40° N and 80° W. You might also use a relative address, telling where one place is by referring to another place. *Between school and the mall* and *eight miles east of Pleasant City* are examples of relative locations.

REGIONS

Regions are areas that share at least one common feature. Geographers divide the world into many types of regions. For example, countries, states, and cities are political regions. The people in any one of these places live under the same government. Other features, such as climate and culture, can be used to define regions. Therefore the same place can be found in more than one region. For example, the state of Hawaii is in the political region of the United States. Because it has a tropical climate, Hawaii is also part of a tropical climate region.

MOVEMENT

Movement answers the question, "How do people, goods, and ideas move from place to place?" Remember that what happens in one place often affects what happens in another. Use the theme of movement to help you trace the spread of goods, people, and ideas from one location to another.

PLACE

Place identifies the natural and human features that make one place different from every other place. You can identify a specific place by its landforms, climate, plants, animals, people, language, or culture. You might even think of place as a geographic signature. Use the signature to help you understand the natural and human features that make one place different from every other place.

INTERACTION

Human-environment interaction focuses on the relationship between people and the environment. As people live in an area, they often begin to make changes to it, usually to make their lives easier. For example, they might build a dam to control flooding during rainy seasons. Also, the environment can affect how people live, work, dress, travel, and communicate.

◀ **Interaction**
These Congolese women interact with their environment by gathering wood for cooking.

PRACTICE YOUR GEOGRAPHY SKILLS

1 Describe your town or city, using each of the five themes of geography.

2 Name at least one thing that comes into your town or city and one that goes out. How is each moved? Where does it come from? Where does it go?

Understanding Movements of Earth

The planet Earth is part of our solar system. Earth revolves around the sun in a nearly circular path called an orbit. A revolution, or one complete orbit around the sun, takes 365¼ days, or one year. As Earth orbits the sun, it also spins on its axis, an invisible line through the center of Earth from the North Pole to the South Pole. This movement is called a rotation.

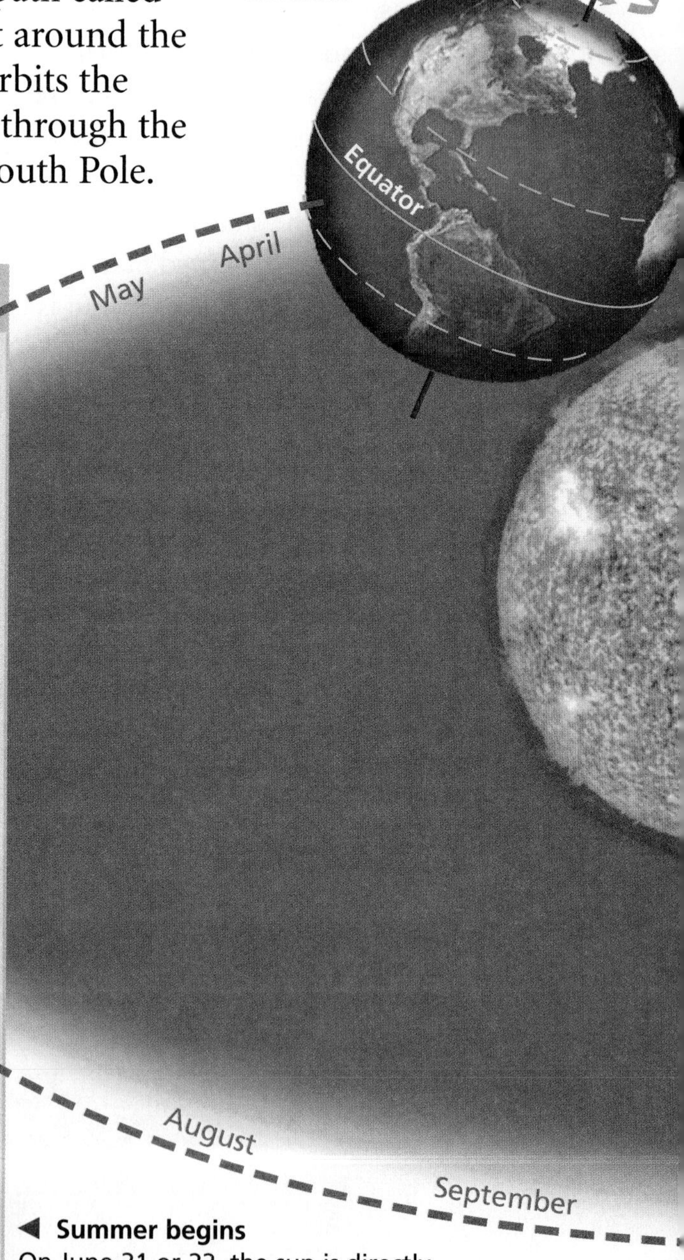

How Night Changes Into Day

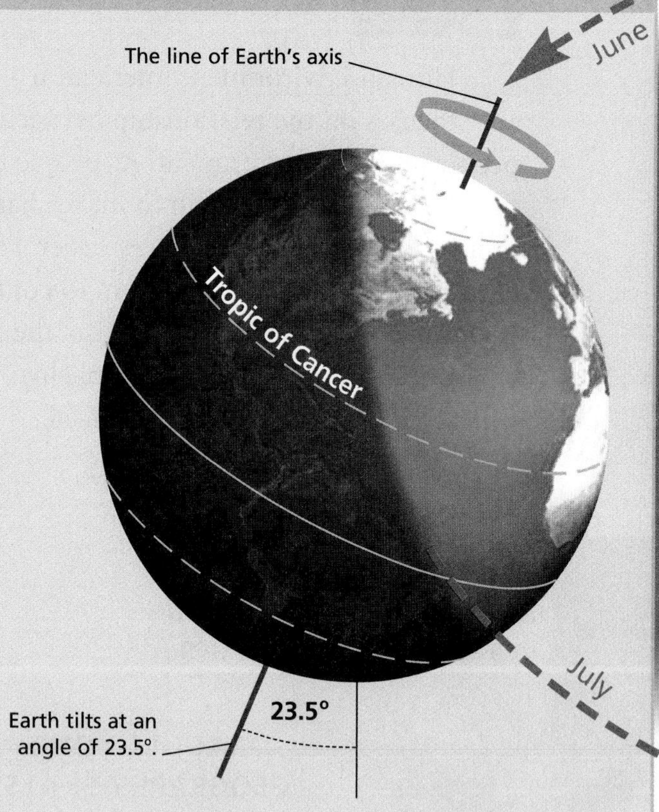

The line of Earth's axis

Tropic of Cancer

Earth tilts at an angle of 23.5°.

23.5°

Earth takes about 24 hours to make one full rotation on its axis. As Earth rotates, it is daytime on the side facing the sun. It is night on the side away from the sun.

▼ **Spring begins**
On March 20 or 21, the sun is directly overhead at the Equator. The Northern and Southern Hemispheres receive almost equal hours of sunlight and darkness.

Equator

May   April

June

July

August

September

◄ **Summer begins**
On June 21 or 22, the sun is directly overhead at the Tropic of Cancer. The Northern Hemisphere receives the greatest number of sunlight hours.

The Seasons

Earth's axis is tilted at an angle. Because of this tilt, sunlight strikes different parts of Earth at different times in the year, creating seasons. The illustration below shows how the seasons are created in the Northern Hemisphere. In the Southern Hemisphere, the seasons are reversed.

PRACTICE YOUR GEOGRAPHY SKILLS

1 What causes the seasons in the Northern Hemisphere to be the opposite of those in the Southern Hemisphere?

2 During which two days of the year do the Northern Hemisphere and Southern Hemisphere have equal hours of daylight and darkness?

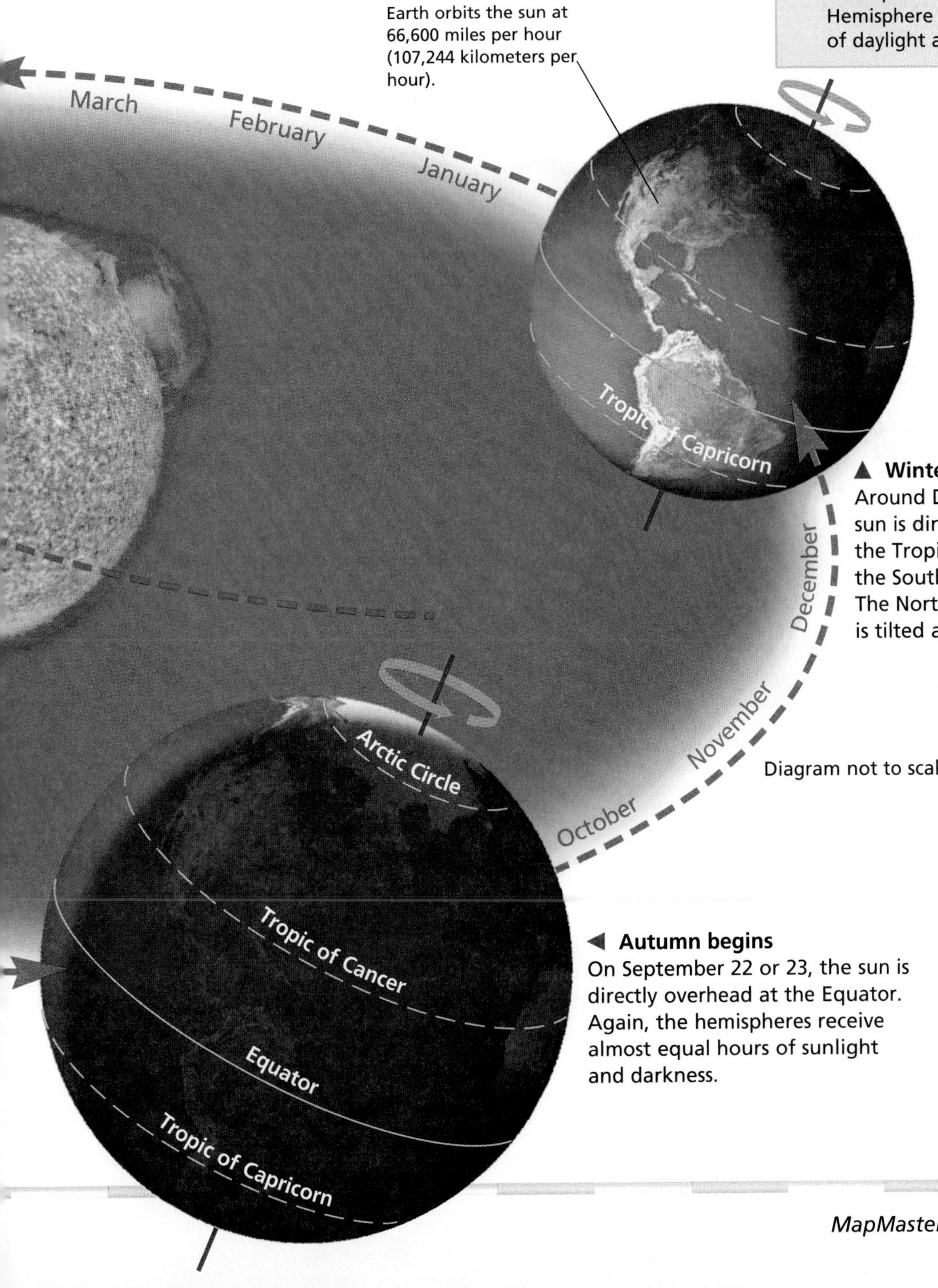

Earth orbits the sun at 66,600 miles per hour (107,244 kilometers per hour).

March

February

January

Tropic of Capricorn

December

November

October

Diagram not to scale

Arctic Circle

Tropic of Cancer

Equator

Tropic of Capricorn

▲ Winter begins
Around December 21, the sun is directly overhead at the Tropic of Capricorn in the Southern Hemisphere. The Northern Hemisphere is tilted away from the sun.

◀ Autumn begins
On September 22 or 23, the sun is directly overhead at the Equator. Again, the hemispheres receive almost equal hours of sunlight and darkness.

Understanding Globes

A globe is a scale model of Earth. It shows the actual shapes, sizes, and locations of all Earth's landmasses and bodies of water. Features on the surface of Earth are drawn to scale on a globe. This means that a small unit of measure on the globe stands for a large unit of measure on Earth.

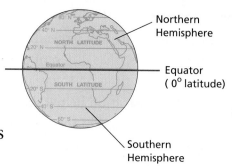

Northern Hemisphere

Equator (0° latitude)

Southern Hemisphere

Parallels of Latitude

Geographers divide the globe along imaginary horizontal lines called parallels of latitude. One of these latitude lines is the Equator, located halfway between the North and South Poles. Parallels of latitude are measured in degrees (°). One degree of latitude represents a distance of about 69 miles (111 kilometers).

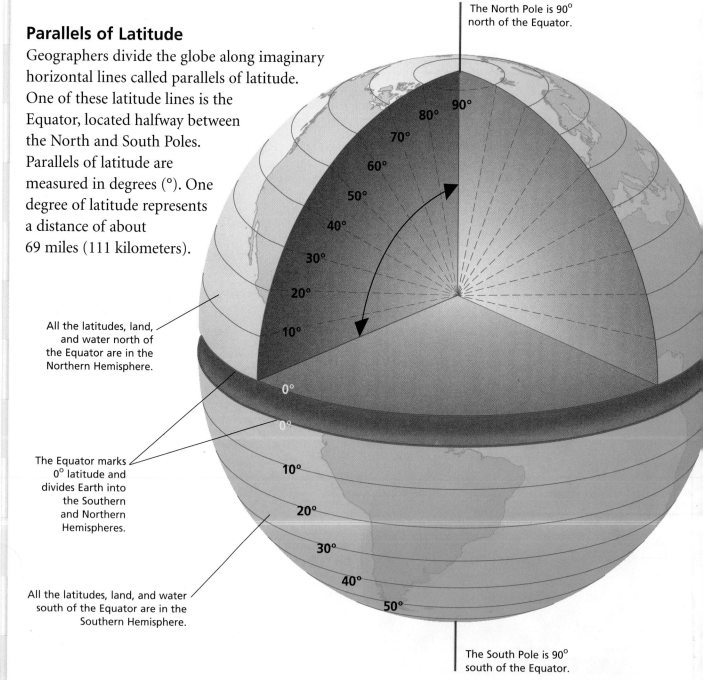

The North Pole is 90° north of the Equator.

All the latitudes, land, and water north of the Equator are in the Northern Hemisphere.

The Equator marks 0° latitude and divides Earth into the Southern and Northern Hemispheres.

All the latitudes, land, and water south of the Equator are in the Southern Hemisphere.

The South Pole is 90° south of the Equator.

Meridians of Longitude

Geographers also divide the globe along imaginary vertical lines called meridians of longitude, which are measured in degrees (°). The longitude line called the Prime Meridian runs from pole to pole through Greenwich, England. All meridians of longitude come together at the North and South Poles.

PRACTICE YOUR GEOGRAPHY SKILLS

1 Which continents lie completely in the Northern Hemisphere? In the Western Hemisphere?

2 Is there land or water at 20° S latitude and the Prime Meridian? At the Equator and 60° W longitude?

All the longitudes, land, and water west of the Prime Meridian are in the Western Hemisphere.

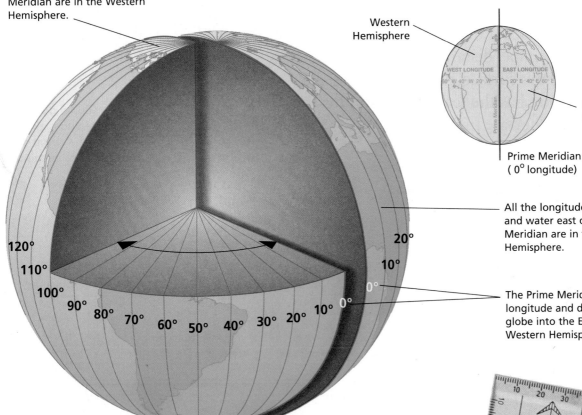

Western Hemisphere

Eastern Hemisphere

Prime Meridian (0° longitude)

All the longitudes, land, and water east of the Prime Meridian are in the Eastern Hemisphere.

The Prime Meridian marks 0° longitude and divides the globe into the Eastern and Western Hemispheres.

The Global Grid

Together, the pattern of parallels of latitude and meridians of longitude is called the global grid. Using the lines of latitude and longitude, you can locate any place on Earth. For example, the location of 30° north latitude and 90° west longitude is usually written as 30° N, 90° W. Only one place on Earth has these coordinates—the city of New Orleans, in the state of Louisiana.

▲ **Compass**
Wherever you are on Earth, a compass can be used to show direction.

Map Projections

Maps are drawings that show regions on flat surfaces. Maps are easier to use and carry than globes, but they cannot show the correct size and shape of every feature on Earth's curved surface. They must shrink some places and stretch others. To make up for this distortion, mapmakers use different map projections. No one projection can accurately show the correct area, shape, distance, and direction for all of Earth's surface. Mapmakers use the projection that has the least distortion for the information they are presenting.

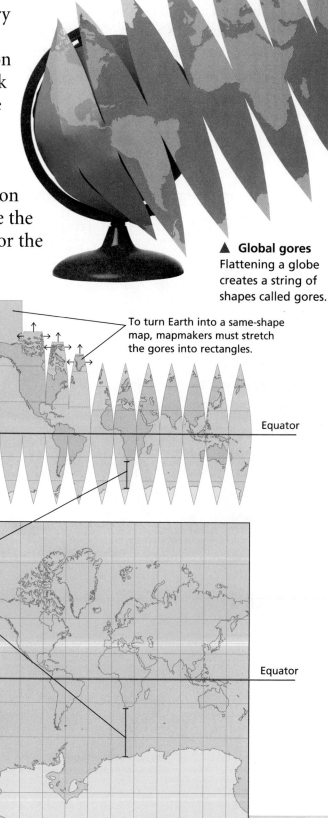

▲ **Global gores**
Flattening a globe creates a string of shapes called gores.

To turn Earth into a same-shape map, mapmakers must stretch the gores into rectangles.

Equator

Same-Shape Maps

Map projections that accurately show the shapes of landmasses are called same-shape maps. However, these projections often greatly distort, or make less accurate, the size of landmasses as well as the distance between them. In the projection below, the northern and southern areas of the globe appear more stretched than the areas near the Equator.

Stretching the gores makes parts of Earth larger. This enlargement becomes greater toward the North and South Poles.

Mercator projection ▶
One of the most common same-shape maps is the Mercator projection, named for the mapmaker who invented it. The Mercator projection accurately shows shape and direction, but it distorts distance and size. Because the projection shows true directions, ships' navigators use it to chart a straight-line course between two ports.

Equator

Equal-Area Maps

Map projections that show the correct size of landmasses are called equal-area maps. In order to show the correct size of landmasses, these maps usually distort shapes. The distortion is usually greater at the edges of the map and less at the center.

PRACTICE YOUR GEOGRAPHY SKILLS

1 What feature is distorted on an equal-area map?

2 Would you use a Mercator projection to find the exact distance between two locations? Tell why or why not.

To turn Earth's surface into an equal-area map, mapmakers have to squeeze each gore into an oval.

Equator

The tips of all the gores are then joined together. The points at which they join form the North and South Poles. The line of the Equator stays the same.

North Pole

Equator

South Pole

Robinson Maps

Many of the maps in this book use the Robinson projection, which is a compromise between the Mercator and equal-area projections. The Robinson projection gives a useful overall picture of the world. It keeps the size and shape relationships of most continents and oceans, but distorts the size of the polar regions.

The entire top edge of the map is the North Pole.

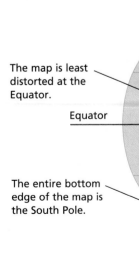

The map is least distorted at the Equator.

Equator

The entire bottom edge of the map is the South Pole.

How to Use a Map

Mapmakers provide several clues to help you understand the information on a map. Maps provide different clues, depending on their purpose or scale. However, most maps have several clues in common.

Locator globe
Many maps are shown with locator globes. They show where on the globe the area of the map is located.

Title
All maps have a title. The title tells you the subject of the map.

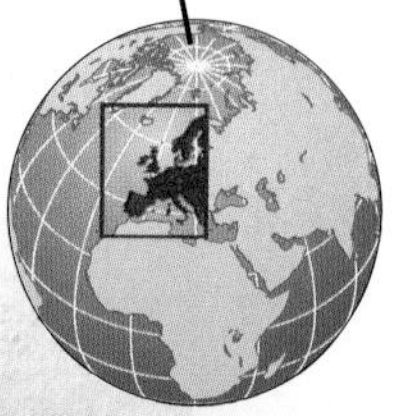

Compass rose
Many maps show direction by displaying a compass rose with the directions north, east, south, and west. The letters N, E, S, and W are placed to indicate these directions.

Key
Often a map has a key, or legend. The key shows the symbols and colors used on the map, and what each one means.

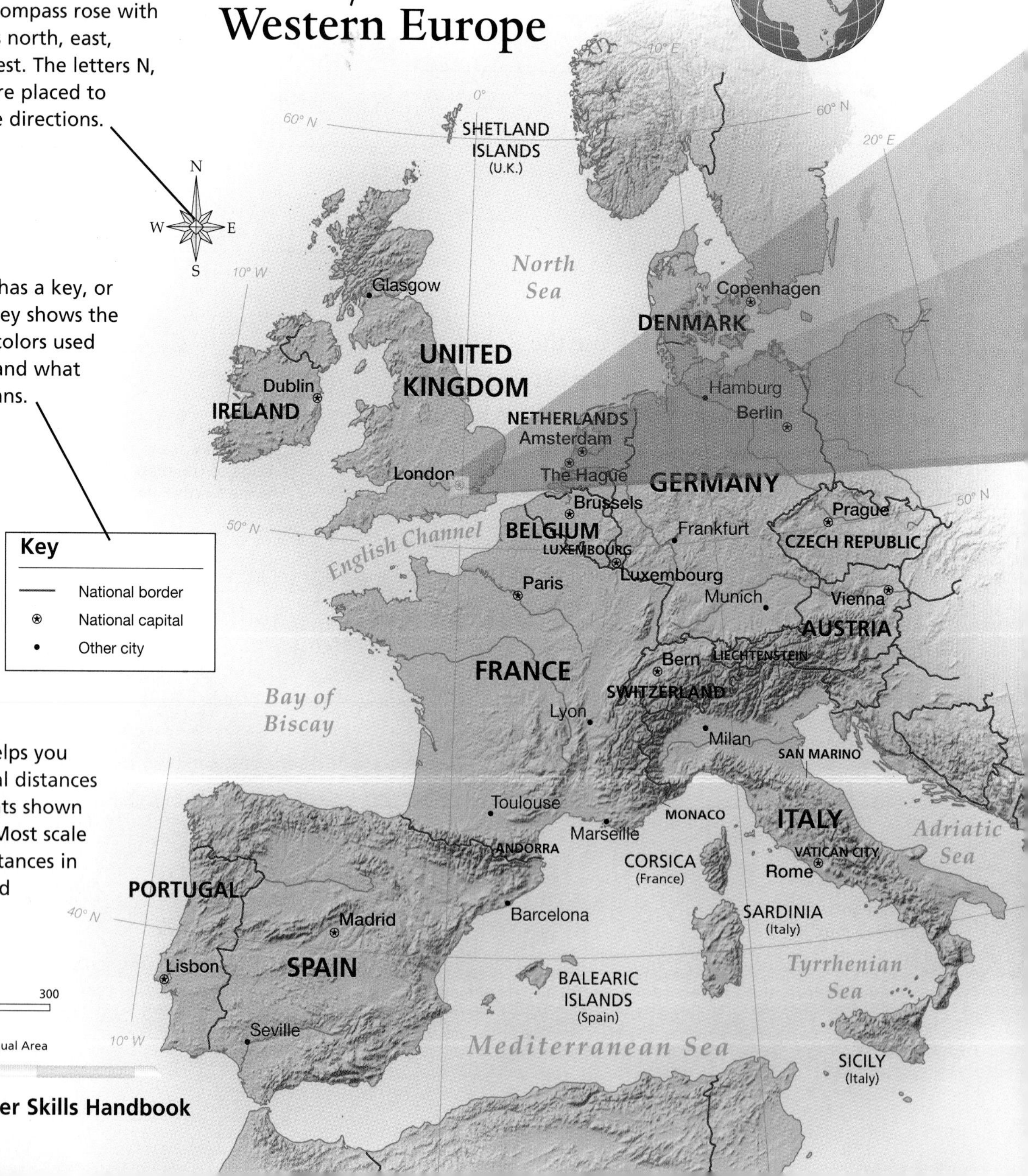

Western Europe

Key

——	National border
⊛	National capital
•	Other city

Scale bar
A scale bar helps you find the actual distances between points shown on the map. Most scale bars show distances in both miles and kilometers.

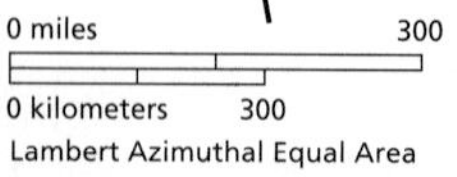

0 miles   300
0 kilometers   300
Lambert Azimuthal Equal Area

60° N   SHETLAND ISLANDS (U.K.)
10° W   Glasgow
North Sea
Copenhagen
DENMARK
UNITED KINGDOM
Dublin
IRELAND
NETHERLANDS
Amsterdam
Hamburg
Berlin
London
The Hague
GERMANY
Brussels
BELGIUM
Frankfurt
Prague
CZECH REPUBLIC
50° N
English Channel
LUXEMBOURG
Luxembourg
Paris
Munich
Vienna
AUSTRIA
Bay of Biscay
FRANCE
Bern
LIECHTENSTEIN
SWITZERLAND
Lyon
Milan
SAN MARINO
Toulouse
MONACO
ITALY
Adriatic Sea
Marseille
ANDORRA
CORSICA (France)
VATICAN CITY
Rome
PORTUGAL
40° N
Madrid
Barcelona
SARDINIA (Italy)
Tyrrhenian Sea
Lisbon
SPAIN
BALEARIC ISLANDS (Spain)
Seville
Mediterranean Sea
SICILY (Italy)

Maps of Different Scales

Maps are drawn to different scales, depending on their purpose. Here are three maps drawn to very different scales. Keep in mind that maps showing large areas have smaller scales. Maps showing small areas have larger scales.

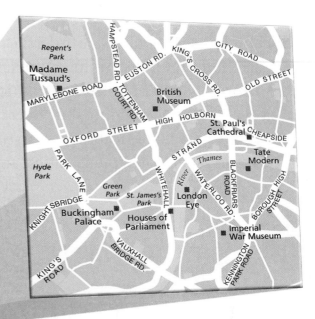

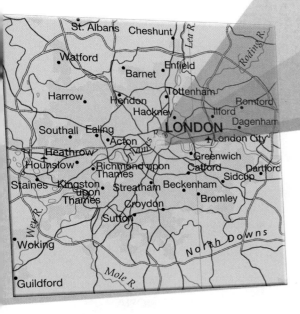

▲ **Greater London**
Find the gray square on the main map of Western Europe (left). This square represents the area shown on the map above. It shows London's boundaries, the general shape of the city, and the features around the city. This map can help you find your way from the airport to the center of town.

▲ **Central London**
Find the gray square on the map of Greater London. This square represents the area shown on the map above. This map moves you closer into the center of London. Like the zoom on a computer or a camera, this map shows a smaller area but in greater detail. It has the largest scale (1 inch represents about 0.9 mile). You can use this map to explore downtown London.

Key

■ Point of interest

⬠ Park

0 miles   0.5   1
0 kilometers   1

Key

▨ Built-up area   ✈ Airport

─ City or county border

⊛ National capital

• Town or neighborhood

0 miles   10   20
0 kilometers   20
Lambert Conformal Conic

PRACTICE YOUR GEOGRAPHY SKILLS

1 What part of a map explains the colors used on the map?

2 How does the scale bar change depending on the scale of the map?

3 Which map would be best for finding the location of the British Museum? Explain why.

Political Maps

Political maps show political borders: continents, countries, and divisions within countries, such as states or provinces. The colors on political maps do not have any special meaning, but they make the map easier to read. Political maps also include symbols and labels for capitals, cities, and towns.

PRACTICE YOUR GEOGRAPHY SKILLS

1 What symbols show a national border, a national capital, and a city?

2 What is Angola's capital city?

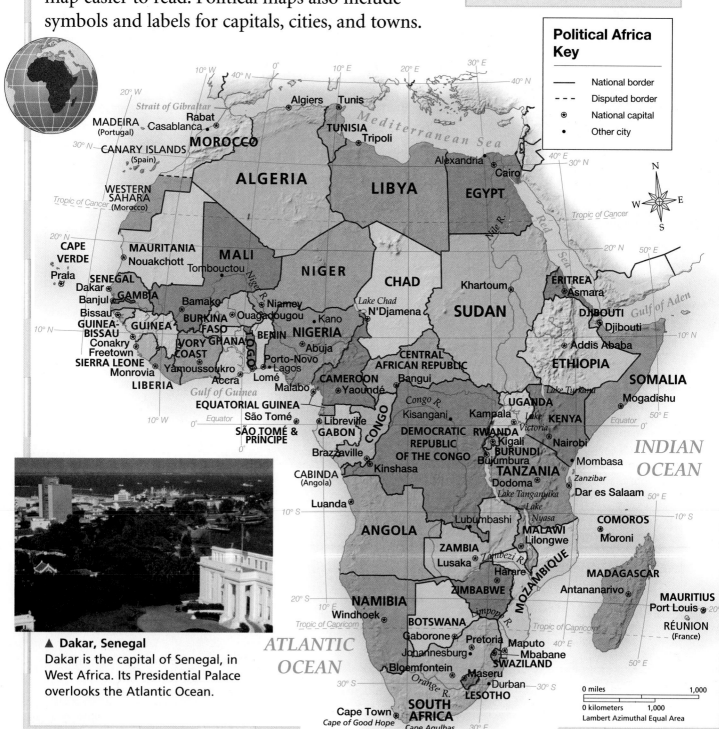

Political Africa Key

———	National border
- - -	Disputed border
⊛	National capital
•	Other city

▲ **Dakar, Senegal**
Dakar is the capital of Senegal, in West Africa. Its Presidential Palace overlooks the Atlantic Ocean.

Physical Maps

Physical maps represent what a region looks like by showing its major physical features, such as hills and plains. Physical maps also often show elevation and relief. Elevation, indicated by colors, is the height of the land above sea level. Relief, indicated by shading, shows how sharply the land rises or falls.

PRACTICE YOUR GEOGRAPHY SKILLS

1 Which areas of Africa have the highest elevation?

2 How can you use relief to plan a hiking trip?

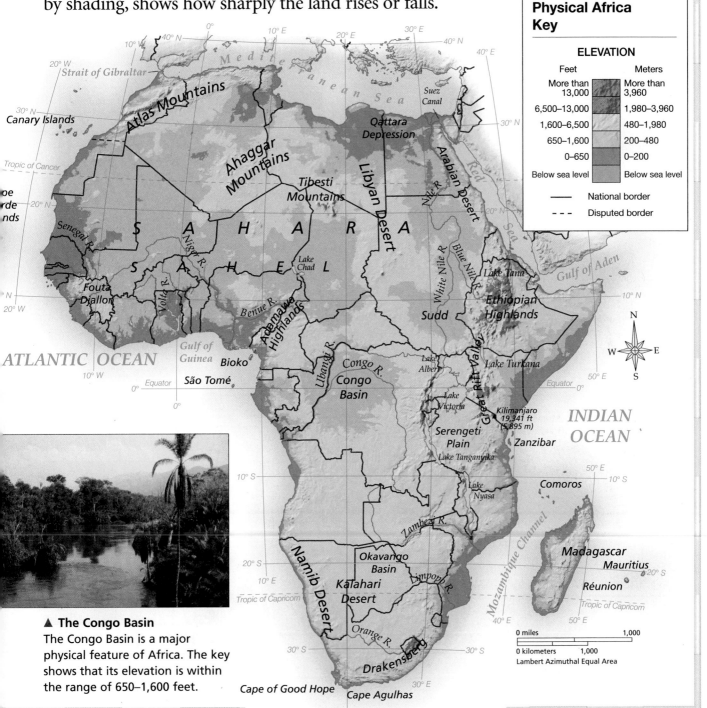

Physical Africa Key

ELEVATION

Feet		Meters
More than 13,000		More than 3,960
6,500–13,000		1,980–3,960
1,600–6,500		480–1,980
650–1,600		200–480
0–650		0–200
Below sea level		Below sea level

—— National border

- - - Disputed border

0 miles 1,000
0 kilometers 1,000
Lambert Azimuthal Equal Area

▲ **The Congo Basin**
The Congo Basin is a major physical feature of Africa. The key shows that its elevation is within the range of 650–1,600 feet.

Special-Purpose Maps: Climate

Unlike the boundary lines on a political map, the boundary lines on climate maps do not separate the land into exact divisions. For example, in this climate map of India, a tropical wet climate gradually changes to a tropical wet and dry climate.

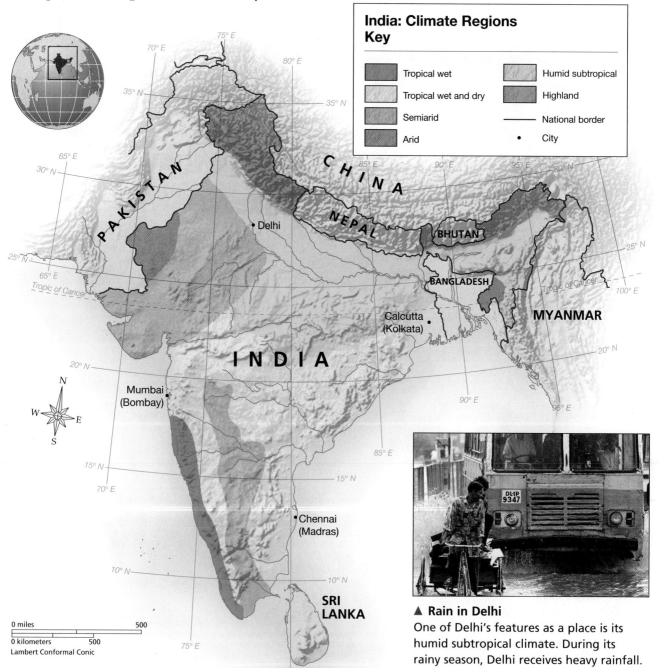

India: Climate Regions Key

- Tropical wet
- Tropical wet and dry
- Semiarid
- Arid
- Humid subtropical
- Highland
- ——— National border
- • City

▲ **Rain in Delhi**
One of Delhi's features as a place is its humid subtropical climate. During its rainy season, Delhi receives heavy rainfall.

Special-Purpose Maps: Language

This map shows the official languages of India. An official language is the language used by the government. Even though a region has an official language, the people there may speak other languages as well. As in other special-purpose maps, the key explains how the different languages appear on the map.

PRACTICE YOUR GEOGRAPHY SKILLS

1 What color represents the Malayalam language on this map?

2 Where in India is Tamil the official language?

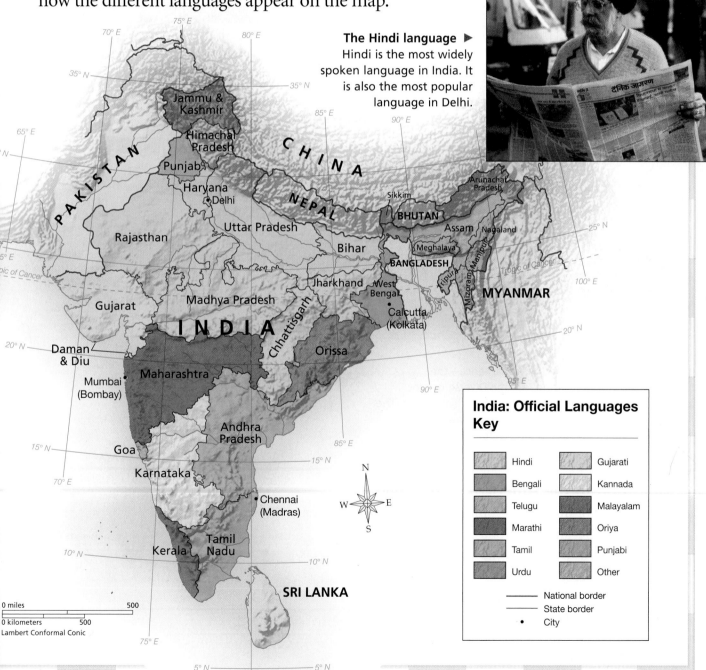

The Hindi language ▶
Hindi is the most widely spoken language in India. It is also the most popular language in Delhi.

India: Official Languages Key

Hindi	Gujarati
Bengali	Kannada
Telugu	Malayalam
Marathi	Oriya
Tamil	Punjabi
Urdu	Other

——— National border
——— State border
• City

0 miles 500
0 kilometers 500
Lambert Conformal Conic

Human Migration

Migration is an important part of the study of geography. Since the beginning of history, people have been on the move. As people move, they both shape and are shaped by their environments. Wherever people go, the culture they bring with them mixes with the cultures of the place in which they have settled.

Explorers arrive ▼
In 1492, Christopher Columbus set sail from Spain for the Americas with three ships. The ships shown here are replicas of those ships.

▲ Native American pyramid
When Europeans arrived in the Americas, the lands they found were not empty. Diverse groups of people with distinct cultures already lived there. The temple-topped pyramid shown above was built by Mayan Indians in Mexico, long before Columbus sailed.

Migration to the Americas, 1500–1800

A huge wave of migration from the Eastern Hemisphere began in the 1500s. European explorers in the Americas paved the way for hundreds of years of European settlement there. Forced migration from Africa started soon afterward, as Europeans began to import African slaves to work in the Americas. The map to the right shows these migrations.

ATLANTIC OCEAN

NEW SPAIN
(Spain)
Mexico City

Caribbean Sea

Panama City

DUTCH GUIANA
(Netherlands)

NEW GRENADA
(Spain)

FRENCH GUIANA
(France)

Amazon R.

PERU
(Spain)
Lima
Cuzco

BRAZIL
(Portugal)

Potosí

RIO DE LA PLATA
(Spain)

Concepción

Buenos Aires

0 miles   1,000
0 kilometers   1,000
Wagner VII

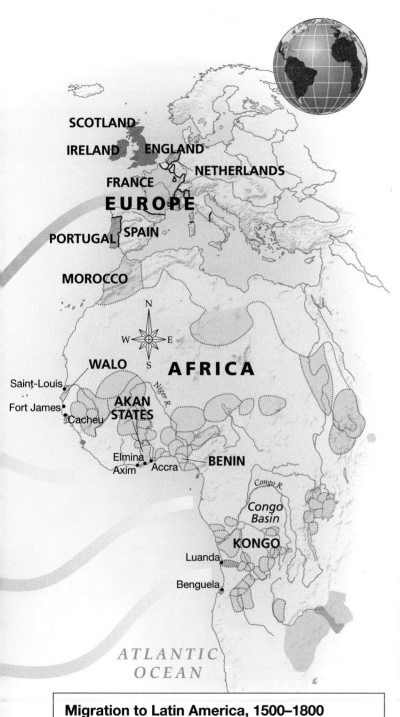

1 Where did the Portuguese settle in the Americas?

2 Would you describe African migration at this time as a result of both push factors and pull factors? Explain why or why not.

"Push" and "Pull" Factors

Geographers describe a people's choice to migrate in terms of "push" factors and "pull" factors. Push factors are things in people's lives that push them to leave, such as poverty and political unrest. Pull factors are things in another country that pull people to move there, including better living conditions and hopes of better jobs.

▲ **Elmina, Ghana**
Elmina, in Ghana, is one of the many ports from which slaves were transported from Africa. Because slaves and gold were traded here, stretches of the western African coast were known as the Slave Coast and the Gold Coast.

Migration to Latin America, 1500–1800
Key

◄ European migration	Spain and possessions
◄ African migration	Portugal and possessions
— National or colonial border	Netherlands and possessions
···· Traditional African border	France and possessions
African State	England and possessions

Map labels: SCOTLAND, IRELAND, ENGLAND, NETHERLANDS, FRANCE, EUROPE, PORTUGAL, SPAIN, MOROCCO, WALO, AFRICA, Saint-Louis, Fort James, Cacheu, AKAN STATES, Niger R., Elmina, Axim, Accra, BENIN, Congo R., Congo Basin, KONGO, Luanda, Benguela, ATLANTIC OCEAN

World Land Use

People around the world have many different economic structures, or ways of making a living. Land-use maps are one way to learn about these structures. The ways that people use the land in each region tell us about the main ways that people in that region make a living.

World Land Use Key

- Nomadic herding
- Hunting and gathering
- Forestry
- Livestock raising
- Commercial farming
- Subsistence farming
- Manufacturing and trade
- Little or no activity
- ——— National border
- - - - Disputed border

▲ **Wheat farming in the United States**
Developed countries practice commercial farming rather than subsistence farming. Commercial farming is the production of food mainly for sale, either within the country or for export to other countries. Commercial farmers like these in Oregon often use heavy equipment to farm.

Levels of Development

Notice on the map key the term *subsistence farming*. This term means the production of food mainly for use by the farmer's own family. In less-developed countries, subsistence farming is often one of the main economic activities. In contrast, in developed countries there is little subsistence farming.

▲ **Growing barley in Ecuador**
These farmers in Ecuador use hand tools to harvest barley. They will use most of the crop they grow to feed themselves or their farm animals.

NORTH AMERICA

SOUTH AMERICA

0 miles
0 kilometers   2,000
Robinson

▲ Growing rice in Vietnam
Women in Vietnam plant rice in wet rice paddies, using the same planting methods their ancestors did.

PRACTICE YOUR GEOGRAPHY SKILLS

1 In what parts of the world is subsistence farming the main land use?

2 Locate where manufacturing and trade are the main land use. Are they found more often near areas of subsistence farming or areas of commercial farming? Why might this be so?

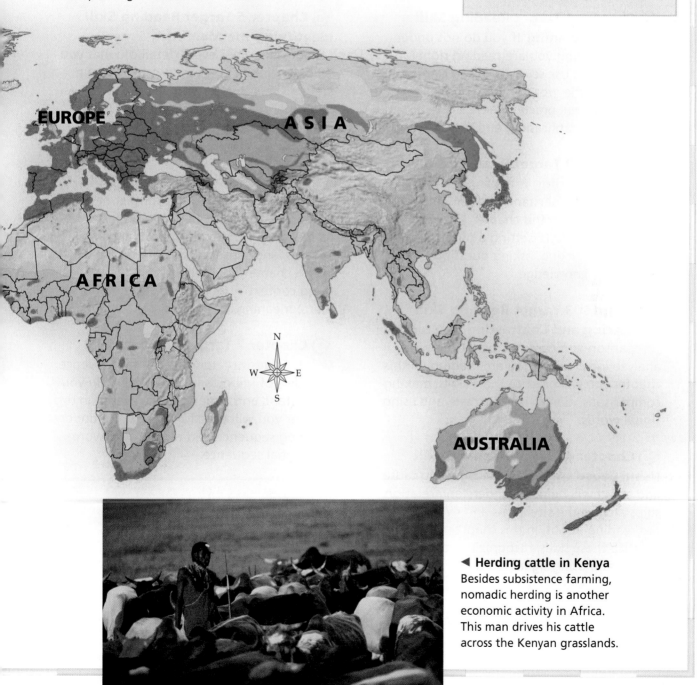

EUROPE

ASIA

AFRICA

N
W E
S

AUSTRALIA

◄ Herding cattle in Kenya
Besides subsistence farming, nomadic herding is another economic activity in Africa. This man drives his cattle across the Kenyan grasslands.

How to Read Social Studies

Target Reading Skills

The Target Reading Skills introduced on this page will help you understand the words and ideas in this book and in other social studies reading you do. Each chapter focuses on one of these reading skills. Good readers develop a bank of reading strategies, or skills. Then they draw on the particular strategies that will help them understand the text they are reading.

Chapter 1 Target Reading Skill

Clarifying Meaning If you do not understand something you are reading right away, you can use several skills to clarify the meaning of the word or idea. In this chapter you will practice these strategies: rereading, paraphrasing, and summarizing.

Chapter 2 Target Reading Skill

Using the Reading Process Previewing can help you understand and remember what you read. In this chapter you will practice these skills: setting a purpose for reading, predicting, asking questions, and using prior knowledge.

Chapter 3 Target Reading Skill

Comparing and Contrasting You can use comparison and contrast to sort out and analyze information you are reading. In this chapter you will practice these skills: making comparisons, identifying contrasts, and using signal words.

Chapter 4 Target Reading Skill

Using Cause and Effect Recognizing cause and effect will help you understand relationships among the situations and events you are reading about. In this chapter you will practice these skills: recognizing causes and effects and using signal words.

Chapter 5 Target Reading Skill

Identifying the Main Idea Since you cannot remember every detail of what you read, it is important to identify the main ideas. In this chapter you will practice these skills: identifying main ideas, identifying implied main ideas, and identifying supporting details.

Chapter 6 Target Reading Skill

Using Context Using the context of an unfamiliar word can help you understand its meaning. Context includes the words, phrases, and sentences surrounding a word. In this chapter you will practice these skills: using context clues and interpreting non-literal meanings.

Chapter 7 Target Reading Skill

Using Sequence Identifying the sequence, or order, of important events can help you understand and remember the events. In this chapter you will practice these skills: understanding sequence and recognizing words that signal sequence.

Target Reading Skills

The Target Reading Skills introduced on this page will help you understand the words and ideas in this book and in other social studies reading you do. Each chapter focuses on one of these reading skills. Good readers develop a bank of reading strategies, or skills. Then they draw on the particular strategies that will help them understand the text they are reading.

Chapter 8 Target Reading Skill
Reading Process When you use the reading process, you set a purpose for reading, predict what you are going to read, and ask questions about what you read.

Chapter 9 Target Reading Skill
Clarifying Meaning If you do not understand something right away, you can use several skills to clarify the meaning of words and ideas. In this chapter, you will practice rereading and reading ahead, paraphrasing, and summarizing.

Chapter 10 Target Reading Skill
Main Idea In this chapter, you will practice these skills: identifying both stated and implied main ideas and identifying supporting details.

Chapter 11 Target Reading Skill
Context Using the context of an unfamiliar word can help you understand its meaning. Context includes the words, phrases, and sentences surrounding a word.

Chapter 12 Target Reading Skill
Word Analysis Word analysis means analyzing a word, or breaking the word into parts to help you recognize and pronounce it. In this chapter, you will analyze words to find roots, prefixes, and suffixes.

Chapter 13 Target Reading Skill
Sequence A sequence is the order in which a series of events occurs. In this chapter, you will practice understanding sequence and recognize words that signal sequences.

Chapter 14 Target Reading Skill
Comparison and Contrast Comparing means examining the similarities between things. Contrasting is looking at differences. In this chapter, you will practice these skills: comparing and contrasting, making comparisons, and identifying contrasts.

Chapter 15 Target Reading Skill
Cause and Effect Identifying cause and effect helps you understand relationships among situations or events. In this chapter, you will practice identifying causes and effects, understanding effects, recognizing multiple causes, and recognizing words that signal cause and effect.

Chapter 16 Target Reading Skill
Main Idea Focusing on main ideas helps you remember the most important information in what you read. In this chapter, you will have another opportunity to practice identifying main ideas and supporting details.

Learning With Technology

You will be making many exciting journeys across time and place in *World Studies*. Technology will help make what you learn come alive.

For: An activity on Confucius
Visit: PHSchool.com
Web Code: ngp-7019

Go Online at PHSchool.com

Use the Web Codes in each Go Online box to access exciting information or activities.

How to Use the Web Code:
1. Go to www.PHSchool.com.
2. Enter the Web Code.
3. Click Go!

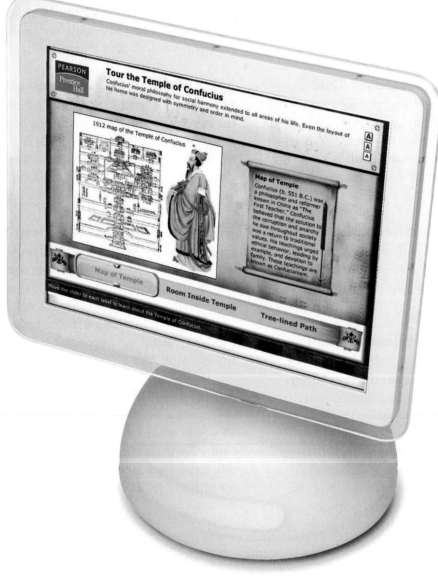

World Desk Reference Online

There are more than 190 countries in the world. To learn about them, you need the most up-to-date information and statistics. The **DK World Desk Reference Online** gives you instant access to the information you need to explore each country.

AFRICA

The name *Africa* may have come from the Latin word *aprica*, which means "sunny." In much of Africa, the sun does shine brightly. Each morning, the African sunrise awakens one eighth of the world's population, in more than fifty different countries. In the chapters that follow, you will spend the day with some of these people.

Guiding Questions

The text, photographs, maps, and charts in this book will help you discover answers to these Guiding Questions.

1 **Geography** What are the main physical features of Africa?

2 **History** How have historical events affected the cultures and nations of Africa?

3 **Culture** What features help define different African cultures?

4 **Government** What factors led to the development of different governments across Africa?

5 **Economics** What factors influence the ways in which Africans make a living?

Project Preview

You can also discover answers to the Guiding Questions by working on projects. Several project possibilities are listed on page 216 of this book.

Investigate Africa

Africa is the second-largest continent in the world after Asia. Africa's climate and physical geography are diverse, ranging from flat, arid deserts to tropical wet rain forests and high mountains. Africa also has a wide range of peoples with their own distinctive languages and cultures. It is a continent potentially rich in natural resources.

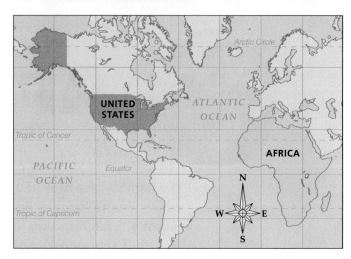

LOCATION

1 Explore Africa's Location

How would you describe Africa's location? One way would be to compare where it is to where the United States is. What ocean lies between Africa and the United States? Find the Equator. What do you know about the climate of countries near the Equator? How do you think the climates of the United States might differ from the climates of Africa?

▲ **Tanzania**
The vast, flat grasslands of the savannas support a diverse population of animals.

REGIONS

2 Estimate the Size of Africa

The United States is 3,500,000 square miles (9,064,958 square kilometers) in land area. How does Africa's size compare to that of the continental United States (all states except Alaska and Hawaii)? Measure mainland Africa at its widest point from east to west. Measure Africa from north to south. Now measure the United States the same way. How do they compare? Estimate Africa's area in square miles.

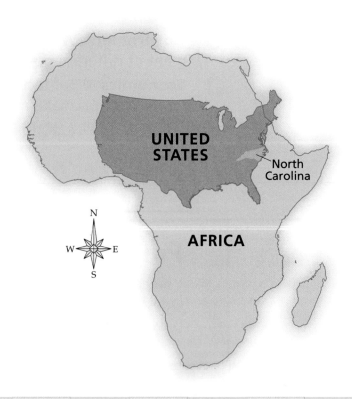

Political Africa

LOCATION

3 Predict How Location Affects Economics

When a country does not border any large body of water, it is called landlocked. Make a list of the African countries that are landlocked. Think about how being landlocked might limit the ability of a country to trade with other countries. How might being landlocked affect the economies of landlocked countries? How might landlocked countries trade in other ways?

▲ **Farafenni Market, Gambia**
This thriving street market is an important part of the local economy. Farmers sell their produce at such local markets, benefiting themselves and the community.

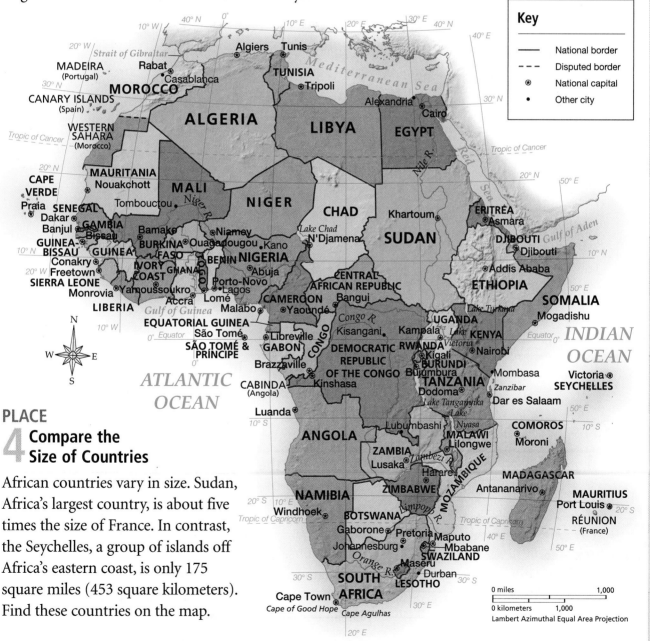

PLACE

4 Compare the Size of Countries

African countries vary in size. Sudan, Africa's largest country, is about five times the size of France. In contrast, the Seychelles, a group of islands off Africa's eastern coast, is only 175 square miles (453 square kilometers). Find these countries on the map.

Physical Africa

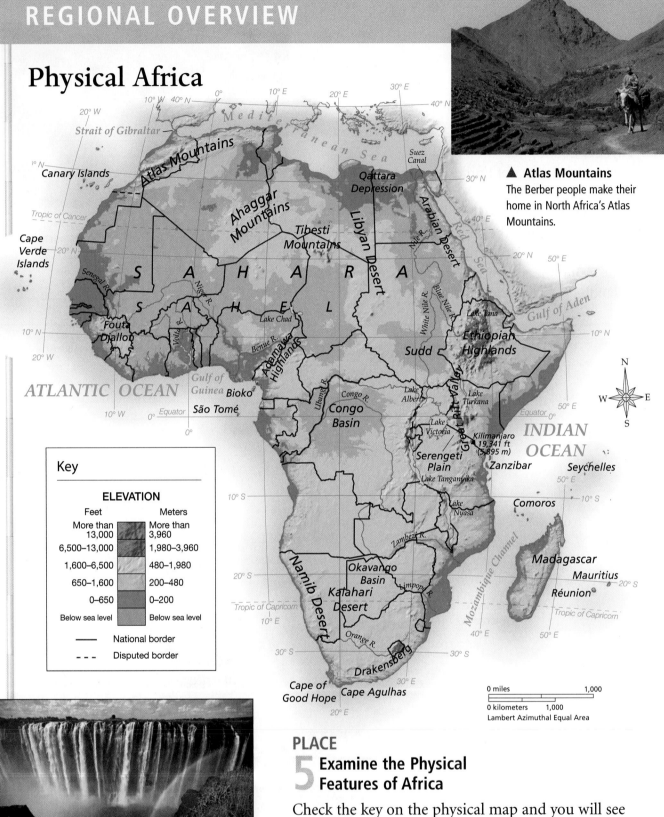

Key

ELEVATION

Feet		Meters
More than 13,000		More than 3,960
6,500–13,000		1,980–3,960
1,600–6,500		480–1,980
650–1,600		200–480
0–650		0–200
Below sea level		Below sea level

— National border
- - - Disputed border

▲ **Atlas Mountains**
The Berber people make their home in North Africa's Atlas Mountains.

0 miles 1,000
0 kilometers 1,000
Lambert Azimuthal Equal Area

▲ **Victoria Falls**
The Zambezi River tumbles over Victoria Falls between Zambia and Zimbabwe in Southern Africa.

PLACE

5 Examine the Physical Features of Africa

Check the key on the physical map and you will see that some of the coastline of Africa has narrow strips of low plains. The interior is a flat plateau covered by the Sahara in the north. On the coast of Southern Africa there are many steep cliffs. Find other places where the plateau comes close to the ocean.

Africa: Land Use

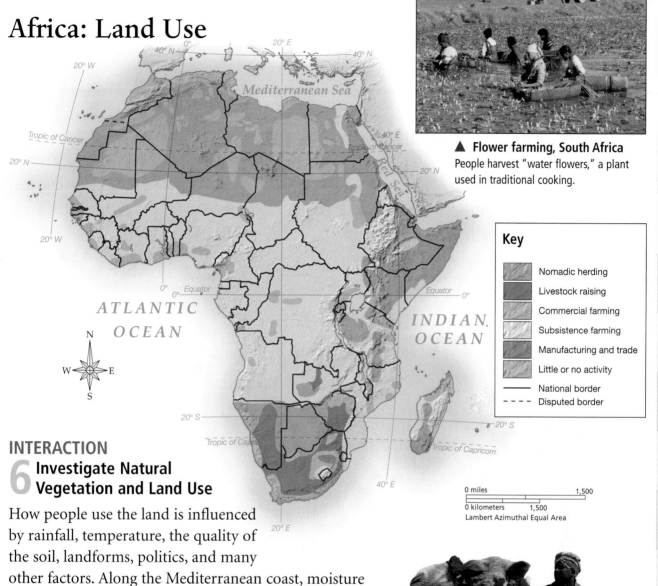

▲ **Flower farming, South Africa**
People harvest "water flowers," a plant used in traditional cooking.

Key

	Nomadic herding
	Livestock raising
	Commercial farming
	Subsistence farming
	Manufacturing and trade
	Little or no activity
——	National border
- - -	Disputed border

0 miles 1,500
0 kilometers 1,500
Lambert Azimuthal Equal Area

INTERACTION

6 Investigate Natural Vegetation and Land Use

How people use the land is influenced by rainfall, temperature, the quality of the soil, landforms, politics, and many other factors. Along the Mediterranean coast, moisture from the sea makes some agriculture possible. In the vast Sahara, most people live as nomadic herders. Where on the continent is livestock raised?

PRACTICE YOUR GEOGRAPHY SKILLS

1. You are in Egypt. A river meets the sea near the country's capital. What is the name of the river?

2. Flying east from the mouth of the Zambezi River, you come to an island. What is its name, and how is land used there?

3. Now you are traveling west by ship toward the southern tip of Africa. You stop at a port near the Tropic of Capricorn. What country are you in?

▲ **Camels are still used as a means of transportation in parts of Egypt.**

Focus on Countries in Africa

Now that you've investigated the geography of Africa, take a closer look at some of the countries that make up this continent. The map shows all of the countries of Africa. The ten countries you will study in depth in the second half of this book are shown in yellow on the map.

Go Online
PHSchool.com Use Web Code **ngp-5020** for the **interactive maps** on these pages.

▲ **Nigeria**
The Hausa-Fulani, Igbo, Yoruba, and a number of other, smaller ethnic groups make up Nigeria, where more than 200 languages are spoken. Nigeria is a major oil-producing country.

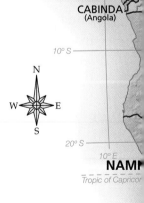

Democratic Republic of the Congo ▶
The Democratic Republic of the Congo is Africa's third-largest country. It is rich in minerals including diamonds, petroleum, cobalt, and copper.

◀ Egypt
Almost all of the people of Egypt live in the fertile valley of the Nile. The vast desert on either side of this river is almost completely unpopulated.

Key

——	National border
----	Disputed border
▨	Countries with in-depth coverage
▨	Non-feature countries

Mediterranean Sea
LIBYA
EGYPT
Nile R.
Red Sea
Tropic of Cancer
CHAD
SUDAN
ERITREA
DJIBOUTI
Gulf of Aden
CENTRAL AFRICAN REPUBLIC
ETHIOPIA
SOMALIA
Congo R.
UGANDA
Lake Turkana
Lake Victoria
KENYA
Equator
DEMOCRATIC REPUBLIC OF THE CONGO
RWANDA
BURUNDI
TANZANIA
INDIAN OCEAN
SEYCHELLES
Lake Tanganyika
Lake Nyasa
COMOROS
ANGOLA
ZAMBIA
MALAWI
MOZAMBIQUE
Zambezi R.
ZIMBABWE
MADAGASCAR
MAURITIUS
RÉUNION (France)
BOTSWANA
Limpopo R.
Tropic of Capricorn
SWAZILAND
Orange R.
SOUTH AFRICA
LESOTHO

0 miles 1,000
0 kilometers 1,000
Lambert Azimuthal Equal Area

▲ Kenya
Two thirds of Kenya's people live in the countryside. Many Kenyan women raise cash crops or work on plantations, while the men work in the cities.

▲ South Africa
South Africa, at Africa's southern tip, is bordered by oceans on three sides. It is a resource-rich country with a strong economy.

Chapter Preview

 NC Standard Course of Study

7.1.02 Use tools to answer geography questions

7.2.01 Influence of physical features and climate on cultures

7.2.02 Factors that influence distribution of population, resources, and climate

7.5.01 How the location of natural resources affects development

7.5.04 Relationship between specialization and interdependence

7.6.03 Effects of over-specialization

SS.1.01 Read for literal meaning

SS.1.02 Summarize to select main ideas

Sections

1. Land and Water
   7.1.02, 7.2.01, 7.2.02, SS.1.01

2. Climate and Vegetation
   7.2.01, 7.2.02, SS.1.01

3. Resources and Land Use
   7.5.01, 7.5.04, 7.6.03, SS.1.02

 Target Reading Skill

Clarifying Meaning In this chapter you will focus on clarifying, or better understanding, the meaning of what you read. Rereading, paraphrasing, and summarizing can help you better understand sentences and passages.

▶ Elephants walk across the plains below Africa's tallest mountain, Mount Kilimanjaro.

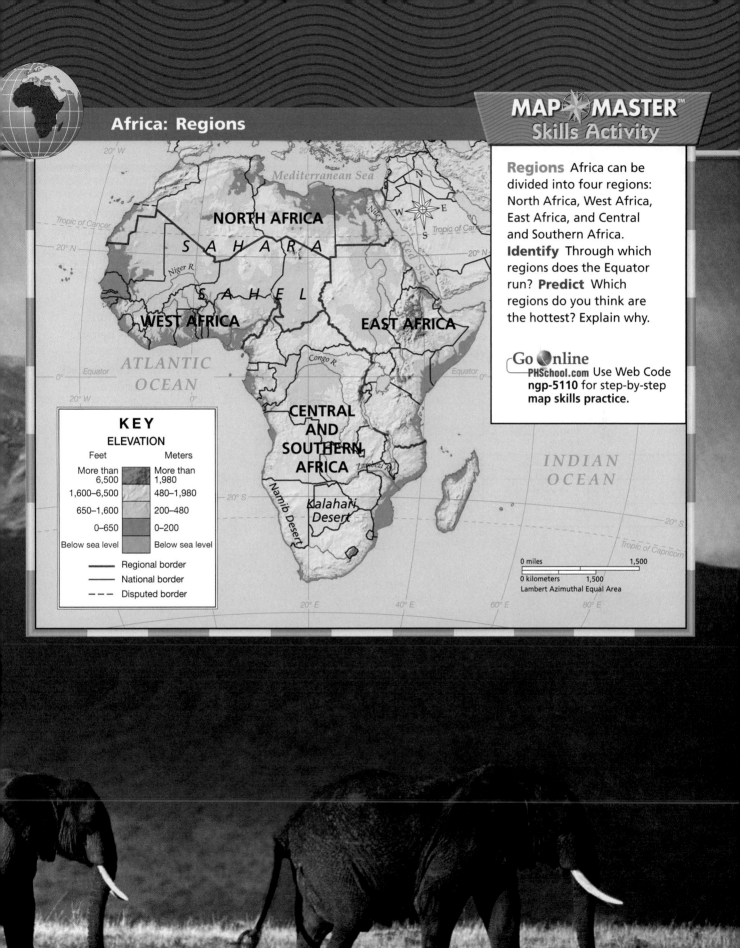

MAP MASTER™
Skills Activity

Regions Africa can be divided into four regions: North Africa, West Africa, East Africa, and Central and Southern Africa. **Identify** Through which regions does the Equator run? **Predict** Which regions do you think are the hottest? Explain why.

Go Online
PHSchool.com Use Web Code **ngp-5110** for step-by-step **map skills practice.**

NORTH AFRICA

SAHARA

SAHEL

WEST AFRICA

EAST AFRICA

CENTRAL AND SOUTHERN AFRICA

Mediterranean Sea

Nile R.

Red Sea

Niger R.

Congo R.

Zambezi R.

Namib Desert

Kalahari Desert

ATLANTIC OCEAN

INDIAN OCEAN

Tropic of Cancer

Tropic of Cancer

Equator

Equator

Tropic of Capricorn

20° W

20° N

0°

20° S

20° W

0°

20° E

40° E

60° E

80° E

KEY
ELEVATION

Feet		Meters
More than 6,500		More than 1,980
1,600–6,500		480–1,980
650–1,600		200–480
0–650		0–200
Below sea level		Below sea level

—— Regional border
—— National border
- - - Disputed border

0 miles 1,500
0 kilometers 1,500
Lambert Azimuthal Equal Area

Prepare to Read

Objectives

In this section you will
1. Learn about Africa's four regions and its major landforms.
2. Find out about Africa's major rivers.

Taking Notes

As you read, look for details about the land and waterways of the four regions of Africa. Copy the table below, and use it to record your findings.

Region of Africa	Physical Features
North	• Land: • Water:

Target Reading Skill

Reread Rereading is a strategy that can help you clarify words and ideas in the text. If you do not understand a certain passage, reread it to look for connections among the words and sentences.

In the following example, you may not know what *level* means. "Much of Africa is made up of raised, mostly level areas of land. Not all of Africa is level, however. Each of Africa's four regions has mountains." If you reread, you will see that level land is land without mountains.

Key Terms

• **plateau** (pla TOH) *n.* a large, level area that rises above the surrounding land; has at least one side with a steep slope
• **elevation** (el uh VAY shun) *n.* the height of land above or below sea level
• **rift** (rift) *n.* a deep crack in Earth's surface
• **tributary** (TRIB yoo tehr ee) *n.* a river or stream that flows into a larger river
• **fertile** (FUR tul) *adj.* rich in the substances plants need to grow well

Dinosaurs like this allosaurus once lived in Africa.

Scientists believe that more than 200 million years ago, dinosaurs were able to walk from Africa to South America. They could do that because Africa and South America were connected then. Turn to page 220 of the Atlas. Find Africa on the map titled The World: Physical. As you can see, it would be impossible to walk from Africa to South America today.

How did Africa and South America become separated? At least 65 million years ago, forces on our planet's surface caused South America and Africa to move apart, forming the southern part of the Atlantic Ocean. In the process, Africa became the second-largest continent on Earth. To learn more about this vast continent, first examine the geography of Africa's regions.

Africa's Regions and Landforms

Africa includes more than 50 countries. This large continent can be divided into four regions: North Africa, West Africa, East Africa, and Central and Southern Africa. Each region contains several different climates and landforms. Turn to the map on page 9 to see the physical features of the four regions.

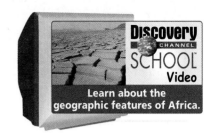

Discovery CHANNEL **SCHOOL** Video
Learn about the geographic features of Africa.

The Four Regions   The region of North Africa is marked in places by rocky mountains. It is also home to seemingly endless stretches of the world's largest desert, the Sahara (suh HA ruh). West Africa, the continent's most populated region, consists mostly of grassland. The soil in the grassland is good for farming. The region of East Africa has many mountains and a few **plateaus,** which are large, raised areas of mostly level land. Grasslands and hills are also found there. Much of Central and Southern Africa is flat or rolling grassland. The region also has thick rain forests, mountains, and swamps. The Namib (NAH mib) Desert and the Kalahari (kah luh HAH ree) Desert are in Southern Africa.

The Plateau Continent   Africa is often called the plateau continent because much of the continent is made up of raised, mostly level areas of land that drop off sharply near the sea. Much of this land has a high **elevation,** or height above or below sea level.

Mountains   Not all of Africa is level, however. All of Africa's four regions have mountains. The highest are in East Africa. Mount Kilimanjaro in Tanzania is Africa's tallest mountain. It rises to a height of 19,341 feet (5,895 meters).

Rising Up From Flat Land
The Kassala Mountains in the East African country of Sudan rise up from flat land that the people farm. **Analyze Images** *Do these mountains prevent people from farming the land?*

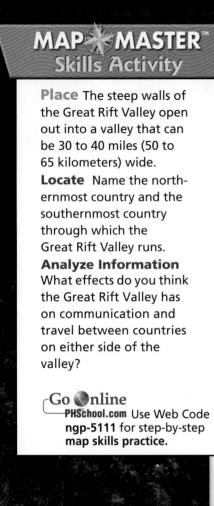

Place The steep walls of the Great Rift Valley open out into a valley that can be 30 to 40 miles (50 to 65 kilometers) wide.

Locate Name the northernmost country and the southernmost country through which the Great Rift Valley runs.

Analyze Information What effects do you think the Great Rift Valley has on communication and travel between countries on either side of the valley?

Go Online
PHSchool.com Use Web Code **ngp-5111** for step-by-step map skills practice.

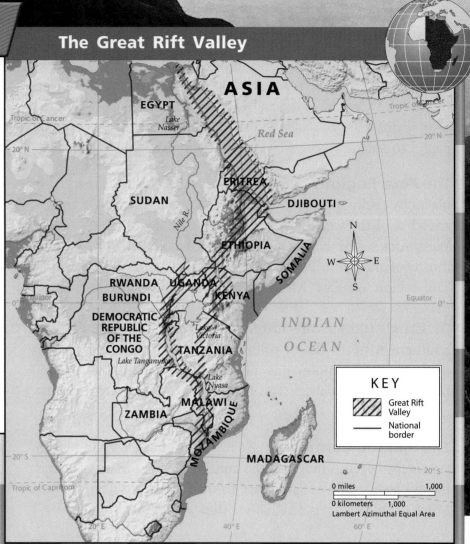

KEY

Great Rift Valley

National border

0 miles 1,000
0 kilometers 1,000
Lambert Azimuthal Equal Area

Coastal Plains Edge the Continent There is a strip of coastal plain that runs along much of Africa's coast. This land is dry and sandy in some places and marshy and moist in other places. Turn to the political map of Africa on page 3 of the Regional Overview. Find the West African country of Ghana (GAH nuh). The western edge of the coastal strip in Ghana is only about 5 miles (8 kilometers) wide. There, the coastal strip ends in a long, steep slope that rises to a plateau.

The Great Rift Valley Mount Kilimanjaro, Africa's highest peak, is located in East Africa on the edge of the Great Rift Valley. This valley was formed millions of years ago, when the continents pulled apart and left a **rift,** or deep trench. The rift that cuts through East Africa is 4,000 miles (6,400 kilometers) long. Most of Africa's major lakes are located in or near the Great Rift Valley.

✓ **Reading Check** Why is Africa called the plateau continent?

The Great Rift Valley

Africa's Rivers

Four large rivers carry water from the mountains of Africa's plateaus to the sea. They are the Nile (nyl), the Congo (KAHNG goh), the Zambezi (zam BEE zee), and the Niger (NY jur). Turn to page 4 and find these rivers on the physical map of Africa. Sections of these four rivers may be used for travel. But the rivers are broken in places by large waterfalls or steep rapids. These obstacles make it impossible for ships to sail the whole way between Africa's interior and the sea.

The Nile River The Nile is the longest river in the world. Its length, more than 4,000 miles (6,400 kilometers), is almost twice the length of the Mississippi River. The White Nile in Sudan and the Blue Nile in the highlands of Ethiopia are tributaries of the Nile. **Tributaries** are rivers and streams that flow into a larger river. After the White Nile and Blue Nile combine to form the Nile, the river flows north into the Mediterranean Sea.

Target Skill

Reread
Reread to clarify what *Africa's interior* means. When you read the paragraph at the left again, look for connections to other words.

Farming on the Banks
Farmers planted the crops shown above near the banks of the Nile River. **Summarize** *What are the benefits of farming near a river?*

Farming Along the Nile   People have farmed the land surrounding the Nile for thousands of years. At one time, the Nile flooded its banks regularly. Farmers planted their crops to match the flood cycle of the river. The floods provided water for the crops and left behind a layer of silt, tiny bits of rock and dirt carried downstream by the river. Silt helps make soil **fertile,** or rich in the substances that plants need to grow well.

In the 1960s, Egypt's government built the Aswan High Dam to control the flooding of the Nile. As the water backed up behind the dam, Lake Nasser was created. Waters from the lake are channeled to water crops that grow in the desert. Water rushing through the dam produces electricity. Since the dam was built, the Nile no longer floods the land.

The Congo River   The Congo River flows through the rain forests of the Central African countries of the Congo and the Democratic Republic of the Congo. At 2,900 miles (4,677 kilometers), the Congo River is Africa's second-longest river. It is fed by hundreds of tributaries. Many farmers in this region grow yams and cassava (kuh SAH vuh), a starchy plant that is a bit like a potato. They also catch many different types of fish in the Congo River.

The Niger River   The third-longest river in Africa, the Niger, begins its journey in Guinea (GIH nee). For 2,600 miles (4,180 kilometers), the river flows north and then bends south. It provides water for farms in the river valley. Many people make their living fishing in the river.

The Zambezi River   Africa's fourth-longest river, the Zambezi, is in Southern Africa. It runs through or forms the border of six countries: Angola (ang GOH luh), Zambia (ZAM bee uh), Namibia (nuh MIB ee uh), Botswana (baht SWAH nuh), Zimbabwe (zim BAHB way), and Mozambique (moh zum BEEK). The river is 2,200 miles (3,540 kilometers) long, but boats can travel only on about 460 miles (740 kilometers) of it because of its waterfalls and rapids.

People have used the Zambezi's strong current to produce electricity. About halfway to its outlet in the Indian Ocean, the Zambezi plunges into a canyon, creating the spectacular waterfall known as Victoria Falls. Tourists from around the world visit these falls. People can sometimes see the mist and spray of Victoria Falls from as far away as 40 miles (65 kilometers).

✓ **Reading Check**   What effect has the Aswan High Dam had on Egypt and on the waters of the Nile?

Victoria Falls is located on the border between Zambia and Zimbabwe.

Section 1 Assessment

Key Terms
Review the key terms at the beginning of this section. Use each term in a sentence that explains its meaning.

Target Reading Skill
Name a word or an idea that you were able to clarify on your own by rereading. Explain it in your own words.

Comprehension and Critical Thinking
1. (a) **Identify** Name the four regions of Africa.

(b) **Compare** What physical features do all of the regions have in common?
(c) **Draw Conclusions** Why might West Africa be the continent's most populated region?
2. (a) **Describe** Describe the course traveled by each of Africa's major rivers.
(b) **Identify Effects** How do Africa's four major rivers affect the lives of its people?
(c) **Draw Inferences** How did farming on the Nile change after the Aswan High Dam was built?

Writing Activity
List several landforms and rivers in Africa that you would like to visit. Explain why you would like to visit them and what you would do on your trip.

Writing Tip Use vivid details to describe your trip. These will help support your explanation of the reasons you chose the landforms you did.

Climate and Vegetation

Prepare to Read

Objectives

In this section you will

1. Discover the factors that influence Africa's climate.
2. Learn the characteristics of each of Africa's vegetation regions.
3. Find out how climate can affect the health of people in Africa.

Taking Notes

Copy the outline below. As you read, find details about Africa's climate and vegetation, and record them in your outline.

```
I. Africa's climate factors
   A. Distance from the Equator
      1.
      2.
   B.
II. Vegetation regions
```

Target Reading Skill

Paraphrase Paraphrasing can help you understand what you read. You paraphrase by restating what you have read in your own words.

For example, you could paraphrase the first paragraph on page 20 this way: "Africa has different kinds of vegetation in different parts of the continent. It has rain forests, savannas, and deserts."

As you read this section, paraphrase, or restate, the information following each red or blue heading.

Key Terms

- **irrigate** (IHR uh gayt) *v.* to supply with water through a ditch, pipe, channel, or sprinkler
- **drought** (drowt) *n.* a long period of little or no rain
- **oasis** (oh AY sis) *n.* a fertile place in a desert where there is water and vegetation
- **savanna** (suh VAN uh) *n.* a region of tall grasses with scattered trees
- **nomad** (NOH mad) *n.* a person who has no permanent, settled home and who instead moves from place to place

A home in a forest region of Uganda

If you were to travel throughout Africa, you would experience many different climates. Deserts would feel hot and dry. The highlands would feel cool and moist. In some places close to the Equator, hot weather and rainfall would occur throughout the year.

Africa's vegetation is as diverse as its climate. Forest regions are filled with trees and a great variety of plant life. Grasslands are dotted with low trees and scrub bushes. Low mountain areas support plant life, while the highest mountains are covered with snow and ice. A region's climate has a great influence on its vegetation. But what influences climate?

What Influences Climate?

Although people sometimes think of Africa as a hot place, not all parts of it are hot. That is because there are several geographic factors that influence climate. Some key factors are distance from the Equator and elevation. Nearness to large bodies of water and major landforms also affects climate.

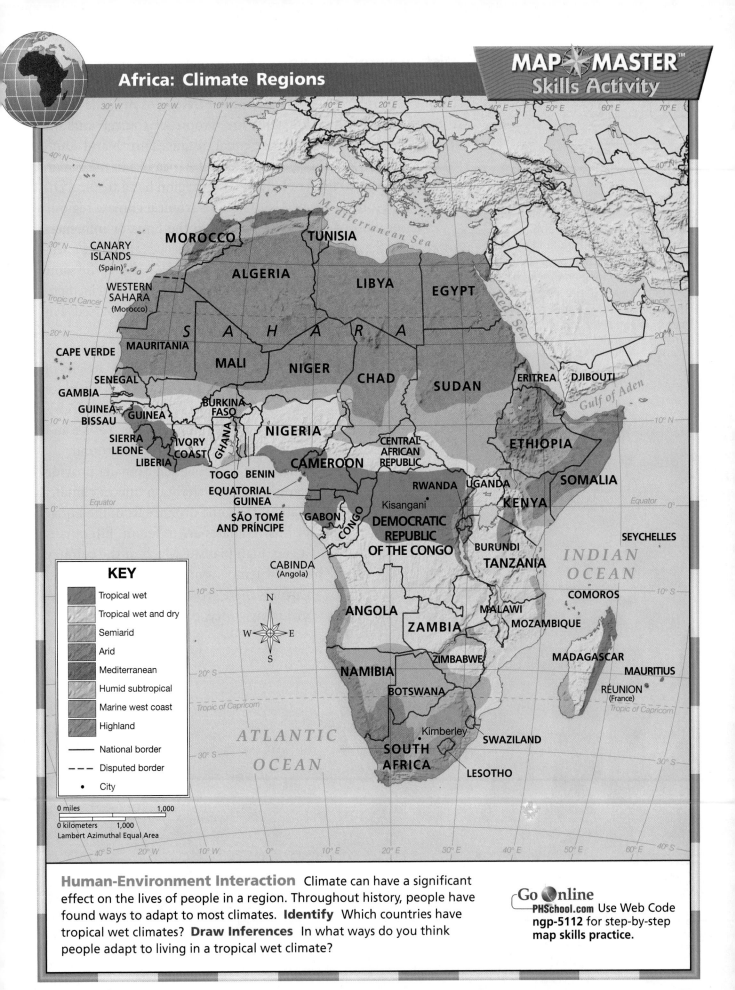

MAP MASTER™
Skills Activity

KEY

Tropical wet
Tropical wet and dry
Semiarid
Arid
Mediterranean
Humid subtropical
Marine west coast
Highland

— National border
– – – Disputed border
• City

0 miles 1,000
0 kilometers 1,000
Lambert Azimuthal Equal Area

Human-Environment Interaction Climate can have a significant effect on the lives of people in a region. Throughout history, people have found ways to adapt to most climates. **Identify** Which countries have tropical wet climates? **Draw Inferences** In what ways do you think people adapt to living in a tropical wet climate?

Go Online
PHSchool.com Use Web Code ngp-5112 for step-by-step map skills practice.

Distance From the Equator Look at the map on page 17 titled Africa: Climate Regions. Notice that the Equator runs through the midsection of the continent. Regions near the Equator are usually hot. Now find the Tropic of Cancer and the Tropic of Capricorn, which are equal distances north and south of the Equator. As you can see, much of Africa lies in the region between these two lines of latitude. This region has a tropical climate. Therefore, much of Africa lies in a tropical climate region.

The location of a place in relation to the Equator influences more than the place's climate—it also influences the place's seasons. North of the Equator, winter and summer occur at the same time as they do in the United States and the rest of the Northern Hemisphere. South of the Equator, the seasons are reversed. For example, July in South Africa is the middle of winter.

The Role of Elevation Recall that elevation is the height of land above sea level. The higher the elevation, the cooler a place tends to be. For example, Mount Kilimanjaro, Africa's highest peak, is located close to the Equator. Yet ice and snow blanket the peak of Kilimanjaro year-round.

The countries of Ethiopia and Somalia provide another example of how elevation affects climate. They are about the same distance from the Equator, yet their climates are different. Ethiopia is on a very high plateau. Much of the country has mild temperatures and abundant rain. Farmers there grow a wide range of crops, including coffee, dates, and cereals.

Home to Many Animals
The open grasslands of Tanzania's Tarangire National Park are home to many thousands of large animals. Elephants may be seen in herds of 500 or more at a time. **Infer** *Given that animals thrive in this environment, do you think it has a mild or a harsh climate?*

Because Ethiopia usually gets plenty of rain, many farmers there do not irrigate their crops. To **irrigate** is to supply with water through a ditch, pipe, channel, or sprinkler. Even so, the country sometimes goes through a **drought** (drowt), or a long period of little or no rain. With little water, crops and livestock are harder to raise, and food becomes scarce. Ethiopia has suffered severe droughts several times since the 1980s.

Somalia is at a much lower elevation than Ethiopia is. The Somalian climate is hot and dry. Farming is possible only near a river or in or near an oasis, where crops can be irrigated. An **oasis** is a fertile place in a desert, with water and vegetation. Fresh underground water can support life in a region that gets little rain.

Unpredictable Rainfall Rainfall varies greatly from one region of Africa to another. Along parts of the west coast, winds carry moisture from the warm ocean over the land. Rainfall there averages more than 100 inches (250 centimeters) per year. Compare that with your own height. Forty inches (100 centimeters) of rain might fall during June alone. But in parts of the Sahara in the north and the Namib Desert in the south, rain may not fall at all for several years in a row.

Farmers who live in dry regions can never be sure whether there will be enough rain for their crops. Some farmers choose to plant a variety of crops, each needing a different amount of rainfall. These farmers hope they will have at least one successful crop.

✓ **Reading Check** How does elevation affect the climate of regions in Africa?

Graph Skills

The city of Kimberley is located in a desert region, while the city of Kisangani is located in a tropical region. **Identify** Which city has higher temperatures throughout the year? Which city gets more total rainfall in a year? **Synthesize Information** How does location help explain the differences in temperature and in rainfall?

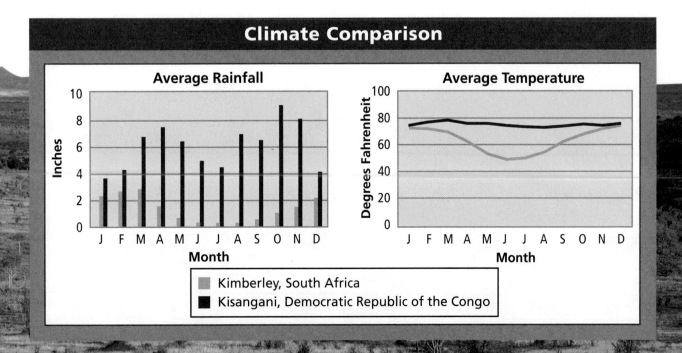

Climate Comparison

Kimberley, South Africa
Kisangani, Democratic Republic of the Congo

Vegetation Regions of Africa

Africa's vegetation varies across the land. Near the Equator, there are rain forests. North and south of the rain forests lie **savanna, a region of tall grasses with scattered trees.** Beyond the savanna, many parts of northern Africa, as well as the southwestern coast of the continent, are covered in desert.

Tropical Rain Forests Tropical rain forests are regions where rain falls often throughout the year. Rain forests exist in parts of West and Central Africa, covering close to 20 percent of the continent. Rain forests are well known for supporting a great number and variety of life forms. Forest moisture provides a rich environment of trees and plants that supports animals such as gorillas and chimpanzees.

People in rain forest regions live in towns, cities, or on farms built on cleared land. Cacao (kuh KAY oh), the plant from which chocolate is made, and cassava grow well in these regions. People also fish, hunt, and harvest timber in the rain forests. However, logging threatens these forests and the many species that live in them.

Tropical Savannas The most common vegetation in Africa is tropical savanna. Tall grasses, thorny bushes, and scattered trees grow in the savanna region. It is also home to large herd animals such as lions, elephants, and zebras. Tropical savannas cover more of Africa than any other type of vegetation.

The savanna has two seasons: dry and wet. During the dry season, farming is impossible. Trees lose their leaves and rivers run dry. Farmers use this time to trade, build houses, and visit friends. In the wet season, the land turns green and farmers plant crops.

World's Largest Desert
The Sahara is famous for sand dunes like the ones shown below. However, most of the Sahara is rock plateau or gravel. Mountains exist there as well.
Apply Information *Do you think the Sahara is an easy place for people and animals to live?*

Deserts in Africa Beyond the savanna lie the deserts. The immense Sahara extends across most of North Africa. This desert covers almost as much land as the entire United States. A journalist traveling in the Sahara described what she saw:

> **❝**[H]orizon-to-horizon vistas [views] of sand in a palette of colors, luxurious arches of palm trees swaying in the wind . . . heaving mountains of rough stone unbroken by the slightest sign of vegetation, vast expanses of sand obscured [hidden] by a veil of dust.**❞**
>
> —*Christine Negroni,* The New York Times

The southern edge of the Sahara meets the savanna in a region called the Sahel (sah HEL), which is the Arabic word for "shore" or "border." The Sahel is very hot and dry. Each year it receives only 4 to 8 inches (10 to 20 centimeters) of rain. Small shrubs, grass, and some trees grow there.

The Namib and Kalahari deserts reach across Namibia and Botswana in Southern Africa. Large parts of the Kalahari are covered in scrub and small bushes, while the smaller Namib has more sand dunes.

The fennec fox, the world's smallest fox, lives in the Sahara.

The Sahara and the Sahel

MAP★MASTER™ Skills Activity

Regions Unlike the Sahara, the Sahel does receive some rain. However, rain falls in the Sahel only during the summer months. **Locate** In what direction does the Sahel lie in relation to the Sahara? **Analyze Information** How does this location help explain why the Sahel gets more rain than the Sahara does?

KEY
- Sahara
- Sahel

ATLANTIC OCEAN
Mediterranean Sea
Tropic of Cancer
Tropic of Cancer
Red Sea
Equator
Equator

0 miles 1,000
0 kilometers 1,000
Lambert Azimuthal Equal Area

20° W
40° N
40° N
20° N
20° N
0°
0°
20° E
40° E

Go Online
PHSchool.com Use Web Code **ngp-5122** for step-by-step map skills practice.

A desert nomad traveling through the Sahara with his camel

Desert Living Few people live in Africa's deserts. Most of those who do are **nomads,** or people who have no permanent, settled home. Nomads move around to various places, often following the same route each year, to make their living. Most nomads are herders who also take part in trade. They travel to places where they know they can find water and food for their herds of goats, camels, or sheep.

Some nomadic herders live mainly in Africa's mountainous areas. In spring, they leave their winter grazing grounds in the foothills and head up into the mountains. Other nomadic herders live mainly in the flat desert areas. During the dry season, they set up tents near oases (oh AY seez). When the rainy season comes, they move their goats and camels to pastures that are better for grazing.

Desert nomads have herded camels for hundreds of years because the animals are well suited to desert life. They are large, strong animals that can transport goods on their backs over long distances. In addition, when a camel eats, it stores fat in the hump on its back. If no food or water is available, a camel can survive for several days by using the stored fat as food.

✓ **Reading Check** **What kinds of vegetation are found in Africa's savanna regions?**

Climate and Health

The climate people live in can affect their health. Throughout Africa, there are regions that present health risks to livestock and people. In rain forest regions, the moist environment is home to many disease-carrying insects. Even in the drier grasslands, disease and illness take their toll.

Sleeping Sickness Nearly one fifth of Africa is home to the tsetse (TSET see) fly, a pest that makes raising cattle almost impossible. A tsetse bite can kill cattle and can cause a disease called sleeping sickness in humans. African researchers, together with cattle herders, have worked to find ways to control the spread of the tsetse fly. Cattle herders in Kenya are setting traps for flies. Herders in the country of Uganda catch flies by sewing into tents netting that contains poison.

Malaria Another disease, malaria (muh LEHR ee uh), is spread to humans by the bite of an infected mosquito. Mosquitoes thrive in warm, moist climates and breed in swamps, ponds, and pools of standing water. These conditions make malaria a particular problem in parts of Africa south of the Sahara. Researchers continue to look for ways of fighting the spread of malaria. Protective clothing and insecticide can help prevent infection.

✓ **Reading Check** What is being done to control the spread of the tsetse fly?

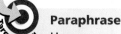
Paraphrase Use your own words to paraphrase the paragraph at the left. What would be a good way to restate *take their toll*? In your own words, you might say "disease and illness cause serious problems."

Section 2 Assessment

Key Terms
Review the key terms at the beginning of this section. Use each term in a sentence that explains its meaning.

Target Reading Skill
Read the paragraphs under Desert Living on page 22. Then, paraphrase the paragraphs in 25 words or fewer.

Comprehension and Critical Thinking
1. (a) Identify Name three factors that influence climate.

(b) Summarize Give an example of how one of these factors can influence the climate of an area.

2. (a) Name Identify the types of vegetation found in each of Africa's four regions.

(b) Identify Effects How do climate and vegetation affect the ways Africans make a living?

3. (a) Recall What health risks do people and animals in different climate regions of Africa face?

(b) Draw Conclusions In which of Africa's climate regions do you think you would be least likely to contract malaria?

Writing Activity
Choose a region of Africa that you would like to live in or visit. Write a short essay about the climate and vegetation. Include several reasons why the region is of interest to you.

For: An activity on vegetation in Africa
Visit: PHSchool.com
Web Code: ngd-5102

Africa makes up about one fifth of all the land on Earth. It is a plateau continent with sloping coastal plains, a broad central basin, towering mountains, and a deep rift, or crack, in Earth's surface. If you could drive across the widest stretch of Africa, going 65 miles (105 kilometers) per hour and not stopping for gas or sleep, the trip would take about three full days.

An effective way to learn about Africa's landforms is by looking at a cross-sectional diagram. A cross section is what you would see if you sliced through the continent from its highest point to its lowest point and looked at it from the side.

NC SS.3.02 Interpret graphs and charts

Learn the Skill

To interpret information in any type of diagram, including a cross-sectional diagram, follow the steps below.

1 **Study the diagram.** Notice the various parts of the diagram. What can you learn from the title? What details are shown?

2 **Read the labels.** Notice the lines that lead from each label to the cross section. Make sure you understand what all the labels refer to.

3 **Summarize the information in the diagram.** Describe what you learned from studying the diagram and its labels.

Cross-Sectional Diagram of Africa South of the Sahara

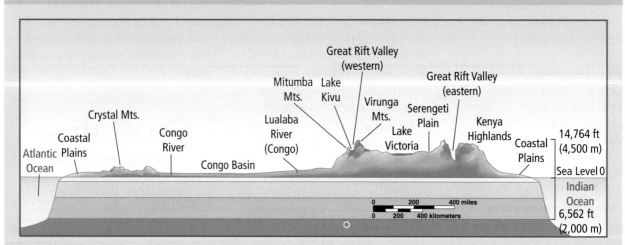

Practice the Skill

Study the cross section of Africa on page 24. Use the steps below to interpret the diagram and learn about Africa's landforms.

1 Look at the diagram. What information can you learn from the title? What kinds of landforms are shown?

2 Examine the labels. Name the mountain ranges and bodies of water shown in the diagram. Identify the elevation of at least three features in the diagram.

3 Write a sentence or two describing the ways in which the elevation of Africa changes as you travel from the Atlantic Ocean to the Indian Ocean.

Apply the Skill

Study the diagram of Earth's movements on pages M2–M3 of the MapMaster Skills Handbook. In a sentence or two, summarize the information given in the diagram.

The Virunga Mountains of East Africa

Resources and Land Use

Prepare to Read

Objectives

In this section you will
1. Discover the ways in which Africans make use of their agricultural resources.
2. Learn about the mineral and energy resources found in Africa.
3. Find out what African countries are doing to improve their economic health.

Taking Notes

As you read, look for details about Africa's natural resources. Copy the chart below, and use it to record your findings.

```
              Land Use and Economy
    ┌──────────────┬──────────────┬──────────────┐
    │ Agriculture  │   Minerals   │   Economic   │
    │              │  and Energy  │    Health    │
    │    •         │      •       │      •       │
    │    •         │      •       │      •       │
    └──────────────┴──────────────┴──────────────┘
```

Target Reading Skill

Summarize When you summarize, you review what you have read so far. Then you state the main points in the correct order. Summarizing what you read is a good technique to help you comprehend and study. As you read, pause occasionally to summarize what you have read.

Key Terms

- **subsistence farming** (sub SIS tuns FAHR ming) *n.* raising just enough crops to support one's family
- **cash crop** (kash krahp) *n.* a crop that is raised for sale
- **economy** (ih KAHN uh mee) *n.* a system for producing, distributing, consuming, and owning goods and services
- **diversify** (duh VUR suh fy) *v.* to add variety to; to expand a country's economy by increasing the variety of goods produced

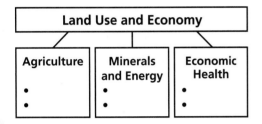

Cacao beans (inset photo) grow on trees as shown below.

"Here, in this load, I bear the seeds of a wonderful tree which, if cultivated in this land, will bless its sons everlastingly with wealth, and people far and near with health. These are the seeds of the cacao tree which I have brought with me from across the sea. . . . Would you, therefore, be kind enough to grant me a mere acre of land in this neighborhood to try my luck, and yours, and that of this country as a whole?"

—from the play Cocoa Comes to Mampong
by Michael Francis Dei-Anang

In the excerpt above, the character Tete Quarshie (TEH tay KWAWR shee) asks for land on which to plant cacao trees in Ghana. These trees, from which cocoa and chocolate are made, originally grew only in Central and South America. As Americans, Europeans, and Africans began to trade with one another, they found that cacao trees could grow in West Africa. In the play, the people grant Tete Quarshie the land, who then raises the first crop of cacao beans in Ghana. Cacao is now one of Africa's many agricultural resources.

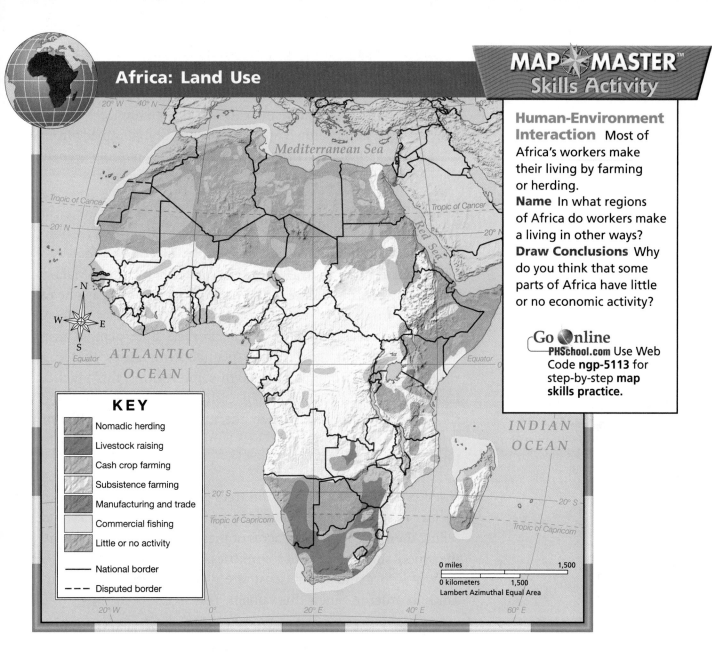

MAP★MASTER™
Skills Activity

Human-Environment Interaction Most of Africa's workers make their living by farming or herding.
Name In what regions of Africa do workers make a living in other ways?
Draw Conclusions Why do you think that some parts of Africa have little or no economic activity?

Go Online
PHSchool.com Use Web Code **ngp-5113** for step-by-step **map skills practice.**

KEY

- Nomadic herding
- Livestock raising
- Cash crop farming
- Subsistence farming
- Manufacturing and trade
- Commercial fishing
- Little or no activity

—— National border
– – – Disputed border

Mediterranean Sea
Tropic of Cancer
Red Sea
ATLANTIC OCEAN
Equator
INDIAN OCEAN
Tropic of Capricorn

0 miles 1,500
0 kilometers 1,500
Lambert Azimuthal Equal Area

Agricultural Resources

Most Africans are farmers. Some of these farmers live in areas with fertile soil and much rain. But most live on land that is difficult to farm because of poor soil or too little rain. Others lack enough land or tools to make a good living.

Farming to Live On the map above, you can see how much of Africa's land is used for **subsistence farming,** or raising just enough crops to support one's family. Subsistence farmers may sell or trade a few crops for other items they need.

In North African countries such as Morocco, subsistence farmers raise barley and wheat. They also irrigate fields to grow fruits and vegetables. Farms at Saharan oases in Egypt produce dates and small crops of barley and wheat.

In countries with dry tropical savanna, such as Burkina Faso (bur KEE nuh FAH soh) and Niger, subsistence farmers grow grains. In regions with more rainfall, farmers also grow vegetables, fruits, and root crops such as yams and cassava. Tapioca (tap ee OH kuh), which is used in the United States to make pudding, is made from cassava. In West Africa, corn and rice are important crops. People in many of Africa's cultures fish or raise goats or poultry.

Crops for Sale In all regions of Africa, farmers grow cash crops, or crops that are raised for sale. Farmers in Ivory Coast, Ghana, and Cameroon grow cash crops of coffee and cacao beans. Farmers in Kenya, Tanzania (tan zuh NEE uh), Malawi (MAH lah wee), Zimbabwe, and Mozambique grow tea as one of their cash crops.

In recent years, more and more farmers have planted cash crops. As a result, less land is planted with crops that can completely meet a family's needs. In some regions, this practice has led to food shortages when cash crops have failed. Food shortages can also occur when the market prices of coffee or other cash crops fall steeply. Then families receive less money to buy the things they need.

Harvesting Trees Hardwood trees grow in all four regions of Africa. People can earn money by cutting down the trees and selling them. Thousands of acres of these trees have been cut and the wood shipped to other countries. A number of countries, such as Kenya and Ivory Coast, are planting trees by the thousands in order to renew this valuable resource.

✓ **Reading Check** What are some of the crops grown in Africa, and where are they grown?

Summarize
To summarize the paragraph at the right, first state the main points. An important point is that more African farmers have started to plant cash crops. Which point follows that one?

Replanting the Forest
Thousands of Kenyan women have responded to the cutting down of trees in their country. Like the women shown here, they have prepared millions of young trees for local families to plant. **Predict** *How easy do you think it will be for people in Kenya to replace all the cut trees?*

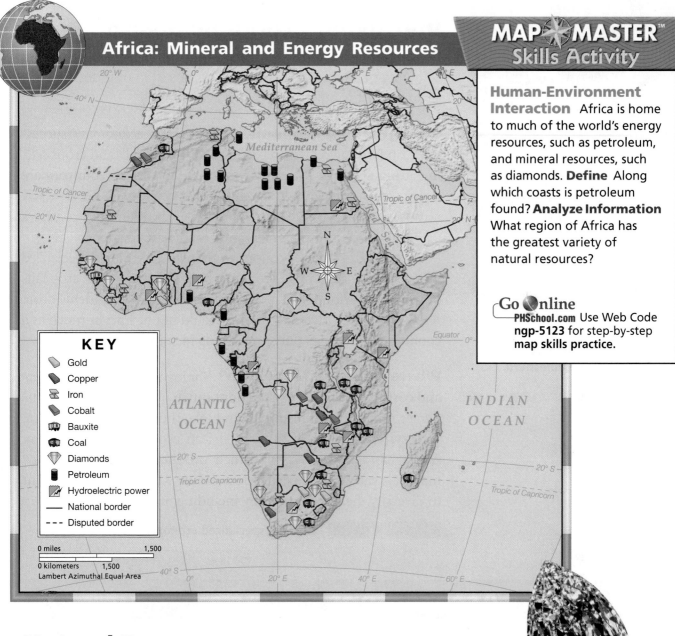

Africa: Mineral and Energy Resources

MAP MASTER™
Skills Activity

Human-Environment Interaction Africa is home to much of the world's energy resources, such as petroleum, and mineral resources, such as diamonds. **Define** Along which coasts is petroleum found? **Analyze Information** What region of Africa has the greatest variety of natural resources?

Go Online
PHSchool.com Use Web Code **ngp-5123** for step-by-step map skills practice.

KEY

- Gold
- Copper
- Iron
- Cobalt
- Bauxite
- Coal
- Diamonds
- Petroleum
- Hydroelectric power
- — National border
- - - - Disputed border

0 miles   1,500
0 kilometers   1,500
Lambert Azimuthal Equal Area

Mediterranean Sea

Tropic of Cancer

Red Sea

Tropic of Cancer

Equator

ATLANTIC OCEAN

INDIAN OCEAN

Tropic of Capricorn

Tropic of Capricorn

Natural Resources

Each African country has its own economy. An **economy** is a system for producing, distributing, consuming, and owning goods and services. You have read that farming is an important part of many African economies. The same is true of mining. Look at the map above. Notice how many countries conduct mining operations.

Parts of Africa are rich in mineral resources. Some African countries have large amounts of petroleum, which is used to make oil and gasoline. Major oil producers include Libya and Algeria in North Africa, and Nigeria, Cameroon, Gabon, and Angola along the west coast of Africa. Ghana is a leading exporter of gold. Other mineral resources from Africa include copper, silver, uranium, titanium, and diamonds.

Diamonds that have just been mined (bottom photo) are not nearly as dazzling as ones that have been cut (top photo).

✓ **Reading Check** How is petroleum used?

A man assembling electronic equipment in Johannesburg, South Africa

Improving Economic Health

As you have read, most of Africa's workers are farmers. When an economy of a nation is dependent on one kind of industry, such as farming, it is called a specialized economy.

Strengthening Economies In Africa, economic success relies on farming regions receiving enough rainfall, and crops selling at high enough prices. For that reason, African countries are trying to diversify (duh VUR suh fy) their economies. To **diversify means to add variety.** These countries are working to produce a variety of crops, raw materials, and manufactured goods.

In general, a diverse economy is more flexible than a specialized economy is. For example, suppose a country's major cash crop fails or world prices for one of its major mineral exports suddenly drop. A country with a diverse economy would not be hurt as much as a country that depends only on farming or mining.

Where Does the Money Go? Mining requires many workers and costly equipment. Throughout much of Africa, foreign companies mine African resources and take the profits out of Africa. This system does little to help African economies. In addition, Africa has few factories in which products from its own raw materials can be made. Therefore, many African countries want to diversify their economies by including manufacturing.

✓ **Reading Check** What is a specialized economy?

Section 3 Assessment

Key Terms
Review the key terms at the beginning of this section. Use each term in a sentence that explains its meaning.

Target Reading Skill
Reread the paragraphs under Improving Economic Health. Then write a summary of them. Include at least two main points.

Comprehension and Critical Thinking
1. (a) Recall What makes most land Africans live on hard to farm?

(b) Compare and Contrast Compare subsistence farming with farming to raise cash crops. How are they similar? How are they different?

2. (a) Identify What are some of the important natural resources found in Africa?

(b) Draw Conclusions What do you think happens to most of Africa's mineral resources after they are mined?

3. (a) Recall What kind of work is done by most Africans?

(b) Predict In what ways could African countries benefit from diversifying their economies?

Writing Activity
List some of Africa's natural resources that you and your family use. Which resource would you miss most if you did not have it? Write a paragraph explaining why.

For: An activity on natural resources in Africa
Visit: PHSchool.com
Web Code: ngd-5103

Review and Assessment

◆ Chapter Summary

Section 1: Land and Water

- Africa can be divided into four regions: North, West, East, and Central and Southern. Africa's major landforms include plateaus, mountains, coastal plains, and a rift valley.
- Africa's four major rivers are the Nile, the Congo, the Zambezi, and the Niger.

Section 2: Climate and Vegetation

- Distance from the Equator and elevation are both factors that influence climate.
- Africa's vegetation regions include tropical rain forests, tropical savannas, and deserts.
- Disease-carrying insects thrive in some of Africa's climate regions, threatening the health of the people who live there.

Section 3: Resources and Land Use

- Africa's agricultural resources are used for subsistence farming and cash crops.
- Natural resources, such as minerals, are an important part of African economies.
- African countries are working to improve their economic health by diversifying their specialized economies.

Taka Mountains, Sudan

◆ Key Terms

Choose the key term from the list that best completes each sentence.

1. _____ is the height of land above or below sea level.

2. A(n) _____ is a deep crack in the surface of Earth.

3. A(n) _____ flows into a river.

4. People who practice _____ raise just enough crops to support their families.

5. A(n) _____ is a region of tall grasses with scattered trees.

6. In areas that receive plenty of rain, many farmers do not need to _____ their crops.

7. A nomad traveling through the Sahara would probably visit a(n) _____ for water.

8. A(n) _____ is a system for producing, distributing, consuming, and owning goods and services.

9. To _____ is to add variety.

10. A period of little or no rainfall is a(n) _____.

Key Terms

plateau
elevation
drought
rift
fertile
tributary
irrigate
oasis
savanna
nomad
subsistence farming
cash crop
economy
diversify

Review and Assessment (continued)

◆ Comprehension and Critical Thinking

11. (a) Describe Describe the physical features of each of the major rivers in Africa.
(b) Identify Cause and Effect How did the regular flooding of the Nile in the past affect farmers in the Nile Valley? How did the building of the Aswan High Dam change life for farmers?

12. (a) Recall What do elevation and distance from the Equator have to do with climate?
(b) Explain Why are some parts of Africa cold even though they are near the Equator?
(c) Compare and Contrast Compare the climates of Ethiopia and Somalia. Explain why their climates are similar or different.

13. (a) Locate Where in Africa can you find tropical savannas? Tropical rain forests? Deserts?
(b) Describe What characterizes the climate and plant life of each vegetation region?
(c) Apply Information Choose one of these regions and describe how the people who live there adapt to their environment. Give examples.

14. (a) Name List three cash crops raised in Africa.
(b) Identify Causes Why is there little or no farming in much of North Africa and parts of Southern Africa?
(c) Summarize Why and in what ways are many African nations trying to strengthen and diversify their economies?

◆ Skills Practice

Interpreting Diagrams You have learned how to interpret diagrams in this chapter's Skills for Life activity. You have also learned how to summarize information found in diagrams.

Review the steps you followed to learn this skill. Then turn to the diagram of Earth's longitude on page M5 of the MapMaster Skills Handbook. Identify and summarize the main ideas in the diagram.

◆ Writing Activity: Math

Make a bar graph that shows the lengths of rivers in Africa. Include the four rivers mentioned in the chapter as well as at least three others that you research on your own. Then write a short paragraph comparing the lengths of the various rivers.

MAP ✦ MASTER™ Skills Activity

Place Location For each place listed, write the letter from the map that shows its location.

1. Nile River
2. Congo River
3. Sahara
4. Namib Desert
5. Zambezi River
6. Kalahari Desert
7. Niger River
8. Great Rift Valley

Go Online
PHSchool.com Use Web Code **ngp-5120** for an **interactive map.**

Africa

Standardized Test Prep

Test-Taking Tips

Some questions on standardized tests ask you to analyze parts of maps. Study the map key below. Then follow the tips to answer the sample question.

KEY

	Nomadic herding
	Livestock raising
	Commercial farming
	Subsistence farming
	Manufacturing and trade
	Little or no activity

TIP On a map key, the color column lines up with the data in the information column. To find the information you need, move from a given color to the data on the right.

Pick the letter that best answers the question.

On a land-use map, Angola is colored mostly yellow with a small amount of light green. Using the key at the left, you can determine that the people of Angola

A make a great deal of money.

B use the land mainly to support themselves.

C export many products.

D use their land in many different ways.

TIP Restate the question in your own words to make sure you understand it: *What conclusion can you draw from the map key about the people of Angola and their land?*

Think It Through Yellow on the map stands for subsistence farming. Light green stands for commercial farming. Subsistence farmers grow just enough food to feed and support their families. Since most of Angola is colored yellow, you can rule out A and D. Commercial farmers may raise their crops for export. However, since most of Angola is yellow, you can rule out C also. The correct answer is B.

Practice Questions

Use the tips above and other tips in this book to help you answer the following questions.

1. Most of North Africa is along the border of the

  A Mediterranean Sea.

  B Indian Ocean.

  C Atlantic Ocean.

  D Red Sea.

2. Areas that are higher in elevation

  A tend to be closer to the Equator.

  B tend to be cooler than places lower in elevation.

  C have very mild climates.

  D have little or no rainfall.

3. African economies

  A are based largely on manufacturing.

  B could benefit from increased diversification.

  C rely solely on exports.

  D are usually dependent on a wide variety of industries.

Study the map key below, and then answer the question that follows.

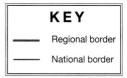

KEY

——	Regional border
——	National border

4. The boundaries of Egypt are marked by black and red lines. Using the key, you can conclude that

  A Egypt is part of two regions of Africa.

  B Egypt borders other nations of Africa but not other regions.

  C Egypt borders other regions of Africa but not other nations.

  D Egypt borders other regions and nations.

Go Online PHSchool.com

Use Web Code **nga-5100** for **Chapter 1 self-test.**

Chapter 2 Africa: Shaped by Its History

Chapter Preview

 Standard Course of Study

7.2.01 Influence of physical features and climate on cultures

7.3.03 Examine the development and use of tools and technologies

7.4.01 Describe patterns of and motivations for migrations

7.4.02 Commodities of trade and their significance for cultures and regions

7.6.01 Connection between economic development and standard of living

7.7.01 Relationship between historical events and cultures

7.7.02 Cause and effects of historical events

7.8.02 Impact of key groups on historical and contemporary societies

Sections

1. **African Beginnings**
   7.3.03, 7.4.01
2. **Kingdoms, City-States, and Empires**
   7.4.02, 7.8.02
3. **European Conquest of Africa**
   7.4.02, 7.7.01
4. **Kingdoms, City-States, and Empires**
   7.7.01, 7.7.02
5. **Issues for Africa Today**
   7.2.01, 7.6.01

 Target Reading Skill

Reading Process In this chapter you will focus on processes that help you understand and remember what you read. Setting a purpose, predicting, asking questions, and using prior knowledge are all processes that will help you learn as you read.

▶ This ancient Egyptian mural, painted on an interior wall of a tomb, is more than 3,000 years old.

MAP★MASTER
Skills Activity

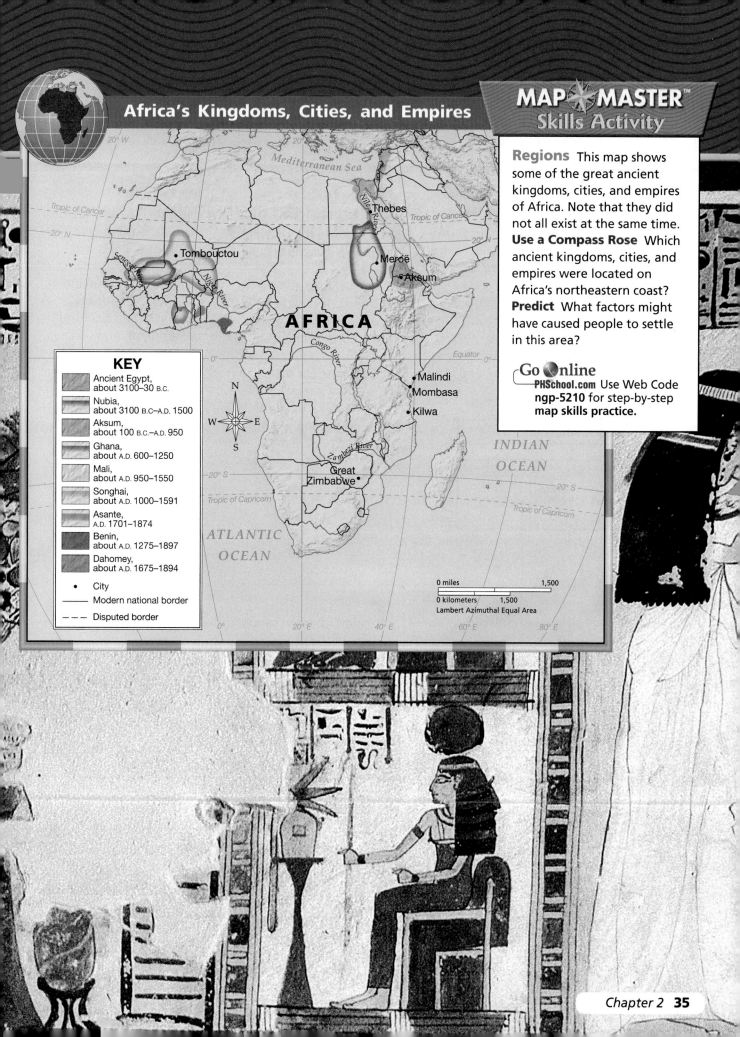

Regions This map shows some of the great ancient kingdoms, cities, and empires of Africa. Note that they did not all exist at the same time. **Use a Compass Rose** Which ancient kingdoms, cities, and empires were located on Africa's northeastern coast? **Predict** What factors might have caused people to settle in this area?

Go Online
PHSchool.com Use Web Code **ngp-5210** for step-by-step map skills practice.

KEY

- Ancient Egypt, about 3100–30 B.C.
- Nubia, about 3100 B.C.–A.D. 1500
- Aksum, about 100 B.C.–A.D. 950
- Ghana, about A.D. 600–1250
- Mali, about A.D. 950–1550
- Songhai, about A.D. 1000–1591
- Asante, A.D. 1701–1874
- Benin, about A.D. 1275–1897
- Dahomey, about A.D. 1675–1894
- • City
- — Modern national border
- - - - Disputed border

Mediterranean Sea

Thebes
Meroë
Aksum

AFRICA

Tombouctou

Senegal River
Niger River
Congo River

Equator

Malindi
Mombasa
Kilwa

Zambezi River

Great Zimbabwe

INDIAN OCEAN

ATLANTIC OCEAN

Tropic of Cancer
Tropic of Capricorn

0 miles 1,500
0 kilometers 1,500
Lambert Azimuthal Equal Area

Section 1

African Beginnings

Prepare to Read

Objectives

In this section you will
1. Examine the ways in which the survival skills of early Africans changed over time.
2. Find out about early civilizations that arose along the Nile River.
3. Learn about the Bantu migrations.

Taking Notes

As you read, look for details about Africa's first people. Copy the chart below, and use it to record your findings.

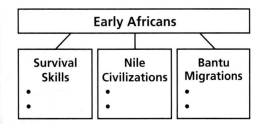

```
                Early Africans
    ┌──────────────┬──────────────┬──────────────┐
    │   Survival   │     Nile     │    Bantu     │
    │    Skills    │ Civilizations│  Migrations  │
    │     •        │      •       │      •       │
    │     •        │      •       │      •       │
    └──────────────┴──────────────┴──────────────┘
```

Target Reading Skill

Set a Purpose for Reading When you set a purpose for reading, you give yourself a focus. Before you read this section, look at the headings and illustrations to see what the section is about. Then set a purpose for reading this section. Your purpose might be to learn about the people who lived in Africa long ago. Finally, read to meet your purpose.

Key Terms

- **domesticate** (duh MES tih kayt) v. to adapt wild plants or animals and breed them for human use
- **civilization** (sih vuh luh ZAY shun) n. a society that has cities, a central government, and social classes and that usually has writing, art, and architecture
- **migrate** (MY grayt) v. to move from one place to settle in another
- **ethnic group** (ETH nik groop) n. a group of people who share the same ancestors, culture, language, or religion

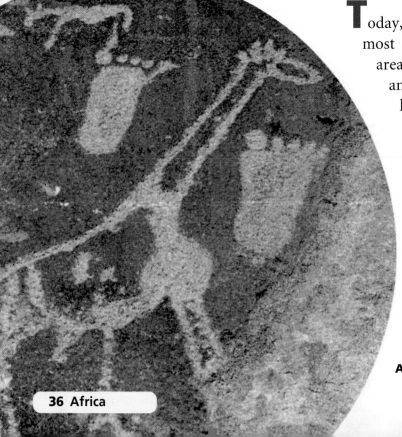

Today, the dry sands and rocks of the Sahara cover most of North Africa. But 10,000 years ago, this area was wet enough to support many people and animals. Scientists think Africa's first farmers lived in what is now the Sahara. Ancient rock paintings tell their story.

The history of humans in Africa goes back even further in time than the history of those early farmers. Scientists believe that our early human ancestors lived in East Africa at least 2 million years ago. Today, scientists study the stone tools and bones that these ancestors left behind. By doing so, they learn about the ways our early human ancestors found to survive.

Ancient cave painting from Namibia

36 Africa

Changing Survival Skills

What skills did our early human ancestors need to survive? Like people today, they needed to find food, water, and shelter to live. Survival skills changed and developed over the course of many thousands of years.

Hunting and Gathering Our early human ancestors were hunter-gatherers. A hunter-gatherer is someone who hunts animals and gathers food in the wild to survive. Hunter-gatherers hunted animals to use the meat for food and the hides and fur for clothing and shelter. They ate foods such as fruits, nuts, and roots. They made tools out of wood, animal bones, and eventually stone. The first use of stone tools marks the beginning of a time period scientists call the Stone Age.

The stone tools made by our early human ancestors worked very well. The scientist Louis Leakey found some of the first evidence of human ancestors in East Africa. He also taught himself how to make and use their tools. Using a two-inch, 25,000-year-old stone knife, Leakey could skin and cut up a gazelle in just 20 minutes.

Studying Early Human Ancestors
This stone tool (above) was made by one of our early human ancestors. For more than 30 years, Louis Leakey studied finds like this one at Olduvai Gorge (left) in Tanzania. His family (below) also studied them. **Analyze Images** *Do you find it easy or hard to tell this stone tool from an ordinary stone?*

Target Skill

Set a Purpose
What purpose did you set for the section? Has the text you have read so far helped you toward achieving this purpose? If not, set a new purpose for the rest of the section.

African Farmers Today
In African communities that practice agriculture today, women play a variety of roles. Here, Central African women carry firewood to their homes. **Predict** *What activities are essential to a successful agricultural community?*

Farming and Herding Between 10,000 and 6,000 years ago, some hunter-gatherers began to farm and to herd animals. As you read earlier, farming in Africa probably began in North Africa, when the area that is now the Sahara offered more water than is available there today. The first farmers probably planted wild grains such as barley. At first, gatherers just protected the areas where these grains grew best. Then they began to save some seeds to plant for the next year's crop.

Later, people began to **domesticate** plants, or adapt them for their own use. They threw away seeds from weaker plants and saved seeds from stronger ones. People also domesticated certain wild animals by taming and breeding them.

Early Settlements Domesticating plants and animals meant people could have better control over their food supply. They did not have to travel to places where grains were already growing. Instead, they planted the crops they wanted. As a result, they could settle in one place. Most early farmers settled on fertile land near a water supply. Some communities produced a food surplus, or more than what was needed. Surpluses allowed some people in the community to do work other than farming.

✓ **Reading Check** **What was the Stone Age?**

Civilizations on the Nile

Over a period of hundreds of thousands of years, some Stone Age groups became civilizations. A **civilization** is a society with cities, a government, and social classes. A social class is a group that is made up of people with similar backgrounds, wealth, and ways of living. Social classes form when people do different jobs. The types of jobs people do determine whether they are rich, poor, or in the middle. Civilizations also usually have architecture, writing, and art. A few thousand years ago, two important African civilizations—Egypt and Nubia—arose along the Nile River.

Egypt Each summer, the Nile River used to flood its banks. The flooding waters would cover the ground with a layer of fertile silt that was ideal for farming because it enriched the soil. Around 5000 B.C., people began farming along the river's banks. They settled in scattered villages. Over many years, these villages grew into the civilization of ancient Egypt.

Ancient Egypt was ruled by kings and queens. The kings of Egypt were called pharaohs (FEHR ohz). The people believed that their pharaohs were also gods. When kings and queens died, they were buried in tombs. Some of the tombs were built as large pyramids. People painted murals and picture-writing symbols called hieroglyphs (HY ur oh glifs) on the inner walls of the tombs. The ancient Egyptians became skilled in paper-making, architecture, medicine, and astronomy.

Nubia In about 6000 B.C., settled hunting and fishing communities began to arise along the Nile south of Egypt. About 1,000 years later, these communities began farming. This area was called Nubia. Scientists believe the formation of Nubian kingdoms may have started around 3100 B.C.

One of the greatest Nubian kingdoms was centered in the city of Napata. Around 724 B.C., the Nubians of Napata conquered Egypt. Nubians ruled Egypt for about 60 years. A later Nubian kingdom was based farther south, in the city of Meroë (MEHR oh ee). Meroë began to weaken in the A.D. 200s. It was finally conquered in A.D. 350 by invading forces from the Ethiopian kingdom of Aksum (AHK soom).

Leftover From Ancient Times
The Nubian mural (top) was painted inside a tomb more than 3,000 years ago. The pair of Egyptian leather sandals (above), which are similar to the ones shown in the mural, are more than 5,000 years old. **Infer** *What kind of information can objects like these teach us about ancient civilizations?*

✓ **Reading Check** **What are social classes, and how are they formed?**

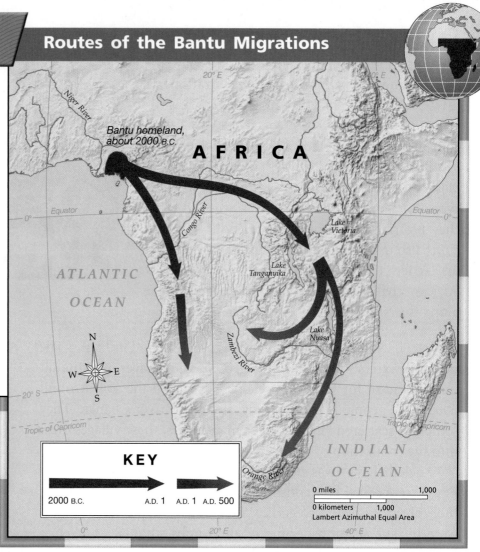

Movement The Bantu migrations were some of the largest movements of people in history. As a result, millions of Africans today speak Bantu languages. **Identify** Where did the Bantu migrations begin? **Analyze Information** Notice that the arrows on the map change color to show time passing. Which place did the migrations reach first, Lake Tanganyika or the Orange River?

Go Online
PHSchool.com Use Web Code **ngp-5211** for step-by-step **map skills practice.**

KEY

2000 B.C.   A.D. 1   A.D. 1   A.D. 500

0 miles   1,000
0 kilometers   1,000
Lambert Azimuthal Equal Area

The Bantu Migrations

About 4,000 years ago, people in Africa began one of the largest migrations that has ever taken place. To **migrate** is to move from one place to resettle in another. Around that time, a group of people who spoke Bantu (BAN too) languages began to migrate out of the region that today forms the border between Nigeria and Cameroon.

Why Migrate? No one knows for certain why the migrations began. Some experts believe that a new ability to grow certain crops in the tropical rain forest made the migrations possible. For example, yams and oil palms became a larger part of people's diet. Then increased food supplies may have led to overpopulation, or overcrowding of people living in one area. As a result, Bantu-speaking farmers migrated, perhaps looking for new land to farm. Over hundreds of years, settlements of Bantu speakers spread across Central and Southern Africa.

Bantus Spread Their Language People had been living in most parts of Africa before the Bantu speakers arrived. As the Bantu-speaking farmers settled, their language became the one that most people spoke. Not everyone agrees on how the Bantu languages spread. People who investigate the migrations have found evidence of various routes Bantu speakers took across Africa. By studying cultural clues and modern African languages, experts may eventually understand how many people followed each route and when.

Language and Ethnic Groups Today, people in Central and Southern Africa belong to hundreds of **ethnic groups**, or groups that share languages, religions, family ties, and customs. People in an ethnic group share an identity separate from others. Most often, this identity is based on a shared history or culture. An ethnic group may also share a distinct language. Most of the ethnic groups living in Central and Southern Africa today are Bantu speakers. In fact, more than 200 million people in the region speak one of the many Bantu languages. The most widely spoken of these languages include Zulu, Xhosa (KOH sah), Shona, and Swahili.

✓ **Reading Check** How many people in Central and Southern Africa speak Bantu languages today?

Links Across The World

Ethnic Groups Ethnic groups can be found around the world. French Canadians are a major ethnic group in Canada. Hispanics, African Americans, and Irish Americans are just a few of the many ethnic groups found in the United States. Below, members of various ethnic groups gather in Paris, France.

Section 1 Assessment

Key Terms
Review the key terms at the beginning of this section. Use each term in a sentence that explains its meaning.

Target Reading Skill
How did having a purpose help you understand the important ideas in this section?

Comprehension and Critical Thinking
1. (a) Locate Where in Africa did farming most likely begin?
(b) Identify Causes Why did people give up hunting and gathering for farming and herding?

(c) Identify Effects What effects did farming have on people?
2. (a) Recall What were some characteristics of the civilizations that arose along the Nile River?
(b) Predict How might the Egyptian and Nubian civilizations have been affected if the Nile River did not regularly flood its banks?
3. (a) Identify What were the Bantu migrations?
(b) Draw Conclusions How do you think the Bantu-speaking farmers adapted to different environments during the hundreds of years of migrations?

Writing Activity
Make a poster that illustrates, step by step, an important idea from this section. For example, your poster could show how scientists learn about early people or how languages spread from one part of Africa to another.

Go Online
PHSchool.com
For: An activity on early human ancestors in Africa
Visit: PHSchool.com
Web Code: ngd-5201

Kingdoms, City-States, and Empires

Prepare to Read

Objectives

In this section you will
1. Learn how trade affected the development of early East African civilizations.
2. Examine the forces that shaped the history of the North African trading powers.
3. Find out how West African kingdoms gained wealth and power.

Taking Notes

As you read, look for details about important African kingdoms and city-states. Copy the table below, and use it to record your notes.

Early African Civilizations		
Kingdom or City-State	Location	Historical Events

Target Reading Skill

Predict Making predictions before you read helps you set a purpose for reading and remember what you read. First, preview the section by looking at the headings. Then note illustrations or anything else that stands out. Finally, predict what might be discussed in the text. For example, after previewing this section, you might predict that the text will explain the history of trade in Africa. As you read, compare what you read to your prediction.

Key Terms

- **Swahili** (swah HEE lee) *n.* a Bantu language spoken in much of East Africa; also an ethnic group
- **city-state** (SIH tee stayt) *n.* a city that is also an independent state, with its own traditions, government, and laws
- **pilgrimage** (PIL gruh mij) *n.* a religious journey
- **Tombouctou** (tohm book TOO) *n.* a city in Mali near the Niger River; also spelled *Timbuktu*

Aksum was the first African kingdom to make coins for trade.

In the decades before A.D. 100, a Greek writer made a list of goods for sale in the markets of Adulis, East Africa. The list included the following:

> **Cloth made in Egypt . . . many articles of flint glass . . . and brass, which is used for ornament and in cut pieces instead of coin; sheets of soft copper, used for cooking utensils and cut up for bracelets and anklets for the women; iron, which is made into spears used against the elephants and other wild beasts, and in their wars.**
>
> —*anonymous Greek trader*

Adulis was a bustling trade center along the Red Sea. It was also the main port of the wealthy and powerful kingdom of Aksum.

East African Trading Civilizations

Early East African civilizations grew strong from trade. Turn to the map titled Africa: Regions on page 9. Notice that the boundaries of East Africa include the Red Sea and the Indian Ocean. East Africa's early trading civilizations developed on or near a coastline, providing access to important markets in Arabia, India, and East Asia.

Aksum The kingdom of Aksum was located in East Africa, where the present-day countries of Ethiopia and Eritrea lie. Around 1000 B.C., African and Arab traders began settling along the west coast of the Red Sea. They were the ancestors of the people of Aksum. Over time, Aksum came to control trade in the Red Sea area. By the A.D. 200s, the kingdom controlled a trade network that stretched from the Mediterranean Sea to India.

Ideas, as well as goods, traveled along trade routes. In the A.D. 300s, many people in Aksum became Christian as news about the religion spread. Aksum became a center of the early Ethiopian Christian Church. During the A.D. 600s, Aksum began to decline as Arabs took control of much of the region's trade.

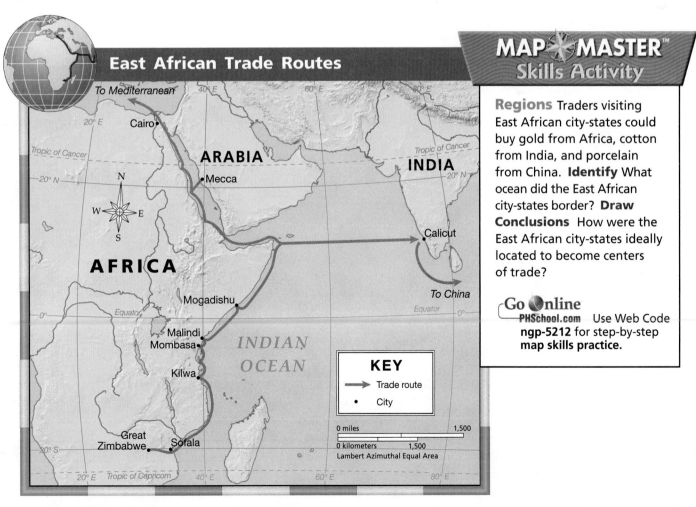

East African Trade Routes

MAP MASTER™
Skills Activity

Regions Traders visiting East African city-states could buy gold from Africa, cotton from India, and porcelain from China. **Identify** What ocean did the East African city-states border? **Draw Conclusions** How were the East African city-states ideally located to become centers of trade?

Go Online
PHSchool.com Use Web Code **ngp-5212** for step-by-step **map skills practice.**

Ivory comes from elephant tusks such as the one the men below are holding. Although it is no longer legal to trade ivory, a monument (bottom) in Mombasa, Kenya, commemorates the role ivory played in African trade. **Draw Conclusions** *Why do you think it is no longer legal to trade ivory?*

Cities of Trade Around the time that Aksum declined, trading cities arose along East Africa's coast. Traders from these cities used seasonal winds to sail northeast to India and China. The traders carried animal skins, ivory, and gold and other metals. When the winds changed direction, the traders sailed back. They brought many goods, including cotton, silk, and porcelain.

Trade affected the culture of coastal East Africa. Some of the traders who visited the area or settled in it were Muslim. They introduced the religion of Islam to East Africa. As well, a new language, called Swahili (swah HEE lee), developed in the area. **Swahili** is a Bantu language that includes some Arab words. Today, it is the most widely spoken Bantu language in Africa.

Rise of City-States Some East African trading cities grew into powerful city-states. A **city-state** is a city that has its own traditions, government, and laws. It is both a city and an independent state. City-states often control much of the surrounding land. Among the greatest of the East African city-states were Malindi (muh LIN dee), Mombasa (mahm BAH suh), Great Zimbabwe (grayt zim BAHB way), and Kilwa (KEEL wah).

Kilwa Ibn Battutah (IB un bat TOO tah) was a Muslim from North Africa who became famous for traveling to and writing about many countries. He visited Kilwa in 1331. He had seen great cities in China, India, and West Africa. Ibn Battutah wrote that Kilwa was "one of the most beautiful and best-constructed towns in the world." In Kilwa, people lived in three- and four-story houses made of stone and sea coral.

Kilwa and other East African city-states grew rich from trade and taxes. Traders had to pay huge taxes on goods they brought into the city. "Any merchant who wished to enter the city paid for every five hundred pieces of cloth, no matter what the quality, one gold [piece] as entrance duty," reported one visitor. "After this, the king took two thirds of all the merchandise, leaving the trader one third."

In the early 1500s, Kilwa and the other East African city-states were conquered and destroyed by the European country of Portugal. The Portuguese wanted to build their own trading empire.

Southern and East African Trade Ties Inland and south from the East African city-states, another great trading civilization developed. Great Zimbabwe was located near the bend of the Limpopo (lim POH poh) River in Southern Africa. It was connected to the trade civilizations of East Africa through a trade network that extended to the coast of the Indian Ocean. Great Zimbabwe reached the peak of its power in about the year 1300. At one time, thousands of people lived in the gigantic stone buildings that covered the area. Today, ruins of Great Zimbabwe remain, including city walls, a fortress, and homes.

Many tall walls of Great Zimbabwe still stand today.

✓ **Reading Check** What kinds of goods traveled to and from East Africa's trading cities?

Predict
Is the text saying what you predicted it would? If not, look over the headings and illustrations again, and then revise your prediction.

North African Trading Powers

North Africa's history was shaped in part by its location. The region's major boundaries are the Sahara and the Mediterranean Sea. Its long Mediterranean coastline attracted sea traders. As early as 1000 B.C., ships from Phoenicia (fuh NISH uh) began searching the North African coast for ports that would connect them to Africa's riches. Phoenicia included present-day Lebanon and parts of Syria and Israel.

The Rise and Fall of Carthage By 800 B.C., the Phoenicians had established the city of Carthage (KAHR thij) as a trading post in present-day Tunisia. In time, Carthage became a powerful city-state that controlled the coast of North Africa. Carthage grew rich from the trade of textiles, metals, slaves, and food products. Possibly the wealthiest city in the world at the time, Carthage maintained control over Mediterranean trade from the late 500s B.C. through the 200s B.C. However, wars with the Roman Republic weakened the Carthaginians. In 146 B.C., Carthage fell to the Roman Empire, and the city was destroyed.

Roman and Islamic Influences Under Roman rule, cities grew up in areas that are parts of present-day Morocco, northern Algeria, and Tunisia. Christianity also spread to North African cities. The Romans built thousands of miles of roads throughout the territory, and North Africa's ports flourished.

After the Roman Empire fell in A.D. 476, invading forces competed for control of parts of North Africa. During the A.D. 600s, Arabs took control of Egypt and began to invade areas to the west of it. Thus began a long period of Arab control of North Africa. With Arab rule came the spread of Islam, the major religion of the Arabs. Soon many North Africans became Muslim. Then through trade, North Africa's Muslims helped spread Islam to people in West Africa, many of whom also accepted the religion.

Islam and Art
As Islam spread into North Africa, so did Islamic art styles. The gate shown above, which leads into the city of Fès, Morocco, is Islamic in design.
Analyze Images *How would you describe Islamic art from looking at this gate?*

✓ **Reading Check** Why did the Phoenicians establish Carthage?

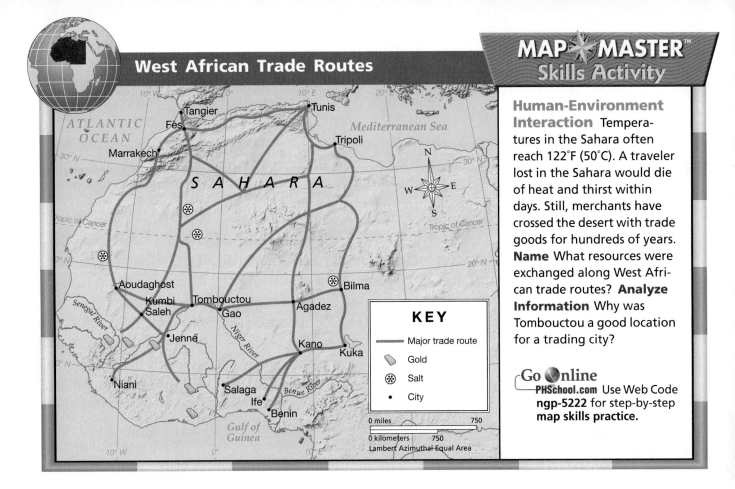

ATLANTIC OCEAN

Tangier
Fés
Tunis
Marrakech
Tripoli

Mediterranean Sea

S A H A R A

Aoudaghost
Kumbi Saleh
Tombouctou
Gao
Agadez
Bilma

Senegal River

Jenné
Kano
Kuka
Niger River

Niani
Salaga
Ife
Benin
Benue River

Gulf of Guinea

KEY

— Major trade route
▱ Gold
✿ Salt
• City

0 miles 750
0 kilometers 750
Lambert Azimuthal Equal Area

Human-Environment Interaction Temperatures in the Sahara often reach 122°F (50°C). A traveler lost in the Sahara would die of heat and thirst within days. Still, merchants have crossed the desert with trade goods for hundreds of years. **Name** What resources were exchanged along West African trade routes? **Analyze Information** Why was Tombouctou a good location for a trading city?

Go Online
PHSchool.com Use Web Code **ngp-5222** for step-by-step map skills practice.

West African Kingdoms

Around the time that East and North African city-states were developing, great trading kingdoms arose on the west side of the continent. The power of the West African kingdoms was based on the trade of salt and gold. People need salt to survive, especially in areas with hot climates such as West Africa. But there were no local sources of salt in the region. However, West Africa had plenty of gold. In North Africa, the opposite was true. There was salt, but no gold.

A brisk trade between North Africa and West Africa quickly grew. Control of this trade brought power and riches to three West African kingdoms: Ghana (GAH nuh), Mali (MAH lee), and Songhai (SAWNG hy). Forest kingdoms such as Benin (beh NEEN) also grew wealthy from trade.

Ghana You can see on the map titled Africa's Kingdoms, Cities, and Empires on page 35 that the kingdom of Ghana was located between the Senegal and Niger rivers. From that location Ghana controlled much of the trade across West Africa. Ghana's kings grew rich from the taxes they charged on the salt, gold, and other goods that flowed through their land. The flow of gold was so great that Arab writers called Ghana "land of gold."

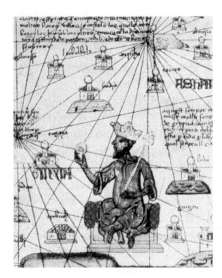

Mansa Musa was so famous that he was portrayed on a Spanish map of the world from the 1300s.

Links Across
The World

The Spread of Islam In the A.D. 600s, Islam began to spread west from Arabia through Southwest Asia and North Africa. Later, it reached West Africa. Islam also spread east—to Central Asia, India, Pakistan, Bangladesh, and Indonesia. About one billion people around the world practice Islam today. On some days, millions of Muslims visit the holy site of Mecca, as shown below.

Mali In time, Ghana lost control of its trade routes to a new power, the kingdom of Mali. This kingdom arose in the mid-1200s in the upper Niger valley. Mali's kings controlled the gold mines of the south and the salt supplies of the north.

In Mali, the king was called *Mansa,* which means "emperor." Mali's most famous king, Mansa Musa (MAHN sah MOO sah), gained the throne in about 1312. His 20-year reign brought peace and order to the kingdom.

Mansa Musa and the Spread of Islam Over hundreds of years, Muslim traders had spread their religion, Islam, into much of Africa. Mansa Musa and many of his subjects were Muslim. Mansa Musa based his laws on the teachings of Islam.

In 1324, Mansa Musa made a **pilgrimage,** or a religious journey, to the Arabian city of Mecca. Muslims consider Mecca a holy place. It is the birthplace of Muhammad, the founder of Islam. Mansa Musa brought 60,000 people with him on his pilgrimage. Each of 80 camels carried 300 pounds (136 kilograms) of gold, which Mansa Musa gave to people as gifts along the way. Mansa Musa's pilgrimage brought about new trading ties with other Muslim states. It also displayed Mali's wealth. Hearing the reports, Europe's rulers eagerly sought Mali's gold.

Songhai After Mansa Musa's death in about 1332, the Songhai empire became West Africa's most powerful kingdom. Songhai's rulers controlled important trade routes and wealthy cities. The wealthiest Songhai trading city was **Tombouctou** (tohm book TOO), an important caravan stop located along the Niger River. People considered Tombouctou a great Muslim learning center.

> **❝**Salt comes from the north, gold from the south, and silver from the city of white men. But the word of God and the treasures of wisdom are only to be found in Tombouctou.**❞**
>
> *—West African proverb*

Invaders from North Africa defeated Songhai in 1591. However, Songhai people still live near the Niger River, and Islam remains important in the region.

Forest Kingdoms Songhai traded with kingdoms located to the south in the forested region of West Africa. One such kingdom, Benin, arose in the late 1200s. Trade in ivory, palm oil, and pepper made the kingdom of Benin wealthy. Benin's artisans worked in ivory, bronze, brass, and wood in a distinctive style. They created some of the finest sculptures and carvings of the time.

Because it was located on the coast, Benin also traded with other African kingdoms as well as with Europeans arriving by sea. In the 1500s, Europeans began to trade guns for slaves from coastal forest kingdoms such as Benin, Asante (uh SAHN tee), and Dahomey (duh HOH mee). Many African Americans are descendants of enslaved people from those kingdoms.

✓ **Reading Check** Who was Mansa Musa?

Bronze sculpture from the forest kingdom of Owo

Section 2 Assessment

Key Terms

Review the key terms at the beginning of this section. Use each term in a sentence that explains its meaning.

Target Reading Skill

What did you predict about this section? Did your prediction help you remember what you read?

Comprehension and Critical Thinking

1. (a) Name Identify two city-states that were important to East African trade.
(b) Identify Effects How did trade affect the coastal culture of East Africa?

(c) Analyze Information Why do you think East African traders had to pay taxes for the right to bring goods into Kilwa?
2. (a) Identify Sequence What forces influenced North Africa throughout its history?
(b) Analyze Information How did Islam become a major religion in North Africa?
3. (a) Describe How did location affect the various kingdoms of West Africa?
(b) Draw Conclusions How did Ghana, Mali, and Songhai become wealthy from gold and salt?

Writing Activity

Suppose you are a traveler visiting one of Africa's ancient kingdoms or city-states during the time that it thrived. Write a short letter home about some of the things that you see and the people that you meet. Explain what your favorite part of the visit has been.

For: An activity on the empire of Ghana
Visit: PHSchool.com
Web Code: ngd-5202

European Conquest of Africa

Prepare to Read

Objectives

In this section you will

1. Discover what motivated Europeans to explore the African coast.
2. Find out how the Atlantic slave trade developed in the 1500s.
3. Learn how Europeans colonized regions of Africa.

Taking Notes

As you read, find important details about the European conquest of Africa. Copy the flowchart below, and use it to record your findings.

> The Portuguese explore West Africa's coast, looking for better access to African gold.

Target Reading Skill

Ask Questions Before you read this section, preview the headings and illustrations to see what the section is about. Write one question that will help you understand or remember something important in the section. For example, you could write this question: "Why did Europeans originally go to Africa?" Then read to answer your question.

Key Terms

- **Cape of Good Hope** (kayp uv good hohp) *n.* a former province of the Republic of South Africa; the point of land at the southern end of Cape Peninsula, South Africa
- **plantation** (plan TAY shun) *n.* a large farm where cash crops are grown
- **Olaudah Equiano** (oh LOW duh ek wee AHN oh) *n.* an antislavery activist who wrote an account of his enslavement
- **colonize** (KAHL uh nyz) *v.* to settle in an area and take control of its government

Many Africans stayed in cells like this one at Gorée.

On the island of Gorée (goh RAY), off the coast of the West African country of Senegal, stands a museum called the House of Slaves. It honors the millions of Africans who were enslaved and then shipped across the Atlantic Ocean. Many Africans passed through the building that now houses the museum. Their last view of Africa was an opening called "The Door of No Return." Beyond it lay the ocean and the slave ships bound for the Americas.

The Atlantic slave trade began in the 1500s and continued through the late 1800s. But contact between Europeans and Africans began long before that. In North Africa, Europeans traded for gold from the empires of Ghana and Mali. Why do you think Europeans' first contacts with Africans took place in North Africa?

Europeans on the Coast

After 1500, Europe's relationship with Africa changed. It had begun as trade between equals. But it turned into the enslavement and forced migration of millions of Africans. The African slave trade eventually ended in the 1800s. Afterward, Europeans became more interested in Africa's natural resources. By 1900, European countries had divided Africa among themselves.

Portuguese Exploration In the mid-1400s, the Portuguese began sailing along the West African coast in search of gold. For centuries, gold from West Africa had been transported across the Sahara to North African ports. It was then shipped across the Mediterranean to arrive at European markets. But the Portuguese and other Europeans wanted to trade directly for West African gold and ivory, instead of dealing with North African merchants. They also wanted to trade with Asia.

Many inventions helped the Portuguese explore Africa's coast. The Portuguese used a lateen sail, a triangle-shaped sail designed in North Africa. The lateen sail allowed ships to sail against the wind as well as with it. And better instruments, such as the astrolabe (AS troh layb), helped sailors navigate at sea. With these improvements, Portuguese sailors became the first Europeans to travel south along Africa's coasts.

A Change in Trade Relations At first, Africans and Europeans traded with one another as equals. Africans traded gold, cotton, ivory, skins, metal objects, and pepper. In return, Europeans traded copper, brass, and clothing. Europeans also introduced corn, cassava, and yams from the Americas. These plants became food crops in Africa. Africans in turn introduced Europeans to okra, watermelon, and the best type of rice for growing in the Americas.

Over time, however, the trade relationship changed. In 1498, three Portuguese ships rounded the tip of Southern Africa and sailed north along Africa's east coast. The wealth of the East African city-states amazed the Portuguese. More Portuguese ships followed—not to trade but to seize the riches of the city-states. Portugal controlled the wealth of East Africa's coast until well into the 1600s.

Portuguese Ship, African Sails
This illustration shows a typical Portuguese sailing ship of the 1400s, called a caravel. It used lateen sails. **Synthesize** *How does this ship show that Europeans adopted elements of African culture?*

Europeans in Africa

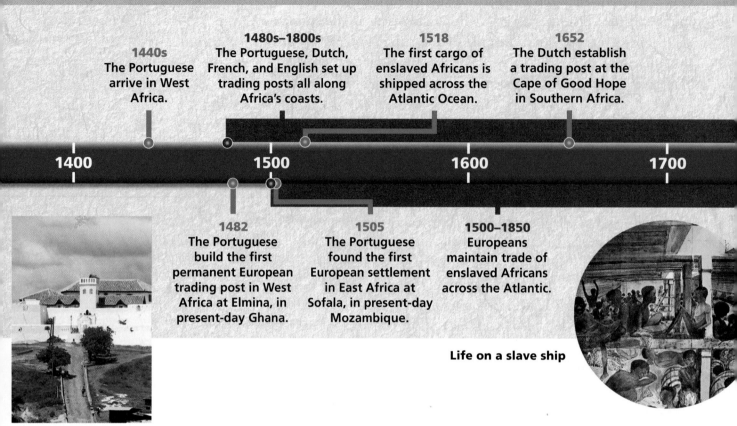

1440s
The Portuguese arrive in West Africa.

1480s–1800s
The Portuguese, Dutch, French, and English set up trading posts all along Africa's coasts.

1518
The first cargo of enslaved Africans is shipped across the Atlantic Ocean.

1652
The Dutch establish a trading post at the Cape of Good Hope in Southern Africa.

1400   1500   1600   1700

1482
The Portuguese build the first permanent European trading post in West Africa at Elmina, in present-day Ghana.

1505
The Portuguese found the first European settlement in East Africa at Sofala, in present-day Mozambique.

1500–1850
Europeans maintain trade of enslaved Africans across the Atlantic.

Life on a slave ship

Trading post at Elmina

European Trade Spreads The Dutch, French, and English soon followed the Portuguese. They set up trading posts along Africa's coasts, where sailors could get supplies. The Dutch built a trading post on the **Cape of Good Hope,** a point of land at Africa's southern tip. Soon, settlers arrived. They moved inland, building homes and farms.

As Europeans spread out, sometimes by force, their relations with Africans worsened. But it was the growing trade in enslaved Africans that poisoned future relations between Africans and Europeans the most.

√ Reading Check   **What advantages allowed the Portuguese to be the first Europeans to trade directly with West Africans?**

The Atlantic Slave Trade

Before the 1500s, slavery was common in some parts of Africa. There, enslaved people became the property of their owners and were forced to work for them. Slaves could win their freedom after a few years. Some became important citizens among the people who had enslaved them. Slaves could even be bought out of slavery by their own people.

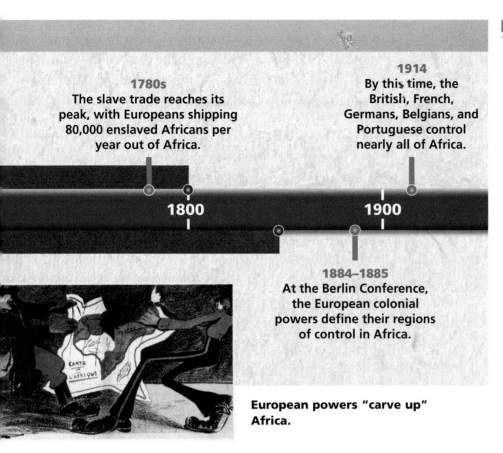

1780s
The slave trade reaches its peak, with Europeans shipping 80,000 enslaved Africans per year out of Africa.

1914
By this time, the British, French, Germans, Belgians, and Portuguese control nearly all of Africa.

1800

1900

1884–1885
At the Berlin Conference, the European colonial powers define their regions of control in Africa.

European powers "carve up" Africa.

■ **Timeline Skills**

Over the course of 500 years, Europeans had a strong influence on Africa. **Note** When did Europeans establish their first trading post in Africa? **Identify Effects** What were the effects of European trade interests on Africa?

Then the European powers began to establish colonies in North, South, and Central America, as well as the Caribbean. The Europeans practiced a different type of slavery in the Americas. They treated the enslaved Africans as property that they shipped across the Atlantic to the Americas. The Europeans rarely freed their slaves. When the African slave trade ended in the mid-1800s, millions of Africans had been taken from their homelands, most never to return.

The Demand for Slaves European settlers in the Americas needed workers for their mines and plantations. A **plantation** is a large farm where cash crops are grown. Instead of paying plantation workers, the settlers preferred to use enslaved laborers. At first the settlers enslaved Native Americans. But many Native Americans became sick and died from diseases or brutal working conditions. Others ran away.

Therefore the European settlers decided to enslave Africans instead. The settlers knew Africans were skilled farmers, miners, and metal workers. They also thought Africans would easily adapt to the climate of the American tropics, which is similar to that of Africa. And since Africans would be in unfamiliar territory, they would not be able to escape easily.

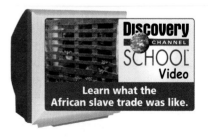

DISCOVERY CHANNEL **SCHOOL** Video
Learn what the African slave trade was like.

The Slave Trade Begins By the 1600s, Portuguese traders were exchanging goods, such as guns, for African slaves. Some African nations refused to take part. But others sold people they captured during battles. By 1780, about 80,000 African slaves were being shipped across the Atlantic each year.

The Horrors of Slavery Captured Africans were often branded with hot irons to identify them as slaves. On the journey across the Atlantic, captives lay side by side on filthy shelves stacked from floor to ceiling. They received little food or water. As many as 20 percent of the slaves died during each crossing. To make up for these losses, ships' captains packed in even more people.

Olaudah Equiano (oh LOW duh ek wee AHN oh) was a slave who bought his own freedom and then fought against slavery. Equiano had been captured and sold at a slave auction in 1756, at about age 11. He felt sure he would die. In a book he later wrote about his experience, Equiano explained,

❝[W]hen I looked around the ship and saw a large furnace of copper boiling and a multitude of black people of every description chained together . . . I no longer doubted of my fate. ❞

—*The Interesting Narrative of the Life of Olaudah Equiano, or Gustavus Vassa, the African*, by Olaudah Equiano

Equiano proved luckier than most African slaves. In time, he was able to buy his freedom. For most enslaved people, freedom was little more than a distant dream.

The Effects of Slavery on Africa Some Africans grew wealthy from the slave trade. Overall, however, the slave trade was a disaster for Africa. West Africa lost much of its population. Robbed of skilled workers, and with many families torn apart, many African societies broke down.

√ Reading Check **What fueled the European demand for slaves?**

The Trials of Slavery
Olaudah Equiano (top right) was a slave who bought his own freedom. He traveled to America in cramped quarters on a slave ship similar to this model (above). **Analyze Images** *Do you think it would have been bearable to live on a ship like this one?*

Europeans Colonize Africa

In the mid-1800s, the African slave trade ended. Europeans then began to raid Africa's interior for its natural resources. They wanted the resources in order to run factories all across Europe. They also viewed Africa as a place to build empires. Many Africans fiercely resisted European conquest. But their old guns proved no match for modern European weapons.

MAP★MASTER™
Skills Activity

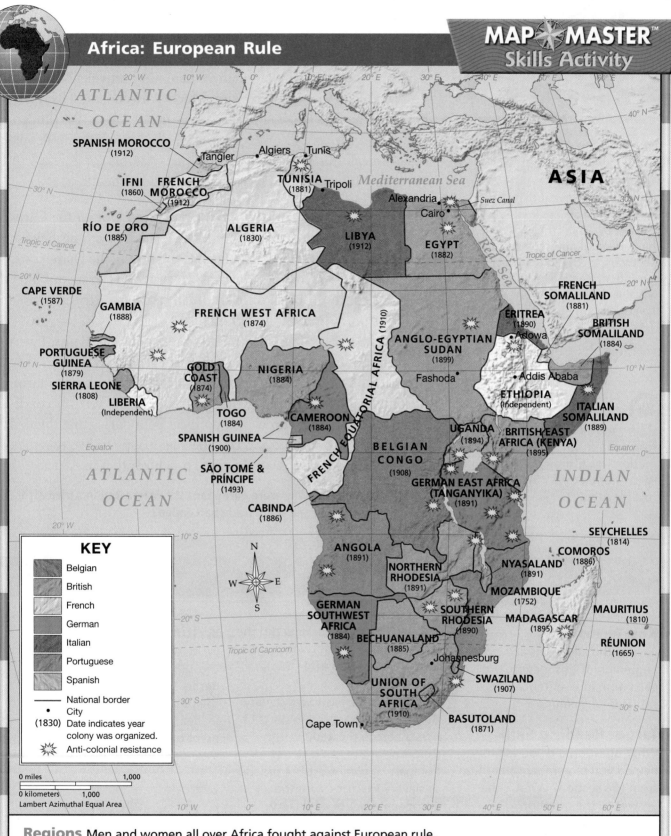

ATLANTIC OCEAN

ASIA

SPANISH MOROCCO (1912)
Tangier
Algiers
Tunis
Mediterranean Sea
IFNI (1860)
FRENCH MOROCCO (1912)
TUNISIA (1881)
Tripoli
Alexandria
Suez Canal
Cairo
RÍO DE ORO (1885)
ALGERIA (1830)
LIBYA (1912)
EGYPT (1882)
Tropic of Cancer
Tropic of Cancer
Red Sea

CAPE VERDE (1587)
FRENCH SOMALILAND (1881)
GAMBIA (1888)
FRENCH WEST AFRICA (1874)
ERITREA (1890)
Adowa
BRITISH SOMALILAND (1884)
ANGLO-EGYPTIAN SUDAN (1899)
PORTUGUESE GUINEA (1879)
SIERRA LEONE (1808)
GOLD COAST (1874)
NIGERIA (1884)
Fashoda
ETHIOPIA (Independent)
LIBERIA (Independent)
TOGO (1884)
CAMEROON (1884)
FRENCH EQUATORIAL AFRICA (1910)
Addis Ababa
ITALIAN SOMALILAND (1889)
SPANISH GUINEA (1900)
UGANDA (1894)
BRITISH EAST AFRICA (KENYA) (1895)
Equator
SÃO TOMÉ & PRÍNCIPE (1493)
BELGIAN CONGO (1908)
Equator
ATLANTIC OCEAN
CABINDA (1886)
GERMAN EAST AFRICA (TANGANYIKA) (1891)
INDIAN OCEAN

ANGOLA (1891)
NORTHERN RHODESIA (1891)
NYASALAND (1891)
SEYCHELLES (1814)
COMOROS (1886)
N
W E
S
MOZAMBIQUE (1752)
GERMAN SOUTHWEST AFRICA (1884)
SOUTHERN RHODESIA (1890)
MADAGASCAR (1895)
MAURITIUS (1810)
BECHUANALAND (1885)
Tropic of Capricorn
RÉUNION (1665)
Johannesburg
UNION OF SOUTH AFRICA (1910)
SWAZILAND (1907)
BASUTOLAND (1871)
Cape Town

KEY
Belgian
British
French
German
Italian
Portuguese
Spanish
National border
• City
(1830) Date indicates year colony was organized.
✷ Anti-colonial resistance

0 miles 1,000
0 kilometers 1,000
Lambert Azimuthal Equal Area

Regions Men and women all over Africa fought against European rule. However, by 1914, Europeans ruled almost all of Africa. Only Liberia and Ethiopia remained independent. **Identify** Name two African countries that were not yet ruled by Europeans in 1900. **Draw Conclusions** Why do you think most of the regions that resisted colonization were near the coasts?

Go Online
PHSchool.com Use Web Code
ngp-5213 for step-by-step **map skills practice.**

How Stamps Reveal History
These postage stamps were printed in the early 1900s. They are from the German colony in present-day Cameroon and the British colony in present-day Kenya, Uganda, and Tanzania. **Infer** *Did Europeans view their colonies as African or European?*

Ask Questions
Ask yourself why the competition among European nations for African territory was referred to as "the scramble for Africa."

The Scramble for Africa European nations competed with one another to gain African territory. But they did not want this competition to lead to war. In 1884, leaders of several European countries met in Berlin, Germany. There, they set rules for which European countries could claim which African land. By 1900, European nations had colonized many parts of Africa. To **colonize** means to settle an area and take control of its government. People began to call this rush for territory "the scramble for Africa." By 1914, only Ethiopia and Liberia remained independent.

Effects of European Control on Africa Not all the European countries ruled their colonies the same way. The Belgian government directly ran the Belgian Congo (now the Democratic Republic of the Congo). Africans governed Nigeria, but they took orders from British officials. In all cases, the African people had little power in their governments.

The scramble for Africa caused long-lasting problems. Europeans had gained power in part by encouraging rivalries among African ethnic groups. Europeans also took the best land to farm. In some areas, they forced Africans to labor under terrible conditions. Europeans also drew new political boundaries that divided some ethnic groups and forced differing groups to live together. Later, these boundaries would cause much conflict in Africa.

✓ **Reading Check** Why were Europeans still interested in Africa after the slave trade had ended?

Section 3 Assessment

Key Terms
Review the key terms at the beginning of this section. Use each term in a sentence that explains its meaning.

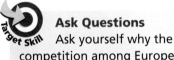 **Target Reading Skill**
What question did you ask that helped you remember something from this section? What is the answer to the question?

Comprehension and Critical Thinking
1. (a) Recall What region of Africa did most Europeans trade with before the mid-1400s?

(b) Identify Causes How did the trade relationship between Europe and Africa change after the late 1400s?
2. (a) Describe How was slavery traditionally practiced in parts of Africa before the 1500s?
(b) Compare and Contrast Compare and contrast the practice of slavery in Africa with the European practice of slavery.
3. (a) Recall In what different ways did the Europeans govern their African colonies?
(b) Identify Sequence How did relations between Africa and Europe change over time?

Writing Activity
Write two brief editorials about the 1884 European conference in Berlin. Write one editorial from the point of view of an African leader. Write the other from the point of view of a European leader attending the conference.

For: An activity on the Boers
Visit: PHSchool.com
Web Code: ngd-5203

Section 4
Independence and Its Challenges

Prepare to Read

Objectives

In this section you will
1. Learn about the growth of nationalism in Africa.
2. Find out about the effects of World War II on Africa and on the growing independence movement.
3. Examine the different challenges faced by African nations on their paths to independence.

Taking Notes

As you read, find details on the causes and effects of the African movement for independence. Copy the flowchart below, and use it to record your findings.

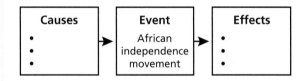

Causes		Event		Effects
• • •	→	African independence movement	→	• • •

Target Reading Skill

Use Prior Knowledge Prior knowledge is what you already know about a topic before you begin to read. Building on what you already know can give you a head start on learning new information.

Before you begin to read, page through your reading assignment, looking at the headings and illustrations to spark your memory. Write down what you know about a certain topic, such as World War II. As you read, connect what you learn to what you already know.

Key Terms

- **nationalism** (NASH uh nul iz um) *n.* a feeling of pride in one's homeland; a group's identity as members of a nation
- **Pan-Africanism** (pan AF rih kun iz um) *n.* the belief that all Africans should work together for their rights and freedoms
- **boycott** (BOY kaht) *n.* a refusal to buy or use certain products or services
- **democracy** (dih MAHK ruh see) *n.* a government over which citizens exercise power

On April 18, 1980, the people of Rhodesia took to the streets. They had recently elected Robert Mugabe (muh GAH bee) prime minister in Rhodesia's first free election. People waited excitedly through the evening. Then, at midnight, the British flag came down for the last time. At that moment, the British colony of Rhodesia became the independent country of Zimbabwe.

The fight for independence had been difficult and sometimes violent. Now, Prime Minister Mugabe asked all the people to work together. They would have to build a new nation. Zimbabwe was one of the last African countries to win independence. But the movement for freedom there had begun many years before.

People in Zimbabwe celebrate the country's independence.

A Lasting Legacy

Some 80 years after it was founded, the African National Congress, led by Nelson Mandela (below), won an end to South Africa's domination by the descendants of European colonists. People cheer for Mandela during South Africa's 1994 presidential campaign (bottom).

Evaluate *Based on this information, when did South Africa begin to overcome the effects of colonization?*

The Growth of Nationalism

After "the scramble for Africa," many Africans dreamed of independence. In 1897, Mankayi Sontanga (mun KY ee sun TAHN guh) put this dream to music. His song, called "Bless, O Lord, Our Land of Africa," expressed the growing nationalism of Africans. **Nationalism** is a feeling of pride in one's homeland.

Political Parties and Nationalism Most European colonial rulers did not view Africans as their equals. For that reason, many African leaders knew they would have to work hard at developing pride in being African. The colonial powers had drawn political borders that combined many nations and ethnic groups. Some of these groups were old rivals. African leaders saw that to end colonial rule, they would have to build a spirit of unity.

Nationalism grew during the early 1900s. In 1912, Africans in South Africa formed a political party called the South African Native National Congress. (Today this party is the African National Congress, or the ANC.) Party members protested laws that limited the rights of black South Africans. In 1920, African lawyers in British West Africa formed the National Congress of British West Africa. This group also worked to gain rights for Africans, including the right to vote.

A better life for all

ANC

Pan-Africanism In the 1920s, Africans formed a movement based on **Pan-Africanism,** the belief that all Africans should work together for their rights and freedoms. This movement stressed unity and cooperation among all Africans, whether they lived in Africa or not. Their slogan was "Africa for Africans." The movement won many supporters.

One of the greatest leaders of the Pan-African movement was Léopold Senghor (lay oh POHLD sahn GAWR) of Senegal. Senghor was a poet and a political leader. He encouraged Africans to study their traditions and be proud of their culture. Senegal became independent in 1960, with Senghor as its first president.

✓ Reading Check **Name two African political parties. What work did these parties do?**

Africa and World War II

A major boost to African independence came unexpectedly in the 1930s and 1940s, when World War II unfolded. The war would inspire many people throughout Africa to seek freedom for their own nations.

The Invasion of North Africa During World War II, Great Britain, France, and the United States formed a group called the Allies. Together, the Allies fought the armies of Germany, Italy, and Japan, which were invading much of the world. German and Italian forces invaded North Africa, much of which was under British or French colonial control. Italian forces also invaded Ethiopia.

These men from Ghana fought in the British Army during World War II.

Some African nations played a major role in supporting the Allies. Countries such as Liberia and the Belgian Congo supplied the Allies with rubber and other needed resources. Allied planes were allowed to use African airfields to move supplies into Asia. Many thousands of African soldiers fought and died to help free Europe from conquest. About 170,000 soldiers from West Africa and 280,000 soldiers from East Africa and Southern Africa served in the British Army.

An Inspirational Victory Africans came home victorious. After the sacrifices they made, however, they wanted their own freedom. One soldier said, "We have been told what we fought for. That is 'freedom.' We want freedom, nothing but freedom."

✓ Reading Check **What parts of Africa were invaded during World War II?**

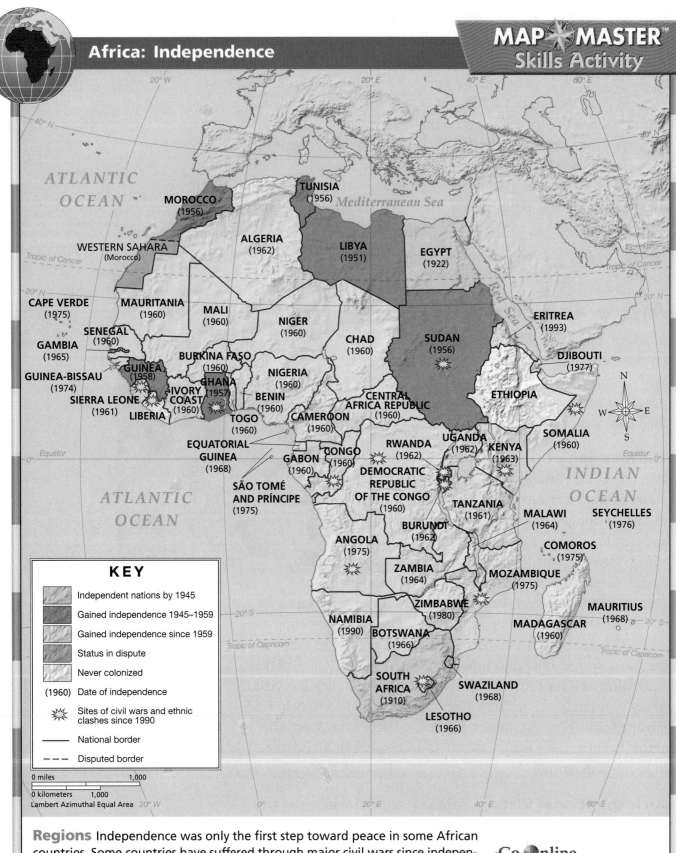

ATLANTIC
OCEAN

MOROCCO
(1956)

TUNISIA
(1956)   *Mediterranean Sea*

WESTERN SAHARA
(Morocco)

ALGERIA
(1962)

LIBYA
(1951)

EGYPT
(1922)

CAPE VERDE
(1975)

MAURITANIA
(1960)

MALI
(1960)

NIGER
(1960)

SUDAN
(1956)

ERITREA
(1993)

SENEGAL
(1960)

GAMBIA
(1965)

CHAD
(1960)

DJIBOUTI
(1977)

BURKINA FASO
(1960)

GUINEA-BISSAU
(1974)

GUINEA
(1958)

GHANA (1957)

NIGERIA
(1960)

SIERRA LEONE
(1961)

IVORY
COAST
(1960)

BENIN
(1960)

CENTRAL
AFRICA REPUBLIC
(1960)

ETHIOPIA

LIBERIA

TOGO
(1960)

CAMEROON
(1960)

EQUATORIAL
GUINEA
(1968)

GABON
(1960)

CONGO
(1960)

RWANDA
(1962)

UGANDA
(1962)

KENYA
(1963)

SOMALIA
(1960)

SÃO TOMÉ
AND PRÍNCIPE
(1975)

DEMOCRATIC
REPUBLIC
OF THE CONGO
(1960)

BURUNDI
(1962)

TANZANIA
(1961)

MALAWI
(1964)

SEYCHELLES
(1976)

ANGOLA
(1975)

ZAMBIA
(1964)

COMOROS
(1975)

MOZAMBIQUE
(1975)

ZIMBABWE
(1980)

MAURITIUS
(1968)

NAMIBIA
(1990)

BOTSWANA
(1966)

MADAGASCAR
(1960)

SOUTH
AFRICA
(1910)

SWAZILAND
(1968)

LESOTHO
(1966)

ATLANTIC
OCEAN

INDIAN
OCEAN

KEY

Independent nations by 1945

Gained independence 1945–1959

Gained independence since 1959

Status in dispute

Never colonized

(1960)   Date of independence

⟡   Sites of civil wars and ethnic
clashes since 1990

———   National border

– – –   Disputed border

0 miles   1,000

0 kilometers   1,000

Lambert Azimuthal Equal Area

Regions Independence was only the first step toward peace in some African countries. Some countries have suffered through major civil wars since independence. **Identify** During what period of time did the most African countries gain independence? **Analyze Information** Why do you think there was an increase in the number of countries that became independent after a certain time?

Go Online
PHSchool.com Use Web Code
ngp-5214 for step-by-step
map skills practice.

Different Paths to Independence

World War II did not only inspire Africans to win their freedom. The war also weakened the economies of colonial powers such as France and Great Britain. Colonialism was about to come to an end in Africa.

Winds of Change Public opinion began to turn against the practice of colonialism as well. Many people in Britain felt they could no longer afford a colonial empire. Even the United States and the Soviet Union—Britain's allies during the war—began to speak out against colonialism.

British leader Harold Macmillan realized that Britain would not be able to keep its African colonies. "The winds of change are blowing across Africa," he said. As more and more Africans demanded freedom, European countries began to give up their African colonies. Some colonial powers gave up their colonies peacefully, while others fought to maintain control. Ghana was granted its independence from Britain. But Algeria, a French colony, had to fight for its freedom.

Independence Across Africa
Women in Mauritius in 1965 hold up signs asking for independence from Britain (bottom). Prince Philip of Britain and Prime Minister Jomo Kenyatta of Kenya shake hands at an independence ceremony in 1963 (below). **Predict** *Do you think Mauritius and Kenya gained independence peacefully or through fighting?*

From Gold Coast to Ghana In the Gold Coast colony, Kwame Nkrumah (KWAH mee un KROO muh) organized protests against British rule in the early 1950s. The protests were peaceful strikes and boycotts. In a **boycott,** people refuse to buy or use certain products or services. The British jailed Nkrumah several times for his actions, but the protests continued. In 1957, the people achieved their goal: independence. The new country took on the name Ghana, and Nkrumah became its president.

War in Algeria The French people who had settled in Algeria thought of it as more than a colony. To them, it was part of France. Algerians disagreed. They were willing to fight for the right to govern themselves. A bloody war began in Algeria in 1954. The eight-year struggle cost the lives of 100,000 Algerians and 10,000 French. But by 1962, the Algerians had won.

Challenges of Independence The new leaders of Africa had spent many years working for independence. But the colonial powers had rarely allowed Africans to gain experience in government. After agreeing to independence, the colonial powers did little to prepare the new leaders to govern. As a result, many new governments in Africa were unstable.

The Right to Vote
A key part of democracy is allowing all citizens to vote. An elderly woman casts her vote in an election in Mali (below). Voters line up for miles to cast votes in South Africa's first democratic elections in 1994 (bottom). **Apply Information** *Why do you think South Africans were willing to walk miles in order to cast a vote?*

In some African countries, African military leaders took control of the government by force. Military governments do not always govern fairly. The people often have few rights. Further, citizens may be jailed if they protest. But military governments have held together some African countries that otherwise might have been torn apart by war.

Building Democracy In many parts of Africa, there is a long history of democracy. A **democracy** is a government over which citizens exercise power. In a democracy, citizens influence governmental decisions. Some countries have made traditional ways a part of governing. For example, in Botswana, lively political debates take place in "freedom squares." These outdoor meetings are like the traditional kgotla (GOHT lah), in which people talk with their leaders.

Most African countries are less than 50 years old. In contrast, the stable, democratic country of the United States is more than 200 years old. Many Africans feel that building stable countries will take time. As one leader said, "Let Africa be given the time to develop its own system of democracy."

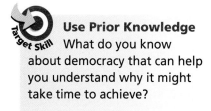

Use Prior Knowledge What do you know about democracy that can help you understand why it might take time to achieve?

✓ **Reading Check** How did Algeria gain independence?

Section 4 Assessment

Key Terms
Review the key terms at the beginning of this section. Use each term in a sentence that explains its meaning.

Target Reading Skill
Look back at what you wrote down about what you already knew. How did what you learned relate to what you already knew?

Comprehension and Critical Thinking
1. (a) Recall How did Africans respond to years of colonial rule?

(b) Infer Why did African leaders encourage people to feel pride about being African?

2. (a) Describe What was Africa's role in World War II?

(b) Identify Effects How did World War II boost the independence movement in Africa?

3. (a) Identify Causes What pressures forced European countries to give up their colonies?

(b) Compare and Contrast How was Ghana's road to independence similar to that of Algeria? How was it different?

Writing Activity
Use a book, an encyclopedia, or the Internet to research an African country that won its independence after 1950. Write a headline and a short newspaper article that might have appeared on the day that country became independent.

Writing Tip Be sure to write a good headline for your newspaper article. The headline should identify the main point of the article. It should also be catchy so that the reader wants to read on.

Mr. DeNoto's class had just finished reading about the ways African countries gained independence. Then the class formed groups. Each group was going to build a float to celebrate the independence of an African country.

"Let's make the flag first," said Tamika.

"No, no, we need to build the float frame first," cried Ari.

"Well, I don't see how we can do anything until we buy the materials we need!" complained Sarah.

Mr. DeNoto held up a hand to quiet the class. "Building a float is complicated. The first thing you have to do is make a plan," he said. "Otherwise, you might cover the same ground more than once. You might even forget an important step. Adam, why don't you come up to the board and be our scribe? We're going to make a flowchart to help us plan."

A flowchart shows sequence, or the order in which actions or events happen. Understanding sequence can help you plan an activity or remember what you have read. A flowchart usually uses arrows to show which step or event happens when. A diagram such as a timeline uses dates to show the order of events.

SS.4.06 Draw conclusions

Learn the Skill

Use these steps when you read a diagram for sequence.

1. **Read the title first.** The title will help you understand what the diagram is about. Mr. DeNoto's class titled its flowchart Building a Float. From the title, you know that the flowchart shows how the class plans to build a float.

2. **Find clues that show the order of events.** On a flowchart, the arrows tell you the order in which you should read the chart. Find the beginning and start there. Mr. DeNoto's class decided that their first step would be "Choose a country."

3. **Read the diagram carefully for connections.** Think about how one step leads to the next step. What are the connections? If there are no illustrations, try imagining each step in your head to help you understand the sequence.

Practice the Skill

Follow the steps below to read the flowchart about Ghana.

1 Read the title. What does it tell you the flowchart will be about?

2 Find the beginning of the chart and identify the first step. Start there and follow the arrows through each step.

3 Now reread the flowchart and answer these questions: (a) What is the first step on the flowchart? (b) What step leads to Nkrumah being jailed? (c) What step comes after Nkrumah being jailed? (d) What is the final result of the Gold Coast colony's struggle for independence?

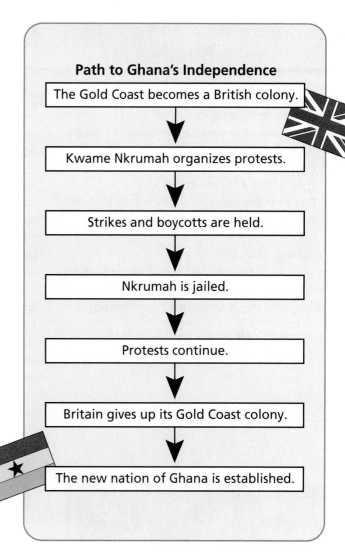

Path to Ghana's Independence

The Gold Coast becomes a British colony.

↓

Kwame Nkrumah organizes protests.

↓

Strikes and boycotts are held.

↓

Nkrumah is jailed.

↓

Protests continue.

↓

Britain gives up its Gold Coast colony.

↓

The new nation of Ghana is established.

After Ghana was established, its government created this coat of arms to represent the nation.

Apply the Skill

Turn to pages 52–53 and study the timeline. Use the steps in this skill to understand what events are shown on the timeline as well as what the sequence of events was.

Issues for Africa Today

Prepare to Read

Objectives

In this section you will

1. Learn about the economic issues faced by African nations today.
2. Find out about major social issues and how they affect Africans today.
3. Discover the ways in which Africa is facing current environmental challenges.

Taking Notes

As you read, find details about issues faced by people in Africa today. Copy the outline below, and use it to record your findings.

I. Economic issues
  A. Farming and mining
    1.
    2.
  B.
II.

Target Reading Skill

Predict As you have learned, making predictions before you read helps you set a purpose for reading and helps you remember what you read.

Before you read this section, think about what you know about Africa's history. Then predict some issues the region might face today. As you read, connect what you read to your prediction. If what you learn doesn't support your prediction, revise the prediction.

Key Terms

- **commercial farming** (kuh MUR shul FAHR ming) *n.* the large-scale production of crops for sale
- **hybrid** (HY brid) *n.* a plant that is created by breeding different types of the same plant
- **literate** (LIT ur it) *adj.* able to read and write
- **life expectancy** (lyf ek SPEK tun see) *n.* the average length of time a person can expect to live

A young man digs an irrigation ditch in Niger.

In the past, nothing grew during the dry season in the Sahel. Farmers had to travel to cities to find work. Now, the West African country of Niger has a new irrigation program for its part of the Sahel. Irrigation allows farmers to grow a second crop during the dry season, in addition to their usual crop in the wet season. One farmer says that raising two crops a year means he can stay on village land.

❝Dry-season crops are such a normal practice now that everyone grows them. Before, each year after the harvest, I went to the city to look for work. But today, with the dry-season crops, I have work in the village. Truly it is a good thing.❞

—*Adamou Sani, farmer*

Niger's irrigation program is one way Africans are improving their lives. Africans are also finding ways to meet economic, social, and environmental challenges.

Economic Issues

The colonial powers saw Africa as a source of raw materials and a market for their own manufactured goods. They did little to build factories in Africa. Today, African countries still have little manufacturing. Most economies are based on farming and mining.

Farming Farming is the most important economic activity in Africa. About 60 percent of workers are farmers. And more than half of the goods that African countries sell overseas are farm goods. Africans practice two kinds of farming—subsistence farming and commercial farming. Recall that subsistence farmers work small plots of land. They try to raise as much food as their families need. **Commercial farming** is the large-scale production of cash crops for sale. In Africa, commercial farmers grow cash crops such as coffee, cacao, and bananas.

Mining Many African nations have rich mineral resources. They export minerals to other countries. Nigeria has oil and coal. The Democratic Republic of the Congo and Zambia have copper, while South Africa has gold and diamonds.

Farming for Food or for Profit?
A man bicycles through a banana farm in Ivory Coast (bottom). A woman picks coffee in Zambia (below). **Analyze Information** *Do you think the farms shown are commercial or subsistence farms? Explain why.*

South African Gold Mine

In South Africa's deep-level gold mines, miners work as far down as two miles (3.2 kilometers) underground. The mines run 24 hours a day. Because it is so hot at that depth, deep-level mining requires ventilation and cooling. In addition to tunnels, there are shafts, elevators to lift the ore to the surface, and surface processing plants. South Africa produces almost half of the world's gold.

Working in the Mines
Miners like this man train for their jobs by stepping up and down on blocks for hours in a very hot room.

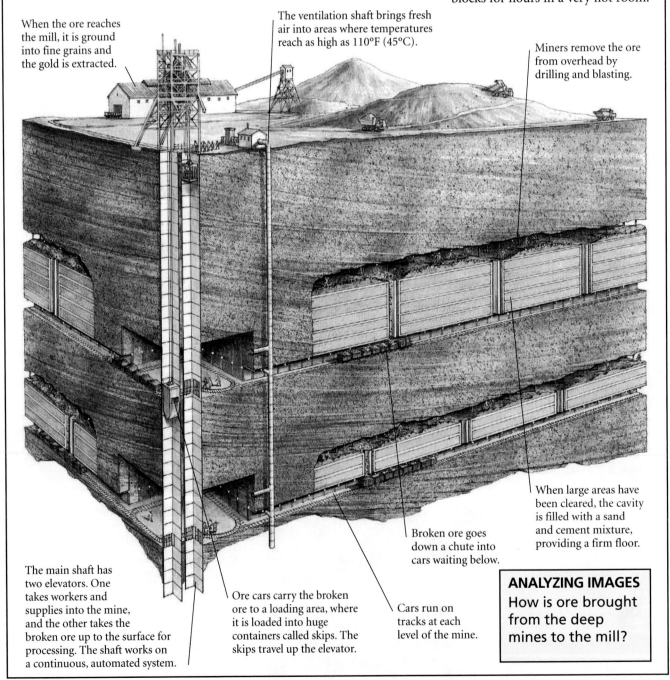

When the ore reaches the mill, it is ground into fine grains and the gold is extracted.

The ventilation shaft brings fresh air into areas where temperatures reach as high as 110°F (45°C).

Miners remove the ore from overhead by drilling and blasting.

When large areas have been cleared, the cavity is filled with a sand and cement mixture, providing a firm floor.

Broken ore goes down a chute into cars waiting below.

Cars run on tracks at each level of the mine.

Ore cars carry the broken ore to a loading area, where it is loaded into huge containers called skips. The skips travel up the elevator.

The main shaft has two elevators. One takes workers and supplies into the mine, and the other takes the broken ore up to the surface for processing. The shaft works on a continuous, automated system.

ANALYZING IMAGES
How is ore brought from the deep mines to the mill?

Economic Challenges About 75 percent of African countries have specialized economies—they depend on exporting one or two products. Gambia depends on peanuts, while Zambia relies on the export of copper. As a result, African economies are especially sensitive to the rise and fall of world prices. A fall in prices hurts economies that depend on the sale of one crop or mineral.

African countries are now trying to reduce their dependence on one export by diversifying their economies. For example, Senegal became independent in 1960. At that time, more than 70 percent of Senegal's people worked in the peanut industry. Today, Senegal has other major export industries, such as fishing, fish processing, and mining. Peanuts now account for only a small percent of the money Senegal earns from exports.

Farming Improvements African nations face another economic problem—how to feed a growing population. Several governments are trying to help farmers increase the size of their crops. One method they use is to develop hybrid plants. A **hybrid** is a plant created by breeding different types of the same plant. The goal is that the best qualities of each type of plant will show up in the hybrid. Since the late 1990s, West Africans have been planting hybrid rice that combines the best aspects of African and Asian rices. As a result, these farmers have been able to produce more rice.

✓ **Reading Check** Which two activities do most African economies depend upon?

Predict
Based on what you know about specialized economies, predict whether more African countries are likely to change their economies.

Expanding Economies
Today, fish markets like the ones below are helping Senegal's economy succeed. Fish products have become Senegal's major export. **Generalize** *What advantages do you think the fishing industry offers to a country with a specialized economy?*

A South African girl focuses on her schoolwork.

Social Issues

In addition to making economic improvements, African nations also must provide social services to their growing populations. Many Africans need better access to education and health care.

Education African children must often contribute to their family's income by working on family farms or by selling goods in the market. When girls and boys go to school, families sacrifice. But most Africans are willing to make this sacrifice because they know education can improve their children's lives.

It has long been a tradition in Africa for communities to actively support their schools. If needed, people will construct new schools. For example, parents in South Africa have often helped to build new schools when the government could not do it alone. Even so, many of the schools are overcrowded, so students must take turns attending classes.

The headmaster at one such school said that students "who couldn't cram into the desks knelt on the floor or stood on their toes so as not to miss a word the teacher was saying." African students are often expected to help keep their school and its grounds clean. The students might do this by sweeping the floors or disposing of the trash.

Reading and Writing The number of Africans who are literate varies from country to country. Being **literate** means being able to read and write. In all African countries, more people have learned to read and write since independence. When Mozambique gained independence from Portugal in 1975, less than 7 percent of its people were literate. Today, about 48 percent of the people in Mozambique are literate. In Tanzania, progress with literacy has been even more dramatic. When the country gained independence from Britain in 1961, only 15 percent of Tanzania's people were literate. Today, about 78 percent of Tanzanians can read and write.

Health Another social issue that differs from country to country in Africa is **life expectancy**—the average length of time a person can expect to live. In Morocco, life expectancy is between 67 and 72 years. In Southern Africa, however, the average life expectancy is less than 50 years. In the Southern African country of Botswana, people only live an average of 32 years.

The main reason for low life expectancy in Africa is childhood disease. There are many diseases for which children have low resistance. For example, insects spread diseases such as malaria. Unclean drinking water and living conditions help spread other diseases. The virus called HIV causes AIDS. Millions of African children have been born with HIV, and millions more adults have died of AIDS before age 50.

Preventing Disease Although the problem of AIDS exists around the world, it is worst in Southern Africa. One reason is that many Southern Africans who are poor cannot afford drugs that might help them. Also, many people have not had access to education, so they have not learned how to prevent the disease. African governments are working with groups such as the World Health Organization to prevent and treat health problems. Some progress has been made. For example, individuals and organizations in Uganda have worked hard to reduce the number of HIV infections there. Because of its success, Uganda may serve as a model for preventing and controlling HIV in other countries.

✓ **Reading Check** What is the main reason for low life expectancy in Africa?

Health Concerns in Africa
Children surround a health worker at a clinic in Gambia as she writes down information about their health.
Predict *In what ways do you think the health worker can help this community?*

The Environment

Like other countries around the world, the countries of Africa face a number of environmental challenges. About two thirds of Africa is desert or dry land. High-quality farmland is scarce, and rainfall may vary greatly over the year. These environmental factors make farming especially challenging in parts of Africa.

Soil Problems People in Africa's rural areas often struggle to make a living. Much of the land in Africa is poor for farming. People thus need great areas of land to raise enough crops to support their families. They may cut down trees to use or sell the wood and to clear land for farming. With no cover from trees, soil is exposed to wind and rain. The soil then erodes, or wears away. Soil erosion reduces the amount of land on which food can grow. Without enough farmland, many Africans face starvation.

Solutions From Science Improvements in science can help feed Africans and protect Africa's environment. Irrigation projects, hybrids, and plants that hold water in the ground have all increased crop harvests. To fight soil erosion, Nigerian farmers now plant traditional crops like yams in long rows. Between the rows they plant trees that hold the soil in place. African nations still face many challenges, but they are trying to meet these challenges by using their resources and improving education.

Men plant trees in Madagascar to help prevent erosion.

✓ **Reading Check** How have Nigerian farmers fought soil erosion?

Section 5 Assessment

Key Terms
Review the key terms at the beginning of this section. Use each term in a sentence that explains its meaning.

Target Reading Skill
What did you predict about this section? How did your prediction guide your reading?

Comprehension and Critical Thinking
1. (a) Recall Do many African nations today have specialized economies?

(b) Draw Conclusions Why are African nations trying to diversify their economies?

2. (a) Identify What social issues are people facing in Africa today?

(b) Infer Literacy rates in most African countries have increased since independence. Education has also improved. From these facts, what can you infer that people value in Africa?

3. (a) Name Give an example of an environmental challenge African nations face today.

(b) Analyze How is that challenge being addressed?

Writing Activity
Suppose you are the economic advisor to the president of an African country. Write a brief report on some steps the president might take to improve the economy.

Go Online
PHSchool.com

For: An activity on environmental issues in Africa
Visit: PHSchool.com
Web Code: ngd-5205

Review and Assessment

◆ Chapter Summary

Section 1: African Beginnings

- Our ancestors were originally hunters and gatherers and became herders and farmers.
- The early African civilizations of Egypt and Nubia arose along the Nile River.
- When Bantu-speaking farmers migrated, Bantu languages spread throughout much of Africa.

Section 2: Kingdoms, City-States, and Empires

- Along East Africa's coast, civilizations grew strong from trade.
- North Africa was shaped by the Carthaginians, the Romans, and the Arabs.
- West African kingdoms grew rich from trade with North Africa.

Bronze head

Section 3: European Conquest of Africa

- Europeans explored Africa's coast to expand their trade ties beyond North Africa.
- Europeans expanded their trade with Africa to include slaves, whom they sent to work on plantations in the Americas.
- European countries claimed African lands for themselves, which had lasting effects on Africa.

Section 4: Independence and Its Challenges

- Fueled by increased feelings of African nationalism, African political parties and leaders worked for the rights of Africans.
- Africans who fought in World War II returned home seeking freedom and independence for their own countries.
- After World War II, African nations gradually gained independence from colonial powers.

Section 5: Issues for Africa Today

- To increase economic stability, African countries are trying to diversify their economies.
- Africans today are working to increase literacy rates and life expectancy.
- Africans are trying to address environmental issues, such as soil erosion, through the help of science, education, and the sensible use of land and other resources.

South Africa

◆ Reviewing Key Terms

Use each key term below in a sentence that shows the meaning of the term.

1. domesticate
2. civilization
3. migrate
4. ethnic group
5. city-state
6. pilgrimage
7. plantation
8. colonize
9. nationalism
10. Pan-Africanism
11. boycott
12. democracy
13. commercial farming
14. hybrid
15. literate
16. life expectancy

◆ Comprehension and Critical Thinking

17. (a) List Identify some of the skills early Africans used to survive.
(b) Draw Conclusions How did the onset of farming affect early civilizations in Africa?

18. (a) Name Identify an ancient trading civilization from each of the following areas: East Africa, North Africa, and West Africa.
(b) Explain Why was trade important to ancient African civilizations?
(c) Analyze Information What was the relationship between trade and the spread of Islam in Africa?

19. (a) Recall How did the relationship between Europeans and Africans begin?
(b) Identify Sequence How did the relationship between Europeans and Africans change over time?
(c) Identify Effects Describe the effects of the Atlantic slave trade on Africa.

20. (a) Define What is meant by the phrase "the scramble for Africa"?

(b) Describe What challenges have African nations faced since independence?
(c) Make Inferences In what ways did colonial rule cause problems for African countries after independence?

21. (a) Identify What economic, social, and environmental issues challenge Africans today?
(b) Explain How are Africans working to improve their economies and social conditions?

◆ Skills Practice

Sequencing In the Skills for Life activity in this chapter, you learned how to show sequence. Review the steps you followed to learn this skill. Then make a timeline of key events in this chapter.

◆ Writing Activity: Language Arts

In the 1800s, many people in the United States spoke out against slavery. They were called abolitionists because they wanted to abolish, or put an end to, slavery. Using what you have learned about the slave trade, write a speech that could be used by an abolitionist to help end slavery.

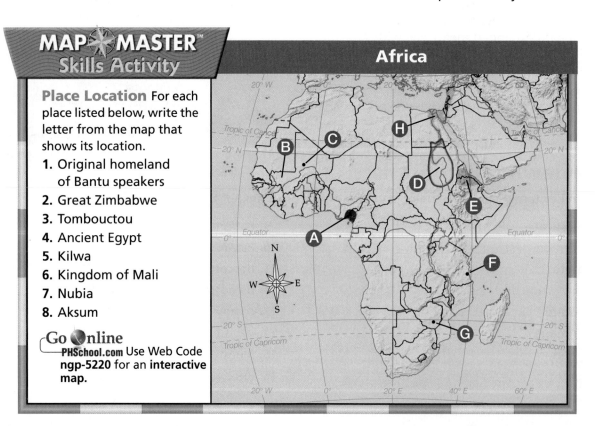

MAP✦MASTER™ Skills Activity

Africa

Place Location For each place listed below, write the letter from the map that shows its location.

1. Original homeland of Bantu speakers
2. Great Zimbabwe
3. Tombouctou
4. Ancient Egypt
5. Kilwa
6. Kingdom of Mali
7. Nubia
8. Aksum

Go Online
PHSchool.com Use Web Code **ngp-5220** for an **interactive map.**

Standardized Test Prep

Test-Taking Tips

Some questions on standardized tests ask you to analyze a reading selection. Study the passage below. Then follow the tips to answer the sample question.

> In A.D. 1312, Mansa Musa became emperor of Mali. As emperor, he controlled huge supplies of gold and salt. Mansa Musa brought laws based on Islam to his land. Mali became a safe place to live and travel. The emperor also promoted trade with North Africa. His fame spread to Europe.

TIP Try to identify the main idea, or most important point, in the paragraph. Every sentence in a paragraph helps to support this idea.

Pick the letter that best answers the question.

From this paragraph, it is clear that Mansa Musa

A ~~became too powerful for the good of his people~~.

B ~~was the most powerful ruler in the world at that time~~.

C brought order and prosperity to his land.

D traveled to Europe to promote trade.

TIP Cross out answer choices that don't make sense. Then choose the BEST answer from the remaining choices.

Think It Through You can rule out A and B. Mansa Musa was powerful, but the paragraph doesn't suggest that he was too powerful or that he was the world's most powerful ruler. That leaves C and D. It is true that Mansa Musa's travels promoted trade, but the paragraph doesn't mention a trip to Europe. The correct answer is C.

Practice Questions

Use the tips above and other tips in this book to help you answer the following questions.

1. An early civilization formed in which area along the Nile River?

   A Mali   B Ghana

   C Nubia   D Great Zimbabwe

2. During the time of the Atlantic slave trade,

   A Europeans traded weapons for African slaves.

   B slaves in the European colonies usually won their freedom after a few years.

   C almost all slaves survived the voyage across the Atlantic.

   D Africans did not profit from slavery.

3. What was the goal of the Pan-African movement?

   A bringing all Africans together in one nation

   B bringing all Africans living around the world together to work for their rights and freedoms

   C bringing only Africans living in Africa together to work for their rights and freedoms

   D bringing all Africans living outside of Africa back to Africa

Read the passage below, and then answer the question that follows.

> European countries competed with one another to gain African territory. Instead of going to war over territory, they set rules for how they could claim African land. By 1900, European nations had colonized many parts of Africa.

4. What can you conclude from this passage about the colonization of Africa?

   A Africans did not resist colonization.

   B Africa was colonized sometime after 1900.

   C European nations believed they could benefit from controlling Africa's resources.

   D European nations were not good at fighting wars with one another.

Go Online
PHSchool.com

Use Web Code **nga-5200** for **Chapter 2 self-test.**

Chapter Preview

 Standard Course of Study

7.11.01 How culture links and separates society

7.11.02 Influence of environment and beliefs in creating cultural responses

7.11.03 Compare and contrast institutions in different cultures

7.11.04 Impact of economic, political, and social changes on individuals and cultures

7.12.01 Impact of belief system on practices and institutions

7.12.03 Cultural borrowing and the development of societies

SS.1.06 Use social studies terms in reports

SS.1.08 Use context clues and appropriate sources to gain meaning

Sections

 **Target Reading Skill**

Comparison and Contrast In this chapter you will focus on comparing and contrasting ideas to help you understand the text that you read. Making comparisons, identifying contrasts, and using signal words are all ways for you to learn as you read.

▶ **A dancer leaps through the air to the rhythm of the drums at a performance in Burundi.**

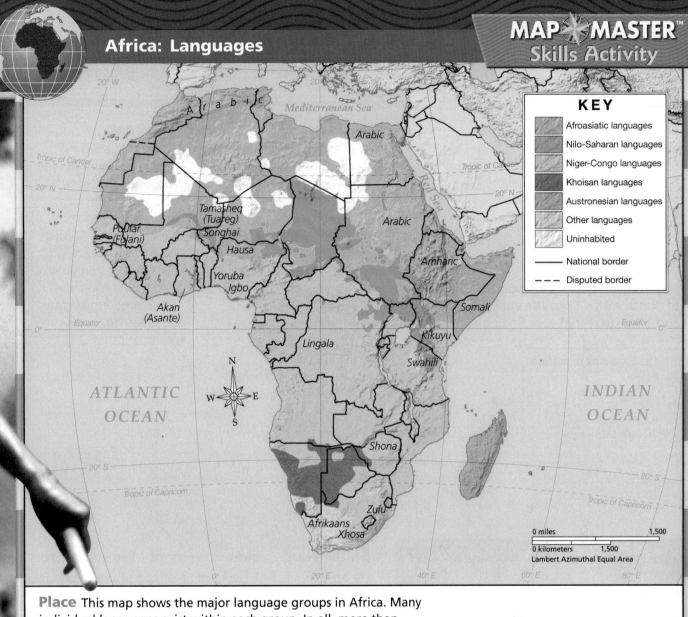

KEY

Afroasiatic languages
Nilo-Saharan languages
Niger-Congo languages
Khoisan languages
Austronesian languages
Other languages
Uninhabited

—— National border
- - - Disputed border

Mediterranean Sea

Arabic

Arabic

Arabic

Tamasheq
(Tuareg)
Songhai

Poular
(Fulani)

Hausa

Amharic

Yoruba
Igbo

Akan
(Asante)

Somali

Lingala

Kikuyu

Swahili

ATLANTIC
OCEAN

INDIAN
OCEAN

Shona

Zulu

Afrikaans
Xhosa

Tropic of Cancer

20° N

Equator
0°

20° S

Tropic of Capricorn

Red Sea

0 miles   1,500
0 kilometers   1,500
Lambert Azimuthal Equal Area

Place This map shows the major language groups in Africa. Many individual languages exist within each group. In all, more than 1,500 languages are spoken in Africa. **Identify** Name the two African language groups that are the largest. **Draw Conclusions** Why do you think large numbers of people who live near one another tend to speak languages from the same language group?

Go Online
PHSchool.com Use Web Code
ngp-5310 for step-by-step
map skills practice.

The Cultures of North Africa

Prepare to Read

Objectives

In this section you will
1. Learn about the elements of culture.
2. Discover how Islam influences life in North Africa.
3. Find out about cultural change in North Africa.

Taking Notes

As you read, find details about the cultures of North Africa. Copy the outline below, and use it to record your findings.

```
I. The Elements of culture
   A.
      1.
      2.
   B.
II. Islamic influence
```

Target Reading Skill

Make Comparisons
Making comparisons between groups or situations can help you see what they have in common. As you read this section, compare the ways of life of different peoples in North Africa. Look for similarities among ethnic groups, among people who live in different locations, or among other groups that are logical to compare.

Key Terms

- **culture** (KUL chur) *n.* the way of life of people who share similar customs and beliefs
- **Quran** (koo RAHN) *n.* the sacred book of Islam; also spelled *Koran*
- **cultural diffusion** (KUL chur ul dih FYOO zhun) *n.* the spread of customs and ideas from one culture to another

A carpet salesman in Marrakech

In the North African country of Morocco, carpets are an export. But they are also part of everyday life. In some Moroccan homes, carpets serve as more than just floor coverings. People may use them as places to sit and to sleep. People also use special carpets as prayer mats.

Suppose your family lives in the Moroccan city of Marrakech (ma ruh KESH). A typical day might unfold in the following way. After breakfast, your mother spends the day weaving carpets. She learned this skill from her mother, who learned it from her mother. Her workday ends at sunset, when she hears the crier who calls out from the nearby mosque (mahsk), the Muslim house of worship. When she hears the call, your mother joins many others in reciting this prayer in Arabic: "There is no god but God, and Muhammad is His messenger."

The Elements of Culture

The way of life you just read about is different in some ways from yours. In other words, Morocco's culture is somewhat different from yours. **Culture** is the way of life of a group of people who share similar customs and beliefs.

What Defines Culture? Culture has many elements. Culture includes food, clothing, homes, jobs, and language. It also includes things that are not so easy to see, such as how people view their world and what their beliefs are. These views and beliefs shape the way people behave. In Morocco, for example, many people take time from their activities to pray several times each day.

Shared Elements Different cultures may have elements in common. People in different places sometimes share the same language, although they may speak different dialects, or versions of that language. Similarly, cultures sometimes share the same religion, although people may practice it in different ways.

Some shared elements of culture are easy to notice. People of different cultures might wear similar clothing or live in similar housing. In many rural villages in Morocco, for example, houses are made of thick adobe (uh DOH bee), a type of brick made from sun-dried clay. Far from Morocco, in Mexico and in the southwestern United States, many people in rural areas also live in adobe houses.

✓ **Reading Check** Name some cultural elements that are easy to see.

Links to
Science

Building With Adobe
Adobe bricks are made of clay and plant fibers. The fibers strengthen the bricks and keep them from crumbling. People have built with adobe since ancient times in many parts of the world. Native Americans have built with adobe for hundreds of years in the southwestern United States, where it is still used today.

Adobe is a good building material because it acts as an insulator, a material that helps keep outside heat from traveling inside. This insulating quality is especially important in hot climates, such as Morocco's (below).

Religion and Culture in North Africa

The peoples of North Africa are spread out over a large area that includes the following countries: Egypt, Libya, Tunisia, Algeria, and Morocco. North Africans have many different backgrounds and ways of life. The Arabic language helps unify the different peoples of North Africa. So does Islam.

Muslim Beliefs Religion is an important part of North African culture. More than 95 percent of North Africans are Muslims. Muslims believe in God, whom they call by the Arabic word *Allah* (AL uh). The founder of Islam was a man named Muhammad. Muslims believe that Muhammad was a prophet, or a religious teacher who speaks for God or a god. In Islam, Jesus and the prophets of the Hebrew Bible, or Christian Old Testament, are also believed to be God's messengers. However, Muhammad is considered God's final messenger.

The sacred book of Islam is called the **Quran** (koo RAHN). Muslims consider the Quran to be the word of God. They believe that God revealed the verses of the Quran to the prophet Muhammad. Like the Hebrew and Christian Bibles, the Quran contains many kinds of writing, including stories, promises, and instructions. The Quran teaches about God, and it also provides a guide to living. The Quran forbids lying, stealing, and murder. It also prohibits gambling, eating pork, and drinking alcohol.

■ Chart Skills

Muslims call Muhammad's most essential teachings the Five Pillars of Islam. These pillars are duties that all Muslims are expected to follow, such as praying daily, as shown above. **Define** What are alms? **Infer** Why do you think Muhammad wanted Muslims to regularly declare their belief in God?

The Five Pillars of Islam

Pillar	Description
Declaration of Faith	Muslims must regularly declare the belief that there is only one God and Muhammad is God's messenger.
Prayer	Muslims must pray five times each day, facing in the direction of the holy city of Mecca.
Almsgiving	Muslims must give alms, or money that goes to the needy.
Fasting	Muslims must fast during daylight hours in the month of Ramadan.
Pilgrimage	Muslims must make a pilgrimage to Mecca at least one time in their lives if they are able.

Islam and Law The Islamic system of law is based on the Quran. Islamic law governs many aspects of life, including family life, business practices, banking, and government. Because so many North Africans are Muslims, Islamic law influences the cultures of the region.

Ethnic Groups of North Africa Most North Africans are Arabs. Because the Arab influence is so strong, North Africa is sometimes seen as a part (the western end) of the Arab world. But the region has other ethnic groups besides the Arabs. The largest of these groups is the Berbers, who live mainly in Algeria and Morocco. Most Berbers speak both Berber and Arabic, and almost all are Muslim.

Many Berbers live in cities, while others live in small villages in rugged mountain areas. They make their living by herding and farming. The Tuareg (TWAH reg) are a group of Berbers who live in the Sahara, the enormous desert that stretches across the southern part of North Africa. The Tuareg herd camels, goats, and other livestock and also engage in long-distance trade.

Mixing Old and New
As is traditional for Muslim women, these Moroccan girls are wearing head scarves. At the same time, one is using a cell phone. **Analyze Images** *Do you think these girls would say it is easy or difficult to blend old and new ways?*

Traditional and Modern Lifestyles In parts of rural North Africa, some people live traditionally, or in ways similar to those of their parents and grandparents. But traditional and modern ways of life mix in towns and large cities such as Cairo (KY roh), in Egypt, and Tunis (TOO nis), in Tunisia.

Some city people work at traditional crafts such as carpet weaving. Others work as architects, scientists, bus drivers, or bankers. Some sell baskets in outdoor markets. Others sell television sets, books, and other items in modern stores. The peoples of North Africa may live vastly different lives, yet Islam helps form a common bond of culture among them.

✓ **Reading Check** **What are the two largest ethnic groups of North Africa?**

Make Comparisons The people who live in North Africa's cities practice a variety of lifestyles. What element of culture do they have in common?

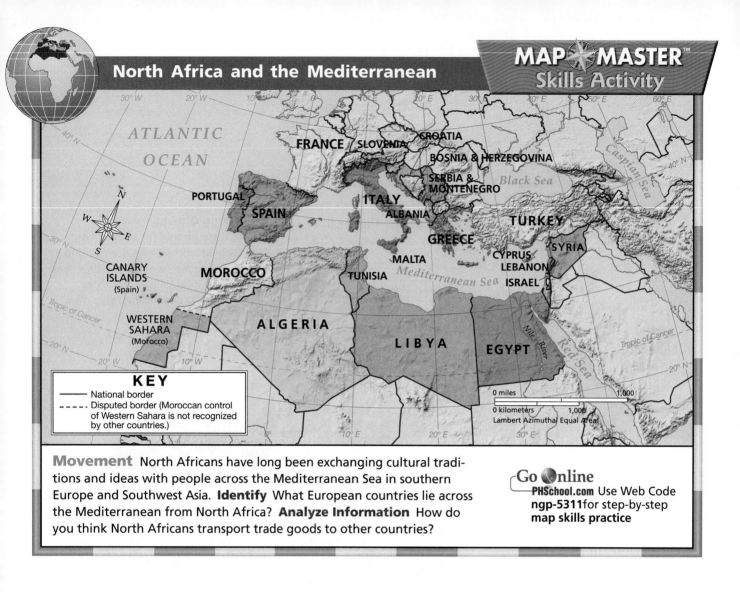

MAP MASTER™
Skills Activity

ATLANTIC OCEAN

FRANCE
SLOVENIA
CROATIA
BOSNIA & HERZEGOVINA
SERBIA & MONTENEGRO
Black Sea
Caspian Sea
PORTUGAL
SPAIN
ITALY
ALBANIA
GREECE
TURKEY
CYPRUS
SYRIA
LEBANON
MALTA
CANARY ISLANDS (Spain)
MOROCCO
TUNISIA
Mediterranean Sea
ISRAEL
Tropic of Cancer
WESTERN SAHARA (Morocco)
ALGERIA
LIBYA
EGYPT
Nile River
Red Sea
Tropic of Cancer

KEY
—— National border
- - - - Disputed border (Moroccan control of Western Sahara is not recognized by other countries.)

0 miles 1,000
0 kilometers 1,000
Lambert Azimuthal Equal Area

Movement North Africans have long been exchanging cultural traditions and ideas with people across the Mediterranean Sea in southern Europe and Southwest Asia. **Identify** What European countries lie across the Mediterranean from North Africa? **Analyze Information** How do you think North Africans transport trade goods to other countries?

Go Online
PHSchool.com Use Web Code ngp-5311 for step-by-step map skills practice

Cultural Change in North Africa

North Africa's mix of traditional and modern ways of life shows that culture does not stay the same forever. It changes all the time. Cultural changes often occur when people move from one place to another. As they travel, people share their customs and ideas with others. They also learn about new ideas and customs. The result is **cultural diffusion,** or the spread of customs and ideas to new places. *Diffusion* means "spreading out."

Tunisian pottery

A Hub of Trade Study the map above. An important factor in the diffusion of culture in North Africa is location. Because of its location, North Africa has been a hub, or center, of trade for people from Europe, Asia, North Africa, and other parts of Africa. Thus, the peoples of these regions have come into contact with one another's cultures. Many customs and ideas have spread into and out of North Africa.

Conquering Empires The mixing of cultures in North Africa did not occur only through trade. It also occurred through conquest. North Africa was home to the ancient Egyptians, one of the world's oldest civilizations. Once the ancient Egyptians had developed trade links with ancient civilizations in both Europe and Southwest Asia, these civilizations competed with one another for power. The ancient Egyptians both conquered and were conquered by other empires. Through these conquests, more cultural diffusion occurred.

Western and Muslim Cultures One of the more recent influences on North Africa is Western culture, meaning the cultures of Europe and North America. Some Muslims are concerned that their countries are becoming too Westernized. More people are wearing Western clothes, buying Western products, seeing films produced by the West, and adopting Western ideas. Some Muslims fear that these influences will lead to the loss of Muslim values and traditions. They want to preserve their way of life. All over Africa, people face the challenge of how to preserve the traditions they value as their countries change.

In Algeria, women in traditional Muslim clothes walk alongside women and men in Western dress.

 **Reading Check** With what regions have North Africans traditionally traded?

Section 1 Assessment

Key Terms
Review the key terms at the beginning of this section. Use each term in a sentence that explains its meaning.

Target Reading Skill
Other than religion, what is an element of culture that most North Africans have in common?

Comprehension and Critical Thinking
1. (a) Name What are some elements of culture?

(b) Draw Conclusions How do you think cultural beliefs shape the way people behave?

2. (a) Recall What are the beliefs of the followers of Islam?

(b) Analyze Information How has Islam influenced the cultures of North Africa?

3. (a) Locate Describe North Africa's location.

(b) Cause and Effect How has North Africa's location contributed to cultural diffusion?

(c) Analyze Information Do you think that adding new elements to a culture has to lead to the loss of old ones?

Writing Activity
What is your culture? What traditions in your culture do you think are the most important ones to preserve? Write an essay describing these customs and explaining why you value them.

Writing Tip To help you get started, write a list of traditions and customs you practice throughout the year.

The Cultures of West Africa

Prepare to Read

Objectives

In this section you will
1. Learn about West Africa's ethnic diversity.
2. Find out about the importance of family ties in West African culture.
3. Examine the West African tradition of storytelling.

Taking Notes

As you read, look for details about the cultures of West Africa. Copy the flowchart below, and use it to record your findings.

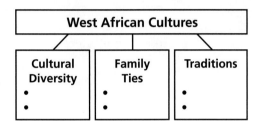

West African Cultures		
Cultural Diversity • •	**Family Ties** • •	**Traditions** • •

Target Reading Skill

Identify Contrasts
Identifying contrasts between two groups or situations can help you see what is unique about each one. As you read this section, contrast the cultures in West Africa with the cultures in the United States. List the differences that relate to language and to family life.

Key Terms

- **cultural diversity** (KUL chur ul duh VUR suh tee) *n.* a wide variety of cultures
- **kinship** (KIN ship) *n.* a family relationship
- **nuclear family** (NOO klee ur FAM uh lee) *n.* the part of a family that includes parents and children
- **extended family** (ek STEN did FAM uh lee) *n.* the part of a family that includes parents, children, and other relatives
- **lineage** (LIN ee ij) *n.* a group of families descended from a common ancestor
- **clan** (klan) *n.* a group of lineages

Mauritanian students in school

In Mauritania (mawr uh TAY nee uh), North Africa meets West Africa. There, the Sahara merges into the tree-dotted grasslands of the savanna. But geography is not the only part of Mauritanian life that reveals major contrasts. Culture does, too. If you were to attend school in one of the small villages in southern Mauritania, you could see this firsthand. You would hear teachers speaking in French, even though they probably also know the country's official language, Arabic. Outside the classroom, students would speak the local language of their ethnic group, which might differ from town to town.

Cultural Diversity of West Africa

Being able to speak more than one language is useful in West Africa, which is home to hundreds of ethnic groups. The region is famous for its **cultural diversity, or wide variety of cultures.** Unlike the ethnic groups of North Africa, those of West Africa are not united by a single religion or a common language.

A Region of Many Languages

Think about your community. Imagine that the people who live nearby speak a different language. How could you communicate with them? Suppose you want to shop in a store, eat in a restaurant, or attend a sports event taking place in the next town. It might seem like visiting another country.

This situation is exactly what many West Africans experience. The hundreds of ethnic groups in West Africa speak different languages. Sometimes groups in neighboring villages speak different languages. In order to communicate, most West Africans speak more than one language. Some speak four or five languages. This practice helps unify countries with many ethnic groups. People use these various languages when they travel or conduct business. They often use French, English, Portuguese, or a local language called Hausa to communicate among various ethnic groups.

Rural and Urban Workers

The ethnic groups in West Africa differ in more than just the languages they speak. Like North Africans, West Africans make a living in various ways. Many West Africans live in rural areas. A typical village consists of a group of homes surrounded by farmland. The villagers grow food for themselves as well as cash crops to sell. In the Sahara and the dry Sahel just south of it, many people herd cattle, goats, sheep, or camels. Along the coast, most West Africans make a living by fishing. Some West Africans live in large cities where they may work in hospitals, hotels, or office buildings.

Many Languages in One Place
If you were shopping at this market in West Africa, you might hear a number of languages being spoken. **Draw Conclusions** *How do you think people communicate in situations like this?*

✓ **Reading Check** How does cultural diversity affect the people of West Africa?

West African Families

Like North Africans, West Africans see themselves as members of a number of groups. Just as you belong to a family, one or more ethnic groups, and a country, so do West Africans.

Identify Contrasts A nuclear family and an extended family are similar. Contrast them to understand the important differences between them.

West African Family Ties
Members of an extended family in Nigeria gather in front of their home (bottom). A woman in Ivory Coast cares for her granddaughter (below). **Identify Effects** *What effects do you think the strong kinship ties of West Africa have on communities?*

Kinship and Customs One of the strongest bonds that West Africans have is the bond of **kinship,** or family relationship. The first level of kinship is the **nuclear family,** which consists of parents and their children. The next level is the **extended family,** a group consisting of the nuclear family plus other relatives. It may include grandparents, aunts, uncles, and cousins. Often, members of a West African extended family all live together. They also work together and make decisions together. Family members care for the elderly, the sick, and the less well-off. They also watch over the children of other families in the village and willingly help neighbors.

Larger Kinship Groups In many rural areas, kinship reaches beyond extended families to larger groups. One such group is a **lineage,** or a group of families that can trace their descent back to a common ancestor. Some people also recognize larger kinship groups called clans. A **clan** is a group of lineages. As with a lineage, the people in a clan can all trace their roots back to a common ancestor. Members of a clan may be more distantly related to one another than members of a lineage because the group of members is larger in a clan.

Kinship

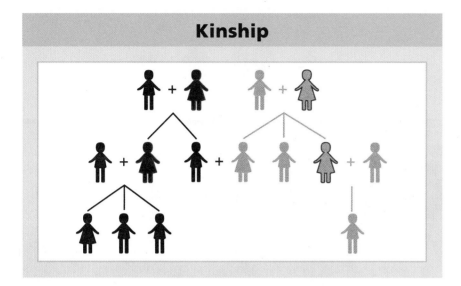

Diagram Skills

The diagram shows the extended family of the married couple at the center. The husband's lineage is in purple, and the wife's is in orange. In a matrilineal society, this family would trace descent through the women who are outlined in red. **Identify** How many nuclear families exist in the extended lineage? **Synthesize** What is the relationship of the woman at the top of the purple lineage to the three siblings at the bottom of it?

Tracing Lineage Different traditions govern the ways West African groups trace their ancestry. Some groups are matrilineal (mat ruh LIN ee ul), meaning that they trace their descent through female ancestors. In matrilineal societies, a person's father is not considered part of the person's lineage. Within the lineage, children consider their mother's brother their closest adult male relative. Their father is a member of another lineage. Most groups, however, are patrilineal (pat ruh LIN ee ul)—they trace their descent through the male side of the family.

Changes in Family Life Although traditional family ties are still strong in West Africa, family life is changing. More and more people are moving from rural villages to urban areas. This trend, known as urbanization, is occurring not only in Africa but throughout the world.

Many young men are looking for work to support themselves and their families. They travel long distances to West Africa's cities to find jobs. The women often stay in the rural homes. They raise the children and farm the land. The men come home from time to time to visit their families and to share what they have earned.

Families live close together in West African villages such as this one in Mali.

✓ **Reading Check** What responsibilities do extended family members have toward one another?

Master of Storytelling
Boys from an Ivory Coast village listen intently as a griot tells them a legend about their ethnic group's history. **Synthesize** *How does oral storytelling help preserve a culture's history?*

Keeping Traditions Alive

Cultural changes, such as urbanization, affect different families in different ways. As they adapt to these changes, most West Africans try to maintain strong family ties. They pass their history, values, and traditions on to the young.

Storytelling Traditions One important way in which West African traditions are being preserved is through the art of vivid and exciting storytelling. Traditional West African stories are spoken aloud rather than written down. A storyteller called a griot (GREE oh) passes a group's oral traditions on from one generation to another.

Stories of tricksters, animal fables, proverbs, riddles, and songs are all part of West Africa's oral tradition. The details in the stories tell about the histories of ethnic groups and kinships. At the same time, they teach children cultural values. An African proverb reflects the value that West Africans place on handing down traditions from generation to generation: "The young can't teach traditions to the old."

African musicians perform around the world, from Massachusetts (left) to Ivory Coast (right).

Cultural Influence The traditions of West Africa have greatly influenced other cultures, especially American culture. Many of the enslaved Africans who were brought to the United States came from West Africa. They brought with them the only things they could: their ideas, stories, dances, music, and customs. The trickster tales of Br'er Rabbit, as well as blues and jazz music, have their roots in West Africa.

Today, West African culture—its stories, music, dances, art, cooking, and clothing—is popular in many countries outside of Africa. Griot guitarists and other musicians from West Africa have international followings. In recent years, four Africans have won the Nobel Prize for literature. One of them is West African— the Nigerian writer Wole Soyinka (WOH lay shaw YING kuh).

✓ **Reading Check** What does a griot do?

Section 2 Assessment

Key Terms
Review the key terms at the beginning of this section. Use each term in a sentence that explains its meaning.

Target Reading Skill
Identify one contrast between the way West Africans use language and the way Americans do.

Comprehension and Critical Thinking
1. (a) Recall In what ways is West Africa culturally diverse?

(b) Identify Effects How does cultural diversity create communication challenges for West Africans?

2. (a) Describe What kinds of kinship ties are found in West African societies?

(b) Draw Conclusions How do you think living together with members of one's extended family helps build a sense of community?

3. (a) Explain What purpose does storytelling serve in West African culture?

(b) Analyze What is the meaning of the proverb "The young can't teach traditions to the old"?

Writing Activity
Suppose you live with your extended family in a small village in West Africa. Make a list of the advantages and disadvantages of your way of life. Indicate which are most important to you.

For: An activity on the cultures of West Africa
Visit: PHSchool.com
Web Code: ngd-5302

Skills for Life

Comparing and Contrasting

Nathan and Antonio went to the mall to buy CDs. When Antonio saw the CD Nathan had chosen, he commented, "I like that CD. But I think the band's new CD is better. They use more drums on the new CD."

Nathan argued. "I disagree. I like the way the band sounded on the old CD. They had two singers, and the two voices together sounded better than this one singer's voice alone." The girl working at the register smiled. She couldn't hear any differences in the CDs. She thought they were both great.

When you look for differences between two or more items, you *contrast* them. To *compare,* you do one of two things: you look for similarities between two or more items, or you look for similarities *and* differences between two or more items. If you are asked to compare, ask if you should find similarities only, or similarities and differences.

Learn the Skill

 SS.4.06 Draw conclusions

Follow these steps to learn how to compare and contrast.

1. **Identify a topic and purpose.** What do you want to compare or contrast, and why? Some purposes for comparing and contrasting are to make a choice, to understand a topic, or to discover patterns.

2. **Select some categories for comparison and contrast.** For example, if you wanted to choose between two bikes, your categories might be color, cost, and types of tires.

3. **Make notes—or a chart—about the categories you are comparing or contrasting.** Some categories call for a yes or no answer. Other categories, such as color or cost, require that you note specific details.

4. **Notice the similarities and differences.** Are the details the same or different for each item?

5. **Draw conclusions.** Write a few sentences explaining whether the items are more similar or more different.

Practice the Skill

Use the steps below, plus your own knowledge, to compare and contrast the two scenes from Africa that are shown in the photographs on this page. Use what you find to determine a pattern in the photographs.

1 What is your topic? What is the purpose?

2 Study the photographs. Then write down at least three categories for comparison and contrast.

3 For each category, take notes on what the photographs show.

4 Now study your notes to see what is similar and what is different about the two photographs.

5 Write a conclusion that explains whether the scenes in the photographs are mostly similar or mostly different. Include a description of one pattern you see in the photographs. Can you describe a third photograph that would fit the pattern?

Chimpanzees in Tanzania

Giraffes in Kenya

Apply the Skill

Reread Sections 1 and 2 of this chapter. Use the steps you learned in this skill to compare and contrast the cultures of North Africa and West Africa.

Prepare to Read

Objectives

In this section you will

1. Find out how geography has affected the development of East African cultures.
2. Learn how and why ideas about land ownership are changing in East Africa.

Taking Notes

As you read, find details about the cultures of East Africa. Copy the concept web below, and use it to record your findings.

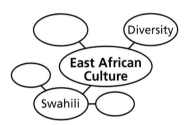

Target Reading Skill

Use Signal Words

Signal words point out relationships among ideas or events. Certain words or phrases, such as *like* and *as with*, can signal a comparison or a contrast. As you read this section, notice the comparisons between East Africa and other parts of Africa.

Key Terms

- **Swahili** (swah HEE lee) *n.* an ethnic group in East Africa that resulted from the mixing of African and Arab ways more than 1,000 years ago; also a language
- **heritage** (HEHR uh tij) *n.* the values, traditions, and customs handed down from one's ancestors

A woman in Lamu gets her hand decorated with henna.

In the neighborhood square, old friends often sit together playing dominoes. A man on a donkey may wander past amidst the occasional roar of motorcycles. Down the street, there is a store that sells spices next to a shop that offers fax services and Internet connections. Nearby, behind shuttered windows that filter the hot sun, women take turns making intricate designs on one another's hands using a natural dye called henna. In former East African city-states such as Lamu (LAH moo), in Kenya, and Zanzibar (ZAN zuh bahr), in Tanzania, such traditional and modern ways are interwoven.

Geography and Cultural Diversity

Like West Africa, East Africa is a region of great cultural diversity. In some parts of the region, such as Lamu and Zanzibar, the diversity reveals itself in the contrast between old and new ways. In other parts, it is reflected in the diversity of languages spoken or religions practiced.

Indian Ocean Connections Much of the cultural diversity of East Africa comes from contact among people from many cultures. Like other Africans, the people of East Africa have often been exposed to other cultures through trade. Turn to the political map of Africa on page 3 of the Regional Overview. Notice how much of East Africa's long coastline borders the Indian Ocean. This ocean provides a trade and travel route for East Africans as well as for the people living across the ocean to the east. These people include Arabs, Indians, and other Asians, even those from countries as far away from Africa as China and Malaysia.

Swahili Culture The connection across the Indian Ocean dates back to early times. Nearly 2,000 years ago, Arab traders began to settle in the coastal villages of East Africa. Members of various African cultures took on elements of Arab culture from the newcomers. The Arabs took on elements of African culture as well. The **Swahili** are an ethnic group that resulted from this mixing of African and Arab ways.

Most people who live in Lamu or Zanzibar are Swahili. A professor in Zanzibar described the history of the Swahili to a reporter in this way:

> **❝**We have always been middlemen—between the land and the sea, the producers and the buyers, the African and the Arabian. That is not a concern; it is our strength. We will survive. Swahili culture may not be quite the same tomorrow as today, but then nothing living is.**❞**
>
> —*Professor Abdul Sheriff*

Swahili Arts and Crafts
Swahili craftsmen are known for carving front doors with detailed decoration on their frames. This one is in Zanzibar, Tanzania. **Analyze Images** *Why do you think people would choose a front door as a place to show their craft?*

One important strength of the Swahili people is their ability to adapt to other cultures. To adapt is to adjust to new things or circumstances. At the same time, the Swahilis try to preserve their **heritage,** or the values, traditions, and customs handed down from their ancestors.

Widespread Swahili Language Swahilis live along East Africa's coast from Somalia to Tanzania. Recall from Chapter 2 that the Swahili language is a Bantu language that contains many Arabic words. Although the Swahili are just one of hundreds of ethnic groups in East Africa, their language is used among ethnic groups throughout the region for business and communication. In Tanzania, children are educated in Swahili through the primary grades. Later, they learn English as well. By promoting the use of Swahili, East African nations are helping to preserve their African heritage and to establish unity among different peoples.

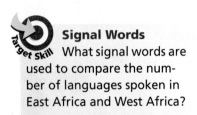

Signal Words What signal words are used to compare the number of languages spoken in East Africa and West Africa?

Other Languages As is true of West Africa, East Africa is home to many ethnic groups who speak different languages. It is not unusual for people in the region to know three languages or more. For example, in Ethiopia more than 80 languages are spoken, and in Kenya about 40 are spoken. About 1,000 languages can be heard in Sudan alone. The variety of languages spoken in the region is largely due to the long history of migrations of ethnic groups from other parts of the continent. For example, the Bantu migration that you read about earlier brought many Bantu-speaking peoples from West Africa to East Africa.

Religion As with languages, religious beliefs in East Africa reflect the cultural diversity of the region. Both Islam and Christianity have large followings there. Islam was introduced to East Africa by Arab traders. Christianity spread into Ethiopia in the A.D. 300s after being introduced to North Africa when the area was a part of the Roman Empire. During the 1800s, Europeans pushed into Africa and spread Christianity even farther. In addition, traditional religions are still practiced in East Africa.

√ **Reading Check** What religions are practiced by East Africans?

Changing Ideas About Land

In East Africa, as in the rest of Africa, most people live in rural areas, where they farm and tend livestock. The ways in which they work the land and view land ownership are part of the culture of East Africans.

Before Land Was Owned Before Europeans took over parts of Africa in the 1800s, individual Africans did not buy or sell land. The very idea of owning land did not exist. Families had the right to farm plots of land, but the size and location of the plots might change over time.

Traditionally in Africa, extended families farmed the land to produce food for the whole group. Men cleared the land and broke up the soil. Women then planted the seeds, tended the fields, and harvested the crops. Meanwhile, the men herded livestock or traded goods.

The Rise and Fall of Plantations The practice of owning land privately was introduced into much of Africa by European settlers. In parts of East Africa, the British set up plantations. When many African countries became independent, their governments broke up the colonial plantations and sold the land to individual Africans.

Some land in East Africa is still available to buy. But much of it is poor farmland in areas where few people live. In fertile areas such as the Ethiopian Highlands and the Great Rift Valley, most of the land good for farming is already taken. Many people live in these fertile areas. In densely populated countries such as Rwanda (roo AHN duh) and Burundi (boo ROON dee), conflicts have developed over land.

The Legacy of Land
Agriculture is part of life all over East Africa. Farmers work fields of a large plantation (bottom). An Ethiopian farmer tends his fields (inset).
Synthesize Information *Why has farmland caused conflicts in some East African countries?*

Where Is Home? Traditionally, Africans feel a strong bond to the land where they grew up. Like the rest of Africa, East Africa is becoming increasingly urban. Yet even people who spend most of their time in a city often do not call it home. If asked where home is, an East African will usually name the village of his or her family or clan. Most people consider their life in the city temporary. They expect to return to their villages at some point.

Tanzania's former president Julius Nyerere (JOOL yus nyuh REHR uh) is one example. After he stepped down as president in 1985, Nyerere moved back to his home village. Although he was far from Dar es Salaam (DAHR es suh LAHM), one of Tanzania's two capital cities, Nyerere continued to be involved in world affairs. Until his death in 1999, he spent his mornings working in the fields, where he grew corn and millet on his farm.

In an interview in 1996, Nyerere said: "In a sense I am a very rural person. I grew up here, and [working in] Dar es Salaam was a duty. I did my duty and after retiring in 1985, I came back here and said, 'Ah, it's good to be back.'" Many other East Africans feel the same. They do their duty by earning money in the city, but they never forget their rural roots.

Julius Nyerere, Tanzania's first president

√ **Reading Check** How did East Africans farm before Europeans arrived?

Section 3 Assessment

Key Terms
Review the key terms at the beginning of this section. Use each term in a sentence that explains its meaning.

 ## Target Reading Skill
Make a list of all the signal words you found as you read this section. Describe the comparison that each signal word indicates.

Comprehension and Critical Thinking
1. (a) Locate Where in East Africa do the Swahilis live?

(b) Summarize How did East Africa become a region with great diversity of language and religion?
(c) Make Inferences What is the importance of the Swahili language in East Africa?
2. (a) Recall When was private land ownership introduced to East Africa?
(b) Summarize How have ideas about land ownership changed over time in East Africa?
(c) Identify Point of View How did traditional East African ideas about land differ from those of Europeans who took over parts of Africa?

Writing Activity
Write a description of the place that you consider home. Tell what home means to you and explain why. How does your meaning of home compare to Julius Nyerere's feelings about his homeland?

Writing Tip Before you begin, think of important details about your home that you can use in your description. Use vivid language to make your description come to life.

The Cultures of Southern and Central Africa

Prepare to Read

Objectives

In this section you will

1. Learn about the cultural diversity of Southern Africa.
2. Examine different ways of life in Central Africa and learn about the diverse cultures of the region.

Taking Notes

As you read, look for details about the cultures of Southern and Central Africa. Copy the table below, and use it to record your findings.

Southern Africa	Central Africa
•	•
•	•
•	•

Target Reading Skill

Compare and Contrast Comparing and contrasting can help you sort out and analyze information. When you compare, you examine the similarities between things. When you contrast, you look at the differences.

As you read this section, compare and contrast the cultures of Southern and Central Africa. Look for similarities and differences in ethnic groups and in economic conditions.

Key Terms

- **migrant worker** (MY grunt WUR kur) *n.* a laborer who travels away from where he or she lives to find work
- **compound** (KAHM pownd) *n.* a fenced-in group of homes

Soccer is a popular sport all around the world. It is no surprise, then, that it is a favorite sport of people in the country of South Africa. But the fact that the sport is played there reveals more than just that South Africans love fun and recreation. It is proof of the changing political times in South Africa.

Soccer came to South Africa from Europe. As you will read in Chapter 7, Europeans settled in the region from the mid-1600s through the 1800s. After the country gained independence in 1910, the white minority of the population took charge of the government. As part of their rule, the white population denied other members of society certain basic rights. For example, black South Africans were not allowed to play on many of the nation's sports teams.

In 1994, the South African government was restructured, and equal rights were extended to all. Today, when black and white soccer players run onto the field, all South Africans have reason to cheer.

A member of South Africa's national soccer team

Diversity in Southern Africa

Like the rest of Africa, Southern Africa has a great deal of cultural diversity. Most of the people of Southern Africa are black Africans. They belong to a variety of ethnic groups, many of which speak separate languages. In addition, there are certain ethnic groups that have greater numbers of members in Southern Africa than in other parts of Africa—for example, people of European descent.

European Influence Southern Africa attracted Europeans for a variety of reasons. The Portuguese arrived in Mozambique in the 1500s and soon began transporting slaves out of Africa. In the 1600s, Dutch and British settlers moved to the Cape of Good Hope at the southern tip of Africa. They grew wheat and herded cattle. Many of the Dutch eventually spread to the north to places such as Malawi, where they started up a mining industry and enlisted local people as laborers. The British also moved north, to Zimbabwe and Zambia.

European Ethnic Groups Southern Africa is home to three main groups of people with European ancestry. One group is descended from the British settlers. These Africans speak English. Another group is Afrikaners (af rih KAHN urz), who are descendants of the Dutch settlers. They speak Afrikaans (af rih KAHNZ), a language related to Dutch. The third group, descended from the Portuguese settlers, speaks Portuguese.

Urbanization The cultural diversity of Southern Africa extends beyond ethnic differences. It is also represented by the contrast between rural and urban lifestyles. For hundreds of years, people in the region lived in villages or small cities. European settlers started a process of urbanization in Southern Africa. The region now includes a number of cities inhabited by more than 1 million people. The largest are Cape Town and Johannesburg in South Africa and Maputo in Mozambique.

Effects of Urbanization
Even though it sits nestled between ocean and mountains, Cape Town has grown to be one of South Africa's largest cities. Its population is about 3 million people. **Infer** *How do you think the presence of numerous large cities changes the culture of a region?*

Industry in South Africa South Africa is the richest, most urban, and most industrialized country in Africa. During the 1900s, South African industries created a great demand for labor. Hundreds of thousands of people came from nearby countries in Southern Africa to work on South African mines. They formed a large force of **migrant workers,** or laborers who travel away from where they live to find work. These migrant workers had to live together in **compounds,** or fenced-in groups of homes. They were far from their families, clans, and ethnic groups. They worked long hours in dangerous conditions for low wages.

A woman in Zimbabwe spreads fertilizer on corn plants.

New Roles for Women The workers who migrated to South Africa for work were mostly men. While they were gone, the women had to take on the men's responsibilities. Traditionally, women had raised the children and farmed the land. Men had cared for the animals, dealt with local matters, and headed the households. Once the men were gone for a year or two at a time, the women began to make the household and community decisions. For most women, this change was a challenge. For example, many of the women had no training for the new tasks. But the change was also rewarding for many women because they gained new rights, responsibilities, and skills.

✓ **Reading Check** Name two cities in Southern Africa that have a population of more than one million people.

Life in Central Africa

Like the people of Southern Africa and the rest of Africa, Central Africans went through many cultural changes in the 1900s. But many people in the region still follow old traditions as well.

Economics and Culture In some ways, Central Africa's cultural diversity is a result of sharp economic contrasts that exist in the region. On the Atlantic coast, the countries of Angola, Congo, Gabon, Cameroon, and Equatorial Guinea have large oil reserves. The cities in these coastal areas tend to benefit most from the oil wealth. People living near the coast also gain more exposure to cultures outside of Africa, allowing for the exchange of traditions and customs.

Compare and Contrast
Target Skill Compare and contrast the ways industry affects culture in Southern and Central Africa. Are there more similarities or more differences?

Mbuti Art The lives of the Mbuti (em BOO tee) are very different from the lives of most people in Central Africa. They are hunter-gatherers who live in the rain forests of Congo. The Mbuti live off the land the way their ancestors have for more than 3,000 years.

For example, they make some of their cloth out of tree bark. Men pound the bark with mallets until it is almost as soft as velvet. Then women draw shapes and patterns on the cloth. Many art galleries in the United States and Europe collect Mbuti barkcloth drawings for their shapes and patterns.

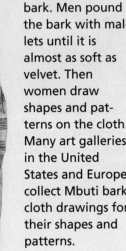

In contrast, living conditions get poorer as you move in from the coast to the interior areas of Angola, Congo, the Democratic Republic of the Congo, and the Central African Republic. There, village societies are organized by kinship groups, and land is owned by clans. In less-populated rural areas, individual families live and work on their own land.

Diverse Ways of Life Like the rest of the continent, Central Africa contains great cultural diversity. The Democratic Republic of the Congo alone has about 200 ethnic groups.

Millions of people live in crowded shantytowns or cinder-block apartments in Kinshasa, the largest city in the Democratic Republic of the Congo. They walk or take buses or trucks to work in factories, offices, and hotels. Millions of others live in rural areas. Some Central African people are Roman Catholic or Protestant. Others practice religions that blend Christian and traditional African beliefs. Still others are Muslim.

What one writer said about North Africa applies to Central and Southern Africa as well. To define the real North African, he said, "you have to define which one you mean: the rich or the poor, the Berber women of the mountains or the college girls on motorbikes. . . ." Old, new, and mixtures of the two live on in all regions of Africa.

✓ **Reading Check** What are some examples of cultural diversity in Central Africa?

Section 4 Assessment

Key Terms
Review the key terms at the beginning of this section. Use each term in a sentence that explains its meaning.

Target Reading Skill
Name two similarities between Southern Africa and Central Africa. Name two differences.

Comprehension and Critical Thinking
1. (a) Identify When did the process of urbanization in Southern Africa begin?

(b) Explain Why did people from all over Southern Africa migrate to South Africa?
(c) Identify Causes How were the lives of many Southern African women affected by South Africa even though the women never moved there?
2. (a) Recall What industry has brought wealth to some of the countries on Central Africa's Atlantic coast?
(b) Contrast How do the economics and culture of Central Africa's Atlantic coast differ from the economics and culture of its interior areas?

Writing Activity
Write a short report summarizing the ways in which economics have affected culture in Southern Africa and Central Africa. Point out any similarities or differences.

For: An activity on the region of Southern Africa
Visit: PHSchool.com
Web Code: ngd-5304

Review and Assessment

◆ Chapter Summary

Section 1: The Cultures of North Africa

- Culture has many elements, such as food, language, and beliefs.
- Islam has greatly influenced life in North Africa.
- Because of North Africa's location, the people of the region have been exposed to the cultures of its trading partners, including Europe, Asia, and other parts of Africa.

Morocco

Section 2: The Cultures of West Africa

- West Africa has great ethnic diversity. Most West Africans speak several languages.
- West Africans are bound by strong kinship ties.
- West Africans have kept their cultural values alive by passing them on to younger generations.

Section 3: The Cultures of East Africa

- East Africa's location has contributed to the region's cultural diversity.
- Ideas about land use and ownership have changed over time, but even urban East Africans still feel a bond to their rural villages.

Section 4: The Cultures of Southern and Central Africa

- Southern Africa's diverse culture includes people with three types of European ancestry—Dutch, British, and Portuguese.
- South Africa has had strong economic and cultural influences on Southern Africa.
- Central Africa has great cultural diversity and economic contrasts.

Zimbabwe

◆ Key Terms

Match the definitions in Column I with the key terms in Column II. There are more terms than definitions.

Column I

1. the spread of customs and ideas from one culture to another

2. a group of families descended from a common ancestor

3. the values, traditions, and customs handed down from one's ancestors

4. the part of a family that includes parents and children only

5. an ethnic group in East Africa

6. a laborer who travels away from where he or she lives to find work

Column II

A Quran

B culture

C cultural diffusion

D cultural diversity

E nuclear family

F extended family

G lineage

H heritage

I Swahili

J migrant worker

◆ Comprehension and Critical Thinking

7. (a) Recall What is culture?
(b) Describe What are some elements of North Africa's culture?

8. (a) Identify What is the role of kinship in West African cultures?
(b) Explain How is urbanization changing traditional family life in West Africa?

9. (a) Locate Describe East Africa's location.
(b) Analyze Explain how location has affected East African cultures.
(c) Summarize How does the Swahili language help unite the people of East Africa?

10. (a) Recall What were the traditional African ideas about owning and using land before European rule in the 1800s?
(b) Make Generalizations How do East Africans view land use and land ownership today?

11. (a) Recall In what economic activities did Europeans in Southern Africa take part?
(b) Identify Causes What economic activity in South Africa caused many Southern Africans to migrate to that country?
(c) Make Inferences Is the life of a migrant worker an easy one?

12. (a) Note Describe the cultures of Central Africa.
(b) Compare In what ways are the cultures of Central Africa like those in other parts of Africa?

◆ Skills Practice

Comparing and Contrasting In the Skills for Life activity in this chapter, you learned how to compare and contrast. You learned how to note similarities and differences and then draw a conclusion based on your findings.

Review the steps you followed to learn this skill. Then reread the part of Section 1 called Cultural Change in North Africa and the part of Section 3 called Geography and Cultural Diversity. List the similarities and differences between the cultures of these two regions. Draw a conclusion about these cultures based on your findings.

◆ Writing Activity: Language Arts

Suppose an exchange student from an African country has come to stay at your home for six weeks. You and your family are sharing your first dinner with this visitor. Write a dialogue in which you ask your visitor about African culture and the visitor asks you similar questions about your culture. Use what you have learned in this chapter to write your visitor's answers to questions.

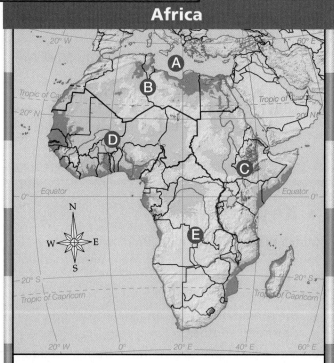

MAP ★ MASTER™
Skills Activity

Africa

Place Location For each place listed, write the letter from the map that shows its location.

1. Mediterranean Sea
2. North Africa
3. West Africa
4. East Africa
5. Southern and Central Africa

Go Online
PHSchool.com Use Web Code **ngp-5320** for an **interactive map.**

Standardized Test Prep

Test-Taking Tips

Some questions on standardized tests ask you to analyze a graphic organizer. Study the concept web below. Then follow the tips to answer the sample question.

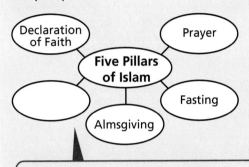

TIP When you study a concept web, notice the kind of information that goes in each oval. The main idea is in the center oval, and the supporting details are in the outer ovals.

Pick the letter that best answers the question.

What is the fifth Pillar of Islam that belongs on this concept web?

  A The Quran

  B Pilgrimage

  C Duties of a Muslim

  D The influence of Islam

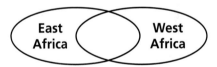

TIP Use logic, or good reasoning, to be sure you choose an answer that makes sense.

Think It Through The center of the web says "Five Pillars of Islam"—meaning duties required by the religion—and each of the outer ovals shows one duty. What other pillar, or duty, belongs in an outer oval? You can rule out C and D because both are general ideas rather than specific duties. That leaves A and B. Even if you're not sure of the answer, you can see that the other outer ovals involve actions. Because pilgrimage involves an action, you can guess that B is the correct answer.

Practice Questions

Use the tips above and other tips in this book to help you answer the following questions.

1. Which of the following statements is true?

  A Cultural diffusion only occurs on coasts.

  B In general, Africa has little cultural diversity.

  C Cultural changes often occur during travel.

  D Cultural diffusion and cultural diversity are the same thing.

2. Which of the following best explains the meaning of the proverb "The young can't teach traditions to the old"?

  A Traditions do not interest young people.

  B Only adults know customs and traditions.

  C Young people are not the best teachers.

  D Adults must pass traditions on to young people.

3. A cultural group that lives in Southern Africa is the

  A Swahili.   **B** Afrikaners.

  C Berbers.   **D** Tuareg.

Use the Venn diagram below to answer Question 4. Choose the letter of the best answer.

East Africa   West Africa

4. Which of the following could be listed in the part of the diagram where *East Africa* and *West Africa* intersect?

  A Cultures affected by coastal trade

  B Indian Ocean location

  C Br'er Rabbit tales

  D Swahili culture

Chapter

4 North Africa

Chapter Preview

Standard Course of Study

7.3.01 How cultures and regions are influenced by human interaction with the environment

7.3.03 How tools and technologies influence human use of the environment

7.7.01 Relationship between historical events and current issues

7.11.03 Compare and contrast institutions in different cultures

7.12.01 Examine major belief systems

7.12.03 Cultural borrowing and the development of societies

SS.1.04 Detect cause and effect

SS.1.08 Use context clues and appropriate sources to gain meaning

Country Databank

Sections

1. **Egypt: A Nation on the Nile**
   7.3.01, 7.3.03, 7.11.03, 7.12.01, SS.1.04

2. **Algeria: Varied Geography, Varied History**
   7.3.01, 7.7.01, 7.12.03, SS.1.08

 Target Reading Skill

Cause and Effect In this chapter you will focus on understanding causes and effects. Identifying causes and effects and recognizing signal words for causes and effects will help you learn as you read.

▶ Some North Africans live in the Sahara in oasis towns, such as Ghardaia, Algeria, shown here.

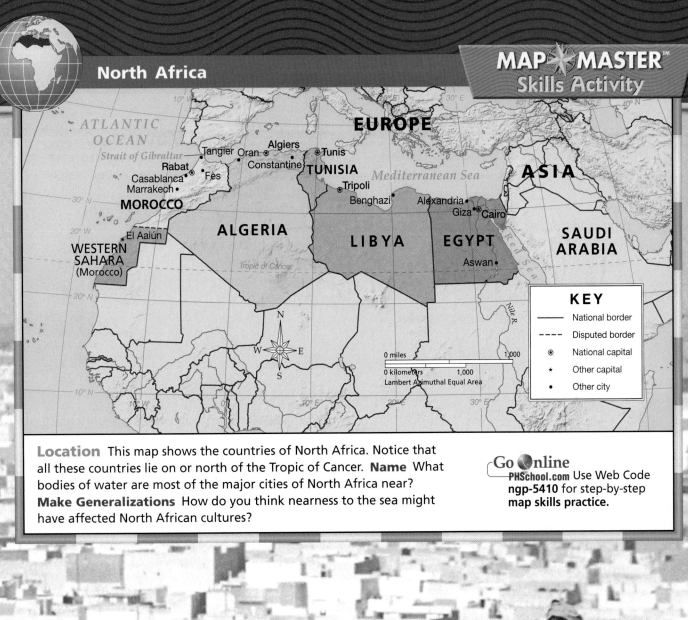

MAP★MASTER™
Skills Activity

ATLANTIC OCEAN

EUROPE

Strait of Gibraltar

Tangier • Oran ⊛ Algiers • ⊛ Tunis
Rabat • Constantine **TUNISIA**
Casablanca • • Fès Tripoli •
Marrakech • Benghazi

MOROCCO

Mediterranean Sea

ASIA

Alexandria •
Giza ⊛ • Cairo

30° N

20° W

El Aaiún •

ALGERIA

LIBYA

EGYPT

SAUDI ARABIA

WESTERN SAHARA
(Morocco)

Tropic of Cancer

Aswan •

20° N

Nile R.

N
W   E
S

0 miles   1,000
0 kilometers   1,000
Lambert Azimuthal Equal Area

KEY
——— National border
- - - Disputed border
⊛ National capital
★ Other capital
• Other city

Location This map shows the countries of North Africa. Notice that all these countries lie on or north of the Tropic of Cancer. **Name** What bodies of water are most of the major cities of North Africa near? **Make Generalizations** How do you think nearness to the sea might have affected North African cultures?

Go Online
PHSchool.com Use Web Code **ngp-5410** for step-by-step **map skills practice.**

Guide for Reading

This section provides an introduction to the five countries that make up the region of North Africa.

- Look at the map on the previous page and then read the paragraphs below to learn about each nation.
- Analyze the data to compare the countries.
- What are the characteristics that most of the countries share?
- What are some key differences among the countries?

Viewing the Video Overview

View the World Studies Video Overview to learn more about each of the countries. As you watch, answer these questions:

- What are some common features of the region?
- How does the availability of water influence where the people of North Africa live?

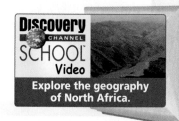

Explore the geography of North Africa.

Algeria

Capital	Algiers
Land Area	919,590 sq mi; 2,381,740 sq km
Population	32.3 million
Ethnic Group(s)	Arab, Berber, white
Religion(s)	Muslim, Christian, Jewish
Government	republic
Currency	Algerian dinar
Leading Exports	petroleum, natural gas, petroleum products
Language(s)	Arabic (official), Tamazight (official), Kabyle, Shawia, Tamashek, French

Algeria (al JIHR ee uh) is Africa's second-largest country. It is bordered on the west by Mauritania and Morocco, on the north by the Mediterranean Sea, on the east by Tunisia and Libya, and on the south by Niger and Mali. Algeria has long acted as a bridge between Europe and other African lands to the south. Much of Algeria is covered by the Sahara. Most Algerians live in the north, where summers are hot and dry and winters are warm and wet. Following independence from France in 1962, Algeria made improvements in education and literacy. Since the 1990s, Algeria has struggled with economic troubles and civil war.

Algerian girl preparing food

Egypt

Capital	Cairo
Land Area	384,343 sq mi; 995,450 sq km
Population	70.7 million
Ethnic Group(s)	Eastern Hamitic, Nubian, white
Religion(s)	Muslim, Christian
Government	republic
Currency	Egyptian pound
Leading Exports	crude oil and petroleum products, cotton, textiles, metal products, chemicals
Language(s)	Arabic (official), French, English, Berber

Egypt (EE jipt) is bordered on the west by Libya, on the north by the Mediterranean Sea, Israel, and the Gaza Strip, on the east by the Red Sea, and on the south by Sudan. Most of the people live in the fertile valley and delta regions of the Nile River. The rest of Egypt is hot desert. Egypt is famous for the ancient civilization that developed there along the Nile. The ancient Egyptians built pyramids and monuments that today draw tourists and scholars from around the world. Egypt's capital, Cairo, is an important cultural center for the Arabic world.

The Great Pyramids (left) and the Sphinx (below) at Giza, Egypt

Introducing **North Africa** (continued)

Libya

Capital	Tripoli
Land Area	679,358 sq mi; 1,759,540 sq km
Population	5.4 million
Ethnic Group(s)	Arab, Berber, white, Southwest Asian, South Asian
Religion(s)	Muslim
Government	local councils in theory; military dictatorship in practice
Currency	Libyan dinar
Leading Exports	crude oil, refined petroleum products
Language(s)	Arabic (official), Tuareg

Libya (LIB ee uh) is bordered on the west by Algeria and Tunisia, on the north by the Mediterranean Sea, on the east by Egypt and Sudan, and on the south by Chad and Niger. Each year, an average of four inches (10 centimeters) of rain falls in Libya. The country has no rivers that flow year-round. Instead, it relies on groundwater from desert oases and man-made wells. Most Libyans live in urban areas. Large oil and natural gas reserves are important to Libya's economy. Libya gained independence from Italy in 1951. Revolution followed in 1969, leading to the establishment of a military dictatorship.

Morocco

Capital	Rabat
Land Area	172,316 sq mi; 446,300 sq km
Population	31.2 million
Ethnic Group(s)	Arab, Berber
Religion(s)	Muslim, Christian, Jewish
Government	constitutional monarchy
Currency	Moroccan dirham
Leading Exports	phosphates and fertilizers, food and beverages, minerals
Language(s)	Arabic (official), Tamazight, French, Spanish

Morocco (muh RAH koh) is a mountainous country in which earthquakes are common. It is bordered on the west by the Atlantic Ocean, on the north by the Strait of Gibraltar and the Mediterranean Sea, on the east by Algeria, and on the south by Western Sahara. In 1956, Morocco gained independence from France. A year later, Morocco claimed the Spanish colony of Western Sahara as its territory. Today, Morocco occupies Western Sahara, but most countries do not recognize the region as Morocco's possession. Morocco's largest city, Casablanca, lies in the west, along the Atlantic.

Moroccan pottery

Tunisia

Capital	Tunis
Land Area	59,984 sq mi; 155,360 sq km
Population	9.8 million
Ethnic Group(s)	Arab, Berber, white
Religion(s)	Muslim, Christian, Jewish
Government	republic
Currency	Tunisian dinar
Leading Exports	textiles, mechanical goods, phosphates and chemicals, agricultural products, hydrocarbons
Language(s)	Arabic (official), French

SOURCES: DK World Desk Reference Online; CIA World Factbook Online, 2002; *The World Almanac*, 2003

The famed ancient port city of Carthage was founded on the Gulf of Tunis, in the land of present-day Tunisia (too NEE zhuh). In A.D. 698, Carthage fell to the Arabs, who then established Tunis. Tunisia is North Africa's smallest country. It is wedged between Algeria on the west and Libya on the east. It is bordered on the north and east by the Mediterranean Sea. Tunisia is one of the Arab world's most liberal countries, where women make up about one third of the workforce. The importance of education is stressed in Tunisia. Since 1995, enrollment in colleges has doubled.

Berber drummers in Tunisia

Assessment

Comprehension and Critical Thinking

1. Compare and Contrast Compare and contrast the physical characteristics of the countries that make up North Africa.

2. Draw Conclusions What are some characteristics that most of the countries share?

3. Analyze Information What are some key differences among the countries?

4. Categorize What kinds of products are the major exports of North Africa?

5. Infer What part of North Africa's history can you infer from reading the list of languages that are spoken in each country?

6. Make a Bar Graph Create a bar graph showing the population of the countries in the region.

Keeping Current

Access the **DK World Desk Reference Online** at **PHSchool.com** for up-to-date information about all five countries in this chapter.

Web Code: **nge-5400**

Egypt
A Nation on the Nile

Prepare to Read

Objectives
In this section you will
1. Find out how Islam influences Egyptian culture.
2. Learn about daily life in Egypt.

Taking Notes
As you read this section, look for details about life in Egypt. Copy the table below, and use it to record your findings.

| Islam in Egypt | •
 • |
| Everyday Life in Egypt | •
 • |

Target Reading Skill

Identify Causes and Effects Determining causes and effects can help you understand the relationships among situations or events. A cause makes something happen. An effect is what happens. As you read this section, note the effects Islam and the Nile River have had on life in Egypt.

Key Terms
- **Cairo** (KY roh) n. the capital of Egypt
- **Sharia** (shah REE ah) n. Islamic law, based on the words and deeds of Muhammad and on comments written by Muslim scholars and lawmakers
- **bazaar** (buh ZAHR) n. a traditional open-air market with shops or rows of stalls
- **fellaheen** (fel uh HEEN) n. peasants or agricultural workers in Egypt and other Arab countries

Egyptian boy at Ramadan evening meal

For one month of the year, the restaurants in **Cairo,** Egypt's capital, stand empty at noon. Egyptian teenagers try not to think about foods such as pita bread or sweet dates. Only certain people, such as the very young or those who are sick, eat regular meals. It is the Muslim holy month of Ramadan (ram uh DAHN). During this month, followers of Islam fast from dawn to dusk. To fast is to go without food for a period of time. During Ramadan, Muslims eat only after the sun has set.

But Muslims do more than fast during the month of Ramadan. They also focus on prayer and obedience to God. They try to avoid thinking unkind thoughts. And they help the poor and other people who are less fortunate than themselves.

Islam in Egypt

Egypt is located in North Africa. It lies across the Red Sea from Saudi Arabia, where Muhammad, the founder of Islam, was born. As you have read, Islam spread from Arabia across North Africa. Today, most North Africans are Muslim. This is true in Egypt, where Islam is the religion that most people practice. However, a minority of Egypt's population is Christian. Most Egyptian Christians are members of the Coptic Church, which is one of the oldest branches of Christianity in the world. Coptic Christianity existed in Egypt for a few hundred years before Islam did.

Islamic Practices Recall from Chapter 3 that the Quran is the sacred book of Islam. One of the Quran's requirements is that Muslims pray five times each day. Many Egyptians pray in mosques. While they pray, they face southeast so that they pray in the direction of the Muslim holy city of Mecca, in Saudi Arabia. Egyptians also often send their children to mosques to receive religious training. There, young students learn to read and memorize the Quran.

Links to Math

Muslim Mathematicians
Beginning around A.D. 800, Muslims throughout the Arab world began developing and using important mathematical concepts. Much of the work done by these Muslim mathematicians has formed the basis of mathematics as it exists today. A number of Muslim mathematicians came from North Africa. For example, Abu Kamil (born A.D. 850) and Ibn Yusun (born A.D. 950) were Egyptian, while Ibn al-Banna (born A.D. 1256) is thought to have been Moroccan.

Islam and the Law The Quran is one of the main sources of **Sharia** (shah REE ah), or Islamic law. Sharia is based on the words and deeds of Muhammad, as well as on comments written by Muslim scholars and lawmakers. Muslims in North Africa and Southwest Asia try to renew their faith by living each day according to Sharia.

Most Muslims in Egypt agree that, in general, the laws of their country should be based on the laws of Islam. In 1980, the Egyptian government adopted a new constitutional amendment. This amendment identified Sharia as the main source of the laws of Egypt. Still, not all of Egypt's laws are based on Sharia. In recent years, some Egyptians have argued that all of Egypt's laws should match Islamic law exactly. On this issue, however, many Egyptian Muslims disagree.

Muslim men praying in a mosque in Cairo

✓ **Reading Check** Why do Egyptian Muslims face southeast when they pray each day?

Egypt

The most important body of water in Egypt is the Nile River, which flows from the mountains of East Africa north to the Mediterranean Sea. Nearly all of Egypt's people live on the 4 percent of the land that is closest to the Nile's shores. Irrigation with Nile water allows agriculture to thrive, and one third of Egypt's workforce is employed in agriculture. Each month, however, thousands of Egyptians leave crowded farm communities to begin new lives in the cities. Study the map and charts to learn more about Egypt's changing society.

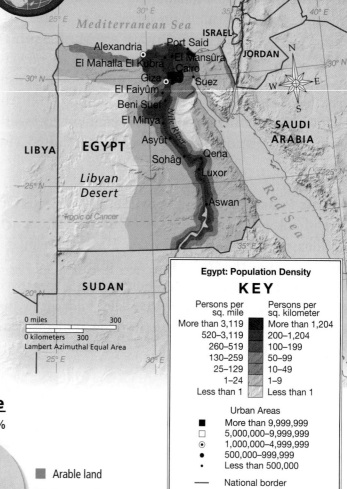

Egypt: Population Density

KEY

Persons per sq. mile	Persons per sq. kilometer
More than 3,119	More than 1,204
520–3,119	200–1,204
260–519	100–199
130–259	50–99
25–129	10–49
1–24	1–9
Less than 1	Less than 1

Urban Areas

■ More than 9,999,999
□ 5,000,000–9,999,999
◉ 1,000,000–4,999,999
• 500,000–999,999
· Less than 500,000

— National border

0 miles 300
0 kilometers 300
Lambert Azimuthal Equal Area

Urban and Rural Population

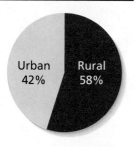

Urban 42%
Rural 58%

SOURCE: *United Nations Population Division*

Land Use

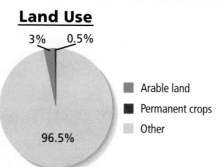

3%   0.5%
96.5%

■ Arable land
■ Permanent crops
■ Other

SOURCE: CIA World Factbook Online, 2003

The Nile River

Map and Chart Skills

1. **Locate** In what part of Egypt are most of the major cities located?
2. **Explain** How does Egypt's geography affect where in the country people live?
3. **Predict** What changes could Egyptians make that would allow them to live in areas where currently few people live?

Go Online
PHSchool.com

Use Web Code **nge-5401** for **DK World Desk Reference Online.**

Daily Life in Egypt

As you can see from the circle graph in the Country Profile on page 112, Egypt's population is fairly evenly divided between people who live in cities and people who live in villages. City dwellers and villagers live very different lives. One thing they have in common, however, is their dependence on the life-giving waters of the Nile River.

Egypt's Water Source Look at the map of Egypt on page 112 in the Country Profile. You can see that Egypt is most densely populated along the Nile River and in the Nile Delta region. Now turn to page 114 and read about the Aswan High Dam. With the help of this dam, the Nile River allows Egypt's crops to be irrigated year-round. The river supplies water to people in the cities and in rural areas.

But farming practices and population pressures threaten Egypt's water supply. The Aswan High Dam blocks the Nile's rich silt from reaching farmland downstream. Without the silt, the Nile Delta has been shrinking. Farmers have to use more fertilizer to grow their crops. The fertilizers they use, along with waste that comes from urban areas, threaten the safety of Egypt's water supply.

City Life Nearly half of all Egyptians live in cities. Cairo is the nation's capital and also its largest city. It is home to more than 10 million Egyptians. Some parts of Cairo are more than 1,000 years old. Other parts are very modern. Most people live in apartment buildings with electric fans or air conditioning. However, they frequently shop in traditional open-air markets called **bazaars.**

Many people move to the cities from rural areas. They hope to find a better education and jobs. As a result, Cairo is very crowded. There are traffic jams and housing shortages. Some people live in tents that they have set up on boats on the Nile. Others live in homes they have built in the huge cemeteries on the outskirts of Cairo. Overcrowding in Egypt's cities has even affected agriculture. Some farmland has been lost because people have built on it instead of farming on it.

Identify Causes and Effects
What effects of the Aswan High Dam are described in this section?

Outdoor Markets
At a bazaar in Cairo, people buy goods from vendors who set up stands beneath umbrellas along the streets. **Contrast** *How do you think open-air markets are different from indoor shopping centers?*

Aswan High Dam

The Aswan High Dam is one of the modern world's greatest engineering projects. A force of 30,000 workers labored for ten years to build the dam out of layers of rock, clay, and cement. The dam serves three major purposes: it controls flooding, it provides electricity, and it supplies water for crops and drinking year-round.

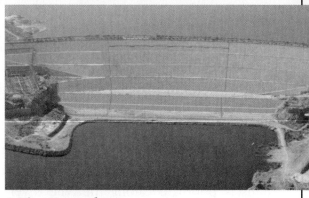

A View From Above
Located on the Nile River near Aswan, Egypt, the dam created the world's third-largest reservoir–Lake Nasser. The lake is 310 miles (500 kilometers) long.

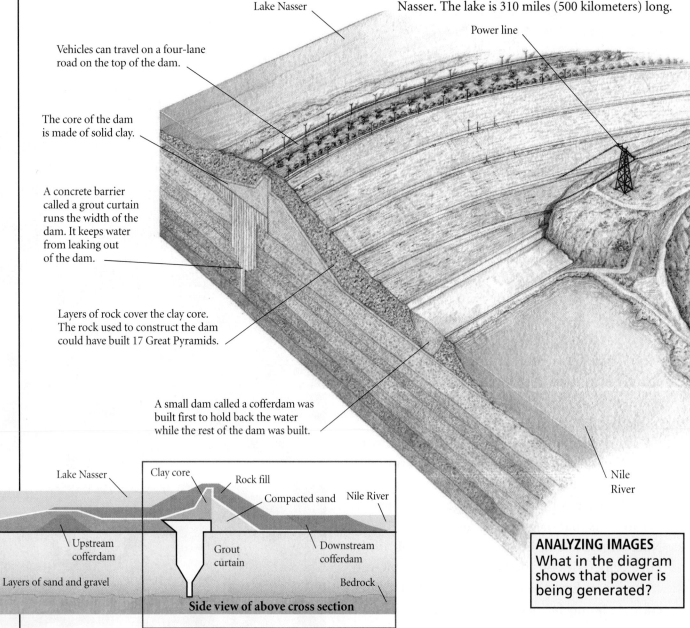

Lake Nasser

Vehicles can travel on a four-lane road on the top of the dam.

The core of the dam is made of solid clay.

A concrete barrier called a grout curtain runs the width of the dam. It keeps water from leaking out of the dam.

Layers of rock cover the clay core. The rock used to construct the dam could have built 17 Great Pyramids.

A small dam called a cofferdam was built first to hold back the water while the rest of the dam was built.

Power line

Nile River

Lake Nasser

Clay core

Rock fill

Compacted sand

Nile River

Upstream cofferdam

Grout curtain

Downstream cofferdam

Layers of sand and gravel

Bedrock

Side view of above cross section

ANALYZING IMAGES
What in the diagram shows that power is being generated?

Rural Life Most of the people in Egypt's rural areas live in villages along the banks of the Nile River or in the Nile Delta region. In Egyptian villages, most of the people make their living by farming. Egypt's rural farmers are called **fellaheen** (fel uh HEEN). Most of the fellaheen do not own the land they farm. Good farmland is scarce because the riverbanks are so narrow. Some fellaheen farm small rented plots of land. Others work in the fields of rich landowners.

Many of the fellaheen live in homes built of mud bricks or of stones. Most of these homes are small. They may have from one to three rooms and a courtyard, which the family often shares with its animals. The roofs of the houses are typically flat. Therefore, the fellaheen can use their roofs as places to store food and firewood, to spread dates or other fruits out to dry, and to dry their laundry after washing it.

Learn about farming along the Nile in Egypt.

Fellaheen working near the Great Pyramids at Giza

✓ **Reading Check** What land do the fellaheen farm?

Section 1 Assessment

Key Terms
Review the key terms at the beginning of this section. Use each term in a sentence that explains its meaning.

Target Reading Skill
Many Egyptians are Muslim. What are two effects that Islam has had on life in Egypt?

Comprehension and Critical Thinking
1. (a) Recall Describe Egypt's location.

(b) Identify Cause and Effect How did location affect the spread of Islam into North Africa?
(c) Draw Conclusions In what ways does Islam influence Egyptian culture?
2. (a) Identify Where do most people in Egypt live?
(b) Compare How do the lives of city dwellers compare with the lives of villagers in Egypt?
(c) Analyze What is the importance of the Nile River to the people of Egypt?

Writing Activity
Write a letter from the point of view of a rural Egyptian visiting Cairo for the first time. You may want to include observations of things that a rural person would find unfamiliar or familiar.

For: An activity on Egypt
Visit: PHSchool.com
Web Code: ngd-5401

Distinguishing Fact and Opinion

When Aretha got to class, she looked at the chalkboard. Every day, Mr. Copeland began class by writing a discussion topic on the board. On this day, he had written,

Life in Egyptian cities is better than life in rural Egypt.

Aretha wondered how someone decided this and raised her hand. "That statement doesn't tell the whole story! Whose life is it referring to? Are they wealthy or poor? And when did they live?"

Mr. Copeland smiled. "Exactly, Aretha! The statement cannot be proved. It's somebody's opinion."

Distinguishing between fact and opinion is something you need to do almost every day. Doing it helps you reach your own decisions about what you read, see, or hear.

Learn the Skill

To distinguish fact and opinion, use the following steps.

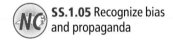
SS.1.05 Recognize bias and propaganda

1 **Look for facts by asking what can be proved true or false.** A fact usually tells who, what, when, where, or how much.

2 **Ask how you could check whether each fact is true.** Could you do your own test, such as measuring or counting, or could you find information in a reliable source, such as an encyclopedia?

3 **Look for opinions by identifying personal beliefs or value judgments.** An opinion cannot be proved true *or* false. Look for words that signal personal feelings, such as *I think*. Look for words that judge, such as *better* and *worse* or *should* and *ought to*.

4 **Ask whether each opinion is supported by facts or good reasons.** A well-supported opinion can help you make up your own mind—as long as you recognize it as an opinion and not a fact.

Practice the Skill

Read the letter below from an American student who is traveling in Egypt with her father. Then use the following steps to analyze the letter for facts and opinions.

1 Identify the facts given about the writer's father.

2 Explain how each fact could be proved true or false.

3 Identify statements within the letter that express opinions. Explain whether each opinion signals a personal feeling or a judgment.

4 Which opinion in the letter do you think has the best factual support?

Dear Brenda,

    I'm sure my dad will help you with your report on ancient Egypt. He has spent years researching the Valley of Kings, where many ancient Egyptian tombs have been found. Scientists like my dad have learned a lot about ancient Egypt because it had a system of writing, called hieroglyphics. Nobody knows more about hieroglyphics than my dad!

    If you could visit while we are here, I know my dad would take you into places that most tourists don't get to see. You would be amazed to see the magnificent tombs. Grave robbers stole many of the mummies and much of the furniture from the tombs. The tomb paintings, which are still there, are unbelievably beautiful. Dad says that the bright colors have faded over time. But I still love looking at them and thinking of how those people lived. You would enjoy it, too, since you like ancient history so much. Please think about coming!

Your friend,
Dominique

Egyptian hieroglyphs

Apply the Skill

Find the editorial page of a daily newspaper. Read through the editorials and select one that interests you. List several facts and several opinions from the editorial. Can the facts be proved? Are the opinions well supported? Explain what you find.

Section 2

Algeria
Varied Geography, Varied History

Prepare to Read

Objectives

In this section you will

1. Learn about the history and people of Algeria.
2. Find out about life in Algeria's different geographic regions.
3. Examine life in Algeria today.

Taking Notes

As you read, find details about Algeria's past and present. Copy the outline below, and use it to record your findings.

```
I. Algeria's history and people
   A. Algeria's past
      1.
      2.
   B.
II.
```

Target Reading Skill

Use Signal Words Signal words point out the relationships among ideas or events. To help identify the causes and the effects described in this section, look for words like *because, influence,* or *for that reason* that signal a cause or an effect.

Key Terms

- **souq** (sook) *n.* an open-air marketplace in an Arab city
- **casbah** (KAHZ bah) *n.* an old, crowded section of a North African city
- **terrace** (TEHR us) *n.* a flat platform of earth cut into the side of a slope, used for growing crops in steep places

An Algerian desert home

The Sahara covers all of Algeria south of the Atlas Mountains, which cross the northern portion of Algeria from east to west. Water is in short supply in Algeria's desert lands. For that reason, fewer than 3 percent of Algeria's people live there. Because so much of Algeria is desert, more than 90 percent of Algerians live near the coast, where the weather is milder than in the Sahara.

Algeria's Mediterranean coast, its mountains, and its great desert lands are all part of the country's rich history. Algerians live in modern cities, in rural areas, and in the harsh desert. Geography, history, and culture all influence the way people live in Algeria today.

Algeria's History and People

Algeria has had a long and eventful history. Its Mediterranean location provided easy access to the markets of Europe. Algeria has also participated in trade with other parts of Africa for hundreds of years. Because of its location and resources, Algeria has been a treasure both to its people and to foreign invaders.

Early Foreign Occupations Parts of Algeria have long been occupied by outside groups. The earliest known invaders were the Phoenicians (fuh NISH unz), who were sea traders from the region of present-day Lebanon. The Phoenicians were attracted to Algeria's coast as early as two to three thousand years ago. With help from the Berbers, a North African ethnic group, the Phoenicians set up a trading post on the site of Algiers (al JEERZ). Today, Algiers is the capital of Algeria.

In the A.D. 100s, the Romans invaded Algeria. Berber farmers paid Roman taxes in grain and rented their land from Roman nobles. In the A.D. 600s, Arabs began to spread across North Africa. The Arabs conquered North Africa gradually, over hundreds of years. As a result, the Berber way of life began to change. For example, peace came to the region only after most Berbers accepted the religion of Islam.

Recent Occupations At different times, Algeria's valuable port cities have been commanded by the Spanish, by local pirates, and by the Ottoman Turks. In 1830, the French captured Algiers. The capture resulted in a long period of French colonial rule. Algeria gained independence from France in 1962.

Algeria's People Today, about 75 percent of Algeria's population is Arab, about 24 percent is Berber, and most of the rest is of European descent. Arabs and Berbers alike are Muslim, but many Berbers have combined Islam with their own traditional religious beliefs.

Arabic, several Berber languages, and French are the country's main languages. Many Algerians speak more than one of these languages. Arabic and Tamazight (TAHM uh zyt), a Berber language, are the country's two official languages.

✓ **Reading Check** What foreign influences have been felt in Algeria?

Target Skill

Use Signal Words
What word or phrase in the paragraph at the left signals a cause or an effect? Which does it signal?

City on the Sea
The city of Algiers sits on hills overlooking a bay in the Mediterranean Sea. It has long served as one of Algeria's main ports.
Draw Conclusion *Why do you think the Phoenicians chose the site of Algiers for a trading post?*

Algeria

Both the climate and the physical geography of Algeria vary from place to place. The climate is very different in the south, where the Sahara lies, and along the Mediterranean coast of the north. The Sahara covers most of Algeria's land, but the desert climate is too harsh for most uses. Only northern Algeria, near the Mediterranean Sea, receives enough rainfall to grow crops. Algeria's population is concentrated in the north, in a narrow band of cities and farmland. Study the map and charts to learn more about Algeria's geography.

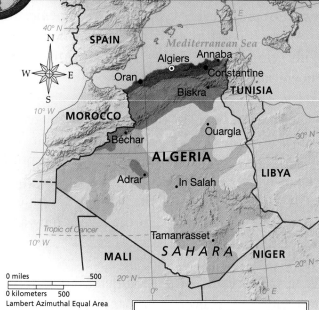

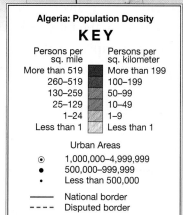

Algeria: Population Density

KEY

Persons per sq. mile	Persons per sq. kilometer
More than 519	More than 199
260–519	100–199
130–259	50–99
25–129	10–49
1–24	1–9
Less than 1	Less than 1

Urban Areas
- ◉ 1,000,000–4,999,999
- • 500,000–999,999
- • Less than 500,000

— National border
---- Disputed border

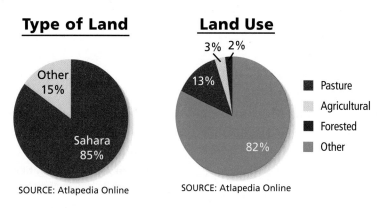

Type of Land

Other 15%
Sahara 85%

SOURCE: Atlapedia Online

Land Use

3% 2%
13%
82%

- ■ Pasture
- Agricultural
- ■ Forested
- Other

SOURCE: Atlapedia Online

Weather Chart for Algiers

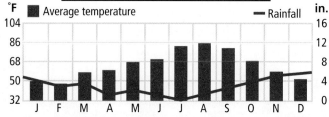

SOURCE: DK World Desk Reference

Map and Chart Skills

1. **Identify** In which three months does Algiers receive the greatest amount of rainfall?
2. **Draw Conclusions** Why do you think such a small percent of Algeria's land is used for agriculture?
3. **Synthesize Information** Why do most Algerians live near the Mediterranean Sea?

Use Web Code **nge-5402** for **DK World Desk Reference Online.**

Algeria's Geography

Most Algerians live in the country's coastal region, called the Tell. Algeria's best farmland is located in this region, as are most of its cities. More than half of Algeria's people live in cities.

Urban Living Many of the Algerians who live in cities are Arab, while some of them are Berber. At the heart of the cities are mosques and open-air marketplaces called **souqs** (sooks). In these souqs, merchants sell food, traditional crafts, and a variety of other goods from their stalls. Older parts of the cities are called **casbahs** (KAHZ bahz). The houses and stores in the casbahs are close together. Children play outside on the narrow, winding streets. Newer parts of the cities are modern, with wide streets and tall buildings made of steel and glass.

Rural Areas Most Berbers and many Arabs live in the countryside. Although the farmland tends to be of poor quality, about one third of Algerians are farmers. Algeria's farmers grow wheat and barley and raise livestock. In the mountains, they build **terraces,** or flat platforms of earth cut into a slope, one above another, for their crops. The terraces increase the amount of farmland and prevent the soil from washing away in the rain.

Traditionally, Algerians live with their extended families. In both urban and rural areas, homes feature several rooms with high walls surrounding an inner courtyard. Family members gather in the courtyard, which might have a garden or fountain.

Desert Dwellers Algeria is more than 80 percent desert. Among the small number of Algerians living in the desert, most settle in oasis towns, where water is available. There, people grow dates or citrus fruits.

Some people who live in the desert work for companies that produce oil and natural gas, Algeria's two main resources. Other desert dwellers are nomads, herding camels and other livestock suited to the climate. Like people in many parts of the world, these nomadic Algerians adapt to their climate by resting during the hottest hours of the day. By being resourceful, Berber and Arab nomads are able to survive the harsh desert conditions.

✓ **Reading Check** How do Algerian desert dwellers make a living?

Finding Land to Farm
Much work goes into building terraces for farming, but the benefits are enormous in areas that are hilly or mountainous. Here, Algerian farmers work the fields below a terraced hillside. **Compare** How do you think farming on flat land is different from farming on terraced hillsides?

DISCOVERY CHANNEL SCHOOL Video
Learn how people farm in a desert oasis.

Algeria Today

Throughout the long periods of outside rule, native Algerians preserved many of their traditions. For example, while French was Algeria's official language, many people kept Arabic and Berber languages alive in their homes. Today, Algerians continue to express their customs and traditions.

Modern Home Life In both urban and rural areas, Algerians continue to value family. Many Algerians live with their extended families. However, young couples in urban areas are having fewer children than people did in previous generations. Urban Algerians also tend to live in smaller family groups.

Educating Algeria's Youth While under French rule, few non-European children received a good formal education. Since gaining independence, the Algerian government has worked hard to improve education for its children and young people. Most instruction is in Arabic. Children from ages 6 to 15 are required by law to attend school. Attendance is high in city schools but is lower in rural areas. New universities have been built to educate Algeria's young people. Some students attend colleges in other countries.

An Algerian family

✓ **Reading Check** Which language is used in most Algerian classrooms today?

 Section 2 Assessment

Key Terms
Review the key terms at the beginning of this section. Use each term in a sentence that explains its meaning.

Target Reading Skill
Review the section Algeria's History and People on pages 118 and 119. Find the words that signal causes or effects related to the foreign occupation of Algeria.

Comprehension and Critical Thinking
1. (a) Name What foreign groups have played a role in the history of Algeria?

(b) Explain What roles did Arabs and Berbers play in the history of Algeria?

2. (a) Identify In which geographic area do most Algerians live?

(b) Compare and Contrast Compare life for Algerians living in urban, rural, and desert areas. How are their lives similar? How are they different?

3. (a) Recall Describe education in Algeria today.

(b) Draw Conclusions What do you think is the importance of the language that is spoken in schools?

Writing Activity
Write an interview that you could conduct with someone living in Algeria today. Think of five questions you would like to ask this person. Try to ask questions that cover a number of different topics.

> **Writing Tip** Try to avoid questions that could be answered with a *yes* or a *no*. Questions that begin with words such as *why* or *how* often lead to more interesting answers.

Review and Assessment

◆ Chapter Summary

Section 1: Egypt

- Islam influences many parts of daily life in Egypt, including daily practices and the country's laws.
- Most of Egypt's population is centered along the Nile River, the country's main source of water in both urban and rural areas.

Section 2: Algeria

- At times over thousands of years, a variety of foreign groups have occupied Algeria.
- Most Algerians live in modern cities or in rural areas. A small number of Algerians, however, live in the desert.
- Family and education are both valued by Algerians today.

Cairo, Egypt

Algerian desert

◆ Key Terms

Each of the statements below contains a key term from the chapter. If the statement is true, write *true*. If it is false, change the highlighted term to make the statement true.

1. A traditional Egyptian open-air market is called a casbah.
2. Egypt's rural farmers are called fellaheen.
3. Souqs are platforms cut into the side of a slope.
4. Islamic law is called Cairo.
5. In Algeria, open-air markets may be called terraces.
6. The old section of Algiers is called the bazaar.
7. Sharia is the capital of Egypt.

Review and Assessment (continued)

◆ Comprehension and Critical Thinking

8. (a) **Recall** What are some common Islamic religious practices in Egypt?
(b) **Analyze Information** What is the importance of Sharia to Muslims in Egypt?

9. (a) **Identify** What is the main source of Egypt's water supply?
(b) **Conclude** How does the Aswan High Dam affect Egypt's water supply?

10. (a) **Describe** What is life like in Cairo?
(b) **Make Generalizations** Why do so many Egyptians move from rural areas to cities such as Cairo?
(c) **Identify Effects** What are some of the effects of overcrowding in Cairo?

11. (a) **Recall** Describe the geography of Algeria.
(b) **Explain** How have people adapted to the geography and climate of Algeria?
(c) **Summarize** What has been the importance of Algeria's coastal location throughout its history?

12. (a) **Identify** What languages are spoken in Algeria today?
(b) **Apply Information** How do these languages reflect the history of Algeria?

13. (a) **Explain** How has the traditional view of family changed for urban Algerians?
(b) **Predict** Do you think rural Algerians will change their view of family in a similar way? Explain why or why not.

◆ Skills Practice

Distinguishing Fact and Opinion In the Skills for Life activity in this chapter, you learned how to distinguish fact from opinion.

Review the steps you followed to learn this skill. Next, read a magazine article. List several facts and several opinions that are given in the article. Write down a way that each fact you listed can be proved. Then explain whether facts or reasons are given to support each opinion.

◆ Writing Activity: Science

Do research to learn about how people have used science to help them live in desert climates. Find out about nomadic living as well as life in an oasis town. Write a report describing your findings.

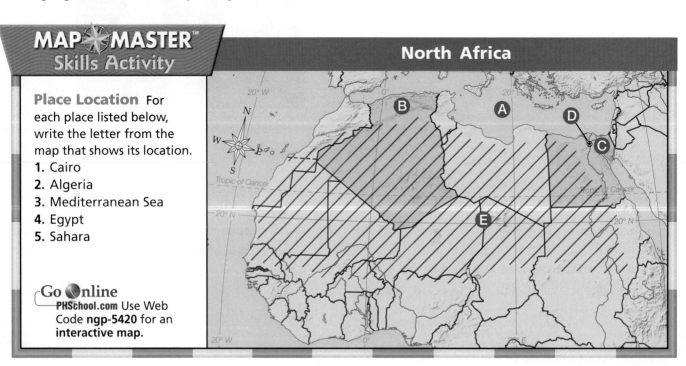

MAP MASTER™ Skills Activity

Place Location For each place listed below, write the letter from the map that shows its location.
1. Cairo
2. Algeria
3. Mediterranean Sea
4. Egypt
5. Sahara

Go Online
PHSchool.com Use Web Code ngp-5420 for an interactive map.

North Africa

Standardized Test Prep

Test-Taking Tips

Some questions on standardized tests ask you to identify main ideas. Read the paragraph below. Then follow the tips to answer the sample question.

> A Berber household can include grandparents, parents, sons, daughters, and cousins. Family members all share one courtyard. Each married couple within the family has a house that opens onto the courtyard. All the windows of the house face the courtyard. The head of each family is a member of the village assembly that makes village laws.

TIP Some paragraphs have a topic sentence that states the main idea. Every sentence in the paragraph supports this idea.

Pick the letter that best answers the question.

Which topic sentence is missing from this passage?

TIP The best way to be sure you have picked the right answer is to read all four answer choices before deciding on one.

A The Berbers and the Arabs are Algeria's two main ethnic groups.

B An extended Berber family includes more than just a mother, a father, and children.

C Most Berbers from Algeria live in villages.

D Family is central to every part of Berber village life.

Think It Through By reading the paragraph, you will find that every sentence tells about Berber life. You can rule out A because the paragraph is not about Arabs. You can rule out C because the paragraph is not mainly about villages. That leaves B and D. B is about Berber families, but it could be a detail sentence in the paragraph; not all the sentences are about family members. The correct answer is D.

Practice Questions

Use the tips above and other tips in this book to help you answer the following questions. Read the paragraph below to answer Question 1. Choose the letter of the best answer.

> Some desert dwellers work for companies that produce oil and natural gas. Others are nomads who herd camels and other livestock that are suited to the hot, dry climate. Like people in many parts of the world, these Algerians adapt to their climate by resting during the hottest hours of the day.

1. Which topic sentence is missing from the paragraph above?

   A Oil and natural gas are Algeria's two most important natural resources.

   B Algerians have found ways to work and survive in the desert.

   C It is difficult to live in the desert.

   D Agriculture and fuel industries thrive in the desert.

2. In Egypt, most people live

   A in Cairo.

   B in Alexandria.

   C in the valley and delta regions of the Nile.

   D in the Nile delta region.

3. Which of the following statements is true?

   A In Algeria, all Arabs and Berbers are Muslims.

   B In Algeria, Arabs and a small percentage of Berbers are Muslims.

   C In Egypt, most people are Coptic Christians.

   D In Egypt, almost half of the people are Coptic Christians.

Go Online PHSchool.com

Use Web Code **nga-5400** for **Chapter 4 self-test.**

Chapter Preview

 Standard Course of Study

7.2.01 Influence of physical features and climate on cultures

7.3.02 Environmental impact and global effects of regional activities

7.5.01 How the location of natural resources affects economic development

7.9.01 Historical developments of types of governments

7.9.02 How different types of governments function

7.9.04 Compare how different governments select leaders and establish laws

7.10.02 Identify sources of citizens' rights and responsibilities

7.11.01 How culture links and separates societies

7.11.04 Impact of economic, political, and social changes and cultures

Country Databank

Sections

1. **Nigeria: Land of Diverse Peoples**
   7.9.01, 7.10.02, 7.11.01, 7.11.04

2. **Ghana: Leading Africa to Independence**
   7.5.01, 7.9.01, 7.9.02, 7.9.04

3. **Mali: Desert Living**
   7.2.01, 7.3.02

 Target Reading Skill

Main Idea In this chapter you will focus on understanding main ideas. Identifying main ideas and their supporting details will help you learn as you read.

▶ The large, mud-brick Great Mosque in Djenné, Mali, is a source of pride for many West Africans.

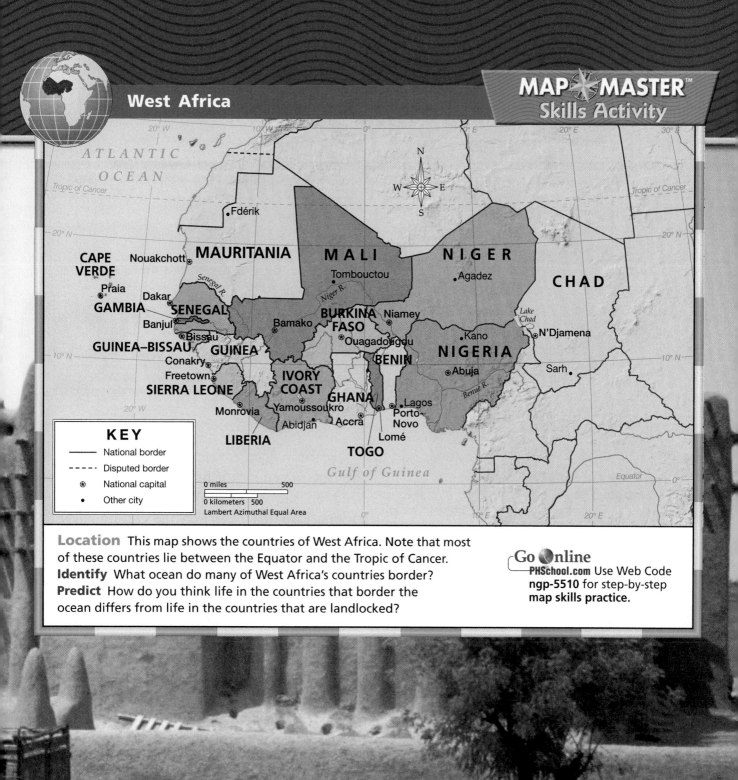

MAP★MASTER™
Skills Activity

ATLANTIC OCEAN

Tropic of Cancer

N
W ★ E
S

20° W   10° W   0°   10° E   20° E   30° E

•Fdérik

20° N

CAPE VERDE   Nouakchott⊛   MAURITANIA   MALI   NIGER   CHAD

•Praia   Dakar⊛   Senegal R.   Tombouctou•   •Agadez

GAMBIA   SENEGAL   Niger R.   Lake Chad

Banjul⊛   Bamako⊛   BURKINA FASO   Niamey•   •Kano   •N'Djamena

GUINEA-BISSAU   ⊛Bissau   GUINEA   Ouagadougou⊛   NIGERIA

Conakry⊛   BENIN   •Abuja   Sarh•

10° N   Freetown⊛   IVORY COAST   Benue R.   10° N

SIERRA LEONE   GHANA   Lagos•

20° W   Monrovia•   Yamoussoukro•   Accra⊛   Porto-Novo

LIBERIA   Abidjan•   Lomé•

TOGO   Gulf of Guinea   Equator   0°

KEY
—— National border
----- Disputed border
⊛ National capital
• Other city

0 miles   500
0 kilometers   500
Lambert Azimuthal Equal Area

0°   10° E   20° E

Location This map shows the countries of West Africa. Note that most of these countries lie between the Equator and the Tropic of Cancer.
Identify What ocean do many of West Africa's countries border?
Predict How do you think life in the countries that border the ocean differs from life in the countries that are landlocked?

Go Online
PHSchool.com Use Web Code ngp-5510 for step-by-step map skills practice.

Guide for Reading

This section provides an introduction to the 17 countries that make up the region of West Africa.

- Look at the map on the previous page and then read the paragraphs below to learn about each nation.
- Analyze the data to compare the countries.
- What are the characteristics that most of the countries share?
- What are some key differences among the countries?

Viewing the Video Overview

View the World Studies Video Overview to learn more about each of the countries. As you watch, answer these questions:

- What are some common features of the region?
- How does the climate of West Africa affect the people living there?
- What natural resources are important to the countries of West Africa?

Explore the geography of West Africa.

Benin

Capital	Porto-Novo
Land Area	42,710 sq mi; 110,620 sq km
Population	6.9 million
Ethnic Group(s)	42 ethnic groups, including Fon, Adja, Yoruba, Bariba
Religion(s)	traditional beliefs, Muslim, Christian
Government	republic
Currency	CFA franc
Leading Exports	cotton, crude oil, palm products, cocoa
Language(s)	French (official), Fon, Bariba, Yoruba, Adja, Houeda, Somba

The narrow country of Benin (beh NEEN) is bordered on the west by Togo, on the north by Burkina Faso and Niger, on the east by Nigeria, and on the south by the Atlantic Ocean. Seasons are rainy or dry. More than two thirds of Benin's people live in the south. Most live in or near either Porto-Novo, the capital, or Cotonou, the center of business. Present-day Benin was formed by the French in the late 1800s. Since it gained independence in 1960, it has been on a shaky path to democracy and stability. In 1990, Benin successfully opened politics to multiple parties.

Near Porto-Novo, Benin

Burkina Faso

Capital	Ouagadougou
Land Area	105,714 sq mi; 273,800 sq km
Population	12.6 million
Ethnic Group(s)	Mossi, Gurunsi, Senufo, Lobi, Bobo, Mande, Fulani
Religion(s)	traditional beliefs, Muslim, Christian
Government	parliamentary republic
Currency	CFA franc
Leading Exports	cotton, animal products, gold
Language(s)	French (official), Mossi, Fulani, Tuareg, Dyula, Songhai

Burkina Faso (bur KEE nuh FAH soh) is bordered on the west and north by Mali, on the east by Niger and Benin, and on the south by Togo, Ghana, and Ivory Coast. The hot, dry north receives plentiful sunshine. The south is tropical, with more rainfall and a greater range of temperatures. Ninety percent of the population is rural—a higher percentage than in any other West African country. A French colony beginning in the 1890s, it gained independence as Upper Volta in 1960. Its name changed to Burkina Faso in 1984.

Cape Verde

Capital	Praia
Land Area	1,557 sq mi; 4,033 sq km
Population	408,760
Ethnic Group(s)	Creole, black, white
Religion(s)	Roman Catholic, Protestant
Government	republic
Currency	Cape Verde escudo
Leading Exports	fuel, shoes, garments, fish, hides
Language(s)	Portuguese (official), Portuguese Creole

West Africa's smallest nation, Cape Verde (kayp vurd), lies in the Atlantic Ocean, west of Senegal. It consists of ten islands and five islets. One of them, Fogo Island, is home to an active volcano that last erupted in 1995. Throughout its history, periods with little rainfall have brought hardship on the nation. Cape Verde has been inhabited since 1462, when its first settlers arrived from Portugal. They brought enslaved Africans as well. In 1975, Cape Verde gained independence. Today, about half of Cape Verdeans live on the island of São Tiago.

Chad

Capital	N'Djamena
Land Area	486,177 sq mi; 1,259,200 sq km
Population	9 million
Ethnic Group(s)	200 distinct groups, including Arab, Sara
Religion(s)	Muslim, Christian, traditional beliefs
Government	republic
Currency	CFA franc
Leading Exports	cotton, cattle, gum arabic
Language(s)	Arabic (official), French (official), Sara, Maba

Chad (chad) is Africa's fifth-largest country. It is bordered on the west by Cameroon, Nigeria, and Niger; on the north by Libya; on the east by Sudan; and on the south by the Central African Republic. Its northern lands are covered by the Sahara and are spotted with extinct volcanoes. In the south, the Sahel gets slightly more rain. Lake Chad, in the west, was historically a stop for traders crossing the Sahara. The French controlled the region from 1900 to 1960, when it became independent. Chad has since faced civil wars and military takeovers of the government.

Introducing **West Africa**

Gambia

Capital	Banjul
Land Area	3,861 sq mi; 10,000 sq km
Population	1.5 million
Ethnic Group(s)	Mandinka, Fulani, Wolof, Jola, Serahuli
Religion(s)	Muslim, Christian, traditional beliefs
Government	republic
Currency	dalasi
Leading Exports	peanuts and peanut products, fish, cotton lint, palm kernels
Language(s)	English (official), Mandinka, Fulani, Wolof, Jola, Sonike

At 295 miles (475 kilometers) in length and 15 to 30 miles (24 to 48 kilometers) in width, Gambia (GAM bee uh) is a narrow country. It is surrounded by Senegal except on the west, where it borders the Atlantic Ocean. The Gambia River flows the entire length of the country. Gambia's economy depends on peanuts as a cash crop. Great Britain ruled Gambia from the early 1600s until 1965. In the early years after independence, Gambia's smooth transition from colonial rule to stable democracy stood as a model for other African nations. Although the government was overthrown in 1994, Gambia has since returned to a stable democracy.

Ghana

Capital	Accra
Land Area	89,166 sq mi; 230,940 sq km
Population	20.2 million
Ethnic Group(s)	Akan, Moshi-Dagomba, Ewe, Ga, Gurma, Yoruba, white
Religion(s)	Christian, traditional beliefs, Muslim
Government	constitutional democracy
Currency	cedi
Leading Exports	gold, cocoa, timber, tuna, bauxite, aluminum, manganese ore, diamonds
Language(s)	English (official), Twi, Fanti, Ewe, Ga, Adangbe, Gurma, Dagomba (Dagbani)

Ghana (GAH nuh) is bordered on the west by Ivory Coast, on the north by Burkina Faso, on the east by Togo, and on the south by the Atlantic Ocean. Ghana is rich in natural resources. It was originally referred to as the Gold Coast because of its abundant supply of gold. In addition, Ghana is viewed as a leader in African politics. The country became independent in 1957, making it the first African nation south of the Sahara to achieve independence as well as the first former European colony to be governed by black leaders.

Gold ornaments from Ghana

Guinea

Capital	Conakry
Land Area	94,925 sq mi; 245,857 sq km
Population	7.8 million
Ethnic Group(s)	Peuhl, Malinke, Soussou
Religion(s)	Muslim, Christian, traditional beliefs
Government	republic
Currency	Guinea franc
Leading Exports	bauxite, alumina, fish, diamonds, coffee, gold, agricultural products
Language(s)	French (official), Fulani, Malinke, Soussou

Guinea (GIH nee) is neighbored by Guinea-Bissau, Senegal, Mali, Ivory Coast, Sierra Leone, and Liberia. The western border of the country runs along the Atlantic Ocean. Three major rivers—the Gambia, the Senegal, and the Niger—all have their sources in Guinea. The country is rich in natural resources. At least one third of the world's supply of bauxite comes from Guinea, which is the world's second-largest producer of the mineral, after Australia. Farming is also a dominant industry in Guinea, where many people produce cash crops as well as crops to support their families.

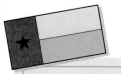

Guinea-Bissau

Capital	Bissau
Land Area	10,811 sq mi; 28,000 sq km
Population	1.4 million
Ethnic Group(s)	Balanta, Fula, Manjaca, Mandinga, Papel, white, mixed white and black
Religion(s)	traditional beliefs, Muslim, Christian
Government	republic
Currency	CFA franc
Leading Exports	cashew nuts, shrimp, peanuts, palm kernels, sawn lumber
Language(s)	Portuguese (official), Portuguese Creole, Balante, Fulani, Malinke

The mainland of Guinea-Bissau (GIH nee bih SOW) is bordered by the Atlantic Ocean on the west, Senegal on the north, and Guinea on the east and south. The country also includes a group of islands off its Atlantic coast. Guinea-Bissau's economy revolves mostly around farming. Rice is the main food crop, and cashews are the country's main export. Guinea-Bissau is one of the world's poorest countries. It gained independence from Portugal in 1975 after years of warfare. Since then, it has suffered from civil war and a series of military takeovers. Guinea-Bissau's instability has made it more difficult for the country to escape poverty.

Ivory Coast

Capital	Yamoussoukro
Land Area	122,780 sq mi; 318,000 sq km
Population	16.8 million
Ethnic Group(s)	Akan, Voltaiques (Gur), Northern Mandes, Krous, Southern Mandes
Religion(s)	Muslim, Christian, traditional beliefs
Government	republic
Currency	CFA franc
Leading Exports	cocoa, coffee, timber, petroleum, cotton, bananas, pineapples, palm oil, cotton, fish
Language(s)	French (official), Akan, Kru, Voltaic

Ivory Coast (EYE vur ee kohst) is one of the largest countries on West Africa's coast. It is bordered on the west by Liberia and Guinea, on the north by Mali and Burkina Faso, on the east by Ghana, and on the south by the Gulf of Guinea. Mountains cover most of its western edge. Cocoa and coffee are major agricultural products. Since a 1999 coup, Ivory Coast has faced political instability and violence. A civil war between the government and rebel forces lasted from 2002 to 2003. Despite the presence of African, UN, and French peacekeeping troops, the country remains unstable.

Introducing West Africa

Spot-nosed monkey in Liberia

Liberia

Capital	Monrovia
Land Area	37,189 sq mi; 96,320 sq km
Population	3.3 million
Ethnic Group(s)	Kpelle, Bassa, Gio, Kru, Grebo, Mano, Krahn, Gola, Gbandi, Loma, Kissi, Vai, Dei, Bella, Mandingo, Mende, Americo-Liberians, Congo People
Religion(s)	traditional beliefs, Christian, Muslim
Government	republic
Currency	Liberian dollar
Leading Exports	rubber, timber, iron, diamonds, cocoa, coffee
Language(s)	English (official), Kpelle, Vai, Kru Bassa, Grebo, Kissi, Gola, Loma

Liberia (ly BIHR ee uh) never experienced European rule. It was Africa's first republic, founded in 1847 by freed slaves from the United States. It is bordered on the northwest by Sierra Leone, on the north by Guinea, on the east by Ivory Coast, and on the south and west by the Atlantic Ocean. It has rain forests in which animals such as monkeys and crocodiles live. Beginning in 1990, a chaotic civil war engulfed Liberia. A peace deal was signed in 2003, but about 15,000 UN peacekeeping soldiers remain in the country. Today, 95 percent of Liberians are of African descent. The rest are mostly Americo-Liberians, descendants of the country's American-born founders.

Mali

Capital	Bamako
Land Area	471,042 sq mi; 1,220,000 sq km
Population	11.3 million
Ethnic Group(s)	Mande, Peul, Voltaic, Songhai, Tuareg, Moor
Religion(s)	Muslim, traditional beliefs, Christian
Government	republic
Currency	CFA franc
Leading Exports	cotton, gold, livestock
Language(s)	French (official), Bambara, Fulani, Senufo, Soninke

Mali (MAH lee) is one of West Africa's few land-locked countries. It is bordered on the west by Senegal and Mauritania, on the north by Algeria, on the east by Niger and Burkina Faso, and on the south by Ivory Coast and Guinea. The northern third of Mali is covered by the Sahara. To the south lies the Sahel, where cattle graze widely. The Senegal and Niger rivers flow through Mali. The country is named after an empire that flourished there 700 years ago.

Cattle herders in Mali

Mauritania

Capital	Nouakchott
Land Area	397,837 sq mi; 1,030,400 sq km
Population	2.8 million
Ethnic Group(s)	Maur, black, mixed
Religion(s)	Muslim
Government	republic
Currency	ouguiya
Leading Exports	iron ore, fish, fish products, gold
Language(s)	Arabic (official), Hassaniyah Arabic, Wolof, French

Mauritania (mawr uh TAY nee uh) is bordered on the west by the Atlantic Ocean, on the north by Western Morocco and Algeria, on the east and south by Mali, and on the south by Senegal. About two thirds of the country is covered by the Sahara. Many nomads once lived in the desert, but frequent droughts prevented many of them from staying there. For that reason, the population of the city of Nouakchott (nwahk SHAHT) has grown to around one million people.

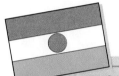

Niger

Capital	Niamey
Land Area	489,073 sq mi; 1,226,700 sq km
Population	11.3 million
Ethnic Group(s)	Hausa, Djerma, Songhai, Fula, Tuareg, Beri Beri, Arab, Toubou, Gourmantche
Religion(s)	Muslim, traditional beliefs, Christian
Government	republic
Currency	CFA franc
Leading Exports	uranium ore, livestock products, cowpeas, onions
Language(s)	French (official), Hausa, Djerma, Fulani, Tuareg, Teda

Niger (NY jur) is bordered on the west by Burkina Faso and Mali, on the north by Algeria and Libya, on the east by Chad, and on the south by Nigeria and Benin. Much of the country is arid Sahara or Sahel, although there are savannas in the south. Niger has often faced drought. Also, the country has faced long-term conflict between the northern and southern ethnic groups. Although politically stable after gaining independence in 1960, Niger has struggled to establish democracy. In 1990, seeking fairer treatment, the Tuareg people of the north rebelled against the government. The signing of a peace treaty in 1995 resolved the conflict.

Nigeria

Capital	Abuja
Land Area	351,648 sq mi; 910,768 sq km
Population	129.9 million
Ethnic Group(s)	250 distinct groups, including Hausa, Fulani, Yoruba, Igbo, Ijaw, Kanuri, Ibibio, Tiv
Religion(s)	Muslim, Christian, traditional beliefs
Government	republic
Currency	naira
Leading Exports	petroleum and petroleum products, cocoa, rubber
Language(s)	English (official), Hausa, Yoruba, Igbo

Nigeria (ny JIHR ee uh) has the largest population of any African country. It is bordered on the west by Benin, on the north by Niger, on the east by Chad and Cameroon, and on the south by the Atlantic Ocean. Members of at least 250 ethnic groups live in Nigeria. The country is one of the world's largest oil producers. It is also one of Africa's leaders in education. About 98 percent of Nigerian children attend elementary school, and the country is home to more than 50 colleges and universities. Still, corrupt government, ethnic conflict, and religious conflict have all troubled modern Nigeria.

Introducing West Africa

Senegal

Capital	Dakar
Land Area	74,131 sq mi; 192,000 sq km
Population	10.6 million
Ethnic Group(s)	Wolof, Pular, Serer, Jola, Mandinka, Soninke, white, Southwest Asian
Religion(s)	Muslim, Christian, traditional beliefs
Government	republic
Currency	CFA franc
Leading Exports	fish, peanuts, petroleum products, phosphates, cotton
Language(s)	French (official), Wolof, Fulani, Serer, Diola, Malinke, Soninke, Arabic

Senegal (SEN ih gawl) is bordered on the west by the Atlantic Ocean, on the north by Mauritania, on the east by Mali, and on the south by Guinea and Guinea-Bissau. Its capital, Dakar, is located on the westernmost reach of the African continent and is an important port for West Africa. Senegal was colonized by the French, and it became independent in 1960. The first president of the country, Léopold Senghor, is known as one of the great African poets.

Léopold Senghor

Sierra Leone

Capital	Freetown
Land Area	27,652 sq mi; 71,620 sq km
Population	5.6 million
Ethnic Group(s)	20 distinct groups, including Temne, Mende, Creole
Religion(s)	Muslim, traditional beliefs, Christian
Government	constitutional democracy
Currency	leone
Leading Exports	diamonds, rutile, cocoa, coffee, fish
Language(s)	English (official), Mende, Temne, Krio

Sierra Leone (see EHR uh lee OHN) is bordered on the west by the Atlantic Ocean, on the north and east by Guinea, and on the south by Liberia. Its capital city, Freetown, lies beside a huge natural harbor surrounded by low mountains. In 1787, the British established Sierra Leone as a place for freed African slaves to live. It later became a British colony and then gained independence in 1961. Since the 1990s, the country has suffered through intense civil wars. The people of Sierra Leone are known for the carved wooden masks they wear during performances, as well as for their carved ivory figures.

Carved wooden mask from Sierra Leone

Togo

Capital	Lomé
Land Area	20,998 sq mi; 54,385 sq km
Population	5.2 million
Ethnic Group(s)	37 distinct groups, including Ewe, Mina, Kabre, white, Southwest Asian
Religion(s)	traditional beliefs, Christian, Muslim
Government	republic
Currency	CFA franc
Leading Exports	cotton, phosphates, coffee, cocoa
Language(s)	French (official), Ewe, Kabye, Gurma

Togo (TOH goh) is bordered on the west by Ghana, on the north by Burkina Faso, on the east by Benin, and on the south by the Atlantic Ocean. The small country includes coastal lands, mountains, rivers, and plateaus. Many trees cover the southern plateaus, including baobab (BAY oh bab) trees, which are famous for their huge trunks. Togo is one of the world's largest producers of the mineral phosphate. Politically, one party has dominated since 1967. In the 1990s, however, the country made the formation of other political parties legal.

SOURCES: DK World Desk Reference Online; CIA World Factbook Online, 2002; *The World Almanac,* 2003

Baobab tree

Assessment

Comprehension and Critical Thinking

1. Compare and Contrast Compare and contrast the histories of these countries.

2. Summarize What are some characteristics that most of the countries share?

3. Analyze Information What are some key differences among the countries?

4. Categorize What kinds of products are the major exports of this region?

5. Predict How might the region be affected by the presence of a great number of ethnic groups?

6. Make a Circle Graph Create a circle graph showing the forms of government held by the countries of West Africa and the percentage each form represents.

Keeping Current

Access the **DK World Desk Reference Online** at **PHSchool.com** for up-to-date information about all 17 countries in this chapter.

Web Code: **nge-5500**

Nigeria
Land of Diverse Peoples

Prepare to Read

Objectives

In this section you will

1. Learn to identify Nigeria's three main ethnic groups.
2. Understand the major events in Nigeria's history.
3. Find out about the conflicts Nigeria faced on its path to democracy.

Taking Notes

As you read this section, look for details about Nigeria's three main ethnic groups. Copy the chart below, and use it to record your findings.

Nigeria's Ethnic Groups		
Hausa-Fulani	**Yoruba**	**Igbo**
•	•	•
•	•	•

🎯 Target Reading Skill

Identify Main Ideas It is impossible to remember every detail that you read. Therefore, good readers identify the main idea in every paragraph or section.

The main idea is the most important point in the section. For example, on page 141, the main idea of the paragraph under the heading Oil is stated here: "Another notable source of tension in Nigeria is the country's wealth of oil resources." All the other information in the paragraph supports this main idea.

Key Terms

- **multiethnic** (mul tee ETH nik) *adj.* having many ethnic groups living within a society
- **Hausa-Fulani** (HOW suh foo LAH nee) *n.* Nigeria's largest ethnic group
- **Yoruba** (YOH roo buh) *n.* Nigeria's second-largest ethnic group
- **Igbo** (IG boh) *n.* Nigeria's third-largest ethnic group

Nigerian youth

If you were planning to travel to Spain, you might learn Spanish. If you were planning to travel to Greece, you might try to learn Greek. But if you were traveling to Nigeria, would you study Nigerian? No, you would not even try to, because there is no such language. In fact, out of the more than 1,000 languages spoken in Africa, at least 200 are spoken in Nigeria alone.

If you find it hard to believe that so many languages can be heard in just one country, picture this: Nigeria is a little larger than the states of California, Oregon, and Washington combined. That means Nigeria could fit inside the United States about 11 times. But Nigeria has nearly half the population of the whole United States. At about 130 million people, Nigeria's population is the largest in Africa.

Ethnic Groups of Nigeria

Nigeria is **multiethnic,** which means that many ethnic groups live within its borders. In fact, it is home to more than 250 ethnic groups—most of whom speak different languages. English is the official language of Nigeria. However, the languages of Nigeria's major ethnic groups dominate the country.

These ethnic groups have inhabited Nigeria for many centuries. As you can see on the map in the Country Profile on page 139, the people of each group tend to live in certain parts of the country. Most members of Nigeria's largest ethnic group, the **Hausa-Fulani** (HOW suh foo LAH nee), live in the northwest. Nigeria's second-largest ethnic group, the **Yoruba** (YOH roo buh), make their home in the southwest. And the **Igbo** (IG boh), Nigeria's third-largest ethnic group, live mainly in the southeast. In addition, many smaller ethnic groups live in central Nigeria, and others are scattered throughout the country.

The Hausa-Fulani In the early 1800s, the Fulani entered northern Nigeria and conquered the Hausa there. The Fulani then ruled over the Hausa. But instead of imposing their own culture, many of the Fulani adopted the Hausa's language and practices. Over time, many Hausa and Fulani have intermarried, and the two groups have come to be known as the Hausa-Fulani.

The majority of Hausa-Fulani live in the countryside. Some herd cattle, while others farm crops such as peanuts and a grain called sorghum (SAWR gum). Still others produce crafts that are traded in markets. Trade has been an important part of the Hausa economy for hundreds of years—since long before the Fulani arrived. The Hausa built trading cities in northern Nigeria, each of which was enclosed by walls and housed a central market. Today, some of these cities, such as Kano, still thrive as centers of commerce.

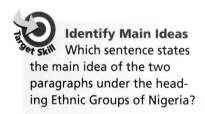

Identify Main Ideas Which sentence states the main idea of the two paragraphs under the heading Ethnic Groups of Nigeria?

Trading City Still Thrives
Kano has been a center of trade for more than 1,000 years. Today, people from around the world visit Kano's Kurmi Market. Vendors sell everything from fabrics (below right) to carved calabash bowls (below left). **Draw Conclusions** *Why do you think trading centers such as Kano have been able to last so long?*

A Yoruba farming family

The Yoruba Historically, the Yoruba have been the most urban of Nigeria's major ethnic groups. The Yoruba tradition of building cities began around 1100 and continued for hundreds of years. Each Yoruba city was ruled by a king and was densely populated, including traders and many skilled artisans. Currently, the majority of residents of one of Africa's largest cities, Lagos, are Yoruba. The city was founded in the 1400s and served as the capital of Nigeria from 1960 to 1991.

Today, many Yoruba also live outside cities. Often they are farmers, traders, or craftspeople. The farmers tend to grow cash crops such as cacao. They also grow food for their own families. Yoruba families live in large compounds made up of several houses built around a shared yard. A Yoruba community has many of these compounds.

The Igbo The Igbo have traditionally been rural. They have not built large cities but rather live in small farming villages. The people in a village work closely together. Each village is ruled democratically by a council of elders that the people select. Council members work together to solve problems.

Today, many Igbo also live in cities. Throughout much of the past century, they have served as members of Nigeria's local and federal governments. As you will read, Nigeria became an independent country in 1960, and its first president, Benjamin Nnamdi Azikiwe (NUM dee ah ZEE kway), was Igbo.

✓ **Reading Check** Which of Nigeria's ethnic groups is known as the most urban?

Nigeria

Nigeria is Africa's most heavily populated country and one of its most diverse. The country is rich in culture, but the differences can result in clashes. With more than 250 ethnic groups, tensions between the different groups have been hard to avoid. In addition, Muslim communities in the north and Christian communities in the south often face conflict today. Many northern states have adopted Islamic law. At the same time, Christian churches have drawn millions of new members. Study the map and charts to learn more about Nigeria's diverse population.

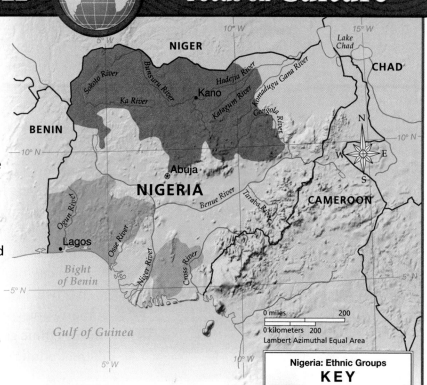

Nigeria: Ethnic Groups
KEY

Hausa-Fulani

Igbo

Yoruba

Other

—— National border

⊛ National capital

• Other city

Ethnic Groups

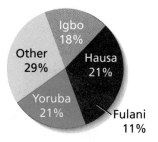

Igbo 18%
Other 29%
Hausa 21%
Yoruba 21%
Fulani 11%

SOURCE: DK World Desk Reference

Religions

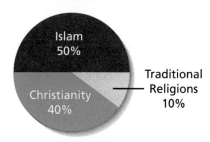

Islam 50%
Christianity 40%
Traditional Religions 10%

SOURCE: *DK World Desk Reference*

Tall, carved drums like these are made by Igbo people in Nigeria.

Map and Chart Skills

1. **Identify** What are two factors that make Nigeria a diverse country?
2. **Infer** Using the information given in the paragraph and the map above, which of Nigeria's ethnic groups can you infer are Muslim?
3. **Evaluate** Southern Nigeria has large oil reserves. How could this oil wealth play a role in the country's tensions?

Use Web Code **nge-5501** for **DK World Desk Reference Online.**

Nigeria's History

For thousands of years, the region of present-day Nigeria was ruled by many different African peoples who formed their own governments. In the late 1400s, however, Portugal began trading for slaves in West Africa. Soon, Great Britain and the Netherlands began trading in the region as well. By 1914, Great Britain had taken over Nigeria's government.

In 1960, Nigeria became an independent nation, with Lagos as its capital. Ethnic groups that had always lived separately had to learn to live and work together as one nation. In 1991, to help unify the country, Nigeria's government moved its capital from Lagos, in the south, to the city of Abuja (uh BOO juh). The new capital has two advantages. It is located in the middle of the country, relatively close to each of the three major ethnic groups. In addition, members of many different ethnic groups live in Abuja.

✓ **Reading Check** What city became Nigeria's new capital in 1991?

Lagos, Nigeria

The Path to Democracy

Unifying Nigeria's many ethnic groups has not been easy. These groups live in different areas, speak different languages, practice different religions, and sometimes have access to different amounts of economic resources. Only a few years after independence, conflicts began to arise. In 1966, a military group took over the government. The next year, civil war broke out as the Igbo tried to separate from Nigeria and form their own country. In 1970, after thousands had been killed or injured, the Igbo surrendered. The fighting ended, and Nigeria remained united. However, tensions remained high, and military control of the country continued for years.

Religion A key source of the tension in Nigeria is the religious diversity among the various ethnic groups. Most of the Hausa-Fulani practice Islam, while some Yoruba practice Islam and others practice Christianity. The Igbo are primarily Christian. Some members of these groups, as well as members of hundreds of others, also practice traditional African religions. Such religious diversity makes Nigeria rich in culture, but it also challenges national unity.

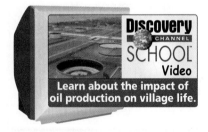

DISCOVERY CHANNEL **SCHOOL** Video
Learn about the impact of oil production on village life.

Oil Another notable source of tension in Nigeria is the country's wealth of oil resources. Nigeria's economy, which is one of the strongest in Africa, revolves around oil. Ninety-five percent of the income Nigeria earns from its exports to other countries comes from oil. However, while the government and the oil companies earn large profits from oil, the people who live on the oil-rich land do not. That is because most of the oil companies are foreign and use foreign workers. Many Nigerians want to gain a share of the work or income generated by the oil industry.

Democracy for Nigeria Since Nigeria gained its independence in 1960, many Nigerians have struggled to create a democratic government free of military rule. Finally, Nigeria's military leaders gave up their power. On May 29, 1999, an election was held for the first time in more than 15 years. Olusegun Obasanjo (oh loo SEG oon oh bah SAHN joh) was elected president of Nigeria. He was re-elected in 2003.

Oil workers in Port Harcourt, Nigeria

✓ **Reading Check** Which different religions do people in Nigeria practice?

Section 1 Assessment

Key Terms
Review the key terms at the beginning of this section. Use each term in a sentence that explains its meaning.

 **Target Reading Skill**
State three main ideas from Section 1. Tell whether each is the main idea of a paragraph or of a section under a red heading.

Comprehension and Critical Thinking
1. (a) Recall What are the three largest ethnic groups in Nigeria, and in which region does each group live?

(b) Evaluate Information Identify one feature that is unique to each of Nigeria's three major ethnic groups.

2. (a) Locate In what part of Nigeria is the country's capital, Abuja, located?

(b) Identify Causes Why did Nigeria's government think it was necessary to move the country's capital to Abuja?

3. (a) Name Which ethnic group tried to separate itself from Nigeria in 1967?

(b) Synthesize Information How is being a multiethnic country both good and bad for Nigeria?

(c) Predict What can Nigerians do in the future to resolve the conflicts in their country?

Writing Activity
Suppose that you are a Nigerian newspaper editor. Write an editorial supporting a movement for all Nigerians to use one common language. Be sure to say whether you think the common language should be English or another language, and explain why you think so.

For: An activity on Nigeria
Visit: PHSchool.com
Web Code: ngd-5501

Section 2

Ghana
Leading Africa to Independence

Prepare to Read

Objectives

In this section you will
1. Learn about the years of British colonial rule in the area that is now called Ghana.
2. Find out about the beliefs that helped move Ghana toward independence.
3. Discover how Ghana changed after achieving independence.

Taking Notes

As you read this section, look for details about events in the history of Ghana's government. Copy the timeline below, and use it to record your findings.

```
1874                          2000
```

Target Reading Skill

Identify Implied Main Ideas Identifying main ideas can help you remember the most important ideas in your text. Sometimes the main ideas are not stated directly. In those cases, you must add up all the details in a paragraph or section, and then state the main idea yourself.

Key Terms

- **Kwame Nkrumah** (KWAH mee un KROO muh) *n.* founder of Ghana's independence movement and Ghana's first president
- **sovereignty** (SAHV run tee) *n.* political control
- **coup d'état** (koo day TAH) *n.* the sudden overthrow of a government by force

Kwame Nkrumah

In 1935, a 26-year-old student traveled by ship from Ghana to the United States. At that time, Ghana was called the Gold Coast because of its abundant supply of gold. The region had been ruled by Great Britain for more than 60 years. The student's visit to the United States was a turning point in his life. He was well aware that the people of his country did not have true freedom or equality. When he saw the Statue of Liberty for the first time, he felt determined to bring freedom to both his country and his whole continent. As he looked at the statue, he thought to himself, "I shall never rest until I have carried your message to Africa." The student's name was **Kwame Nkrumah**, and in 1957, he would become the leader who steered Ghana to independence.

Links Across

Time

Asante Legacy The Asante did not submit to colonial rule without a struggle. In 1900, Yaa Asantewa (YAH ah uh sahn TEE wah), the Asante king's mother (at the right), led a war against the British. Even with more powerful weapons, the British took four months to defeat the queen mother's troops. After the war, the British began to treat the Asante more respectfully. Asante children still sing a song about "Yaa Asantewa, the warrior woman who carries a gun and a sword of state into battle."

The Colonial Years

For hundreds of years, many Africans in the Gold Coast had wanted their people to be free to rule themselves. While the Europeans were trading gold and slaves on the Gold Coast, some members of a large local ethnic group called the Akan (AH kahn) formed the Asante (uh SAHN tee) kingdom. This kingdom became very rich from trade. It controlled parts of the northern savanna and the coastal south. The Asante used their wealth and power to try stopping the European takeover of their kingdom. Despite these efforts, in 1874 Great Britain succeeded in colonizing the Gold Coast. Great Britain then ruled the colony through chiefs it appointed or who already held authority.

Effects of British Control When the British colonized the Gold Coast, their main interest was controlling the colony's economy. They encouraged farmers to grow cacao beans, from which they produced cocoa. The British then sent the cocoa to factories in Britain where it was made into chocolate. The British also exported timber and gold.

The export of raw materials led to problems that became common throughout colonial Africa. For example, people began growing fewer food crops for themselves and more cash crops such as cacao, which brought in more money. Soon, Gold Coast Africans could no longer supply enough food for their own needs, so they had to import it.

A related problem was that processing cacao brought in more money than growing it did. Therefore, most of the profit was gained in Britain, not in the Gold Coast. Yet another concern was that people began spending more time farming and less time making traditional crafts. As a result, Gold Coast people began to depend on buying factory-made goods from the British.

A Symbol of Pride
Colorful kente (KEN tay) cloth was invented in Ghana in the 1100s as a cloth to be worn by royalty. Over time, it became common for all people in Ghana to wear kente. Many West Africans and African Americans wear kente today with great pride.
Analyze Information *Why would a piece of cloth serve well as a way to show pride in one's heritage?*

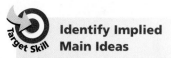
Mixing Old and New The British brought changes to some aspects of Gold Coast culture. For example, they built schools in the Gold Coast. Foreign missionaries ran the schools. Christianity began to replace traditional religions in many areas. Over the years, new ideas and ways of doing things came to traditional communities. Many people blended the new ways with the old African ways. For example, Kwame Nkrumah was born a Christian. But he also believed in parts of the traditional African religion. Nkrumah's respect for the old and the new ways helped him govern when Ghana became independent.

✓ **Reading Check** What goods did the British export from the Gold Coast?

Moving Toward Independence

During the 1900s, Africans whose countries were under colonial rule organized to demand independence. The European countries, however, resisted giving up their colonies. Some Europeans claimed that the colonies were not ready to rule themselves. Nkrumah challenged this argument with a reminder that traditional African governments had ruled Africa's lands for thousands of years. The Akan, for example, had long governed much of the Gold Coast.

Traditional Government The Akan are the largest ethnic group in Ghana today. Historically, Akan elders selected their rulers from members of the royal family. If the leader did not rule fairly, the elders had the right to choose another ruler. Each new ruler received this warning about how to behave:

A Symbolic Seat
Stools such as this one carry important symbolism for the Akan. When a new ruler takes office, the people say he has been "enstooled." They believe the stool the ruler sits on contains the soul of the nation.
Draw Conclusions *Why do you think people would consider a seat an important symbol?*

> **❝Tell him that**
> **We do not wish greediness**
> **We do not wish that he should curse us**
> **We do not wish that his ears should be hard of hearing**
> **We do not wish that he should call people fools**
> **We do not wish that he should act on his own initiative [act alone] . . .**
> **We do not wish that it should ever be said 'I have no time. I have no time.'**
> **We do not wish personal abuse**
> **We do not wish personal violence.❞**
>
> —*Akan statement of political expectation*

Nkrumah Takes Action In 1947, after more than a decade of schooling in the United States and England, Nkrumah returned home. He found a region that was poor, despite an abundance of natural resources. Nkrumah believed that people should benefit from the wealth of their land. He traveled throughout the Gold Coast, convincing people to demand independence.

✔ **Reading Check** How did the Akan system of government aim to assure good government?

COUNTRY PROFILE   Focus on Economics

Ghana

Ghana began its period of independence in the late 1950s with a wealth of natural resources. At the time, few people in Ghana had benefited from this wealth. As it has moved from a colony to an independent country with new priorities, Ghana has worked to change its economy. Mining has become much more important than farming. Ghana trades extensively with countries in Europe, North America, and Africa. Study the map and charts to learn more about the economy of Ghana.

Export Destinations

- Netherlands — 15%
- United Kingdom — 10%
- United States — 7%
- Germany — 6%
- France — 6%
- Other — 56%

SOURCE: DK World Desk Reference

Income From Mining, 2000

Percent of Income

- Diamonds — 2%
- Maganese — 2%
- Other Minerals — 24%
- Gold — 71%
- Bauxite — 1%

SOURCE: United States Geological Survey

Ghana: Natural Resources KEY

- Gold
- Iron
- Manganese
- Bauxite
- Diamonds
- Natural gas
- Hydroelectric power
- National border
- ⊛ National capital
- • Other city

BURKINA FASO
Bolgatanga
Tamale
GHANA
Lake Volta
Kumasi
Accra
Sekondi-Takoradi
Volta River
TOGO
BENIN
Gulf of Guinea
ATLANTIC OCEAN

0 miles 100
0 kilometers 100
Lambert Azimuthal Equal Area

Map and Chart Skills

1. **Locate** Where is most of Ghana's gold located?
2. **Analyze** How much of Ghana's income comes from gold?
3. **Summarize** Explain whether Ghana sells most of its exports to one country or to a variety of countries.

Go Online
PHSchool.com

Use Web Code **nge-5502** for **DK World Desk Reference Online.**

Learn about challenges facing Ghana's environment.

Independence Achieved

In 1957, some 22 years after making his pledge at the Statue of Liberty, Nkrumah gave a moving speech to his people. Great Britain, he said, had finally agreed to grant them **sovereignty** (SAHV run tee), or political control of their own country. Cheering, the people carried Nkrumah through the streets. Crowds sang victory songs to celebrate a dream come true.

Nkrumah became the leader and later the president of the new country. The government named the country Ghana after an African kingdom that flourished hundreds of years ago. Ghana was the first West African colony to gain independence. It was also the second country in all of Africa to become independent of European rule, after South Africa. The achievement of Ghana's independence would soon inspire many other Africans to push hard for—and achieve—freedom.

Nkrumah Overthrown   Nine years after he had been carried through the streets a hero, Nkrumah was removed from office by a military **coup d'état** (koo day TAH), or takeover. Most Ghanaian (guh NAY un) citizens did not protest. In fact, many celebrated. Some even pulled down statues of Nkrumah.

How did a hero become an enemy? Nkrumah had formed great plans for Ghana. He borrowed huge amounts of money to make those plans happen quickly. For example, he spent millions of dollars on the construction of a conference center and a superhighway. In addition, he made an agreement with a United States company to build a dam on the Volta River. The dam would provide electricity and irrigation for people in rural areas. But when world prices of Ghana's chief export, cocoa, fell, Ghana could not pay back its loans. Many people blamed Nkrumah for the country's economic problems.

Nkrumah Toppled
Pulled down by angry citizens, the headless statue of Nkrumah lies on the ground in Accra, Ghana. After his overthrow, Nkrumah lived in Guinea and did not return to Ghana before his death. **Draw Inferences** *What do you think Ghanaians thought when they looked at the toppled statue of Nkrumah?*

A Hero Again Nkrumah's downfall did not end Ghana's problems. The country alternated between military and democratically elected governments. Few were successful. Over time, people began to think well again of Nkrumah. Many felt that he had done his best to help the country, especially by leading Ghana to independence. When he died in 1972, he was hailed as a national hero. Leaders around the world mourned his death.

Ghana's Government and Economy Today In 1981, Jerry Rawlings seized power, becoming Ghana's second long-term president. Rawlings, an Air Force pilot, had previously overthrown the government and ruled for a few months. As president from 1981 to 2000, Rawlings tried to reform the politics and economy of Ghana. He stressed the importance of Ghana's traditional values of hard work and sacrifice. Ghanaians supported Rawlings, and Ghana's economy began to grow.

Today, Ghana's economy continues to be dependent on the sale of cocoa. Even so, the economy has grown strong enough that Ghana has been able to build better roads and irrigation systems. The government under John Kufuor, who was democratically elected president in 2000, has continued implementing improvements in Ghana.

✔ **Reading Check** How did Nkrumah lose his position as president?

After Nkrumah's death, this mausoleum was built as a national monument in his honor.

Section 2 Assessment

Key Terms
Review the key terms at the beginning of this section. Use each term in a sentence that explains its meaning.

Target Reading Skill
State an implied main idea from Section 2 other than the one you identified on page 144.

Comprehension and Critical Thinking
1. (a) Explain How did the Gold Coast's economy change after the British began encouraging farmers to grow cacao beans?
(b) Summarize While the British ruled the Gold Coast, did traditional ways stay the same, disappear, or blend with the new?
2. (a) Recall When arguing for independence, how did Kwame Nkrumah respond to the European claim that the African colonies were not ready to rule themselves?
(b) Identify Causes Why did the economic conditions of the Gold Coast under colonial rule lead Africans there to believe they should rule themselves?
3. (a) Note Compared to other African colonies, when did Ghana gain independence?
(b) Identify Cause and Effect What caused people's attitudes toward Nkrumah to change before and after his death?

Writing Activity
Work with a partner to write about one or two changes you would like to see happen in your country or community. Consider obstacles to making these changes. Then write a plan that explains each change, how you would make it, and how you would overcome any obstacles.

Go Online PHSchool.com
For: An activity on Ghana
Visit: PHSchool.com
Web Code: ngd-5502

Skills for Life — Decision Making

Julia's neighbor, Mrs. Gonzalez, owns a dog that Julia loves to play with. One day Mrs. Gonzalez offered to pay Julia for walking the dog every morning and afternoon. That sounded to Julia like a fun way to earn some money. But she was already considering joining the swim team. Walking the dog twice a day as well as going to swim practice seemed like too many commitments. Julia realized she would have to decide between the two—but how?

Playing with Buster in the backyard

 SS.4.07 Offer solutions

Some decisions are easy to make because one choice clearly has more to offer than the other. On the other hand, many decisions are difficult to make because all the choices have both positive and negative outcomes. Making good decisions means considering all the options before you decide.

Learn the Skill

Use these steps to make a good decision.

1. **Identify the issue.** Write a question explaining what needs to be decided.

2. **List the alternatives.** When you make a decision, you are choosing between at least two alternatives, or choices.

3. **For each alternative, list the likely outcomes, both positive and negative.** Every decision has outcomes, or effects. Use a decision-making grid like the one on page 149 to list the possible outcomes.

4. **Put a check mark (✓) next to the most important outcomes.** Marking the outcomes that matter most to you can help you reach your decision.

5. **Choose the option that seems best.** Write your decision in a sentence.

My Decision-Making Grid

Decision: Should I take the dog-walking job or join the swim team?

Alternatives	Likely Positive Outcomes	Likely Negative Outcomes
Take the dog-walking job.	Earn money. Get to play with a dog. Help my neighbor.	Don't have time for other activities. Don't get to spend time with friends.
Join the swim team.	Get exercise. Have fun. Meet new people.	Don't have time for other activities. Don't get to spend time with animals.

Practice the Skill

Suppose you win a contest at school and receive money as a prize. There is a certain item you have wanted to buy, and now you can afford it. But in three months your class is taking a field trip, and you know you will need to have some money for the trip. Follow the steps below to decide what to do with your prize money.

1 What is the decision you will make? Write down a question explaining what needs to be decided.

2 List the alternatives that you have to choose from. Are there two alternatives, or more?

3 Create a decision-making grid like the one above. Fill in the likely outcomes.

4 Put a check mark next to the outcomes that are most important to you.

5 Decide which alternative seems best to you. Write down an explanation of your reasoning.

Apply the Skill

Think of an important decision that you might have to make in the near future. It might have to do with school, friends, family, or something else. Create a decision-making grid to analyze the alternatives and outcomes. Then state your decision and your reasons for making it.

Prepare to Read

Objectives

In this section you will

1. Discover how Mali's environment affects its economy.
2. Find out how desert can spread across the land.
3. Learn about the importance of preserving Mali's environment.

Taking Notes

As you read this section, look for details about the role of the Sahel in the life of the people of Mali. Copy the diagram below, and use it to record your findings.

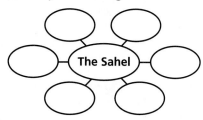

The Sahel

Target Reading Skill

Identify Supporting Details The main idea of a paragraph or section is supported by details that give further information about it. These details may explain the main idea by giving examples or reasons. As you read, note the details that support each main idea in the text.

Key Terms

- **desertification** (dih zurt uh fih KAY shun) *n.* the process by which fertile land becomes too dry or damaged to support life
- **overgrazing** (oh vur GRAYZ ing) *n.* allowing too much grazing by large herds of animals

Tombouctou, Mali

These days in Tombouctou (tohm book TOO), Mali, sand piles up against buildings. It coats the fur of camels. It gives a yellowish tint to everything in sight. Inside a hotel, a fine layer of red sand coats the lobby. Only a few of the rooms are taken. The manager is waiting for the river to rise, hoping it will bring customers.

But each year, as the climate slowly changes, the river rises a little later. "Ten years ago the first boat arrived on July 1," says Tombouctou politician Moulaye Haidara (moo LAH ee HY dah rah). "Five years ago it was July 15. Now, we're lucky if it's here by early August. In another five years, who knows?"

Mali's Environment

Tombouctou is located in the partly dry lands of the Sahel. As you can see on the map in the Country Profile on page 153, the Sahel lies between the Sahara and the savanna. The Sahara stretches over much of West Africa, and it is expanding all the time. In Mali, the Sahara covers about one third of the land. Few Malians inhabit the Sahara. Some live in the Sahel, while others live in the savanna, the one area of the country that receives abundant rainfall.

Resources of the Sahel The Sahel extends across Africa from Mauritania in the west to Ethiopia in the east. People have lived in the Sahel for thousands of years. They have long used its resources to earn their living. Malians in the Sahel herd animals and raise food crops to feed their families. Many earn extra money by raising cash crops as well. The rainy season, which lasts from May to October, is an ideal time for farming. During the rest of the year, farming is still possible in the Sahel thanks to water sources that exist year-round, such as the Niger River.

A Crossroads Location In the past, the Sahel's location as a crossroads between the Sahara and the savanna helped its economy flourish. For example, the city of Tombouctou was once a convenient stopping point for many camel caravans traveling between North Africa and the savanna. From the 1300s through the 1500s, Tombouctou thrived as one of Africa's wealthy centers of trade.

Today, people still live in Tombouctou, but they no longer practice trade on a large scale. Once European ships began trading along Africa's coast, trade through the Sahel decreased. Transporting goods by ship was faster and easier than sending them by camel. However, Tombouctou is still a crossroads for people traveling through the area.

✓ **Reading Check** Which months are the best for farming in the Sahel?

Table Skills

The table shows some of the groups of people who pass through Tombouctou and the ways they typically make a living. Below, a trader's camels carry salt to Tombouctou. **Identify** Which groups are traders? **Analyze Information** Based on the way they earn their living, what reasons do you think these groups have for passing through Tombouctou?

Activity in Tombouctou

Ethnic Group	Activities
Bambara	Farmers, traders
Berbers	Nomads
Fulani	Cattle herders
Mandingo	Farmers, traders
Songhai	Traders, gardeners
Tuareg	Nomads

Identify Supporting Details

The main idea under the red heading The Desert Spreads is that desertification is threatening the ways people in Mali make a living. Which details in the paragraphs at the right tell about this problem?

Diagram Skills

Overgrazing in the Sahara is the result of too much grazing by animals such as sheep, goats, camels, and cattle. **Identify** How does the soil become loosened when animals graze? **Predict** Do you think there are ways in which the people of the Sahara could avoid overgrazing their animals?

The Desert Spreads

Mali has little industry. Most people make their living through trading, farming, or herding. However, these types of work are being threatened by **desertification,** the change of fertile land into land that is too dry or damaged to support life. In Mali and other countries of the Sahel, the desert is spreading south. Even the wetter lands in southwest Mali are at risk of becoming desert. But how does fertile land turn into desert? Scientists have identified two causes of desertification that may be at work in Mali.

Overgrazing One cause of desertification is **overgrazing,** or allowing too much grazing by large herds of animals. When animals graze, they often eat the roots of plants, which hold the soil in place. With the roots gone, the fierce winds of the Sahara erode the soil. The soil then blows into the air, creating yellow dust clouds. This loose soil is one reason that Tombouctou is slowly being covered in sand—the desert is taking over the land.

Drought Another cause of desertification is drought, which you will recall is a long period of little or no rain. Droughts can turn land into desert. Over the last 30 years, the Sahel has received much less rain than it did before. Some scientists argue that a few years of good rainfall could stop desertification.

✓ **Reading Check** What does desertification do to fertile land?

Overgrazing

The roots of a plant hold the soil in place.

As a camel eats the plant and pulls up the roots, the soil is loosened.

Wind lifts the loosened soil from the ground and into the air.

Mali

From north to south, Mali's climate changes from the dry desert of the Sahara to the moderately wet savanna. In between lies the Sahel, a zone where farmers and herders face challenges from year to year due to unpredictable rainfall. The boundaries of the three regions are shifting as the Sahel grows drier and the desert expands southward. Human activity has also endangered farmland and vegetation in the Sahel. Study the map and charts to learn more about the importance of water in shaping the human geography of Mali.

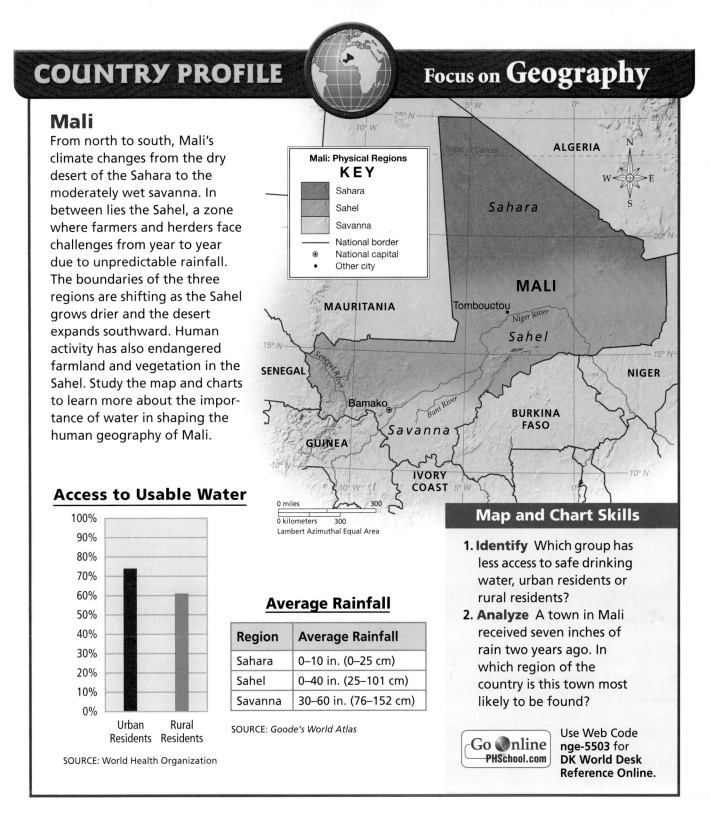

Mali: Physical Regions
KEY
- Sahara
- Sahel
- Savanna
- —— National border
- ⊛ National capital
- • Other city

0 miles 300
0 kilometers 300
Lambert Azimuthal Equal Area

Access to Usable Water

SOURCE: World Health Organization

Average Rainfall

Region	Average Rainfall
Sahara	0–10 in. (0–25 cm)
Sahel	0–40 in. (25–101 cm)
Savanna	30–60 in. (76–152 cm)

SOURCE: *Goode's World Atlas*

Map and Chart Skills

1. **Identify** Which group has less access to safe drinking water, urban residents or rural residents?
2. **Analyze** A town in Mali received seven inches of rain two years ago. In which region of the country is this town most likely to be found?

Go Online
PHSchool.com

Use Web Code
nge-5503 for
DK World Desk Reference Online.

Preserving the Environment

Many people around the world are concerned about the future of the Sahel. The United Nations has created a committee to help prevent desertification. Before the problem of desertification can be resolved, however, people living in the Sahel must learn how to avoid practices that make the problem worse.

Like this woman, most Tuaregs wear blue from head to toe.

Learn about government changes to farming.

A Way of Life in Danger Many people who live in the Sahel are nomads. The Tuareg (TWAH reg), for example, have lived in the desert and in the Sahel for many hundreds of years. They move their herds of goats, sheep, and camels south in the dry season and north in the wet season. The desertification of countries like Mali is threatening the Tuareg way of life. Moreover, during the 1970s and 1980s, Mali experienced several major droughts. Facing water and food shortages, some of the nomadic Tuareg have settled on farms or moved to cities. Others have built camps outside Tombouctou.

Finding Solutions Desertification has hurt Mali's economy by making it harder for farmers to grow cash crops. To help the economy, Mali's government has encouraged businesses to come to Mali and people to start their own businesses. Also, to help the environment, Mali's government has been studying the problem of desertification and is implementing programs to combat it. With the help of the United Nations, the government is working to educate people about better ways to use land. The government is also sponsoring irrigation and farming projects that will offset the effects of desertification.

✓ **Reading Check** Why did many Tuareg settle on farms, move to cities, or build camps?

Section 3 Assessment

Key Terms
Review the key terms at the beginning of this section. Use each term in a sentence that explains its meaning.

Target Reading Skill
 State the details that support the main idea of the paragraphs under the red heading Preserving the Environment.

Comprehension and Critical Thinking
1. (a) Identify Name two ways in which the environment of the Sahel makes farming in the region possible.

(b) Compare Compare the effects of the environment on farming and on trade.

2. (a) Recall What are two possible causes of desertification in Mali?

(b) Draw Conclusions How much control do humans have in preventing desertification?

3. (a) Describe How has Mali's government responded to the negative effects of desertification on the economy?

(b) Predict If the government's efforts succeed, do you think some of the Tuareg will be able to return to their nomadic way of life?

Writing Activity
Overgrazing is one possible cause of desertification in the Sahel. In North America, what common activities may present a threat to its environment? Do you think those activities should be discouraged? Write a persuasive essay explaining why or why not.

Writing Tip Be sure to use persuasive language in your essay. Include reasons and examples that clearly support your argument.

◆ Chapter Summary

Section 1: Nigeria

- Nigeria is home to more than 250 ethnic groups. The largest are the Hausa-Fulani, the Yoruba, and the Igbo.
- After thousands of years of self-rule, Nigeria became a British colony in 1914. It gained independence from Great Britain in 1960.
- During Nigeria's move toward democracy, Nigerians have faced conflicts over religion and over the wealth gained by the oil industry.

Section 2: Ghana

- In 1874, the British colonized the Gold Coast. They took control of the economy, built schools, and brought Christianity to the region.
- During the 1900s, Africans under colonial rule began organizing for independence. Kwame Nkrumah led the independence movement in the Gold Coast.
- In 1957, Ghana became the first West African country to become independent.

Section 3: Mali

- People in the Sahel have long relied on its resources and its location as a crossroads for trade.
- Desertification is occurring in Mali and other countries of the Sahel. Two possible causes are overgrazing and drought.
- Desertification threatens the ways of life of many people living in the Sahel. Mali's government is working to find solutions to this problem.

Tuareg woman

Kano, Nigeria

◆ Key Terms

Match the definitions in Column I with the key terms in Column II.

Column I

1. Nigeria's second-largest ethnic group
2. having many ethnic groups living within a society
3. the process by which fertile land becomes too dry or damaged to support life
4. Ghana's first president
5. a sudden overthrow of a government by force
6. political control

Column II

A Kwame Nkrumah
B Yoruba
C sovereignty
D coup d'état
E desertification
F multiethnic

◆ Comprehension and Critical Thinking

7. (a) Name List the three largest ethnic groups that live in Nigeria.
(b) Explain What are two sources of conflict in Nigeria today?
(c) Predict How might Nigeria's government help resolve the country's conflicts?

8. (a) Recall During the colonial years, why did people in the Gold Coast have to start importing their food?
(b) Synthesize Information When the British changed the structure of the Gold Coast's economy, how did the lifestyles of the people living there also change?
(c) Infer According to Kwame Nkrumah's beliefs, did those lifestyle changes matter in the discussion of independence?

9. (a) Explain How did Tombouctou's location in the Sahel allow it to develop as a major trading center in the 1300s?
(b) Summarize Did large-scale trading in Tombouctou end because of environmental change or because of social change? Explain.

◆ Skills Practice

Decision Making In the Skills for Life activity in this chapter, you learned how you can make good decisions.

Review the steps you followed to learn this skill. Then suppose that you have to make a choice between two after-school activities, such as writing for the school newspaper and acting in the school play. Create a decision-making grid. Put check marks next to the most important outcomes. Review the check marks and choose the option that seems best. Write a sentence stating your decision.

◆ Writing Activity: Geography

In the Sahel, overgrazing may be a cause of desertification. It might seem that a simple solution is to stop overgrazing. However, many people of the Sahel make their living from the animals that they graze. To prevent overgrazing, these people would have to change their ways of life. They would have to stop herding animals, herd fewer animals, or move elsewhere to herd their animals. Write a newspaper editorial explaining how you think this problem could be solved.

MAP MASTER™ Skills Activity

Place Location For each place listed below, write the letter from the map that shows its location.
1. Nigeria
2. Ghana
3. Liberia
4. Tombouctou
5. Lagos
6. Abuja
7. Senegal
8. Mali

Go Online
PHSchool.com Use Web Code ngp-5520 for an interactive map.

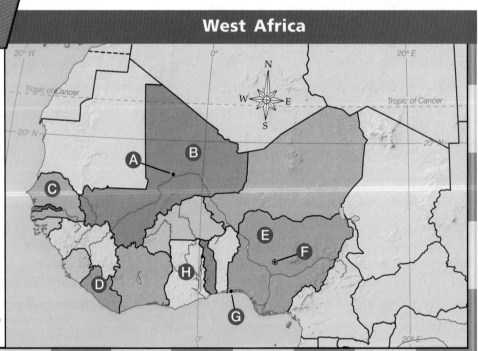

West Africa

Standardized Test Prep

Test-Taking Tips

Some questions on standardized tests ask you to analyze an outline. Study the outline below. Then follow the tips to answer the sample question.

> I. The Hausa-Fulani
>   A. Cattle herders, farmers, craftspeople
>   B. Built trading cities
> II. The Yoruba
>   A. Very urban
>   B. Also many farmers, traders, craftspeople
> III. _____
>   A. Rural farmers
>   B. Governed by democratic councils

TIP Pay attention to the organization of the outline. Use that information to help you answer the question.

Pick the letter that best answers the question.

Which of the following major topics belongs next to III?

A The Nigerians
B Ethnic groups of Nigeria
C The Igbo
D Christians

TIP Use what you know about history, geography, or government to find the BEST answer.

Think It Through This outline is organized by major topics and details. The question asks you to find major topic III. Answer B is too general; it could be the subject of an entire outline. Answer D is not an ethnic group. That leaves A and C. You can use your knowledge of geography to help you. Nigerians are a general group—citizens of a country. The Hausa-Fulani and the Yoruba are specific groups—ethnic groups in Nigeria. The Igbo are also a Nigerian ethnic group, so the correct answer is C.

Practice Questions

Use the tips above and other tips in this book to help you answer the following questions. Use the outline below to answer Question 1. Choose the letter of the best answer.

> I. Nkrumah overthrown
>   A. Nkrumah removed from office by a coup d'état
>   B. Nkrumah blamed for economic problems
> II. _____
>   A. Continuing economic problems
>   B. Improvement of public opinion about Nkrumah
> III. Government and economy today

1. According to the outline, which of the following belongs next to II?
   A Independence achieved
   B A hero again
   C Traditional government
   D Mixing old and new

2. Which of the following was Nigeria's first capital after independence?
   A Kano
   B Abuja
   C Lagos
   D Tombouctou

3. How does Mali's savanna differ from the Sahel and the Sahara?
   A It gets less rain.
   B It has a more northern location.
   C It gets more rain.
   D It is inhabited by fewer people.

Go Online
PHSchool.com

Use Web Code **nga-5500** for
Chapter 5 self-test.

Chapter
6 East Africa

Chapter Preview

 Standard Course of Study

7.2.03 Factors that influence migration

7.6.01 Connection between economic development and standard of living

7.7.02 Causes and effects of historical events

7.8.02 Impact of key groups on historical and contemporary societies

7.9.02 How different types of governments function

7.9.04 Analyze strengths and weaknesses of different governments

7.11.01 How culture links and separates societies

7.11.04 Impact of economic, political, and social changes on cultures

7.12.01 Impact of belief systems on practices and institutions

Country Databank

Sections

1. **Ethiopia: Religious Roots**
   7.7.02, 7.8.02, 7.12.01, SS.1.08
2. **Tanzania: Determined to Succeed**
   6.6.01, 7.9.02, 7.9.04, 7.11.01
3. **Kenya: Ties That Bind**
   7.2.03, 7.11.01, 7.11.04

Target Reading Skill

Context In this chapter you will focus on understanding context. Using context clues and recognizing nonliteral meanings will help you learn as you read.

▶ **Many of the world's fastest runners are Kenyan. This man is training on the plains of Kenya.**

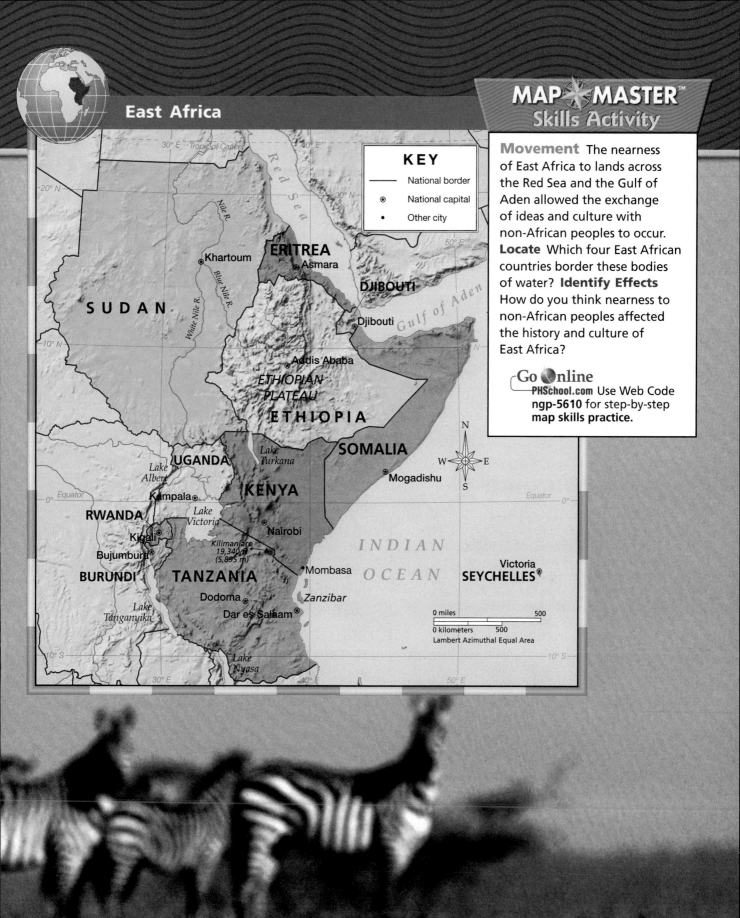

East Africa

MAP★MASTER™
Skills Activity

Movement The nearness of East Africa to lands across the Red Sea and the Gulf of Aden allowed the exchange of ideas and culture with non-African peoples to occur. **Locate** Which four East African countries border these bodies of water? **Identify Effects** How do you think nearness to non-African peoples affected the history and culture of East Africa?

Go Online
PHSchool.com Use Web Code **ngp-5610** for step-by-step **map skills practice.**

KEY

— National border
⊛ National capital
• Other city

30° E Tropic of Cancer 40° E

Red Sea

20° N   20° N

Nile R.

• Khartoum   **ERITREA**
                ⊛ Asmara

Blue Nile R.   **DJIBOUTI**

S U D A N   • Djibouti   Gulf of Aden

10° N   White Nile R.   10° N

              ⊛ Addis Ababa

              ETHIOPIAN
              PLATEAU

              E T H I O P I A

        Lake   **SOMALIA**
        Turkana
UGANDA   N
Lake   W ⊛ E
Albert   **KENYA**   ⊛ Mogadishu   S

0° Equator Kampala ⊛   Equator 0°

RWANDA Lake
          Victoria   • Nairobi   *INDIAN*
Kigali ⊛
Bujumbura ⊛ Kilimanjaro   *OCEAN*   Victoria
            19,340 ft   **SEYCHELLES** ⊛
BURUNDI (5,895 m)   • Mombasa

        TANZANIA
Lake   Dodoma ⊛   • Zanzibar
Tanganyika
          Dar es Salaam ⊛

10° S   10° S

                                    0 miles   500

Lake   0 kilometers   500
Nyasa   Lambert Azimuthal Equal Area

30° E   40° E   50° E

Guide for Reading

This section provides an introduction to the eleven countries that make up the region of East Africa.

- Look at the map on the previous page and then read the paragraphs below to learn about each nation.
- Analyze the data to compare the countries.
- What are the characteristics that most of the countries share?
- What are some key differences among the countries?

Viewing the Video Overview

View the World Studies Video Overview to learn more about each of the countries. As you watch, answer these questions:

- What are some common features of the region?
- What are some of the geographic points of interest in East Africa?
- What accounts for the blend of cultures in this region?

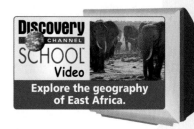

DISCOVERY CHANNEL **SCHOOL** Video

Explore the geography of East Africa.

Burundi

Capital	Bujumbura
Land Area	9,903 sq mi; 25,650 sq km
Population	6.4 million
Ethnic Group(s)	Hutu, Tutsi, Twa
Religion(s)	Roman Catholic, Protestant, traditional beliefs, Muslim
Government	republic
Currency	Burundi franc
Leading Exports	coffee, tea, sugar, cotton, hides
Language(s)	French (official), Kirundi (official), Kiswahili

The small country of Burundi (boo ROON dee) is bordered on the west by the Democratic Republic of the Congo, on the north by Rwanda, and on the east and south by Tanzania. Beginning in the 1970s, the country faced fierce fighting between two ethnic groups, the Hutu and the Tutsi. In 2002, a new government signed a peace treaty to help end the conflict. However, the country remains unstable, with small conflicts continuing and the economy weakened from the many years of fighting.

Djibouti

Capital	Djibouti
Land Area	8,873 sq mi; 22,980 sq km
Population	472,810
Ethnic Group(s)	Issa, Afar, Somali, white, Arab, Ethiopian
Religion(s)	Muslim, Christian
Government	republic
Currency	Djibouti franc
Leading Exports	reexports, hides and skins, coffee (in transit)
Language(s)	Arabic (official), French (official), Somali, Afar

Djibouti (jih BOO tee) is bordered on the south by Somalia, on the south and west by Ethiopia, on the north by Eritrea and the Red Sea, and on the east by the Gulf of Aden. It was established in 1977, when it gained independence from France. Its capital, Djibouti, is an important port city for the country's economy. Otherwise, the economy is weak because the country has few natural resources. In the early 1990s, fighting broke out between the nation's two main ethnic groups. In 2000, a peace treaty ended the fighting.

Eritrea

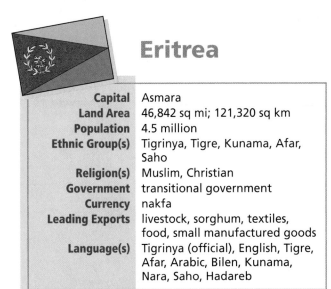

Capital	Asmara
Land Area	46,842 sq mi; 121,320 sq km
Population	4.5 million
Ethnic Group(s)	Tigrinya, Tigre, Kunama, Afar, Saho
Religion(s)	Muslim, Christian
Government	transitional government
Currency	nakfa
Leading Exports	livestock, sorghum, textiles, food, small manufactured goods
Language(s)	Tigrinya (official), English, Tigre, Afar, Arabic, Bilen, Kunama, Nara, Saho, Hadareb

Eritrea (ehr uh TREE uh) is bordered on the west and north by Sudan, on the north and east by the Red Sea, and on the south by Djibouti and Ethiopia. After being ruled by the Italians and then the British during the 1800s and early 1900s, Eritrea was taken over by Ethiopia in 1952. After thirty years of fighting, Eritrea gained its independence in 1993. Then, from 1998 to 2000, Eritrea and Ethiopia fought another destructive war over border disputes. Tensions in the region continue, and Eritrea's economy is weak from many years of war.

An Eritrean girl

Ethiopia

Capital	Addis Ababa
Land Area	432,310 sq mi; 1,119,683 sq km
Population	67.7 million
Ethnic Group(s)	Oromo, Amhara, Tigre, Sidamo, Shankella, Somali, Afar, Gurage
Religion(s)	Muslim, Christian, traditional beliefs
Government	federal republic
Currency	Ethiopian birr
Leading Exports	coffee, qat, gold, leather products, oilseeds
Language(s)	Amharic (official), Tigrinya, Galla, Sidamo, Somali, English, Arabic

Ethiopia (ee thee OH pea uh) is bordered on the west by Sudan, on the north by Eritrea and Djibouti, on the east and south by Somalia, and on the south by Kenya. It is one of the oldest countries in the world. Unlike most African countries, it was never colonized by a European power—at each European attempt, the Ethiopians proved victorious. In the 1990s, Ethiopia became a federal republic with a constitution and free elections. In the past 50 years, the country has experienced war and severe famine, or lack of food. Establishing a stable economy has therefore been difficult.

Introducing East Africa

Cheetahs in a Kenyan national park

Kenya

Capital	Nairobi
Land Area	219,787 sq mi; 569,250 sq km
Population	31.3 million
Ethnic Group(s)	Kikuyu, Luhya, Luo, Kalenjin, Kamba, Kisii, Meru
Religion(s)	Protestant, Roman Catholic, traditional beliefs, Muslim
Government	republic
Currency	Kenya shilling
Leading Exports	tea, horticultural products, coffee, petroleum products, fish, cement
Language(s)	Kiswahili (official), English (official), Kikuyu, Luo, Kamba

Located along the Equator, Kenya (KEN yuh) is bordered on the west by Lake Victoria and Uganda, on the north by Sudan and Ethiopia, on the east by Somalia and the Indian Ocean, and on the south by Tanzania. The Great Rift Valley runs through the western half of the country. Kenya is home to the Kenyan Highlands, one of the most successful farming regions in Africa. The country is also a major center of business and trade in East Africa. In addition, many rare animals and numerous national parks have made tourism a strong industry in Kenya.

Rwanda

Capital	Kigali
Land Area	9,632 sq mi; 24,948 sq km
Population	7.4 million
Ethnic Group(s)	Hutu, Tutsi, Twa
Religion(s)	Christian, Muslim, traditional beliefs
Government	republic
Currency	Rwanda franc
Leading Exports	coffee, tea, hides, tin ore
Language(s)	French (official), English (official), Kinyarwanda (official), Kiswahili

Rwanda (roo AHN duh) is bordered on the west by the Democratic Republic of the Congo, on the north by Uganda, on the east by Tanzania, and on the south by Burundi. It is the most densely populated country in Africa. Fierce civil war erupted in the early 1990s when nearly 1 million Tutsi were massacred by the majority Hutu. As a result of the war, about 2 million Hutus migrated to neighboring countries. After the war's end, many of them returned to Rwanda. The country's economy is slowly improving.

Seychelles

Capital	Victoria
Land Area	176 sq mi; 455 sq km
Population	80,098
Ethnic Group(s)	white, black, South Asian, East Asian, Arab
Religion(s)	Christian
Government	republic
Currency	Seychelles rupee
Leading Exports	canned tuna, cinnamon bark, copra, petroleum products (reexports)
Language(s)	Seselwa (French Creole) (official), English, French

The 115 islands of Seychelles (say SHEL) are located in the Indian Ocean, northwest of Madagascar. The islands are known for their natural beauty and unique plants and animals. They are home to the coco de mer (KOH koh duh mehr), a plant that produces a coconut-like fruit that is one of the largest fruits in the world. In addition, some of the last giant tortoises in the world live there. In 1976, Seychelles gained its independence from the United Kingdom, and in 1993 it became a democracy. Tuna fishing and tourism are the leading economic activities of these islands.

Fishing near Seychelles (left); a giant tortoise (below)

Somalia

Capital	Mogadishu
Land Area	242,215 sq mi; 627,337 sq km
Population	7.8 million
Ethnic Group(s)	Somali, Bantu, Arab
Religion(s)	Muslim
Government	transitional government
Currency	Somali shilling
Leading Exports	livestock, bananas, hides, fish, charcoal, scrap metal
Language(s)	Somali (official), Arabic (official), English, Italian

Somalia (soh MAH lee uh) occupies the Horn of Africa, the easternmost point of the continent. It is bordered on the west by Kenya, Ethiopia, and Djibouti; on the north by the Gulf of Aden; and on the east by the Indian Ocean. Much of Somalia is semiarid desert. There is some fertile land along the coast and in the south near the capital, Mogadishu (moh gah DEE shoo). Most Somalis are farmers or nomadic herders. In recent years, Somalia has faced many severe problems, such as civil war, the collapse of its government, and famine.

Introducing **East Africa**

Sudan

Capital	Khartoum
Land Area	917,374 sq mi; 2,376,000 sq km
Population	37.1 million
Ethnic Group(s)	black, Arab, Beja
Religion(s)	Muslim, traditional beliefs, Christian
Government	authoritarian regime
Currency	Sudanese pound or dinar
Leading Exports	oil and petroleum products, cotton, sesame, livestock, groundnuts, gum arabic, sugar
Language(s)	Arabic (official), Dinka, Nuer, Nubian, Beja, Zande, Bari, Fur, Shilluk, Lotuko

In land area, Sudan (soo DAN) is the largest country in Africa. It is bordered on the west by the Central African Republic, Chad, and Libya; on the north by Egypt; on the east by the Red Sea, Eritrea, and Ethiopia; and on the south by Kenya, Uganda, and the Democratic Republic of the Congo. Both the Blue Nile and White Nile rivers flow through Sudan. Nearly 50 years of civil war have led to millions of deaths, migrations out of the country, and economic problems.

An ancient pyramid at Meroë, in present-day Sudan

Tanzania

Capital	Dar es Salaam and Dodoma
Land Area	342,099 sq mi; 886,037 sq km
Population	37.2 million
Ethnic Group(s)	Bantu, Asian, white, Arab
Religion(s)	Muslim, traditional beliefs, Christian
Government	republic
Currency	Tanzanian shilling
Leading Exports	gold, coffee, cashew nuts, manufactured goods, cotton
Language(s)	English (official), Kiswahili (official), Sukuma, Chagga, Nyamwezi, Hehe, Makonde, Yao, Sandawe

Tanzania (tan zuh NEE uh) is bordered on the west by Zambia, the Democratic Republic of the Congo, Burundi, and Rwanda; on the north by Uganda and Kenya; on the east by the Indian Ocean; and on the south by Mozambique and Malawi. It is home to Mount Kilimanjaro, Africa's tallest mountain. The Great Rift Valley forms the country's south-western border. In 1964 the newly independent regions of Tanganyika and Zanzibar joined to become Tanzania. It is one of the world's poorest nations, but today Tanzania's manufacturing and mining industries are helping the economy boom.

Uganda

Capital	Kampala
Land Area	77,108 sq mi; 199,710 sq km
Population	24.7 million
Ethnic Group(s)	18 distinct groups, including Baganda, Ankole, Basoga, Iteso, Bakiga, Langi, Rwanda, Bagisu
Religion(s)	Roman Catholic, Protestant, traditional beliefs, Hindu, Muslim
Government	republic
Currency	New Uganda shilling
Leading Exports	coffee, fish and fish products, tea, gold, cotton, flowers, horticultural products
Language(s)	English (official), Luganda, Nkole, Chiga, Lango, Acholi, Teso, Lugbara

SOURCES: DK World Desk Reference Online; CIA World Factbook Online; *The World Almanac,* 2003

Uganda (yoo GAN duh) is bordered on the west by the Democratic Republic of the Congo, on the north by Sudan, on the east by Kenya, and on the south by Tanzania, Lake Victoria, and Rwanda. Uganda gained independence from Britain in 1962. It has since faced difficult political challenges. During the 1970s and 1980s, civil war led to hundreds of thousands of deaths as well as the destruction of the country's economy. Since the 1990s, Uganda has been celebrated for its return to economic success. The country has many natural resources, including copper and cobalt, as well as fertile soil and plentiful rain.

Lake Victoria

Assessment

Comprehension and Critical Thinking

1. Draw Conclusions What are some characteristics that most East African countries share?

2. Analyze Information What are some key differences among the countries?

3. Compare Compare the land areas and populations of Burundi and Sudan.

4. Categorize What kinds of products are the major exports of this region?

5. Summarize Which languages are spoken in more than one country in this region?

6. Make a Bar Graph Create a bar graph showing the land area, in square miles, of each of the countries in this region.

Keeping Current

Access the **DK World Desk Reference Online** at **PHSchool.com** for up-to-date information about all eleven countries in this chapter.

Web Code: **nge-5600**

Prepare to Read

Objectives

In this section you will

1. Learn about the two major religions practiced in Ethiopia.
2. Understand the contrasts in the daily lives of rural and urban Ethiopians.

Taking Notes

As you read this section, look for details about religion and daily life in Ethiopia. Copy the table below, and use it to record your findings.

Culture of Ethiopia	
Religion	**Daily Life**
•	•
•	•

Target Reading Skill

Use Context Clues When you come across an unfamiliar word, you can sometimes figure out its meaning from clues in the context. The context refers to the surrounding words and sentences. As you read, look at the context for the word *isolated* in the last paragraph on page 167. Use the sentence that follows it as a clue. What do you think *isolated* means?

Key Terms

- **monastery** (MAHN uh stehr ee) *n.* a place where people, especially men known as monks, live a religious life
- **Geez** (gee EZ) *n.* an ancient Ethiopian language that was once used to write literature and religious texts but is no longer spoken

As a young boy, Iyasus Mo'a (ee YAH soos MOH uh) learned to read and write. Around the year 1241, he traveled from his home in Wag to Tigray (tee GRAY), both in northern Ethiopia. He walked a distance that today would take three days to drive.

Did he plan to enter a university in Tigray? No—at that time there were no universities in Ethiopia. Iyasus entered a Christian monastery. A **monastery** is a place where people, especially men known as monks, live a religious life. As a monk, Iyasus studied hard for many years and eventually also became a famous teacher. His students built monasteries and schools all over the region.

The monastery of Debre Damo, where Iyasus Mo'a became a monk in the 1200s

Christianity in Ethiopia Today
An Ethiopian man takes part in a Christian celebration, wearing colorful silk clothing and carrying an elaborate gold cross.
Analyze Images *What details in the picture provide clues that this man is involved in an important ceremony?*

Major Religions of Ethiopia

Iyasus Mo'a learned Ethiopia's ancient traditions. He studied a language called Geez (gee EZ). **Geez** is one of the world's oldest languages. Much of Ethiopia's history was preserved by monks like Iyasus, who copied books in Geez by hand.

The religion Iyasus studied—Christianity—had spread to Ethiopia along trade routes. Ethiopia was a center of trade. It once included present-day Eritrea as well. These lands border the Red Sea. Look at the physical map of Africa on page 4 of the Regional Overview. Find the Red Sea. As people traded goods along the Red Sea, they also learned about one another's religions. The Red Sea connected Ethiopia with Egypt and Palestine, which were early centers of Christianity.

Establishment of Christianity in Ethiopia Alexandria, a city in Egypt, was one of the first centers of Christianity. By the year A.D. 350, missionaries from Alexandria had brought Christianity to Ethiopia. Over time, Christians in Egypt and Ethiopia came to differ with Christians in Rome and Constantinople about certain beliefs. In A.D. 451, Egyptian Christians separated from the rest of the Christian Church. They formed an Egyptian branch of Christianity called the Coptic Christian Church. Ethiopia's Christians also practiced Coptic Christianity.

Over time, Ethiopian Christians became isolated from Christians in other parts of the world. Ethiopia's mountains made it difficult for people who lived in the interior to travel to other areas. Some people did travel overland or along the Red Sea. However, Ethiopian Christians were cut off from these travel routes in the A.D. 600s, when Muslim Arabs arrived in the region.

Links to
Language Arts

Written Language Ethiopians began writing in Geez by the A.D. 300s. They used Geez to write literature and religious texts such as the one shown below. Ethiopia and Egypt were the only ancient African countries to develop their own writing systems. Many Islamic kingdoms in Africa did produce written documents for religious and government purposes. However, these texts were written in Arabic, which was developed in Arabia.

Underground Churches
Here you see St. George's Church of Lalibela from a side view (above left) and an overhead view (above right). The church was built in the shape of a cross. **Compare** *Compare the effects of looking at the church from the side and from above.*

Target Skill **Use Context Clues** If you do not know what *reigned* means, consider the word's context. You know that Lalibela reigned for a few decades. You also know that he was the ruler of Roha. You could conclude that *reigned* means "was the ruler of."

Spread of Islam Into Ethiopia The Muslim Arabs who had begun to settle across North Africa did not attempt to take over Ethiopia. But they did move into nearby areas. Over time, Arab traders built cities along the trade routes of the Red Sea coast. Eventually, Muslim Arabs came to control trade in the entire region. And, in time, some Ethiopians adopted the Muslim faith.

A Unique Form of Christianity As Muslim Arabs took control of Ethiopia's coastal regions, Ethiopian Christians began moving farther inland. Finally, Christian Ethiopia became surrounded by Muslim-controlled areas. As a result, Christians in Ethiopia had very little contact with Christians elsewhere. The Ethiopian Christian Church developed into a unique form of Christianity with its own traditions and language, Geez.

Also unique to Ethiopian Christianity are the churches of a town called Lalibela (lah lee BAY lah). Once called Roha, it was the capital of Christian Ethiopia for about 300 years. It was renamed for its most famous ruler, Lalibela, who reigned during the late 1100s and early 1200s. The ruler Lalibela sponsored the construction of eleven churches unlike any others—they were built below the ground and cut out of solid rock. Many Christians today travel to Lalibela to visit the churches and celebrate their faith.

Christian-Muslim Interaction Throughout most of Ethiopia's history, Christians and Muslims have coexisted peacefully. However, they have sometimes fought over religious issues. For example, they went to war with each other in the 1500s. Today, about 35 percent of Ethiopians are Christians and about 45 percent are Muslims. Most other Ethiopians practice traditional African religions, although a small number practice Judaism.

✓ **Reading Check** **How did Christianity first come to Ethiopia?**

Ethiopia

People have lived in Ethiopia longer than in most other countries on Earth. And for most of its history, the nation has ruled itself. Except for a short period of time before World War II, Ethiopia was never colonized by a European country.

Today, as for thousands of years, Ethiopian cultures have been centered mainly in the country's highlands. Many ethnic groups exist, but a few are much larger than the rest. Members of each ethnic group tend to live near one another. Study the map and charts to learn more about Ethiopia's people today.

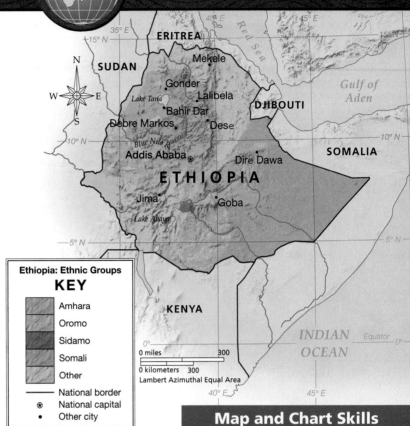

Ethiopia: Ethnic Groups
KEY

- Amhara
- Oromo
- Sidamo
- Somali
- Other

— National border
⊛ National capital
• Other city

0 miles 300
0 kilometers 300
Lambert Azimuthal Equal Area

Population by Age*

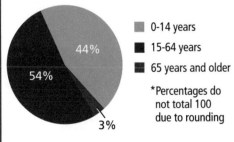

- 0-14 years
- 15-64 years
- 65 years and older

44%
54%
3%

*Percentages do not total 100 due to rounding

SOURCE: *CIA World Factbook*

Ethnic Groups

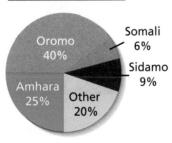

Oromo 40%
Somali 6%
Sidamo 9%
Amhara 25%
Other 20%

SOURCE: *DK World Desk Reference*

Map and Chart Skills

1. **Name** What is the largest ethnic group in Ethiopia?
2. **Identify** What percentage of Ethiopia's population is under 14 years of age?
3. **Analyze** What does this percentage tell you about Ethiopian society?

 Go Online PHSchool.com

Use Web Code **nge-5601** for **DK World Desk Reference Online.**

Contrasts in Daily Life

Today, most Ethiopians, regardless of their religious background, live in rural areas. In fact, only about 16 percent of the population lives in cities. How do rural and urban life in Ethiopia differ? A look at the village of Gerba Sefer reveals many clues about rural life in Ethiopia. The capital city of Addis Ababa (ad is AB uh buh), on the other hand, represents the urban life that some Ethiopians know.

Learn about life in
an Ethiopian village.

Rural Ethiopia Public services such as electricity and running water are rare in rural Ethiopia. For example, no one in the village of Gerba Sefer has electricity, and more people own donkeys than cars. The people who live in the areas surrounding Gerba Sefer make a living by farming. In some rural areas, people make a living by herding cattle or by fishing. Some families specialize in jobs such as woodworking and beekeeping.

A street in Addis Ababa

Urban Ethiopia Addis Ababa, the capital of Ethiopia, has a population of almost 3 million people. It is located in the center of the country. People in Addis Ababa have access to all the conveniences of city life—for example, running water, electricity, and modern hospitals. The city also has a university and a museum, as well as palaces built by ancient emperors. And Addis Ababa is a center of business and trade that reflects a diverse population, which includes ethnic groups such as the Amhara, Tigrey, Galla, and Gurage. The city also houses the headquarters of several international organizations that work for the economic, political, and social well-being of Africa.

✓ **Reading Check** Do most Ethiopians live in rural or in urban settings?

Section 1 Assessment

Key Terms
Review the key terms at the beginning of this section. Use each term in a sentence that explains its meaning.

 Target Reading Skill
Find the word *coexisted* in the last paragraph on page 168. Use context to figure out its meaning. What do you think it means? What clues helped you arrive at its meaning?

Comprehension and Critical Thinking
1. (a) **Recall** When did Christianity first come to Ethiopia?
(b) **Summarize** What led to the unique nature of the Christianity practiced in Ethiopia?
(c) **Predict** What do you think helps Christians and Muslims exist peacefully in Ethiopia today?
2. (a) **Identify** In what ways do rural Ethiopians make a living?
(b) **Contrast** How is life in Ethiopia's rural areas different from life in Addis Ababa?

Writing Activity
Write a paragraph encouraging travelers to visit the historic churches of Lalibela, Ethiopia. In it, explain how the Ethiopian Christian Church has been affected by the country's history.

For: An activity on Ethiopia
Visit: PHSchool.com
Web Code: ngd-5601

Tanzania
Determined to Succeed

Prepare to Read

Objectives
In this section you will
1. Find out about early reforms that the government of Tanzania made after independence.
2. Learn about continued social, economic, and political progress and reforms that have been made in Tanzania.

Taking Notes
As you read this section, look for details about social, economic, and political reforms in Tanzania. Copy the chart below, and use it to record your findings.

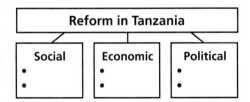

Reform in Tanzania

Social	Economic	Political
•	•	•
•	•	•

Target Reading Skill
Use Context Clues You can sometimes clarify the meaning of a word or phrase by using context—the surrounding words, phrases, and sentences. Sometimes the context will give a clear definition or explanation of the word. For example, each word highlighted in blue in this book is followed by a definition. As you read, look for other words that are accompanied by definitions or explanations.

Key Terms
- **lingua franca** (LING gwuh FRANG kuh) *n.* a language used for communication among people who speak different first languages
- **privatization** (pry vuh tih ZAY shun) *n.* the sale of government-owned industries to private companies
- **multiparty system** (MUL tee PAHR tee SIS tum) *n.* a political system in which two or more parties compete in elections

In October 1995, Dar es Salaam (DAHR es suh LAHM), Tanzania, looked ready for a celebration. Flags hung from buildings. People sang in the streets. Was it a holiday? Had a sports team become champions? No—an election was about to start. It would be the first election in more than 30 years to include more than one political party. Finally, voters would have a real choice among candidates with differing views. Tanzanians felt joyful, but they did not know what the future would hold. Other reforms their country had gone through had met with different levels of success.

Early Reforms After Independence

Tanzania lies on the Indian Ocean. This location has made it an important center of trade. Arab traders settled along the coast around 1,200 years ago. In the late 1800s, Germans colonized the entire region. The British took over in the early 1900s. The British named the mainland area Tanganyika (tan guh NYEE kuh). Tanganyika became independent in 1961. In 1964, it joined with the island state of Zanzibar to form Tanzania.

Tanzanians cast their votes.

Use Context Clues If you do not know what a one-party system is, look at the context. In the paragraph at the right, the phrase is followed by an explanation. Use this explanation to write a sentence describing a one-party system in your own words.

Challenges for the New Nation When Tanzania became independent, most of its people were poor. Few were literate. According to Tanzania's then president, Julius Nyerere, the new republic had serious problems:

> **❝We had 12 medical doctors in a population of 9 million. About 45 percent of children of schoolgoing age were going to school, and 85 percent of the adult population was illiterate.❞**
>
> —*Julius Nyerere*

A problem Nyerere wanted to avoid was tension among Tanzania's 120 ethnic groups. In many other African nations, ethnic groups fought against one another after independence. To ensure that ethnic conflicts would not occur in Tanzania, Nyerere adopted unusual social policies. Although some of these policies met with approval both at home and abroad, others were sharply criticized. Even today, debate continues over whether or not Nyerere made good choices for Tanzania.

A National Language One of Nyerere's social policies had to do with language. Various languages are spoken in East African homes, but many people also speak Swahili. As you read in Chapter 2, Swahili is one of Africa's most widely spoken languages. In East Africa, Swahili is a lingua franca (LING gwuh FRANG kuh). A **lingua franca** is a language used for communication among people who speak different first languages. To help unite all of Tanzania's ethnic groups, Nyerere made Swahili the national language.

A One-Party System Nyerere also established a new political system. He feared that political parties in Tanzania would be based on ethnic groups. If so, competition among parties could lead to competition or hatred among ethnic groups. This had happened in other newly independent African nations. Therefore, Nyerere established a one-party system. Elections still involved several candidates, but they were all members of the same party. Critics complained that having just one party encouraged corruption in the government.

Economic Changes Next, Nyerere turned to the economy. He told Tanzanians that independence meant *uhuru na kazi* (oo HOO roo nah KAH zee)—"freedom and work." By this he meant that only hard work could end poverty. Nyerere said that Tanzania should be self-reliant. He did not want the country to depend on other nations for economic support.

To promote self-reliance, Nyerere established a program of *ujamaa* (oo JAH mah), which is Swahili for "togetherness" or "being a family." Tanzania's economy is based on farming. Nyerere called for all farmers to live in ujamaa villages, where they could work together and share resources. He believed this would help boost farm production. It would also make it easier for the government to provide clean water, education, and other services in an organized way.

✓ **Reading Check** What language is the lingua franca of Tanzania?

Progress and Continued Reform

By the time Nyerere stepped down as president in 1985, Tanzania had changed greatly. The country had a national language and very little ethnic conflict. Education and literacy had improved greatly. Proud of his success, Nyerere commented,

> **"When I stepped down, 91 percent of the adult population was literate, 100 percent of the children of school-going age were going to school. . . . We did not have enough engineers, but we had thousands . . . trained by ourselves. We did not have enough doctors, but we had . . . thousands trained by ourselves. That is what we were able to do . . . in a short period of independence. "**
>
> —*Julius Nyerere*

However, Tanzania was still one of the poorest countries in the world. The ujamaa program had failed, and the economy was suffering. Many farm families had refused to move to the new villages. Crop production had decreased throughout the nation.

Tanzania

Like many African nations, Tanzania grows cash crops for export to other countries. The price of these cash crops on the world market greatly influences whether Tanzania's economy improves or declines. When the world price of coffee dropped from about $1.00 per pound in 1996 to less than $.40 per pound in 2003, many Tanzanians suffered. At the same time, the world price of tea rose, helping other Tanzanian farmers. Study the map and charts to learn more about the economy of Tanzania.

Economic Activity

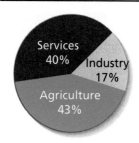

Services 40%
Industry 17%
Agriculture 43%

SOURCE: *CIA World Factbook*

Tanzania: Farming and Land Use

KEY

- Pasture
- Cropland
- Tea
- Coffee
- Cattle
- National border
- ⊛ National capital

Major Cash Crops, 2001

Crop	Exports (billions of Tanzanian shillings*)
Cashews	50.9
Coffee	49.6
Cotton seeds	29.2
Sisal	5.9
Tobacco	32.3

* $1 = approximately 1,000 Tanzanian shillings
SOURCE: Tanzanian Ministry of Agriculture and Food Security

Map and Chart Skills

1. **Identify** (a) Which of Tanzania's cash crops was the most valuable export in 2001? (b) Which was least valuable?

2. **Draw Conclusions** You can see that agriculture makes up the largest part of Tanzania's economy. Name one advantage and one disadvantage of basing an economy on selling cash crops to other countries.

Use Web Code nge-5602 for DK World Desk Reference Online.

A New Era in Economics After Nyerere retired, Ali Hassan Mwinyi (AH lee hah SAHN um WEEN yee) was elected president. His government replaced some of Nyerere's unsuccessful programs. For example, the government ended Nyerere's failing ujamaa program. The government then encouraged farmers to use new farming methods and types of seeds in order to produce more cash crops. It also asked foreign countries for more help, and a number of them have since loaned money to Tanzania.

Discover how people make a living on Lake Victoria.

The government also decided to try privatization. **Privatization** is the sale of government-owned industries to private companies. Private companies, including some that are foreign-owned, now manage Tanzania's telephone and airline industries. The result of the new economic policies is that Tanzania's economy is improving more quickly and more smoothly than the economies of most other African nations.

Attempts at Political Reform Tanzania's new government also changed the election system. In 1992, the government began to allow new political parties to form. When a country has two or more political parties, it has a **multiparty system.** Tanzania's first elections under the multiparty system were held in October 1995.

But the 1995 and 2000 elections raised some issues that divided people. For example, in both elections, Nyerere's party won the most votes, so power remained with that party. Also, another party suggested that the island of Zanzibar should no longer be part of Tanzania. That would cause exactly the type of social split that Nyerere worried about. Whether Tanzania can achieve the same progress in politics as it has with its economy is still to be seen.

Cashews: A New Cash Crop
Cashew nuts are one of the cash crops that Tanzanian farmers now produce for export to other countries. Coffee and cotton are also major export items. **Summarize** *How can producing cash crops for export help improve a country's economy?*

 **Reading Check** **What political change occurred in 1992?**

Section 2 Assessment

Key Terms
Review the key terms at the beginning of this section. Use each term in a sentence that explains its meaning.

Target Reading Skill
Find the word *self-reliant* on page 172. From its context, what do you think it means?

Comprehension and Critical Thinking
1. (a) Explain Why did Julius Nyerere decide to establish a one-party political system in Tanzania?

(b) Analyze Information In what ways can having a national language help prevent ethnic conflict in a country?
(c) Draw Conclusions If people had not had to move away from their homes, do you think the ujamaa program would have succeeded? Explain.
2. (a) Identify What improvements were made in Tanzania during Nyerere's presidency?
(b) Contrast Contrast the views Nyerere had on foreign involvement in Tanzania with the views that later government leaders had.

Writing Activity
How does Nyerere's slogan *uhuru na kazi*, or "freedom and work," apply to the kind of independence that you develop as you grow up? Write a paragraph explaining your response to this question.

For: An activity on the Ngorongoro Crater
Visit: PHSchool.com
Web Code: ngd-5602

Writing a Summary

Early each morning, the President of the United States listens to a news briefing prepared just for him. His staff members put the briefing together by reading and listening to news from dozens of newspapers, radio stations, and television networks. They then select the most important stories and write a summary of each one.

W riting a summary of any kind of information involves identifying the main ideas and weaving them together based on what they have in common. Knowing how to write a summary will help you take tests, write essays, and understand what you read.

NC SS.1.02 Summarize to select main ideas

Learn the Skill

Use these steps to summarize information.

1. **Find and state the main idea of each paragraph or section you want to summarize.** You can often find a main idea in the topic sentence of a paragraph.

2. **Identify what the main ideas have in common.** Look for the ways the ideas are presented—for example, in chronological order, as causes and effects, as comparisons, or as a progression of ideas from simple to complex. Doing this will help you identify the overall focus of the information.

3. **Write a summary paragraph that begins with a topic sentence.** The summary should draw together the main ideas into a broad description of the information. The main ideas will be the supporting details of your topic sentence.

U.S. President George W. Bush discusses the day's events with his staff.

Practice the Skill

Read the section titled Major Religions of Ethiopia on pages 167–168. Then follow the steps below to summarize what you read.

1 Read the heading and subheadings in the section. These titles give you a general idea of the content. You can see that both Christianity and Islam are practiced in Ethiopia. Now read each paragraph and list its main idea.

2 The main ideas in this passage are in chronological order. They cover these dates: 350, 451, the 600s, the 1500s, and today. In what other ways are the main ideas related? What overall idea holds these paragraphs together?

3 You might use this topic sentence for your summary: *Ethiopia's location as a crossroads of trade and ideas has shaped its unique religious history.* Use this topic sentence, or write your own, and then complete the summary paragraph by adding explanations and details. The details will come from the main ideas on your list.

Ethiopian places of worship: the Church of St. Mary of Zion (above) and the Nagash mosque (below)

Apply the Skill

Read the section titled Early Reforms After Independence on pages 171–173. Use the steps in this skill to summarize the information.

Kenya
Ties That Bind

Prepare to Read

Objectives

In this section you will
1. Learn about the peoples of Kenya.
2. Discover what life is like in rural Kenya.
3. Find out what life is like in urban Kenya.

Taking Notes

As you read this section, look for details about daily life in rural and urban Kenya. Copy the chart below, and use it to record your findings.

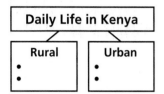

Daily Life in Kenya	
Rural	**Urban**
•	•
•	•

Target Reading Skill

Interpret Nonliteral Meanings Literal language is language that means exactly what it says. Nonliteral language uses images or comparisons to communicate an idea.

In this section you will read about "ties that bind" Kenyans together. When you see these words, ask yourself: Are Kenyans really tied together by something physical, or do the words have another meaning?

Key Terms

- **Kikuyu** (kee KOO yoo) *n.* the largest ethnic group in Kenya
- **Maasai** (mah SY) *n.* a seminomadic ethnic group in Kenya
- **seminomadic** (seh mee noh MAD ik) *adj.* combining nomadic wandering and farming in settlements
- **harambee** (hah RAHM bay) *n.* a social policy started by Jomo Kenyatta and meaning "let's pull together" in Swahili

A Maasai family in Kenya standing in front of their land

"**W**here is your shamba?" is a question that two Kenyans usually ask each other when they first meet. A shamba is a small farm owned and run by a Kenyan family. Even Kenyans who move to the city think of the land where they were born as home. They return to it throughout their lives. Land is very important to Kenyans.

Peoples of Kenya

Kenya's highest mountain, Mount Kenya, lies just south of the Equator. Southwest of Mount Kenya is a region of highlands that receives plenty of rain, so the land is good for farming. Most of Kenya's people are farmers. Many of them live in shambas dotting the countryside of the highlands. Others live along Kenya's coast, a warmer area that also has good farmland.

Kenya's Shared Culture Although some Kenyans are of European, Asian, or Arab descent, most come from families that have always lived in Africa. Kenya has plenty of cultural diversity—including more than 40 ethnic groups. Each ethnic group has distinct cultural features. But many groups have features in common, too. For example, some groups speak the same language as one another, and most Kenyans are either Christian or Muslim. Language and religion are some of the ties that bind the peoples of Kenya together.

Many Kenyans also share common values. Most Kenyans value their families as much as they value the land. Some families have six or more children. Members of extended families can be very close, often considering their cousins to be like brothers and sisters.

Kenya's Ethnic Groups The Kikuyu (kee KOO yoo) are Kenya's largest ethnic group. Many Kikuyu live in shambas in the highlands near Mount Kenya. They build round homes with mud walls and thatched roofs. The Kikuyu grow food and cash crops such as coffee and sisal, a fiber used to make rope. The Maasai (mah SY) are another ethnic group in Kenya, who traditionally make a living by farming and herding. The Maasai are seminomadic, which means they sometimes wander as nomads and sometimes live in settlements where they farm.

✓ **Reading Check** How many ethnic groups live in Kenya?

Ethnic Groups of Kenya
These women are Samburu people who, like the Maasai, are seminomadic herders. The women wear traditional Samburu dress—brightly patterned cloths and jewelry made of many colorful beads. **Evaluate** *Why do you think many peoples around the world dress traditionally?*

Life in Rural Kenya

As elsewhere in Africa, the majority of Kenya's farmers are women. They grow fruits and vegetables and herd livestock. Men also farm, but they usually raise cash crops, such as coffee and tea.

The way of life of many Kenyans is changing. As the population increases, many men and some women are moving to the cities to find work. Most women and children, however, stay in rural areas. Women are the primary caretakers of children, and it is expensive for women with children to move to a city. Many find it easier to support their families by farming.

Learn how growing beans has helped Kenya's economy.

Kenyans Working Together Kenya gained independence from the British in 1963. The first president, Jomo Kenyatta (JOH moh ken YAH tuh), began a social policy he called **harambee** (hah RAHM bay), which in Swahili means "let's pull together." Kenyatta encouraged harambee in many forms, including politics, farming, and education. For example, he had the government pay for a part of each child's education. In response, many villagers worked together to build and support their schools.

COUNTRY PROFILE   Focus on Geography

Kenya

Most Kenyans live in the countryside. The majority of the country's agricultural products are grown in the highlands region, where rainfall is sufficient for farming. An increasing number of Kenyans have moved to major cities. Nairobi, the largest business center in East Africa, is home both to very wealthy families and to people who live in slums. Study the map and charts to learn more about Kenya's land and people.

Major Agricultural Products, 2005

Production (in metric tons)	
Corn	2,800,000
Cassava	910,000
Plantains	452,000
Sugar cane	489,000
Coffee	1,080,000

SOURCE: USDA Foreign Agricultural Service, 2005

Kenya: Yearly Precipitation
KEY

Inches		Millimeters
More than 59		More than 1,499
40–59		1,000–1,499
20–39		500–999
10–19		250–499

— National border
⊛ National capital
• Other city

0 miles 250
0 kilometers 250
Lambert Azimuthal Equal Area

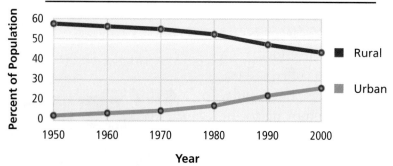

Urban and Rural Population, 1950–2000

SOURCE: United Nations Food and Agriculture Organization

Map and Chart Skills

1. **Identify** What products did Kenya produce more than one million metric tons of in 2005?
2. **Infer** In what region do you think Kenyans farm the least?
3. **Synthesize** Study the population graph. How do you think the trend shown has affected Kenya's agriculture?

Go Online PHSchool.com Use Web Code **nge-5603** for **DK World Desk Reference Online.**

Women's Self-Help Groups One of the best examples of how harambee is successful in Kenya is the rise of women's self-help groups in rural areas. Women in rural areas all over Kenya have formed these groups to solve problems in their communities. For example, many women felt it was not easy to farm, chop firewood, haul water, and take care of children all in one day. One woman commented, "My children were educated through the sweat of my brow."

These self-help groups do a great variety of work. Some women's groups grow cash crops in addition to the crops they grow for their families to eat. Then they sell the cash crops and save the money as a group. The women meet to decide what to do with the money they have saved. In the mountain village of Mitero, Kikuyu women's groups have built a nursery school and installed water pipes for the community. They also loan money to women who want to start small businesses. Sometimes they give money to women who need to buy such necessities as a cow or a water tank. They also save money individually and use it to educate their children.

✓ **Reading Check** **What is the purpose of women's self-help groups in Kenya?**

Life in Urban Kenya

Kenya's capital, Nairobi (ny ROH bee), is an important business center and one of the largest cities in East Africa. It is also East Africa's most important center of industry and manufacturing. Much of East Africa's banking and trade is centered there as well.

Working in the City Because Nairobi is a thriving city, many Kenyans move there looking for jobs. Every day, people arrive in Nairobi by train, bus, or *matatu* (muh TAH too)—minibus. Nairobi's population grew from one million in 1985 to more than two million in 2000. Many of Nairobi's newcomers walk to their jobs from the outskirts of the city. They may walk as far as ten miles each way because they cannot afford the cost of taking the bus to work.

When men move to Nairobi without their families, they often feel homesick for their loved ones in rural villages. Meanwhile, the women who remain in the villages must do much more work. Many people in Kenya have responded to this situation in the spirit of harambee—by working together.

Interpret Nonliteral Meanings

What does the woman mean by saying that her children were educated through the sweat of her brow? Did she use the sweat to teach the children or to pay for their schooling? Restate what she means in your own words.

These Kikuyu women have formed a savings and loan club to support local businesses.

Nairobi, Kenya

City Life Men who move to the city also work together. Many are saving money to buy land in the countryside. Men in Nairobi from the same ethnic group often welcome one another, share rooms, and help one another. Take Moses Mpoke (MOH zuz um POH kay) as an example. Mpoke is a Maasai. He owns land that is too dry for farming or grazing, but he could not move his livestock to find better grazing. After finishing high school, Mpoke moved to Nairobi to work.

Living in the city, Mpoke could have forgotten about his Maasai roots. But every weekend, he returns to his village to see his family and friends. When a visitor in his village asked Mpoke which is the real Moses Mpoke, the one in the city or the one in the village, he answered,

> **"This is the real Moses Mpoke, but the other is also me. In the week, I can live in the city and be comfortable. At weekends, I can live here [in my village] and be comfortable. The city has not stopped me from being a Maasai. "**
>
> —*Moses Mpoke*

✓ **Reading Check** How do Kenyans living in the city support one another?

Section 3 Assessment

Key Terms
Review the key terms at the beginning of this section. Use each term in a sentence that explains its meaning.

Target Reading Skill
Find the phrase "in shambas dotting the countryside" on page 179. Explain in your own words what this means.

Comprehension and Critical Thinking
1. (a) Recall In what way do most Kenyans make their living?

(b) Compare What other traits do Kenya's different ethnic groups have in common?

2. (a) Explain Why do most Kenyan women stay in rural villages rather than move to the city?

(b) Summarize How have Kenya's government and Kenya's village women used harambee to help benefit village families?

3. (a) Describe What do many Kenyans who live in the city plan to do with the money they earn?

(b) Analyze Information What different hardships do men and women in Kenya face if the men decide to work in Nairobi?

Writing Activity
Consider the concept of harambee. It means that people work together for a common good. Write an account of how you have seen or would like to see harambee in your community or school.

> **Writing Tip** Start your account with an explanation of what harambee is, so that readers can easily understand how your example fits into the concept.

Review and Assessment

◆ Chapter Summary

Section 1: Ethiopia

- Ethiopia has two major religions—Christianity and Islam. At times Ethiopian Christians and Muslims have fought each other, but today they live together peacefully.
- Most Ethiopians live in rural areas. Their daily lives are very different from those of Ethiopians in urban areas.

Ethiopia

Section 2: Tanzania

- After independence, Tanzania's president Julius Nyerere established Swahili as the country's lingua franca, created a one-party political system, and encouraged farmers to live in ujamaa villages.
- Since Nyerere retired in 1985, Tanzania's government has encouraged privatization and other economic reforms as well as a multiparty political system.

Section 3: Kenya

- Kenyans come from 40 ethnic groups that are distinct but also share some values and characteristics. Many Kenyans are farmers.
- Most Kenyan farmers are women. To help solve community problems, many Kenyan women have formed various self-help groups.
- Many Kenyan men have had to move to the city to find work, but they often return to their villages on weekends or when they retire.

Kenya

◆ Key Terms

Each of the statements below contains a key term from the chapter. If it is true, write *true*. If it is false, change the highlighted term to make the statement true.

1. The Swahili word that means "let's pull together" is harambee.

2. Kikuyu is an ancient Ethiopian language.

3. A place where people live a religious life is a multiparty system.

4. People who speak different languages often communicate by speaking a lingua franca.

5. A country with two or more political parties has a monastery.

Review and Assessment (continued)

◆ Comprehension and Critical Thinking

6. (a) Describe How did Christianity and Islam spread into Ethiopia?
(b) Identify Effects How did the spread of Islam cause Ethiopian Christians to become more isolated?

7. (a) Identify What public services are lacking in Ethiopia's rural areas?
(b) Make Generalizations Do you think the prosperity of Addis Ababa could spread into rural Ethiopia? If it did, how would life change in rural areas?

8. (a) Explain Why did Julius Nyerere establish a lingua franca for Tanzania?
(b) Identify What changes did Julius Nyerere make to Tanzania's economic and political systems?
(c) Contrast What are some advantages of a one-party political system? Of a multiparty system?

9. (a) Recall Has Tanzania had greater success in economics or in politics?
(b) Analyze Information Why has establishing a multiparty political system in Tanzania been a challenge?

10. (a) Recall What are some ties that bind the people of Kenya together?
(b) Summarize How have rural Kenyans worked together to improve their lives?
(c) Identify Effects The movement of men from Kenya's countryside to Nairobi can cause some hardship. How can it also help improve village life?

◆ Skills Practice

Writing a Summary In the Skills for Life activity in this chapter, you learned how to write a summary.

Review the steps you followed to learn this skill. Then reread the part of Section 3 titled Life in Rural Kenya. Find the main idea of each paragraph. Then identify what the main ideas have in common, and write a summary paragraph.

◆ Writing Activity: Language Arts

Think about the community you live in. Is it growing or becoming smaller? Think of reasons why your community may have developed in the way that it has. What are some positive changes that have occurred? What are some negative ones? Use your answers to write a newspaper editorial explaining your opinion on whether your community is developing in a way that benefits its citizens.

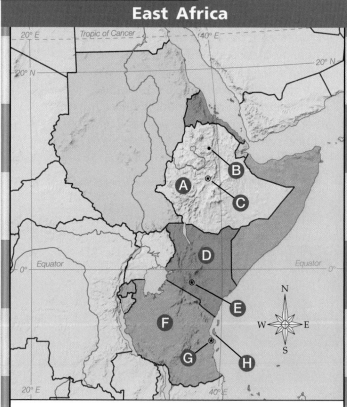

MAP✶MASTER™
Skills Activity

East Africa

Place Location For each place listed, write the letter from the map that shows its location.
1. Ethiopia
2. Nairobi
3. Tanzania
4. Dar es Salaam
5. Zanzibar
6. Kenya
7. Addis Ababa
8. Lalibela

Go Online
PHSchool.com Use Web Code **ngp-5620** for an **interactive map.**

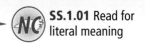
Standardized Test Prep

Test-Taking Tips

Some questions on standardized tests ask you to analyze a reading selection. Read the passage below. Then follow the tips to answer the sample question.

> Julius Nyerere became the first president of Tanzania in 1964. He made Swahili the national language to help unite his country's many ethnic groups. He encouraged farmers to live together in organized villages and to cooperate. Many more schools were built, and literacy improved dramatically after independence. Many more Tanzanians were trained to be engineers, doctors, and teachers.

TIP Look for topics that are shared by all the sentences in the passage.

Pick the letter that best answers the question.

Which kind of resources in Tanzania does this passage describe?

  A natural resources

  B human resources

  C capital resources

  D entrepreneurial resources

TIP Before you read the paragraph, preview the question. Think about it as you read.

Think It Through The question asks what kind of resources the paragraph describes. Skim over each sentence of the paragraph. Each one mentions something about the people of Tanzania. You can eliminate answer A, natural resources, because those are materials found in the environment. You may not know the words *capital* or *entrepreneurial* in C and D, but you probably know that *human* has to do with people. The correct answer is B.

Practice Questions

Use the tips above and other tips in this book to help you answer the following questions. Use the passage below to answer Question 1. Choose the letter of the best answer.

> Lalibela is a town in Ethiopia. People travel there to visit a group of churches for which Lalibela is famous. Many people who live there, however, do not have electricity. Most of them do not own cars. Most of them earn a living by farming.

1. Which is a detail that is described in this passage?

  A The people who live in Lalibela love the churches there.

  B The tourists who visit Lalibela cannot bring cars.

  C Most of the people who live in Lalibela are farmers.

  D Most of Lalibela's visitors are farmers.

2. Which of the following was NOT true of Tanzania's ujamaa program?

  A The program's goal was to boost farm production.

  B People had to work together to make the program successful.

  C The government had to help out with the program.

  D All farm families in Tanzania agreed to take part.

3. Which is the word for a family farm in Kenya?

  A Maasai

  B shamba

  C harambee

  D Kikuyu

Use Web Code **nga-5600** for **Chapter 6 self-test.**

A Promise to the Sun
By Tololwa M. Mollel

Prepare to Read

Background Information

Not all stories were written down when they were first told. Myths like the one you are about to read were originally told aloud. They were part of an oral tradition that people passed down from generation to generation.

These myths are meant to entertain the listener. They are also meant to explain something to the listener. Usually, they explain why aspects of the world are as they are. Myths often provide a moral lesson to the listener as well.

This story was written by Tololwa M. Mollel in the style of Maasai myths heard in his youth in Tanzania. Mollel is a well-known storyteller and author.

Objectives
In this section you will
1. Explore the natural world from a point of view that may not be familiar to you.
2. Learn how a storyteller can use animals and natural forces as characters to make a story more meaningful.

savannah alternate spelling of *savanna*

maize (mayz) *n.* corn

shrivel (SHRIH vul) *v.* to wrinkle as moisture is lost

wilt (wilt) *v.* to droop

withered (WITH urd) *adj.* shriveled and shrunken from drying out

Long ago, when the world was new, a severe drought hit the land of the birds. The savannah turned brown, and streams dried up. Maize plants died, and banana trees shriveled in the sun, their broad leaves wilting away. Even the nearby forest grew withered and pale.

The birds held a meeting and decided to send someone in search of rain. They drew lots to choose who would go on the journey. And they told the Bat, their distant cousin who was visiting, that she must draw, too. "You might not be a bird," they said, "but for now you're one of us." Everyone took a lot, and as luck would have it, the task fell to the Bat.

Over the trees and the mountains flew the Bat, to the Moon. There she cried, "Earth has no rain, Earth has no food, Earth asks for rain!"

A full moon rises over the Kenyan landscape.

The Moon smiled. "I can't bring rain. My task is to wash and oil the night's face. But you can try the Stars."

On flew the Bat, until she found the Stars at play. "Away with you!" they snapped, angry at being interrupted. "If you want rain, go to the Clouds!"

The Clouds were asleep but awoke at the sound of the Bat arriving. "We can bring rain," they yawned, "but the Winds must first blow us together, to hang over the Earth in one big lump."

At the approach of the Bat, the Winds howled to a stop.

"We'll blow the Clouds together," they said, "but not before the Sun has brought up steam to the sky."

As the Bat flew toward the Sun, a sudden scream shook the sky:

"Stop where you are, foolish Bat, before I burn off your little wings!"

The Bat shrank back in terror, and the Sun smothered its fire in rolls of clouds. Quickly the Bat said, "Earth has no rain, Earth has no food, Earth asks for rain!"

"I'll help you," replied the Sun, "in return for a favor. After the rain falls, choose for me the greenest patch on the forest top, and build me a nest there. Then no longer will I have to journey to the <u>horizon</u> at the end of each day but will rest for the night in the cool and quiet of the forest."

The Bat quickly replied, "I'm only a Bat and don't know how to build nests, but the birds will happily make you one. Nothing will be easier—there are so many of them. They will do it right after the harvest, I promise—all in a day!"

And down the sky's sunlit paths the Bat flew, excited to bring the good news to the birds.

The birds readily promised to build the nest.

"The very day after the harvest," said the Sparrow.

"All in a day," said the Owl.

"A beautiful nest it'll be," said the Canary.

"With all the colors of the rainbow," said the Peacock.

So the Sun burnt down upon the earth, steam rose, Winds blew, and Clouds gathered. Then rain fell. The savannah bloomed, and streams flowed. Green and thick and tall, the forest grew until it touched the sky. Crops flourished and ripened— maize, bananas, cassava, millet, and peanuts—and the birds harvested. The morning after the harvest, the Bat reminded the birds about the nest. Suddenly the birds were in no mood for work. All they cared about was the harvest celebrations, which were to start that night and last several days.

Clouds fill the East African sky.

horizon (huh RY zun) *n.* the place where Earth and sky appear to meet

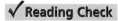

✓ **Reading Check**

What promise does the Bat make to the Sun?

"I have to adorn myself," said the Peacock.

"I have to practice my flute," said the Canary.

"I have to heat up my drums," said the Owl.

"I have to help prepare the feast," said the Sparrow.

"Wait until after the celebrations," they said. "We'll do it then." But their hearts were not in it, and the Bat knew they would never build the nest.

What was she to do? A promise is a promise, she firmly believed, yet she didn't know anything about making a nest. Even if she did, how could she, all on her own, hope to make one big enough for the sun?

The Sun set, and the Moon rose. The celebrations began. The drums <u>throbbed,</u> the flutes wailed, and the dancers pounded the earth with their feet.

Alone with her thoughts and tired, the Bat fell fast asleep.

She awoke in a panic. The Moon had vanished, the Stars faded. Soon the Sun would rise!

Slowly, the Sun peered out over the horizon in search of the nest.

Certain the Sun was looking for her, the Bat scrambled behind a banana leaf. The Sun moved up in the sky. One of its rays glared over the leaf. With a cry of fear, the Bat fled to the forest.

But even there, she was not long at peace. There was a gust of wind, and the forest opened for a moment overhead. The Bat looked up anxiously. Peeking down at her was the Sun.

She let out a <u>shriek</u> and flew away.

As she flew, a cave came into view below. She dived down and quickly darted in.

There, silent and out of reach, she hid from the glare of the Sun.

She hid from the shame of a broken promise, a shame the birds did not feel.

Outside, the celebrations went on. The Owl's drums roared furiously. The Canary's flute pierced the air. And the Sparrow cheered the Peacock's wild dancing.

The Sun inched down toward the horizon. It lingered over the forest and cast one more glance at the treetops, hoping for a miracle. Then, disappointed, it began to set. The birds carried on unconcerned, the sounds of their festivities reaching into the cave.

throb (thrahb) *v.* to beat

shriek (shreek) *n.* a sharp, shrill sound

Sunrise in Kenya

The Bat did not stir from her hiding place that night. Nor the next day. For many days and nights she huddled in the cave. Then gradually she got up enough courage to <u>venture</u> out—but never in daylight! Only after sunset with Earth in the <u>embrace</u> of night.

Days and months and years went by, but the birds didn't build the nest. The Sun never gave up wishing, though. Every day as it set, it would linger to cast one last, hopeful glance at the forest top. Then, slowly, very slowly, it would sink away below the horizon.

Year after year the Sun continued to drag up steam, so the Winds would blow, the Clouds gather, and rain fall. It continues to do so today, hoping that the birds will one day keep their promise and build a nest among the treetops.

As for the Bat, . . . she made a home in the cave, and there she lives to this day. Whenever it rains, though, she listens eagerly. From the dark silence of her perch, the sound of the downpour, ripening the crops and renewing the forest, is to her a magical song she wishes she could be out dancing to.

And as she listens, the trees outside sway and bow toward the cave. It is their thank-you salute to the hero who helped turn the forests green and thick and tall as the sky.

venture (VEN chur) *v.* to move forward in the face of danger

embrace (em BRAYS) *n.* hug

About the Selection

A Promise to the Sun is a children's book written by Tololwa M. Mollel and published in 1992.

✓ Reading Check

How does the Bat's life change as a result of what happens in the story?

About the Author

Tololwa M. Mollel (b. 1952) is an Arusha-Maasai born in northern Tanzania. He was educated and has taught writing and theater in Tanzania and Canada. Mollel has written more than 15 children's books. He has based his books on African folklore, including traditional Maasai tales and themes from his childhood.

Review and Assessment

Thinking About the Selection

1. (a) Recall What favor did the Sun ask of the Bat?

(b) Explain Why did the Bat not keep her promise?

(c) Analyze What aspects of how a bat lives are explained by this story? What other natural events are explained by this story?

2. (a) Respond Why do you think that the birds did not feel as ashamed as the Bat did?

(b) Analyze What moral lesson does the story teach about making and keeping promises?

Writing Activity

Write a Myth Using this story as a model, write your own myth. You might want to write a myth in which the Bat makes peace with the Sun, or one in which another animal makes a promise to the Moon.

Chapter

7 Central and Southern Africa

Chapter Preview

NC Standard Course of Study

7.3.01 How cultures and regions are influenced by human interaction with environment

7.7.01 Relationship between historical events and current issues

7.9.01 Historical development of types of governments

7.9.02 Evaluate effectiveness of different types of governments

7.9.03 Influence of values on how governments deal with issues of justice

7.10.01 Development of relationships between individuals and their governments

7.10.02 How citizens' roles are incorporated into government structures

7.10.04 Rights, roles, and status of individuals in selected countries

Country Databank

Sections

1. **Democratic Republic of the Congo: A Wealth of Possibilities**
   7.3.01, 7.9.01, 7.9.02, 7.10.04

2. **South Africa: Struggle for Equality**
   7.7.01, 7.9.03, 7.10.01, 7.10.02

 Target Reading Skill

Sequence In this chapter you will focus on understanding sequence. Identifying sequence and recognizing sequence signal words will help you learn as you read.

▶ **Cape Town, South Africa, is an important port and center of industry in Southern Africa.**

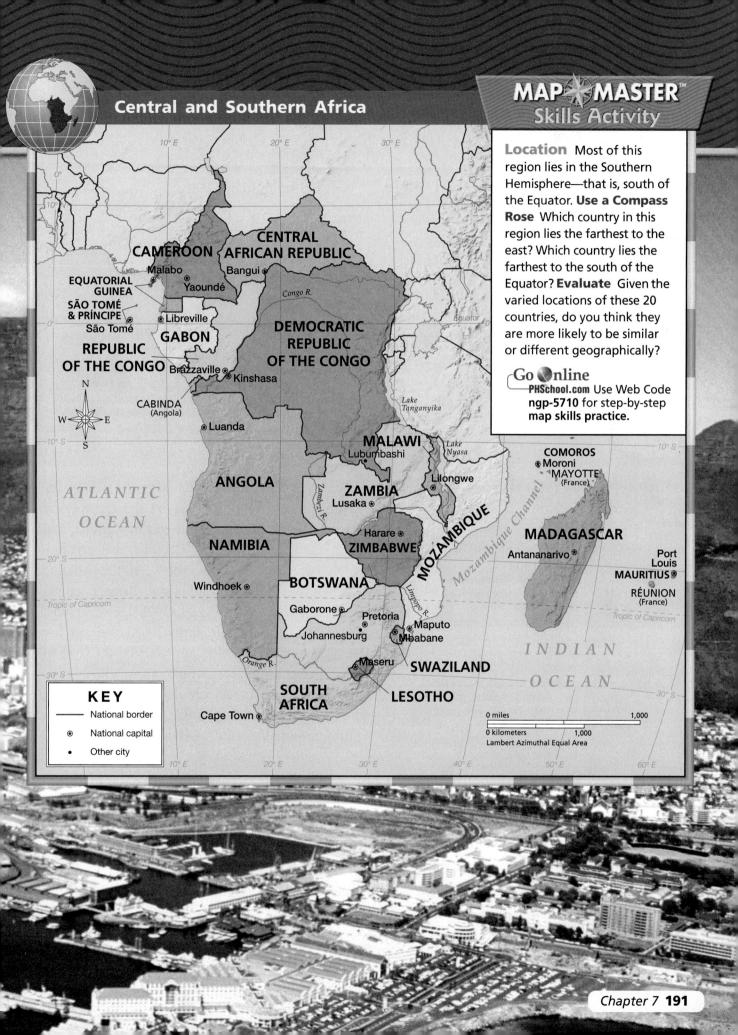

Central and Southern Africa

Location Most of this region lies in the Southern Hemisphere—that is, south of the Equator. **Use a Compass Rose** Which country in this region lies the farthest to the east? Which country lies the farthest to the south of the Equator? **Evaluate** Given the varied locations of these 20 countries, do you think they are more likely to be similar or different geographically?

Go Online
PHSchool.com Use Web Code **ngp-5710** for step-by-step map skills practice.

10° E · 20° E · 30° E

0°

10° S

20° S

CAMEROON
Malabo
EQUATORIAL GUINEA
Yaoundé
SÃO TOMÉ & PRÍNCIPE
São Tomé
Libreville
GABON
REPUBLIC OF THE CONGO
Brazzaville
Kinshasa
CABINDA (Angola)
Luanda

CENTRAL AFRICAN REPUBLIC
Bangui
Congo R.

DEMOCRATIC REPUBLIC OF THE CONGO

Equator

Lake Tanganyika

MALAWI
Lubumbashi
Lake Nyasa
Lilongwe

ANGOLA

ZAMBIA
Lusaka
Zambezi R.

Harare
ZIMBABWE

MOZAMBIQUE
Mozambique Channel

COMOROS
Moroni
MAYOTTE (France)

MADAGASCAR
Antananarivo

Port Louis
MAURITIUS
RÉUNION (France)

N
W E
S

ATLANTIC OCEAN

NAMIBIA
Windhoek

BOTSWANA
Gaborone
Pretoria
Johannesburg
Maputo
Mbabane
Maseru
SWAZILAND
LESOTHO

Tropic of Capricorn

Limpopo R.

Orange R.

SOUTH AFRICA
Cape Town

INDIAN OCEAN

Tropic of Capricorn

10° S
20° S
30° S

KEY
— National border
⊕ National capital
• Other city

0 miles · 1,000
0 kilometers · 1,000
Lambert Azimuthal Equal Area

10° E · 20° E · 30° E · 40° E · 50° E · 60° E

Introducing Central and Southern Africa

Guide for Reading

This section provides an introduction to the 20 countries that make up the region of Central and Southern Africa.

- Look at the map on the previous page and then read the paragraphs below to learn about each nation.
- Analyze the data to compare the countries.
- What are the characteristics that most of the countries share?
- What are some key differences among the countries?

Viewing the Video Overview

View the World Studies Video Overview to learn more about each of the countries. As you watch, answer these questions:

- What are some common features of the region?
- What obstacles do children in the Democratic Republic of the Congo face to get an education?

DISCOVERY CHANNEL SCHOOL Video
Explore the geography of Central and Southern Africa.

Angola

Capital	Luanda
Land Area	481,551 sq mi; 1,246,700 sq km
Population	10.6 million
Ethnic Group(s)	Ovimbundu, Kimbundu, Bankongo, mixed white and black, white
Religion(s)	traditional beliefs, Roman Catholic, Protestant
Government	republic
Currency	kwanza
Leading Exports	crude oil, diamonds, refined petroleum products, gas, coffee, sisal, fish and fish products, timber, cotton
Language(s)	Portuguese (official), Umbundu, Kimbundu, Kikongo

Angola (ang GOH luh) is bordered on the west by the Atlantic Ocean, on the north by the Democratic Republic of the Congo, on the east by Zambia, and on the south by Namibia. Cabinda is a separate region of Angola that lies between the Atlantic Ocean and the Congo republics. Angola gained independence from Portugal in 1975. However, civil war gripped the country until 2002. The war left many thousands homeless and claimed the lives of an estimated 1.5 million people. Although Angola's economy has been severely damaged by the war, economic recovery is possible. Angola is rich in natural resources, including oil and diamonds.

Thatched-roof houses in Angola

Botswana

Capital	Gaborone
Land Area	226,011 sq mi; 585,370 sq km
Population	1.6 million
Ethnic Group(s)	Tswana, Kalanga, Basarwa, Kgalagadi, white
Religion(s)	traditional beliefs, Christian
Government	parliamentary republic
Currency	pula
Leading Exports	diamonds, copper, nickel, soda ash, meat, textiles
Language(s)	English (official), Tswana, Shona, San, Khoikhoi, Ndebele

Botswana (baht SWAH nuh) is bordered on the west and north by Namibia, on the north and east by Zambia and Zimbabwe, and on the east and south by South Africa. When it was a British colony, Botswana was known as Bechuanaland (bech WAH nah land). After gaining independence in 1966, Botswana's government transformed the economy into one of the fastest-growing in the world. Diamond mining is Botswana's largest industry. AIDS poses a severe health threat to the country. Hundreds of thousands of people have the disease.

Cameroon

Capital	Yaoundé
Land Area	181,251 sq mi; 469,440 sq km
Population	16.1 million
Ethnic Group(s)	Cameroon Highlanders, Bantu, Kirdi, Fulani, Eastern Nigritic
Religion(s)	traditional beliefs, Christian, Muslim
Government	unitary republic
Currency	CFA franc
Leading Exports	crude oil and petroleum products, lumber, cacao beans, aluminum, coffee, cotton
Language(s)	French (official), English (official), Bamileke, Fang, Fulani

Cameroon (kam uh ROON) is bordered on the west by the Atlantic Ocean and Nigeria, on the north by Chad, on the east by the Central African Republic, and on the south by the Republic of the Congo, Gabon, and Equatorial Guinea. It has many forests and rivers and good farmland. Present-day Cameroon was formed in 1961 by merging French Cameroon and a part of British Cameroon. The government has spent the last several decades improving farming conditions and building roads and railways. In terms of oil and agricultural resources, Cameroon is one of Africa's richest countries.

Central African Republic

Capital	Bangui
Land Area	240,534 sq mi; 622,984 sq km
Population	3.6 million
Ethnic Group(s)	Baya, Banda, Mandjia, Sara, Mbouri, M'Baka, Yakoma
Religion(s)	traditional beliefs, Protestant, Roman Catholic, Muslim
Government	republic
Currency	CFA franc
Leading Exports	diamonds, timber, cotton, coffee, tobacco
Language(s)	French (official), Sango, Banda, Gbaya

The Central African Republic (SEN trul AF rih kun rih PUB lik) is bordered on the west by Cameroon, on the north by Chad, on the north and east by Sudan, and on the south by the Democratic Republic of the Congo and the Republic of the Congo. It sits on a low plateau at the southern edge of the Sahel. Once a French colony called Ubangi-Shari (yoo BANG gee SHAH ree), the Central African Republic gained independence in 1960. Since 1993, the government has faced several rebellions. Despite the country's history of instability, the elections of 2005 raised hopes for a more stable future.

Introducing Central and Southern Africa

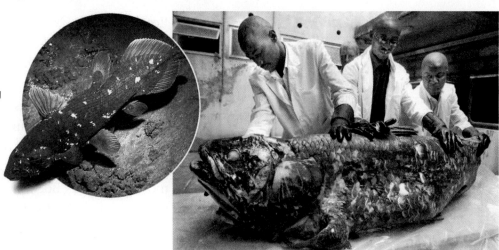

A live coelacanth (left); African scientists studying a dead coelacanth (right)

Comoros

Capital	Moroni
Land Area	838 sq mi; 2,170 sq km
Population	614,382
Ethnic Group(s)	Antalote, Cafre, Makoa, Oimatsaha, Sakalava
Religion(s)	Muslim, Roman Catholic
Government	independent republic
Currency	Comoros franc
Leading Exports	vanilla, ylang-ylang, cloves, perfume oil, copra
Language(s)	Arabic (official), French (official), Comoran (official)

Comoros (KAH muh rohz) is made up of three islands in the Indian Ocean, off the east coast of Mozambique. Numerous species of birds, animals, and fish live on and around the islands. The most famous of these is the coelacanth (SEE luh kanth), an extremely rare fish. Since gaining its independence from France in 1975, Comoros has experienced several major rebellions and civil wars. It is an extremely poor country. The population is growing rapidly, but the country has few natural resources or economic opportunities. Most of the people of Comoros are subsistence farmers.

Congo, Democratic Republic of the

Capital	Kinshasa
Land Area	875,520 sq mi; 2,267,600 sq km
Population	55.2 million
Ethnic Group(s)	more than 200 distinct ethnic groups, including Bantu, Hamitic
Religion(s)	Roman Catholic, Protestant, Muslim, traditional beliefs
Government	dictatorship
Currency	Congolese franc
Leading Exports	diamonds, copper, coffee, cobalt, crude oil
Language(s)	French (official), Kiswahili, Tshiluba, Kikongo, Lingala

The Democratic Republic of the Congo (dem uh KRAT ik rih PUB lik uv thuh KAHNG goh) lies on the Equator. It is bordered on the west by the Republic of the Congo; on the north by the Central African Republic and Sudan; on the east by Uganda, Rwanda, Burundi, and Tanzania; and on the south by Zambia. The rain forests of the Congo River basin cover much of the country. The country has suffered through years of civil war, which led to the deaths of about 3.5 million people. The nation has the potential for a strong economy, with many mineral resources, farmable land, and good soil.

Congo, Republic of the

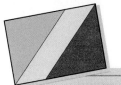

Capital	Brazzaville
Land Area	131,853 sq mi; 341,500 sq km
Population	3.3 million
Ethnic Group(s)	Kongo, Sangha, M'Bochi, Take
Religion(s)	Christian, traditional beliefs, Muslim
Government	republic
Currency	CFA franc
Leading Exports	petroleum, lumber, plywood, sugar, cocoa, coffee, diamonds
Language(s)	French (official), Kongo, Teke, Lingala

The Republic of the Congo (rih PUB lik uv thuh KAHNG goh) lies on the Equator. It is bordered on the west by Gabon, on the north by Cameroon and the Central African Republic, on the east and south by the Democratic Republic of the Congo, and on the south by Angola. The Congo River forms the border with the Democratic Republic of the Congo. The Republic of the Congo gained independence from France in 1960. Since then, it has faced years of civil war. The nation has large supplies of oil and timber, and sales of oil have brought the country some wealth.

Equatorial Guinea

Capital	Malabo
Land Area	10,830 sq mi; 28,051 sq km
Population	498,144
Ethnic Group(s)	Bioko, Rio Muni
Religion(s)	Christian, traditional beliefs
Government	republic
Currency	CFA franc
Leading Exports	petroleum, timber, cocoa
Language(s)	Spanish (official), French (official), Fang, Bubi

Equatorial Guinea (ee kwuh TAWR ee ul GIH nee) lies just north of the Equator. It consists of five islands and a mainland area. The mainland is bordered on the west by the Atlantic Ocean, on the north by Cameroon, and on the east and south by Gabon. Many species of animals live on the mainland, including gorillas, leopards, antelopes, crocodiles, and snakes. After almost two hundred years as a Spanish colony, Equatorial Guinea gained independence in 1968. The economy is strong due to recently discovered oil reserves. Forestry, farming, and fishing are also important industries.

Gabon

Capital	Libreville
Land Area	99,489 sq mi; 257,667 sq km
Population	1.2 million
Ethnic Group(s)	Bantu, Fang, Bapounou, Nzebi, Obamba
Religion(s)	Christian, traditional beliefs, Muslim
Government	republic
Currency	CFA franc
Leading Exports	crude oil, timber, manganese, uranium
Language(s)	French (official), Fang, Punu, Sira, Nzebi, Mpongwe

Gabon (gah BOHN) is bordered on the west by the Atlantic Ocean, on the north by Equatorial Guinea and Cameroon, and on the east and south by the Republic of the Congo. The country gained its independence from France in 1960, and it became a democracy in 1990. Oil resources have made Gabon's economy very strong in comparison to the economies of other African countries. People live on only a small portion of Gabon's land. More than three quarters of the country is covered by rain forests that are inhabited by many kinds of animals and plants.

Introducing Central and Southern Africa

Lesotho

Capital	Maseru
Land Area	11,720 sq mi; 30,355 sq km
Population	2.2 million
Ethnic Group(s)	Sotho, white, Asian
Religion(s)	Christian, traditional beliefs
Government	parliamentary constitutional monarchy
Currency	loti
Leading Exports	manufactured goods, wool, mohair, food, live animals
Language(s)	English (off.), Sesotho (off.), Zulu

Lesotho (leh SOO too) is a tiny, mountainous country surrounded on all sides by South Africa. In 1966, the country became independent as a monarchy, or a government led by a king or a queen. Since that time, its government has been unstable. The country has been ruled by a king, by military leaders, and by elected leaders. Lesotho's economy depends heavily on South Africa. Many of Lesotho's men find work in the mines of South Africa. Despite widespread poverty, a large percentage of people in Lesotho are literate.

Madagascar

Capital	Antananarivo
Land Area	224,533 sq mi; 581,540 sq km
Population	16.5 million
Ethnic Group(s)	Malayo-Indonesian, Cotier, white, South Asian, Creole, Comoran
Religion(s)	traditional beliefs, Christian, Muslim
Government	republic
Currency	Malagasy franc
Leading Exports	coffee, vanilla, shellfish, sugar, cotton cloth, chromite
Language(s)	French (off.), Malagasy (off.)

Madagascar (mad uh GAS kur) is the world's fourth-largest island. It lies in the Indian Ocean, east of Mozambique. Before the French colonized Madagascar in 1886, it was an independent kingdom. The nation regained its independence in 1960 and became a democracy in the early 1990s. The nation's economy is based mainly on farming, fishing, and forestry. Madagascar is famous for plants and animals that cannot be found anywhere else on Earth. It is also well known for its spices, including vanilla. A larger percentage of people in Madagascar are literate than in most other African countries.

Malawi

Capital	Lilongwe
Land Area	36,324 sq mi; 94,080 sq km
Population	10.7 million
Ethnic Group(s)	Chewa, Nyanja, Tumbuka, Yao, Lomwe, Sena, Tonga, Ngongi, Ngonde, Asian, white
Religion(s)	Protestant, Roman Catholic, Muslim, traditional beliefs
Government	multiparty democracy
Currency	Malawi kwacha
Leading Exports	tobacco, tea, sugar, cotton, coffee, peanuts, wood products, apparel
Language(s)	English (official), Chichewa (official), Lomwe, Yao, Ngoni

Malawi (MAH lah wee) is bordered on the west, east, and south by Mozambique, on the west by Zambia, and on the north by Tanzania. The dominant geographical feature of this tiny country is Lake Nyasa (NYAH sah), Africa's third-largest body of water. In addition, Malawi lies alongside the Great Rift Valley. Malawi was called Nyasaland while under British rule. It became an independent nation in 1964. Malawi then became a democracy in the mid-1990s. The country's economy is mostly agricultural. Almost 90 percent of Malawians live in rural areas.

Mauritius

Capital	Port Louis
Land Area	784 sq mi; 2,030 sq km
Population	1.2 million
Ethnic Group(s)	Indo-Mauritian, Creole, Sino-Mauritian, Franco-Mauritian
Religion(s)	Hindu, Roman Catholic, Muslim, Protestant
Government	parliamentary democracy
Currency	Mauritian rupee
Leading Exports	iron ore, fish, fish products, gold
Language(s)	English (official), French Creole, Hindi, Urdu, Tamil, Chinese, French

Mauritius (maw RISH ee us) is made up of islands in the Indian Ocean east of Madagascar. The islands were colonized by Portugal in the 1500s. The country was claimed by the Dutch, the French, and the British before it gained independence in 1968. Since that time, it has turned a weak economy based on agriculture into a healthy economy based on manufacturing, banking, and tourism. Mauritius has a stable, democratic government. A majority of the people of Mauritius are descended from Indians who moved to the islands to work on sugar plantations in the 1800s.

Mozambique

Capital	Maputo
Land Area	302,737 sq mi; 784,090 sq km
Population	19.6 million
Ethnic Group(s)	Shangaan, Chokwe, Manyika, Sena, Makha, white, mixed white and black, South Asian
Religion(s)	traditional beliefs, Christian, Muslim
Government	republic
Currency	metical
Leading Exports	prawns, cashews, cotton, sugar, citrus, timber, electricity
Language(s)	Portuguese (official), Makua, Tsonga, Sena, Lomwe

Mozambique (moh zum BEEK) is bordered on the west by South Africa, Zimbabwe, Zambia, and Malawi; on the north by Tanzania; and on the east and south by the Indian Ocean. The Zambezi River divides the country into dry savanna in the south and fertile lands in the north. When it gained independence from Portugal in 1975, Mozambique was one of the world's poorest countries. It suffered through civil war from 1977 to 1992. Heavy flooding in 1999 and 2000 made the poor economy even worse. The people of Mozambique are relying on economic aid from other countries and new policies to improve their situation.

Namibia

Capital	Windhoek
Land Area	318,694 sq mi; 825,418 sq km
Population	1.8 million
Ethnic Group(s)	Ovambo, Kavango, Herero, Damara, Nama, Caprivian, Bushman, Baster, Tswana
Religion(s)	Christian, traditional beliefs
Government	republic
Currency	Namibian dollar
Leading Exports	diamonds, copper, gold, zinc, lead, uranium, cattle, fish
Language(s)	English (official), Ovambo, Kavango, Bergdama, German, Afrikaans

Namibia (nuh MIB ee uh) is bordered on the west by the Atlantic Ocean, on the north by Angola and Zambia, on the east by Botswana, and on the south by South Africa. Its land includes both the Namib and Kalahari deserts. Its economy is dependent on mining. Once a German colony, Namibia fell under South African rule after World War I. It became an independent country in 1990. Namibia still suffers from the effects of the system of racial inequality that South Africa imposed on it for decades. Its government and people are working to overcome these effects.

Introducing Central and Southern Africa

São Tomé and Príncipe

Capital	São Tomé
Land Area	386 sq mi; 1,001 sq km
Population	170,372
Ethnic Group(s)	mixed white and black, angolares, forros, servicais, tongas, white
Religion(s)	Christian
Government	republic
Currency	dobra
Leading Exports	cocoa, copra, coffee, palm oil
Language(s)	Portuguese (official), Portuguese Creole

São Tomé and Príncipe (sow toh MEE and PRIN suh pea) is made up of islands in the Gulf of Guinea, west of Gabon. The Portuguese discovered the uninhabited islands in the 1400s. They immediately built plantations and imported slaves to grow the islands' major resource, sugar cane. The islands began exporting coffee and cocoa in the 1800s. The nation gained independence in 1975. The first free elections were held in 1991. Although a poor country, São Tomé and Príncipe has very fertile land and is working to diversify its crops. It is also hoping to make use of oil reserves located in the Gulf of Guinea.

South Africa

Capital	Pretoria, Cape Town, Bloemfontein
Land Area	471,008 sq mi; 1,219,912 sq km
Population	43.6 million
Ethnic Group(s)	black, white, mixed white and black, South Asian
Religion(s)	Christian, traditional beliefs
Government	republic
Currency	rand
Leading Exports	gold, diamonds, platinum, other metals and minerals, machinery and equipment
Language(s)	Afrikaans, English, Ndebele, Pedi, Sotho, Swazi, Tsonga, Tswana, Venda, Xhosa, Zulu (all official)

South Africa (sowth AF rih kuh) occupies the southern tip of the African continent. With a wealth of natural resources, including gold and diamonds, it has the continent's strongest economy. Ruled by the Dutch after 1652 and by the British after 1806, South Africa became independent in 1931. From that time until 1990, the country was known for apartheid, a harsh political system under which the races were separated from each other and discrimination against nonwhites was the law. After years of struggle, nonwhites won equality in 1994, when apartheid ended. The country then focused on healing the wounds of the past.

Swaziland

Capital	Mbabane
Land Area	6,642 sq mi; 17,203 sq km
Population	1.1 million
Ethnic Group(s)	black, white
Religion(s)	Christian, traditional beliefs, Muslim, Jewish
Government	monarchy
Currency	lilangeni
Leading Exports	soft drink concentrates, sugar, wood pulp, cotton yarn, fruit
Language(s)	English (official), siSwati (official), Zulu, Tsonga

Swaziland (SWAH zee land) is a small country that is surrounded by South Africa and Mozambique. More than 95 percent of the population belongs to the Swazi ethnic group. Swaziland gained independence from Great Britain in 1968. The country has a very diversified economy. Because it is landlocked, Swaziland depends mainly on South Africa to move goods in and out of the country. Swaziland is ruled by a king. However, many Swazis have been pressuring the government for democratic reforms, such as having a multiparty political system.

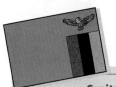

Zambia

Capital	Lusaka
Land Area	285,994 sq mi; 740,724 sq km
Population	10.1 million
Ethnic Group(s)	Bemba, Nyanja, Tonga, Lozi, European, white
Religion(s)	Christian, Muslim, Hindu, traditional beliefs
Government	republic
Currency	Zambian kwacha
Leading Exports	copper, cobalt, electricity, tobacco, flowers, cotton
Language(s)	English (official), Bemba, Nyanja, Tonga, Lunda, Lozi

Zambia (ZAM bee uh) is bordered on the west by Angola, on the north by the Democratic Republic of the Congo and Tanzania, on the east by Malawi and Mozambique, and on the south by Zimbabwe, Botswana, and Namibia. Once a British colony called Northern Rhodesia, Zambia became independent in 1964. For decades, Zambia was under the rule of a single political party. In recent years, it has succeeded in establishing a multiparty democracy. Copper exports have made Zambia prosperous. However, Zambia risks losses if copper prices fall.

Zimbabwe

Capital	Harare
Land Area	149,293 sq mi; 386,670 sq km
Population	11.3 million
Ethnic Group(s)	Shona, Ndebele, Asian, white
Religion(s)	Christian, traditional beliefs, Muslim
Government	parliamentary democracy
Currency	Zimbabwe dollar
Leading Exports	tobacco, gold, ferroalloys, textiles, clothing
Language(s)	English (official), Shona, Ndebele

Zimbabwe (zim BAHB way) is bordered on the west by Botswana and Zambia, on the north by Zambia, on the north and east by Mozambique, and on the south by South Africa. Once the British colony of Southern Rhodesia, Zimbabwe gained independence in 1980. Since then, the country has worked to overcome racial inequality and a troubled economy. Zimbabwe faced additional difficulties under the rule of President Robert Mugabe. These included unfair elections, as well as the destruction of the homes and businesses of about 700,000 people.

SOURCES: DK World Desk Reference Online; CIA World Factbook Online; *The World Almanac*, 2003

Assessment

Comprehension and Critical Thinking

1. Compare and Contrast Compare and contrast the economies of these countries.

2. Summarize What are some characteristics that most of the countries share?

3. Analyze Information What are some key differences among the countries?

4. Infer What can you infer about a country such as South Africa that has eleven official languages?

5. Predict How do you think life in the countries that have no borders on the ocean is different from life in the ones that do?

6. Make a Bar Graph Create a bar graph showing each language that is an official language in this region and how many countries speak that language.

Keeping Current

Access the **DK World Desk Reference Online** at **PHSchool.com** for up-to-date information about all 20 countries in this chapter.

Go Online
PHSchool.com

Web Code: **nge-5700**

Section 1

Democratic Republic of the Congo A Wealth of Possibilities

Prepare to Read

Objectives

In this section you will

1. Discover the physical geography and important natural resources of the Democratic Republic of the Congo.
2. Learn about the country's economic and political challenges since independence.
3. Find out how different groups and leaders have reshaped the nation.

Taking Notes

Copy the outline below. As you read this section, look for details about the geography, natural resources, economics, and politics of the Democratic Republic of the Congo. Use the outline to record your findings.

> I. Physical geography and resources
>   A. Geographic regions
>   1. _____
>   2. _____
>   B. Natural resources

Target Reading Skill

Understand Sequence A sequence is the order in which a series of events occurs. Noting the sequence of important events can help you understand and remember the events. You can track a sequence of events by simply listing the events in the order in which they happened. As you read this section, list the sequence of events in Congo's political history.

Key Terms

- **authoritarian government** (uh thawr uh TEHR ee un GUV urn munt) *n.* a nondemocratic form of government in which a single leader or a small group of leaders has all the power
- **nationalize** (NASH uh nuh lyz) *v.* to transfer ownership of something to a nation's government

An open-pit copper mine in Congo

Copper has been mined in the present-day Democratic Republic of the Congo since ancient times. In the early 1900s, demand for copper brought Europeans to the area. In 1930, a mining company found copper in an area called Kolwezi (kohl WAY zee). The company built a mine and hired miners and a host of other workers. Soon a small city of workers' houses arose. Meanwhile, miners started to dig down into the earth for the copper. They found it, too—right beneath their houses.

The Kolwezi area proved so rich in copper that, at first, miners found they barely had to scratch the surface to find the mineral. As time went on, however, the miners had to dig deeper. Soon they had dug a huge pit in the ground. They built terraces along the sloping walls of the pit. Then they mined each terrace, in a process called open-pit mining. Miners still dig for copper at the Kolwezi mine today.

Physical Geography and Resources

Since the 1930s, the Democratic Republic of the Congo has become one of the world's main sources of copper. Congo, as the country is often referred to, also has many other natural resources. These include gold, diamonds, forests, water, and wildlife. Congo's minerals and other resources have played an important role in the nation's history. (The country's neighbor, the Republic of the Congo, is also referred to as Congo. In this section, all references to Congo are to the Democratic Republic of the Congo.)

Geographic Regions

The Democratic Republic of the Congo is Africa's third-largest country. It is equal in size to the area of the United States east of the Mississippi River. The country has four major geographic regions: the Congo basin, the northern uplands, the eastern highlands, and the southern uplands.

The Congo basin is covered by dense rain forest. Most Congolese (kahng guh LEEZ) live in the other three regions. The northern uplands, which run along the country's northern border, are covered in savanna. Grasslands and occasional thick forests spread across the eastern highlands. The southern uplands are high plains of grasslands and wooded areas. In each of these three regions, many people make a living as subsistence farmers.

Natural Resources

About two thirds of Congo's people are farmers. However, mining produces most of the country's wealth. The Kolwezi and other huge copper deposits exist in the southern province of Katanga (kuh TAHNG guh). Congo is one of the top producers of diamonds in the world. It also has reserves of other valuable minerals such as gold. In addition, Congo has the potential to develop many hydroelectric plants. These are plants that use swiftly flowing river water to generate electricity.

Links to Science

From Water to Electricity
At a hydroelectric plant, electricity is generated by flowing water. For that reason, these plants are usually built at the bottom of a dam. Water that collects behind the dam flows through turbines, which change the energy of the moving water into electricity. The water is not used up in the process—it continues to flow and can be used again for agriculture and other purposes. A large hydroelectric dam (below) sits on Inga Falls, along the Congo River.

Natural Resources in Congo's History Natural resources have dominated much of the history of the Democratic Republic of the Congo. For example, by the 1400s, the kingdoms of Kongo, Luba, and Lunda ruled much of the area. These kingdoms became powerful largely because they had fertile soil and plentiful rain and their people made iron tools that enabled them to farm more productively. Similarly, when the Portuguese arrived in the area in the 1480s, they came in search of a natural resource—gold.

Some 400 years later, during the scramble for Africa, King Leopold II of Belgium took control of present-day Congo. He ruled brutally, forcing Africans to harvest wild rubber without paying them. Belgium grew wealthy while Africans suffered, starved, and died, probably by the millions. Later, because of an international campaign to end Leopold's abuses, the Belgian government ruled less harshly. But it maintained its interest in Congo's resources, especially its copper and diamonds.

✓ **Reading Check** **Which industry produces most of Congo's wealth?**

Economic and Political Challenges

In spite of its abundant natural resources, the Democratic Republic of the Congo has faced major economic and political challenges. During the 1900s, both the economy and the government of Congo faced a series of crises.

Congo Gains Independence As you have read, calls for independence echoed throughout the African continent during the mid-1900s. In 1960, the Democratic Republic of the Congo won its independence from Belgium. However, Congo's first years as an independent country proved to be difficult.

Belgium had done little to prepare Congo for self-rule. In addition, various groups fought one another for power. The foreign companies that controlled Congo's mines feared the unrest would hurt business. In 1965, these foreign companies helped a military leader, Joseph Mobutu (muh BOO too), take power. With a strong ruler in control, they thought their businesses would thrive.

Celebrating Independence
At a celebration of the country's independence in 1960, boys carry the flag of the newly formed Democratic Republic of the Congo. **Predict** *How do you think Congolese people felt when their country gained independence?*

Mobutu Makes Changes Mobutu tried to restore order in the country by setting up an **authoritarian government**—a nondemocratic form of government in which a single leader or small group of leaders has all the power. He also tried to cut ties with the colonial past. First, he renamed the country Zaire (zah IHR), a word that has traditional African roots. And he took on a new name for himself, Mobutu Sese Seko (muh BOO too SAY say SAY koh), which he considered more traditionally African. Then he nationalized foreign-owned industries. To **nationalize** is to transfer ownership to the government.

Target Skill
Understand Sequence
What important events led up to Mobutu's establishing an authoritarian government?

COUNTRY PROFILE   Focus on Economics

Democratic Republic of the Congo

Congo's natural resources play a key role in its economy. The country's total earnings from exports in 2002 were around $1.2 billion. Minerals alone made up about 85 percent of those earnings, as they have in most recent years. Most of the economy's diversity comes from the variety of minerals produced. However, Congo does not use all of its natural resources. Thus, the country has potential for greater economic success. Study the map and charts to learn more about Congo's natural resources and economy.

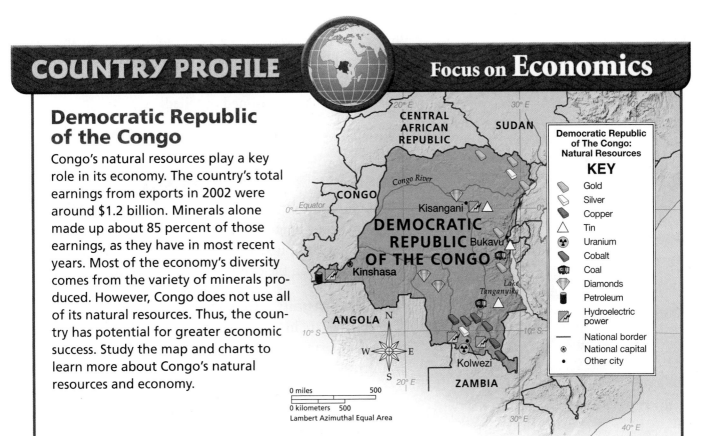

Democratic Republic of The Congo: Natural Resources

KEY

- Gold
- Silver
- Copper
- Tin
- Uranium
- Cobalt
- Coal
- Diamonds
- Petroleum
- Hydroelectric power
- — National border
- ⊛ National capital
- • Other city

0 miles 500
0 kilometers 500
Lambert Azimuthal Equal Area

Export Destinations

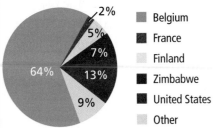

- Belgium 64%
- France
- Finland
- Zimbabwe
- United States
- Other

2%
5%
7%
13%
9%

SOURCE: DK World Desk Reference

Estimated Income From Mining, 2001

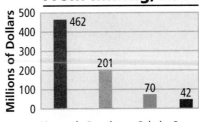

Millions of Dollars

Diamonds	Petroleum	Cobalt	Copper
462	201	70	42

SOURCE: The Economist Intelligence Unit's *Country Profile 2003*

Map and Chart Skills

1. **Name** Which two countries buy most of Congo's exports?
2. **Identify** Which mineral earns the most income for Congo?
3. **Infer** How does the map support the idea that Congo has greater potential for using its natural resources?

Go Online PHSchool.com

Use Web Code **nge-5701** for **DK World Desk Reference Online.**

Find out about education in Congo.

Mobutu also borrowed money from foreign countries, such as the United States, for projects to improve Zaire's economy. But most of Mobutu's economic moves failed. Many government officials who ran the nationalized companies proved to be poor managers. Others stole their companies' profits. Mobutu and his supporters, too, kept much of Zaire's wealth for themselves.

Crisis In the mid-1970s, the world price of copper fell sharply. Suddenly Zaire was earning less and less from its major export. It could not pay back the money it had borrowed, and the economy quickly collapsed. Mobutu responded by cutting the amount of money spent by the government. The cutbacks caused hardship, especially for Zaire's poorest people. Fewer jobs were available, so many people could not earn a living. When political groups challenged Mobutu's policies, Mobutu crushed their efforts. He had many of his opponents imprisoned or killed.

✓ **Reading Check** Why did Mobutu change the country's name?

Reshaping the Nation

Throughout the 1980s, Mobutu ruled harshly, and Zaire's economy continually declined. Calls for reform came from inside and outside the country. In the early 1990s, Mobutu's grip on the country finally began to weaken.

Rebellion Against Government In 1996, a minor uprising began in eastern Zaire. A small ethnic group fought with the government's troops. The neighboring countries of Uganda, Rwanda, and Burundi supported the small group. With their help, the uprising turned into a rebellion against Mobutu's government. Zaire's army was unable to put down the rebellion.

Within months, the rebels gained control of much of eastern Zaire. By May 1997, the rebel army began closing in on the capital, Kinshasa. Alarmed, Mobutu fled to Morocco. He died there four months later. A leader of the rebel army, Laurent Kabila (law RAHN kuh BEEL uh), became the new president.

A New Government Takes Hold The rebel army soon controlled the whole country, which Kabila renamed the Democratic Republic of the Congo. Kabila vowed to establish a new constitution and hold national elections. But months went by without the promised reforms. Criticism quickly erupted. By early 1998, popular support for the new government was fading.

Showing Culture in Currency
The upper bill was printed while the name of the country was Zaire. The lower bill was printed after the name became the Democratic Republic of the Congo. **Analyze Images** *What aspects of the Congo are represented by the images on these bills?*

A Second Rebellion In August 1998, another armed rebellion began, this time against Kabila's government. Supported by Uganda and Rwanda, the new rebels threatened to overthrow the government. Angola, Namibia, and Zimbabwe backed Kabila's government. The civil war continued month after month.

Peace and Reform The war in Congo was the first war in post-independence Africa to involve several African nations. In July 1999, the heads of six of these countries met in Zambia to write a peace agreement. However, neither side fulfilled the agreement. Hostilities continued into 2001, when Kabila was killed. His son, Joseph Kabila, became president.

Rwandan President Paul Kagame (left) and Joseph Kabila sign peace agreements in 2002.

The younger Kabila began making significant reforms. He implemented programs to revive the economy. He replaced many corrupt government officials with well-trained officials. He also allowed the United Nations to send peacekeeping troops to Congo. By the end of 2002, many of the disagreements over the terms of peace had been settled. However, small conflicts did continue in the eastern part of the country. Congo has found that the path to peace is neither smooth nor easy.

 Reading Check How was Congo's civil war unique for Africa?

Section 1 Assessment

Key Terms
Review the key terms at the beginning of this section. Use each term in a sentence that explains its meaning.

Target Reading Skill
Place these events in the correct order: Joseph Kabila becomes president, a rebellion begins, a peace agreement is written.

Comprehension and Critical Thinking
1. (a) List What are some of Congo's natural resources?

(b) Analyze Information What role have these resources played in Congo's history?

2. (a) Describe What changes did Joseph Mobutu make in Congo?

(b) Evaluate What factors prevented Mobutu from bringing stability to Congo?

3. (a) Recall What caused Mobutu to flee the country?

(b) Summarize Once Laurent Kabila became president, how did the civil war in Congo change?

(c) Draw Conclusions In what ways has Joseph Kabila brought positive change to Congo?

Writing Activity
Suppose you are an editor for a newspaper. Write an editorial explaining the challenges Congo has faced and predicting how the country will overcome those challenges once peace returns to the nation.

Writing Tip Be sure to state the opinion you are explaining in your editorial. Then use details to support your opinion.

You have probably played the "telephone game." One person makes up a statement and whispers it to the next person. That person whispers it to the next person, and so on. As the statement is passed along, people do not always hear it correctly and it gets confused. By the end, it might not make any sense.

If a sentence can get distorted in a matter of minutes, think what can happen to a sentence uttered by someone hundreds of years ago! That is one reason why primary sources are important.

Examples of primary sources

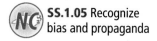
SS.1.05 Recognize bias and propaganda

A primary source is information that comes directly from the person who wrote it, said it, or created it. Diaries, photographs, speeches, and recordings are all examples of primary sources. When information does not come directly from the person who created it, it is a secondary source. Newspapers, history books, and Web sites are examples of secondary sources.

Learn the Skill

Use the steps below to analyze a primary source.

1 **Identify who created the information, when it was created, and why.** Before you use any information, determine the source. Is it a primary source?

2 **Identify the main idea.** Make sure you understand what is being communicated, either in words or in visual form.

3 **Separate facts from opinions.** Facts can be proved or disproved. Opinions indicate personal feelings or judgments. A primary source might contain facts and opinions, and both can be valuable.

4 **Look for evidence of bias, or a one-sided view.** If a person's view is biased, it is influenced by certain factors, such as the person's family, culture, or location.

5 **Evaluate whether the source is reliable and whether it suits your purpose.** For factual evidence, you want a primary source that is believable and accurate. For an opinion, you want one that uses good reasoning.

Practice the Skill

Use the steps below to analyze the source in the box.

1 Read the background information and the quotation. Who is the speaker, and when did he speak these words? Is the quotation a primary source?

2 Write a sentence that summarizes Mandela's main point. What situation is he discussing?

3 Using the background information, identify as many facts and opinions as possible. Overall, is this quotation mostly fact or mostly opinion?

4 Do any parts of Mandela's statement show bias?

5 Would this source be of value if you were writing a history of South Africa? A biography of Nelson Mandela? Explain.

In 1994, democratic elections were held in South Africa for the first time. Never before had all South Africans been allowed to vote. After casting his vote, the man who would be elected president, Nelson Mandela, made this statement:

"This is for all South Africans an unforgettable occasion. It is the realization of hopes and dreams that we have cherished over decades. . . . We are starting a new era of hope, reconciliation [coming together] and nation building. We sincerely hope that by the mere casting of a vote the results will give hope to all South Africans and make all South Africans realize this is our country. We are one nation."

—*Nelson Mandela, April 1994*

Two women in Johannesburg, South Africa, proudly display the identification papers needed for voting in the historic 1994 election.

Apply the Skill

Read the quotation from the South African constitution on page 208.
Follow the steps for analyzing a primary source and answer these questions:
1. What makes the quotation a primary source?
2. What is the main idea?
3. Is the information mostly fact or mostly opinion? Explain.
4. Is the information biased? Explain.
5. For what purpose might you use this source?

South Africa
Struggle for Equality

Prepare to Read

Objectives
In this section you will
1. Understand how white rule in South Africa began.
2. Learn about the system of apartheid.
3. Find out how South Africans built a new nation after apartheid.

Taking Notes
As you read this section, look for details about South Africa before, during, and after apartheid. Copy the chart below, and use to it to record your findings.

South Africa		
Before Apartheid	During Apartheid	After Apartheid
• •	• •	• •

Target Reading Skill

Recognize Words That Signal Sequence Signal words point out relationships among ideas or events. To help keep the order of events clear as you read, look for words like *after, then,* and *in 1994* that signal the order in which events took place.

Key Terms
- **apartheid** (uh PAHR tayt) *n.* the legal system of South Africa in which the rights of nonwhites were greatly restricted
- **discriminate** (dih SKRIM ih nayt) *v.* to treat people differently, and often unfairly, based on race, religion, or sex
- **Nelson Mandela** (NEL sun man DEL uh) *n.* black leader of the African National Congress and South Africa's first president after apartheid ended

A choir celebrates the new constitution.

“ We, the people of South Africa,
Recognize the injustices of our past;
Honour those who suffered for justice and freedom in our land;
Respect those who have worked to build and develop our country; and
Believe that South Africa belongs to all who live in it, united in our diversity. ”

—*Preamble to the South African Constitution*

So begins the constitution of South Africa. It was written in 1996, soon after nearly a century of harsh and unequal treatment of nonwhite South Africans had officially ended. The constitution's words were shaped by South Africans who came from many backgrounds and political parties. As a result, the 1996 constitution represents all South Africans in a new, democratic South Africa.

Beginning of White Rule

People have lived in present-day South Africa for thousands of years. In 1652, the first white Europeans arrived in the region and set up a colony. These Dutch settlers called themselves Boers (bohrz), the Dutch word for farmers. As you read in Chapter 3, the descendants of these settlers called themselves Afrikaners. They spoke a language related to Dutch, called Afrikaans.

British and French settlers arrived in South Africa by the late 1700s. For years, black South Africans fought the white settlers, who took their land. But by the late 1800s, the white settlers had forced the Africans off the best land.

Cultures Clash The Afrikaners founded their own states. After diamonds and gold were discovered there, the British wanted control of the land. British prospectors, or people who explore for minerals, pushed Afrikaners off their farms.

The British and Afrikaners fought over the Afrikaner land from 1899 to 1902. The British proved victorious and took control of the Afrikaner states. In 1910, the British created the Union of South Africa by unifying all the land they controlled in the region.

Unequal Treatment The white-led government of the Union of South Africa passed several laws to keep land and wealth in white hands. For example, the government declared that blacks could live and own land in only 8 percent of the country. Blacks could work in white areas, but for very low wages. Other laws passed in the 1920s separated white and black workers. The best jobs and the highest wages were reserved for whites.

✓ **Reading Check** When did the first white Europeans arrive in present-day South Africa?

System of Apartheid

The British granted independence to South Africa in 1931. But in 1948, the Afrikaners took political control of the country from the English-speaking whites when the Afrikaner political party, the National Party, won the election.

New Laws Take Hold The new Afrikaner leaders named the system of treating whites and nonwhites by different rules apartheid (uh PAHR tayt). In Afrikaans, the word *apartheid* means "apartness." Apartheid laws made it legal to discriminate on the basis of race. To **discriminate** means to treat people differently, and often unfairly, based on race, religion, or sex.

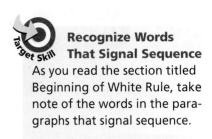

Recognize Words That Signal Sequence
As you read the section titled Beginning of White Rule, take note of the words in the paragraphs that signal sequence.

Keeping People Apart
In this image from the apartheid era, a man sits on a bench designated for Europeans (white South Africans) only. **Analyze Images** *How does this image illustrate discrimination?*

Stephen Biko

Born in 1946 in King William's Town, South Africa, Stephen Biko (BEE koh) studied to become a doctor. Instead, he became a South African hero as a leader of the struggle against apartheid. Biko taught that black South Africans could only become free of white rule if they viewed themselves as equal to whites. His ideas influenced thousands of students and adults throughout South Africa. The white-led government imprisoned Biko for his actions. He died in jail in 1977.

The laws separated South Africans into four groups—blacks, whites, coloreds, and Asians. Coloreds were people of mixed race. Asians were mainly people from India. Coloreds and Asians, who together made up 12 percent of the popuation, had a few rights. Blacks, who made up 75 percent of the population, had practically no rights at all.

Effects of Apartheid Apartheid affected every aspect of the lives of black South Africans. It forced thousands of them to move to ten poor, rural, all-black areas called homelands. These homelands had the driest and least fertile land in the country. There, blacks lived in poverty. Apartheid also strengthened existing laws that required all blacks to stay in homelands unless they could prove that whites would benefit from hiring them.

In addition, apartheid denied blacks citizenship rights, including the right to vote. The system kept blacks, coloreds, and Asians in low-paying jobs and put them in poor schools. It barred these groups from white restaurants, schools, and hospitals. In short, apartheid kept whites in control of the country.

Struggle to End Apartheid Many South Africans fought apartheid. Starting in the 1950s, blacks and some whites led peaceful protests against it. Over the following decades, South Africa's police met the protesters with deadly force many times. Thousands of men, women, and children were wounded, killed, or imprisoned. Protests, even peaceful ones, were banned. But the demonstrations continued. Many people were willing to risk everything for freedom.

In the 1970s, countries around the world joined the movement against apartheid. Many nations stopped trading with South Africa or lending it money. South Africa's athletes were banned from the Olympic Games. In 1990, these international pressures began to have an effect. F. W. de Klerk, an Afrikaner who was South Africa's president, led the government in abolishing the apartheid laws.

Legally ending apartheid was a major accomplishment. But much work lay ahead to make a reality of legal equality. In 1994, **Nelson Mandela** became South Africa's first black president and the leader who would fight to create a new, more equal system.

✓ **Reading Check** What happened to South Africans who protested against apartheid?

In 1993, Nelson Mandela (left) and F. W. de Klerk (right) together won the Nobel Peace Prize for helping end apartheid.

South Africa

South Africa is home to more than 45 million people, and there is a great deal of diversity among them. Numerous black ethnic groups make up almost 90 percent of the population. Of these groups, the Zulu and the Xhosa are the largest. The white population includes people of British, Dutch, German, French, and Portuguese descent. Other South Africans are of Asian descent. Study the map and charts to learn more about the people of South Africa.

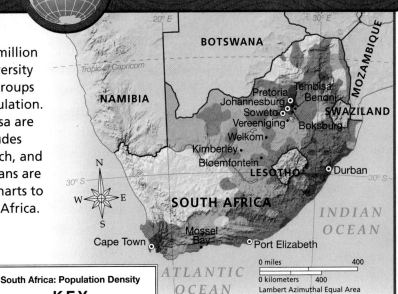

Urban and Rural Population

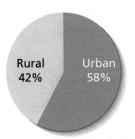

Rural 42%

Urban 58%

SOURCE: The 2003 Revision Population Database

South Africa: Population Density

KEY

Persons per sq. mile	Persons per sq. kilometer
More than 519	More than 199
260–519	100–199
130–259	50–99
25–129	10–49
1–24	1–9
Less than 1	Less than 1

Urban Areas

⊙　1,000,000–4,999,999

·　250,000–999,999

——　National border

Ethnic Groups*

3%

9%

10%

79%

- Black African
- White
- Other Black
- Indian/Asian

SOURCE: *CIA World Factbook*

*Numbers may not equal 100% due to rounding.

Map and Chart Skills

1. **Identify** What single ethnic group makes up the largest part of South Africa's population?
2. **Synthesize** Based on the graph, is the population of South Africa mostly rural, mostly urban, or almost evenly divided between rural and urban? How does the information given on the map support this?

Use Web Code **nge-5702** for **DK World Desk Reference Online.**

Building a New Nation

Since the 1950s, Mandela had been a leader of the African National Congress (ANC), South Africa's first black-led political party. The ANC had long fought for full voting rights for all South Africans. In 1962, Mandela was sent to prison for life for fighting apartheid. After 28 years of public pressure, de Klerk freed Mandela in 1990. Mandela then became president of the ANC. In April 1994, for the first time, all South Africans were allowed to vote. Mandela and the ANC easily won the presidency.

Learn more about the history of apartheid.

Today, South Africans of all races attend school together.

New Challenges Blacks and some whites welcomed the end of apartheid. In some ways, however, South Africa has remained a divided society. For example, blacks and whites usually live in different neighborhoods, and whites control most of the country's biggest businesses. Still, new opportunities have been created for millions of blacks, and tensions have eased. Mandela's government proved it was committed to helping all citizens, regardless of race. In fact, the constitution that Mandela's government wrote in 1996 is considered a world model for human rights.

Democracy Continues In June 1999, South Africa held its second election in which all South Africans were free to vote. Mandela retired, and Thabo Mbeki (TAH boh em BEK ee), also a long-term leader of the ANC, became South Africa's next president. With the equality movement set into motion by Mandela, Mbeki has been able to focus on other important issues as well. He has put great energy into improving the economic situations of all South Africans. In addition, he has continued to strengthen South Africa's new, democratic government. Mbeki was reelected in 2004.

✓ **Reading Check** What was unique about the 1994 election?

 Section 2 Assessment

Key Terms
Review the key terms at the beginning of this section. Use each term in a sentence that explains its meaning.

 Target Reading Skill
Review the section titled Struggle to End Apartheid on page 210. Find the words that signal the sequence of events that helped end apartheid.

Comprehension and Critical Thinking
1. (a) Name Which groups of white Europeans settled in present-day South Africa?

(b) Compare How was the clash between white settlers and black South Africans similar to the clash between the white groups?

2. (a) Describe Describe the system of apartheid.

(b) Draw Conclusions What do you think it was about the system of apartheid that made the struggle to end it take so long?

3. (a) Explain How did apartheid finally end?

(b) Analyze Information Why do you think South Africans chose someone who was black as their first president after apartheid?

Writing Activity
Suppose you live in South Africa. Write a letter to a friend explaining your view of the changes that have taken place there. Include details about what has changed as well as how you think people have responded to the changes.

Go Online
PHSchool.com

For: An activity on South Africa
Visit: PHSchool.com
Web Code: ngd-5702

Review and Assessment

◆ Chapter Summary

Section 1: Democratic Republic of the Congo

- The Democratic Republic of the Congo is rich in natural resources. These resources have helped shape the country's history.
- From the 1960s to the 1990s, Congo suffered under the authoritarian rule of Joseph Mobutu. It also suffered in the 1970s, when world prices of copper fell.
- During the 1990s, Congo faced civil wars that involved rebels in Congo. A number of neighboring countries also took part in the fighting.

Section 2: South Africa

- The Dutch, the British, and the French settled in South Africa. The British won control of the region and unified its lands as the Union of South Africa in 1910. It became independent in 1931.
- In 1948, the Afrikaners won political control of South Africa and legally established the system of apartheid. Many people who fought against this system were imprisoned, injured, or killed.
- Afrikaner president F. W. de Klerk legally ended apartheid in 1990. Nelson Mandela then became South Africa's first black president. He was followed in office by Thabo Mbeki.

Congolese currency

Nelson Mandela and F. W. de Klerk

◆ Key Terms

Match the definitions in Column I with the key terms in Column II.

Column I

1. the legal system of South Africa in which the rights of nonwhites were greatly restricted
2. black leader of the African National Congress and South Africa's first president after apartheid ended
3. a nondemocratic form of government in which a single leader or a small group of leaders has all the power
4. to treat people differently, and often unfairly, based on race, religion, or sex
5. to transfer ownership of something to a nation's government

Column II

A authoritarian government

B nationalize

C apartheid

D discriminate

E Nelson Mandela

Review and Assessment (continued)

◆ Comprehension and Critical Thinking

6. **(a) Recall** What important natural resources exist in the Democratic Republic of the Congo?
(b) Draw Conclusions If mining produces most of Congo's wealth, why do you think so many Congolese are farmers, not miners?

7. **(a) Identify** What kind of government did Joseph Mobutu establish in Congo?
(b) Draw Inferences How might this form of government have helped cause rebellion?
(c) Analyze Information What caused the second rebellion in Congo?

8. **(a) Name** What name did Mobutu give his country? What name did Laurent Kabila give it?
(b) Make Generalizations Why do you think a leader might want to change a country's name?

9. **(a) Recall** When did the system of apartheid in South Africa begin?
(b) Summarize How did apartheid affect different groups of South Africans?

10. **(a) Define** What was an important form of protest that black South Africans used against apartheid?
(b) Analyze Information How did the South African government respond to these protests?

11. **(a) Explain** How did the legal end to apartheid come about?
(b) Draw Conclusions Why was it significant that South Africa's first president after apartheid was not white?
(c) Predict Now that apartheid is over, do you think that South Africans will stop focusing on racial issues in politics? Explain.

◆ Skills Practice

Analyzing Primary Sources In the Skills for Life activity in this chapter, you learned how to analyze primary sources.

Review the steps you followed to learn this skill. Then reread the quotation from Tanzania's former president, Julius Nyerere, on page 173 of Chapter 6. Explain why the statement was made, what its main idea is, and which details are facts and which are opinions. Then explain whether you can identify any bias based on the background of the speaker.

◆ Writing Activity: History

Choose either South Africa or the Democratic Republic of the Congo. Write a list of five interview questions you would ask someone who has been elected president of the country. Be sure to consider what challenges the new president faces. Then exchange questions with a partner. Pretend that you are the president, and write answers to your partner's questions.

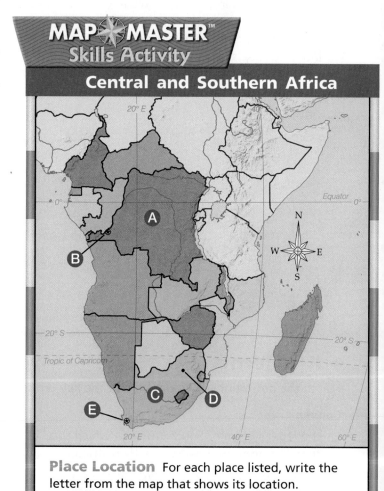

MAP MASTER™
Skills Activity

Central and Southern Africa

Place Location For each place listed, write the letter from the map that shows its location.
1. Cape Town
2. Johannesburg
3. Kinshasa
4. Democratic Republic of the Congo
5. South Africa

Go Online
PHSchool.com Use Web Code **ngp-5720** for an **interactive map.**

Standardized Test Prep

Test-Taking Tips

Some questions on standardized tests ask you to identify a frame of reference. Read the passage below. Then follow the tips to answer the sample question.

> Apartheid separated South Africa into four groups: blacks, whites, coloreds, and Asians. In 1990, apartheid came to an end. In 1994, South Africa elected Nelson Mandela the nation's first black president. Someone hearing the news shouted, "What a happy day. At last my people will have some opportunities. I never believed this would happen in South Africa."

TIP Think about the author's purpose as you read. Is the author trying to give you information, convince you of something, or teach you how to do something?

Pick the letter that best answers the question.

Which onlooker probably made those comments?

A a white businessman who owned a large diamond mine

B a politician in a pro-Afrikaner party

C a black woman living in a rural homeland

D a white woman who left South Africa to protest apartheid

TIP Watch out for careless errors. Be sure you understand the question and consider each answer choice.

Think It Through Start with the author's purpose: to give you information about the end of apartheid. Then ask yourself: Who would be happy about the end of apartheid? You can rule out A and B because neither was denied opportunities under apartheid. That leaves C and D. A white woman who had left South Africa in protest would probably be happy about the end of apartheid but would not say it meant opportunities for *her* people. The correct answer is C.

Practice Questions

Use the passage below to answer Question 1. Choose the letter of the best answer. Use the tips above and other tips in this book to help you answer the following questions.

> "We need a new government. The one we have now does not rule fairly. It is no better than Mobutu's government. Our neighbors in Rwanda and Uganda agree with us. We must make a change."

1. Who would have been most likely to make this statement?

   A Laurent Kabila

   B Joseph Kabila

   C a member of the first rebellion that occurred in eastern Congo

   D a member of the second rebellion that occurred in eastern Congo

2. Which natural resource did NOT play a role in Congo's history?

   A diamonds

   B silver

   C gold

   D rubber

3. When did South Africa become independent?

   A 1910

   B 1931

   C 1948

   D 1990

Go Online
PHSchool.com

Use Web Code **nga-5700** for **Chapter 7 self-test.**

Projects

Create your own projects to learn more about Africa. At the beginning of this book, you were introduced to the **Guiding Questions** for studying the chapters and special features. But you can also find answers to these questions by doing projects on your own or with a group. Use the questions to find topics you want to explore further. Then try the projects described on this page or create your own.

1 **Geography** What are the main physical features of Africa?

2 **History** How have historical events affected the cultures and nations of Africa?

3 **Culture** What features help define different African cultures?

4 **Government** What factors led to the development of different governments across Africa?

5 **Economics** What factors influence the ways in which Africans make a living?

Project

HOLD AN AFRICA CONFERENCE

Africa in the 2000s

As you read about Africa, organize a conference for the rest of your school about present-day life in Africa. Decide on several major topics for the conference, such as literature, arts, religion, and agriculture. Then form committees to plan the conference. One committee can plan an agenda, or list of events. Another can research the selected topics and give speeches at the conference. A publicity team can make posters to let students in other classes know about the conference. A press committee can write news reports about the speeches given at the conference.

Project

RESEARCH AFRICAN ART

African Masks

As you study Africa, find out about the tradition of mask-making in African countries. Look through books and magazines for information about different African mask-making traditions. Research the kinds of masks people make, the ways of making them, and the meanings that they have. Prepare a mini-museum display with pictures or sketches and detailed explanations of the masks and traditions you research. You may want to try making a mask of your own as well.

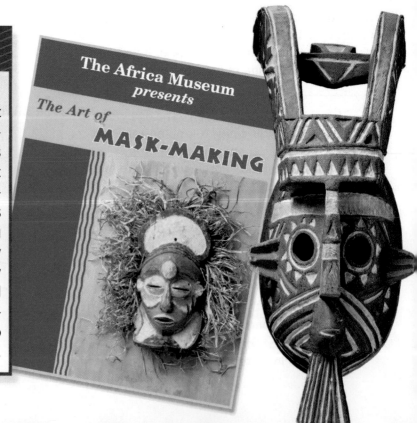

The Africa Museum *presents* The Art of MASK-MAKING

ASIA AND AUSTRALIA

Asia and Australia is a huge region that covers more than one third of Earth's surface. Asia is the largest continent. It includes some of the world's largest and smallest countries. This region also includes the only continent that is also a country—Australia.

Guiding Questions

The text, photographs, maps, and charts in this book will help you discover answers to these Guiding Questions.

1. **Geography** What are the main physical features of Asia and Australia?

2. **History** How have ancient civilizations of Asia and Australia influenced the world today?

3. **Culture** What are the main characteristics of the cultures of Asia and Australia?

4. **Government** What types of government exist in Asia and Australia today?

5. **Economics** How do the people of this region make a living?

Project Preview

You can also discover answers to the Guiding Questions by working on projects. Two projects are listed on page 462 of this book.

Investigate Asia and the Pacific Islands

Asia is the largest continent in the world. The vast Pacific Ocean contains thousands of scattered islands and another continent—the country of Australia. The continent of Asia includes part of Russia. However, Russian Asia is not covered in these pages. Because most of Russia's people live in Europe, Russia is discussed with Europe.

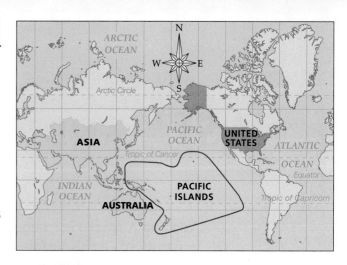

LOCATION

1 Locate Asia and the Pacific Islands

In this book you will read about Asia, Australia, and the islands of the Pacific Ocean. This region is shaded green on the map above. What ocean lies between Asia and the United States? If you lived on the west coast of the United States, in which direction would you travel to reach Asia? If you lived on the most eastern tip of the Pacific islands, in which direction would you travel to reach the west coast of the United States?

▲ **Myanmar, Asia**
Shwedagon Buddhist Temple dates from about A.D. 1000.

REGIONS

2 Estimate Asia's Size

Compare Asia's mainland to the continental United States (all states except Alaska and Hawaii). With a ruler, measure mainland Asia from north to south. Measure the distance from east to west. Now make the same measurements for the continental United States. About how many times longer and wider is mainland Asia (not including Russia) than the continental United States?

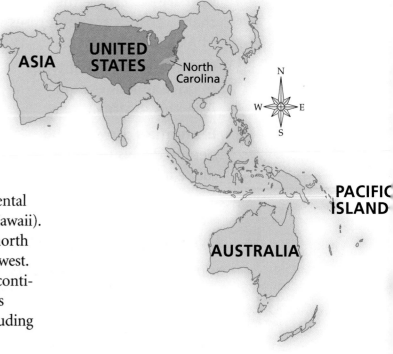

Political Asia

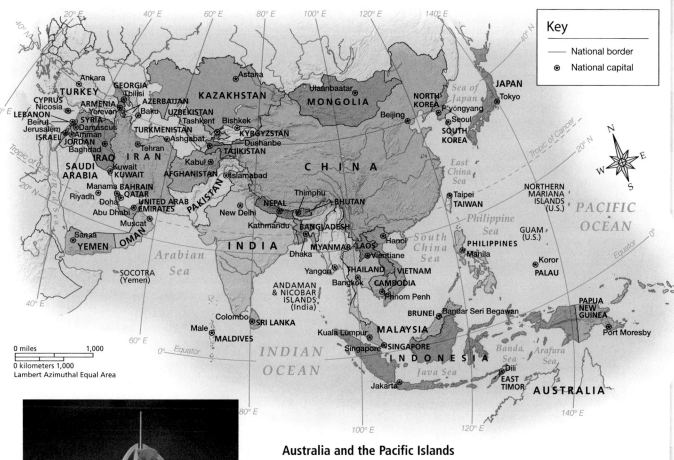

LOCATION

3 Investigate the Countries of Asia and the Pacific

Which Asian country on the map below is the largest? Which country is the second largest? Asia has many countries that are located on islands. Name three of them. Iran is a large country in the western part of Asia. Name three countries that border Iran.

Key

— National border

⊗ National capital

Australia and the Pacific Islands

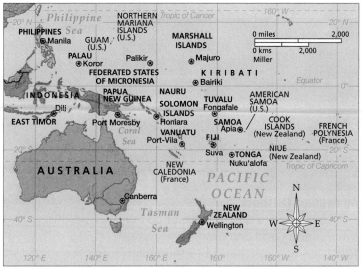

▲ **Dubai, United Arab Emirates**
Wealth from the region's oil resources paid for elaborate buildings like this hotel.

Physical Asia

LOCATION

4 Examine the Physical Features of Asia

Asia is a continent of great physical contrasts, including towering mountains, high plateaus, and low-lying plains. Use the elevation key to identify the highest and lowest areas on the map. Where are they? Describe their physical features.

▲ **Mount Fuji, Japan**
Japan's tallest mountain is actually a volcano, which last erupted in 1707.

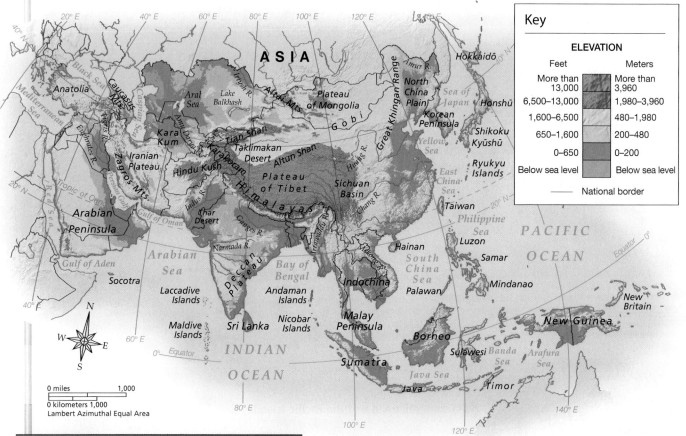

Key

ELEVATION

Feet	Meters
More than 13,000	More than 3,960
6,500–13,000	1,980–3,960
1,600–6,500	480–1,980
650–1,600	200–480
0–650	0–200
Below sea level	Below sea level

— National border

0 miles 1,000
0 kilometers 1,000
Lambert Azimuthal Equal Area

Australia and the Pacific Islands

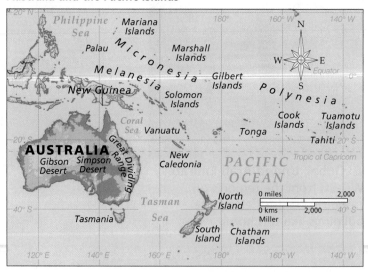

▲ **Australian Outback**
The Outback, in the dry, hot center of the country, is grassland and desert where few people live. Here ranchers raise sheep and cattle.

The Ring of Fire

Earth's crust is made up of plates that ride on top of molten rock called magma. The magma escapes in the form of lava when volcanoes erupt. Ninety percent of the world's active volcanoes circle the Pacific Ocean. Look at the map below. Why is this region described as a "Ring of Fire"?

▲ **Puu Oo Volcano, Hawaii**
The Puu Oo volcano spews molten lava as it erupts. The islands that we call Hawaii are the tops of volcanoes that rest on the ocean floor.

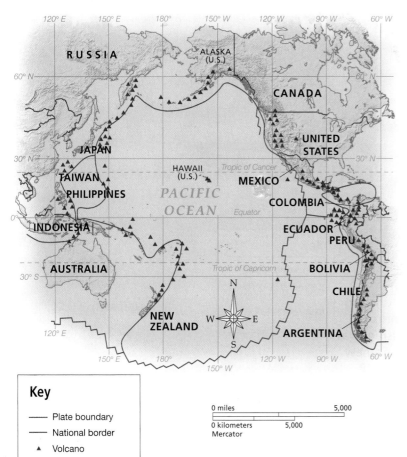

Key

—— Plate boundary
—— National border
▲ Volcano

0 miles 5,000
0 kilometers 5,000
Mercator

INTERACTION

5 Investigate the Ring of Fire

Where Earth's plates meet, plate boundaries are formed. With your finger, trace the plate boundaries on the map at left. Notice where the volcanoes are located in relation to the plate boundaries. Compare the location of volcanoes to the location of cities on the political maps on page 219. Where might volcano eruptions cause the most harm to people?

PRACTICE YOUR GEOGRAPHY SKILLS

1 You begin your boat trip from Australia's north coast and travel west through Indonesia. After you pass Borneo and Java, you cross the Equator and enter a large body of water. What is its name?

2 Today you fly from the Himalayas along the 30° N parallel across the Indus River to the Zagros Mountains. What body of water are you near?

3 There are many volcanoes to the east of this island nation north of the East China Sea. What is the name of this country?

▲ **Boats moored in Indonesia**

Focus on Countries in Asia

Now that you've investigated the geography of Asia and the Pacific, take a closer look at some of the countries that make up this vast region. The map shows the countries of Asia and the Pacific. The countries that you will study in depth in the second half of this book appear in yellow on the map.

Go Online
PHSchool.com
Use Web Code **ngp-6000** for the **interactive maps** on these pages.

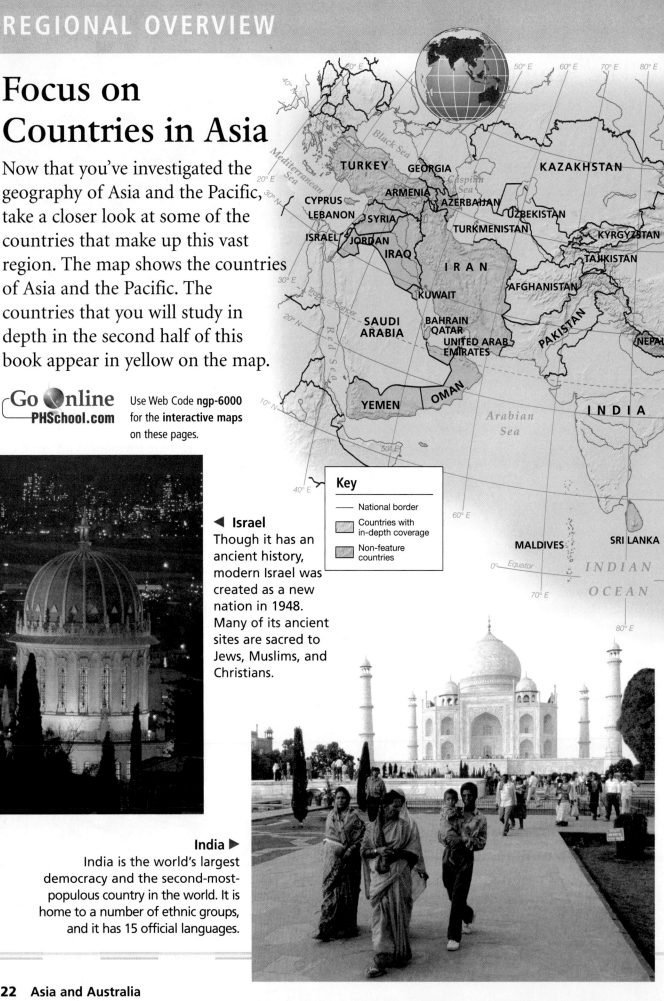

Key

——	National border
▨	Countries with in-depth coverage
▨	Non-feature countries

◀ Israel
Though it has an ancient history, modern Israel was created as a new nation in 1948. Many of its ancient sites are sacred to Jews, Muslims, and Christians.

India ▶
India is the world's largest democracy and the second-most-populous country in the world. It is home to a number of ethnic groups, and it has 15 official languages.

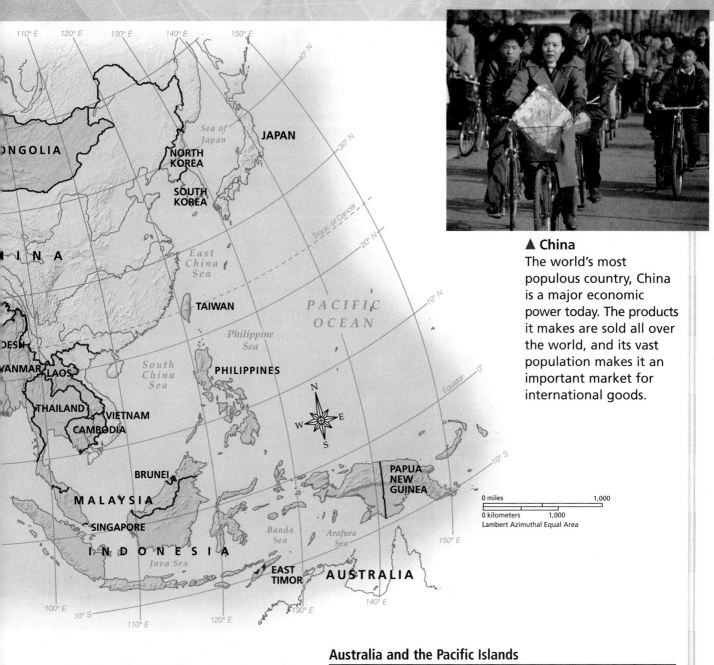

▲ China
The world's most populous country, China is a major economic power today. The products it makes are sold all over the world, and its vast population makes it an important market for international goods.

▲ Seoul, South Korea
The Korean Peninsula is home to one people, but since 1953 they have lived in two separate nations—North Korea and South Korea.

Australia and the Pacific Islands

Chapter

8

East Asia: Physical Geography

Chapter Preview

NC Standard Course of Study

7.1.02 Use tools to answer geography questions

7.2.01 Influence of physical features and climate on cultures

7.2.02 Factors that influence distribution of population, resources, and climate

7.3.01 How people have used their environments

7.3.04 Describe effects of physical processes

7.5.01 How the location of natural resources affects economic development

SS.1.03 Draw inferences

SS.3.01 Use map and globe reading skills

Sections

1. **Land and Water**
   7.2.01, 7.2.02, 7.3.04, SS.3.01
2. **Climate and Vegetation**
   7.1.02, 7.2.01, 7.2.02, SS.1.03
3. **Natural Resources and Land Use**
   7.3.01, 7.5.01, SS.1.03

 Target Reading Skill

Reading Process In this chapter you will focus on using the reading process to improve your reading skills. When you use the reading process, you set a purpose for reading, predict what you are going to learn, and ask questions about what you read.

▶ **The Great Wall of China stretches across the mountains of northern China.**

MAP MASTER™
Skills Activity

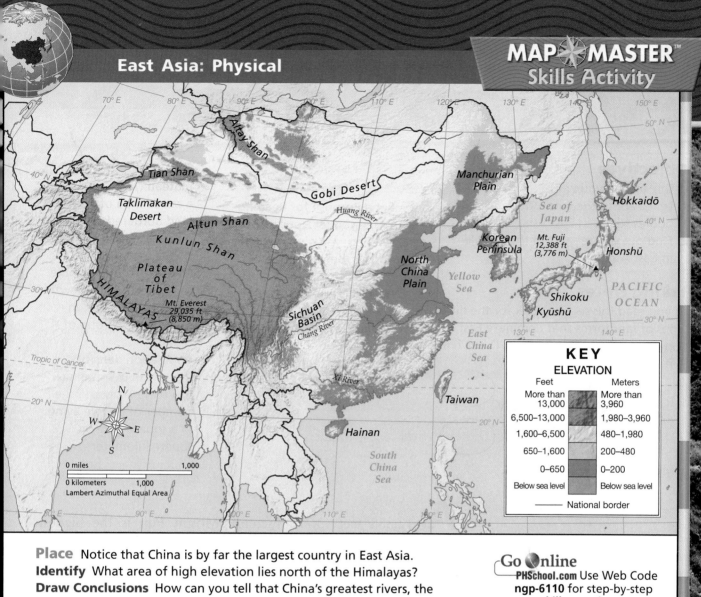

KEY
ELEVATION

Feet		Meters
More than 13,000		More than 3,960
6,500–13,000		1,980–3,960
1,600–6,500		480–1,980
650–1,600		200–480
0–650		0–200
Below sea level		Below sea level
	National border	

Place Notice that China is by far the largest country in East Asia.
Identify What area of high elevation lies north of the Himalayas?
Draw Conclusions How can you tell that China's greatest rivers, the Chang and the Huang, flow toward the east? Explain your answer.

Go Online
PHSchool.com Use Web Code **ngp-6110** for step-by-step **map skills practice.**

Prepare to Read

Objectives

In this section you will

1. Learn about the landforms and water bodies found in East Asia.
2. Find out where most of the people in East Asia live.

Taking Notes

As you read this section, look for the different types of landforms that dominate East Asia. Copy the web below and record your findings in it.

East Asia's Landforms

Target Reading Skill

Set a Purpose for Reading
When you set a purpose for reading, you give yourself a focus. Before you read this section, look at the headings and pictures. Then set a purpose for reading. In this section, your purpose is to learn about the landforms and water bodies of East Asia.

Key Terms

- **plateau** (pla TOH) *n.* a raised area of level land bordered on one or more sides by steep slopes or cliffs
- **fertile** (FUR tul) *adj.* able to support plant growth
- **archipelago** (ahr kuh PEL uh goh) *n.* a group of islands
- **population density** (pahp yuh LAY shun DEN suh tee) *n.* the average number of people living in a square mile or square kilometer

A view of Mount Fuji, Japan

At 12,388 feet (3,776 meters), Mount Fuji is the highest mountain in Japan. Each year, 150,000 to 200,000 people reach its summit. Visitors heading to the top can stay in mountain lodges and browse in souvenir shops that sell canisters of oxygen to make breathing easier at the high altitude.

Landforms and Water Bodies

Mount Fuji is one of the many spectacular landforms that make up East Asia. A single nation, China, takes up most of East Asia's land. Mountains, highlands, and **plateaus,** or raised areas of level land bordered on one or more sides by steep slopes or cliffs, make up much of China's landscape. The other countries of this region are mountainous, like China. But only China and Mongolia also have wide plains and plateaus. Japan, Taiwan, North Korea, and South Korea have narrow plains that lie mainly along coasts and rivers.

The Himalayas Powerful natural forces created the rugged landscape of East Asia. About 50 million years ago, a huge piece of a continent collided with Asia. The collision caused Earth's surface to fold and buckle, forming the Himalayas and the Plateau of Tibet. The Himalayas are the highest mountains in the world. They include Mount Everest, the highest peak in the world. The Himalayas extend along the border of China and Nepal. The Plateau of Tibet is a huge highland area that lies north of the Himalaya mountains.

Island Landscapes Natural forces also shaped the islands that make up Japan. Earthquakes forced some parts of the country to rise and others to sink. Erupting volcanoes piled up masses of lava and ash, forming new mountains. Japan's Mount Fuji is actually a volcano that has not erupted since 1707. Today, earthquakes and volcanoes are still changing the landscape in many parts of East Asia.

China: More Than One Billion People China is home to one of the oldest civilizations on Earth. With a population of more than one billion people, it also has more people than any other nation in the world.

Mountains and deserts make up more than two thirds of China's land. A desert is a dry region with little vegetation. The area of western and southwestern China has some of the highest mountains in the world. China's Gobi is the northernmost desert on Earth.

China's most important rivers, the Chang and the Huang, begin in Tibet and flow east. The Chang River is deep enough for cargo ships to sail on. More than 100 million people live along the banks of the Huang River. It runs through one of the most fertile regions of China, the North China Plain. **Fertile** soil is capable of supporting abundant plant growth. The North China Plain is covered with deposits of loess (LOH es), a brownish-yellow soil that is very fertile.

The Plateau of Tibet
The Plateau of Tibet is a vast, high area in China that includes the region of Tibet. These Tibetan women make their living by herding livestock.
Infer *The Plateau of Tibet is called "the roof of the world." Why do you think this is so?*

Set a Purpose for Reading
If your purpose is to learn about East Asia's landforms and water bodies, how does this paragraph help you meet your goal?

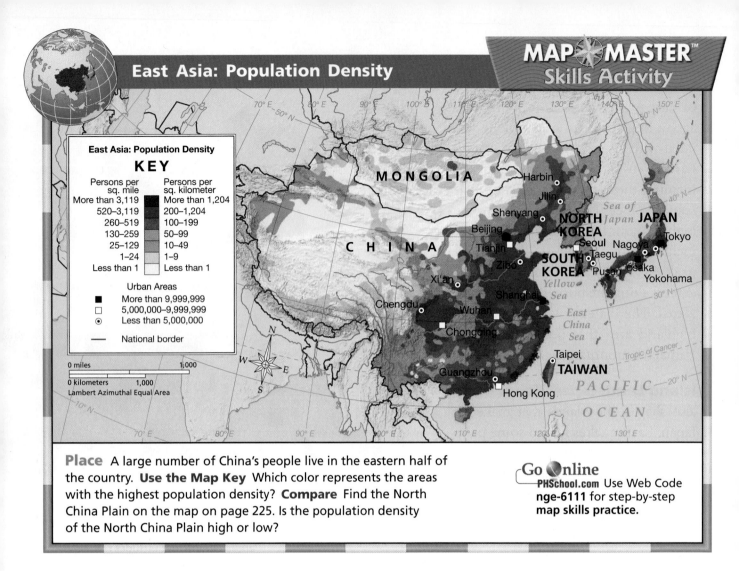

East Asia: Population Density

MAP MASTER™ Skills Activity

East Asia: Population Density
KEY

Persons per sq. mile	Persons per sq. kilometer
More than 3,119	More than 1,204
520–3,119	200–1,204
260–519	100–199
130–259	50–99
25–129	10–49
1–24	1–9
Less than 1	Less than 1

Urban Areas
- ■ More than 9,999,999
- ☐ 5,000,000–9,999,999
- ⊙ Less than 5,000,000

— National border

0 miles 1,000
0 kilometers 1,000
Lambert Azimuthal Equal Area

Place A large number of China's people live in the eastern half of the country. **Use the Map Key** Which color represents the areas with the highest population density? **Compare** Find the North China Plain on the map on page 225. Is the population density of the North China Plain high or low?

Go Online
PHSchool.com Use Web Code
nge-6111 for step-by-step
map skills practice.

Discovery CHANNEL SCHOOL Video
Learn about the key geographic features in East Asia.

Japan: An Island Country Japan is an archipelago (ahr kuh PEL uh goh), or group of islands, in the western Pacific Ocean. Japan has four main islands and more than 3,000 smaller ones. Every major Japanese city is located on the coast. As the map above shows, most of Japan's people live in coastal areas. Nearly 80 percent of the country is mountainous.

Japan's four main islands are Hokkaidō (hoh ky doh), Honshū (hahn shoo), Shikoku (shee koh koo), and Kyūshū (kyoo shoo). The largest and most populated of these is Honshū. Most of Japan's major cities, including its capital city of Tokyo, are located on Honshū.

The Koreas: Two Countries, One Peninsula The Korean Peninsula extends south into the Yellow Sea between China and Japan. A peninsula is a piece of land nearly surrounded by water. Since 1953, Korea has been divided into two separate countries, North Korea and South Korea.

✓ **Reading Check** Which type of landform dominates Japan—mountains or plains?

228 Asia and Australia

Population in East Asia

As you can see on the map on the previous page, the population of East Asia is spread unevenly across the land. Few people live in the deserts, plateaus, and mountains. Yet almost 1.5 billion people make their homes in East Asia. Most of the people live in the plains and coastal areas, where living and growing food are easier. These parts of East Asia have a very high **population density,** or average number of people living in a square mile (or square kilometer).

Look at the physical map of East Asia on page 225 and find the North China Plain. Now look at the population density map of East Asia on page 228. You can see that this area of China has a very high population density. That is because the land in the North China Plain is better suited for human settlement than the mountains and deserts of China. For example, the North China Plain is level and has fertile soil.

In East Asia, level ground must be shared by cities, farms, and industries. Almost half the population of Japan is crowded onto less than 3 percent of the country's land. In China, most of the population is located in the eastern half of the country, where the plains and coastal areas are located.

A crowded street in Seoul, the capital of South Korea

 **Reading Check** **Why does the North China Plain have such a high population density?**

 Section 1 Assessment

Key Terms

Review the key terms at the beginning of this section. Use each term in a sentence that explains its meaning.

Target Reading Skill

How did having a purpose help you understand important ideas in this section?

Comprehension and Critical Thinking

1. (a) Recall What are the major landforms in East Asia?

(b) Locate In what part of China is the Plateau of Tibet?
(c) Contrast How are the landforms in eastern China different from the landforms in western China?
2. (a) Identify Name one type of landform in China where there is a high population density. You may refer to the maps in the section to answer.
(b) Draw Conclusions How does the physical geography of East Asia help explain why the eastern part of China is the most densely populated part of the country?

Writing Activity

Suppose that you are a travel agent helping a customer who wants to visit East Asia. Which landforms would you suggest that your customer visit? In which countries are these landforms located? Record your suggestions.

For: An activity on East Asia
Visit: PHSchool.com
Web Code: ngp-6101

Section 2 Climate and Vegetation

Prepare to Read

Objectives

In this section you will
1. Examine the major climate regions in East Asia.
2. Discover how climate affects people and vegetation in East Asia.

Taking Notes

As you read this section, look for details about how climate affects the people and vegetation in East Asia. Copy the table below and record your findings in it.

| East Asia's Climates ||
Effect on Vegetation	Effect on People
•	• Rice is the main food in southern China.

Target Reading Skill

Predict Making predictions about your text helps you set a purpose for reading and helps you remember what you read. Preview the section by looking at the headings, pictures, and maps. Then predict what the text might discuss about climate and vegetation in East Asia.

Key Terms

- **monsoon** (mahn SOON) *n.* a wind that changes direction with the change of season
- **typhoon** (ty FOON) *n.* a tropical storm that develops over the Pacific Ocean, with winds that reach speeds greater than 74 miles per hour
- **deciduous** (dee SIJ oo us) *adj.* falling off or shedding, as in leaves, seasonally or at a certain stage of development

Y ou and your family are visiting Japan in the middle of February. All of you are trying to decide where to go for a long weekend. Your brother wants to go north to the island of Hokkaidō, where the skiing is perfect. Your parents, though, have had enough of winter. They would like to go to the island of Okinawa (oh kee nah wuh). The water there is warm enough for swimming. Which would you prefer—sun or snow?

East Asia's Climate Regions

Look at the climate map on the next page. It shows that East Asia has seven climate regions. Two of them—the tropical wet region and the subarctic region—cover a comparatively small part of the land. The five major climate regions are semiarid, arid, humid subtropical, humid continental, and highland.

Downhill skiing in Japan

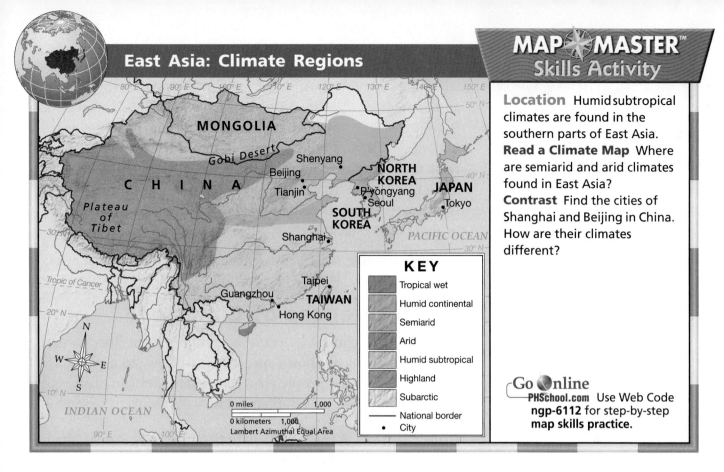

East Asia: Climate Regions

MONGOLIA

Gobi Desert

Shenyang

Beijing

Tianjin

CHINA

Plateau
of
Tibet

NORTH
KOREA

P'yŏngyang
Seoul

SOUTH
KOREA

JAPAN

Tokyo

Shanghai

PACIFIC OCEAN

Tropic of Cancer

Taipei

Guangzhou

TAIWAN

Hong Kong

INDIAN OCEAN

0 miles   1,000
0 kilometers   1,000
Lambert Azimuthal Equal Area

KEY

Tropical wet
Humid continental
Semiarid
Arid
Humid subtropical
Highland
Subarctic
—— National border
• City

Location Humid subtropical climates are found in the southern parts of East Asia.
Read a Climate Map Where are semiarid and arid climates found in East Asia?
Contrast Find the cities of Shanghai and Beijing in China. How are their climates different?

Go Online
PHSchool.com Use Web Code **ngp-6112** for step-by-step map skills practice.

A Variety of Climates A large part of eastern China has a humid subtropical climate—cool winters and hot summers with plenty of rain. To the north is a humid continental area of warm summers and cold winters. Because South Korea and Japan are almost completely surrounded by water, summers are a bit cooler and winters are a bit warmer than in other places at the same latitude.

In contrast, the northern interior of China is very dry, with arid and semiarid climate regions. There, temperatures can range from very hot to very cold. To the south, the Plateau of Tibet has a cool, dry, highland climate.

Monsoons Monsoons strongly affect the climates of East Asia. Monsoons are winds that change direction with the change of season. In summer, Pacific Ocean winds blow northwest toward the Asian continent. They bring rainfall that starts in June as a drizzle. The Japanese call this the "plum rain" because it begins just as the plums begin to ripen on the trees. The winds cause hot, humid weather and heavier rain in July.

In winter, the winds blow toward the east. The winds that begin in the interior of northern Asia are icy cold and very dry. In parts of China, the winds produce dust storms that can last for days. Where they cross warm ocean waters, these monsoons pick up moisture. Farther inland, they drop it as rain or snow.

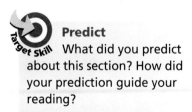

Predict
What did you predict about this section? How did your prediction guide your reading?

Links Across
Time

Divine Winds Typhoons twice saved Japan from invaders. In 1274, Kublai Khan, a great leader of China's Mongol people, sent a fleet of warships to Japan. The Mongols got only as far as the island of Kyūshū. A typhoon frightened them back to China. When Kublai Khan tried again in 1281, a typhoon destroyed his huge fleet. The Japanese called this typhoon *kamikaze*, or "divine wind."

Typhoons East Asia has hurricanes like those that sometimes strike the southern coastline of the United States during August and September. These violent storms, which develop over the Pacific Ocean, are called **typhoons.** Whirling typhoon winds blow at speeds of 74 miles an hour or more. The winds and heavy rains they bring can cause major damage. Killer typhoons have brought great devastation and death to some countries in East Asia. For example, a typhoon that struck China in 1922 resulted in about 60,000 deaths.

✓ **Reading Check** **Name and describe two types of storms that occur in East Asia.**

The Influences of Climate

In East Asia, climate governs everything from the natural vegetation, which is shown on the map below, to agriculture. Climate affects what people grow, how often they can plant, and how easily they can harvest their fields.

How Climate Affects Vegetation in East Asia Much of the plant life in East Asia is strong enough to stand seasonal differences in temperature and rainfall. Bamboo, for example, grows remarkably quickly during the wet season in southern China and Japan. Yet it can also survive dry spells by storing food

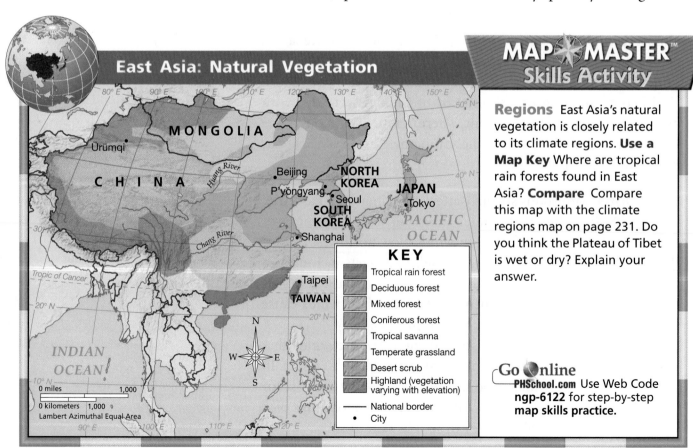

East Asia: Natural Vegetation

KEY

Tropical rain forest
Deciduous forest
Mixed forest
Coniferous forest
Tropical savanna
Temperate grassland
Desert scrub
Highland (vegetation varying with elevation)
— National border
• City

0 miles 1,000
0 kilometers 1,000
Lambert Azimuthal Equal Area

MAP MASTER
Skills Activity

Regions East Asia's natural vegetation is closely related to its climate regions. **Use a Map Key** Where are tropical rain forests found in East Asia? **Compare** Compare this map with the climate regions map on page 231. Do you think the Plateau of Tibet is wet or dry? Explain your answer.

Go Online
PHSchool.com Use Web Code **ngp-6122** for step-by-step map skills practice.

in its huge root system. Shrubs and many small flowering plants in the deserts of China spring up rapidly after summer rains. **Deciduous** (dih SIJ oo us), or leaf-shedding, trees change with the seasons. Maples, birches, and other trees turn the hillsides of Japan and the Koreas gold, orange, and red, once summer gives way to fall.

How Climate Affects People in East Asia

Climate greatly affects life in East Asia. The region around the Huang River in China is a good example. The Chinese word *Huang* means "yellow." The river gets its name from the brownish-yellow loess that is blown by the desert winds. The river picks up the loess and deposits it to the east on the North China Plain. The loess covers a huge 125,000-square-mile (324,000-square-kilometer) area around the river. This plain is one of the best farming areas in China.

The Huang River also floods. A system of dams helps control the waters. But the river can still overflow during the monsoons. Floods gave the Huang River its nickname, "China's Sorrow."

The diet of East Asians is also affected by climate. Because rice grows best in warm weather, it is the main crop—and food—of people in southern China. In the cooler north, wheat and other grains grow better than rice. This means that people in the north eat more flour products, such as noodles.

Brilliant Fall Colors in Japan
Most parts of Japan have spring, summer, fall, and winter. At this teahouse in the city of Nara, it is still warm enough to sit outdoors in October and November. **Analyze Images** *How can you tell the trees in the photo are deciduous trees?*

✓ **Reading Check** How does bamboo survive during dry spells in southern China and Japan?

Section 2 Assessment

Key Terms
Review the key terms at the beginning of this section. Use each term in a sentence that explains its meaning.

Target Reading Skill
What did you predict about this section? How did your prediction guide your reading?

Comprehension and Critical Thinking
1. (a) Recall What are the five major climate regions in East Asia?

(b) Summarize What kind of winters and summers are found in a humid subtropical climate?

2. (a) Identify Name three ways climate affects agriculture in East Asia.

(b) Generalize How does the climate affect what people eat in China?

Writing Activity
Write a letter to a friend who is planning a long trip to East Asia. Explain what climate conditions can occur in different areas. Include suggestions for clothing.

For: An activity on East Asia's climate
Visit: PHSchool.com
Web Code: ngd-6102

Using Reliable Information on the Internet

Your teacher has given you an assignment to write a report about the Gobi Desert in Mongolia and China. To research your report, you are asked to find articles, photos, and statistics about the Gobi Desert.

"Use a variety of good sources on the Internet," your teacher urges. "An encyclopedia article is a good start for basic facts. But if you search further, you might find stories from people who live there. You might also find photographs that will help you to describe the land in your own words."

You enter the word *Gobi* on an Internet search engine, and receive 123,000 "hits"—that is, Web sites that contain the word *Gobi*. How can you find reliable, useful information among all these sites?

Learn the Skill

To find information from Web sites you can trust, follow the steps below.

1. **Decide on your search terms.** Make a list of what you are looking for. For example, try *Gobi Desert* or *Gobi climate.*

2. **Notice the Web site's Internet address.** The address, or URL, will include a period followed by a three-letter abbreviation. Among the most common are ".com," ".edu," ".gov," and ".org." Just about anyone can set up a Web site with a .com (commercial) address. Schools and universities use a .edu (education) address. Nonprofit organizations such as museums use .org. Official government sites carry a .gov address.

3. **Try to identify the author and date of information on a Web site.** The author and date often appear on the Web page. But many sites are anonymous—they do not identify the author. Do not use information from anonymous sites. It may be out of date or it may be written by an author who has no particular expertise about the topic.

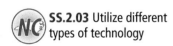

SS.2.03 Utilize different types of technology

4. **Choose a reliable source, or use more than one source, if needed.** Encyclopedias are reliable. They are written by people who have knowledge about a wide range of subject areas and they present facts. Sources with .gov and .edu are generally reliable, as are newspapers, magazines, and television network news sites.

Practice the Skill

Use the steps in the skill to do some research on a computer.

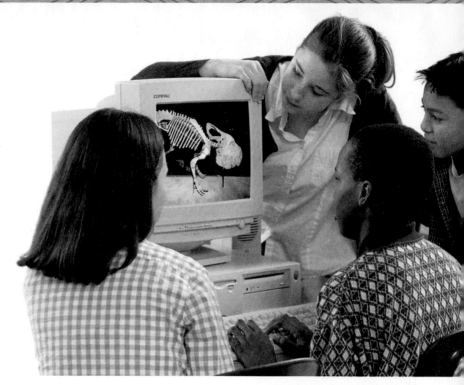

1. If a search for *Gobi* gives you thousands of results, what additional search terms could you use to narrow the search?

2. Look for a site with a .gov address from the government of China or Mongolia. Or try a United States government Web site for statistics about the location and size of the Gobi. Why is it a good idea to go to an .edu address to research the Gobi?

Reliable Web sites can help you research Gobi dinosaurs—or any school assignment.

3. Would it matter if an online map of the Gobi was created this year or 50 years ago? Would it matter if a graph of average rainfall in the Gobi was from this year or 50 years ago? Explain.

4. Say you read about a recent discovery of dinosaur bones in the Gobi. The news appears on an archaeology Web site, but the author and date are unidentified. Where would you find a reliable source of this news?

Apply the Skill

Suppose your neighbor writes a letter to the editor of the Internet edition of your local newspaper. In the letter, she writes, "The population in our community has doubled in the last year." Is this reliable information? Then you go to your local government's Web site and read this: "Town population doubles in just one year, according to government statistics." Is this information reliable? Name two Web sites you could go to in order to find the actual statistics. Explain why each is reliable.

Section 3
Natural Resources and Land Use

Prepare to Read

Objectives

In this section you will
1. Learn about East Asia's major natural resources.
2. Find out how the people of East Asia use land to produce food.

Taking Notes

Copy the table below. As you read, look for the headings that appear in large red type. Turn these headings into questions. Use the table to record your answers to these questions.

Natural Resources and Land Use in East Asia	
Questions	Answers

Target Reading Skill

Ask Questions Preview the headings, pictures, and maps to see what this section is about. Find the main headings in this section. (They appear in large red type.) Turn these headings into questions. Then read to answer your questions. Write your questions and answers in the Taking Notes table.

Key Terms

- **developing country** (dih VEL up ing KUN tree) *n.* a country that has low industrial production and little modern technology
- **developed country** (dih VEL upt KUN tree) *n.* a country with many industries and a well-developed economy
- **terrace** (TEHR us) *n.* a level area in a hillside
- **double-cropping** (DUB ul KRAHP ing) *v.* to grow two or more crops on the same land

When planning their economies, all countries ask these three basic questions: What will be produced? How will it be produced? For whom will it be produced? For the countries of East Asia, the answers to these questions depend largely on factors surrounding these two things: natural resources and land use.

Natural resources are materials found in nature. They include fertile land, minerals, water, and forests. Natural resources can be used to produce all sorts of goods, from cars to sweatshirts. Land use is linked to natural resources. To improve their economies, governments have to decide how to use the land and the natural resources they contain.

East Asia's Natural Resources

East Asia's lands and waters are filled with abundant natural resources. As the map on the next page shows, East Asia has natural resources that can be used to produce energy, such as coal, oil, and water for hydroelectric power. Other resources in East Asia are the raw materials for manufactured goods, such as electronic equipment. The water bodies and fertile land of East Asia are also important resources.

Coal miners in China

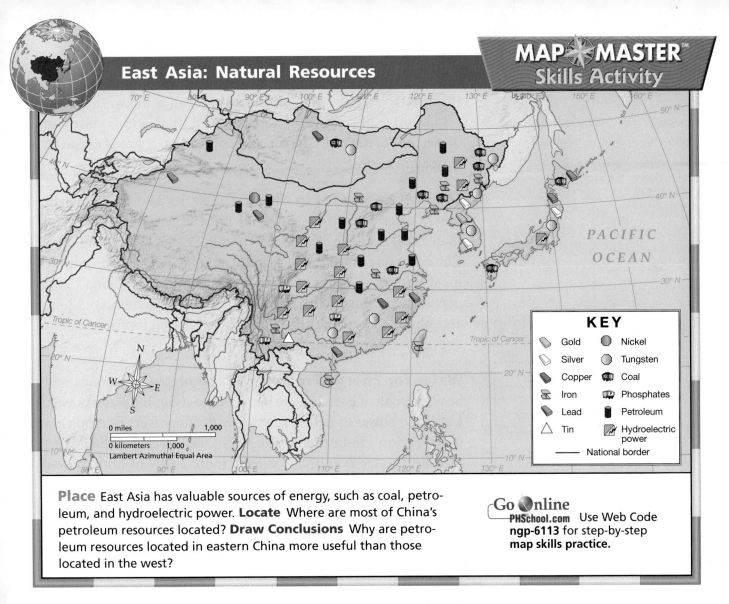

KEY

Gold		Nickel	
Silver		Tungsten	
Copper		Coal	
Iron		Phosphates	
Lead		Petroleum	
Tin		Hydroelectric power	
		National border	

PACIFIC OCEAN

Place East Asia has valuable sources of energy, such as coal, petroleum, and hydroelectric power. **Locate** Where are most of China's petroleum resources located? **Draw Conclusions** Why are petroleum resources located in eastern China more useful than those located in the west?

Go Online
PHSchool.com Use Web Code **ngp-6113** for step-by-step **map skills practice.**

Mineral Resources in the Two Koreas East Asia has plenty of mineral resources, but they are unevenly distributed. Some countries have more and other countries have less. The two Koreas, for example, have limited mineral resources. Coal and iron, which are used in manufacturing, are plentiful in North Korea. But there is little coal or iron in South Korea, where much more manufacturing takes place. The only minerals that are in large supply in the South are tungsten and graphite.

If South Korea could share North Korea's coal and iron, both countries would benefit. But the two do not share resources, since they are hostile toward each other. North Korea is a **developing country**—one that has low industrial production and little modern technology. South Korea is a **developed country**—one with many industries and a well-developed economy. Because of its limited resources, South Korea must import the iron, crude oil, and chemicals it needs for its industries. Nevertheless, it has become one of East Asia's richest economies. It exports, or sells, many manufactured goods to other nations.

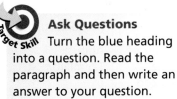

Ask Questions
Target Skill Turn the blue heading into a question. Read the paragraph and then write an answer to your question.

Mineral Resources in Japan Japan is a modern industrial society. Yet Japan—like South Korea—has few mineral resources. It imports vast quantities of minerals. Japan is the world's largest importer of coal, natural gas, and oil. It also imports about 95 percent of the iron ore, tin, and copper that it needs to run its major industries.

Mineral Resources in China Unlike its East Asian neighbors, China has a large supply of mineral resources. For more than 2,000 years, the Chinese have mined copper, tin, and iron. China has one of the world's largest supplies of coal, which is the most important of its mineral resources. Most of China's coal deposits are found in the northern part of the country. China also has oil deposits. China uses most of the oil it produces, but does export some crude oil and oil products.

Water for Energy Production The rugged mountains and heavy rainfall of East Asia are perfect for developing water power. Using the power of East Asia's swiftly flowing rivers is important to the region's industrial development. However, building dams to collect water is costly. It is even more costly to build power plants that produce hydroelectricity. Hydroelectricity is electricity produced by using the power of flowing water.

The Three Gorges Dam

Location	Chang River
Width	1.4 miles (2,309 meters)
Height	607 feet (185 meters)
Start date	1994
Expected completion date	2009
Number of construction workers	About 250,000
Purpose	Flood control, hydroelectricity
Number of people displaced	About 1.5 million

In 2004, China produced about 20 percent of its electricity from hydroelectric power. The Chinese government expects this figure to increase when China finishes building the Three Gorges Dam across the Chang River. The Three Gorges Dam will be one and a half miles wide and more than 600 feet high. China is building the dam not only to produce electricity but also to control the frequent floods on the Chang River.

Water for Aquaculture East Asia's ocean and inland waters have been an important source of food for the region's people. Aquaculture, or fish farming, has been practiced in Asia for centuries. During the 1980s and 1990s, however, aquaculture production in Asia greatly expanded. This was due, in part, to the fact that overfishing and pollution had decreased the supply of saltwater and freshwater fish. The increase was also due to advances in the practice of aquaculture. In East Asia, China is the leading aquaculture producer. Japan, South Korea, and Taiwan are also among the top aquaculture producers in the world. Aquaculture includes farm-raised fish, shrimp, oysters, mussels, clams, and seaweed.

✓ **Reading Check** Based on what you have read, is Japan a developed country or a developing country?

The World's Largest Dam
The bottom photo shows the Three Gorges Dam in China under construction. The top photo shows what the Three Gorges area looked like before construction began. The middle photo shows a model of the completed dam. China is building the dam to produce hydroelectricity. **Contrast** Study the two small photos. How will the dam change the landscape of the Three Gorges area?

A Japanese farmer displays his harvest of rice.

Using the Land to Produce Food

In order to feed its large population, East Asians need to farm every bit of available land. With so many mountains and plateaus, only a small percentage of the land can be cultivated. Only about 14 percent of China, 12 percent of Japan, and 14 percent of North Korea can be farmed. South Korea's 19 percent is about equal to the percentage of land farmed in the United States.

Terrace Farming In China, Japan, and parts of Korea, farmers cut horizontal steps called **terraces** into steep hillsides to gain a few precious yards of soil for crops. Farmers even use the land at the sides of roads and railway lines for planting.

Double-Cropping Where climate and soil allow, farmers practice **double-cropping,** growing two or more crops on the same land in the same season or at the same time. In China, farmers often plant one type of crop between the rows of another crop in order to grow more food. In some parts of southern China, farmers are even able to grow three crops in a year. In southern Japan, rice seeds are sowed in small fields. When the seedlings are about a foot high, they are replanted in a larger field after wheat has been harvested from it.

✓ **Reading Check** What is the difference between terrace farming and double-cropping?

Section 3 Assessment

Key Terms
Review the key terms at the beginning of this section. Use each term in a sentence that explains its meaning.

Target Reading Skill
What questions did you ask about this section?

Comprehension and Critical Thinking
1. (a) **Recall** Name three natural resources in East Asia that can be used to produce energy.

(b) **Contrast** Which country has a larger supply of mineral resources, China or Japan?
(c) **Infer** How could a country develop its economy without a large supply of mineral resources?
2. (a) **Recall** What two farming techniques do East Asian farmers use to make up for a shortage of farmland?
(b) **Infer** Why might East Asian farmers be interested in learning about faster-growing crops?

Writing Activity
Suppose you are a reporter for a television news program. Write a report that tells how the waters of East Asia are an important resource for its people. Include at least two ways water is used in East Asia.

For: An activity on East Asia
Visit: PHSchool.com
Web Code: ngd-6103

Review and Assessment

◆ Chapter Summary

Section 1: Land and Water

- Mountains, plains, and plateaus are the main landforms in East Asia. The Chang and Huang rivers are major bodies of water.
- Most people in East Asia live in the plains and coastal areas.

China

Section 2: Climate and Vegetation

- East Asia's five major climate regions are semi-arid, arid, humid subtropical, humid continental, and highlands. Monsoons have a strong effect on the climate of East Asia.
- The climate of East Asia supports vegetation, such as bamboo, that is strong enough to stand seasonal differences in temperature and rainfall. Winds blow fertile soil, which is then carried by the Huang River to the North China Plain.

Japan

Section 3: Natural Resources and Land Use

- China has more mineral resources than its neighbors. Water in East Asia is used to produce hydroelectricity and to support aquaculture.
- East Asia's physical landscape leaves a small amount of land available for farming. Terraces and double-cropping are two ways East Asian farmers get the most food out of the land that is used for farming.

◆ Key Terms

Each of the statements below contains a key term from the chapter. If the statement is true, write *true*. If the statement is false, rewrite the statement to make it true.

1. A **plateau** is a dry region with little vegetation.

2. When soil is **fertile,** it is capable of supporting abundant plant growth.

3. **Population density** measures the average number of people living in a square mile or square kilometer.

4. A **monsoon** is a tropical storm that occurs over the Pacific Ocean.

5. **Deciduous** trees shed their leaves in the fall.

6. A **developed country** has a low level of industrial production.

7. A **developing country** has many industries and a well-developed economy.

8. When farmers use **double-cropping,** they build steps into hillsides to increase farmland.

Review and Assessment (continued)

◆ Comprehension and Critical Thinking

9. (a) Recall Which East Asian countries have mountains, wide plains, and plateaus?
(b) Locate Where are the Himalayas located?

10. (a) Name Name two major rivers in China.
(b) Recall Which of these rivers flows through the North China Plain?
(c) Identify Effect How does this river make the North China Plain a fertile region?

11. (a) List What are Japan's four main islands?
(b) Compare and Contrast How is the physical geography of Japan different from the physical geography of the Koreas?

12. (a) Identify Which parts of East Asia have a very high population density?
(b) Summarize Why does most of the population in China live in the eastern half of the country?

13. (a) Explain How does water affect the climates of the Koreas and Japan?
(b) Summarize What does the summer monsoon do in East Asia and in what direction does it blow?

14. (a) Define What three basic questions do countries ask when planning their economies?

(b) Summarize How do Japan and South Korea make up for their lack of mineral resources?

15. (a) Locate Where is the Three Gorges Dam?
(b) Predict How might the Three Gorges Dam affect energy production in China?

16. (a) Explain How have the farmers of East Asia made the best use of the land for farming?
(b) Apply Information Which farming method is linked to the physical landscape of East Asia?

◆ Skills Practice

Using Reliable Information on the Internet
Review the steps you followed to learn this skill. Then explain why an Internet encyclopedia is a reliable source.

◆ Writing Activity: Geography

Create a geographic dictionary of these items: plateau, plain, volcano, monsoon, mountain, peninsula. Arrange the list in alphabetical order. Write a definition, using your textbook to find a real-life example of each term. The example must be located in East Asia. Include the country where your example is located.

MAP MASTER™
Skills Activity

East Asia

Place Location For each place listed below, write the letter from the map that shows its location.

1. Himalayas
2. North China Plain
3. Huang River
4. Plateau of Tibet
5. Chang River
6. Mount Fuji

Go Online
PHSchool.com Use Web Code **ngp-6120** for an interactive map.

Standardized Test Prep

Test-Taking Tips

Some questions on standardized tests ask you to identify the main topic of a reading passage. Study the passage below. Then follow the tips to answer the sample question.

> Desert winds blow silt into the Huang River. The Huang, or Yellow, River gets its name from this brownish-yellow loess. The river carries and deposits loess to the east. The loess covers 125,000 square miles (324,000 square kilometers) on the North China Plain. This great plain is one of China's best farming regions.

TIP Some paragraphs contain a topic sentence that states its main idea. All other sentences in the paragraph support this point.

Pick the letter of the statement that best answers the question.

Which is the best topic sentence for this paragraph?

A ~~Climate influences everything from natural vegetation to agriculture.~~

B ~~Loess is rich yellow-brown silt or clay.~~

C Climate affects life in the region around the Huang River.

D The Huang River is known as China's Sorrow because of its damaging floods.

TIP Rule out answer choices that don't make sense. Then pick the best answer from the remaining choices.

Think It Through You can rule out A because the statement is too general. It could be the topic for a paragraph on any region of the world. However, B is too specific; it could be another detail in the paragraph. Similarly, D is another detail, one that might be included in a different paragraph about flooding on the Huang. The correct answer is C.

Practice Questions

Use the passage below to answer Question 1. Use the tips above to help you.

> In summer, the monsoon blows northwest from the Pacific Ocean toward the Asian continent. The summer monsoon brings hot, humid weather and rainfall to East Asia. In winter, the monsoon blows toward the east. Where they cross warm ocean waters, such as the South China Sea, these monsoons pick up moisture. Later, they drop it as rain or snow.

1. Which is the best topic sentence for the above paragraph?

   A People need rain to grow crops.

   B Monsoons have a strong effect on climate in East Asia.

   C The South China Sea is located off China's southern coast.

   D The Pacific Ocean is the deepest ocean in the world.

Use the tips above and other tips in this book to help you answer the following questions.

2. Which country takes up most of East Asia's land?

   A Japan   B Mongolia

   C China   D South Korea

3. Most of the people in Japan live

   A in coastal areas.

   B in mountainous areas.

   C on Japan's wide plains.

   D on plateaus.

4. The Huang River runs through a fertile region of East Asia called

   A Mongolia.

   B Taiwan.

   C the North China Plain.

   D Tibet.

Go Online
PHSchool.com

Use Web Code **nga-6100** for a **Chapter 8 self-test**.

Chapter

9

South, Southwest, and Central Asia: Physical Geography

Chapter Preview

 Standard Course of Study

7.2.02 Factors that influence distribution of population, resources, and climate

7.2.03 Factors that influence human migration

7.3.01 How cultures and regions are influenced by human interaction with their environment

7.5.01 How the location of natural resources affects economic development

7.5.03 Evaluate impact of economic decisions on standard of living

7.6.03 Impact of over-specialization on standard of living

SS.1.02 Summarize to select main ideas

SS.1.03 Draw inferences

SS.1.08 Use context clues and appropriate sources to gain meaning

Sections

1. **South Asia: Physical Geography**
   7.2.02, 7.2.03, SS.1.08

2. **Southwest Asia: Physical Geography**
   7.5.01, 7.5.03, 7.6.03, SS.1.03

3. **Central Asia: Physical Geography**
   7.5.01, 7.3.01, SS.1.02

 Target Reading Skill

Clarifying Meaning In this chapter, you will focus on understanding what you read by rereading and reading ahead, paraphrasing, and summarizing.

▶ **An American climbing team below the summit of Mount Everest, the world's tallest peak**

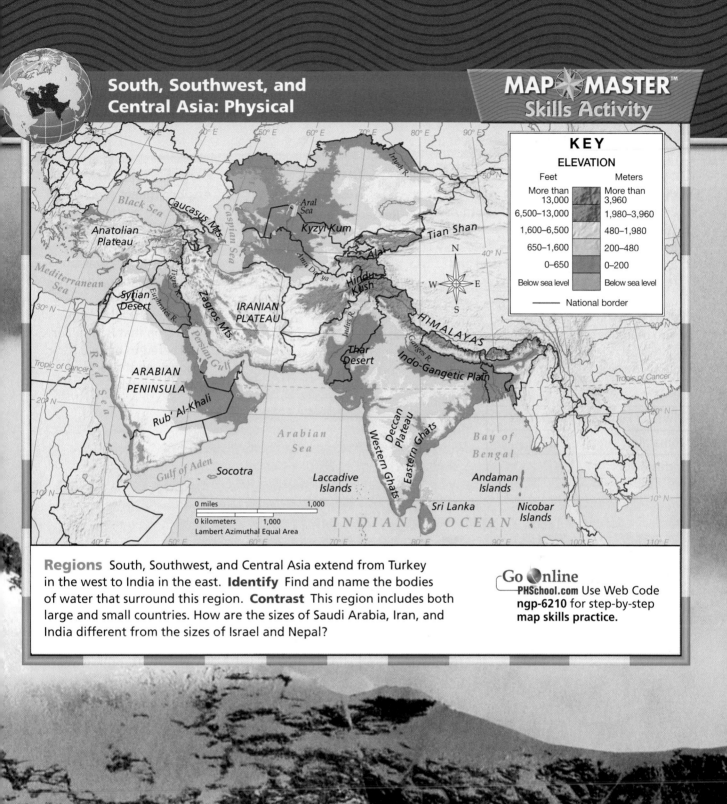

KEY

ELEVATION

Feet		Meters
More than 13,000		More than 3,960
6,500–13,000		1,980–3,960
1,600–6,500		480–1,980
650–1,600		200–480
0–650		0–200
Below sea level		Below sea level
——— National border		

Black Sea
Caucasus Mts.
Anatolian Plateau
Mediterranean Sea
Sytian Desert
Tigris R.
Euphrates R.
Zagros Mts.
IRANIAN PLATEAU
Persian Gulf
ARABIAN PENINSULA
Rub' Al-Khali
Red Sea
Gulf of Aden
Socotra
Arabian Sea
Laccadive Islands
Caspian Sea
Aral Sea
Kyzyl Kum
Amu Darya
Alai
Hindu Kush
Indus R.
Thar Desert
Western Ghats
Deccan Plateau
Eastern Ghats
Sri Lanka
Irtysh R.
Tian Shan
HIMALAYAS
Ganges R.
Indo-Gangetic Plain
Bay of Bengal
Andaman Islands
Nicobar Islands
INDIAN OCEAN
Tropic of Cancer

0 miles 1,000
0 kilometers 1,000
Lambert Azimuthal Equal Area

Regions South, Southwest, and Central Asia extend from Turkey in the west to India in the east. **Identify** Find and name the bodies of water that surround this region. **Contrast** This region includes both large and small countries. How are the sizes of Saudi Arabia, Iran, and India different from the sizes of Israel and Nepal?

Go Online
PHSchool.com Use Web Code
ngp-6210 for step-by-step
map skills practice.

Section 1

South Asia
Physical Geography

Prepare to Read

Objectives

In this section, you will

1. Learn about the landforms of South Asia.
2. Discover the most important factor that affects climate in South Asia.
3. Examine how people use the land and resources of South Asia.

Taking Notes

As you read this section, look for details about the physical features of South Asia. Copy the table below and record your findings in it.

Physical Features	Details
Himalayas	
Indus River	

Target Reading Skill

Rereading or Reading Ahead If you do not understand a certain passage, reread it to look for connections among the words and sentences. It might also help to read ahead, because a word or an idea may be explained further on.

Key Terms

- **subcontinent** (SUB kahn tih nunt) *n.* a large landmass that is a major part of a continent
- **alluvial** (uh LOO vee ul) *adj.* made of soil deposited by rivers
- **cash crop** (kash krahp) *n.* a crop that is raised or gathered to be sold for money on the local or world market

Mountain climbing in the Himalayas

Two hundred million years ago, the Indian subcontinent was attached to the east coast of Africa. A **subcontinent** is a large landmass that is a major part of a continent. Scientists believe that at that time, all of Earth's continents were joined. Starting about 200 million years ago, the Indian subcontinent broke apart from Africa and slid slowly toward Asia. About 50 million years ago, the Indian subcontinent collided with Asia. Northern India and southern Asia crumpled where they met, forming the mountains of the Himalayas. The Himalayas contain the tallest peaks in the world.

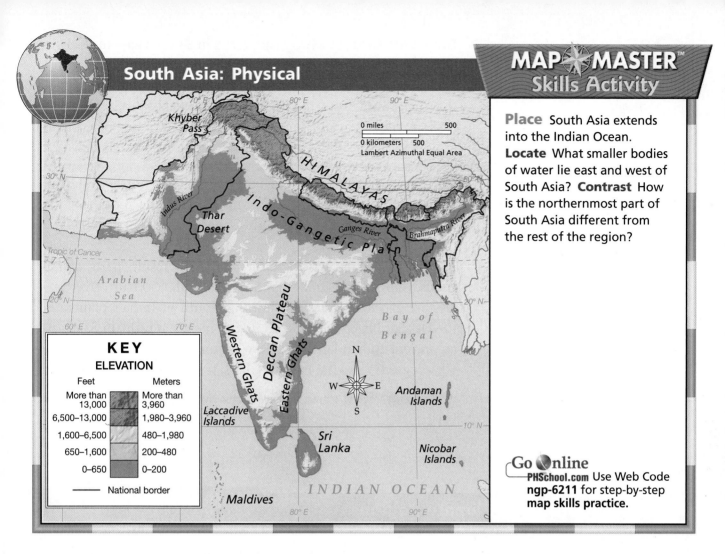

South Asia: Physical

MAP★MASTER™
Skills Activity

Place South Asia extends into the Indian Ocean. **Locate** What smaller bodies of water lie east and west of South Asia? **Contrast** How is the northernmost part of South Asia different from the rest of the region?

Go Online
PHSchool.com Use Web Code **ngp-6211** for step-by-step map skills practice.

KEY
ELEVATION

Feet	Meters
More than 13,000	More than 3,960
6,500–13,000	1,980–3,960
1,600–6,500	480–1,980
650–1,600	200–480
0–650	0–200

——— National border

Major Landforms of South Asia

The largest nation in South Asia is India. It extends from the Himalayas down to the narrow tip of the Indian subcontinent in the south. Pakistan (PAK ih stan) and Afghanistan (af GAN ih stan) lie to the west of India. Along India's northern border, the kingdoms of Nepal (nuh PAWL) and Bhutan (BOO tahn) lie along the slopes of the Himalayas. To the east is Bangladesh (BAHNG luh DESH). The island nations of Sri Lanka (sree LAHNG kuh) and the Maldives (MAL dyvz) lie off the southern tip of India.

A Natural Barrier Find the Himalayas on the map above. Notice that they form a barrier between South Asia and the rest of Asia. This huge mountain range stretches some 1,550 miles (2,500 kilometers) from east to west. Mount Everest, the world's tallest mountain, is located in the Himalayas. Mount Everest rises to 29,035 feet (8,850 meters). That's about five and a half miles high! More than 100 mountains in the Himalayas soar above 24,000 feet (7,300 meters). The Himalayas present the greatest challenge in the world to mountain climbers.

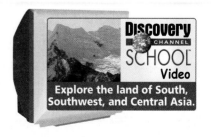

DISCOVERY CHANNEL
SCHOOL Video
Explore the land of South, Southwest, and Central Asia.

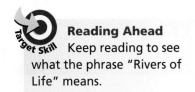

Reading Ahead
Keep reading to see what the phrase "Rivers of Life" means.

Rivers of Life The two major rivers in South Asia—the Ganges and the Indus—begin in the Himalayas. The Ganges flows across northern India and empties into the Bay of Bengal. The Indus flows westward from the Himalayas into Pakistan. South Asia's rivers carry water and minerals to support farming. The plains around the rivers, therefore, are fertile and heavily populated.

Plains and Plateaus Huge plains cover the northern part of the Indian subcontinent. They stretch from the mouth of the Indus River to the mouth of the Ganges River. These plains are **alluvial,** which means they are made of soil deposited by rivers. Alluvial plains have rich, fertile soil. As a result, parts of the Indus, Ganges, and Brahmaputra (brah muh POO truh) river valleys are excellent areas for farming. South of India's plains lies the Deccan Plateau. The word *deccan* means "south" in Sanskrit, an ancient Indian language. Two mountain ranges, the Western Ghats (gawts) and the Eastern Ghats, frame the Deccan Plateau.

✓ **Reading Check** Name the two major rivers in South Asia.

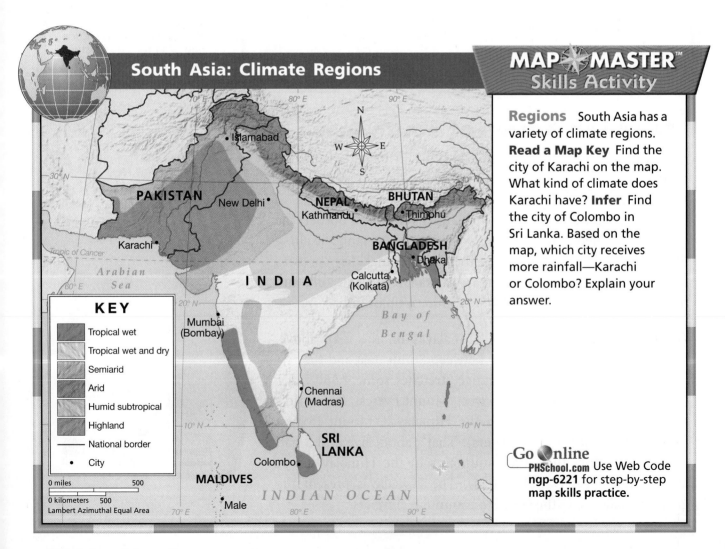

South Asia: Climate Regions

MAP MASTER™
Skills Activity

Regions South Asia has a variety of climate regions. **Read a Map Key** Find the city of Karachi on the map. What kind of climate does Karachi have? **Infer** Find the city of Colombo in Sri Lanka. Based on the map, which city receives more rainfall—Karachi or Colombo? Explain your answer.

KEY

- Tropical wet
- Tropical wet and dry
- Semiarid
- Arid
- Humid subtropical
- Highland
- National border
- • City

0 miles 500
0 kilometers 500
Lambert Azimuthal Equal Area

Go Online
PHSchool.com Use Web Code ngp-6221 for step-by-step map skills practice.

The Climates of South Asia

Monsoons are the single most important factor that affects the climate of South Asia. Monsoons are winds that change direction with the change of seasons. The summer monsoons blow across South Asia from the southwest. During the winter, the winds change direction and blow from the northeast.

The Summer Monsoons From June to early October, steady winds blow over the surface of the Arabian Sea and the Indian Ocean. The air picks up a great deal of moisture. Then, the air passes over the hot land along the western tip of India. As the moist air passes over the hot land, it rises and loses its moisture in the form of rain. The rains that fall along the coastline cool the land somewhat. When the next air mass blows in, it travels farther inland before losing its supply of moisture. In this way, the monsoon rains work their way inland until they finally reach the Himalayas.

The Winter Monsoons During the winter months, the monsoons change direction, and the winds blow from the frigid northeast. These winds move dry, cold air toward South Asia. The Himalayas block the cold air. The countries of South Asia enjoy dry winter weather, with temperatures averaging 70°F (21°C).

✓ **Reading Check** What are monsoons?

Land Use in South Asia

About 70 percent of the population in South Asia live in rural areas. Most of these people are crowded into fertile river valleys. Here, they grow whatever crops the soil and climate of their particular region will allow.

Links to
Science

India's Salt Lake During the hot months, the 90-square-mile (230-square-kilometer) Sambhar (SAM bar) Lake in northwestern India is dry. Oddly, during this time the lake bed looks as though it is covered in snow. The white blanket is not snow but a sheet of salt. This salt supply has been harvested as far back as the 1500s. It is still an important resource for the region today.

Tea Harvest in India
Tea is a major crop in India. Workers harvest fresh tea leaves by hand. The leaves are then processed and dried. Dried tea is sometimes packed in tea bags. **Infer** *How can you tell harvesting leaves is labor-intensive?*

The densely populated city of Dhaka is Bangladesh's capital.

Cash Crops Some countries of South Asia produce cash crops such as tea, cotton, coffee, and sugar cane. A **cash crop** is one that is raised or gathered to be sold for money on the local or world market. Growing cash crops often brings in a great deal of money, but it can also cause problems. The economy of a region can become dependent on world prices for the crops. When prices fall, the cash crops do not bring in enough money. When cash crops fail, farmers may not earn enough money.

Mineral Resources The earth beneath India holds a vast supply of mineral wealth. Iron ore and coal are plentiful. Other important minerals include copper, limestone, and bauxite—an ore that contains aluminum. India has only a small amount of oil. Because of this, India relies heavily on hydroelectricity and nuclear power plants.

Population and Land Use South Asia is one of the most densely populated regions in the world. Most of the people live in areas that have plenty of rainfall. These include coastal areas, as well as northeastern India and the country of Bangladesh. The population is lower in areas where it is more difficult for people to live.

✓ **Reading Check** Where do most of the people in South Asia live?

Section 1 Assessment

Key Terms

Review the key terms at the beginning of this section. Use each term in a sentence that explains its meaning.

Target Reading Skill

What words were you able to clarify by rereading?

Comprehension and Critical Thinking

1. (a) Recall Which landform forms a natural barrier between South Asia and the rest of Asia?

(b) Connect How do the Ganges and the Indus rivers relate to this landform?

2. (a) Identify From which direction does the summer monsoon blow across South Asia?

(b) Contrast How is the winter monsoon different from the summer monsoon in South Asia?

3. (a) List Give some examples of the cash crops raised in South Asia.

(b) Summarize Why may cash crops cause problems for the economies of South Asian countries?

Writing Activity

Write a two-paragraph description of a television show about the geography and resources of South Asia. In your description, include at least three locations in South Asia. Tell what your camera crew will film in each location.

For: An activity on South Asia
Visit: PHSchool.com
Web Code: ngd-6201

Southwest Asia
Physical Geography

Prepare to Read

Objectives

In this section, you will

1. Learn about the major landforms of Southwest Asia.
2. Find out what the two most important resources in Southwest Asia are.
3. Examine how people use the land in Southwest Asia.

Taking Notes

As you read this section, look for details about Southwest Asia's major physical features, including climate. Copy the table below and record your findings in it.

Physical Features of Southwest Asia	Details
Desert	
Persian Gulf	
Arabian Peninsula	
Dry climate	

Target Reading Skill

Paraphrasing When you paraphrase, you state what you have read in your own words. Here is a paraphrase of the first paragraph under the red heading on page 257: "Land in Southwest Asia is used mainly for agriculture, nomadic herding, and producing oil. The region has a small percentage of arable land. Most farming takes place in the northern part of the region."

As you read this section, paraphrase the first paragraph after each red heading.

Key Terms

- **oasis** (oh AY sis) *n.* an area in a desert region where fresh water is usually available from an underground spring or well
- **petroleum** (puh TROH lee um) *n.* an oily liquid formed from the remains of ancient plants and animals; a fuel
- **nonrenewable resource** (nahn rih NOO uh bul REE sawrs) *n.* a natural resource that cannot be quickly replaced once it is used
- **standard of living** (STAN durd uv LIV ing) *n.* a measurement of a person's or a group's education, housing, health, and nutrition

A parachutist lands in the Rub' al-Khali desert in Saudi Arabia.

The Rub' al-Khali (roob ahl KHAH lee), or "Empty Quarter," of the Arabian Peninsula is the largest all-sand desert in the world. Almost nothing lives in this flat, hot territory. Ten years may pass between rainfalls. The sand dunes do not stay in one place—they gradually move as they are blown by the wind.

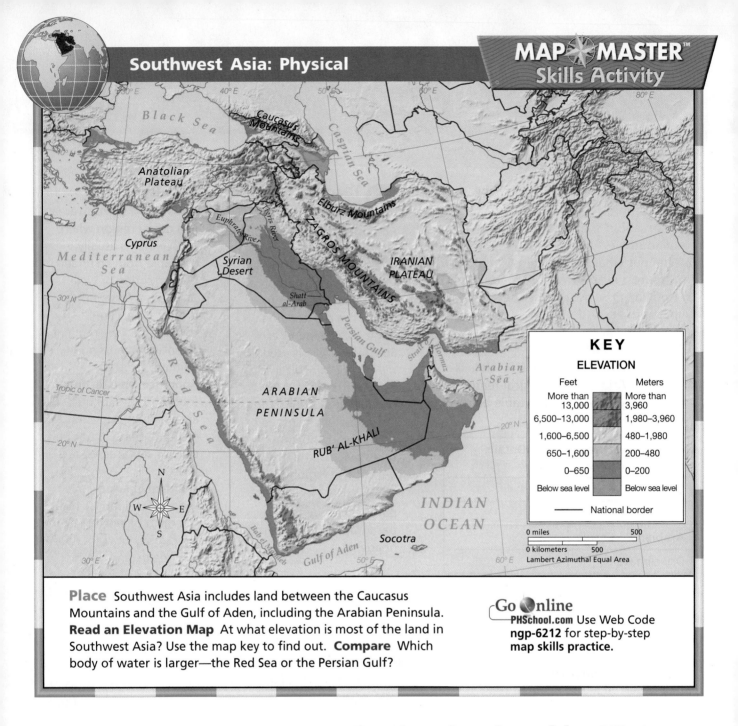

Black Sea

Caucasus Mountains

Anatolian Plateau

Caspian Sea

Cyprus

Euphrates River

Tigris River

Elburz Mountains

ZAGROS MOUNTAINS

IRANIAN PLATEAU

Mediterranean Sea

Syrian Desert

Shatt al-Arab

Persian Gulf

Strait of Hormuz

Arabian Sea

Tropic of Cancer

Red Sea

ARABIAN PENINSULA

RUB' AL-KHALI

INDIAN OCEAN

Gulf of Aden

Bab el Mandeb

Socotra

KEY
ELEVATION

Feet		Meters
More than 13,000		More than 3,960
6,500–13,000		1,980–3,960
1,600–6,500		480–1,980
650–1,600		200–480
0–650		0–200
Below sea level		Below sea level

—— National border

0 miles 500
0 kilometers 500
Lambert Azimuthal Equal Area

Place Southwest Asia includes land between the Caucasus Mountains and the Gulf of Aden, including the Arabian Peninsula. **Read an Elevation Map** At what elevation is most of the land in Southwest Asia? Use the map key to find out. **Compare** Which body of water is larger—the Red Sea or the Persian Gulf?

Go Online
PHSchool.com Use Web Code **ngp-6212** for step-by-step map skills practice.

A Dry Region Bordered by Water

Southwest Asia contains some of Earth's largest deserts. The Rub'al-Khali is almost as big as the state of Texas. Deserts also cover much of the country of Iran, Syria, and Iraq. Many parts of Southwest Asia receive little rain. Water is very valuable here.

Some of the region's deserts are covered with sand. In others, the land is strewn with pebbles, gravel, and boulders. Travelers passing through these dry areas are relieved when they find an oasis (oh AY sis). An **oasis** is a small area in a desert region where fresh water is usually available from an underground spring or well. Sometimes, an oasis can support a community of people. Farmers can grow crops. Nomadic shepherds can raise livestock.

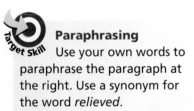

Paraphrasing
Use your own words to paraphrase the paragraph at the right. Use a synonym for the word *relieved*.

Two Historic Rivers Few plants grow in most Southwest Asian deserts. Some of the most fertile soil in the world, however, lies along the Tigris (TY gris) and Euphrates (yoo FRAY teez) rivers. When these rivers flood, they deposit rich soil along their banks. The Tigris and the Euphrates rivers begin in Turkey and flow south through Iraq. They join to form the Shatt-al-Arab, which flows into the Persian Gulf. In ancient times, the land between these two rivers supported one of the world's first civilizations. The region was known as Mesopotamia. Here, people learned to raise plants and animals for food, relying on the rich soil provided by the rivers.

Mountains and Plateaus As you can see on the physical map of Southwest Asia, the Tigris and Euphrates rivers begin in the mountains of Turkey. Iran also has mountains. The Zagros Mountains extend along the western part of Iran. The Elburz Mountains extend along the northern coast of Iran. The mountains give way to large plateaus in both Turkey and Iran.

Seas and Gulfs Much of the land of Southwest Asia borders bodies of water that separate countries within the region. These bodies of water also separate Southwest Asia from other regions. The Red Sea separates Southwest Asia and Africa. The Mediterranean Sea forms Southwest Asia's western border. The Black Sea forms Turkey's northern border. The Caspian Sea forms part of the boundary between Southwest Asia and Central Asia. The Persian Gulf separates Iran from the Arabian Peninsula.

Iraq's capital, Baghdad, lies on both banks of the Tigris River. The small photo shows a mosque, or Islamic place of worship, in Istanbul, Turkey.

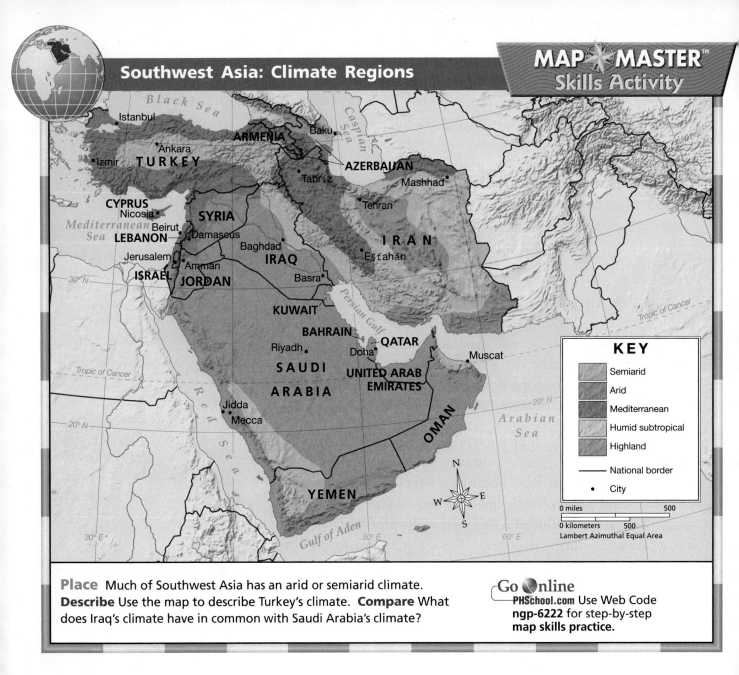

Place Much of Southwest Asia has an arid or semiarid climate. **Describe** Use the map to describe Turkey's climate. **Compare** What does Iraq's climate have in common with Saudi Arabia's climate?

KEY

	Semiarid
	Arid
	Mediterranean
	Humid subtropical
	Highland
——	National border
•	City

0 miles 500
0 kilometers 500
Lambert Azimuthal Equal Area

Go Online
PHSchool.com Use Web Code
ngp-6222 for step-by-step
map skills practice.

A Hot, Dry Climate Most of Southwest Asia has an arid or a semiarid climate. Much of the region receives less than 10 inches (25 centimeters) of rain each year. It is no wonder, then, that nearly two thirds of Southwest Asia is desert!

Because the desert air contains little moisture, few clouds form over the dry land. As a result, temperatures may reach as high as 125°F (52°C) during the day. At night, they may drop to as low as 40°F (4°C).

Some parts of Southwest Asia have a Mediterranean climate, with hot, dry summers and mild, rainy winters. The coasts of the Mediterranean, Black, and Caspian seas as well as the mountainous areas of the region have a Mediterranean climate.

✓ **Reading Check** **Which two countries in Southwest Asia have mountains?**

Southwest Asia's Major Natural Resources

The two most important natural resources in Southwest Asia are petroleum and water. **Petroleum** (puh TROH lee um) is an oily, flammable liquid formed from the remains of ancient plants and animals. It is found under Earth's surface. Petroleum deposits take millions of years to form. Petroleum is a **nonrenewable resource**—a natural resource that cannot be quickly replaced once it is used.

Petroleum is the source of gasoline and other fuels. People all over the world depend on petroleum to fuel cars and trucks, provide energy for industry, and heat homes. Petroleum is the natural resource that brings the most money into Southwest Asia. Water, however, is the resource that people there need most. Since much of Southwest Asia has a dry climate, the water in the region must be used carefully.

Petroleum Large deposits of petroleum, also called oil, can be found in only a few places on Earth. As a result, petroleum-rich countries play a key role in the world's economy. Southwest Asia is the largest oil-producing region in the world. Petroleum is Southwest Asia's greatest export.

Oil wealth allows many Southwest Asian countries to increase the standard of living of their people. **Standard of living** is a measurement of a person's or a group's education, housing, health, and nutrition. These countries have enough money to build schools and hospitals and to import goods from other countries. They can also import workers. Most of the people living in oil-rich Kuwait are citizens of other countries, including Pakistan, India, and Bangladesh.

Southwest Asia has more than half of the world's oil reserves. But some countries in the region have little or no oil. These countries tend to have a lower standard of living than their oil-rich neighbors. They do not have the income that petroleum brings.

Oil pipelines in Saudi Arabia

Water To grow crops in this dry region, people usually must irrigate their land. Saudi Arabia, for example, has no permanent rivers. It has wadis (WAH deez), or stream beds that may hold water when seasonal rains fall but are dry much of the year. People there irrigate their crops by pumping water from deep underground wells. In other parts of Southwest Asia, wells are not as necessary. People use water from rivers and streams to irrigate the dry areas of the country.

The nations of Southwest Asia have continued to build irrigation systems. But irrigation cannot solve the problem of water scarcity. Too much irrigation can use up the water that is available. In an area with little rainfall, water that is taken from a river is not soon replaced. When a river runs through more than one nation, each nation is affected by the others' irrigation systems.

Water from the Sea of Galilee is carried to southern Israel by the National Water Carrier.

✓ **Reading Check** What benefits has petroleum brought to the countries of Southwest Asia?

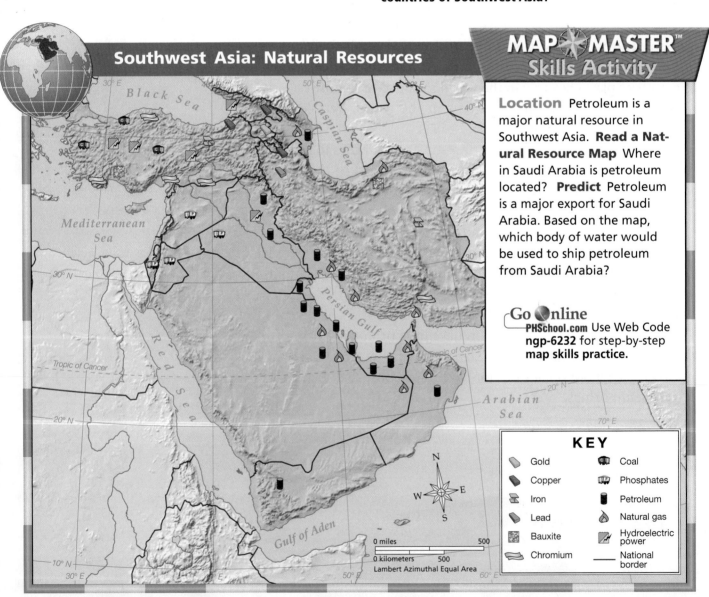

Southwest Asia: Natural Resources

MAP MASTER™
Skills Activity

Location Petroleum is a major natural resource in Southwest Asia. **Read a Natural Resource Map** Where in Saudi Arabia is petroleum located? **Predict** Petroleum is a major export for Saudi Arabia. Based on the map, which body of water would be used to ship petroleum from Saudi Arabia?

Go Online
PHSchool.com Use Web Code **ngp-6232** for step-by-step map skills practice.

KEY

◇	Gold	🚃	Coal
▱	Copper	🚛	Phosphates
⬛	Iron	▮	Petroleum
◇	Lead	◒	Natural gas
▦	Bauxite	◿	Hydroelectric power
⬭	Chromium	—	National border

Using the Land in Southwest Asia

People use the land in Southwest Asia in three major ways: for agriculture, for nomadic herding, and for producing oil. Because of the region's climate, only a small percentage of the region is made up of arable land. Most of this farmland is located in the northern part of the region, with commercial farming taking place along the coasts. There, the Mediterranean climate makes it possible for people to grow a wide variety of crops.

Various commercial farm products are raised in Israel and Turkey. In Israel, these include citrus fruits, cotton, peanuts, and sugar cane. Turkey's commercial farms produce such crops as wheat, barley, cotton, sugar beets, fruits, olives, and corn.

For centuries, Arabic-speaking nomadic herders known as Bedouins (BED oo inz) have lived in Southwest Asia's deserts herding camels, goats, and sheep. Instead of settling in one place, Bedouins moved over a large area of land, seeking grass and water for their animals. Today the Bedouin make up about 10 percent of the population of Southwest Asia. In recent times, settlement policies of countries in Southwest Asia have forced many Bedouins to settle in one place.

✔ **Reading Check** What are some of Turkey's commercial farming crops?

Section 2 Assessment

Key Terms
Review the key terms at the beginning of this section. Use each term in a sentence that explains its meaning.

Target Reading Skill
Reread the first paragraph after the heading Two Historic Rivers on page 253. Then, using your own words, paraphrase the paragraph. Begin your paraphrase with the sentence, "Rich soil lies along the banks of the Tigris and Euphrates rivers."

Comprehension and Critical Thinking

1. (a) Recall What kind of land covers much of Southwest Asia?

(b) Identify Name one major desert, two seas, and one mountain range in Southwest Asia.

(c) Explain Give a location for the desert, the seas, and the mountain range in the previous question.

2. (a) Identify What are the two most important natural resources in Southwest Asia?

(b) Explain Why are irrigation systems important in Southwest Asia?

3. (a) Recall What are three major ways that people use the land in Southwest Asia?

(b) Summarize What are some commercial farm products of Southwest Asia?

Writing Activity
Write a paragraph that describes water from the point of view of a person living in the United States on the coast of the Atlantic Ocean. Then write another paragraph from the point of view of a person living in a desert region in Southwest Asia. Exchange your paragraphs with a partner. How are your paragraphs similar to or different from those of your partner?

Go Online
PHSchool.com

For: An activity on Southwest Asia
Visit: PHSchool.com
Web Code: ngd-6202

Skills for Life

Identifying Main Ideas

Keith was just starting his homework when his mother popped her head into the room.

"What assignment are you working on?" she asked.

"I'm reading an article on petroleum mining in Southwest Asia," Keith replied. "Did you know that more than half of Saudi Arabia's oil reserves are found in just eight oil fields, including the largest onshore oil field in the world?"

"That's a fascinating detail," Keith's mother said. "What's the main idea of the article?"

"That's the assignment," Keith answered. "We have to read the article and identify the main idea."

 SS.1.02 Summarize to select main ideas

Identifying main ideas is an essential study skill.

A main idea is the most important information in a paragraph or reading passage. A main idea is not the same as a topic. Knowing how to identify main ideas will make you a better reader and a better student.

Learn the Skill

To identify the main idea in a paragraph, follow these steps:

1. **Identify the topic of the paragraph.** The topic of a paragraph tells what the paragraph is about. Look for a sentence that identifies the topic. It is called a "topic sentence," and it is often the first sentence of a paragraph. Also, it sometimes—but not always—states the main idea.

2. **Look for an idea that all the sentences in the paragraph have in common.** In a well-written paragraph, most of the sentences provide details that support or explain the main idea.

3. **State the main idea in your own words.** Write what you think is the main idea in your own words. Write a complete sentence. Avoid writing a sentence that is too broad or too specific. Remember that a main idea focuses on the most important information about the topic. Even if a detail is interesting, it may not be the most important information. A main idea should always be a complete sentence.

Practice the Skill

Now turn to page 253 and study the first paragraph under the heading Southwest Asia's Major Natural Resources. Use the steps on the previous page to find the main idea of the paragraph.

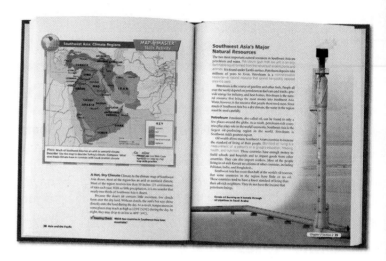

1 What is the topic of the paragraph? Remember that the topic of a paragraph is not necessarily the same as a main idea. For example, the topic of a paragraph is usually a subject, such as petroleum mining in Southwest Asia.

2 In a word or phrase, write down what you think each sentence is about. Then look at the words you've listed and find a common idea among them.

3 Look for the most important information about the topic. Write a complete sentence that states the most important information. Be sure your sentence focuses on the most important information. Why is the following statement too broad? *Southwest Asia has many natural resources.* Why is the following statement too specific? *Petroleum is found under Earth's surface.*

Apply the Skill

Read the following paragraph. Use the steps you learned to write a statement giving the main idea of this paragraph.

With about one fourth of the world's oil, Saudi Arabia is the leading country in the Organization of Petroleum Exporting Countries (OPEC). OPEC is an organization of countries with economies that rely on money from oil exports. As a group, OPEC decides how much oil its members will produce and at what price to sell it. Besides Saudi Arabia, members consist of Algeria, Indonesia, Iran, Iraq, Kuwait, Libya, Nigeria, Qatar, the United Arab Emirates, and Venezuela. OPEC produces about 40 percent of the world's crude oil.

Prepare to Read

Objectives

In this section, you will

1. Learn about the main physical features of Central Asia.
2. Discover which natural resources are important in Central Asia.
3. Find out how people use the land in Central Asia.

Taking Notes

As you read this section, look for details about the physical geography of Central Asia. Copy the diagram below and record your findings in it.

Land	Climate	Natural Resources
• •	• •	• •

Target Reading Skill

Summarizing When you summarize, you review and state the main points you have read. Summarizing is a good technique to help you better understand a text. A good summary identifies the main ideas, states them in the order in which they appear, and notes when one event causes another to happen. As you read, pause occasionally to summarize what you have read.

Key Term

• **steppe** (step) *n.* vast, mostly level, treeless plains that are covered in grasses

On the treeless plains of Central Asia sprawls the Baikonur (by kuh NOOR) Cosmodrome, the largest space-launch center in the world. Baikonur is the site of several historic spaceflights. In 1957, the first artificial satellite was launched from Baikonur. The first mission to put a human in space blasted off from Baikonur in 1961. In 2003, the *Mars Express,* a European mission to send a spacecraft to Mars, was launched from Baikonur.

Baikonur is located in Kazakhstan (kah zahk STAHN), the largest and northernmost country in Central Asia. To its south are Uzbekistan (ooz BEK ih stan), Kyrgyzstan (kihr gih STAN), Turkmenistan (turk MEN ih stan), and Tajikistan (tah jik ih STAN). Afghanistan forms the southern border of Central Asia. Except for Afghanistan, the countries of Central Asia were once part of the Soviet Union.

This rocket, carrying the *Mars Express,* was launched from Baikonur in 2003.

Central Asia's Main Physical Features

Central Asia's main physical features are highlands, deserts, and steppes. **Steppes** are vast, mostly level, treeless plains covered with grassland vegetation. Central Asia's mountains are in the southeastern part of the region. The Tian Shan and Pamir mountain ranges cover much of Kyrgyzstan and Tajikistan. The Tian Shan range also extends into China. The Pamir extend into Afghanistan, where they meet the Hindu Kush mountains.

To the west of these mountain ranges, the elevation drops and the land flattens. The Kara Kum desert covers much of the land in Turkmenistan. The Kyzyl Kum desert covers much of neighboring Uzbekistan. The Kirghiz Steppe is located in Kazakhstan.

Steppes in Central Asia

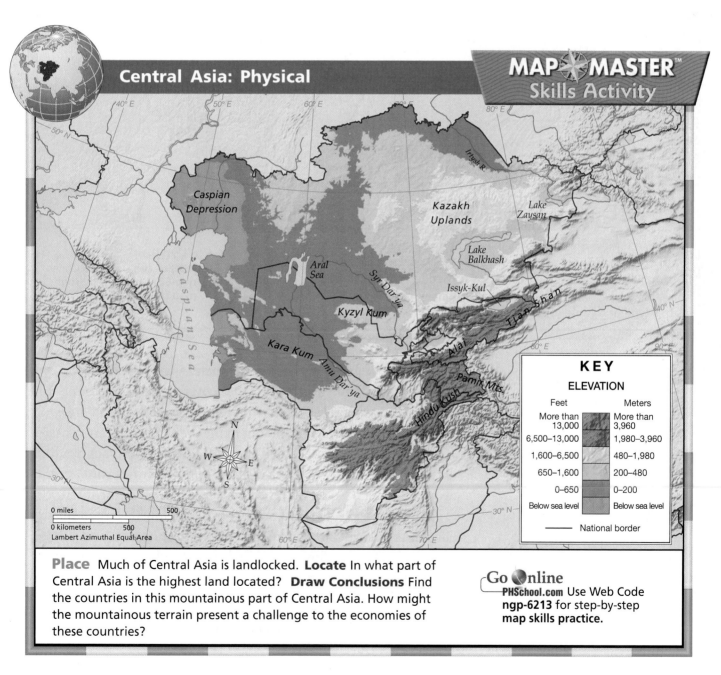

Central Asia: Physical

MAP MASTER™ Skills Activity

KEY
ELEVATION

Feet		Meters
More than 13,000		More than 3,960
6,500–13,000		1,980–3,960
1,600–6,500		480–1,980
650–1,600		200–480
0–650		0–200
Below sea level		Below sea level

——— National border

0 miles 500
0 kilometers 500
Lambert Azimuthal Equal Area

Place Much of Central Asia is landlocked. **Locate** In what part of Central Asia is the highest land located? **Draw Conclusions** Find the countries in this mountainous part of Central Asia. How might the mountainous terrain present a challenge to the economies of these countries?

Go Online
PHSchool.com Use Web Code **ngp-6213** for step-by-step map skills practice.

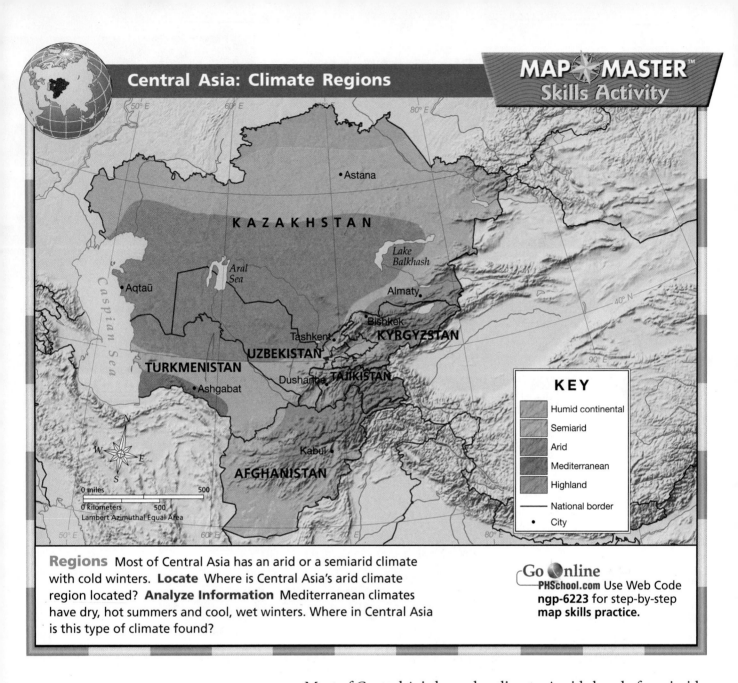

Central Asia: Climate Regions

KAZAKHSTAN

• Astana

Lake
Balkhash

Aral
Sea

• Aqtaū

Caspian Sea

Almaty •

Bishkek

Tashkent •

KYRGYZSTAN

UZBEKISTAN

TURKMENISTAN

Dushanbe • **TAJIKISTAN**

• Ashgabat

Kabul •

AFGHANISTAN

0 miles 500
0 kilometers 500
Lambert Azimuthal Equal Area

N
W E
S

KEY

Humid continental
Semiarid
Arid
Mediterranean
Highland
—— National border
• City

Regions Most of Central Asia has an arid or a semiarid climate with cold winters. **Locate** Where is Central Asia's arid climate region located? **Analyze Information** Mediterranean climates have dry, hot summers and cool, wet winters. Where in Central Asia is this type of climate found?

Go Online
PHSchool.com Use Web Code
ngp-6223 for step-by-step
map skills practice.

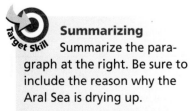

Summarizing
Summarize the paragraph at the right. Be sure to include the reason why the Aral Sea is drying up.

Most of Central Asia has a dry climate. A wide band of semiarid land surrounds the arid region that covers much of the interior. The arid areas receive less precipitation than the semiarid areas.

Two bodies of water stand out in the dry region of Central Asia. They are the Caspian Sea and the Aral Sea. The Caspian Sea, the largest lake in the world, is actually a salt lake. It has some of the world's largest oil reserves. The Aral Sea is located in the interior.

Also a salt lake, the Aral Sea was once the fourth-largest inland lake in the world. Now many boats there rest on dry land. In the 1960s, the former Soviet Union began to channel water from rivers that feed the sea to irrigate crops. As a result, the Aral Sea began to dry up.

✓ **Reading Check** What type of climate does most of Central Asia have?

Natural Resources in Central Asia

As in Southwest Asia, petroleum is a major natural resource in Central Asia. Another major natural resource in the region is natural gas. Kazakhstan is one of three Central Asian countries that have large oil and gas reserves. The other two are Uzbekistan and Turkmenistan. Turkmenistan has the fifth-largest reserve of natural gas in the world. These countries are working to develop the oil and gas industry.

Central Asia has other valuable minerals in addition to petroleum and natural gas. Kazakhstan has rich deposits of coal, much of which it exports to Russia, Ukraine, and Kyrgyzstan. Kazakhstan is the largest exporter of coal to other former Soviet republics as well. Kyrgyzstan, Tajikistan, and Uzbekistan are important gold producers. Other major mineral resources in the region are copper, iron ore, lead, and uranium.

✓ **Reading Check** What are two major natural resources in Central Asia?

Drilling for oil in Kazakhstan

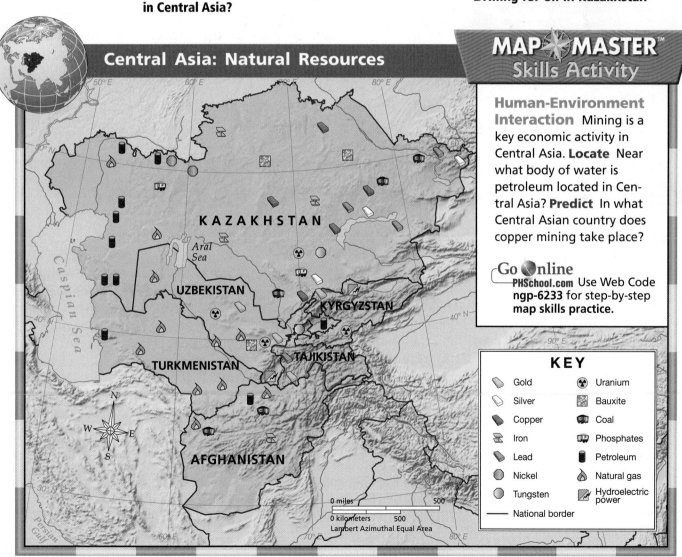

Central Asia: Natural Resources

MAP MASTER™ Skills Activity

Human-Environment Interaction Mining is a key economic activity in Central Asia. **Locate** Near what body of water is petroleum located in Central Asia? **Predict** In what Central Asian country does copper mining take place?

Go Online
PHSchool.com Use Web Code **ngp-6233** for step-by-step map skills practice.

KEY

Gold		Uranium	
Silver		Bauxite	
Copper		Coal	
Iron		Phosphates	
Lead		Petroleum	
Nickel		Natural gas	
Tungsten		Hydroelectric power	
— National border			

0 miles 500
0 kilometers 500
Lambert Azimuthal Equal Area

Abandoned boats lie rusting on land that was once the bottom of the Aral Sea.

Land Use in Central Asia

Most of the land in Central Asia is used for agriculture, especially livestock raising and commercial farming. People in Central Asia have raised sheep, horses, goats, and camels for thousands of years. Cotton is a major crop in Uzbekistan, Turkmenistan, and Tajikistan.

Agriculture in Central Asia depends on irrigation. In the 1960s, the Soviet Union started a huge irrigation project to bring water to Central Asia. The Soviet Union wanted to increase cotton production. Canals were built to carry fresh water from two rivers to irrigate the cotton fields. Between 1960 and 1980, cotton production in the Soviet Union more than tripled.

The irrigation projects turned Central Asia into a leading cotton producer. But they also caused major damage to the Aral Sea. The Amu Darya and Sry Darya rivers flow into the Aral Sea. Over the decades, heavy irrigation has taken great amounts of water from these two rivers. As a result, the Aral Sea is drying up. The land around the Aral Sea is affected, too. Huge quantities of pesticides were used on the cotton crops. These chemicals have polluted the soil. The destruction of the Aral Sea has been called one of the world's worst environmental disasters.

✓ **Reading Check** How has irrigation affected the land in Central Asia?

Section 3 Assessment

Key Terms
Review the key terms at the beginning of the section. Use each term in a sentence that explains its meaning.

Target Reading Skill
Write a summary of the first paragraph under the heading Natural Resources in Central Asia on page 263. Be sure to use your own words and include the main idea and details in the order in which they appeared.

Comprehension and Critical Thinking
1. (a) Recall What are Central Asia's three main physical features?

(b) Transfer Information If you were to draw a map of Central Asia, where would these main physical features be located?

2. (a) Identify What are two important natural resources in Central Asia?

(b) Draw Inferences With which Central Asian country might an American energy company want to work to develop natural gas resources? Explain why.

3. (a) Explain What major crop raised in Uzbekistan, Turkmenistan, and Tajikistan depends on irrigation?

(b) Identify Cause and Effect What were the effects of irrigation on the Aral Sea?

Writing Activity
As in many regions around the world, the economies of Central Asian countries depend on the availability of water. Write a paragraph suggesting ways in which your community can wisely conserve water.

For: An activity on Central Asia
Visit: PHSchool.com
Web Code: ngd-6203

◆ Chapter Summary

Section 1: South Asia: Physical Geography

- The Himalayas are a major landform in South Asia. The region also includes the Ganges and Indus rivers, fertile plains, and a plateau framed by the Western Ghats and the Eastern Ghats.
- The climate of South Asia is greatly affected by the monsoons.
- South Asia is a densely populated and generally rural region. Most of the people work in agriculture, and most of the land is used for farming.

Section 2: Southwest Asia: Physical Geography

Israel

- Much of Southwest Asia is a peninsula. The region has a dry climate and contains some of Earth's largest deserts.
- Petroleum and water are Southwest Asia's most important and valuable natural resources.
- Land in Southwest Asia is used mainly for agriculture, for nomadic herding, and for producing oil.

Section 3: Central Asia: Physical Geography

- Highlands, deserts, steppes, and a generally dry climate are Central Asia's main physical features. Much of the region is located inland.
- Central Asia's most valuable natural resources are oil and natural gas.
- Most of the land in Central Asia is used for agriculture, especially livestock raising and commercial farming. Because the region is dry, agriculture in Central Asia depends on irrigation.

India

◆ Key Terms

Match the definitions in Column I with the key terms in Column II.

Column I

1. a large landmass that is a major part of a continent
2. a crop that is raised to be sold for money on the local or world market
3. an oily liquid used as a fuel
4. an area in a desert region where fresh water is usually found
5. a natural resource that cannot be quickly replaced once it is used up
6. a measurement of a person's or group's education, housing, health, and nutrition
7. a vast, mostly level, treeless plain

Column II

A standard of living

B oasis

C steppe

D petroleum

E subcontinent

F nonrenewable resource

G cash crop

◆ Comprehension and Critical Thinking

8. (a) Define What are the two most important rivers in South Asia?
(b) Identify Effects How do the rivers of South Asia affect farmland?

9. (a) Recall What percentage of the population in South Asia lives in rural areas?
(b) Apply Information How does rainfall relate to population patterns in South Asia?

10. (a) Locate Where are the Tigris and Euphrates rivers located?
(b) Analyze Information What are some of the factors that explain why one of the world's first civilizations grew in Mesopotamia rather than on the Arabian Peninsula?

11. (a) Identify What is Southwest Asia's greatest export?
(b) Infer Southwest Asia has more than half of the world's oil reserves. Why might the United States have an interest in this region?

12. (a) Name Name one way that people use the land in Southwest Asia.

(b) Predict Where would you expect to find a commercial farm in Southwest Asia—in Saudi Arabia or in Turkey? Give at least two reasons to support your answer.

13. (a) List What are three facts about the geography of Central Asia?
(b) Summarize Why is the Aral Sea shrinking?

◆ Skills Practice

Identifying Main Ideas Review the steps you followed on page 258 to learn how to identify main ideas. Then re-read the first paragraph on page 263. Write a sentence that states the main idea.

◆ Writing Activity: Science

Suppose that you are a science reporter assigned to write about the Aral Sea. Do research to learn more about how the area around the Aral Sea has been affected by heavy irrigation. Write a brief article about the current situation.

MAP MASTER™
Skills Activity

South, Southwest, and Central Asia

Place Location For each place listed below, write the letter from the map that shows its location.

1. Rub' al-Khali
2. Mediterranean Sea
3. Euphrates River
4. Himalayas
5. Indian Ocean
6. Aral Sea

Go Online
PHSchool.com Use Web Code
ngp-6220 for step-by-step
map skills practice.

Standardized Test Prep

Test-Taking Tips

Some questions on standardized tests ask you to analyze parts of a map. Study the map key below. Then follow the tips to answer the sample question.

KEY

Feet	Elevation	Meters
Over 13,000		Over 3,960
6,500–13,000		1,980–3,960
1,600–6,500		480–1,980
650–1,600		200–480
0–650		0–200
Below sea level		Below sea level

TIP On a map key, the color column lines up with the data on the information column or columns. To find the required information, move from a given color to the data on the left or right.

Pick the letter that best answers the question.

On an elevation map, most of the area around the Ganges River is colored green. According to the key at the left, how many meters is the elevation in that area?

A below sea level

B 0–200

C 0–650

D 650–1,600

TIP Preview the question. Keep it in mind as you study the information on the map key.

Practice Questions

Use the tips above and other tips in this book to help you answer the following questions.

1. Scientists think that about 50 million years ago, the Indian subcontinent slowly collided with Asia to form
   A the island nation of Sri Lanka.
   B the Western Ghats.
   C the Himalayas.
   D Mesopotamia.

2. The alluvial plains in northern India make the area ideal for
   A mining.
   B farming.
   C aquaculture.
   D hydroelectricity.

3. South Asian countries have climates with warm, dry winters because
   A they are located along the Equator.
   B they are located in a desert region.
   C the Himalayas block cold air blown by the winter monsoon.
   D the Eastern Ghats block cold air blown by the winter monsoon.

Use the passage below to answer Question 4.

In the winter, the people of eastern Kazakhstan wrap themselves in fur to brave the freezing temperatures. Snow covers the ground as far as the eye can see. Livestock must dig through the ice to feed on the tough grass underneath. But the straight roads of the countryside never need to be plowed. Engineers built the roads slightly higher than the surrounding land. The strong winds keep the roads free of snow.

4. This paragraph is missing a topic sentence. What is the best topic sentence for this paragraph?
   A Winters in eastern Kazakhstan are extremely cold and snowy.
   B Engineers in Kazakhstan are among the best in the world.
   C Some people in eastern Kazakhstan raise livestock for a living.
   D Summers in Kazakhstan are extremely hot.

Go Online
PHSchool.com

Use Web Code **nga-6200** for **Chapter 9** self-test.

Southeast Asia and the Pacific Region: Physical Geography

Chapter Preview

Standard Course of Study

7.2.01 Influence of physical features and climate on cultures

7.2.02 Factors that influence distribution of population, resources, and climate

7.2.03 Factors that influence human migration

7.3.01 How cultures and regions are influenced by human interaction with environment

7.3.02 Environmental impact and global effects of regional activities

7.3.04 Describe effects of physical processes

7.5.01 How the location of natural resources affects economic development

SS.1.02 Summarize to select main ideas

Sections

1. **Southeast Asia: Physical Geography**
   7.3.01, 7.3.02, SS.1.02
2. **Australia and New Zealand: Physical Geography**
   7.2.01, 7.2.02, 7.2.03, SS.1.02
3. **The Pacific Islands: Physical Geography**
   7.2.01, 7.3.04, 7.5.01, SS.1.02

🎯 Target Reading Skill

Main Idea In this chapter, you will focus on identifying the main ideas in the sections and paragraphs you read. You will also focus on identifying the details that support each main idea.

▶ **A lush rain forest in the Philippines**

Southeast Asia and the Pacific Region: Physical

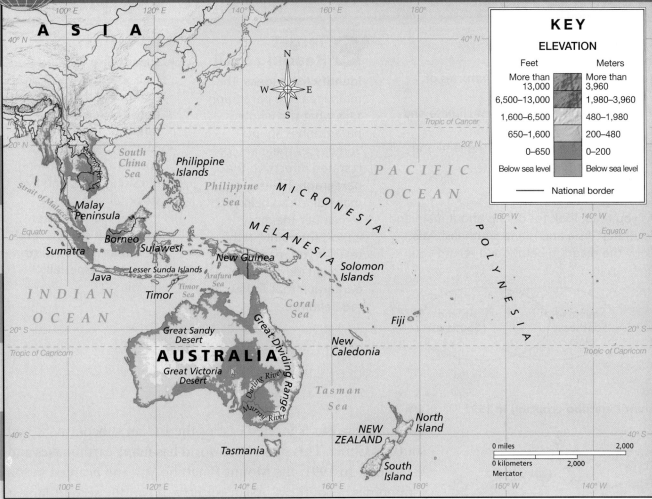

ASIA

40° N .... 40° N

Tropic of Cancer

20° N .... 20° N

South China Sea

Philippine Islands

Philippine Sea

MICRONESIA

PACIFIC OCEAN

Strait of Malacca

Malay Peninsula

MELANESIA

Borneo

Sulawesi

New Guinea

Solomon Islands

P O L Y N E S I A

Equator .... 0° .... Equator .... 0°

Sumatra

Lesser Sunda Islands

Java

Timor

Arafura Sea

Timor Sea

Coral Sea

Fiji

INDIAN OCEAN

Great Sandy Desert

20° S .... 20° S

Tropic of Capricorn .... Tropic of Capricorn

AUSTRALIA

Great Victoria Desert

Great Dividing Range

New Caledonia

Darling River

Murray River

Tasman Sea

North Island

Murray River

NEW ZEALAND

40° S .... 40° S

Tasmania

South Island

Mercator

KEY

ELEVATION

Feet		Meters
More than 13,000		More than 3,960
6,500–13,000		1,980–3,960
1,600–6,500		480–1,980
650–1,600		200–480
0–650		0–200
Below sea level		Below sea level

—— National border

0 miles 2,000
0 kilometers 2,000

Place Much of Southeast Asia and the Pacific Region is located between the Tropic of Cancer and the Tropic of Capricorn. **Identify** Name the continents in Southeast Asia and the Pacific Region. **Draw Conclusions** What kind of climate would you expect most of these countries to have? Explain your answer.

Go Online
PHSchool.com Use Web Code ngp-6310 for step-by-step map skills practice.

Southeast Asia
Physical Geography

Prepare to Read

Objectives

In this section, you will
1. Learn about the major landforms of Southeast Asia.
2. Find out about the kinds of climate and vegetation in Southeast Asia.
3. Examine how people use the land and resources of Southeast Asia.

Taking Notes

As you read, look for details about mainland Southeast Asia and island Southeast Asia. Copy the diagram below, and record your findings in it.

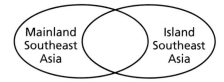

Mainland Southeast Asia — Island Southeast Asia

Target Reading Skill

Identify Main Ideas The main idea of a paragraph tells what the whole paragraph is about. Sometimes the main idea is stated directly in the paragraph. Identifying main ideas can help you remember the most important points in the text. As you read, identify the main idea of each paragraph that follows a red heading.

Key Terms

- **subsistence farming** (sub SIS tuns FAHR ming) *n.* farming that provides only enough food for a family or for a village
- **commercial farming** (kuh MUR shul FAHR ming) *n.* raising crops and livestock for sale on the local or world market
- **paddy** (PAD ee) *n.* a level field that is flooded to grow rice, especially in Asia

Mount Pinatubo erupting in 1991

Southeast Asia is located east of the Indian subcontinent and south of China. This part of the world has many earthquakes and volcanoes. In 1991, the Mount Pinatubo volcano erupted in the Philippines, a Southeast Asian country. It was the second-largest volcanic eruption of the twentieth century. About 58,000 people moved to safety, but about 800 people died. The eruption threw nearly 20 millions tons of gas and ash 21 miles (34 kilometers) into the atmosphere. The gas cloud spread around Earth. For two years, this gas cloud caused global temperatures to drop by about 1°F (0.5°C). Volcanoes are one physical feature of Southeast Asia. What are other major physical features of Southeast Asia? How do they affect land use in the region?

The Land of Southeast Asia

Southeast Asia is divided into mainland and island areas. The mainland is a peninsula that juts south from the main area of Asia. The islands extend east and west between the Indian and the Pacific oceans. Locate the mainland and the islands on the map on the next page.

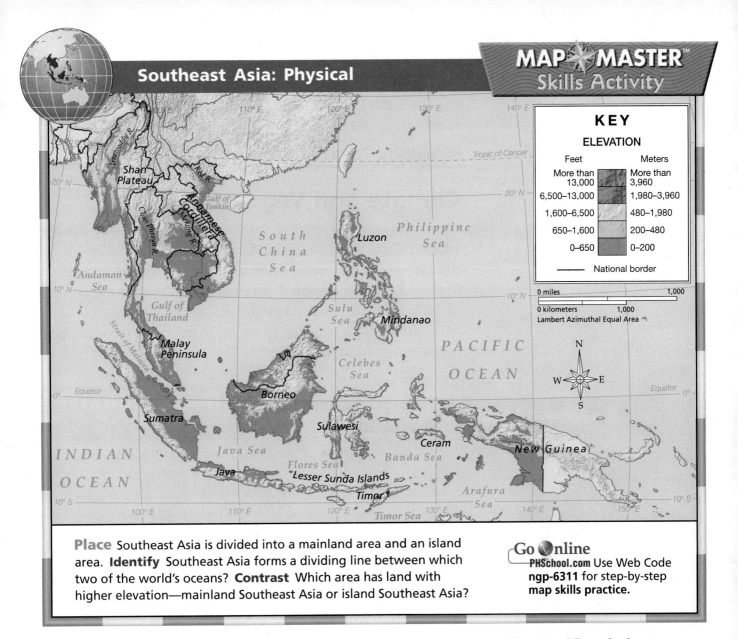

KEY

ELEVATION

Feet		Meters
More than 13,000		More than 3,960
6,500–13,000		1,980–3,960
1,600–6,500		480–1,980
650–1,600		200–480
0–650		0–200
——		National border

0 miles 1,000
0 kilometers 1,000
Lambert Azimuthal Equal Area

Place Southeast Asia is divided into a mainland area and an island area. **Identify** Southeast Asia forms a dividing line between which two of the world's oceans? **Contrast** Which area has land with higher elevation—mainland Southeast Asia or island Southeast Asia?

Go Online
PHSchool.com Use Web Code **ngp-6311** for step-by-step map skills practice.

Mainland Southeast Asia

The nations of mainland Southeast Asia are Cambodia, Laos (LAH ohs), Malaysia (muh LAY zhuh), Myanmar (MYUN mahr), Thailand (TY land), and Vietnam. Note that Malaysia is part of mainland Southeast Asia as well as of island Southeast Asia. Much of this area is covered by forested mountains. Most people live in the narrow river valleys between mountain ranges.

Island Southeast Asia

Five major nations make up island Southeast Asia: Singapore, Malaysia, Brunei (broo NY), Indonesia, and the Philippines. The largest of the island nations is Indonesia. Indonesia's biggest island is Sumatra. Singapore is a tiny nation, located at the tip of the Malay Peninsula. The country of Malaysia lies partly on the mainland and partly on the island of Borneo. The Philippines is a country made up of some 7,000 islands.

Tourists riding elephants through the forests of Thailand

The Ring of Fire The islands of Southeast Asia are part of the Ring of Fire. That is a region of volcanoes and earthquakes surrounding the Pacific Ocean. Most of the mountainous islands there are actually the peaks of underwater volcanoes.

✓ **Reading Check** Name the largest nation in island Southeast Asia.

Climate and Vegetation

Look at the climate map of Southeast Asia below. The climate regions in mainland Southeast Asia between Myanmar and Vietnam are similar to those in South Asia. On the west coast of Myanmar, there is a tropical wet climate, just as on the west coast of India. As you move eastward through mainland Southeast Asia, the climate changes to tropical wet and dry and then becomes humid subtropical.

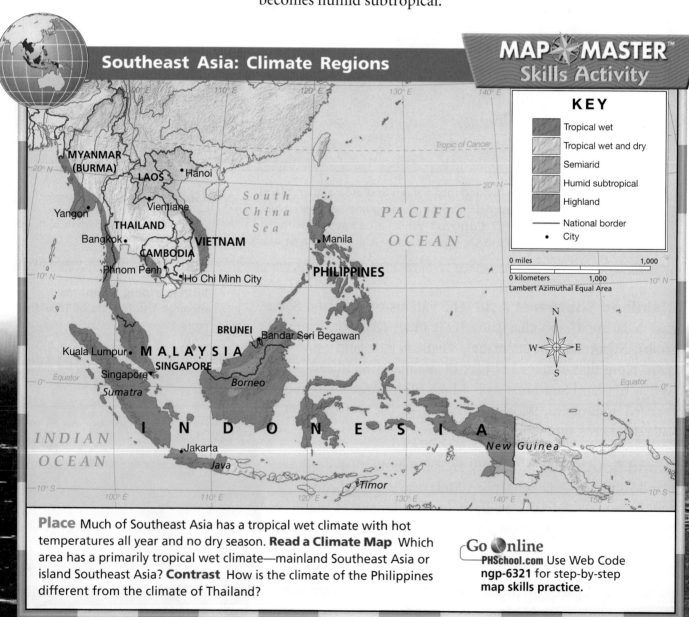

Southeast Asia: Climate Regions

MAP MASTER™
Skills Activity

KEY
- Tropical wet
- Tropical wet and dry
- Semiarid
- Humid subtropical
- Highland
- —— National border
- • City

0 miles / 1,000
0 kilometers / 1,000
Lambert Azimuthal Equal Area

Place Much of Southeast Asia has a tropical wet climate with hot temperatures all year and no dry season. **Read a Climate Map** Which area has a primarily tropical wet climate—mainland Southeast Asia or island Southeast Asia? **Contrast** How is the climate of the Philippines different from the climate of Thailand?

Go Online
PHSchool.com Use Web Code
ngp-6321 for step-by-step
map skills practice.

Multiple Monsoons However, when you get to the southeastern coast of Vietnam, the pattern changes. The climate is again tropical wet. It supports tropical rain forests—thick forests that receive at least 60 inches (152 centimeters) of rain a year. Why is this area so wet? The answer is that summer monsoons bring rains to this coast just as they do to the western coast.

In fact, there are two separate summer monsoons. An Indian Ocean monsoon blows from the southwest, and a Pacific Ocean monsoon blows from the southeast. Each brings heavy summer rain to the Southeast Asian coast that it hits. Also, during the Northern Hemisphere's winter, winds off the central Pacific Ocean blow from the northeast. This winter monsoon brings heavy rains to the southern Philippines and Indonesia. Because most of Indonesia is in the Southern Hemisphere, the heavy rain from December to March is a summer monsoon there.

Effects of a Tropical Wet Climate Most of island Southeast Asia has a tropical wet climate that supports tropical rain forests. Southeast Asia contains the second-largest tropical rain forest region in the world.

The rain forests of Southeast Asia are lush and thick with vegetation. However, there are disadvantages to living in the tropical climate of Southeast Asia—typhoons. When typhoons hit land, the high winds and heavy rain often lead to widespread property damage and loss of life.

✓ Reading Check **How does the northeast monsoon affect the southern Philippines and Indonesia?**

Monsoons in Southeast Asia
The photos below show the effect of monsoons in Cambodia. Monsoons bring rains that can sometimes flood streets. **Analyze Images** *How do people get around when monsoon flooding is severe?*

Using the Land and Resources of Southeast Asia

Growing Rice in Indonesia
In most of Southeast Asia, people grow rice by hand. Farmers use water buffalo to plow the fields. Rice seedlings are transplanted by hand to the fields, which have been flooded with water. **Analyze Images** *Which photo shows people transplanting rice seedlings to the fields?*

Many of the people in Southeast Asia make their living from the land. Some live in villages, where they build their own houses and grow their own food. Farming that provides only enough for a family or for a village is called **subsistence farming.** Many use the same building and farming methods that their ancestors relied upon thousands of years ago. Other people in Southeast Asia work on plantations—large farming operations designed to raise crops for profit, or cash crops. Plantation agriculture is a type of commercial farming. **Commercial farming** is the raising of crops and livestock for sale on the local or world market.

Farming Farming is a major economic activity in Southeast Asia, even though the region's cities and industries have been growing rapidly. In most Southeast Asian countries, more than 40 percent of the population work in agriculture. People farm—and live—in the river valleys of mountainous mainland Southeast Asia and on the lowland plains of island Southeast Asia. Crops include cash crops such as coffee, tea, and rubber. In Indonesia and Malaysia, rubber is grown on plantations and is a major export crop. Other major crops are soybeans, sugar cane, fruit, and, most important, rice.

The Importance of Rice Rice has been the chief crop in Southeast Asia for centuries. Rice needs a hot climate and plenty of water to grow. In fact, rice grows best when it is planted in the water. In Southeast Asia, farmers use the paddy system to grow rice. A **paddy** is a level field that is flooded to grow rice. Indonesia and Thailand are among the top rice-producing countries in the world. In Southeast Asia, rice is also an important part of the people's diet. It is a food crop as well as a cash crop.

MAP MASTER™
Skills Activity

KEY

Extent of rain forest, 3000 B.C.

Present-day extent of rain forest

National border

• City

0 miles 600
0 kilometers 600
Lambert Azimuthal Equal Area

Human-Environment Interaction Rain forests have a thin layer of topsoil. When people clear rain forests for farms, heavy rains often wash the topsoil away. Then people must clear more land for crops. **Locate** Where are rain forests located in Southeast Asia today? **Compare** On which island has rain forest destruction been greater—Sumatra or Java?

Go Online
PHSchool.com Use Web Code **ngp-6331** for step-by-step map skills practice.

Rain Forest Resources Southeast Asia's tropical rain forests cover large areas in the region. Rain forests contain a great variety of plant and animal life. In Southeast Asia, rain forests are a source of lumber, medicines, and chemicals used in industry. Tropical rain forests once covered nearly all of Southeast Asia. Over the years, huge sections have been cut down to provide lumber and to create farmland. On the island of Java in Indonesia, more than 90 percent of the rain forest has been cleared.

One challenge for the nations of Southeast Asia is balancing the need for economic growth with the need for rain forests. Thailand has made some progress toward conserving its rain forests. In 1988, hundreds of people in Thailand were killed by huge mudslides. The mudslides occurred because trees that had held the soil on the hillsides had been cut down. In 1989, Thailand banned logging in natural forests.

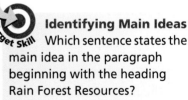

Identifying Main Ideas Which sentence states the main idea in the paragraph beginning with the heading Rain Forest Resources?

Target Skill

Bamboo as a Resource One forest resource that Southeast Asian people have long used for shelter is bamboo. Bamboo is a type of fast-growing grass that produces a woody stem. Giant bamboo can grow to about 100 feet (30 meters) tall. Millions of people in Southeast Asia live in houses made of bamboo. It is also used to make irrigation pipes, ropes, and bridges. Bamboo is important to the economies of several Southeast Asian countries. The Philippines is one of the world's largest suppliers of bamboo to the world market.

Mineral Resources The countries of Southeast Asia are rich in minerals. Indonesia, Myanmar, and Brunei have large deposits of oil. Even more plentiful, however, are the region's reserves of natural gas. Among the Southeast Asian countries, Indonesia and Malaysia have the largest reserves of natural gas. Thailand has large natural gas reserves in the Gulf of Thailand. These countries are using their own supplies of natural gas to generate electricity instead of importing oil.

✓ **Reading Check** Why does Southeast Asia now have fewer areas of tropical rain forests than in the past?

Bamboo stems being used as scaffolding in Laos

Section 1 Assessment

Key Terms
Review the key terms at the beginning of this section. Use each term in a sentence that explains its meaning.

Target Reading Skill
Write the main idea of each paragraph that follows a red heading in this section.

Comprehension and Critical Thinking
1. (a) Recall What kind of landform makes up mainland Southeast Asia?

(b) Compare and Contrast How is mainland Southeast Asia similar to and different from island Southeast Asia?
2. (a) Recall What kind of climate does most of island Southeast Asia have?
(b) Synthesize Information Why does the southeastern coast of Vietnam have the same climate as most of island Southeast Asia?
3. (a) List Give some examples of cash crops raised in Southeast Asia.
(b) Contrast What is the difference between subsistence farming and commercial farming?
(c) Draw Conclusions How can rice be a product of both commercial and subsistence farming?

Writing Activity
Write a paragraph that explains why commercial logging and commercial farming have a destructive effect on tropical rain forests.

For: An activity about Southeast Asia's geography
Visit: PHSchool.com
Web Code: ngd-6301

Prepare to Read

Objectives
In this section, you will
1. Find out why Australia and New Zealand have unique physical environments.
2. Learn about Australia's physical geography.
3. Explore New Zealand's physical geography.

Taking Notes
As you read, look for details about the physical geography of Australia and New Zealand. Copy the table below, and record your findings in it.

Physical Geography	
Australia	**New Zealand**

🎯 Target Reading Skill
Identify Supporting Details The main idea of a paragraph is supported by details that give further information about it. These details may explain the main idea or give examples or reasons. Look at the first paragraph on page 278. The first sentence is the main idea. The rest of the sentences support this main idea. How do the details about marsupials support the main idea?

Key Terms
- **marsupial** (mahr SOO pea ul) *n.* an animal, such as a kangaroo, that carries its young in a body pouch
- **tectonic plate** (tek TAHN ik playt) *n.* a huge slab of rock that moves very slowly over a softer layer beneath the surface of Earth's crust
- **geyser** (GY zur) *n.* a hot spring that shoots a jet of water and steam into the air
- **fiord** (fyawrd) *n.* a long, narrow inlet or arm of the sea bordered by steep slopes created by glaciers

What bird is strange looking, has a long bill, does not fly, and only comes out at night to hunt? If you said a kiwi, you are right. The people of New Zealand are so proud of this unusual bird that they have made it their national symbol. The people even call themselves "Kiwis." The bird is one of many unique animals found in New Zealand and its neighbor to the west, Australia.

Unique Physical Environments
Australia lies between the Pacific Ocean and the Indian Ocean. New Zealand lies in the Pacific Ocean to the east of Australia. Both countries are in the Southern Hemisphere, south of the Equator. This means that their seasons are the opposite of those in the United States. They are far from other continents, which has made them unique.

The kiwi has appeared on New Zealand stamps since 1898.

Unique Plants and Animals   New Zealand and Australia are so far from other continents that many of their animals and plants are found nowhere else on Earth. Only in New Zealand can you find kiwis and yellow-eyed penguins. Eighty-four percent of the plants in New Zealand's forests grow nowhere else. Australia has many unique creatures, such as the kangaroo and the koala. They are **marsupials** (mahr SOO pea ulz), or animals that carry their young in a body pouch. Marsupials *are* found elsewhere in the world. The opossum of North America, for instance, is a marsupial. But in Australia, almost all mammals are marsupials. This is not true anywhere else on Earth.

Moving Plates of Rock   The uniqueness of New Zealand and Australia is the result of forces beneath Earth's surface. According to the theory of plate tectonics, the outer "skin," or crust of Earth, is broken into huge, moving slabs of rock called **tectonic plates.** These plates move independently, sometimes colliding and sometimes sliding against one another. Australia, New Zealand, and the Pacific islands are all part of the Indo-Australian plate. Once, it was part of a landmass that included Africa. Then, several hundred million years ago, the Indo-Australian plate broke away. Slowly—at a rate of an inch or two each year—it moved northeast toward Asia.

Ayers Rock, known in the Aboriginal language as Uluru, is located in central Australia. Kangaroos are common in Australia.

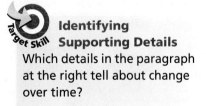 **Identifying Supporting Details**
Which details in the paragraph at the right tell about change over time?

Movement and Change Over Time   As the plates moved, Australia and the Pacific islands moved farther from Africa. Over the centuries, small changes have occurred naturally in the animals and plants of Australia and the islands. For instance, many birds have lost the ability to fly, even though they still have small wings. Because Australia and the islands are so isolated, these animals have not spread to other regions.

✓ **Reading Check**   **In which hemisphere are Australia and New Zealand located?**

Australia's Physical Geography

Australia is Earth's smallest continent. It is about as large as the continental United States (the part of the United States located between Canada and Mexico, not including Alaska and Hawaii). Most Australians live along Australia's eastern and southeastern coasts. Australia's physical geography explains why.

Find the region along Australia's east coast on the map below. This region receives ample rain. Winds blowing westward across the Pacific Ocean pick up moisture. As the winds rise to cross the Great Dividing Range, the moisture falls as rain. These winds also help make the climate mild and pleasant. Most Australians live here, in cities. Australia's most important rivers, the Murray and the Darling, flow through the region. They flow across a vast plain that contains Australia's most fertile farmland.

✓ **Reading Check** **How does the physical geography of Australia explain where the people live?**

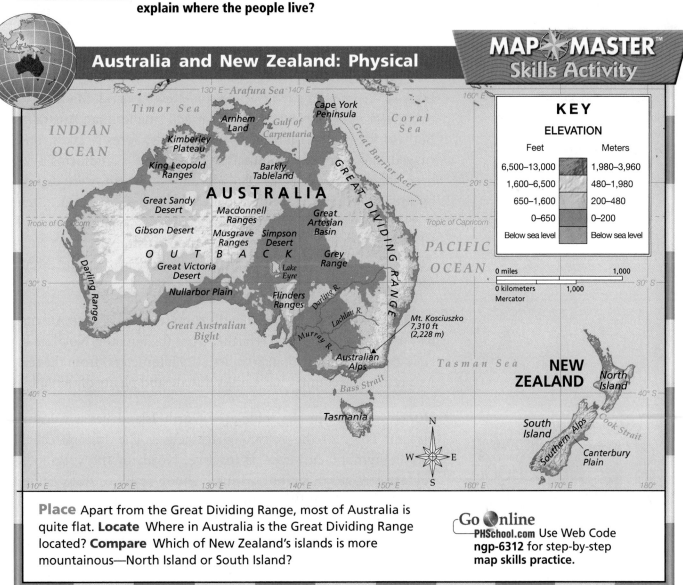

MAP MASTER™
Skills Activity

Australia and New Zealand: Physical

KEY
ELEVATION

Feet		Meters
6,500–13,000		1,980–3,960
1,600–6,500		480–1,980
650–1,600		200–480
0–650		0–200
Below sea level		Below sea level

Place Apart from the Great Dividing Range, most of Australia is quite flat. **Locate** Where in Australia is the Great Dividing Range located? **Compare** Which of New Zealand's islands is more mountainous—North Island or South Island?

Go Online
PHSchool.com Use Web Code
ngp-6312 for step-by-step
map skills practice.

Mount Cook National Park
New Zealand's Mount Cook National Park, located in the Southern Alps, is popular with hikers and mountain climbers. **Infer** *Is this group of people out to climb a mountain or enjoy a day hike?*

Explore the land of Southeast Asia and the Pacific Region.

New Zealand's Physical Geography

Look at the map on page 279 and find New Zealand. Made up of two major islands, New Zealand is much smaller than Australia. Both of its major islands have highlands, forests, lakes, and rugged, snowcapped mountains. New Zealand's landforms have been shaped by volcanoes. The volcanoes, in turn, were caused by the movement of tectonic plates. Where plates meet, often there are earthquakes and volcanoes. New Zealand is located where the Pacific plate meets the Indo-Australian plate. New Zealand's major islands, North Island and South Island, were formed by volcanoes when these plates collided.

A Mild Climate   New Zealand's climate is cooler than Australia's because New Zealand is farther from the Equator. No place in New Zealand is more than 80 miles (129 kilometers) from the sea. As a result, the country has a mild climate and plenty of rainfall.

North Island   In the middle of North Island lies a volcanic plateau. Three of the volcanoes are active. The volcano called Mount Egmont, however, is inactive. North of the volcanoes, **geysers** (GY zurz), or hot springs, shoot scalding water more than 100 feet (30.5 meters) into the air. New Zealanders use this energy to produce electricity. North Island is where New Zealand's capital city of Wellington is located. The country's largest city, Auckland, is also located on North Island.

South Island   South Island has a high mountain range called the Southern Alps. Mount Cook, the highest peak in the range, rises to 12,349 feet (3,764 meters). Glaciers cover the mountainsides. Below, crystal-clear lakes dot the landscape. **Fiords** (fyawrds), or narrow inlets bordered by steep slopes, slice the southwest coastline. Here, the mountains reach the sea. To the southeast lies a flat, fertile land called the Canterbury Plain. This is where farmers produce most of New Zealand's crops. Ranchers also raise sheep and cattle here.

Comparing Australia and New Zealand   New Zealand is like Australia in several ways. In both countries, most of the population lives in cities along the coast. More than four out of five New Zealanders live in towns and cities. Both Australia and New Zealand have important natural resources such as coal, iron ore, and natural gas. The two countries also raise sheep and cattle and grow similar crops.

New Zealand is different from Australia in a number of ways, too. New Zealand is much smaller but has higher mountains than those in Australia. New Zealand has glaciers, while Australia does not. The two countries also have different climates.

 **Reading Check**   Where do most people in New Zealand live—in urban areas or in rural areas?

Links Across
The World

Steam Heat   Geysers are found in three places in the world: the northwestern United States, Iceland, and New Zealand. In these places, movements of tectonic plates have created deep cracks in Earth's crust. Water seeps down into the cracks until it reaches very hot rocks. The heat raises the temperature of the water until it is so hot that it bursts upward in a shower of water and steam.

Section 2 Assessment

Key Terms
Review the key terms at the beginning of this section. Use each term in a sentence that explains its meaning.

Target Reading Skill
The main idea of the last paragraph in this section is that Australia and New Zealand are different in many ways. State the details that support this main idea.

Comprehension and Critical Thinking
1. (a) Recall   Where do most of the people in Australia live?

(b) Identify Cause and Effect   How have Australia's geography and climate affected where Australians live?

2. (a) Recall   How were New Zealand's North Island and South Island formed?

(b) Compare and Contrast   How is the physical geography of New Zealand different from that of Australia? How is it similar?

3. (a) Explain   How are the population patterns similar in Australia and New Zealand?

(b) Draw Conclusions   Why do most of the people in New Zealand live near the coasts?

Writing Activity
Write a list of adjectives that describe Australia. Then write a list of adjectives that describe New Zealand. Include at least three adjectives for each country. Using the information in this section, write a fact related to each adjective on your list.

For: An activity about Australia
Visit: PHSchool.com
Web Code: ngd-6302

Identifying Cause and Effect

Have you ever tossed a stone into a pond and watched what happens? As soon as that stone hits the surface and sinks, circles of ripples, or waves, begin to move away from that spot in ever-widening circles. This is one case of cause and effect. Tossing the stone started the waves moving away from the spot where the stone landed. Understanding this relationship between cause and effect is useful in school and in daily life.

Learn the Skill

Being able to identify causes and effects helps you to understand what you read. To learn this skill, follow the steps below.

NC **SS.1.04** Detect cause and effect

1 **Look for a cause-and-effect relationship.** Remember the pebble in the pond. As you read, ask yourself, "Why did this happen?" or "How did this happen?" Look for words such as *because, so,* and *as a result.* These words sometimes signal a cause-and-effect relationship.

2 **Identify the effect or effects.** Like the ripples that appear in a pond, an effect is what happens. A cause may have more than one effect. List the effect(s) you have identified.

3 **Identify the cause or causes.** A cause makes something happen. An effect may have more than one cause. List the cause(s) of the effect(s) you identified in Step 2.

4 **State the cause and effect.** A simple cause-and-effect statement might read, "A caused B." A is the cause, and B is the effect. A cause that produced three effects might be stated as, "A caused B, C, and D." A is the cause; its effects are B, C, and D.

A stone tossed into this pond caused the ripples to form. The stone is the cause, and the ripples are the effect.

Practice the Skill

To practice identifying a cause-and-effect relationship, read the paragraph below, using the steps on the previous page.

1 What words signal a possible cause-and-effect situation?

2 Identify the effect by filling in the blank in the following sentence: "Why do _____ happen?" The word you use to fill in the blank is the effect.

3 The effect you identified is triggered by two causes. What are the two causes?

4 State the cause-and-effect relationship in a sentence. Your sentence should give an answer to this question: What causes tsunamis?

A Japanese woodblock print of a tsunami

Tsunamis (soo NAH mees) are powerful waves caused by earthquakes or volcanic eruptions that take place underwater. When an earthquake happens under the ocean floor or when an underwater volcano erupts, both of these actions cause circles of waves like the ones that form when you throw a stone into a pond. The result is a wave that is extremely forceful and fast. In deep water, tsunamis can move as fast as 500 to 600 miles (800 to 960 kilometers) per hour. As a tsunami approaches land, the speed slows down and the wave grows in height, sometimes as high as a ten-story building. The wave pushes inland, carrying boulders, boats, and buildings along until its energy is gone. In 2004, a huge tsunami struck at least 12 countries along the Indian Ocean. Entire villages were destroyed, and at least 225,000 people were killed.

Apply the Skill

Read the passages titled Moving Plates of Rock and Movement and Change Over Time on page 278. Use the steps in the skill to identify one cause that explains why New Zealand and Australia are unique.

Prepare to Read

Objectives

In this section, you will

1. Examine features of high islands and low islands.
2. Learn about the three main island groups.
3. Find out what kind of climate and vegetation the islands have.
4. Discover how land is used in the Pacific islands.

Taking Notes

As you read this section, look for details about the three major Pacific island groups. Copy the diagram below, and record your findings in it.

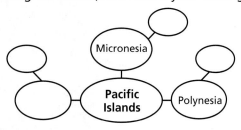

Target Reading Skill

Identify Main Ideas
Sometimes the main idea in a paragraph or reading passage is not stated directly. All the details add up to a main idea, but you must state the main idea yourself. As you read, look for main ideas that are not stated directly.

Key Terms

- **high island** (hy EYE lund) *n.* an island formed from the mountainous top of an ancient volcano
- **low island** (loh EYE lund) *n.* an island formed from coral reefs or atolls
- **atoll** (A tawl) *n.* a small coral island in the shape of a ring
- **coral** (KAWR ul) *n.* a rock-like material made up of the skeletons of tiny sea creatures, most plentiful in warm ocean water

Scuba diving in the Pacific islands

The Pacific Ocean, which covers nearly one third of Earth's surface, is dotted with thousands of islands. Some are barely large enough for a person to stand on. Others cover thousands of square miles. The Pacific islands include the second-largest island in the world. This is New Guinea. Half of this island is actually part of Indonesia. The other half is the independent country of Papua New Guinea (PAP yoo uh noo GIH nee). The Pacific islands also include the world's smallest independent island nation. This is the country of Nauru (NAH oo roo), which has a total land area of just 8 square miles (21 square kilometers).

Geographers divide these thousands of islands into three main groups. Melanesia (mel uh NEE zhuh) means "black islands." Micronesia (my kruh NEE zhuh) means "small islands." Polynesia (pahl uh NEE zhuh) means "many islands." Each of these groups covers a particular area, and any island that falls inside the boundaries of one of these areas belongs to that group.

High Islands and Low Islands

Geographers also divide the Pacific islands into high islands and low islands. **High islands** are mountainous and have been formed by volcanoes. The soil, which consists of volcanic ash, is very fertile. Because of their size and because people can grow crops there, high islands can support more people than low islands.

Low islands are made up of coral reefs or atolls. An **atoll** (A tawl) is a small coral island in the shape of a ring. The ring encloses a shallow pool of ocean water called a lagoon. Often, the lagoon has one or more openings to the sea. An atoll may rise only a few feet above the water. Low islands have this shape and low elevation because they are coral reefs. **Coral** is a rocklike material made up of the skeletons of tiny sea creatures. A reef develops until it nears the surface. Then sand and other debris accumulate on the reef's surface, raising the island above the level of the water.

Far fewer people live on low islands than on high islands. In part, this is because low islands are quite small. Also, low islands have poor, sandy soil and little fresh water, so it is difficult to raise crops. Most low islanders survive by fishing. They may also grow coconuts, yams, and a starchy root called taro.

A traditional house on a high island in Polynesia

✓ **Reading Check** **On which type of island do most Pacific island people live?**

A Coral Atoll

A South Pacific Atoll
The diagram below shows how a coral atoll is formed. **1** It begins as a fringe of coral around a volcanic island. **2** The coral continues to build as the island is worn away. **3** Eventually, only a ring of coral remains. The aerial view of an atoll at the left shows the ring structure of the coral.

Melanesia, Micronesia, and Polynesia

The island group with the most people is Melanesia, which is north and east of Australia. Most of Melanesia's large islands are high islands. New Guinea, for example, has two ranges of high mountains. The western half of New Guinea is called Irian Jaya (IHR ee ahn JAH yuh). It is part of the country of Indonesia. The eastern half is Papua New Guinea, the largest and most populated Melanesian country. Some smaller Melanesian islands are Fiji, the Solomon Islands, and New Caledonia.

Made up largely of low islands, Micronesia covers an area of the Pacific as large as the continental United States. Most of the islands of Micronesia lie north of the Equator. Some of Micronesia's 2,000 islands are less than 1 square mile (2.6 square kilometers) in area. The largest is Guam, which is 209 square miles (541 square kilometers). Most of Micronesia's islands are divided into groups. The largest are the Caroline, Gilbert, Marshall, and Mariana islands. Guam is part of the Marianas.

Polynesia is the largest island group in the Pacific. It includes the fiftieth state of the United States, Hawaii. Polynesia consists of a great many high islands, such as Tahiti and Samoa. Dense rain forests cover their high volcanic mountains. Along the shores are palm-fringed, sandy beaches. The Tuamotus and Tonga are examples of Polynesia's few low islands and atolls.

✓ **Reading Check**   **Which island group contains Hawaii?**

Living in the Pacific Islands
The bottom photo on the opposite page shows a traditional canoe in Fiji. Below left, fishers haul nets in the waters of Fiji. Below right, some people in Papua New Guinea farm for a living. The inset photo on the opposite page shows children playing volleyball in Vanuatu.

Climate and Vegetation of the Pacific Islands

The Pacific islands lie in the tropics. Temperatures are hot year-round. Daytime temperatures can reach as high as the 80s and mid-90s in degrees Fahrenheit (around 30°C). Nighttime temperatures average about 75°F (24°C). The ocean winds keep the temperatures from getting too high.

Some Pacific islands have wet and dry seasons. Most islands, however, receive heavy rainfall all year long. In Hawaii, for example, volcanic peaks such as Mauna Kea (MOW nuh KAY uh) receive 100 inches (250 centimeters) of rain each year. Usually the rain falls in brief, heavy downpours. Some low islands, however, receive only scattered rainfall.

Because of high temperatures, plentiful rainfall, and fertile soil, high islands such as Papua New Guinea and the Hawaiian Islands have rich vegetation. Tropical rain forests cover the hills. Savanna grasses grow in the lowlands. Low islands, on the other hand, have little vegetation. The poor soil supports only palm trees, grasses, and small shrubs.

✓ Reading Check **Why do low islands have little vegetation?**

Target Skill **Identify Main Ideas** In one sentence, state what the paragraph at the left is about.

Natural Resources and Land Use

The Pacific island region has few natural resources. The coconut palm is its most important resource. It provides food, clothing, and shelter. Another important resource is fish.

Cash Crops Some Pacific island countries, such as the nation of Fiji, grow cash crops. Fiji is a nation of some 300 islands in Melanesia. The Fiji islands' fertile, volcanic soil and hot, wet climate are good for growing sugar cane. Sugar is a major export for Fiji. Another important cash crop for many Pacific island countries is copra. Copra, or dried coconut, is used in margarine, cooking oils, soaps, and cosmetics. The people in Fiji also work as subsistence farmers, growing their own food crops such as taro, yams, and sweet potatoes.

Tourism The Pacific islands' most valuable resource may be their natural beauty. Tourism provides a key source of income in the region. Many Pacific island nations are working to develop their tourist industries. The greatest number of visitors to the Pacific islands come from Australia. Nearly as many come from the United States.

A worker harvests ripe coconuts in Fiji.

✓ **Reading Check** Give two examples of cash crops grown in the Pacific islands.

Section 3 Assessment

Key Terms

Review the key terms at the beginning of this section. Use each key term in a sentence that explains its meaning.

Target Reading Skill

Read the paragraph titled Tourism, above. Write a sentence that states the main idea.

Comprehension and Critical Thinking

1. (a) Explain Tell the difference between high islands and low islands in the Pacific.

(b) Make Generalizations The people on high islands often have a better standard of living than people on low islands. Explain why this might be so.

2. (a) Recall Name the three Pacific island groups.

(b) Apply Information Why do most of the people in the Pacific islands live in Melanesia?

(c) Draw Conclusions Most Pacific islands have few natural resources. How might this affect trade between these islands and industrial nations around the world?

Writing Activity

Suppose that you have decided to live on one of the Pacific islands. Write a paragraph explaining why you have decided to move. How will you handle the challenges of island life? Will you live on a high island or a low island?

For: An activity on the Pacific islands
Visit: PHSchool.com
Web Code: ngd-6303

Review and Assessment

◆ Chapter Summary

Section 1: Southeast Asia Physical Geography

- Southeast Asia is divided into mainland and island areas. Mainland Southeast Asia is a peninsula. Island Southeast Asia is part of the Ring of Fire, a region of volcanoes and earthquakes.
- Most of Southeast Asia has a tropical wet climate.
- Farming is a major economic activity in Southeast Asia, although the region's cities and industries have been growing rapidly.
- Southeast Asian rain forests are a source of lumber, medicines, and materials used in industry. The region's remaining rain forests are in danger of destruction from commercial logging and farming.

Section 2: Australia and New Zealand Physical Geography

- Because Australia and New Zealand are far from other landmasses, many of their plants and animals are found nowhere else on Earth.
- Australia is the smallest continent. Most people live along its eastern and southern coasts.
- New Zealand is made up of two mountainous islands.

Cambodia

Section 3: The Pacific Islands Physical Geography

- The Pacific islands are divided into three main groups: Melanesia, Micronesia, and Polynesia.
- Within these groups, there are high islands and low islands.
- Because the Pacific islands lie in the tropics, temperatures are hot all year.
- The Pacific islands have few natural resources, but some island countries are able to grow cash crops such as sugar and copra, or dried coconut. Tourism is growing in importance in the region.

Australia

◆ Key Terms

Use each key term in a sentence that explains its meaning.

1. fiord
2. paddy
3. subsistence farming
4. commercial farming
5. marsupial

6. tectonic plate
7. geyser
8. high island
9. low island
10. coral

Review and Assessment (continued)

◆ Comprehension and Critical Thinking

11. **(a) List** Which countries make up mainland Southeast Asia?
(b) Explain Why is Malaysia part of both mainland Southeast Asia and island Southeast Asia?

12. **(a) Explain** Why does Southeast Asia have more than one summer monsoon?
(b) Summarize Describe the effects of summer monsoons in Southeast Asia.

13. **(a) Name** Which two Southeast Asian countries are among the world's leading rice producers?
(b) Analyze Information Why would a subsistence farmer in Southeast Asia raise rice instead of rubber?

14. **(a) Name** What is one mountain range in Australia?
(b) Locate Where is this mountain range located relative to Australia's east coast?

15. **(a) Recall** Describe the major features of New Zealand's geography.
(b) Compare and Contrast How are Australia and New Zealand different from and similar to each other?

16. **(a) Identify** Where do most people in the Pacific islands live—on high islands or on low islands?
(b) Draw Conclusions You have read about high islands and low islands. What conclusion can you reach about why more people live on one kind than another?

◆ Skills Practice

Identifying Cause and Effect Review the steps you followed to learn this skill. Then reread the first paragraph on page 270. Identify three effects of the eruption of Mount Pinatubo.

◆ Writing Activity: Math

Suppose that it is Monday at 12 noon where you live. Calculate what day and time it is in Bangkok, Thailand; in Jakarta, Indonesia; and in Sydney, Australia. You will need to use a world time zones map, which you can find in an atlas. Do research to learn more about time zones and the International Date Line. Then write a paragraph about the International Date Line.

MAP MASTER™ Skills Activity

Southeast Asia and the Pacific

Place Location For each place listed below, write the letter that shows its location on the map.

1. Malay Peninsula
2. South China Sea
3. Philippine Islands
4. Australia
5. New Guinea
6. Micronesia

Go Online
PHSchool.com Use Web Code **ngp-6320** for an **interactive map.**

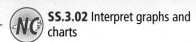
Standardized Test Prep

Test-Taking Tips

Some questions on standardized tests ask you to analyze graphic organizers. Study the Venn diagram below. Then follow the tips to answer the sample question.

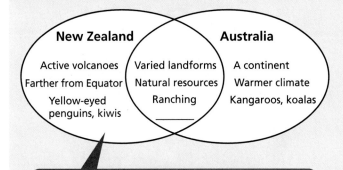

TIP A Venn diagram lists ways that two things are the same and different. This kind of chart is good for writing or note-taking.

Pick the letter that best answers the question.

Which of the following belongs in the blank in the overlapping space?

- **A** compare and contrast
- **B** population mostly in cities
- **C** Great Dividing Range
- **D** geysers

Think It Through The question asks you to choose another example for the overlapping space—in other words, ways that both countries are the same. You can rule out C and D because the Great Dividing Range is in Australia and geysers are only in New Zealand. You can eliminate A, because it describes the chart—not an example in the chart. The correct answer is B, because the population of both countries is mostly in cities.

Practice Questions

Use the tips above and other tips in this book to help you answer the following questions.

1. Thailand, Cambodia, and Vietnam are part of
   - **A** island Southeast Asia.
   - **B** Polynesia.
   - **C** Micronesia.
   - **D** mainland Southeast Asia.

2. Most Australians live along Australia's eastern and southeastern coasts. Based on this information, what conclusion can be drawn about the location of Australia's cities?
   - **A** Most of Australia's cities are located in the interior of the continent.
   - **B** Most of Australia's cities are located along Australia's eastern and southeastern coasts.
   - **C** Most of Australia's cities are located along Australia's northern coast.
   - **D** Most of Australia's cities are located along Australia's western coast.

3. New Zealand's North Island and South Island were formed by
   - **A** volcanoes.   **B** coral.
   - **C** earthquakes.   **D** geysers.

Use the Venn diagram below to answer Question 4.

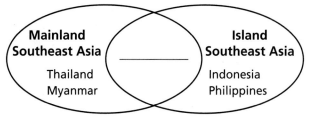

4. Which of the following belongs in the blank in the overlapping space?
   - **A** Vietnam   **B** Australia
   - **C** Malaysia   **D** Cambodia

Use Web Code **nga-6300** for **Chapter 10 self-test.**

Chapter 10 **291**

Chapter Preview

Standard Course of Study

7.3.03 Examine the development and use of tools and technology

7.4.03 Influence of ideas and values on development of societies

7.7.01 Relationship between historical events and current issues

7.7.02 Causes and effects of historical events

7.8.01 Impact of historical figures on past and present societies

7.8.03 Influence of discoveries, innovations, and inventions on societies

7.9.01 Historical development of types of governments

7.11.01 How culture links and separates societies

7.11.04 Impact of economic, political, and social changes on individuals and cultures

Sections

1. **Historic Traditions**
   7.3.03, 7.4.03, 7.7.01, 7.8.01, 7.8.03, 7.9.01

2. **People and Cultures**
   7.7.02, 7.9.01, 7.11.01, 7.11.04

Target Reading Skill

Context In this chapter, you will focus on using context to help you understand the meanings of unfamiliar words. Context includes the words, phrases, and sentences surrounding a particular word.

▶ **The Great Buddha of Kamakura is the second-largest statue of Buddha in Japan.**

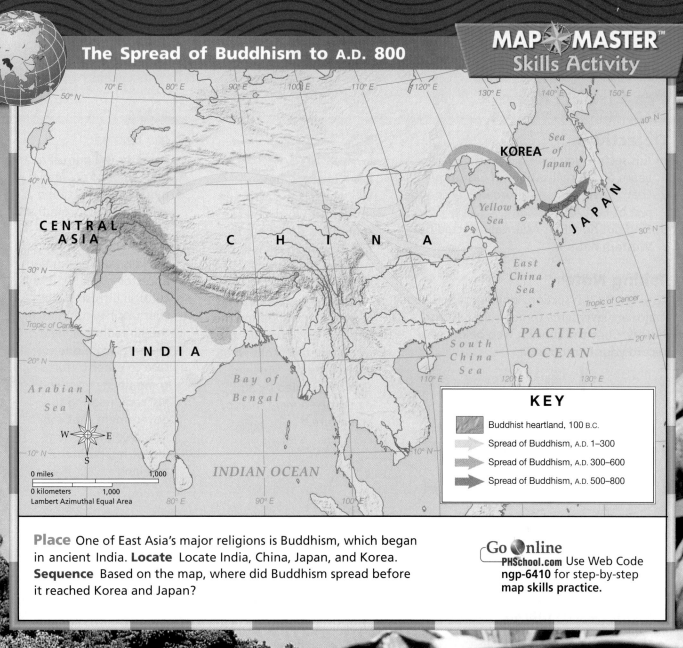

The Spread of Buddhism to A.D. 800

KOREA

Sea of Japan

JAPAN

CENTRAL ASIA

C H I N A

Yellow Sea

East China Sea

PACIFIC OCEAN

Tropic of Cancer

I N D I A

Arabian Sea

Bay of Bengal

South China Sea

N
W   E
S

0 miles   1,000
0 kilometers   1,000
Lambert Azimuthal Equal Area

INDIAN OCEAN

KEY

Buddhist heartland, 100 B.C.

Spread of Buddhism, A.D. 1–300

Spread of Buddhism, A.D. 300–600

Spread of Buddhism, A.D. 500–800

Place One of East Asia's major religions is Buddhism, which began in ancient India. **Locate** Locate India, China, Japan, and Korea. **Sequence** Based on the map, where did Buddhism spread before it reached Korea and Japan?

Go Online
PHSchool.com Use Web Code **ngp-6410** for step-by-step **map skills practice.**

Prepare to Read

Objectives

In this section you will
1. Learn about civilizations of East Asia.
2. Learn how Chinese culture influenced the rest of East Asia.
3. Find out how East Asia was affected by Western nations.

Taking Notes

As you read this section, look for details about major achievements throughout East Asia's history. Copy the concept web below, and record your findings in it.

World's oldest continuous civilization in China — East Asia's Major Achievements

Target Reading Skill

Use Context Clues

When you come across an unfamiliar word, you can sometimes figure out its meaning from clues in the context. The context refers to the surrounding words and sentences. Sometimes the context will define the word. In this example, the phrase in italics tells what an emperor is: "Ancient China was ruled by an emperor—*a male ruler of an empire.*"

Key Terms

- **emperor** (EM pur ur) *n.* a male ruler of an empire
- **dynasty** (DY nus tee) *n.* a series of rulers from the same family
- **clan** (klan) *n.* a group of families with a common ancestor
- **cultural diffusion** (KUL chur ul dih FYOO zhun) *n.* the spreading of ideas or practices from one culture to other cultures
- **communist** (KAHM yoo nist) *adj.* relating to a government that controls a country's large industries, businesses, and land

In this painting, Confucius is shown standing with his students.

More than two thousand years ago, one of the most important thinkers of ancient times gave this advice:

> "Let the ruler be a ruler and the subject a subject.
>
> A youth, when at home, should act with respect to his parents, and, abroad, be respectful to his elders. He should be earnest and truthful. He should overflow in love to all, and cultivate the friendship of the good.
>
> When you have faults, do not fear to abandon them."

These words are from the teachings of Confucius (kun FYOO shus), who lived in China about 500 B.C. He taught that all individuals have duties and responsibilities. If a person acts correctly, the result will be peace and harmony. Confucius's ideas helped to guide Chinese life for hundreds of years.

Civilizations of East Asia

Regions of Asia and Africa produced civilizations earlier than China's. A civilization has cities, a central government, workers who do specialized jobs, and social classes. Of the world's early civilizations, however, only China's has survived. This makes it the oldest continuous civilization in the world. Korea and Japan are not as old, but they, too, have long histories.

China's Middle Kingdom For much of its history, China had little to do with the rest of the world. The Great Wall of China first started in the 600s B.C. as many small unconnected walls between warring states. Over time, it became a symbol of China's desire to keep the world at a distance. In fact, Chinese leaders had such pride that they named their country the Middle Kingdom. To them, it was the center of the universe.

Ancient Achievements The Chinese had reason to believe that their civilization was the greatest in the world. They invented paper, gunpowder, silk weaving, the magnetic compass, the printing press, and clockworks. Chinese engineers were experts at digging canals, building dams and bridges, and setting up irrigation systems. Chinese scientists made major discoveries in mathematics and medicine.

Dynasties in China Starting in ancient times, China was governed by an **emperor**—a male ruler of an empire. An empire is an area of many territories and people that are controlled by one government. A series of emperors from the same family is a **dynasty.** Chinese history is described in terms of dynasties. The chart below lists major dynasties of China.

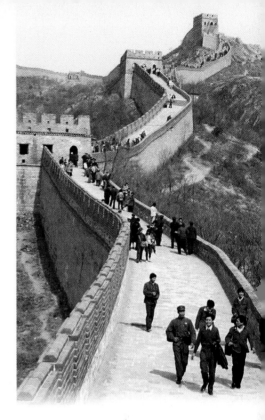

The Great Wall of China

Chart Skills

The chart below shows major dynasties of China. They ruled China from ancient times to A.D. 1911. **Identify** Which dynasty was the first to develop the Chinese calendar? **Sequence** Which was developed in China first—paper money or iron tools?

Major Dynasties of China

Major Dynasty	Major Achievements
Shang (c. 1766–c. 1122 B.C.)	Well-developed writing, first Chinese calendar, bronze casting.
Zhou (c. 1122–c. 256 B.C.)	Writing laws, iron tools and plows in use.
Qin (221 B.C.–206 B.C.)	First great Chinese Empire. Much of the Great Wall built.
Han (206 B.C.–A.D. 220)	Government based on Confucianism. Buddhism introduced.
Tang (A.D. 618–A.D. 907)	Sculpture and poetry flourish.
Song (A.D. 906–A.D. 1279)	Block printing and paper money developed. Gunpowder first used.
Ming (A.D. 1318–A.D. 1644)	Porcelain, the novel, and drama flourish.
Qing (A.D. 1644–A.D. 1911)	Increased trade with Europe. Last Chinese dynasty.

Use Context Clues
If you do not know what *unified* means, look in the surrounding words for a context clue. Here, the phrase following *unified* explains what the term means.

Timeline Skills

Japan has interacted with other countries and regions except for one period in its history. **Note** When did Japan close its borders to the rest of the world?
Analyze Information Which European country introduced Christianity to Japan?

Korea and China Although Korea's original settlers came from north-central Asia, Korea's history is closely tied to China. Around 1200 B.C., during a time of troubles in China, some Chinese moved to the Korean Peninsula. Later, other Chinese settled in the southern part of the peninsula. In this way, Chinese people brought Chinese knowledge and customs to the Koreans.

As in China, dynasties ruled Korea. While China had many dynasties, Korea had only three. The first was the Shilla. The Shilla dynasty unified Korea as one country in A.D. 668.

Years of Isolation in Japan For much of Japan's history, **clans,** or groups of families who claim a common ancestor, fought each other for land and power. Around A.D. 500, one clan, the Yamato (yah MAH toh), became powerful. Claiming descent from the sun goddess, Yamato leaders took the title of emperor. Many emperors sat on Japan's throne. For a long time they had little power. Instead, shoguns (SHOH gunz), or "emperor's generals," made the laws. Warrior nobles, the samurai (SAM uh ry), enforced these laws. Together, the shoguns and samurai ruled Japan for more than 700 years.

Japan was isolated from the outside world from about 1640 to 1853. Japanese leaders believed that isolation, or separation, was the best way to keep the country united. Japan finally was forced to trade with the West in the 1800s.

✓ **Reading Check** **Name at least four major achievements of the Chinese civilization.**

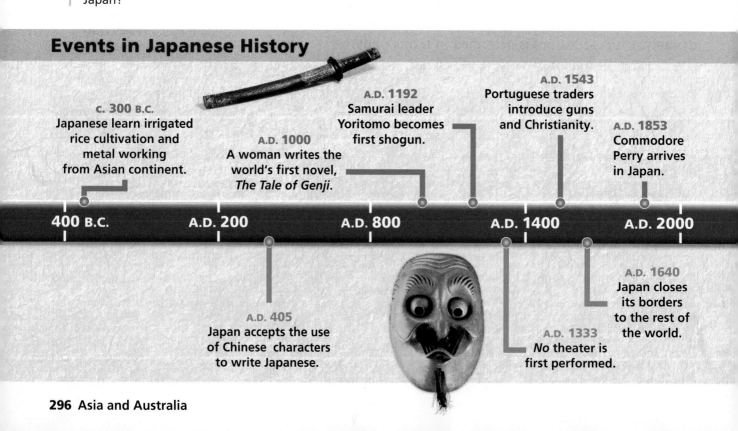

Events in Japanese History

c. 300 B.C.
Japanese learn irrigated rice cultivation and metal working from Asian continent.

A.D. 1000
A woman writes the world's first novel, *The Tale of Genji*.

A.D. 1192
Samurai leader Yoritomo becomes first shogun.

A.D. 1543
Portuguese traders introduce guns and Christianity.

A.D. 1853
Commodore Perry arrives in Japan.

400 B.C.   A.D. 200   A.D. 800   A.D. 1400   A.D. 2000

A.D. 405
Japan accepts the use of Chinese characters to write Japanese.

A.D. 1333
No theater is first performed.

A.D. 1640
Japan closes its borders to the rest of the world.

Paper Making

Civilization developed as people learned first to speak and to draw, and then to write. By the time of the Han dynasty in China, civilization included government, trade, record-keeping, and poetry. Paper was needed for all of these activities. Cai Lun, an official of the Han dynasty, is said to have invented this useful material.

Making paper pulp
People in Xishuangbanna, China, split open bamboo stems to extract pulp.

3 A paper mold—a box with wooden sides and a fine wire screen—is dipped into a vat of pulp and slowly raised.

4 Workers then shake the mold until the water drains off and the wet fibers cover the screen with a thin web of pulp.

2 Workers pound the water-soaked fibers to a pulp.

1 Fibers are gathered from bamboo, mulberry bark, cotton or linen cloth, grass, straw, or wood—and then chopped up, beaten, and soaked in water.

5 While still damp, the sheet of paper is peeled off the mold.

6 The paper sheets are pasted on a wall to dry. A fire might be lit to help the drying process.

Paper dyeing
Women lay out freshly dyed paper to dry in Bhaktapur, Nepal.

ANALYZING IMAGES
Why did it make sense to make paper near a source of water?

Links Across The World

West Meets East The West has been greatly influenced by East Asia. In ancient Rome, wealthy people prized clothing made from Chinese silk. Silk production came to Europe from China. Eastern art influenced the design of Western architecture and furniture. Traders imported porcelain, pottery made from a fine white clay, from East Asia. Europeans and Americans called it "china." All these examples show cultural diffusion, or the spreading of ideas and practices from one culture to others.

Government in Japan
Japan's legislative branch is called the Diet. The Diet elects a prime minister, who heads the executive branch. Members of the Diet are shown in 2001 applauding the election of Junichiro Koizumi as prime minister. **Analyze Images** *Which man in the photo is Koizumi? Explain your answer.*

The Spread of Cultures in East Asia

In ancient times, China was far ahead of the rest of the world in inventions and discoveries. Thus, it is not surprising that many Chinese discoveries spread to Korea and Japan. This process of **cultural diffusion,** or spreading of ideas from one culture to other cultures, happened early. The teachings of Confucius were among the first ideas to be passed along. The religion of Buddhism (BOOD iz um), which China had adopted from India, later spread to Korea and Japan. East Asian culture owes much to the early exchanges among China, Japan, and Korea. In each case, the countries changed what they borrowed until the element of culture became their own.

✓ **Reading Check** **Give an example of cultural diffusion between China and Korea.**

Westerners in East Asia

In the 1800s, Europeans and Americans began to produce great amounts of manufactured goods. East Asia seemed to be a good place to sell these products. Western trading ships began to sail to Asian ports.

The Opening of East Asia In 1853, U.S. Commodore Matthew Perry sailed with four warships to Japan. He forced Japan to grant trading rights to the United States. The opening up of China to Europe was different. The British, French, Germans, Portuguese, Russians, and Japanese gained control over parts of China. Other countries then feared losing the opportunity to share in China's riches. In 1899, the United States announced the policy that China should be open for trade with all nations equally. For a while, nations halted their efforts to divide up China.

New Forces in the 1900s Many Chinese blamed the emperor for the foreign powers in their country. In 1911, revolution broke out in China. The rule of emperors ended, and a republic was set up.

Meanwhile, Japan was becoming more powerful. Its leaders sought to control other Asian countries. One of their reasons was to make sure that Japan would have resources to fuel its growing industries. Japanese attacks on other Asian and Pacific lands led to the start of World War II in East Asia in 1941. In 1945, the United States and its allies defeated Japan.

After World War II ended, civil war broke out in China between two groups, the Nationalists and the Communists. The Communists won the war in 1949 and made China a **communist** nation, one in which the government owns large industries, businesses, and most of the country's land.

After World War II, Korea was divided into two parts. Communists ruled North Korea. South Korea turned to Western nations for support. In 1950, North Korea invaded South Korea. The United States sent 480,000 troops to help South Korea. The Korean War lasted for three years, killing about 37,000 U.S. soldiers and more than 2 million Koreans. Neither side won. The battle line at the end of the war, in 1953, remains the border between the two Koreas today.

✓ **Reading Check** How did Japan's actions lead to the start of World War II in East Asia?

American veterans visiting a memorial in South Korea marking the 50th anniversary of the Korean War

Section 1 Assessment

Key Terms
Review the key terms at the beginning of this section. Use each term in a sentence that explains its meaning.

Target Reading Skill
Find the phrase *foreign powers* on page 298. Use context clues to figure out its meaning. What clues helped you figure out its meaning?

Comprehension and Critical Thinking
1. (a) List Name at least four achievements of the Chinese civilization.
(b) Find Main Ideas How was the Chinese civilization ruled from ancient times to 1911?

2. (a) Identify Give one example of cultural diffusion in East Asia.
(b) Make Generalizations Cultural diffusion can take place when people move from one place to another. When they do, they take their culture with them. Based on what you have read in this section, what are some other ways in which cultural diffusion can happen?
3. (a) Recall Why did U.S. Commodore Matthew Perry sail to Japan in 1853?
(b) Compare and Contrast How was the opening up of China to Europe different from the opening up of Japan?

Writing Activity
Suppose that you are a European merchant traveling through China in the 1300s. Use the chart on page 295 to write three short diary entries about the inventions and achievements you find there.

For: An activity on East Asia's history
Visit: PHSchool.com
Web Code: ngd-6401

Skills for Life

Reading Route Maps

Think of three inventions that had an important effect on human progress. What comes to mind: Farming? Books? Cars?

Did you think of *roads?*

The development of road networks has helped human civilization to grow and spread. Roads have been the lifelines of trade, communication, and human migration for thousands of years. Some of the world's oldest roads are in East Asia.

Learn the Skill

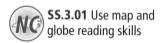

SS.3.01 Use map and globe reading skills

A map that shows roads is called a route map. Follow these steps to learn how to read a route map.

1 **Read the title of the map and become familiar with its features.** First, get a general idea of what region the map shows. Use the compass rose to figure out direction on the map.

2 **Study the key to understand its symbols.** Most modern road maps use colored lines to indicate various types of roads, from country roads to interstate highways. Other maps use colors to show land, sea, and air routes. The colors and what they represent are shown in the key. Notice what other symbols in the key represent, including cities.

3 **Trace routes on the map.** Gather information about the route by studying the features on the map. Use the scale of miles to calculate distances. Notice physical features and landmarks along the journey. Make note of any geographic barriers that would affect speed or comfort on the trip.

4 **Interpret the map.** Use information you gather from the map to draw conclusions about the route. On historical maps you can draw conclusions about why travelers and traders took certain routes and traveled at certain times of the year.

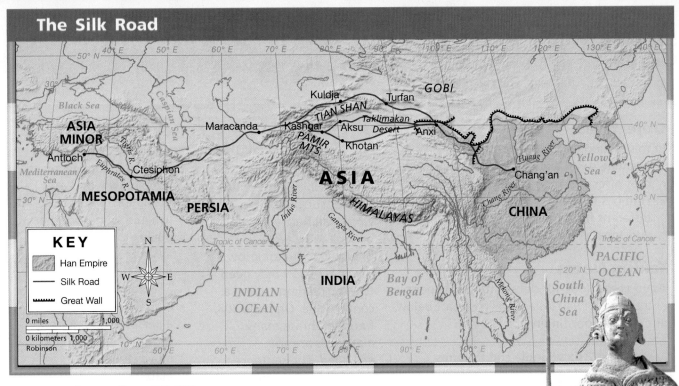

The Silk Road

KEY
- Han Empire
- Silk Road
- Great Wall

0 miles 1,000
0 kilometers 1,000
Robinson

Practice the Skill

Study the map and follow the steps on the previous page to practice reading a route map.

1 Read the title of the map and study the map to observe its main features. What region does it show? What type of map is it—modern or historical, a standard road map, or some other kind? What is its purpose?

2 Look at the key on this map. What features does it identify?

3 With your finger, start at the city of Chang'an, in China, and trace the general paths of the Silk Road. Using the compass rose, determine the direction of the route. What continents or regions did the Silk Road cross? Where did it end? Did it include travel over mountains?

4 The Silk Road was created over time, as local and regional routes became connected to form one long route. Write a paragraph that describes the route and draws conclusions about how and why it took the particular path shown on the map.

Apply the Skill

Find a street map of your community. Use the steps in the Learn the Skill section to trace the route from your house to your school or to some other location you know, such as a park. Write a paragraph that draws conclusions about the route you found.

Section 2

People and Cultures

Prepare to Read

Objectives

In this section you will

1. Examine some ways in which East Asia's past affects its modern-day culture.
2. Find out how the people of China are different from the people of the Koreas and Japan.

Taking Notes

As you read, look for details about the people and culture of East Asia. Copy the chart below, and record your findings in it.

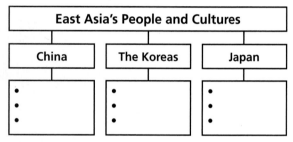

Target Reading Skill

Use Context Clues
Context, the words and phrases surrounding a word, can help you understand a word or phrase you do not know. Sometimes you may need to keep reading to find a context clue. On page 303, find the phrase *many marriages are still arranged.* The sentence that follows this phrase explains what an arranged marriage is.

Key Terms

- **commune** (KAHM yoon) *n.* a community in which people own land as a group and where they live and work together
- **dialect** (DY uh lekt) *n.* a variation of a language that is unique to a region or an area
- **nomad** (NOH mad) *n.* a person who has no settled home but who moves from place to place
- **homogeneous** (hoh moh JEE nee us) *adj.* identical or similar
- **ethnic group** (ETH nik groop) *n.* a group of people who share such characteristics as language, religion, and ancestry

Two men play a game of Go in a small South Korean village.

The Chinese game weiqi (WAY chee) has ancient cultural roots. One player has 181 black stones standing for night. The other has 180 white stones standing for day. The goal is to surround and capture the opponent's stones. But to the Chinese, weiqi is more than a game. For centuries, Buddhists have used it to discipline the mind. Today, you can see people playing this ancient game throughout East Asia. Another name for this traditional Chinese game is Go.

Tradition and Change

In East Asia, tradition mixes with change in a thousand ways. Businesspeople in Western suits greet each other in the traditional way—with a bow. Ancient palaces stand among skyscrapers. Everywhere in Japan, China, and the Koreas, reminders of the past mingle with activities of the present.

Communism Changes Chinese Farming When the Communists took power in 1949, they began to make major changes. The government ended the old system of land ownership. It created **communes,** communities in which land is held in common and where members live and work together.

Many Chinese farmers were bitter at losing their land. They were accustomed to living in family groups that worked together in small fields. The farmers resisted the communes. Food production fell, and China suffered terrible food shortages. Only when the government allowed some private ownership did food production grow.

Changes in Chinese Life Beginning in the 1970s, the Communists also tried to slow China's population growth by attacking the idea of large families. Chinese couples were supposed to wait until their late twenties to marry. They were not supposed to have more than one child per family. Chinese families with only one child could receive special privileges. For example, couples in urban areas could receive a payment of money. In rural areas, the reward could be more land.

Under communism, the position of women improved. One of the first laws the Communists passed allowed a woman to own property, choose her husband, and get a divorce. Today, however, men still hold most of the power, and many marriages are still arranged. That is, parents or other family members decide who will marry whom.

Shanghai at Night
Shanghai, China, is a bustling city with skyscrapers and superhighways. The small photo shows Nanjing Road, one of the principal streets in Shanghai. **Analyze Images** *Do you think Shanghai is a large or a small city? Explain your answer.*

Japan's Capsule Hotels
In densely populated Japan, people have developed unique ways to use space. Capsule hotels are one such example. They are used mainly by businessmen who have missed the last train home. Each capsule usually has a bed, a television, a radio, and an alarm clock. **Analyze Images** *What are most of the people in the photo doing?*

Use Context Clues
Use the last two sentences in this paragraph to help you define *traditional customs.* Check your definition by looking up *traditional* and *custom* in a dictionary.

Old and New in China Old traditions in China are strongest in rural areas. Yet even in the cities, a visitor sees examples of the old China. In cities like Beijing, the capital of China, the streets are filled with three-wheeled cabs pedaled like tricycles. These pedicabs share the roads with buses, cars, and taxis. Tiny shops exist side by side with modern buildings.

Changes in the Koreas In both Koreas, daily life is influenced by long-standing traditions. The family is still important, although the average family is smaller today than before. In rural areas, grandparents, parents, aunts, and uncles may live in one household. In the cities, usually just parents and children live as one household.

As in China, modern ways are much more visible in Korean urban areas. Also, as is true all over the world, the role of women has changed. In the past, Korean women had few opportunities. Today, women can work and vote.

A Blend of Old and New in Japan Japan is the most modern of the East Asian countries. The Japanese use more modern technology than the rest of East Asia. Nearly 80 percent of the population lives in urban areas. Once Japanese workers reach home, however, many still follow traditional customs. For example, they may change into kimonos, or robes. They may sit on mats at a low table to have dinner.

✓ **Reading Check** **Which is the most modern country in East Asia?**

East Asia's People

East Asia is a mix of cultures both old and new. Within each of the area's countries, however, the people tend to share a single culture.

Discovery CHANNEL SCHOOL Video

Learn about the history of China's merchant class.

China: The Han and Other Chinese Ethnic Groups

About 19 of every 20 Chinese people trace their ancestry to the Han ethnic group. As you can see on the map below, the Han live mostly in the eastern half of China. Although they have a common written language, they speak different dialects from region to region. A **dialect** is a variation of a language that is unique to a region or area. The other Chinese come from 55 different minority groups. These groups live mainly in western and southern China. With so many different ethnic groups, China is one of the most ethnically diverse nations in the world.

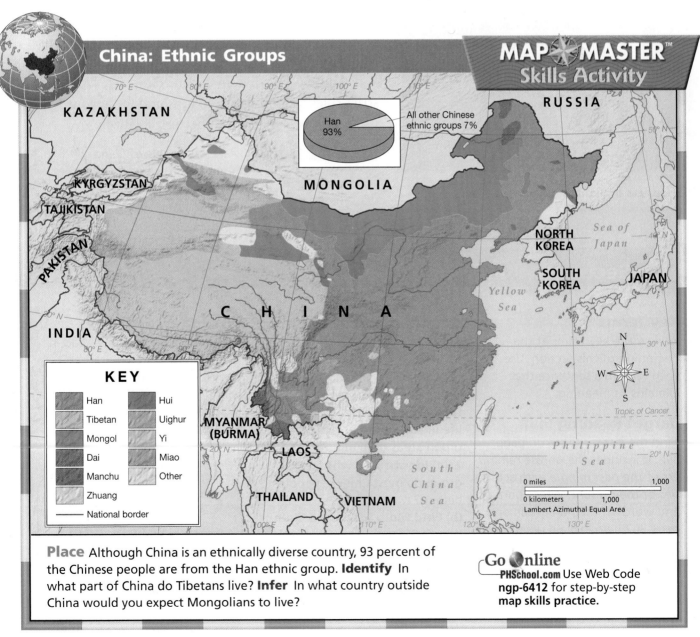

China: Ethnic Groups

MAP MASTER™ Skills Activity

Han 93%

All other Chinese ethnic groups 7%

KEY

- Han
- Tibetan
- Mongol
- Dai
- Manchu
- Zhuang
- Hui
- Uighur
- Yi
- Miao
- Other
- National border

Place Although China is an ethnically diverse country, 93 percent of the Chinese people are from the Han ethnic group. **Identify** In what part of China do Tibetans live? **Infer** In what country outside China would you expect Mongolians to live?

Go Online
PHSchool.com Use Web Code ngp-6412 for step-by-step map skills practice.

Shoppers in Seoul, South Korea

Korea and Japan: Few Minorities Historians believe that the ancient Korean language was brought to Korea by nomads from the north. **Nomads** are people who have no settled home but who move from place to place, usually on a seasonal basis. Over centuries, these groups lost their separate traditions. They formed one **homogeneous** (hoh moh JEE nee us) group, which means identical or similar. Today, even with the division of Korea into two countries, the population is quite homogeneous. There are few minority groups.

Because it is an island nation that isolated itself from the world for a long time, Japan has one of the most homogeneous populations on Earth. Nearly all of the people belong to the same **ethnic group,** a group of people who share such characteristics as language, religion, ancestry, and cultural traditions. Minority groups are few. Small numbers of Koreans and Chinese also live in Japan. However, Japan has strict rules on immigration. It is hard for anyone who is not Japanese by birth to become a citizen.

✓ **Reading Check** How are the people of China different from the people of the Koreas and Japan?

Section 2 Assessment

Key Terms
Review the key terms at the beginning of this section. Use each term in a sentence that explains its meaning.

Target Reading Skill
Find the last sentence on page 302. It includes the phrase *reminders of the past mingle with activities of the present.* Which phrases and words in the paragraph on page 302 help explain what the phrase means?

Comprehension and Critical Thinking
1. (a) Recall In what two major ways did the Communists make changes in the Chinese way of life?
(b) Summarize How is modern life in East Asia more visible in urban areas than in rural areas?
2. (a) Identify To which ethnic group do most Chinese people belong?
(b) Find Main Ideas and Details Why is China said to be an ethnically diverse country?
(c) Summarize Why are the populations of the Koreas and Japan homogeneous?

Writing Activity
Based on what you have read in this section, write a paragraph describing how tradition and change exist together in East Asia. Include at least three supporting details for your topic sentence.

For: An activity on East Asia's culture
Visit: PHSchool.com
Web Code: ngd-6402

Review and Assessment

◆ Chapter Summary

Section 1: Historic Traditions

- China has the oldest continuous civilization in the world. Starting in ancient times, a series of dynasties ruled China.
- Paper, gunpowder, silk weaving, and the magnetic compass are among China's many cultural and technical achievements.
- The Shilla people unified Korea as one country. A series of shoguns ruled Japan for more than 700 years.
- In the 1800s, western nations became interested in East Asia as a market to sell goods.

Japanese *No* mask

Section 2: People and Cultures

- China has been governed under a Communist system since 1949. The Communist party has made major changes in the Chinese way of life.
- Although China is becoming more modern, old traditions are still followed, especially in rural areas of the country.
- As in China, modern ways of life in the Koreas are more visible in urban areas. Japan is the most modern of the East Asian countries but also lives by its historic traditions.
- Most people in China belong to the Han ethnic group. Korea's history resulted in a homogeneous population. As in the Koreas, nearly all Japanese people belong to the same ethnic group.

Shanghai, China

◆ Key Terms

Each of the statements below contains a key term from the chapter. If the statement is true, write *true*. If it is false, rewrite the statement to make it true.

1. An emperor is the male ruler of an empire.

2. A clan is a series of rulers from the same family.

3. A dynasty is a group of families with a common ancestor.

4. Cultural diffusion is the spreading of ideas or practices from one culture to other cultures.

5. People with the same dialect use a variation of a language that is unique to their region or area.

6. A nomad is a community in which people own land as a group and where they live together and work together.

7. A homogeneous group includes people who are identical or similar.

8. An ethnic group shares such characteristics as language, religion, ancestry, and cultural traditions.

◆ Comprehension and Critical Thinking

9. (a) Explain What is a civilization?
(b) Describe What are some achievements of the ancient Chinese civilization?
(c) Make Generalizations Give some examples of how ancient Chinese achievements still affect the world today.

10. (a) Recall To which ethnic group do most of the people in China belong?
(b) Summarize How does China's population differ from the populations of Japan and the Koreas in terms of ethnic diversity?

11. (a) Define What is a dynasty?
(b) Contrast How is China governed today, and how is that government different from China's government in ancient times?

12. (a) Recall About what percentage of people in Japan live in urban areas?
(b) Synthesize Information Give examples of how life in East Asia reflects past traditions and present traditions.
(c) Predict Why might past traditions be followed more in rural areas of East Asia than in urban areas?

13. (a) Recall When did the Communists come into power in China?
(b) Summarize What changes did the Communists make to the Chinese way of life?

◆ Skills Practice

Reading Route Maps In the Skills for Life activity in this chapter, you learned how to read route maps. Review the steps you followed to learn this skill. Then use the map on page 301 to name two rivers in Mesopotamia that the Silk Road crossed. If a traveler was heading west on the Silk Road, which river would he cross first?

◆ Writing Activity: History

As you have read in this chapter, paper was invented in ancient China, as were many other things. Choose one of the inventions named in this chapter, and do research in the library or on the Internet to learn more about it. Find out how it was made and used in ancient China. Also, find out how the invention spread to other parts of the world. Write a paragraph about what you have learned.

MAP★MASTER™ Skills Activity

Place Location For each place listed below, write the letter from the map that shows its location.

1. Mongolia
2. China
3. Taiwan
4. North Korea
5. South Korea
6. Japan

Go Online
PHSchool.com Use Web Code ngp-6420 for an interactive map.

East Asia

Standardized Test Prep

Test-Taking Tips

Some questions on standardized tests ask you to analyze timelines. Study the timeline below. Then follow the tips to answer the sample question.

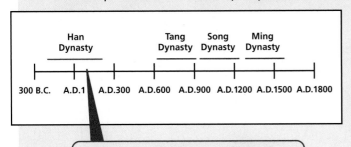

TIP To read a timeline, first figure out the timespan between dates (in this case it is 300 years). Then line up each event or dynasty with the nearest date or dates and estimate.

Pick the letter that best answers the question.

The world's oldest printed book was found in China. It was made around A.D. 868, during the

A Han dynasty.

B Tang dynasty.

C Song dynasty.

D Ming dynasty.

Think It Through The oldest book was made around A.D. 868. You can eliminate Han and Ming (A and D) because they are not near that date. Now look closely at the timeline: A.D. 868 is between A.D. 600 and A.D. 900. The Song Dynasty started *after* A.D. 900. So the correct answer is B, the Tang Dynasty.

TIP Rewrite the sentence in your own words to make sure you understand what it is asking: *During which dynasty was the oldest book made?*

Practice Questions

Use the tips above and other tips in this book to help you answer the following questions.

1. Based on the timeline above, the Tang dynasty lasted about

   A 100 years.

   B 200 years.

   C 300 years.

   D 400 years.

2. The religion of Buddhism, which China adopted from India, is an example of

   A cultural migration.

   B irrigation.

   C cultural diffusion.

   D Communist rule.

3. Which statement correctly describes Chinese culture?

   A Everyone in China belongs to the same ethnic group.

   B Chinese people speak different dialects from region to region.

   C Old traditions and ways of life are illegal in China.

   D There are two ethnic groups in China.

Go Online
PHSchool.com

Use Web Code **nga-6400** for **Chapter 11 self-test.**

Chapter 12

South, Southwest, and Central Asia: Cultures and History

Chapter Preview

 Standard Course of Study

7.4.02 Commodities of trade and their significance for cultures and regions

7.4.03 Influence of ideas and values on development of societies

7.5.01 How the location of natural resources affects economic development

7.5.03 Evaluate impact of economic decisions on standard of living

7.5.04 How specialization and interdependence influence trade patterns

7.7.01 Relationship between historical events and current issues

7.8.01 Impact of historical figures on past and present societies

7.8.02 Impact of key groups on historical and contemporary societies

7.9.01 Historical developments of types of governments

7.10.01 Development of relationships between individuals and their governments

7.12.01 Impact of belief systems on practices and institutions

Sections

1. **South Asia: Cultures and History**
   7.8.01, 7.9.01, 7.10.01, 7.12.01
2. **Southwest Asia: Cultures and History**
   7.4.03, 7.8.02, 7.12.01
3. **Central Asia: Cultures and History**
   7.4.02, 7.5.04, 7.7.01, 7.8.02, 7.9.01

 Target Reading Skill

Word Analysis In this chapter, you will focus on analyzing words. For example, you will learn to break unfamiliar words into parts to understand the words.

▶ **Amber Fort is one of the many forts and palaces of South Asia. It is located in India.**

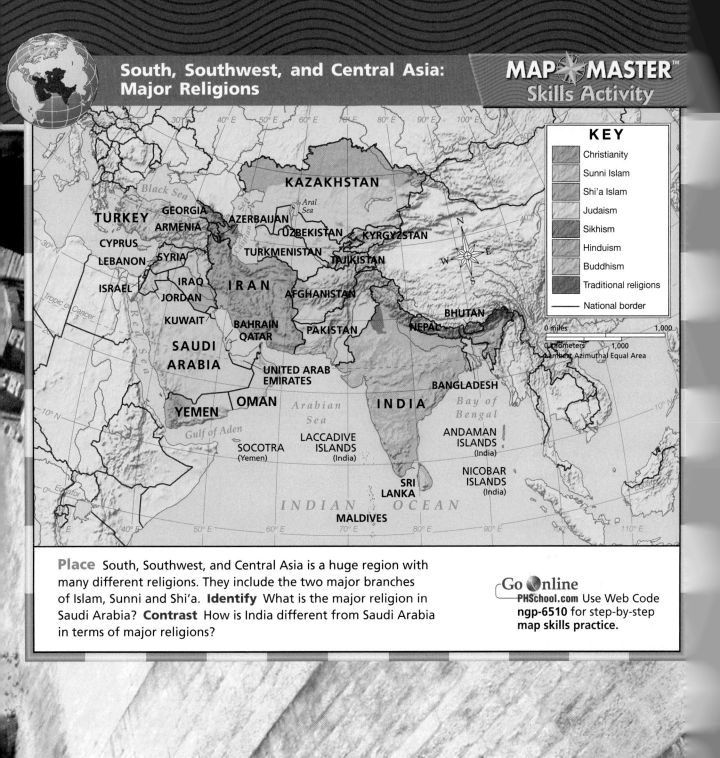

KEY

- Christianity
- Sunni Islam
- Shi'a Islam
- Judaism
- Sikhism
- Hinduism
- Buddhism
- Traditional religions
- National border

KAZAKHSTAN

Black Sea

Aral Sea

TURKEY
GEORGIA
ARMENIA
AZERBAIJAN
UZBEKISTAN
KYRGYZSTAN
CYPRUS
TURKMENISTAN
LEBANON SYRIA
TAJIKISTAN
ISRAEL IRAQ IRAN
JORDAN AFGHANISTAN
KUWAIT
BAHRAIN
QATAR PAKISTAN
BHUTAN
NEPAL
SAUDI
ARABIA
UNITED ARAB
EMIRATES
BANGLADESH
OMAN
YEMEN
Arabian
Sea
INDIA
Bay of
Bengal
Gulf of Aden
SOCOTRA
(Yemen)
LACCADIVE
ISLANDS
(India)
ANDAMAN
ISLANDS
(India)
NICOBAR
ISLANDS
(India)
SRI
LANKA
INDIAN OCEAN
MALDIVES

Red Sea

Tropic of Cancer

Equator

0 miles 1,000
0 kilometers 1,000
Lambert Azimuthal Equal Area

Place South, Southwest, and Central Asia is a huge region with many different religions. They include the two major branches of Islam, Sunni and Shi'a. **Identify** What is the major religion in Saudi Arabia? **Contrast** How is India different from Saudi Arabia in terms of major religions?

Section 1

South Asia
Cultures and History

Prepare to Read

Objectives

In this section, you will

1. Find out which religions became part of South Asian cultures.
2. Understand which empires shaped the history of South Asia.
3. Learn about the present-day religions and languages of South Asian cultures.

Taking Notes

As you read this section, look for main ideas about the history and cultures of South Asia. Copy the web below, and record your findings in it.

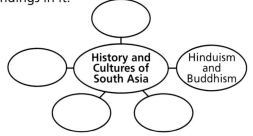

Target Reading Skill

Analyze Word Parts When you come across a word you do not know, break the word into parts to help you recognize it and pronounce it. This may help you find its root and prefix. A root is the part of the word that has meaning by itself. A prefix goes in front of the root and changes its meaning. In this section you will find the word *nonviolent*. Break it into a root and a prefix to learn its meaning.

Key Terms

• **caste** (kast) *n.* in the Hindu religion, a social group into which people are born and which they cannot change; each group with assigned jobs
• **colony** (KAHL uh nee) *n.* a territory ruled by another nation
• **boycott** (BOY kaht) *n.* a refusal to buy or use goods and services to show disapproval or bring about change
• **partition** (pahr TISH un) *n.* a division into parts or portions

In 1921, scientists digging near the Indus River came upon the ruins of an ancient city they called Mohenjo-Daro (moh HEN joh DAH roh). The city was amazingly well planned, with wide, straight streets and large buildings. It had a sewer system and a large walled fortress. Mohenjo-Daro was part of a civilization that developed about 4,500 years ago. The people who lived there were part of the Indus Valley civilization, one of the world's oldest civilizations.

Over the centuries, many other people moved into South Asia. All of them contributed to South Asian culture. South Asian culture, in turn, influenced cultures of other regions. Hinduism (HIN doo iz um) and Buddhism (BOO diz um), two religions that developed in South Asia, are practiced by hundreds of millions of people all over the world.

This ancient statue of a priest-king was unearthed at Mohenjo-Daro.

New Religions

The Indus Valley civilization flourished from about 2500 B.C. to about 1600 B.C. By 1500 B.C., however, the civilization was coming to an end. Scholars are uncertain why this happened.

About the same time that the Indus Valley civilization was weakening, newcomers came to the region, probably from Central Asia. They brought different languages and beliefs to the region. The newcomers merged with the people of the Indus Valley. A new culture combined the ancient languages and beliefs of the region with the language and religion of the newcomers. This mixed culture is known as Aryan culture. The people who practiced this culture are known as Aryans (AYR ee unz).

The Aryans ruled northern India for more than 1,000 years. They divided people into four classes—priests and the educated; rulers and warriors; farmers, artisans, and merchants; and laborers. Europeans later called the division the caste (kast) system. A **caste** is a social group into which people are born and which they cannot change.

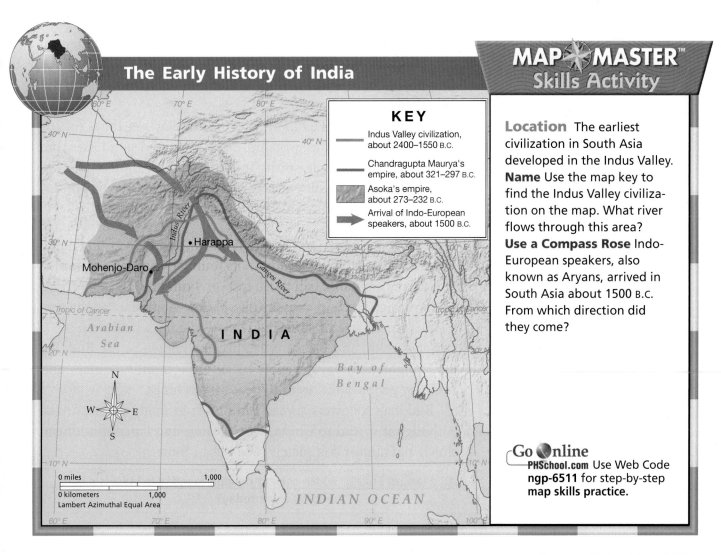

The Early History of India

KEY

Indus Valley civilization, about 2400–1550 B.C.

Chandragupta Maurya's empire, about 321–297 B.C.

Asoka's empire, about 273–232 B.C.

Arrival of Indo-European speakers, about 1500 B.C.

Harappa

Mohenjo-Daro

Indus River

Ganges River

Tropic of Cancer

Arabian Sea

I N D I A

Bay of Bengal

0 miles 1,000
0 kilometers 1,000
Lambert Azimuthal Equal Area

INDIAN OCEAN

MAP★MASTER™
Skills Activity

Location The earliest civilization in South Asia developed in the Indus Valley.
Name Use the map key to find the Indus Valley civilization on the map. What river flows through this area?
Use a Compass Rose Indo-European speakers, also known as Aryans, arrived in South Asia about 1500 B.C. From which direction did they come?

Go Online
PHSchool.com Use Web Code **ngp-6511** for step-by-step map skills practice.

Three Main Hindu Gods
One of the world's oldest religions, Hinduism dates back more than 3,000 years. Shown here are the three main gods in the Hindu trinity

① Brahma is regarded as the creator of the universe.
② Vishnu is worshipped as the preserver of the universe.
③ Shiva appears in many different forms, including the destroyer of the universe.

This lion sculpture originally stood at the top of one of Asoka's pillars.
Decimal Numbers By about A.D. 600, Indian astronomers

Hinduism The caste system was one aspect of a new system of belief that also emerged from Aryan religious ideas and practices. This system of beliefs, Hinduism, is one of the world's oldest living religions.

Hinduism is unlike other major world religions. It has no one single founder. Hindus worship many gods and goddesses, but they believe in a single spirit. To Hindus, the various gods and goddesses represent different parts of this spirit. Today, Hinduism is the main religion of India.

Buddhism Buddhism, like Hinduism, developed in India. According to Buddhist tradition, its founder was a prince named Siddhartha Gautama (sih DAHR tuh GOW tuh muh). He was born in about 560 B.C., in present-day Nepal. Gautama taught that people can be free of suffering if they give up selfish desires for power, wealth, and pleasure. He became known as the Buddha, or "Enlightened One." People of all backgrounds, princes and ordinary people alike, went to hear his teachings.

Buddha's followers spread Buddhism to many parts of Asia. Although it spread to China, Tibet, Korea, and Japan, Buddhism slowly but almost completely died out in India.

✓ **Reading Check** **Which ancient religion founded in India is a main religion there today?**

From Empires to Nations

Today, South Asia is a region of independent countries. Starting in ancient times, however, a series of empires rose and fell in the region. Before South Asian countries became independent in the 1900s, the region was under European control.

The Maurya Empire Around 321 B.C., a leader named Chandragupta Maurya (chun druh GOOP tuh MOWR yuh) conquered many kingdoms. By the time of his death in 298 B.C., the Maurya Empire covered much of the Indian subcontinent.

Chandragupta's grandson, Asoka (uh SOH kuh), became emperor in 268 B.C. After one bloody battle, Asoka gave up war and violence. He changed his beliefs to Buddhism and vowed to rule peacefully. Asoka had stone pillars set up across India. Carved into the pillars were his laws and beliefs in fair and just government.

The Maurya Empire lost power not long after Asoka's death. By about 185 B.C. the empire collapsed as rival leaders fought for power.

The Gupta Empire About 500 years after the Mauryas, the Gupta Empire again united much of the Indian subcontinent. The Guptas ruled from A.D. 320 to about A.D. 550. Gupta emperors set up a strong central government that was supported by trade and farming.

Under Gupta rule, India enjoyed a period of great cultural achievement. Gupta mathematicians developed the system of writing numerals that we use today. These numerals are called "Arabic" numerals. Arabs carried them from India to Southwest Asia and Europe. People built splendid temples of stone decorated with carvings. Artists created wall paintings of Buddhist stories in temples built inside caves at Ajanta (uh JUN tuh) in western India.

Weak rulers and foreign invaders led to the fall of the Gupta Empire. The empire lasted until about A.D. 550.

The Mughal Empire In the A.D. 700s, people from the north began moving into northern India. They introduced the religion of Islam to the area. According to its followers, Islam is the set of beliefs revealed to the prophet Muhammad. He began teaching these beliefs around A.D. 610 in Southwest Asia. Islam eventually spread westward into North Africa and eastward into Central and South Asia.

This lion sculpture originally stood at the top of one of Asoka's pillars.

Links to Math

Decimal Numbers By about A.D. 600, Indian astronomers were using the decimal system—a numbering system based on tens. Their system also had place values and a zero. This made it easy to add, subtract, multiply, and divide. Europeans were using Roman numerals at this time. They later switched to this decimal, or Hindu-Arabic, system, which is used worldwide today.

The Taj Mahal, India
The Taj Mahal is considered to be one of the world's most beautiful buildings. Emperor Shah Jahan had it built as a tomb for his wife. The small photo shows the actual tomb inside the marble structure. **Analyze Images** *How does the large photo show symmetry in the design of the Taj Mahal?*

Analyze Word Parts
Look for the word *subcontinent* in this paragraph. The prefix *sub-* means "under." Now define the word *subcontinent*.

Among these Muslims, or followers of Islam, who settled in India were the Mughals (MOO gulz). They arrived in the 1500s and established an empire. Akbar (AK bahr), who ruled the Mughal Empire from 1556 to 1605, allowed all people to worship freely, regardless of their religion. He also generously supported the arts and literature.

Akbar's grandson, Shah Jahan (shah juh HAHN), built many grand buildings. Perhaps the greatest is the Taj Mahal (tahzh muh HAHL), which still stands today. He had it built as a magnificent tomb for Mumtaz Mahal (mum TAHZ muh HAHL), his wife. The cost of this and other of Jahan's building projects was enormous. It drained the empire of money and, eventually, helped to cause the empire's collapse in the 1700s.

The British in India By the late 1700s, much of the Indian subcontinent had come under British rule. Until 1858, a trading company known as the British East India Company controlled most of India. The British government ended the rule of the British East India Company in 1858. From that time until 1947, India was controlled by Britain as a colony of Britain's empire. A **colony** is a territory ruled by another nation.

Independence and Division In the early 1900s, a strong independence movement emerged in India. Its leader was Mohandas K. Gandhi (GAHN dee). Gandhi called for people to resist British rule. However, Gandhi stressed that they use nonviolent means. For example, he urged a boycott of British goods. A **boycott** means a refusal to buy or use goods and services to show disapproval or bring about change. Gandhi played a major part in forcing Britain to grant India its independence in 1947.

As independence approached, Muslims feared that their rights would not be protected in a land where Hindus were the majority. Fighting erupted as demands arose for a state where Muslims would be the majority. In 1947 this led to the **partition**, or division, of the subcontinent into two nations, Pakistan and India. Muslims would be the majority in Pakistan. Hindus would be the majority in India.

This partition did not stop the fighting. About one million people were killed. Gandhi himself was murdered by a Hindu who was angered at Gandhi's concern for Muslims.

Conflict in South Asia Conflict between India and Pakistan continued throughout the 1900s. In 1971, Indian troops helped East Pakistan break away from Pakistan to form the nation of Bangladesh (BAHNG luh desh). Pakistan and India have fought over the question of which country controls Kashmir (KASH mihr), an area on the border of India and Pakistan. In 1998, both nations tested nuclear weapons. The continuing threat of conflict that might involve nuclear weapons in the region concerns the United States and other countries.

✓ **Reading Check** **What are some contributions from the Maurya, Gupta, and Mughal empires?**

Indian Independence leader Mohandas Gandhi

Republic Day in India
Every January 26, Indians celebrate Republic Day to mark the adoption of the Indian constitution on January 26, 1950.
Infer *Which national flag do you think is shown in the photo?*

Selling spices at an open-air market in India

South Asian Cultures Today

South Asia's long history continues to shape its cultures. Two major examples are religion and languages.

Many Religions Hinduism and Islam are the major religions of South Asia today. About 80 percent of the people in India are Hindus. Hinduism is also the major religion in Nepal. Islam is the main religion in Pakistan and Bangladesh. Other religions in South Asia include Christianity, Sikhism (SEEK iz um), and Jainism (JY niz um). Sikhism began as a religion that combined Hindu and Muslim beliefs. Followers of Jainism believe that violence toward or injury of any living thing is wrong.

Many Languages Many different languages are spoken in South Asia. The languages of South Asia generally belong to two families. Dravidian (druh VID ee un) languages are spoken in southern India. Indo-European languages are spoken in northern India and most of the rest of South Asia. The Aryans who came into South Asia in ancient times spoke Indo-European languages. One of the languages in this group is Hindi (HIN dee). About 30 percent of the people in India speak Hindi. Hindi is one of 22 languages recognized by the Indian government. English is also widely used as an official language in India.

✓ **Reading Check** In which two South Asian countries is Hinduism the major religion?

Section 1 Assessment

Key Terms
Review the key terms at the beginning of this section. Use each term in a sentence that explains its meaning.

Target Reading Skill
Find the word *uncertain* on page 313 in the first paragraph under the heading New Religions. The prefix *un-* means "not." What is the meaning of *uncertain*?

Comprehension and Critical Thinking
1. (a) Recall Which group of people developed the caste system?
(b) Sequence Which developed first, Hinduism or Buddhism?
2. (a) Name Which empire introduced Islam to South Asia?
(b) Identify Effect What major issues led to the partition of India in 1947?
3. (a) Identify What is the main religion in Pakistan?
(b) Make Generalizations How can the movement of people from one place to another affect language in a region?

Writing Activity
Suppose you are traveling throughout South Asia. Write a letter to your family in which you describe ways in which the history of the region is shown in its present-day culture.

Writing Tip Your letter should begin with a greeting and end with a closing and a signature. The body of the letter contains the information you want to communicate to your reader.

Section 2

Southwest Asia
Cultures and History

Prepare to Read

Objectives

In this section, you will

1. Find out that one of the world's earliest civilizations grew in Southwest Asia.
2. Understand that three of the world's great religions began in Southwest Asia.
3. Examine the different ethnic groups and religions of Southwest Asia.
4. Learn about the conflict between Arabs and Israelis in Southwest Asia.

Taking Notes

As you read this section, look for details about the three main religions that developed in Southwest Asia. Copy the chart below, and record your findings in it.

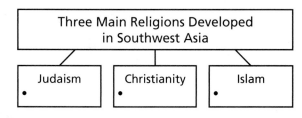

```
Three Main Religions Developed
       in Southwest Asia

  Judaism    Christianity    Islam
  •            •              •
```

Target Reading Skill

Analyze Word Parts Breaking an unfamiliar word into parts can help you understand the word. Word parts include roots and suffixes. A root is the base of a word that has meaning by itself. A suffix comes at the end of a root word. Suffixes change the meanings of root words. In this section you will read the word *creation*. The suffix *-ion* makes the word a noun. If you know what *create* means, you can figure out the meaning of *creation*.

Key Terms

- **monotheism** (MAHN oh thee iz um) *n.* a belief that there is only one god
- **muezzin** (myoo EZ in) *n.* a person whose job is to call Muslims to pray
- **Holocaust** (HAHL uh kawst) *n.* the systematic killing of more than six million European Jews and others by Nazi Germany before and during World War II

Hammurabi's Code was written about 3,800 years ago in Southwest Asia. People have described its laws as demanding "an eye for an eye." But there was more to the code than that.

> **If the robber is not caught, the man who has been robbed shall formally declare whatever he has lost . . . and the city and the mayor . . . shall replace whatever he has lost for him. . . . If a person is too lazy to make the dike of his field strong and there is a break in the dike and water destroys his own farmland, that person will make good the grain [tax] that is destroyed.**
>
> —*from Hammurabi's Code*

The law punished people severely for wrongdoings. But it also offered justice to people who had been hurt through no fault of their own.

In this ancient carving, Hammurabi receives his code of laws from the sun god.

Mesopotamia

Hammurabi ruled the city of Babylon from about 1800 B.C. to 1750 B.C. He united the region along the Tigris and Euphrates rivers. Located in present-day Iraq, this region was called Mesopotamia, which is derived from Greek words meaning "between the rivers." Mesopotamia was one of the world's earliest civilizations.

The people of Mesopotamia developed a system of writing. They also produced ideas about law that still affect people today. For example, they believed that all citizens must obey the same set of laws.

People had lived in Mesopotamia for thousands of years before Hammurabi united it. By 3500 B.C., the area became a center of farming and trade. The Tigris and Euphrates rivers flooded every year, leaving fertile soil along their banks. People dug irrigation ditches to bring water to fields that lay far from the river. Irrigation helped them to produce crop surpluses, or more than they needed for their own use.

Explore the history of trade in Southwest Asia.

✓ **Reading Check** **In what present-day country did Mesopotamia develop?**

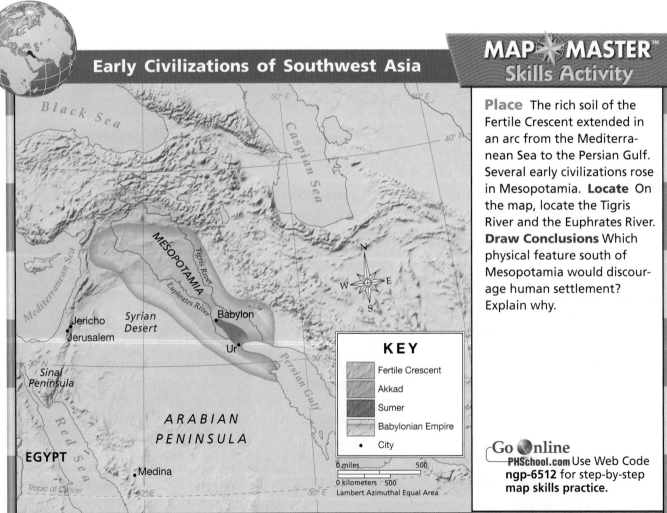

Early Civilizations of Southwest Asia

MAP MASTER™ Skills Activity

Place The rich soil of the Fertile Crescent extended in an arc from the Mediterranean Sea to the Persian Gulf. Several early civilizations rose in Mesopotamia. **Locate** On the map, locate the Tigris River and the Euphrates River. **Draw Conclusions** Which physical feature south of Mesopotamia would discourage human settlement? Explain why.

KEY
- Fertile Crescent
- Akkad
- Sumer
- Babylonian Empire
- • City

0 miles 500
0 kilometers 500
Lambert Azimuthal Equal Area

Go Online
PHSchool.com Use Web Code ngp-6512 for step-by-step map skills practice.

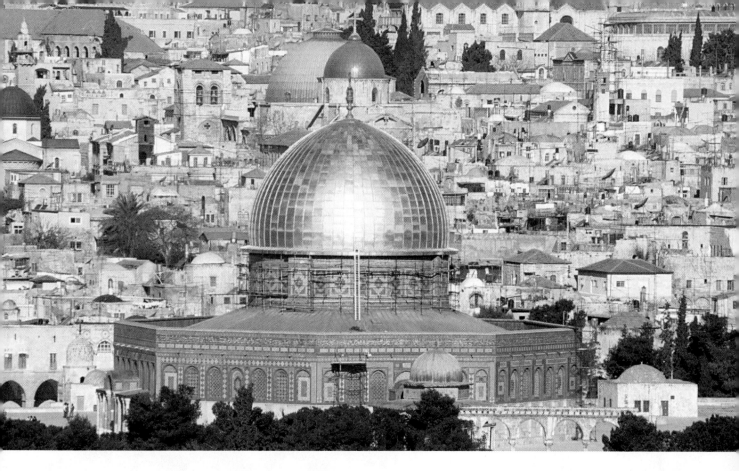

Birthplace of Three Religions

Three of the world's greatest religions—Judaism, Christianity, and Islam—have their roots in Southwest Asia. About 2000 B.C., according to Hebrew religious writings, a man later known as Abraham founded the religion that would become known as Judaism. He lived in present-day Israel. Almost 2,000 years later, Jesus, the founder of Christianity, began preaching in present-day Israel. In about A.D. 600, Islam's founder and prophet, Muhammad, began teaching in present-day Saudi Arabia.

People who practice these three religions share a belief in monotheism. **Monotheism** is a belief in only one god. The followers of these religions also worship the same God—known as Allah in Islam.

Islam Of the three religions, Islam has by far the most followers in Southwest Asia today. They are called Muslims. The sights and sounds of Islam are everywhere in Southwest Asia. One sound is the call of the **muezzin** (myoo EZ in), a person whose job is to call Muslims to pray. Five times a day, Muslims stop what they are doing and pray. In large cities, the call to prayer is broadcast over loudspeakers. Throughout Southwest Asia, as well as other regions in the world, Muslims gather to worship in buildings called mosques. One of the most famous is the Dome of the Rock, shown in the photo on this page.

Jerusalem, A Holy City
Jerusalem is holy to Jews, Christians, and Muslims because events important to their religions took place there. The golden-domed building is the Dome of the Rock. It stands over the rock from which Muslims believe the prophet Muhammad rose into heaven. **Infer** *Why might Muslims from around the world want to visit Jerusalem?*

These women are praying at the Western Wall, held sacred by Jews as the remains of the Second Temple.

The New Testament of the Christian Bible describes Jesus as a good shepherd who lays down his life for his sheep.

Judaism At the heart of Judaism is the Torah (TOH ruh), five books that make up the Jews' most sacred text. According to the Torah, about 2000 B.C. Abraham, a Mesopotamian man, became convinced that there was one god, not many. He migrated to Canaan, where he became the ancestor of the Jewish people. Canaan was an area of land located along the eastern shore of the Mediterranean Sea. Hundreds of years later, it became known as Palestine. From ancient times, Jews saw Palestine as their homeland. The Torah also contains the Ten Commandments. They established religious duties toward God as well as rules for moral and ethical behavior.

Christianity Christianity first developed around A.D. 30. The religion is based on the teachings of Jesus, a Jew who traveled throughout Palestine. Christians later adopted the Torah as the first five books of the Old Testament of the Christian Bible. The first four books of the New Testament of the Christian Bible are the Gospels. They tell about the life and teachings of Jesus. According to the Gospels, Jesus taught that his followers would have eternal life. Like Islam and Judaism, Christianity began in Southwest Asia and spread throughout the world.

✓ Reading Check   Why is Southwest Asia considered the birthplace of Judaism, Christianity, and Islam?

Diverse Cultures in Southwest Asia

More than 3,000 years ago, the land of Southwest Asia was at the center of trading routes that extended across Europe, Africa, and Asia. Time after time, groups from within and outside the region conquered it. The movement of people across Southwest Asia gave the region a unique character. People of many different ethnic groups and religious beliefs settled there.

Arabic-speaking Arabs are the largest ethnic group in the region, and Islam is their main religion. But not all Southwest Asians are Arabs. Many Southwest Asians do not speak Arabic and many people, including Arabic-speaking Arabs, practice religions other than Islam.

A Mix of Ethnic Groups The people in Southwest Asia belong to a mix of ethnic groups. Today, Arabs are the main ethnic group in Saudi Arabia, Jordan, Syria, Iraq, Lebanon, and other countries on the Arabian Peninsula. Arabs also live in territories occupied by Israel. Non-Arab people live mainly in Israel, Turkey, and Iran. In Israel, about 80 percent of the population is Jewish. The remaining 20 percent is mostly Arab. In Turkey, about 80 percent of the population is Turkish. The rest of Turkey's population is Kurdish. Kurdish people also live in communities in Syria, Iraq, and Iran. In Iran, about 50 percent of the people are Persian. The rest belong to a number of different ethnic groups.

About half of Iran's population is Persian.

A Variety of Religions Except for Israel, the majority of the people in each country in Southwest Asia are Muslim. Even within the Islamic religion, however, there are differences. Muslims are divided into two main groups—Sunnis (SOO neez) and Shi'as (SHEE uz). Today, about 90 percent of Muslims are Sunni. Most of the Muslims in both Iran and Iraq, however, are Shi'as.

In Israel, about 80 percent of the people are Jewish. Muslims make up about 20 percent of the population. A small percentage of people in Israel are Christian. Christians also live in Syria, Turkey, Lebanon, and Iraq.

✓ **Reading Check** To which branch of Islam do most Muslims belong?

Scenes of Hope
A Jewish boy and a Palestinian boy walk together in Israel (left). Israeli troops supervise the evacuation of Jewish residents from the Gaza Strip in 2005 (right). **Infer** *Why might friendship and compromise help solve conflict?*

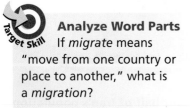

Analyze Word Parts
If *migrate* means "move from one country or place to another," what is a *migration*?

Southwest Asia: Recent History

Differences among various groups of people have led to conflict in Southwest Asia. As you have read, Judaism has ancient roots in Palestine. Over many years, a few Jews continued to live in Palestine. But most had been forced in ancient times to migrate to other parts of the world. In the late 1800s, Jews from around the world began to return to their homeland. This alarmed the Arabs who lived there. For hundreds of years, they had claimed Palestine as their homeland, too.

The Formation of Israel Before and during World War II, Nazi Germany killed more than six million Jews in Europe solely because they were Jewish. This became known as the **Holocaust**. After the war, many of those who had survived decided to migrate to Palestine. On May 14, 1948, Jews declared the formation of their own state, Israel. Their state was recognized by the United Nations.

Arab-Israeli Conflict The day after the state of Israel was declared, the Arab nations of Egypt, Iraq, Jordan, Lebanon, and Syria invaded Israel. These nations supported the Palestinians. Israel drove away the Arab forces. Hundreds of thousands of Palestinians fled from Jewish territory. They lived as refugees in other Arab nations or in territories under Israeli rule. Even larger numbers of Jews were forced to leave Arab countries, and most resettled in Israel. Since 1948, Israel and the Arab nations that border it have fought a number of bloody wars.

Efforts Toward Peace In 1993, Israel and the Palestinian government—known as the Palestine Liberation Organization (PLO)—formally recognized each other. In 2000, fighting broke out between Israel and the Palestinians once again. In 2003, Israeli leaders and the PLO agreed on a new peace plan, which called for the co-existence of Israel and a democratic Palestine. In 2005, Israel withdrew its settlements from the Gaza Strip. Due to renewed fighting in the area, however, future progress is uncertain.

War With Iraq After Iraq's defeat in the 1991 Persian Gulf War, Iraqi leader Saddam Hussein (suh DAHM hoo SAYN) refused to cooperate with United Nations inspectors sent to ensure that Iraq destroyed its most dangerous weapons. In March 2003, U.S. forces attacked Iraq in an invasion supported by Great Britain and several other nations. Three weeks after the start of the war, Saddam fell from power. He was captured by U.S. troops in December 2003. Although Iraq remains unstable, it successfully held democratic national elections and approved a constitution in 2005.

Iraqis line up to vote for new leaders in the city of Suleimaniya in 2005.

✓ **Reading Check** Give one example of conflict in Southwest Asia.

Section 2 Assessment

Key Terms
Review the key terms at the beginning of this section. Use each term in a sentence that explains its meaning.

Target Reading Skill
Define *irrigation*. The root word means "to supply with water by artificial methods." The suffix *–ion* means "act or process."

Comprehension and Critical Thinking
1. (a) Identify Tell where Mesopotamia is located.
(b) Summarize What are two achievements of the civilizations of Mesopotamia?

2. (a) List What three major religions grew in Southwest Asia?
(b) Contrast What do all three religions have in common?
3. (a) Name What is Southwest Asia's main ethnic group today?
(b) Analyze Information Give one example of ethnic or religious diversity in the region of Southwest Asia.
4. (a) Name What area do both Palestinians and Israelis claim as a homeland?
(b) Summarize How has Iraq moved toward establishing a democratic form of government?

Writing Activity
Write a paragraph that begins with this topic sentence: *Southwest Asia is a region with different ethnic groups and religious beliefs.* Include supporting details about at least three countries in the region.

Writing Tip Include at least two sentences about ethnic groups and at least two sentences about religions. Be sure to include supporting details.

Recognizing Bias

A baseball coach chooses his own son over other, better players, to play in a tournament game. The mayor hires her friends to fill important city jobs instead of seeking the most qualified people. The politician who wants to give business to family members says his son-in-law is the best builder to build a new school.

All these situations are examples of bias. Bias is an attitude that favors one way of feeling or acting over any other. Bias prevents someone from making a fair judgment based on facts and reason. Biased speech or writing often contains opinions stated as facts.

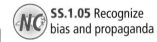

Learn the Skill

NC SS.1.05 Recognize bias and propaganda

Knowing how to recognize bias is an important skill you will need in school and in life. To identify bias in what you read, follow the steps below.

1 **Look for opinions.** Opinions are beliefs that cannot be proved. Biased statements often appear to be facts but are actually opinions.

2 **Look for loaded words and phrases and exaggerations.** Loaded words and phrases cannot be proved. They are intended to produce a strong emotional response. To exaggerate means to enlarge a fact or statement beyond what is actual or true.

3 **Look for missing facts.** Biased speech often leaves out facts that do not support the author's bias.

4 **Determine whether the text presents only one point of view.** Writing that is biased presents only one point of view about an issue or a topic. The point of view may be positive or negative.

5 **Determine whether the text contains bias.** Review the text and draw a conclusion about it.

Traveling Through Turkey by Bus

A group of 150 American tourists spent a busy morning at a market in Istanbul, Turkey, arriving at 7 AM just as sellers opened for business.

The Americans were visiting Istanbul on a tour to study the cultures of Turkey. The tourists spent about an hour shopping at the market.

"We usually don't get such a large group so early in the morning," one shop owner commented.

The tourists arrived so early that some shop owners had not yet opened for business. In a narrow section of the market, four tourists bumped into a display and knocked it over. The visitors stopped to help the shop owner fix the display.

The next stop for the Americans' cultural tour will be Turkey's capital, Ankara. The group is traveling through Turkey by bus.

Greedy Tourists Mob Market

A crowd of greedy American tourists invaded a market in the city of Istanbul, Turkey, buying everything in sight.

In a burst of energy rarely seen from Americans who prefer to drive everywhere instead of walk, the bargain-hunters swarmed out of tour buses to examine the products on display. Shop owners were overwhelmed as the impatient Americans roamed through the market.

One group of tourists overturned tables in their quest for bargains.

Americans should use better manners when they shop in other countries instead of barging into stores and being rude.

The next stop for the mob of American tourists is Turkey's capital city, Ankara.

Practice the Skill

Read the two reports above. Then use the steps on the previous page to determine which report shows bias.

1. Opinions often contain words such as *I believe* and *should*. Which report contains an opinion?

2. Look for loaded words or phrases and exaggerations in the reports. How is the phrase "greedy American tourists" an example of a loaded phrase? Which report contains the phrase "buying everything in sight"? Is this a factual statement or an exaggeration?

3. Which report includes facts, such as the number of tourists and the time of day?

4. Which report presents a point of view about American tourists? Is the point of view negative or positive?

5. Based on your review, which report shows bias? State the bias in a complete sentence.

A market in Istanbul, Turkey

Apply the Skill

Find an article about Turkey in the news, either in a newspaper or a magazine. Use the steps shown here to decide whether the article contains bias. Explain your reasoning.

Central Asia
Cultures and History

Prepare to Read

Objectives
In this section, you will
1. Learn that many cultures and peoples influenced Central Asia in ancient times.
2. Discover how Central Asian nations became independent and why they are a focus of world interest.

Taking Notes
As you read this section, look for details about the topics listed in the outline below. Copy and continue the outline and record your details in it.

I. Meeting Place of Empires
  A. Early history
    1. _____
    2. _____
  B. The Silk Road
    1. _____
    2. _____

Target Reading Skill
Recognize Word Origins A word's origin is where the word comes from. The word *government* contains the root word *govern*, which comes from the Latin word *gubernare*, meaning "to steer." The suffix *-ment* means "act or process." Knowing a word's origin can better help you understand the word's meaning. How is government related to the process of "steering" a country?

Key Term
• **collective farm** (kuh LEK tiv farhm) *n.* in a Communist country, a large farm formed from many private farms collected into a single unit controlled by the government

American fighter planes prepare for takeoff at an airbase in Central Asia. They are part of a new U.S. military force in the region. American soldiers came to fight a war in Afghanistan in 2001. Now they are based in several Central Asian countries.

American troops are not the only foreign visitors in Central Asia these days. Russian soldiers are also there. Political leaders from various countries are making official visits. Investors and business leaders are arriving too. They are coming from the United States, Russia, China, France, Turkey, and other countries. All these foreign visitors reflect Central Asia's growing international importance. The new countries of Central Asia are becoming the focus of world attention.

A growing film industry is one example of change in Central Asia.

Samarkand, Uzbekistan
A Silk Road caravan is the subject of a sculpture near the Registan, an ancient square in Samarkand. Samarkand was a major city along the Silk Road, an ancient trade route crossing Central Asia that linked China and Europe.
Apply Information
Based on what you know about Central Asia's location, how can you be certain the Silk Road was a land route?

Meeting Place of Empires

Long ago, Central Asia was a meeting place for ancient cultures and peoples. Located between East Asia and Europe, Central Asia was a crossroads for trade caravans and conquering armies. Over time, dozens of ethnic groups settled there. Each group brought new ideas and ways of living.

The Silk Road More than 2,000 years ago, a trade route called the Silk Road linked China and Europe. The Silk Road brought Central Asia into contact with East Asia, Southwest Asia, and Europe. For hundreds of years, caravans brought Chinese silk and Asian spices to the West. They carried items such as glass, wool, gold, and silver to the East. Along with goods, the traders exchanged ideas and inventions. Cities like Samarkand (sam ur KAND), in present-day Uzbekistan (ooz BEK ih stan), grew up at oases along the route and became wealthy centers of trade and learning.

Invasion and Conquest The Silk Road generated wealth, but it also attracted invaders. Waves of conquerors fought to control Central Asia. Although some ruled for hundreds of years, each group was eventually replaced by new invaders.

Each conqueror left a mark on the region. For example, about A.D. 700, a Muslim empire spread across large stretches of Central Asia. The Muslims had the greatest impact on the culture of the region. Many of the people of Central Asia adopted Islam. Today, most people in this region are Muslims.

Links Across Time

Lands for Empires In the 1200s, much of Central Asia was part of the largest land empire the world has ever known. Genghis Khan (GEN gis kahn), a leader of the Mongols, united his nomadic people into a strong fighting force. He conquered much of China and then swept west over Central Asia. At his death in 1227, his empire extended from the Sea of Japan to the Caspian Sea.

Ashgabat's Sunday Market
Ashgabat is the capital and largest city of Turkmenistan. Its Sunday market attracts thousands of people. Here, a family displays the traditional dark red carpets of Turkmenistan.
Compare and Contrast *How is shopping at an outdoor market similar to and different from the way most Americans shop?*

By the late 1200s, the rise of sea trade led to the decline of the Silk Road. Ships began carrying goods between China and the seaports of Europe. These sea routes were faster and easier than the overland routes across Asia. As a result, trade declined in Central Asia. This, however, did not stop foreign powers from trying to control the region.

Under Russian Rule In the 1800s, both Russia and Britain tried to expand their empires into Central Asia. Russia was more successful. One of the most important cities Russia captured was the city of Tashkent, Uzbekistan, in 1865.

Russia built railroads, factories, and large farms in Central Asia. Some Russians moved into the region, bringing new ways of life. But most people continued to live as they always had. They practiced Islam and lived as nomadic herders.

The Soviet Union In 1922, Russian Communists formed the Soviet Union. The Soviets extended Communist control over a vast area of Central Asia. They divided the region into five separate states, which they called republics. They also forced people to stop living as nomads and give up their traditional way of life. People had to work on **collective farms**, large farms controlled by the government. The Communist government formed collectives by taking over smaller private farms and livestock herds and combining them into larger units. Soviet collectives did not always produce enough food for people to eat. At least one million Central Asians starved to death during the 1930s.

While the Soviets built new industries, schools, and hospitals in Central Asia, they allowed people few freedoms. The Soviets outlawed the practice of religion and tried to stamp out Muslim culture. Many mosques—places of Islamic worship—were torn down in the mid-1900s.

War in Afghanistan In 1979, the Soviets tried to extend their control over Central Asia by invading Afghanistan. Afghan forces fought the Soviets, and the Afghan fighters called themselves mujahedin (moo jah heh DEEN), or Islamic holy warriors. In ten years of warfare, the Soviet army never defeated the Afghan forces. In 1989, the Soviets finally gave up and withdrew their troops.

War continued, however, as the Afghans fought each other for power. Eventually, in the mid 1990s, a group known as the Taliban took control of most of the country. The brutal regime collapsed in 2001 after a U.S.-led military invasion. Hamid Karzai was elected president of Afghanistan in a 2004 democratic election. Members of the National Assembly were elected the following year.

✓ **Reading Check** What impact did Soviet rule have on Central Asia?

A woman in Kyrgyzstan plays a traditional stringed instrument.

After Independence

The Soviet defeat in Afghanistan helped bring an end to Soviet power. In 1991, the Soviet Union broke up. The five Soviet republics of Central Asia became independent nations.

The New States After independence, each of these countries adopted a name that reflected its main ethnic group. The suffix *-stan* is a Persian term that means "place of, or land." So, for example, Kazakhstan means "place of the Kazakhs," or "Kazakh land." Together with Afghanistan, these countries are sometimes referred to as "the Stans."

The new countries are different in many ways. The largest country, Kazakhstan, is mostly flat and has important natural resources, such as oil and natural gas. The smallest country, Tajikistan, is mountainous and very poor. Nevertheless, the countries have many things in common, including Islamic culture. They also face many of the same challenges as they work to develop their economies.

Children at their desks at a school in Kyrgyzstan

Recognize Word Origins
Find the word *governing* in the first sentence of this paragraph. Compare this word to the word *government*. What is the same? What is different?

Challenges and Opportunities Since independence, the new countries of Central Asia have learned to start governing themselves. Most are weighed down by weak economies. Many people do not have jobs. Health care and education are poor and hard to get.

However, all the countries of Central Asia now proudly celebrate their culture and Islam. Mosques that had fallen into ruin are being rebuilt. The people of Central Asia are teaching their children about their religion. Other benefits of independence include the right to use native languages in schools, literature, and the daily news media.

✓ **Reading Check** What does the suffix *-stan* mean in the names of the Central Asian countries?

Section 3 Assessment

Key Terms
Review the key terms at the beginning of this section. Use each term in a sentence that explains its meaning.

Target Reading Skill
You read about the benefits of independence in Central Asia in this section. The Latin root word *bene* means "good or well." What do you think *benefit* means?

Comprehension and Critical Thinking
1. (a) Recall Where is Central Asia located?

(b) Identify Effects Describe one way that Soviet rule affected Central Asia.
2. (a) Explain How did the Central Asian republics under Soviet control gain their independence?
(b) Identify Central Issues How has Central Asia changed since becoming independent from the former Soviet Union?
(c) Make Generalizations Central Asian countries are now in charge of their own governments. You read that the root word of *governing* means "to steer." How is governing a country related to the idea of steering?

Writing Activity
The countries of Central Asia have many tasks to accomplish as they organize their nations. Using the information in this section, write a list of the challenges facing Central Asian countries. Write a brief explanation of why you think each challenge is an important one to tackle.

For: An activity about Central Asia
Visit: PHSchool.com
Web Code: ngd-6503

12 Review and Assessment

◆ Chapter Summary

Section 1: South Asia Cultures and History

- Two ancient religions, Hinduism and Buddhism, developed in India. Hinduism is a major religion in South Asia today.
- During its long history, South Asia has been shaped by Indian empires and British rule.
- South Asia's religions and languages have been affected by the region's history.

Ancient Indian sculpture

Section 2: Southwest Asia Cultures and History

- One of the world's earliest civilizations grew in Southwest Asia.
- Three of the world's greatest religions have their roots in Southwest Asia.
- People of many different ethnic groups and religious beliefs settled in Southwest Asia.
- Differences among various people, especially over land claims, have led to conflict and struggle in Southwest Asia.

Section 3: Central Asia Cultures and History

- A crossroads between East Asia and Europe, Central Asia was influenced by many cultures and peoples in ancient times.
- After decades of Soviet rule, independent nations emerged in Central Asia and are working to govern themselves.

Samarkand, Uzbekistan

◆ Key Terms

Each of the statements below contains a key term from the chapter. If the statement is true, write *true*. If the statement is false, rewrite the statement to make it true.

1. According to Hinduism, a caste is a social group into which people are born and which they cannot change.

2. A boycott is a refusal to buy or use goods and services to show disapproval or bring about social or political change.

3. A colony is an independent nation that has its own government.

4. Monotheism is the belief that there is only one god.

5. A muezzin is a person whose job is to call Muslims to prayer.

6. More than six million Jews and others died in the Holocaust.

7. A collective farm is owned and operated by one farmer.

◆ Comprehension and Critical Thinking

8. (a) Identify Identify Mohenjo-Daro.
(b) Sequence When did Aryans first come to South Asia?
(c) Identify Effects What new religion grew out of Aryan beliefs and practices?

9. (a) Recall Who is considered the founder of the religion Buddhism?
(b) Summarize Describe the spread of Buddhism after its founder's death.

10. (a) Identify Who was Asoka?
(b) Identify Effects How did Buddhist beliefs affect Asoka?

11. (a) Name Under which empire did India experience a period of great cultural achievement?
(b) Sequence Which empire followed that one?
(c) Contrast How were these two empires different in terms of religious beliefs?

12. (a) Recall Who played a major part in forcing Britain to grant independence to India?
(b) Analyze Why was India's independence followed by heavy fighting between Hindu and Muslim groups?

13. (a) Recall What are the two main religions in South Asia today?

(b) Apply Information What are other religions in South Asia?

14. (a) Identify Of the three religions founded in Southwest Asia, which has the most followers there today?
(b) Sequence Of the three religions founded in Southwest Asia, which is the oldest?

15. (a) Name What is the largest ethnic group in Southwest Asia today?
(b) Synthesize Information Give an example showing that Southwest Asia is a region of many different ethnic groups and religious beliefs.

◆ Skills Practice

Recognizing Bias Review the steps you followed on page 326 to learn this skill. Then write a sentence that explains what bias is.

◆ Writing Activity: Language Arts

The English language includes contributions from the Arabic language. Use a dictionary to research and learn about the history of these words: *admiral, algebra, cipher, cotton, sherbet,* and *zenith.* Write a paragraph on what you learned about the Arabic and English languages.

MAP ✦ MASTER™
Skills Activity

South, Southwest, and Central Asia

Place Location For each place listed below, write the letter from the map that shows its location.
1. Iraq
2. Israel
3. Kazakhstan
4. Indus River
5. Afghanistan
6. Bangladesh

Go Online
PHSchool.com Use Web Code **ngp-6520** for an interactive map.

Standardized Test Prep

Test-Taking Tips

Some questions on standardized tests ask you to analyze a reading selection. Read the passage below. Then follow the tips to answer the sample question.

> The Silk Road was an important trade route across Central Asia that linked China and Europe more than 2,000 years ago. Caravans carried Chinese silk to the west. They also brought glass, wool, gold, and silver eastward. Merchants traded more than just goods. They also exchanged ideas and inventions. Many ancient cities along the Silk Road, including Samarkand, became wealthy centers of trade and learning.

Pick the letter that best answers the question.

One city that sprang up in Central Asia along the Silk Road was

A China.

B Europe.

C Mohenjo-Daro.

D Samarkand.

TIP Use what you know about geography and history to find the BEST answer choice.

Think It Through Reread the question: The answer must be a city in Central Asia. You can rule out A and B as they are not cities. That leaves C and D. In Section 1, you read that Mohenjo-Daro is an ancient city in South Asia. In Section 2, you read that Samarkand is in Central Asia. The correct answer is D.

Practice Questions

Use the reading selection below to answer Question 1.

> The discovery and production of oil in the Arabian Peninsula brought dramatic changes to Riyadh, Saudi Arabia's capital. Once a small country town, Riyadh is now a modern city with wide highways and skyscrapers of steel and glass. It boasts luxury hotels, large hospitals, and one of the biggest airports in the world. By 2003, Riyadh was one of the world's fastest-growing cities.

1. What conclusion can be made from this reading selection?

   A Riyadh benefited from a worldwide increase in air travel.

   B Riyadh is a fast-growing city because it has luxury hotels.

   C Wealth from Arabian oil production has transformed Riyadh.

   D Riyadh was the smallest town in Saudi Arabia.

Use the tips above and other tips in this book to help you answer the following questions.

2. Which of the following events in South Asia happened last?

   A Asoka ruled the Maurya Empire in India.

   B Aryans came to South Asia probably from Central Asia.

   C India became a colony in the British Empire.

   D During the Gupta Empire, mathematicians developed Arabic numerals.

3. People who practice Judaism, Christianity, and Islam share a belief in

   A the caste system.   B monotheism.

   C many gods.   D Buddha.

Use Web Code **nga-6500** for a **Chapter 12 self-test.**

Chapter Preview

 Standard Course of Study

7.4.01 Describe patterns of and motivations for migrations

7.7.02 Causes and effects of historical events

7.9.01 Historical development of types of governments

7.10.01 Development of relationships between individuals and their governments

7.11.01 How culture links and separates societies

7.12.02 Relationship between cultural values and the arts

7.12.03 Cultural borrowing and the development of societies

Sections

1. **Southeast Asia: Cultures and History**
   7.7.02, 7.9.01, 7.10.01, 7.12.03

2. **The Pacific Region: Cultures and History**
   7.4.01, 7.9.01, 7.11.01, 7.12.02

 Target Reading Skill

Sequence In this chapter, you will focus on understanding the order in which a series of events occurs. This is called sequence.

▶ Women sell prepared food and fruits and vegetables at a floating market in Thailand.

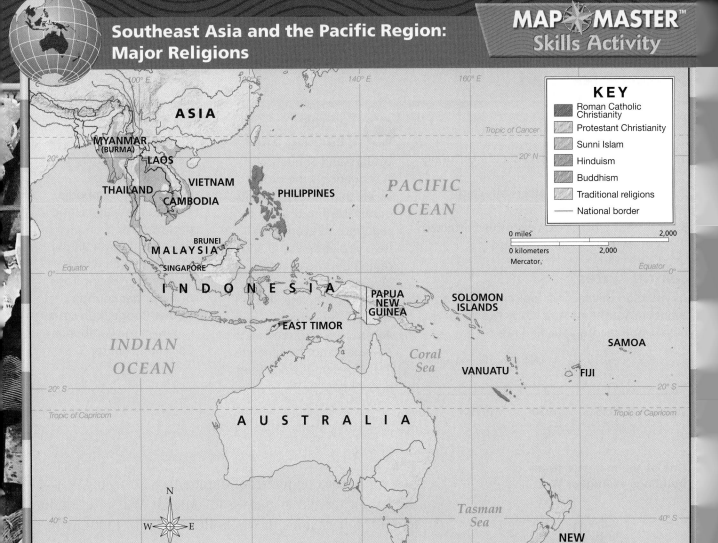

KEY

■ Roman Catholic
  Christianity
▨ Protestant Christianity
▨ Sunni Islam
▨ Hinduism
▨ Buddhism
▨ Traditional religions
— National border

ASIA

MYANMAR
(BURMA)

LAOS

THAILAND   VIETNAM

CAMBODIA

PHILIPPINES

PACIFIC
OCEAN

Tropic of Cancer

20° N

BRUNEI

MALAYSIA

SINGAPORE

Equator   Equator   0°

I N D O N E S I A

PAPUA
NEW
GUINEA

SOLOMON
ISLANDS

SAMOA

EAST TIMOR

INDIAN
OCEAN

Coral
Sea

VANUATU   FIJI

20° S   20° S

Tropic of Capricorn   Tropic of Capricorn

A U S T R A L I A

N
W   E
S

Tasman
Sea

NEW
ZEALAND

40° S   40° S

0 miles   2,000
0 kilometers   2,000
Mercator.

100° E   120° E   140° E   160° E   180°

Place Southeast Asia and the Pacific Region have a mix of religions that reflect the region's diverse history. **Identify** What is the major religion in most of the Philippines? **Infer** The Philippines was a colony held by Spain between the late 1500s and 1898. What do you think is the major religion of Spain?

Go Online
PHSchool.com Use Web Code
ngp-6610 for step-by-step
map skills practice.

Southeast Asia
Cultures and History

Prepare to Read

Objectives

In this section you will
1. Find out why Southeast Asia is a culturally diverse region.
2. Learn how colonial powers affected Southeast Asia.
3. Understand how years of conflict affected Vietnam, Cambodia, and Laos.

Taking Notes

As you read this section, look for details about events in Southeast Asia. Copy the timeline below, and record your findings on it.

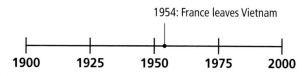

1954: France leaves Vietnam

1900   1925   1950   1975   2000

Target Reading Skill

Understand Sequence
A sequence is the order in which a series of events occurs. Noting the sequence of events can help you understand and remember the events. You can track events by making a timeline, like the one shown at the left. As you read this section, add events to the timeline in the order in which they happened.

Key Terms

- **Khmer Empire** (kuh MEHR EM pyr) *n.* an empire that included much of present-day Cambodia, Thailand, Malaysia, and part of Laos
- **nationalist** (NASH uh nul ist) *n.* a person who is devoted to the interests of his or her country
- **Khmer Rouge** (kuh MEHR roozh) *n.* the Cambodian Communist party

One of the majestic stone buildings at Angkor Wat

Deep in the rain forests of Cambodia lies Angkor Wat— the largest temple in the world. Angkor Wat is a Hindu temple built of stone. It was built in the A.D. 1100s by the Khmer (kuh MEHR) civilization. At its greatest extent, the **Khmer Empire** included much of present-day Cambodia, Thailand, Malaysia, and part of Laos. The empire was at its height from about A.D. 800 to 1434. The Khmer Empire was one of many kingdoms in Southeast Asia.

A Region of Diversity

The peoples of Southeast Asia developed their own cultures before outside influences shaped the region. Southeast Asia's mountains kept groups of people apart from one another. As a result, each group developed its own way of life.

When outside influences came to Southeast Asia, many of them came from India and China. Southeast Asia is located between India and China. Because of this location, the cultures of Southeast Asia were strongly affected by India and China.

The Impact of India and China India affected Southeast Asian cultures mainly through trade. Nearly 2,000 years ago, Indian traders sailed across the Indian Ocean to Southeast Asia. Indians introduced the religion of Hinduism to the region. Later, around A.D. 200, Indians brought Buddhism to Southeast Asia.

Long after Hinduism and Buddhism spread throughout the region, Indians brought Islam to Southeast Asia. Muslim traders from northern India, then under Muslim rule, carried Islam to Indonesia and the Philippines.

China's effect on Southeast Asia was felt primarily in Vietnam. In 111 B.C., the Chinese conquered Vietnam. They ruled the country for more than 1,000 years. During that time, the Vietnamese began using Chinese ways of farming. They also began using the ideas of Confucius, the ancient Chinese philosopher, to run their government.

Major Religions of Southeast Asia Today, there are Hindus in Indonesia and Malaysia. Buddhists and Muslims, however, eventually outnumbered Hindus in the region. Buddhism is the main religion in Myanmar, Thailand, Laos, Vietnam, and Cambodia today. Islam is the religion of the majority of the people in Malaysia and Indonesia. In fact, Indonesia has the largest Muslim population in the world. Singapore has a mix of religions that include Muslims, Buddhists, Hindus, and Christians.

European missionaries brought Christianity to Southeast Asia in the 1500s. Today, most of the people in the Philippines are Christian. There are small groups of Christians in Malaysia and Indonesia, too.

✓ **Reading Check** What are the major religions of Southeast Asia?

Buddhism in Southeast Asia
According to Buddhist tradition, Buddhism was founded in India in the 500s B.C. by Siddhartha Gautama, known as the Buddha. This gigantic sculpture of the Buddha is in Laos. **Apply Information** *Name another Southeast Asian country where Buddhism is the main religion.*

Colonial Rule in Southeast Asia

Europeans brought more than Christianity to Southeast Asia. Traders from Europe arrived in the region in the 1500s. They hoped to gain control of the rich trade in silks, iron, silver, pearls, and spices. At first, Portugal, the Netherlands, and other European nations built trading posts there. From these small posts, Europeans expanded their power. By the 1800s, European nations had gained control of most of Southeast Asia.

As the map below shows, by 1914 Thailand was the only country in Southeast Asia that was not under colonial rule. Thailand was known as Siam until 1939. Spain ruled the Philippines for about 350 years. In 1898, however, the United States defeated Spain in the Spanish-American War. Control of the Philippines passed to the United States.

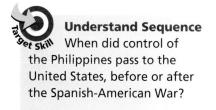

Understand Sequence When did control of the Philippines pass to the United States, before or after the Spanish-American War?

Colonial Rule in Southeast Asia, 1914

MAP MASTER™ Skills Activity

KEY

- Britain
- France
- Portugal
- Netherlands
- United States
- Independent
- National or colonial border
- Internal border

Names of present-day countries are shown in parentheses.

0 miles 1,000
0 kilometers 1,000
Lambert Azimuthal Equal Area

Place Spain ruled the Philippine islands for more than 300 years. In 1898, however, the United States defeated Spain in the Spanish-American War and took control of the colony. **Read a Map Key** Which present-day countries were French colonies in 1914? **Compare** In 1914, which country controlled the most territory in Southeast Asia?

Go Online PHSchool.com Use Web Code ngp-6611 for step-by-step map skills practice.

Singapore has a mix of building styles, from British colonial architecture to modern skyscrapers.

Effects of Colonial Rule Colonial rulers built a network of roads, bridges, ports, and railroads in Southeast Asia. Good transportation was essential for the economic success of the colonies. This new network made moving people and goods across the region much easier. The colonial powers also built schools, which helped to produce skilled workers for colonial industries. Education gave some Southeast Asians the skills to become teachers, doctors, government workers, and more.

The Road to Independence By the early 1900s, nationalists were organizing independence movements throughout the countries of Southeast Asia. A **nationalist** is someone who is devoted to the interests of his or her country. But, by the time World War II broke out in 1939, the Japanese had begun to move into Southeast Asia. During the war, the Japanese invaded mainland Southeast Asia and drove out the European colonial powers.

After the Japanese were defeated in World War II, Western nations hoped to regain power in Southeast Asia. But Southeast Asians had other hopes. They wanted independence.

Southeast Asian countries did gain independence. Some, like the Philippines and Burma (now called Myanmar), won their freedom peacefully. Others, including Laos, Cambodia, Vietnam, Malaysia, and Indonesia, had to fight for it.

✓ **Reading Check** How did the United States gain control of the Philippines?

Citizen Heroes

Aung San Suu Kyi

The country of Myanmar has had a military government since 1962. The key leader in Myanmar's fight for democracy was a woman named Aung San Suu Kyi (awn san soo chee). The government tried to stop her efforts. Suu Kyi was placed under house arrest from 1989 to 1995. In 1991, Suu Kyi won the Nobel Peace Prize for her work to bring democracy and human rights to Myanmar through peaceful means. In spite of the government's efforts to stop her, she stayed in Myanmar and continued to work for freedom and democracy.

Vendors display their fruit on bicycles in Hanoi, Vietnam.

Vietnam, Cambodia, and Laos

The road to independence was especially violent in Laos, Cambodia, and Vietnam. These countries were formerly controlled by France. Together, they were known as French Indochina. After World War II ended in 1945, France tried to take back Indochina from Japan. Nationalist forces in Vietnam fought back against the French. In 1954, they forced France to give up power and leave.

The Vietnam War The Vietnamese forces that defeated France declared Vietnam's independence. They wanted Vietnam to be a Communist country. This concerned leaders in the United States. Since the end of World War II, the United States had worked to prevent communism from spreading. Its main rival, the Soviet Union, had worked to expand communism by bringing other countries under its control.

In 1954, Vietnam was divided into two parts. The government of North Vietnam was Communist. The government of South Vietnam was non-Communist. Communist leaders in North Vietnam used force in an effort to unite the country under Communist rule. Helped by the United States, South Vietnam fought back.

At first, the United States sent military advisers and supplies to South Vietnam. Later, it sent hundreds of thousands of American soldiers to Vietnam. After years of fighting, the United States began to withdraw its forces. In 1975, North Vietnam took over South Vietnam and reunited the country under a Communist government.

Cambodia and Laos Cambodia and Laos had gained independence from France in 1953. Pulled into the conflict over Vietnam, both countries went through years of violence as Communists and non-Communists struggled for power. During the war, the United States bombed Cambodia and Laos to destroy Communist North Vietnamese forces there.

In 1975, the Cambodian Communist party called the **Khmer Rouge** (kuh MEHR roozh) took over the government of Cambodia. Opposed to Western ways of life, the Khmer Rouge moved the entire urban population to rural areas and forced them to work in the fields. Over the next four years, the Khmer Rouge killed more than a million Cambodians. Even after the Khmer Rouge leader, Pol Pot, was driven out in 1979, fighting continued. After Pol Pot died in 1998, the Khmer Rouge surrendered, and the country became more stable. A new coalition government formed in 2004. Local elections are scheduled for 2007 and national elections for 2008.

Cambodian children reading in school

✔ **Reading Check** **Which country did the United States support with troops during the Vietnam War?**

Section 1 Assessment

Key Terms
Review the key terms at the beginning of this section. Use each term in a sentence that explains its meaning.

Target Reading Skill
List these events in the order in which they occurred: Vietnam comes under Communist rule; Nationalists organize independence movements throughout Southeast Asia; elections are held in Cambodia.

Comprehension and Critical Thinking
1. (a) Recall Between which two large Asian countries is Southeast Asia located?

(b) Summarize How did this location affect the development of Southeast Asia's cultures?
(c) Apply Information Give one example showing that Southeast Asia has diverse religions.
2. (a) Explain Why did Europeans begin traveling to Southeast Asia in the 1500s?
(b) Identify Effects What were some positive and negative effects of colonial rule in Southeast Asia?
3. (a) Identify What present-day countries made up French Indochina?
(b) Sequence What happened in Vietnam in 1954?
(c) Identify Point of View Why was the United States concerned about Vietnam in 1954?

Writing Activity
Complete this sentence: *Southeast Asian cultures have been shaped by____.* Use your completed sentence as a topic sentence for a paragraph about Southeast Asian cultures. Use the information in this section to write your paragraph.

Writing Tip To complete the topic sentence, review this section. Choose two or three features that have shaped Southeast Asian cultures. Be sure to include supporting details for your topic sentence.

Ena walked into class wearing a bright red silk dress. Her anklet of tiny bells chimed each time she moved. Smiling, she took some objects out of a large box.

Maria watched as Ena put up a beautiful picture of the full moon. Next, Ena placed a small, handmade boat on the table. Then she put a small dish of rice next to it.

Maria looked at the calendar. The date was April 13. Tonight there would be a full moon.

Maria smiled. "Ena is going to tell us about the Cambodian New Year." "How do you know?" Paul asked. Maria laughed. "Yesterday we read about how Cambodians celebrate the New Year," she reminded Paul. "In April when the moon is full, they send boats down the river and make offerings to relatives. Look at what Ena has in her display." Maria had noticed some important details and drew the correct conclusion.

 **SS.4.06** Draw conclusions

Drawing conclusions means adding clues, or evidence, that you read or see, to what you already know. A conclusion is a judgment.

Learn the Skill

Follow the steps below to learn how to draw a reliable conclusion.

1 **Identify what you know is true.** Use these facts as clues. Maria identified the following facts as clues:

  a. Ena was dressed up and wore an anklet of tiny bells.

  b. Ena displayed a picture of a full moon along with a boat and a bowl of rice.

2 **Add these facts to what you already know.** Maria had heard about the Cambodian New Year. She knew how Cambodians celebrated this special holiday.

3 **Add two or more clues to what you already know to draw a reasoned conclusion.** Maria put together the two clues she saw with what she already knew to reach the conclusion that Ena was going to tell about the Cambodian New Year.

Practice the Skill

Read the passage titled The Vietnam War, on page 342. Then use the steps on the previous page to draw conclusions about why the United States withdrew its troops from Vietnam in 1973.

1 Answer these questions in order to find facts: How did Vietnam become independent after World War II? What country was the main rival of the United States after the end of World War II? Why did the United States send soldiers to Vietnam?

2 Use the facts to build on what you already know. For example, you know that the Vietnamese were successful in driving the French out of their country. If Vietnam had that kind of military success with the French, maybe they could defeat the United States forces, too.

3 Add the clues you have discovered to what you already know. What conclusion can you draw about why the United States withdrew its troops from Vietnam in 1973?

Women dressed in silk clothing attend a New Year's celebration in Hanoi, Vietnam.

Apply the Skill

Turn to page 341 and reread the passage titled Effects of Colonial Rule. Then use the steps in this skill to draw a conclusion about why Southeast Asians fought for independence from their colonial rulers.

The Pacific Region
Cultures and History

Prepare to Read

Objectives

In this section you will
1. Find out how people settled Australia and New Zealand.
2. Learn which groups shaped the cultures of Australia and New Zealand.
3. Understand how Pacific island nations have been affected by other cultures.

Taking Notes

As you read this section, look for details about the cultures and history of Australia, New Zealand, and the Pacific islands. Copy and complete the outline below.

I. Settlement
   A. The Maori of New Zealand
   B. Aborigines in Australia
   C. The Arrival of the British
II. The Cultures of Australia and New Zealand

Target Reading Skill

Recognize Signal Words Signal words point out relationships among ideas or events. To help keep the order of events clear, look for words like *first, before, later, next,* and *recently*. These words help show the order in which events took place. Signal words sometimes, but not always, come at the beginning of a sentence.

Key Terms

- **Maori** (MAH oh ree) *n.* a native of New Zealand whose ancestors first traveled from Asia to Polynesia, and later to New Zealand
- **Aborigine** (ab uh RIJ uh nee) *n.* a member of the earliest people of Australia, who probably came from Asia
- **penal colony** (PEEN ul KAHL uh nee) *n.* a place where people convicted of crimes are sent
- **station** (STAY shun) *n.* in Australia, a large ranch for raising livestock

Stone statues on Easter Island

Hundreds of giant stone statues dot the landscape of Easter Island, a tiny island in the South Pacific. Made of volcanic rock, the statues are from 10 to 40 feet (3 to 12 meters) high. Some weigh more than 50 tons (45 metric tons). A European who saw them in 1722 was amazed:

“ The stone images . . . caused us to be struck with astonishment because we could not comprehend how it was possible that these people, who are devoid of heavy thick timber for making any machines . . . had been able to erect such images. ”

—Dutch explorer Jacob Roggeveen, 1722

Settlement

Easter Island's statues still impress people. Easter Island is part of the island group of Polynesia. The island belongs to Chile, a country in South America. Scientists have wondered how people first came to this faraway island, as well as to the other parts of the Pacific region.

The Maori of New Zealand The earliest people in New Zealand were the Maori (MAH oh ree). **Maori are natives of New Zealand.** Their ancestors first traveled from Asia to Polynesia. Then, about 1,000 years ago, the Maori traveled across the ocean to New Zealand. According to Maori legend, seven groups set out in long canoes to find a new homeland. A storm tossed their boats ashore on New Zealand. The Maori quickly adapted to their new home. They settled in villages, making a living as hunters and farmers. But the Maori also prized fighting and conquering their enemies. They often fought other groups of Maori over the possession of land. The Maori used storytelling to pass on their beliefs and tales of their adventures.

Aborigines in Australia Many scientists think that the earliest settlers in Australia, the **Aborigines** (ab uh RIJ uh neez), came from Asia more than 40,000 years ago. For thousands of years, they hunted and gathered food along the coasts and river valleys.

During this time, the Aboriginal population in Australia flourished. People lived in small family groups that moved from place to place in search of food and water. All had strong religious beliefs about nature and the land.

The Arrival of the British In 1788, the British founded the first colony in Australia as a penal colony. **A penal colony is a remote place where people convicted of crimes are sent.** Soon, other colonists settled in Australia. Some worked for the prison facilities. Others went to find new land. Then, in 1851, gold was discovered. The population soared. Not long after, Britain stopped sending convicts to Australia. In 1901, Australia gained its independence.

The British settled New Zealand at about the same time as Australia. In 1840, the British took control of New Zealand. The colony, with its fine harbors and fertile soil, attracted many British settlers. New Zealand gained independence in 1947.

✓ **Reading Check** How did people settle Australia and New Zealand?

Recognize Signal Words

In the paragraph at the left, which words signal, or tell you, when and how the Maori came to New Zealand?

Links to Art

Maori Canoes The Maori showed their standing in society by the works of art they owned. For instance, a person might own elaborately carved and painted war canoes. Some were as long as 100 feet (30 meters). Human figures were carved along the hull and into the prow, which is the front part of the boat. The figures often had eyes made of mother-of-pearl. Canoes were painted red and decorated with feather streamers. Today these canoes are important artifacts preserved in museums.

The Cultures of Australia and New Zealand

Today, most Australians and New Zealanders are descendants of British settlers. They share British culture, holidays, and customs. Most Australians and New Zealanders enjoy a high standard of living. Employment in farming, mining, manufacturing, and service industries have made the nations prosperous.

Aborigines Since the arrival of Europeans, the Aborigines have suffered great hardships. In the colonial period, settlers forced these native peoples off their lands. Tens of thousands died of European diseases. Others were forced to work on sheep and cattle **stations,** which in Australia are extremely large ranches. The settlers forced Aborigines to adopt European ways. As a result, the Aborigines began to lose their own customs and traditions. More tragically, starting in the 1800s and continuing into the 1960s, Aboriginal children were taken from their families, often by force, to live with non-Aborigines. Today, Aborigines make up less than 1 percent of the country's population.

European and Asian Immigrants People other than the British also settled in Australia. During the gold rush of the 1850s, many people came, including Chinese. Chinese people continue to settle in Australia today. About 2.6 percent of Australia's population is Chinese.

Australians All
About 92 percent of Australians are Caucasian, 7 percent are Asian, and less than 1 percent are Aborigine. Australia's Aborigine heritage was honored at the 2000 Olympic Games when track athlete Kathy Freeman, an Aborigine, lit the Olympic torch.
Summarize *How were Aborigines affected by the arrival of Europeans?*

After World War II, many Europeans migrated to Australia. They came from Ireland, Italy, Yugoslavia, Greece, and Germany. In the 1970s, people fleeing the war in Vietnam settled in Australia. Today, people from all over the world continue to arrive.

The Maori Way of Life When New Zealand became a British colony, Britain promised to protect Maori land. Settlers, however, broke that promise. For many years, the settlers and the Maori clashed violently. The settlers defeated the Maori in 1872. After their defeat, the Maori were forced to adopt English ways. Maori culture seemed in danger of being destroyed. Slowly, however, Maori leaders gained more power. Laws now allow the Maori to practice their customs and ceremonies.

Today about 15 percent of New Zealand's population is Maori. Most Maori now live in urban areas. Many speak both Maori and English. Thanks to their artists, writers, and singers, Maori culture is an important part of New Zealand life.

Other Peoples of New Zealand After World War II, many Europeans migrated to New Zealand. People from Polynesia have settled there as well. Today, more Polynesians live in New Zealand's largest city, Auckland, than in any other city in the world. Although most New Zealanders are of European background, the Asian population has grown rapidly.

✓ Reading Check **What is the main ethnic group in Australia and New Zealand today?**

Girls from the Cook Islands, in Polynesia, wearing flower garlands, or *leis*.

The Cultures of the Pacific Islands

Scientists believe that the first people to inhabit the Pacific islands came from Southeast Asia more than 30,000 years ago.

A Variety of Cultures Because of the distances between islands, groups could not easily communicate with one another. Therefore, each group developed its own language, customs, and religious beliefs. However, the island people did have many things in common. Their ocean environment shaped their lives. It fed them and was their main means of transportation and trade. Most built their lives around their small villages.

From Colonies to Independence In the 1800s, Western nations began to take an interest in the Pacific islands. Britain, France, and Germany set up trading posts and naval bases on many islands. By 1900, the United States, Britain, France, and Germany had claimed nearly every island in the region.

After World War II, most Pacific islands gained independence, and life began to improve. By then, traditional island cultures had blended with cultures from Europe, America, and other countries. Most governments were democratic. Most churches were Christian. Many Pacific islanders read and spoke English.

✓ **Reading Check** What were Pacific island cultures like after World War II?

Section 2 Assessment

Key Terms
Review the key terms at the beginning of this section. Use each term in a sentence that explains its meaning.

Target Reading Skill
Reread the paragraph on page 347 with the heading The Arrival of the British. Find the words that signal time related to the settlement of Australia.

Comprehension and Critical Thinking
1. (a) Apply Information From where do scientists believe the native peoples of Australia came?

(b) Compare In what ways are the histories of the Aborigines and the Maori similar?

2. (a) Recall From which country are most of the people in Australia and New Zealand descended?

(b) Identify Effects How did the settlement of Australia and New Zealand affect native peoples there?

3. (a) Recall From where do scientists believe the first people to live in the Pacific islands came?

(b) Draw Conclusions Why might people who live on an island be able to preserve their culture for a long period without change?

Writing Activity
Write 10 brief entries for a timeline that shows events in the history and cultures of Australia, New Zealand, and the nearby Pacific islands.

Writing Tip Use complete sentences for your timeline entries. This will help make the sequencing of events easier to follow.

◆ Chapter Summary

Section 1: Southeast Asia Cultures and History

- The people of Southeast Asia developed cultures that later blended with influences from India, China, and Europe.
- By the 1800s, European nations had gained control of most of Southeast Asia.
- After World War II ended in 1945, Southeast Asian countries gained independence.
- After Vietnam became independent, it was divided into Communist North Vietnam and non-Communist South Vietnam. In the Vietnam War, the two sides fought for control of the country for nearly 30 years.
- The United States supported South Vietnam during the Vietnam War. Hundreds of thousands of American soldiers fought in Vietnam. Fighting spread to Cambodia and Laos.
- The Vietnam War ended in 1975 when North Vietnam took over South Vietnam and united the country under a Communist government.

The Cook Islands, Polynesia

Section 2: The Pacific Region Cultures and History

- Aborigines first settled Australia, and the Maori first settled New Zealand.
- In 1788, the British set up their first colony in Australia. Australia was a British colony until it became independent in 1901.
- Britain took control of New Zealand in 1840. New Zealand became independent in 1947.
- Most Australians and New Zealanders are descended from the British and share British culture, holidays, and customs.
- Australia's population now includes Aborigines, Asians, and people with European backgrounds. New Zealand's population includes Maori, Asians, and Polynesians.

Buddha sculpture, Laos

◆ Key Terms

Match the definitions in Column I with the key terms in Column II.

Column I

1. a remote place where people convicted of crimes are sent
2. a member of the earliest people of Australia
3. a person who is devoted to the interests of his or her country
4. in Australia, a large ranch for raising livestock
5. a member of the native people of New Zealand

Column II

A nationalist

B Aborigine

C Maori

D penal colony

E station

◆ Comprehension and Critical Thinking

6. **(a) Identify** Identify the Khmer Empire.
   (b) Identify Cause How did Hinduism and Buddhism come to Southeast Asia?

7. **(a) List** What are three religions in Southeast Asia today?
   (b) Apply Information Name three countries in Southeast Asia in which Buddhism is the main religion today.

8. **(a) Identify** Identify French Indochina.
   (b) Identify Causes Why did the French leave Vietnam in 1954?
   (c) Summarize Describe the conflict in Vietnam, including U.S. involvement.

9. **(a) Explain** How did Aborigines live before the British came to Australia?
   (b) Summarize Describe life for the Maori today.

10. **(a) Recall** What happened in Australia in 1788?
    (b) Draw Conclusions How does the history of Australia and New Zealand help explain why their cultures reflect a British heritage?

11. **(a) Name** On what island group do historians believe the people of the Pacific islands first settled?
    (b) Make Generalizations Describe Pacific island cultures after World War II.

◆ Skills Practice

Drawing Conclusions Review the steps you followed on page 344 to learn this skill. Then reread Links to Art on page 347 and draw a conclusion about the level of skill needed to make a Maori canoe.

◆ Writing Activity: Math

Population density is the average number of people living in a square mile or square kilometer. To calculate a country's population density, divide the total population by the total land area. Use an almanac or encyclopedia to find the land areas in square miles and populations for Australia, Thailand, and Vietnam. Be sure to find whole numbers. Calculate the population density of each country to the nearest whole number. Create a table that shows your data. Then write a short paragraph about your findings.

MAP MASTER™
Skills Activity

Place Location For each place listed below, write the letter from the map that shows its location.

1. Thailand
2. Vietnam
3. Indonesia
4. Australia
5. New Zealand
6. The Philippines

Go Online
PHSchool.com Use Web Code **ngp-6620** for an interactive map.

Southeast Asia and the Pacific Region

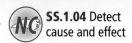
Standardized Test Prep

Test-Taking Tips

Some questions on standardized tests ask you to find cause and effect. Read the passage below. Then follow the tips to answer the sample question at the right.

> In the 1100s, the Khmer Empire extended across much territory. It included lands that are now Cambodia and much of Laos, Thailand, and Vietnam. There were many other kingdoms in Southeast Asia at that time. Because of geography, however, the others were small. The mountains of Southeast Asia isolated people, who had little contact with anybody outside their own valley. Each group developed its unique way of life. The region became rich in cultures.

TIP In a cause-and-effect relationship, the effect is what happens and the cause is what makes it happen.

Pick the letter that best answers the question.

Southeast Asia was rich in cultures because—

A the Khmer Empire extended across much territory.

B mountains isolated groups of people in their own valleys.

C there were many other kingdoms in Southeast Asia in the 1100s.

D the Khmer Empire forced different groups to pull together.

TIP Look for words, such as *because, so,* and *as a result* that point to a cause-and-effect relationship.

Think It Through The fourth sentence in the passage says that "because of geography" many Southeast Asian kingdoms were small. You can eliminate A and D because the Khmer Empire did not produce these small kingdoms. C simply restates the idea that the area is rich in cultures. The correct answer is B.

Practice Questions

Use the passage below to answer Question 1.

> Beginning in the early 1900s, Australia's population grew steadily. Until the end of World War II in 1945, most of Australia's immigrants came from Great Britain. After the war ended, large numbers of immigrants came from other countries in Europe. In recent years, many immigrants have come from East Asia and Southeast Asia because of Australia's nearby location, and because of Australia's high standard of living.

1. Many immigrants recently have come to Australia from Asian countries because

   A they were not welcome in other countries.

   B Australia has a high standard of living.

   C they could afford to travel to Australia.

   D many immigrants from Great Britain were making Asian countries too crowded.

2. During the Vietnam War, fighting spread to

   A Malaysia.

   B Australia.

   C the Philippines.

   D Cambodia.

3. The first colony in Australia was set up by

   A Great Britain.

   B the United States.

   C China.

   D France.

Go Online PHSchool.com

Use Web Code **ngp-6600** for a **Chapter 13 self-test.**

The Clay Marble
By Minfong Ho

Prepare to Read

Background Information

Think of someone you admire. What special gift or quality does that person have? Some people have the ability to show us a new way of looking at things.

In 1980, civil war in Cambodia forced thousands of Cambodians to leave their homes and move to refugee camps near the border of Thailand and Cambodia. Among these refugees were many children. There was very little food, and living conditions were poor. *The Clay Marble* tells the story of twelve-year-old Dara, who lives in one such camp. Dara's friend

Jantu, another girl in the camp, makes toys out of little scraps and trinkets she finds at the camp.

Objectives

In this selection, you will
1. Discover how Jantu deals with the challenge of living in a refugee camp.
2. Find out how the author uses point of view to tell a story.

One of the many refugee camps along the Thai-Cambodian border. The last refugee camp closed in 1999.

I t amazed me, the way she shaped things out of nothing. A knobby branch, in her deft hands, would be whittled into a whirling top. She would weave strips of a banana leaf into plump goldfish or angular frogs. A torn plastic bag and a scrap from some newspaper would be cut and fashioned into a graceful kite with a long tail. A couple of old tin cans and a stick would be transformed into a toy truck.

Whenever Jantu started making something, she would withdraw into her own private world and ignore everything around her. Leaving me to mind her baby brother, she would hunch over her project, her fierce scowl keeping at bay anybody who might come too close or become too noisy. But if I was quiet and kept my distance, she didn't seem to mind my watching her.

And so I would stand a little to one side, holding the baby on my hip, as Jantu's quick fingers shaped, twisted, smoothed, rolled whatever material she happened to be working with into new toys.

"How do you do it?" I asked her one day, after she had casually woven me a delicate bracelet of wild vines.

"Well, you take five vines of about the same length—elephant creeper vines like this work well—and you start braiding them, see. Like this . . ."

"No, I don't mean just this bracelet," I said. "I mean the goldfish, too, and the kites and toy trucks and . . ."

"But they're all different," Jantu said. "You make them different ways."

"But how do you know what to make? Is there some . . . some kind of magic in your hands, maybe?"

Jantu looked puzzled. "I don't know," she said, turning her hands over and examining them with vague interest. They looked like ordinary hands, the fingernails grimy, the palms slightly calloused. "I don't see anything there," she said. "Nothing that looks like magic." She shrugged and dismissed the subject.

Yet the more I watched her, the more convinced I became that Jantu's hands were gifted with some special powers, some magic. How else could anyone explain how she made that wonderful mobile, of two delicate dolls husking rice?

Even from the start, I knew it was going to be something special. For three days Jantu had kept me busy scrounging up a collection of old cloth and string. Then, as I sat cross-legged watching her, she fashioned two straw dolls in <u>sarongs</u> and straw hats and, with dabs of sticky rice, glued their feet onto a smooth branch. Carefully she tied strings connecting the dolls' wrists and waists, so that when one doll bent down, the other one straightened up. Each doll held a long thin club, with which, in turn, one would pound at a tiny <u>mortar</u> as the other doll lifted up its club in readiness. Jantu held up the mobile and showed me how a mere breath of wind would set the two dolls in motion.

About the Selection

This reading selection is from a chapter in *The Clay Marble,* a novel for young readers written by Minfong Ho and published in 1991.

sarong (SUH RAWNG) *n.* a loose garment made of a long strip of cloth wrapped around the body

mortar (MAWRT ur) *n.* a dish in which seed or grain is pounded or ground

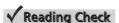 **Reading Check**

What materials does Jantu use to make the dolls?

A Cambodian family leaving their refugee camp to return home

recruit (rih KROOT) *v.* to persuade someone to join
resistance army (rih ZIS tuns AHR mee) *n.* an army of people resisting, or opposing, the group holding political power in a country
saunter (SAWN tur) *v.* to walk in an idle or a casual manner

retrieve (rih TREEV) *v.* to get something back again

Pound and lift, up and down, the two dolls took turns crushing the rice with exactly the same jerky rhythm that real village women pounded it to get the brown husks off. There were even some real grains in the miniature mortar set between the two dolls. It was the cleverest thing I had ever seen.

Children crowded around Jantu, pressing in from all sides to watch her work it. "Let me hold it," I begged, standing next to Jantu. "I helped you find the stuff for the dolls."

Jantu nodded. Breathlessly I held it carefully and blew on it. It worked! One of the dolls bent down and pounded the mortar with its club. The other doll straightened up and waited its turn. I was still engrossed with it when someone shouted a warning: "Watch out, Chnay's coming!"

Even in my short stay at the camp, I'd heard of Chnay. He liked to break things, and he was a bully. An orphan, Chnay made his way to the Border alone. Too young to be <u>recruited</u> into the <u>resistance army</u>, Chnay roamed the fields by himself, scrounging for food and sleeping wherever he liked.

Chnay <u>sauntered</u> up and shoved his way through to us. "What've you got there?" he demanded.

"Nothing," I said, trying to hide the toy behind me.

Laughing, Chnay snatched it away from me. One of the dolls was ripped loose and dropped to the ground.

As I bent over to <u>retrieve</u> it, Chnay pushed me aside. "Leave it," he said. "That's for kids. Look what I have." He thrust his arm out. It was crawling with big red ants, the fierce kind that really sting when they bite. "I'm letting them bite me. See?" he bragged. Already small fierce welts were swelling up on his arm, as some ants kept biting him.

"That's dumb!" I exclaimed. Dodging behind him, I tried to snatch the mobile back from him.

Chnay flung the toy to the ground, scattering straw and red ants into the air.

I grabbed on to his hand, but he was taller than I, and much stronger. He shoved me aside and stomped on the dolls until they were nothing but a pile of crushed sticks and rags. Then, kicking aside a boy who stood in his way, Chnay strode off, angrily brushing red ants off his arm.

I squatted down beside the bits of dolls and tried to fit them together, but it was no use. The delicate mobile was beyond repair. I could feel my eyes smarting with angry tears. "I should've held on to it more tightly," I said bitterly. "I shouldn't have let him grab it away from me."

Jantu knelt next to me and took the fragments of the dolls out of my hands. "Never mind," she said quietly, putting them aside. "We can always start something new."

"But it took you so long to make it," I said.

Idly Jantu scooped up a lump of mud from a puddle by her feet and began to knead it in her hands. "Sure, but the fun is in the making," she said.

She looked down at the lump of mud in her hands with sudden interest. "Have you ever noticed how nice the soil around here is?" she asked. "Almost like clay." She smoothed the ball with quick fingers, then rolled it between her palms.

When she opened her palm and held it out to me, there was a small brown ball of mud cupped in it. "For you," she announced.

I looked at it. Compared to the delicate rice-pounding mobile, this was not very interesting at all. "I don't want it," I said. "It's just a mud ball."

"No, it's not. It's a marble," Jantu said. Her eyes sparkling, she blew on it. "There! Now it's a magic marble."

I took it and held it. Round and cool, it had a nice solid feel to it. I glanced at Jantu. She was smiling. Slowly I smiled back at her.

Maybe, I thought, maybe she did put some magic in the marble. After all, why else would I feel better, just holding it?

✓ **Reading Check**

What happens to Jantu's dolls?

Review and Assessment

Thinking About the Selection

1. (a) Respond How did you feel about Chnay while reading this selection?

(b) Infer How do you think Jantu felt about what Chnay did to the dolls?

2. (a) Recall How would Jantu act when she started to make something?

(b) Analyze For Jantu, what is important, making toys or the toys themselves? Give evidence for your answer.

3. (a) Recall What does Jantu do with the lump of mud she scoops up?

(b) Contrast How is Dara's opinion of the lump of mud different from Jantu's opinion?

(c) Conclude What symbolic meaning might the clay marble have?

Writing Activity

Write an Essay Choose a person who has been important in your life. Write an essay that tells who the person is and what special qualities he or she has. Tell why these qualities are important to you. Include an introduction and a conclusion in your essay.

About the Author

Minfong Ho (b. 1951) was born in Rangoon, Myanmar (Burma). She grew up in Singapore and Thailand and studied at Cornell University in New York. In 1980, Ho worked as a volunteer in a refugee camp on the Cambodian-Thai border. Her experiences helped her write *The Clay Marble*. She is the author of numerous children's fiction books about life in Southeast Asia.

Chapter Preview

 Standard Course of Study

7.3.01 How people have used their environments

7.4.02 Commodities of trade and their significance for cultures and regions

7.5.02 Types of economic systems and their effectiveness in meeting needs

7.6.01 Connection between economic development and standard of living

7.6.02 Influence of education and technology on economic development

7.7.01 Relationship between historical events and current issues

7.8.03 Influence of discoveries, innovations, and inventions on societies

7.9.01 Historical development of types of governments

7.9.02 How different types of governments function

Country Databank

Sections

1. **China: Transforming Itself**
   7.4.02, 7.5.02, 7.9.01
2. **Japan: Tradition and Change**
   7.3.01, 7.6.01, 7.8.03
3. **The Koreas: A Divided Land**
   7.5.02, 7.6.01, 7.7.01

 Target Reading Skill

Comparison and Contrast In this chapter, you will focus on using comparison and contrast to help you analyze information.

▶ Dressed in traditional clothing, a Korean man plays a stringed instrument called a komungo.

MAP MASTER™
Skills Activity

KEY

—— National border

⊛ National capital

• Other city

0 miles   1,000

0 kilometers   1,000

Lambert Azimuthal Equal Area

Regions The region of East Asia is dominated by China. It is the largest country in East Asia and the second-largest in land area in the world.
Identify East Asia has two countries that are islands. What are their names?
Contrast How is Japan different from Taiwan in terms of land area?

Go Online
PHSchool.com Use Web Code
ngp-6710 for step-by-step
map skills practice.

Introducing
East Asia

Guide for Reading

This section provides an introduction to the countries that make up the region of East Asia.

- Look at the map on the previous page and then read the paragraphs below to learn about each nation.
- Analyze the data to compare the countries.
- What are the characteristics that most of the countries share?
- What are some key differences among the countries?

Viewing the Video Overview

View the World Studies Video Overview to learn more about each of the countries. As you watch, answer this question:

- How does the land use in China compare to land use in Japan?

Learn about the key geographic features in East Asia.

China

Capital	Beijing
Land Area	3,600,927 sq mi; 9,326,410 sq km
Population	1.31 billion
Ethnic Group(s)	Han, Zhaung, Uygur, Hui, Tibetan, Miao, Manchu, Mongol, Buyi, Korean
Religion(s)	traditional beliefs, Buddhist, Muslim, Christian
Government	Communist state
Currency	yuan
Leading Exports	machinery and equipment, textiles and clothing, footwear, toys and sporting goods, mineral fuels
Language(s)	Mandarin (official), Wu, Cantonese, Hsiang, Min, Hakka, Kan

With more than one billion people, China (CHY nuh) is the most populous country in the world. The history and culture of China date back about 3,500 years. Since 1949, the country has been governed under a Communist system. In recent years, China has worked to build its economy. In 2005, China had the second-largest economy in the world, after the United States. Expanding private businesses and trade with countries around the world have helped China's economy grow rapidly.

Beijing, China

A priest outside a temple in Japan

Japan

Capital	Tokyo
Land Area	144,689 sq mi; 374,744 sq km
Population	127 million
Ethnic Group(s)	Japanese, Korean, Chinese, Brazilian, Southwest Asian
Religion(s)	traditional beliefs, Buddhist, Christian
Government	constitutional monarchy
Currency	yen
Leading Exports	motor vehicles, semiconductors, office machinery, chemicals
Language(s)	Japanese (official), Korean, Chinese

Japan (juh PAN) is an island country located east of North Korea and South Korea. Japan's four main islands and thousands of small islands lie between the Sea of Japan and the Pacific Ocean. Most of Japan's land is rugged and mountainous. Japan succeeded in building a strong economy in the decades after World War II. Although its economy has declined in recent years, Japan still has one of the largest economies in the world. Japan is among the world's leading producers of motor vehicles and electronic equipment.

Mongolia

Capital	Ulaanbaatar
Land Area	600,540 sq mi; 1,555,400 sq km
Population	2.6 million
Ethnic Group(s)	Mongol, Turkic, Tungusic, Chinese, Russian
Religion(s)	Buddhist, Muslim, traditional beliefs, Christian
Government	parliamentary
Currency	tugrik
Leading Exports	copper, livestock, animal products, cashmere, wool, hides, fluorspar, other nonferrous metals
Language(s)	Khalka Mongolian, Kazakh, Chinese, Russian

Mongolia (mahn GOH lee uh) is a landlocked country bordered by Russia to the north and China to the south. Mongolia has very little land suitable for growing crops. Most of the labor force works in raising and herding livestock. Industry in Mongolia takes place chiefly in the capital city of Ulaanbaatar and consists primarily of livestock products, such as dairy products, meats, and woolen textiles. Mongolia is rich in mineral resources as well. The mining of copper, gold, coal, and other minerals contributes to Mongolia's economy.

Introducing East Asia

North Korea

Capital	Pyongyang
Land Area	46,490 sq mi; 120,410 sq km
Population	22.3 million
Ethnic Group(s)	Korean, Chinese, Japanese
Religion(s)	Buddhist, traditional beliefs, Christian
Government	authoritarian socialist
Currency	North Korean won
Leading Exports	minerals, metallurgical products, manufactured goods (including armaments), agricultural and fishery products
Language(s)	Korean (official), Chinese

North Korea (nawrth kuh REE uh) is located on the northern part of the Korean Peninsula. Before World War II ended in 1945, Korea was one country. From 1910 to 1945, Korea was controlled by Japan. When Japan was defeated in World War II, Korea was divided into two parts. The northern part was occupied by the Soviet Union and the southern part was occupied by the United States. In 1948, North Korea and South Korea were established as separate nations. Since then, North Korea has been governed under a communist system. The government supports a huge military and an extensive weapons program, including weapons of mass destruction.

South Korea

Capital	Seoul
Land Area	37,911 sq mi; 98,190 sq km
Population	48.3 million
Ethnic Group(s)	Korean, Chinese
Religion(s)	Christian, Buddhist, traditional beliefs
Government	republic
Currency	South Korean won
Leading Exports	electronic products, machinery and equipment, motor vehicles, steel, ships, textiles, clothing, footwear, fish
Language(s)	Korean (official), Chinese

The nation of South Korea (sowth kuh REE uh) was established in 1948. South Korea is located on the southern half of the Korean Peninsula. South Korea went through many years of political unrest under a number of different rulers. The country's first democratic elections were held in 1987. Since the 1960s, South Korea has achieved remarkable economic growth. Despite an economic slowdown in the late 1990s, South Korea's economy continued to grow in 2002. Its major industries include car production, electronics, shipbuilding, steel, textiles, and footwear. Political relations between South Korea and North Korea have been strained since the Korean War in the 1950s.

Children eating dinner in South Korea

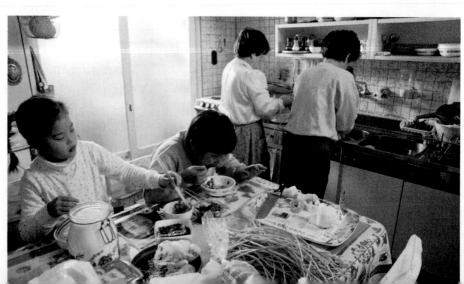

Taiwan

Capital	Taipei
Land Area	12,456 sq mi; 32,260 sq km
Population	22.5 million
Ethnic Group(s)	Taiwanese, Chinese, aborigine
Religion(s)	Buddhist, traditional beliefs, Christian
Government	multiparty democracy
Currency	Taiwan dollar
Leading Exports	machinery and electrical equipment, metals, textiles, plastics, chemicals
Language(s)	Mandarin Chinese (official), Amoy Chinese, Hakka Chinese

SOURCES: DK World Desk Reference Online; CIA World Factbook Online; *World Almanac*, 2003

Taiwan (ty wahn) is an island country located off the southeastern coast of China. The formation of Taiwan as a nation was the result of a power struggle between two political parties in China. One party, the Chinese Communists, gained control of China in 1949. The other party, the Nationalists, fled to Taiwan and set up a government there. During the 1950s and 1960s, Taiwan built a strong economy based on manufacturing industries. Manufacturing is still important in Taiwan today, but growing service industries, such as banking, bring in more money to the nation's economy.

An aerial view of Taipei, Taiwan

Assessment

Comprehension and Critical Thinking

1. Compare Compare the physical size and the population size of China to the other countries in East Asia.

2. Draw Conclusions What are the characteristics that most of the countries share?

3. Contrast What are some key differences among the countries?

4. Categorize What kinds of products are the leading exports of this region?

5. Infer What can you infer about a country if many of its exports are made in factories?

6. Make a Bar Graph Create a bar graph showing the population of the countries in this region.

Keeping Current

Access the **DK World Desk Reference Online** at **PHSchool.com** for up-to-date information about all six countries in this chapter.

Web Code: **nge-6700**

China
Transforming Itself

Prepare to Read

Objectives

In this section, you will
1. Find out how China controlled its economy from 1949 to 1980.
2. Learn about the growth of Taiwan since 1949.
3. Discover how China's government operated after the death of Mao Zedong.
4. Examine aspects of life in China today.

Taking Notes

As you read this section, look for details about how China was governed under the Communist party. Copy the diagram below, and record your findings in it. Write the similarities in the space where the ovals overlap. Write the differences in the space where the ovals do not overlap.

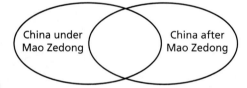

China under Mao Zedong

China after Mao Zedong

Target Reading Skill

Compare and Contrast Comparing and contrasting can help you analyze information. When you compare, you look at the similarities between things. When you contrast, you look at the differences. As you read this section, look for similarities and differences in how China was governed under the Communist party. Write the information in your Taking Notes table.

Key Terms

- **radical** (RAD ih kul) *adj.* extreme
- **Red Guards** (red gahrdz) *n.* groups of students who carried out Mao Zedong's policies during the Cultural Revolution
- **free enterprise system** (free ENT ur pryz SIS tum) *n.* an economic system in which people can choose their own jobs, start private businesses, own property, and make a profit
- **gross domestic product** (grohs duh MES tik PRAHD ukt) *n.* the total value of all goods and services produced in an economy

Bicycles remain a major form of transportation in China.

In 1985, the total number of cars, buses, and trucks in all of China was about 320,000. Most people in cities rode bicycles or walked to get around. In 2005, the number of cars, buses, and trucks had grown to about 25 million. During that time, China had experienced tremendous economic growth.

Changes continue as China works to build its economy. In the past, China's Communist government tightly controlled the economy. Today, however, China is in the process of moving toward an economy with fewer government controls.

China's Economy, 1949–1980

In 1949, the Chinese Communist party set up a new government with leader Mao Zedong (mow dzuh doong) in charge. Under Mao, the government took over China's economy. Factories, businesses, and farmland came under the government's control.

The Great Leap Forward In 1958, Mao began a radical, or extreme, program called the "Great Leap Forward." Its goal was to increase output from farms and factories. The program turned out to be a giant step backward. The Communists rushed to increase production by forcing people to work on large communes. But they ignored the need for experience and planning. For example, they ordered a huge increase in steel production. Thousands of untrained workers built backyard furnaces for making steel and other products. Much of the steel they produced was of poor quality and useless.

The focus on industry took farmers away from farming. At the same time, poor weather destroyed crops, resulting in a severe food shortage. Between 1959 and 1961, an estimated 30 million people died from starvation.

The Cultural Revolution In 1966, Mao introduced another radical policy called the Cultural Revolution. His aim was to create a completely new society with no ties to the past. He began by closing schools and urging students to rebel against their teachers and their families. The students formed bands of radicals called Red Guards. These bands destroyed some of China's most beautiful ancient buildings. They beat and imprisoned many Chinese artists, professors, and doctors. Anyone they considered to be against Mao's policies was attacked.

When the Red Guards raged out of control and began to threaten Mao's government, they were imprisoned, too. The Cultural Revolution kept China in turmoil until its conclusion in 1976. Years of chaos left China in disorder, with hundreds of thousands of its citizens dead. The focus on political revolution disrupted China's economic growth.

China Under Mao
Mao launched the Great Leap Forward in order to improve China's economy. The small photo above shows a poster promoting the program. Mao declared the Cultural Revolution in 1966. In the large photo, Red Guards read a book of Mao's writings. **Summarize** *How did the Great Leap Forward affect China's economy?*

✓ **Reading Check** **What was the purpose of China's Great Leap Forward?**

Links Across Time

China's Government

China's government is a dictatorship. In a dictatorship, the power to govern is held by one person. By contrast, a democracy is a form of government in which the power to govern rests with the people. A dictatorship has complete power over the people. It may also have control of nearly everything people do. Examples of dictatorships in the past include those in the former Soviet Union and Germany. Shown below is Mao Zedong, leader of China's government from 1949 to 1976.

Taiwan Since 1949

After their defeat by the Communists in 1949, the Nationalists fled to Taiwan, an island 100 miles (161 kilometers) off mainland China's southeast coast. They formed a new government and called their country the Republic of China. The Communists on mainland China, however, still claimed the right to rule Taiwan. The Nationalists on Taiwan also claimed the right to rule the rest of China.

In Taiwan, the Nationalists followed the free enterprise system. Under the **free enterprise system,** people can choose their own jobs, start private businesses, own property, and make profits. Taiwan's free enterprise economy quickly became one of Asia's strongest. New programs increased farm output and brought in money to help build new ports and railroads.

Businesses in Taiwan export many goods, such as computer products and electronics, to other countries. These exports, along with new service jobs, have helped the economy grow dramatically. Taiwan has also developed a democratic government. Following the 2000 elections, a new ruling party peacefully took power for the first time in Taiwan's modern history.

✓ **Reading Check** What kind of economic system does Taiwan have?

Changes in China

Meanwhile, many Western countries refused to trade with China. At the same time, some of Mao's policies hurt the country. During the 1970s, the Communists realized that they needed new policies in order to improve China's economy and its relations with the rest of the world.

First, China began repairing relations with the West. In 1971, China was allowed to join the United Nations. In 1972, Richard Nixon became the first American president to visit China. This historic trip opened up trade between the two nations.

China launched the world's first magnetic levitation, or maglev, passenger train system. Powerful magnets work to lift and propel the train.

China

China has a large and complex economy. Much of China's land is devoted to farming to feed its large population. Most of this land is used for subsistence farming, or growing food mainly for the farm family rather than for sale. Now look at the graphs below. China's exports, or sales to other countries, are greater than its imports, or purchases from other countries. These exports have helped China's economy to grow. Many young workers have moved from rural areas to cities to find higher-paying jobs. However, agriculture remains the main source of jobs in China.

China: Land Use
KEY

Commercial farming (without rice)
Commercial farming (with rice)
Subsistence farming (without rice)
Subsistence farming (with rice)
Nomadic herding
Forestry
Manufacturing and trade
Little or no activity
—— National border

Foreign Trade

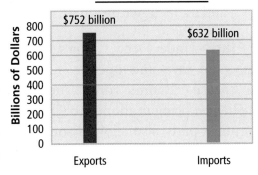

$752 billion — Exports
$632 billion — Imports

Billions of Dollars

SOURCE: *CIA World Factbook*

Labor Force by Sector

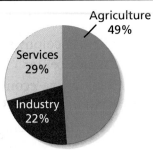

Agriculture 49%
Services 29%
Industry 22%

SOURCE: *CIA World Factbook*

Exports by Sector

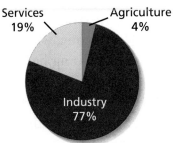

Services 19%
Agriculture 4%
Industry 77%

SOURCE: World Trade Organization

Map and Chart Skills

1. **Identify** Which economic sector in China uses the most land and employs the most people?
2. **Contrast** Which economic sector accounts for most of China's exports?
3. **Infer** How might large population movements from rural to urban areas affect farming?

Use Web Code **nge-6711** for **DK World Desk Reference Online.**

The New China
Sun Dong An Plaza in Beijing, China, includes seven floors of stores, a food court, a multiscreen movie complex, and parking for about 500 cars and about 3,500 bicycles. **Compare and Contrast** *How is Sun Dong An Plaza similar to and different from an American shopping mall?*

New Leaders After Mao died in 1976, moderate leaders gained power in China. By 1981, Deng Xiaoping (dung show ping) was leader of China. Deng carried out a program called the Four Modernizations. This program focused on improvements in farming, industry, science, and defense. During the next 20 years, China gradually allowed some free enterprise. Privately owned Chinese factories began to make electronic equipment, clothes, computer parts, toys, and many other products.

New Economic Plans Under Deng, China set up areas where foreign companies could own and operate businesses. These areas included five "special economic zones" and 14 cities along China's coast. They helped bring in money to China's economy. The Chinese Communist party also allowed some Chinese citizens to run private businesses. By the end of the 1990s, private businesses were producing about 75 percent of China's gross domestic product. **Gross domestic product** is the total value of all goods and services produced in an economy.

Hong Kong Returns to China In 1997, China took back control of Hong Kong, which had been a British colony since the late 1800s. Hong Kong had long been a major center for trade, banking, and shipping. China agreed to allow the economy of Hong Kong to operate without changes for the next 50 years. China also agreed that during this period Hong Kong could largely govern itself.

✓ **Reading Check** What happened to Hong Kong in 1997?

China Today

Today, China is a major economic power. It has formed good relations with many nations. Yet the government has often been criticized for the way it treats its people. China has one political party, which is the Chinese Communist party. Under China's government, its citizens do not have political freedom.

The Chinese government has used violence against people who have called for a democratic government. In 1989, tens of thousands of people gathered in Tiananmen Square in Beijing, China's capital, to demand greater political freedoms. When the people refused to leave, the government sent in tanks and troops. Thousands of people were killed or wounded.

Many nations question how they should relate to a country with such a poor human rights record. Still, most of them continue to remain trade partners with China. China's population makes it a huge market for goods, and China manufactures many items for other countries. In 2003, Hu Jintao became China's president and leader of the Chinese Communist party. Experts on China expected Hu to keep developing an economy with fewer government controls. With the Chinese Communist party firmly in control, however, the country's political system was not expected to change.

✓ **Reading Check** How did China's government respond to the democracy movement in 1989?

Target Skill **Compare and Contrast**
How was China different after Mao Zedong died?

Learn about desertification in China.

Section 1 Assessment

Key Terms
Review the key terms at the beginning of this section. Use each term in a sentence that explains its meaning.

Target Reading Skill
Explain one way China's government was the same and one way it was different after Mao's death.

Comprehension and Critical Thinking
1. (a) Identify Who took control of China in 1949?

(b) Summarize Why did the Chinese government launch the Great Leap Forward?
2. (a) Define What is the Republic of China?
(b) Contrast How is Taiwan different from China?
3. (a) Identify Identify Deng Xiaoping.
(b) Find the Main Idea What economic changes took place under Deng's leadership?
(c) Explain Why has the Chinese government been criticized for the way it treats its people?

Writing Activity
Write a paragraph comparing and contrasting China before and after Mao Zedong's death. Include a description of how China's economy has changed during this time.

> **Writing Tip** Compare and contrast the Great Leap Forward with the Four Modernizations program. How were these programs alike? How were they different?

Japan
Tradition and Change

Prepare to Read

Objectives

In this section, you will

1. Learn about the growth of Japan's economy.
2. Find out about successes and challenges in Japan's economy.
3. Examine aspects of life in Japan.

Taking Notes

As you read this section, look for ways in which tradition and change have helped Japan develop its economy. Copy the web diagram below, and record your findings in it.

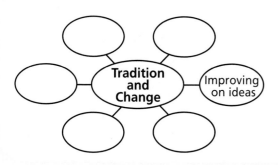

Target Reading Skill

Make Comparisons When you make comparisons, you note how things are alike. As you read this section, compare tradition and change in terms of how they have helped Japan build its economy. Write your information in the Taking Notes web diagram.

Key Terms

- **subsidy** (SUB suh dee) *n.* money given by a government to assist a private company
- **recession** (rih SESH un) *n.* a period during which an economy and the businesses that support it shrink, or make less money
- **birthrate** (BURTH rayt) *n.* the number of live births each year per 1,000 people
- **labor** (LAY bur) *n.* the work people do for which they are paid

A robot demonstration in Japan

In the 1990s, employees of Japanese companies would gather to sing the company song. One song included the words, "Let's put our strength and minds together . . . grow, industry, grow, grow, grow!" A Japanese car company handed out a weekly newsletter that included pep talks to help its employees work more efficiently. Another Japanese car company held an Idea Expo each year. Employees competed in designing unique vehicles. The event reminded workers that each new product is the result of a company-wide team effort.

Harmony and teamwork are important in the Japanese way of life. Tradition and change are also important. Present-day Japan is a modern, urban country where traditional ways blend with the new.

Building a Developed Economy

Once Japan finally opened its ports to other countries in the 1800s, it welcomed new ideas and inventions from the West. For years, the Japanese worked to build major industries. By the 1920s, Japan had become an important manufacturing country.

Japan's Economy After World War II After World War II ended in 1945, however, Japan was in ruins. The United States helped to rebuild Japan's industries. In addition, the Japanese government helped industries by giving them subsidies. A **subsidy** is money given by a government to assist a private company. This allowed companies to build large factories and sell more goods, which boosted the country's economy.

High-Technology Industries Since the 1960s, Japan has produced some of the world's most modern industrial robots. By the 1970s, the Japanese were making more watches and cameras than the Swiss and the Germans. By the 1980s, Japan made and sold a large share of the world's cars, electronic goods, skiing gear, and bicycles. Japan also produced huge amounts of steel, ships, televisions, and CDs.

In addition, Japanese companies improved existing products. For example, the videocassette recorder (VCR) was invented in the United States. But production costs for making VCRs in the United States were thought to be too high. A Japanese company bought the invention. Japan today is a leading maker of VCRs.

Japanese companies also had new ideas of their own. You are probably familiar with portable stereos and small, hand-held electronic games. These products were invented by the Japanese. In 1983, a European company and a Japanese company introduced the first compact disc. Working with European and American companies, Japanese companies also developed the digital video disc (DVD).

✓ **Reading Check** What are some high-technology products made in Japan?

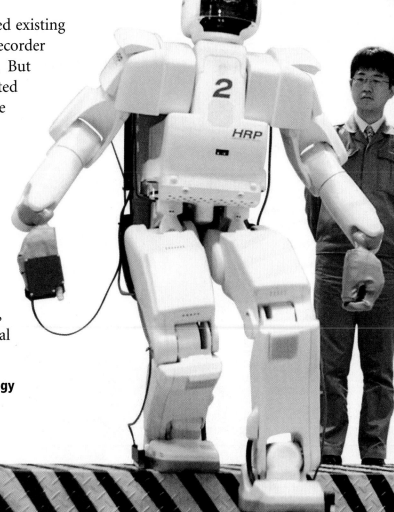

Japan's Robotics Industry
Below, a Japanese robotics designer watches as a humanoid robot steps over a barrier. Increased robot use may be one solution for Japan's labor shortage. **Analyze** *What characteristics does this robot have that would make it suitable as a replacement for a human worker?*

Make Comparisons
In what ways have tradition and change affected Japan's economy?

Successes and Challenges

By the 1980s, Japan had one of the world's largest and strongest economies. Japan's economy depended on exporting its products to the rest of the world. Americans and Europeans eagerly bought Japanese products—particularly cars, television sets, and electronics. Yet Japanese people did not buy many goods from America and Europe.

Other countries grew angry because even though they bought many Japanese products, the Japanese did not buy theirs. This led to poor trade relations between Japan and other countries. On top of that, in the early 1990s, the Japanese economy suffered a severe recession. A **recession** is a period of time when an economy and the businesses that support it shrink, or make less money. To overcome the recession, some companies began laying off their employees. Unemployment in Japan rose.

Since 2004, Japan has experienced improved economic growth, and it still has one of the largest economies in the world. Manufacturing remains an important part of Japan's economy. Today, however, more people work in Japan's service industries than in manufacturing. Service industries include jobs in banking, communications, sales, hotels, and restaurants. More of the country's wealth comes from service industries as well.

✓ **Reading Check** How was Japan affected by the recession in the 1990s?

Inspecting a turbine in Yokohama, Japan (large photo); a Japanese-made electronic book reader (small photo)

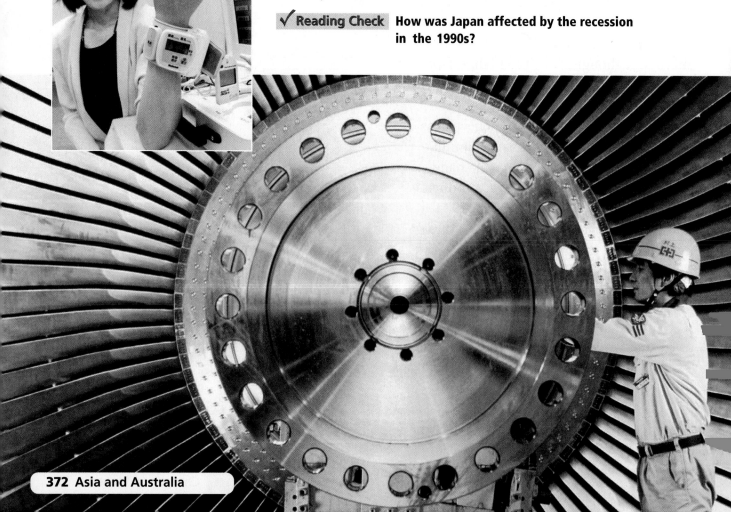

Japan

Japan is one of the world's most densely populated countries. Japan is about the same size as the states of California or Montana. But it has almost half as many people as the entire United States. The bar graph below the map shows that Japan has about the same population density as Massachusetts. Massachusetts is one of the most densely populated U.S. states. Yet, as you can see on the map, forests and farmland cover most of Japan. How is this possible? Japan preserves large areas of forest and farmland because most of its people are crowded into the small part of the country that is urban. Compare the circle graphs below showing land use in Massachusetts and Japan. Even though Japan has nearly the same overall population density as Massachusetts, it devotes much less of its space to urban development. This is mainly because its cities are compact, with little of the sprawling suburban development that we know in the United States.

Population Density Comparison

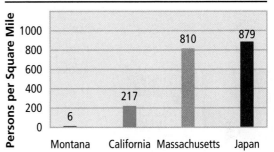

SOURCE: U.S. Census Bureau, Prentice Hall DK World Desk Reference

Land Use

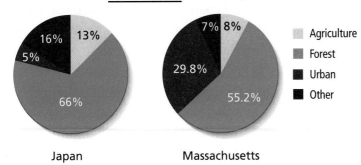

Japan   Massachusetts

SOURCE: Statistics Japan, 2003   SOURCE: U.S. Natural Resources Conservation Service, 1997

Map and Chart Skills

1. **Identify** What percentages of Japan's land are devoted to agriculture and forest?

2. **Compare** Does Japan devote more or less land to agriculture and forest than Massachusetts?

3. **Synthesize** What explains this difference?

Use Web Code **nge-6712** for **DK World Desk Reference Online.**

Life in Japan

Harmony, ceremony, and order have long been important in Japanese culture. Japanese people have generally followed these traditional values. While the past is honored, however, new ways of living and working have been introduced in Japan. The result is a modern culture with features that are unique to the country.

Learn about the ways of the samurai in Japan.

Working Together Working together as a group has long been a tradition in Japan. One way Japanese manufacturing companies have worked together is by forming *keiretsu* (kay ret soo). This is a Japanese term that describes a group of companies that join together to work toward one another's success. Some *keiretsu* included the companies that make goods, the companies that provide the raw materials for those goods, and the companies that sell the goods. The Japanese car industry has followed this model. Although still part of the country's economy, *keiretsu* have been joined by a growing number of small businesses.

Changing Roles The role of marriage is another example of tradition and change in Japan. Marriage has been the most acceptable social position for a Japanese man or woman. Today, however, more and more Japanese men and women are choosing not to marry or to delay marriage. One result is that Japan's birthrate is low. A country's **birthrate** measures the number of live births each year per 1,000 people.

The role of Japanese women in the work force has changed, too. Before World War II, few women in Japan worked outside the home. Today, there are more Japanese women working full time or part time than women who stay at home full time.

Although about half of Japan's work force is made up of women, men hold most of the management positions. In 2005, women headed about 6 percent of the companies in Japan. This compared with some 40 percent of U.S. companies being headed by women.

Japanese Students
Like American schoolchildren, these Japanese students enjoy clowning for the camera. Most public school students in Japan wear uniforms. **Analyze** *What purpose do you think school uniforms serve?*

Facing the Future As Japan heads into the future, its challenge is to find a way of maintaining its wealth. One of the resources a country needs to produce goods and services is labor. **Labor** is the work people do for which they are paid. Japan does not have a growing labor force of young workers. In the United States and Europe, a steady supply of immigrants helps keep the labor force growing. In the past, Japan has limited immigration.

Japan's low birthrate affects the labor force. Fewer and fewer workers have to support an aging population no longer working. This makes the cost of producing goods and services higher in Japan than in countries with growing populations.

✓ **Reading Check** Why is the cost of producing goods and services higher in Japan than in other Asian countries?

Section 2 Assessment

Key Terms
Review the key terms at the beginning of this section. Use each term in a sentence that explains its meaning.

Target Reading Skill
What are two ways in which tradition and change have helped Japan build its economy?

Comprehension and Critical Thinking
1. (a) Recall Describe what Japan's economy was like by the 1920s.

(b) Summarize Tell how Japan's economy grew from the 1960s to the 1980s.
2. (a) Identify What happened that disturbed Japan's economy in the early 1990s?
(b) Identify Effects How did this affect Japan?
3. (a) Explain What tradition helps explain why Japanese companies formed *keiretsu?*
(b) Identify What is one resource a country needs to produce goods and services?
(c) Draw Conclusions How would a low birthrate affect a country's labor force?

Writing Activity
Japan has an aging population. Based on the information in this section, brainstorm a list of what Japan can do to increase its labor force. Write your list and add a short description of each idea.

For: An activity on Japan
Visit: PHSchool.com
Web Code: ngd-6702

James and his family were going to host a Japanese exchange student for the summer. The student, Hiro, would be arriving in three weeks.

James decided to send information about his town to Hiro. First, he got a map that showed the mountains and lakes in the area. Then, James took photos of his favorite places in town. James added photos of his friends at school and playing soccer. His mother gave him a brochure that told about the area. Finally, James made a video showing his family, his apartment, and even his cat.

Soon, James had a mountain of information. He showed it to his dad.

"You've done a great job," his dad said. "But maybe you should synthesize some of this information. After all, Hiro may not have time to digest all of these things."

When you synthesize information, you combine information from several different sources. You find the main ideas and weave them into a conclusion. Synthesizing information is a very important skill in school and in life.

NC **SS.4.06** Draw conclusions

Learn the Skill

Follow these steps to synthesize information.

1 **Identify the main idea in each piece of information.** Main ideas are big, important ideas that are supported by details. You may want to write the main ideas down. The main idea for James is to tell about his town.

2 **Find details that support your main ideas.** Details will give you more information about your main ideas. One detail that James chose to share was that some children in his town like to play soccer.

3 **Look for connections between the pieces of information.** These connections might be similarities, differences, causes, effects, or examples. Jot down these connections.

4 **Draw conclusions based on the connections you found.** What broad, general statements can you make that tie your main ideas together?

Japan's Modern Economy

Main Ideas	Supporting Details	Connections
1. By the 1980s Japan had one of the world's largest and strongest economies.	• Japan loaned large amounts of money to other countries. • Japan exported its products to the rest of the world.	• Japan imported few goods.
2. In the early 1990s Japan suffered a severe recession.		

Practice the Skill

Use the steps on the previous page to synthesize information about Japan's modern economy. Reread the text on page 372 under the heading Successes and Challenges. Then make a table like the partially completed one above.

1. Study the information about Japan's economy from the 1980s to the present. Add one or two main ideas to the two ideas on the table above.

2. Now find details that support each main idea and add them to the chart. The details already listed add more information about Japan's strong economy in the 1980s.

3. Are the pieces of information connected in some way? Consider cause and effect. The connection already included is a possible cause for the decline in Japan's economy. Add other connections to the chart.

4. Draw some conclusions from the connections you find. See whether you can use these conclusions to answer the question, "Why did Japan's economy decline in the early 1990s?"

The Tokyo Stock Exchange is part of Japan's economy. This stock trader is using a hand signal to show he wants to sell stocks.

Apply the Skill

Use the steps on the previous page to synthesize information about how life has changed in modern Japan. Select information from the text and photos in the section Life in Japan on page 374. Focus on a single aspect of Japanese life, such as family life or work life.

Prepare to Read

Objectives

In this section, you will
1. Understand why North Korea has been slow to develop.
2. Find out how South Korea became an economic success.

Taking Notes

As you read this section, look for differences between North Korea and South Korea. Copy the table below, and record your findings in it.

North Korea	South Korea
•	• High economic growth

🎯 Target Reading Skill

Identify Contrasts When you identify contrasts, you examine differences. North Korea and South Korea are very different. As you read, look for differences between these two countries. Write them down in the Taking Notes table.

Key Terms

- **demilitarized zone** (dee MIL uh tuh ryzd zohn) *n.* an area in which no weapons are allowed
- **truce** (troos) *n.* a cease-fire agreement
- **diversify** (duh VUR suh fy) *v.* to add variety to
- **famine** (FAM in) *n.* a huge food shortage

North Korea and South Korea have a border unlike any other in the world. On a map, the border looks like a simple line. In reality, the border runs through the middle of what former President Bill Clinton called "the scariest place on Earth."

The border runs through the DMZ or **demilitarized zone** (dee MIL uh tuh ryzd zohn), an area in which no weapons are allowed. The DMZ is about 2.5 miles (4 kilometers) wide and about 151 miles (248 kilometers) long. Barbed wire, land mines, watchtowers, and thousands of weapons line both sides.

Children in South Korea

On North Korea's side, an estimated one million troops patrol the border. South Korea has about 600,000 troops. Why does the DMZ exist? In 1953, a **truce,** or cease-fire agreement, ended the Korean War. But no peace treaty was signed. Since then, the world's most heavily armed border has divided the two countries.

More than the DMZ divides the Koreas. The two countries have very different economies and governments as well.

A section of the DMZ that divides North Korea and South Korea

North Korea: Economic Challenges

North Korea (the Democratic People's Republic of Korea) is a communist country under a dictatorship. The government runs the economy. The country has kept itself closed to much of the world. This has kept out new technology and fresh ideas. Yet North Korea is rich in mineral resources. Until the end of World War II, it was the industrial center of the Korean Peninsula.

Today, North Korea manufactures poor-quality goods in government-owned factories. Little has been done to **diversify, or add variety to,** the economy. Although the government briefly opened some private markets in 2004, it still controls the economy. Overall, North Korea's economy is in poor shape.

Farming methods, too, are outdated in North Korea. In 1995, North Koreans faced **famine,** or a huge food shortage, and starvation. North Korean officials estimate that about 220,000 people died from famine between 1995 and 1998. Without farming reforms, food shortages have continued. To combat starvation, many countries and international organizations gave humanitarian food aid to North Korea. However, in 2005, the government said that it would stop accepting humanitarian aid.

✓ **Reading Check** **How has North Korea's isolation affected its economy?**

A North Korean man saw his South Korean grandmother for the first time in more than 50 years when North Korea allowed separated families to reunite in 2005.

Soccer is a popular sport in South Korea.

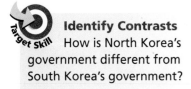

Identify Contrasts
How is North Korea's government different from South Korea's government?

South Korea: Economic Growth

In the mid-1950s, South Korea (the Republic of Korea) had agricultural resources but few industries. Fifty years later, South Korea has become a leading economic power.

South Korea is a democracy with an economy based on free enterprise. After World War II, South Korea's factories focused on making cloth and processed foods. Later, South Korea developed heavy industry. Today, South Korea is among the world's leading shipbuilders. It has a growing electronics industry that exports radios, televisions, and computers. South Korea is a leading producer of the silicon chips used in computers. South Korea also has large refineries, or factories that process oil. The oil products are used to make plastics, rubber, and other goods.

The government of South Korea has focused on the growth of industry. But it has also helped farmers. Some programs helped increase crop production. Other programs improved housing, roads, and water supplies and brought electricity to rural areas.

Despite its successes, South Korea faces a number of challenges. Like Japan, it lacks many natural resources. It must import large amounts of raw materials to keep industry running. Major imports are oil, iron, steel, and chemicals.

✓ Reading Check What are some products made in South Korea?

Years of Tension

Many Koreans hope that one day North Korea and South Korea will once again be one country. But relations between the two Koreas have remained tense since the end of the Korean War. North Korean and South Korean troops have had numerous violent clashes. Better relations seemed possible in 2000. The leaders of the two countries met in Pyongyang, the capital of North Korea, and agreed to work toward peace and cooperation.

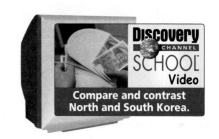
Discovery CHANNEL **SCHOOL** Video
Compare and contrast North and South Korea.

COUNTRY PROFILE · Focus on Economics

The Koreas

The Koreas have very different economies. The map at right shows that North Korea is rich in natural resources. However, its communist system has hurt its economy. The graph below shows that South Korea's gross domestic product, or economic output, has soared, while North Korea's has failed to grow.

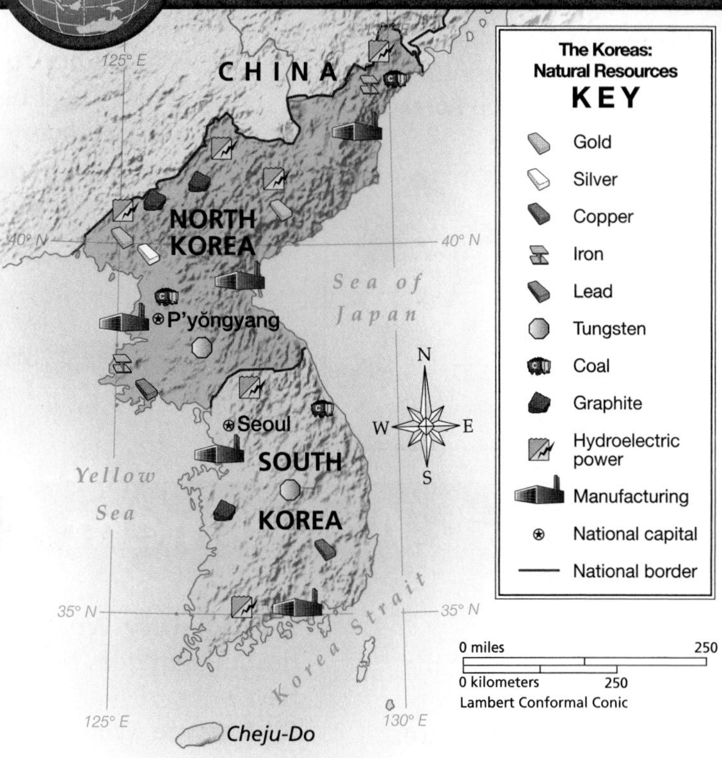

Manufacturing electronics in South Korea

The Koreas: Natural Resources
KEY

- Gold
- Silver
- Copper
- Iron
- Lead
- Tungsten
- Coal
- Graphite
- Hydroelectric power
- Manufacturing
- ⊛ National capital
- — National border

CHINA

NORTH KOREA

P'yŏngyang

Sea of Japan

Seoul

SOUTH KOREA

Yellow Sea

Korea Strait

Cheju-Do

0 miles 250
0 kilometers 250
Lambert Conformal Conic

Gross Domestic Product, 1985–2005

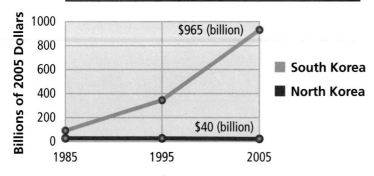

Billions of 2005 Dollars

$965 (billion)

$40 (billion)

■ South Korea
■ North Korea

1985   1995   2005

SOURCE: *CIA World Factbook*

Map and Chart Skills

1. **List** Using the map, name at least three natural resources that are found in North Korea but not South Korea.
2. **Contrast** Based on your reading and the graph at the left, discuss the differences between the economies of North and South Korea.

Go Online PHSchool.com

Use Web Code **nge-6713** for **DK World Desk Reference Online.**

Nature in the DMZ The land inside the DMZ has been untouched by human settlement for more than 50 years. As a result, the DMZ has become a peaceful haven for wildlife. Living in the DMZ are several rare and endangered species. They include eagles, cranes, and bears. Some people believe there are tigers in the DMZ. If North Korea and South Korea ever sign a peace agreement, some people want to preserve the DMZ as a peace park. Other people want to use the land to develop Korea's economy.

In 2002, North Korea's government made a shocking announcement. Even though it had previously agreed not to, North Korea said it had been developing nuclear weapons. The news damaged hopes for peace between the two countries and caused worldwide concern. In 2005, North Korea announced that it had made nuclear weapons. Later that year, "Six-Party Talks" among North Korea, the United States, Russia, China, Japan, and South Korea led to a new agreement. In exchange for giving up its nuclear weapons, North Korea would receive increased aid and diplomatic relations. However, the agreement has not yet been carried out.

In 2005, U.S. President George W. Bush visited several countries in Asia. On that trip, he said,

> **We will not forget the people of North Korea. The 21st century will be freedom's century for all Koreans—and one day every citizen of that peninsula will live in dignity and freedom and prosperity at home, and in peace with their neighbors abroad.**
>
> — *President George W. Bush*

✓ **Reading Check** What happened when North Korea announced it had made nuclear weapons?

Section 3 Assessment

Key Terms
Review the key terms at the beginning of this section. Use each term in a sentence that explains its meaning.

Target Reading Skill
Using your Taking Notes chart, explain ways in which North Korea and South Korea are different.

Comprehension and Critical Thinking
1. (a) Identify What kind of government and economy does South Korea have?
(b) Identify Causes What are some reasons for South Korea's economic success?

2. (a) Identify What kind of government does North Korea have?
(b) Analyze Why has North Korea's economy lagged behind South Korea's?
3. (a) Explain What event seemed to point to better relations between North Korea and South Korea?
(b) Identify Effects What was the effect of North Korea's development of nuclear weapons?
(c) Draw Inferences What did President Bush mean when he said, "We will not forget the people of North Korea."?

Writing Activity
When North Korea and South Korea were divided, families were divided, too. Based on what you have read about the Koreas, write a paragraph that states your viewpoint on the issue of reunifying the two countries.

For: An activity on the Koreas
Visit: PHSchool.com
Web Code: ngd-6703

14 Review and Assessment

◆ Chapter Summary

Section 1: China

- China tried two economic programs from 1949 to 1980, including the Great Leap Forward and the Cultural Revolution.
- Under a free enterprise system, Taiwan developed a successful economy.
- After the death of Chinese leader Mao Zedong, China followed a different path that included many changes to develop the economy.
- China today is a major economic power with a government that has fewer controls over the economy, but that does not allow political freedom for its citizens.

Section 2: Japan

- Japan worked hard to build a successful, highly developed economy.
- After an economic decline in the 1990s, Japan continues its recovery with one of the largest economies in the world.
- Japan has a modern culture that combines traditional Japanese values with new ways of working and living.
- One of Japan's challenges for the future is finding a way of maintaining its wealth, despite an aging population and a low birthrate.

China

Section 3: The Koreas

- South Korea has a democratic government with an economy based on free enterprise.
- North Korea has a communist government that controls the economy.

Japan

◆ Key Terms

Match the definitions in Column I with the key terms in Column II.

Column I

1. an economic system in which people can choose their own jobs, start private businesses, own property, and make a profit
2. extreme
3. a huge food shortage
4. to add variety to
5. the number of live births in a nation each year per 1,000 people

Column II

A radical

B free enterprise system

C birthrate

D diversify

E famine

◆ Comprehension and Critical Thinking

6. (a) Identify What was the purpose of the Cultural Revolution?

(b) Compare and Contrast How was the Cultural Revolution similar to and different from the Great Leap Forward?

7. (a) Define Where and what is Taiwan?

(b) Identify Point of View How does the government of Taiwan view China?

8. (a) Explain What was the Four Modernizations program of the 1990s?

(b) Identify Effects Describe one change in Chia's economy under this program.

9. (a) Note Give examples of some of the high-technology products made in Japan.

(b) Summarize How was the formation of keiretsu an example of th Japanese tradition of working together?

10. (a) Define What is labor?

(b) Summarize What is one reason that Japan has a declining labor force?

11. (a) Describe What was North Korea like before the end of World War II?

(b) Contrast How is North Korea's government and economy different from South Korea's?

12. (a) List Name four products that are made in South Korea.

(b) Compare Why is South Korea similar to Japan in terms of what the country must do to keep industry running?

◆ Skills Practice

Synthesizing Information Review the steps you learned in the Skills for Life lesson in this chapter. Then review the text and pictures in Section 1. Synthesize the information and draw a conclusion about how China has changed since 1949.

◆ Writing Activity: Language Arts

Written Chinese is based on characters, rather than on an alphabet. Each Chinese character represents a word or an idea. The complete Chinese writing system has more than 40,000 characters. Use an encyclopedia to look up information about the Chinese language and the Chinese writing system. Write a brief report that describes Chinese writing.

MAP✷MASTER™ Skills Activity

Place Location For each place listed below, write the letter from the map that shows its location.

1. China
2. Japan
3. Taiwan
4. South Korea
5. North Korea
6. Beijing

Go Online
PHSchool.com Use Web Code **ngp-6720** for an **interactive map.**

East Asia

Standardized Test Prep

Test-Taking Tips

Some questions on standardized tests ask you to analyze graphic organizers. Study the concept web below. Then follow the tips to answer the sample question at the right.

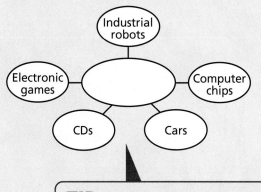

TIP When you study a concept web, think about what kind of information belongs in each part.

Pick the letter that best answers the question.

Which title should go in the center of the web?

  A Skiing Gear

  B Exports

  C Japanese Exports

  D Japanese Imports

TIP Read all four answer choices. Then choose the BEST answer from the remaining choices.

Think It Through The question asks you to choose a title for the center of the web—in other words, an idea that covers the information in all of the outer circles. You can rule out A because it is too specific: skiing gear belongs in an outer circle. However, B is too general. Although it is correct, there is probably a better answer. That leaves C or D. Look over the items in the outer circles. Are they goods that Japan sells to the rest of the world (exports) or buys from other countries (imports)? Look for at least one product on the web that you are sure is an export or import. (For instance, do you know any Americans who own a Japanese car?) The correct answer is C.

Practice Questions

Use the tips above and other tips in this book to help you answer the following questions.

1. How are the governments of China and North Korea similar?

   A They are both ruled by kings.

   B They both have communist governments.

   C They both follow the free enterprise system.

   D They both have democratic governments.

2. In Japan, you could expect to find

   A special economic zones.

   B a high birthrate.

   C a growing labor force.

   D an economy based on manufacturing goods for export.

3. In 1997, Hong Kong was returned to

   A Taiwan.

   B China.

   C Japan.

   D South Korea.

Use the concept web below to answer Question 4.

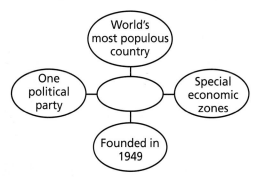

4. Which title should go in the center of the web?

   A Japan

   B North Korea

   C China

   D Taiwan

Use Web Code **nga-6700** for **Chapter 14** self-test.

Chapter

15 South, Southwest, and Central Asia

Chapter Preview

 Standard Course of Study

7.3.02 Environmental impact and global effects of regional activities

7.3.03 How tools and technologies influence human use of the environment

7.4.02 Commodities of trade and their significance for cultures and regions

7.4.03 Influence of ideas and values on development of societies

7.5.03 Evaluate impact of economic decisions on standard of living

7.6.01 Connection between economic development and standard of living

7.6.03 Effects of over-specialization

7.9.02 How different types of governments function

7.10.01 Development of relationships between individuals and their governments

Country Databank

Sections

1. **India: In the Midst of Change**
   7.5.03, 7.6.01
2. **Pakistan: An Economy Based on Agriculture**
   7.5.01, 7.5.03
3. **Israel: Economics and Cultures**
   7.4.03, 7.5.03
4. **Saudi Arabia: Oil and Islam**
   7.3.03, 7.4.02, 7.5.01, 7.6.03
5. **The Stans: A Diverse Region**
   7.3.02, 7.9.02, 7.10.01

Target Reading Skill

Cause and Effect In this chapter, you will practice understanding causes and effects.

▶ **A man docking a small boat in Jordan**

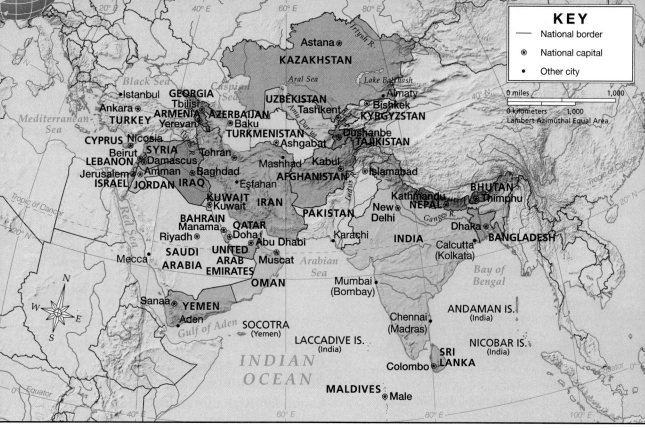

KEY
— National border
⊛ National capital
• Other city

0 miles   1,000
0 kilometers   1,000
Lambert Azimuthal Equal Area

Black Sea
Mediterranean Sea
Caspian Sea
Aral Sea
Lake Balkhash
Irtysh R.

Astana ⊛
KAZAKHSTAN
•Istanbul GEORGIA
Ankara⊛ Tbilisi⊛
TURKEY ARMENIA⊛AZERBAIJAN
Yerevan⊛ ⊛Baku
UZBEKISTAN
•Almaty
⊛Bishkek
⊛Tashkent KYRGYZSTAN
Amu Darya R.
CYPRUS Nicosia⊛
TURKMENISTAN
⊛Dushanbe
⊛Ashgabat TAJIKISTAN
Beirut• SYRIA ≈Tehran
LEBANON ⊛Damascus Mashhad• Kabul
Jerusalem⊛•Amman ⊛Baghdad AFGHANISTAN ⊛Islamabad
ISRAEL JORDAN IRAQ •Eşfahan
Kathmandu BHUTAN
⊛Thimphu
KUWAIT IRAN New NEPAL
⊛Kuwait Delhi *Ganges R.*
BAHRAIN PAKISTAN Dhaka⊛
Manama⊛ ⊛QATAR BANGLADESH
Riyadh⊛ ⊛Doha Karachi• INDIA Calcutta
SAUDI UNITED ⊛Abu Dhabi (Kolkata)
Mecca• ARABIA ARAB ⊛Muscat *Arabian*
EMIRATES *Sea*
OMAN Mumbai•
(Bombay)
Sanaa⊛ YEMEN ANDAMAN IS.
•Aden (India)
Gulf of Aden SOCOTRA Chennai•
(Yemen) (Madras) NICOBAR IS.
LACCADIVE IS. (India)
(India) SRI
Colombo⊛ LANKA
INDIAN
OCEAN MALDIVES•
⊛Male
Equator

Regions Large and small countries make up the region of South, Southwest, and Central Asia. **Locate** Find India on the map. Which country borders India on the northwest? **Contrast** Two of the countries you will read about in this chapter are Israel and Saudi Arabia. Find them on the map. How is Saudi Arabia different from Israel in terms of size?

Go Online
PHSchool.com Use Web Code
ngp-6810 for step-by-step
map skills practice.

COUNTRY DATABANK

Introducing South, Southwest, and Central Asia

Guide for Reading

This section provides an introduction to the countries that make up the region of South, Southwest, and Central Asia.

- Look at the map on the previous page and then read the paragraphs below to learn about each nation.
- Analyze the data to compare the countries.
- What are the characteristics that most of the countries share?
- What are some key differences among the countries?

Viewing the Video Overview

View the World Studies Video Overview to learn more about each of the countries. As you watch, answer this question:

- South, Southwest, and Central Asia encompass many geographic extremes. What are some of them?

Explore the land of South, Southwest, and Central Asia.

Afghanistan

Capital	Kabul
Land Area	250,000 sq mi; 647,500 sq km
Population	27.8 million
Ethnic Group(s)	Pashtun, Tajik, Hazara, Uzbek, Aimaks, Baloch, Turkmen
Religion(s)	Muslim
Government	transitional
Currency	new afghani
Leading Exports	fruits and nuts, handwoven carpets, wool, cotton, hides and pelts, precious and semi-precious gems
Language(s)	Pashtu (official), Dari (official), Tajik, Farsi, Uzbek, Turkmen

Afghanistan (af GAN ih stan) is a landlocked country in Central Asia. Conflict and war have troubled this poor country. A ten-year war with the Soviet Union left Afghanistan in ruins when Soviet forces withdrew in 1989. A group known as the Taliban came to power in 1996 and governed Afghanistan under a very strict interpretation of Islamic law. In 2001, U.S.-led forces drove the Taliban from power. In 2004, Hamid Karzai was elected president, and a new constitution was adopted. Members of the National Assembly were elected in 2005. The new government is working to bring peace to the country.

A girl reading out loud in an Afghanistan classroom

Armenia

Capital	Yerevan
Land Area	10,965 sq mi; 29,400 sq km
Population	3.3 million
Ethnic Group(s)	Armenian, Azeri, Russian, Kurd
Religion(s)	Christian, traditional beliefs
Government	republic
Currency	dram
Leading Exports	diamonds, scrap metal, machinery and equipment, copper ore
Language(s)	Armenian (official), Russian

Located in Southwest Asia east of Turkey, Armenia (ahr MEE nee uh) is a small, landlocked country with an ancient history. Ancient Armenia was the first country in the world to officially adopt Christianity as its religion. The Ottoman Empire conquered Armenia in the 1500s. During World War I, Armenians suffered greatly under Ottoman rule. An estimated 600,000 to 1.5 million Armenians died in what historians called the first genocide in the 1900s. Between 1920 and 1991, Armenia was part of the Soviet Union. Armenia declared its independence from the Soviet Union in 1991.

Azerbaijan

Capital	Baku
Land Area	33,243 sq mi; 86,100 sq km
Population	7.8 million
Ethnic Group(s)	Azeri, Dagestani, Russian, Armenian
Religion(s)	Muslim, Christian
Government	republic
Currency	manat
Leading Exports	oil and gas, machinery, cotton, foodstuffs
Language(s)	Azerbaijani (official), Russian

Azerbaijan (ahz ur by JAHN) is a small country in Southwest Asia located on the west coast of the Caspian Sea. Once part of the Soviet Union, Azerbaijan was the first Soviet republic to declare its independence. Within Azerbaijan is a region called Nagorno-Karabakh (nah GAWR noh kahr ah BAHK). Armenians living in this region wish to become part of Armenia. Between 1988 and 1994, Azerbaijan and Armenia fought a war over which country would control Nagorno-Karabakh. The issue remains a concern today. Azerbaijan has plentiful petroleum and natural gas resources.

Bahrain

Capital	Manama
Land Area	257 sq mi; 665 sq km
Population	656,397
Ethnic Group(s)	Bahraini, Arab, Asian
Religion(s)	Muslim
Government	constitutional hereditary monarchy
Currency	Bahraini dinar
Leading Exports	petroleum and petroleum products, aluminum, textiles
Language(s)	Arabic (official)

Bahrain (bah RAYN) is a tiny island country located in the Persian Gulf east of Saudi Arabia. Bahrain has used its petroleum resources to develop its economy. Aware that it is running out of oil, Bahrain has turned to petroleum processing and refining and has established itself as an international banking center. Unemployment and shrinking oil reserves are major economic problems in Bahrain.

Introducing South, Southwest, and Central Asia

Bangladesh

Capital	Dhaka
Land Area	51,705 sq mi; 133,910 sq km
Population	133.4 million
Ethnic Group(s)	Bengali
Religion(s)	Muslim, Hindu
Government	parliamentary democracy
Currency	taka
Leading Exports	clothing, jute and jute goods, leather, frozen fish and seafood
Language(s)	Bengali (official), Urdu, Chakma, Marma (Magh), Garo, Khasi, Santhali, Tripuri, Mro

Bangladesh (BAHNG luh desh) is located in South Asia. Most of Bangladesh lies on a plain formed by the soil deposited by three powerful rivers that empty into the Bay of Bengal. Most of the country is close to sea level and has a tropical wet climate with heavy rainfall. Low elevation and heavy rainfall contribute to floods that sometimes cause major damage. In 1998, the worst flooding in Bangladesh's history left nearly two thirds of the country underwater. Agriculture is an important part of Bangladesh's economy, and serious flooding can ruin the crops.

Bhutan

Capital	Thimphu
Land Area	18,147 sq mi; 47,000 sq km
Population	2.1 million
Ethnic Group(s)	Bhote, Nepalese, indigenous tribes
Religion(s)	Buddhist, Hindu
Government	monarchy
Currency	ngultrum
Leading Exports	electricity, cardamom, gypsum, timber, handicrafts, cement, fruit, precious stones, spices
Language(s)	Dzongkha (official), Nepali, Assamese

Bhutan (BOO tahn) is a small, landlocked country in South Asia located between India and China. Mountains cover most of Bhutan. These are the Himalayas, the highest mountains in the world. Bhutan's economy is based on agriculture and forestry. Although about 3 percent of Bhutan's land is suitable for growing crops, about 90 percent of the labor force works in farming. Most of the people live in small rural villages. Tourism is an important economic activity in Bhutan. To protect the environment and preserve Bhutan's mostly Buddhist culture, the government limits the number of people who visit Bhutan each year.

Cyprus

Capital	Nicosia
Land Area	3,568 sq mi; 9,240 sq km
Population	767,314
Ethnic Group(s)	Greek, Turkish
Religion(s)	Christian, Muslim
Government	republic
Currency	Cypriot pound and Turkish lira
Leading Exports	citrus, potatoes, grapes, cement, clothing and shoes, textiles
Language(s)	Greek (official), Turkish (official)

Cyprus (SY prus) is an island country located south of Turkey in the Mediterranean Sea. The majority of the people in Cyprus are Greek. About 12 percent of the population is Turkish. In 1974, Turkey invaded Cyprus and won control over a northern region of the island. Today, Greek Cypriots live in the southern two thirds of the island while the Turkish Cypriots occupy the northern third. In 1983, the Turkish region declared independence as a separate nation, which was recognized only by Turkey. The Greek Cypriot region has a prosperous economy.

Georgia

Capital	Tbilisi
Land Area	26,911 sq mi; 69,700 sq km
Population	5 million
Ethnic Group(s)	Georgian, Armenian, Russian, Azeri, Ossetian, Greek, Abkhaz
Religion(s)	Christian, Muslim
Government	republic
Currency	lari
Leading Exports	scrap metal, machinery, tea, chemicals, citrus fruits, other agricultural products
Language(s)	Georgian (official), Abkhazian (official), Russian

Georgia (JAWR juh) emerged as an independent nation in 1991 during the collapse of the Soviet Union. Georgia is located in Southwest Asia between Turkey and Russia. Mountains cover much of the country. Since independence, differences among Georgia's many ethnic groups have led to violence and civil war. Farming is a major economic activity. Georgia is rich in minerals, including copper. An oil pipeline extending from Azerbaijan across Georgia to Turkey is expected to strengthen the economy.

India

Capital	New Delhi
Land Area	1,147,949 sq mi; 2,973,190 sq km
Population	1.05 billion
Ethnic Group(s)	Indo-Aryan, Dravidian, Mongoloid
Religion(s)	Hindu, Muslim, Christian, Buddhist, traditional beliefs
Government	federal republic
Currency	Indian rupee
Leading Exports	textile goods, gems and jewelry, engineering goods, chemicals
Language(s)	Hindi (official), English (official), Urdu, Bengali, Marathi, Telugu, Tamil, Bihari, Gujarati, Kanarese

India (IN dee uh) is the largest country in South Asia and the second-most-populated country in the world. Only China has a larger population than India. India's history dates back to ancient times, with one of the world's earliest civilizations developing in the Indus Valley. A former British colony, India today consists of 28 states governed under a democratic system. A wide range of activities support India's economy. These include farming and modern industries such as textiles, steel, and computer software.

Iran

Capital	Tehran
Land Area	631,660 sq mi; 1,636,000 sq km
Population	66.6 million
Ethnic Group(s)	Persian, Azari, Gilaki and Mazandariani, Kurd, Arab, Lur, Baloch, Turkmen
Religion(s)	Muslim, Jewish, Christian
Government	theocratic republic
Currency	Iranian rial
Leading Exports	petroleum, carpets, fruits and nuts, iron and steel, chemicals
Language(s)	Farsi (official), Azerbaijani, Gilak, Mazanderani, Kurdish, Baluchi, Arabic, Turkmen

Known as Persia until 1935, Iran (ih RAN) became a republic governed under Islamic law in 1979. Islam is the official religion and nearly 100 percent of Iranians are Muslim. Iran's economy depends on the oil industry. Despite recent high oil prices, inflation and unemployment remain high. In 1980, Iraq invaded Iran, beginning an indecisive eight-year war fought over territory claimed by both countries. Iran's commitment to developing nuclear weapons and its support of terrorism have led to tense relations with many countries, including the United States.

Introducing **South, Southwest, and Central Asia**

Iraq

Capital	Baghdad
Land Area	166,858 sq mi; 432,162 sq km
Population	24.7 million
Ethnic Group(s)	Arab, Kurd, Turkoman, Assyrian
Religion(s)	Muslim, Christian
Government	republic
Currency	Iraqi dinar
Leading Exports	crude oil
Language(s)	Arabic (official), Kurdish, Turkic languages, Armenian, Assyrian

Iraq (ih RAHK) became the focus of world attention when it invaded neighboring Kuwait in 1990. The United States led a group of 32 countries in the Persian Gulf War, defeating Iraq. After the war, the United Nations required Iraq to give up its chemical and nuclear weapons programs. Iraq's refusal to do so led to a second U.S.-led invasion in 2003. Dictator Saddam Hussein and his government were quickly removed, and a new government was elected in 2005. Violence remains a problem.

Israel

Capital	Jerusalem
Land Area	7,849 sq mi; 20,330 sq km
Population	6 million
Ethnic Group(s)	Jewish, Arab
Religion(s)	Jewish, Muslim, Christian
Government	parliamentary democracy
Currency	shekel
Leading Exports	machinery and equipment, cut diamonds, software, agricultural products, chemicals, textiles and clothing
Language(s)	Hebrew (official), Arabic (official), Yiddish, German, Russian, Polish, Romanian, Persian

Israel (IZ ree ul) lies between Egypt and Lebanon and borders the Mediterranean Sea. After World War II, the United Nations allowed Israel to form as a Jewish state, but Arab nations in Southwest Asia opposed its formation. They fought a series of wars in which the Israelis were victorious and gained new territories. However, violence beween Israel and Palestinian residents of these areas continued. Peace talks over the last several decades have been hampered by Palestinian terrorist attacks, aggressive Israeli military counter-terrorism operations, and mistrust on both sides. In 2005, Israel began pulling out of the Gaza Strip and parts of the West Bank.

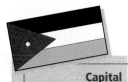

Jordan

Capital	Amman
Land Area	35,510 sq mi; 91,971 sq km
Population	5.3 million
Ethnic Group(s)	Arab, Circassian, Armenian
Religion(s)	Muslim, Christian
Government	constitutional monarchy
Currency	Jordanian dinar
Leading Exports	phosphate, fertilizers, potash, agricultural products, manufactured goods, pharmaceuticals
Language(s)	Arabic (official)

Jordan (JAWRD un) is a Southwest Asian country located northwest of Saudi Arabia. After gaining its independence from the British in 1946, the country was ruled for more than forty years by King Hussein. King Hussein established parliamentary elections and a peace treaty with Israel. After King Hussein's death in 1999, his son, Abdullah, took the throne and worked to bring economic reforms. Recent trade agreements with other countries and increased foreign investment have improved Jordan's economy. The economy is based on tourism, shipping, and the export of phosphate.

Kazakhstan

Capital	Astana
Land Area	1,030,810 sq mi; 2,669,800 sq km
Population	16.7 million
Ethnic Group(s)	Kazakh, Russian, Ukrainian, Uzbek, Uighur
Religion(s)	Muslim, Christian
Government	republic
Currency	tenge
Leading Exports	oil and oil products, ferrous metals, machinery, chemicals, grain, wool, meat, coal
Language(s)	Kazakh (official), Russian, Uighur, Korean, German

Kazakhstan (kah zahk STAHN) is a former Soviet republic, located northwest of China, that struggles to find its national identity. The native people of the area are descendants of Turkic and Mongol tribes who for years did not think of themselves as a nation. Russia conquered these peoples in the 1700s. During the mid-1900s, many Soviet citizens came to cultivate the country's northern pastures as part of a governmental agricultural project. After the country gained independence in 1991, some of these native Russians left. Today, the country is moving quickly to establish a market economy as well as a national identity.

Kuwait

Capital	Kuwait City
Land Area	6,880 sq mi; 17,820 sq km
Population	2.1 million
Ethnic Group(s)	Arab, South Asian
Religion(s)	Muslim, Christian, Hindu, traditional beliefs
Government	nominal constitutional monarchy
Currency	Kuwaiti dinar
Leading Exports	oil and refined products, fertilizers
Language(s)	Arabic (official), English

Kuwait (koo WAYT) is a small country on the Persian Gulf. Its neighbors are Iran, Iraq, and Saudi Arabia. Mainly desert, the country has large oil and gas reserves. Ninety-five percent of its export earnings are from oil. In 1990, Kuwait was invaded by neighboring Iraq. The United States and other countries came to Kuwait's defense in a conflict known as the Persian Gulf War. After the war ended in 1991, Kuwait spent billions on repairs to its oil infrastructure and built a wall on its Iraqi border.

Kuwaitis celebrating the end of the Persian Gulf War

Introducing South, Southwest, and Central Asia

Kyrgyzstan

Capital	Bishkek
Land Area	73,861 sq mi; 191,300 sq km
Population	4.8 million
Ethnic Group(s)	Kyrgyz, Russian, Uzbek, Tatar, Ukrainian
Religion(s)	Muslim, Christian
Government	republic
Currency	som
Leading Exports	cotton, wool, meat, tobacco, gold, mercury, uranium, hydro-power, machinery, shoes
Language(s)	Kyrgyz (official), Russian (official)

Kyrgyzstan (kihr gih STAN) is a mountainous Central Asian country located west of China. In the late 1800s, Kyrgyzstan was annexed by Russia. It gained its independence from the Soviet Union more than one hundred years later. Currently, Kyrgyzstan's rural population is growing faster than its urban population. The country is agriculturally self-sufficient, which gives it an economic advantage. Kyrgyzstan is focused on many of the same issues that face other nations in the region. These include improving its economy and making democratic reforms.

Lebanon

Capital	Beirut
Land Area	3,950 sq mi; 10,230 sq km
Population	3.7 million
Ethnic Group(s)	Arab, Armenian
Religion(s)	Muslim, Christian
Government	republic
Currency	Lebanese pound
Leading Exports	foodstuffs, textiles, chemicals, metal products, electrical products, jewelry, paper products
Language(s)	Arabic (official), French, Armenian, Assyrian

Lebanon (LEB uh nahn) is a Southwest Asian nation on the Mediterranean Sea, bordered by Israel and Syria. Although it only became a nation in modern times, it has some of the world's most ancient human settlements. The country has a Muslim majority and a large minority of Christians. Lebanon has suffered from a 16-year civil war, an invasion by Israel in 1981, and fighting between Hezbollah terrorists based in southern Lebanon and Israel in 2006. It faces many challenges as it tries to rebuild. Lebanon has one of the highest literacy rates in the region and is a vibrant economic and cultural center.

Maldives

Capital	Malé
Land Area	116 sq mi; 300 sq km
Population	320,165
Ethnic Group(s)	South Indian, Sinhalese, Arab
Religion(s)	Muslim
Government	republic
Currency	rufiyaa
Leading Exports	fish, clothing
Language(s)	Dhivehi (Maldivian)

Maldives (MAL dyvz) is a group of about 1,300 islands in the Indian Ocean southwest of India. Today, only about 200 of these small coral islands are inhabited. Located at the center of Arab trade routes, the islands were a stopping place for Arab traders who brought Islam with them. For much of their history, the Maldives were ruled by Muslim sultans, but the islands became a British protectorate in 1887. The country gained independence from the British in 1965. A major economic goal for the Maldives is the growth of a tourist trade.

Nepal

Capital	Kathmandu
Land Area	52,818 sq mi; 136,800 sq km
Population	25.9 million
Ethnic Group(s)	Brahman, Chetri, Newar, Gurung, Magar, Tamang, Rai, Limpu, Sherpa, Tharu
Religion(s)	Hindu, Buddhist, Muslim
Government	parliamentary democracy and constitutional monarchy
Currency	Nepalese rupee
Leading Exports	carpets, clothing, leather goods, jute goods, grain
Language(s)	Nepali (official), Maithilli, Bhojpuri

Nepal (nuh PAWL) is a country with a recent history of troubled leadership. Though a kingdom traditionally ruled by a series of royal families, in 1990 Nepal formed a multiparty government with a modern constitution. This began a period of political turmoil, including the killing of most of the royal family, a dissolved parliament, and the postponement of elections. The current king is working to resolve differences and hold elections once again. One of the poorest nations in the world, Nepal's economy depends on agriculture and the tourists who come to see the Himalayas that dominate the country's physical geography.

Oman

Capital	Muscat
Land Area	82,030 sq mi; 212,460 sq km
Population	2.7 million
Ethnic Group(s)	Arab, Baluchi, South Asian, African
Religion(s)	Muslim, Hindu
Government	monarchy
Currency	Omani rial
Leading Exports	petroleum, reexports, fish, metals, textiles
Language(s)	Arabic (official), Baluchi

Oman (oh MAHN) shares a western border with Yemen, the United Arab Emirates, and Saudi Arabia. To the east, it is bordered by the Arabian Sea, the Gulf of Oman, and the Persian Gulf. The nation is ruled by a monarch. Although the country is the least developed of the Persian Gulf nations, the current sultan's efforts to modernize have increased Oman's standing in the international community. Oil exports have brought some prosperity to Oman. The country also has a large fishing industry.

Pakistan

Capital	Islamabad
Land Area	300,664 sq mi; 778,720 sq km
Population	147.7 million
Ethnic Group(s)	Punjabi, Sindhi, Pashtun (Pathan), Baloch, Muhajir
Religion(s)	Muslim, Christian, Hindu
Government	federal republic
Currency	Pakistani rupee
Leading Exports	textiles (clothing, cotton cloth, and yarn), rice, other agricultural products
Language(s)	Urdu (official), Punjabi, Sindhi, Pashtu, Baluchi, Brahui

Pakistan (PAK ih stan) is a nation with a history of conflict among its many religious and ethnic groups. Pakistan is located on the shores of the Arabian Sea with India to the east, Iran and Afghanistan to the west, and China to the north. Pakistan was created in 1947, when tensions between Muslims and Hindus caused the British to divide British India into Muslim Pakistan and mostly-Hindu India. In 1971, East Pakistan became the separate country of Bangladesh. Tensions with India have continued since Pakistan was created. At the end of the 1900s, Pakistan began testing nuclear weapons.

Introducing South, Southwest, and Central Asia

Qatar

Capital	Doha
Land Area	4,416 sq mi; 11,437 sq km
Population	793,341
Ethnic Group(s)	Arab, South Asian
Religion(s)	Muslim
Government	traditional monarchy
Currency	Qatari riyal
Leading Exports	petroleum products, fertilizers, steel
Language(s)	Arabic (official)

Qatar (kah TAHR) is an oil-rich monarchy on the northeastern tip of the Arabian Peninsula. The country is a small peninsula in the Persian Gulf. A single family has ruled Qatar since the mid-1800s. With plentiful oil and natural gas resources, Qatar is one of the wealthiest nations in Southwest Asia and provides free health care and education to its citizens. It has a large immigrant population, made up of people from northern Africa, the Indian subcontinent, and Iran, who come to Qatar to work in the oil industry.

Saudi Arabia

Capital	Riyadh and Jiddah
Land Area	756,981 sq mi; 1,960,582 sq km
Population	23.5 million
Ethnic Group(s)	Arab, mixed black and Asian
Religion(s)	Muslim
Government	monarchy
Currency	Saudi riyal
Leading Exports	petroleum and petroleum products
Language(s)	Arabic (official)

Saudi Arabia (SAW dee uh RAY bee uh) is an oil-rich nation bordering the Red Sea and the Persian Gulf north of Yemen. Medina and Mecca, two of Islam's holiest cities, are located in Saudi Arabia. This large country is more than 95 percent desert, but oil discovered there in the 1930s quickly brought it into a position of economic power. In 1990, Saudi Arabia received 400,000 Kuwaiti refugees following Iraq's invasion of Kuwait. It played a key role as a launching point for the United States-led military effort to free Kuwait from Iraqi occupation. Today, the royal family of Saudi Arabia faces the issues of a growing population and a petroleum-dominated economy.

Sri Lanka

Capital	Colombo
Land Area	24,996 sq mi; 64,740 sq km
Population	19.6 million
Ethnic Group(s)	Sinhalese, Tamil, Moor, Burgher, Malay, Vedda
Religion(s)	Buddhist, Hindu, Christian, Muslim
Government	republic
Currency	Sri Lankan rupee
Leading Exports	textiles and clothing, tea, diamonds, coconut products, petroleum products
Language(s)	Sinhala (official), Tamil (official), English (official), Sinhalese-Tamil

Sri Lanka (sree LAHNG kuh) is made up of a large island and several small coral islands in the Indian Ocean off the coast of India. This small nation was controlled by other countries until 1948, when it finally gained its independence. Independence did not, however, bring stability to the country. Civil war between the majority Sinhalese group, made up of Buddhists, and the minority Tamil group, made up mainly of Hindus and Muslims, has raged for more than 20 years. A land of great physical and cultural diversity, Sri Lanka is the world's largest exporter of tea.

A lace shop at an outdoor market in Syria

Syria

Capital	Damascus
Land Area	71,062 sq mi; 184,050 sq km
Population	17.2 million
Ethnic Group(s)	Arab, Kurd, Armenian
Religion(s)	Muslim, Christian
Government	republic under military regime
Currency	Syrian pound
Leading Exports	crude oil, textiles, fruits and vegetables, raw cotton
Language(s)	Arabic (official), French, Kurdish, Armenian, Circassian, Turkic languages, Assyrian, Aramaic

Syria (SIHR ee uh) is a Southwest Asian country on the shores of the Mediterranean Sea, between Lebanon and Turkey. After World War I, the French controlled Syria until its independence in 1946. Since that time, Syria has been governed by a series of military leaders. The country opposes its neighbor, Israel, to whom it lost an area known as the Golan Heights in 1967 during the Arab-Israeli War. Though Syria has large oil supplies, much of its income from oil is spent on military defense.

Tajikistan

Capital	Dushanbe
Land Area	55,096 sq mi; 142,700 sq km
Population	6.7 million
Ethnic Group(s)	Tajik, Uzbek, Russian
Religion(s)	Muslim
Government	republic
Currency	somoni
Leading Exports	aluminum, electricity, cotton, fruits, vegetable oil, textiles
Language(s)	Tajiki (official), Russian

Tajikistan (tah jik ih STAN) is a struggling former Soviet republic located in Central Asia. After gaining independence from the Soviet Union in 1991, the nation went through a five-year civil war and three changes in government. The country has 14 percent of the world's uranium reserves, but has not successfully developed this resource. Tajikistan faces many challenges, including an unstable economy, poor health care, and continuing conflict among ethnic groups.

Introducing South, Southwest, and Central Asia

Turkey

Capital	Ankara
Land Area	297,590 sq mi; 770,760 sq km
Population	67.3 million
Ethnic Group(s)	Turkish, Kurd
Religion(s)	Muslim
Government	republican parliamentary democracy
Currency	Turkish lira
Leading Exports	clothing, foodstuffs, textiles, metal manufactured goods, trasport equipment
Language(s)	Turkish (official), Kurdish, Arabic, Circassian, Armenian, Greek, Georgian, Ladino

Turkey (TUR kee) is a primarily Muslim country that straddles two continents—Asia and Europe. Its location on the Black Sea and Mediterranean Sea has always made it a crossroads of trade and culture. Turkey has a strong economy and has great influence in the region. However, a major fault line leaves many Turkish cities vulnerable to earthquakes. The country's two main ethnic groups, Turks and Kurds, are in conflict. Many Kurds seek to form their own state.

Turkmenistan

Capital	Ashgabat
Land Area	188,455 sq mi; 488,100 sq km
Population	4.7 million
Ethnic Group(s)	Turkmen, Uzbek, Russian, Kazakh
Religion(s)	Muslim, Christian
Government	republic
Currency	manat
Leading Exports	gas, oil, cotton fiber, textiles
Language(s)	Turkmen (official), Uzbek, Russian

Turkmenistan (turk MEN ih stan) is a former Soviet republic which borders the Caspian Sea between Kazakhstan and Iran. Turkmenistan is mostly desert. Only 2 percent of the total land area is suitable for agriculture. The country gained its independence in 1991 and formed a democracy, but the president exercises complete control over the government. Culturally, Turkmenistan is dominated by Sunni Muslims. It has abundant natural gas reserves and is currently working to improve its ability to extract and transport this valuable resource.

United Arab Emirates

Capital	Abu Dhabi
Land Area	32,000 sq mi; 82,880 sq km
Population	2.4 million
Ethnic Group(s)	Arab, South Asian
Religion(s)	Muslim
Government	federation
Currency	UAE dirham
Leading Exports	crude oil, natural gas, reexports, dried fish, dates
Language(s)	Arabic (official), Farsi, Indian and Pakistani languages, English

The United Arab Emirates (yoo NYT id AR ub EM ur uts) was created when seven Southwest Asian states united as a single nation. The United Arab Emirates (UAE) is bordered by the Gulf of Oman and the Persian Gulf between Saudi Arabia and Oman. The UAE is mostly desert. With few water resources, the country relies on an extensive irrigation system. The UAE is rich in oil and natural gas resources. It has a strong economy and good health care and education. It has taken on an important role in the affairs of the region.

Uzbekistan

Capital	Tashkent
Land Area	164,247 sq mi; 425,400 sq km
Population	25.5 million
Ethnic Group(s)	Uzbek, Russian, Tajik, Kazakh, Karakalpak, Tatar
Religion(s)	Muslim, Christian
Government	republic
Currency	som
Leading Exports	cotton, gold, energy products, mineral fertilizers, ferrous metals, textiles, food products, automobiles
Language(s)	Arabic (official)

Uzbekistan (ooz bek ih STAN) is a former Soviet republic in Central Asia north of Afghanistan. Conquered by Russia in the late 1800s, it came under Communist control in 1924. Heavy growing of cotton and grain by the Soviet Union depleted its water supplies and polluted the land in many areas. Since it gained its independence in 1991, Uzbekistan has looked to develop its extensive mineral and oil resources. However, the country's economy still depends on agriculture. Uzbekistan is one of the largest exporters of cotton in the world.

Yemen

Capital	Sana
Land Area	203,849 sq mi; 527,970 sq km
Population	18.7 million
Ethnic Group(s)	Arab, mixed black and Arab, South Asian
Religion(s)	Muslim
Government	republic
Currency	Yemeni rial
Leading Exports	crude oil, coffee, dried and salted fish
Language(s)	Arabic

Yemen (YEM un) is located at the southern tip of the Arabian Peninsula. Bordered by Saudi Arabia and Oman, it occupies a fertile strip along the Red Sea. Yemen's recent history is one of conflict, including years of civil war that led to the country being divided in half. In 1990, the country was reunited, but still remains politically unstable. Yemen has large oil, gas, and mineral reserves. Agriculture continues to support most of the population.

SOURCES: DK World Desk Reference Online; CIA World Factbook Online; *World Almanac*, 2003

Assessment

Comprehension and Critical Thinking

1. Identify What is the most common ethnic group in the region?

2. Apply Information What is the language in countries that include this ethnic group?

3. Draw Conclusions What are the characteristics that most of the countries share?

4. Contrast What are some key differences among the countries?

5. Summarize In which region is petroleum a leading export, South Asia or Southwest Asia?

6. Make a Bar Graph Create a bar graph showing the population of the four most populous countries in this region.

Keeping Current

Access the **DK World Desk Reference Online** at PHSchool.com for up-to-date information about the countries in this chapter.

Go Online
PHSchool.com

Web Code: nge-6800

India
In the Midst of Change

Objectives

In this section you will
1. Learn about key features of India's population.
2. Examine the state of India's economy.
3. Understand major challenges facing India.

Taking Notes

As you read this section, look for ways in which India's growing population has an effect on its development. Copy the chart below, and record your findings in it.

CAUSE	EFFECTS
• India's population is growing.	•

Target Reading Skill

Identify Causes and Effects Identifying causes and effects helps you understand how events and situations are related. A cause makes something happen. An effect is what happens as a result. As you read this section, think of India's growing population as a cause. What are the effects of this cause on India's development?

Key Terms

- **textiles** (TEKS tylz) *n.* cloth made by weaving or by knitting
- **malnutrition** (mal noo TRISH un) *n.* poor nutrition caused by a lack of food or an unbalanced diet
- **life expectancy** (lyf ek SPEK tun see) *n.* the average number of years a person is expected to live
- **literacy rate** (LIT ur uh see rayt) *n.* the percentage of a population age 15 and over that can read and write

Students at a private school for boys in Rajasthan, India

In Chapter 7, you read that the gross domestic product (GDP) is the total value of all the goods and services produced in an economy. India's gross domestic product is $3.6 trillion. This makes India's GDP the fourth highest in the world. Yet the standard of living in India is very low compared with many other countries, even though India's GDP is higher. This is because India's $3.6 trillion is shared by more than one billion people. If you divided that $3.6 trillion by India's population, each person would have about $3,300. By comparison, Germany's GDP is about $2.5 trillion. But Germany has a much lower population than India has. If you divided Germany's $2.5 trillion by its population, each person would have about $30,400.

India's large population presents many challenges to the country. At the same time, India's people are an important resource in the drive to develop the country.

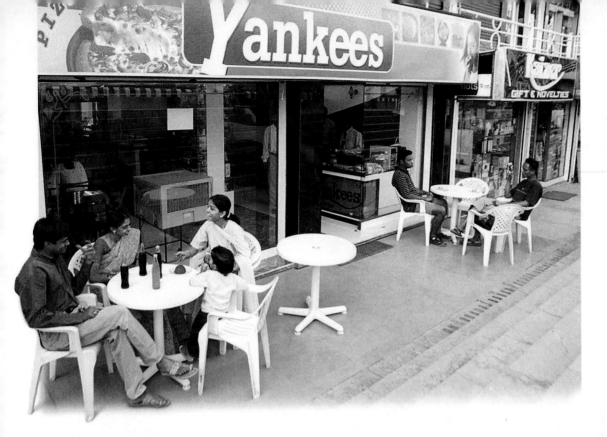

Key Features of India's Population

India is the second-most-populated country in the world. Only China's population is bigger. India's population is changing in ways that affect the country's development.

A Growing Population India has a population of more than one billion people. This large population is growing. India has one of the world's highest population growth rates. By 2050, India is expected to be the world's most populated country.

Growing Urban Areas About 72 percent of India's population lives in rural areas. But with such a large population, that means nearly 300 million people were living in urban areas in 2000. By 2030, the urban population of India is expected to reach more than 600 million. Using 2006 population figures, that equals the combined total populations of the United States, Russia, Mexico, and South Korea.

An Expanding Middle Class About one fourth of India's people lives in poverty. They earn just enough money to buy the food they need to survive. In recent years, however, India's middle class has been growing. People in the middle class are neither very rich nor very poor. They earn enough money to buy goods and services that improve their lives. By some estimates, India's middle class is one of the largest in the world.

✓ **Reading Check** What are some key features of India's population?

India's Middle Class
Although about one fourth of India's population is poor, India has a growing middle class that earns enough money to spend on consumer goods from pizza to cars. The growth of India's middle class is one result of its growing economy. **Analyze Images** *Do you think this photo shows an urban area or a rural area? Explain your answer.*

DISCOVERY CHANNEL **SCHOOL** Video
Learn about the effects of India's caste system.

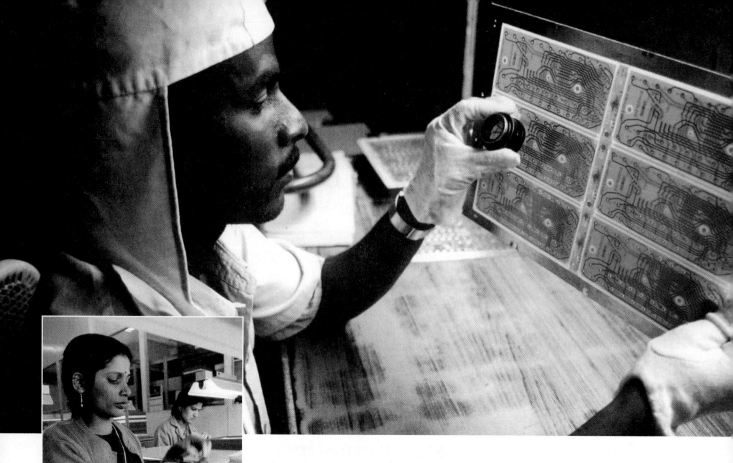

A worker checks electronic circuit boards in Bangalore (large photo); other workers assemble watches (small photo).

A Growing Economy

India has the second-fastest-growing economy in Asia. Only China's economy is growing faster. A democratic government supports India's economy. In the early 1990s, the government made changes to speed economic progress. For example, the government made it easier for foreign companies to do business in India. India's middle class helps the economy, too. The middle class provides a huge market for goods and services produced and sold in India. As the middle class grows, the number of poor people in India is expected to decrease.

Expanding industries in India are also helping the country's economy. One of India's major industries is computer software programming. India has large numbers of highly educated and skilled workers in the computer software industry. India's computer software has become a major export. Products such as electrical appliances are being manufactured in greater numbers. India also has a thriving film industry. More movies are produced in India than in any other country.

India imports more than it exports, but the country can produce all its own food. India exports **textiles, or cloth,** making cotton and silk clothing that are sold worldwide. Gemstones and jewelry are another major export. The United States buys the largest share of India's exports.

✓ **Reading Check** What are some major industries in India?

India

India has great cultural diversity, or variety. Most Indians are Hindus. As you can see on the map, however, Muslims, followers of Islam, are a majority in one of India's states. But there are Muslims in every other state in India. Millions of Indians practice Christianity, Sikhism, and other religions. Indians also speak hundreds of different languages. Hindi has more speakers than any other language in India. However, many other languages have millions of speakers, and most Indians speak a language other than Hindi.

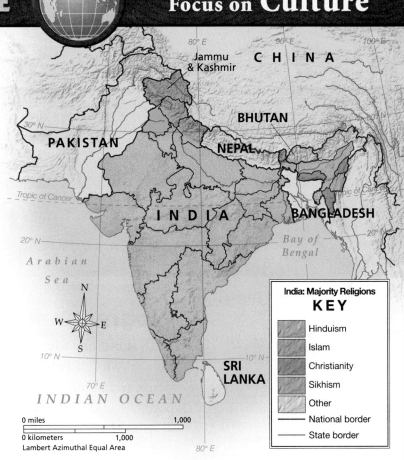

India: Majority Religions
KEY

- Hinduism
- Islam
- Christianity
- Sikhism
- Other
- National border
- State border

0 miles 1,000
0 kilometers 1,000
Lambert Azimuthal Equal Area

Religions

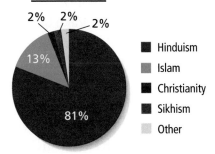

2% 2% 2%
13%
81%

- Hinduism
- Islam
- Christianity
- Sikhism
- Other

SOURCE: *CIA World Factbook*

Where Muslims Live

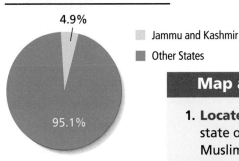

4.9%
95.1%

- Jammu and Kashmir
- Other States

SOURCE: Census of India

Languages

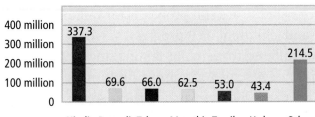

337.3	69.6	66.0	62.5	53.0	43.4	214.5
Hindi	Bengali	Telugu	Marathi	Tamil	Urdu	Other Languages

400 million
300 million
200 million
100 million
0

SOURCE: Census of India, 1991

Map and Chart Skills

1. **Locate** Which is the only state on the map with a Muslim majority?
2. **Note** Based on the graphs, what percentage of India's Muslims live in that state?
3. **Infer** Would you expect states with a Hindu majority to have many people belonging to other religions?

Use Web Code **nge-6801** for **DK World Desk Reference Online.**

Wind Power and Camel Power
India is a world leader in wind energy production. In many rural villages, however, people still use traditional methods to obtain power. At the right, a camel turns a wheel that pumps water.
Identify Effects *India's monsoons bring strong winds to much of the country. How does this affect the potential to create electricity from wind power?*

Identify Causes and Effects
What effects can a growing population have on the need for jobs, education, and housing?

Progress and Challenges

With about one fourth of its people living in poverty, India has a long way to go before all of its people enjoy higher living standards. India must meet the challenge of taking care of its growing population. The millions of people born each year will need jobs, housing, health care, and education. Food, water, and electricity will also be in higher demand. Another challenge facing India is its relations with its neighbor Pakistan.

Tensions Between India and Pakistan Kashmir is an area of land on the northern borders of India and Pakistan. Since becoming independent in 1947, India and Pakistan have both claimed Kashmir as part of their territory. The disagreement over Kashmir has led to fighting between the two countries. Tensions grew worse after India tested nuclear weapons in 1998. Pakistan responded by holding its own nuclear weapons tests. However, a 2004 cease fire and continuing peace talks have brought new hope to the troubled region.

Health Care Disease and **malnutrition,** or poor nutrition caused by a lack of food, are still problems for millions of Indian men, women and children. Yet progress has been made. The country has not suffered from major famine since the 1940s. The government has taken steps to improve health care. More government-paid medical doctors work in rural areas. The government has also launched programs that protect people from certain diseases.

As a result of these efforts, people in India are living longer. The average life expectancy in India has increased from 53 years in 1981 to 63 years in 2003. **Life expectancy** is the average number of years a person is expected to live. It is an important measure of how well a country is caring for its citizens.

Education Another way that is used to measure how well a country is taking care of its people is the literacy rate. A country's **literacy rate** shows the percentage of the population age 15 and over that can read and write. India's literacy rate is far lower than the literacy rate in the United States, but it is rapidly rising. In 1991, just over 50 percent of India's population were literate. In 2001, the literacy rate had risen to about 65 percent. Thanks to ongoing efforts to improve education, India's literacy rate is continuing to rise.

✓ **Reading Check** How has India improved health care and education for its people?

People in India, like these young students, benefit from being educated.

Section 1 Assessment

Key Terms
Review the key terms at the beginning of this section. Use each term in a sentence that explains its meaning.

Target Reading Skill
Using your Taking Notes chart, identify three effects of India's growing population.

Comprehension and Critical Thinking
1. (a) Recall What is the population of India?
(b) Find Main Ideas Why is India expected to be the world's most populated country by 2050?

(c) Identify Effects One effect of rapid urban growth is increased pollution. What might be some other effects of India's rapid urban growth?
2. (a) Note How does India's middle class help the country's economy?
(b) Identify Causes What are some other factors that are helping India's economy?
3. (a) Explain How have changes in health care increased life expectancy in India?
(b) Predict Give some reasons that a nation would want its citizens to read and write.

Writing Activity
Write an entry in your journal describing some of the challenges India must meet to take care of its growing population. Be sure to consider such factors as food and health care. Which of these challenges do you think is most important? Give one or two reasons for your answer.

For: An activity on India
Visit: PHSchool.com
Web Code: ngd-6801

Pakistan
An Economy Based on Agriculture

Prepare to Read

Objectives

In this section you will

1. Find out that Pakistan's economy is based on agriculture.
2. Learn about Pakistan's industries.

Taking Notes

As you read this section, look for ways in which Pakistan's water supply has affected its economy. Copy the chart below, and record your findings in it.

CAUSE	EFFECTS
• Water is in short supply in Pakistan.	•

Target Reading Skill

Understand Effects A cause makes something happen. An effect is what happens as the result of a specific cause. Sometimes one cause may produce several effects. As you read this section, note the effects of Pakistan's water supply on its economy. Write the effects in the Taking Notes chart.

Key Terms

- **drought** (drowt) *n.* a long period of dry weather
- **Green Revolution** (green rev uh LOO shun) *n.* a worldwide effort to increase food production in developing countries
- **self-sufficient** (self suh FISH unt) *adj.* able to supply one's own needs without any outside assistance
- **tributary** (TRIB yoo tehr ee) *n.* a river that flows into a larger river

Rainfall is scarce throughout much of Pakistan. What water the country gets is a precious resource. Pakistan's water supply includes three main sources: the Indus River, monsoon rains, and slow-melting glaciers. To make the most of its water supply, Pakistan built the world's largest irrigation system. Without rainfall, however, the gigantic system of dams, canals, ditches, and reservoirs cannot deliver the water needed for Pakistan's farms.

In 2001, Pakistan was in the middle of an extreme **drought**—a long period of dry weather. The government was so concerned over the lack of water that it considered melting part of the glaciers in northern Pakistan. One idea was to spray on charcoal, which would raise the temperature of the ice. Later that year, however, the government decided to give up the plan due to environmental concerns.

Tarbela Dam on the Indus River provides water for irrigation.

An Agricultural Nation

Pakistan's economy is based mostly on agriculture. That is why water is so important there. About half of Pakistan's labor force works in agriculture.

Farming Most of Pakistan's farming takes place in the Indus River basin, where the irrigation system is located. Cotton, wheat, sugar cane, and rice are grown there. Pakistan is among the world's top ten cotton producers. Farmers in Pakistan grow so much rice that the country exports it to other countries.

Wheat is the major food crop in Pakistan. The green revolution has helped Pakistan's farmers grow more wheat. Starting in the 1940s, **the Green Revolution** was a worldwide effort to increase food production in developing countries, including Pakistan and India. The program introduced modern farming methods and special varieties of wheat, rice, and corn that yielded more grain. The year 2000 was the first year in recent history that Pakistan did not have to import wheat. Instead, the country had enough wheat to export its extra to Afghanistan. Becoming self-sufficient in wheat production and having enough to export are major goals in Pakistan. Being **self-sufficient** means Pakistan can supply its own goods without outside assistance.

Wheat Harvest in Pakistan
Although most of Pakistan's wheat is used for food within the country, Pakistan succeeded in exporting wheat for the first time in 2000. **Analyze Images** *How does the lack of modern farm machinery indicate that this wheat was raised by a subsistence farmer?*

Learn about Pakistan's efforts to improve education.

Understand Effects
In this section, look for details about what happens in Pakistan because of the limited water supply. What are the effects of Pakistan's limited water supply?

Links Across
The World

Cricket One of the most popular sports in Pakistan is cricket. Played with a bat and a ball, cricket is a team sport widely played in Great Britain and in former colonies of the British Empire. Cricket is also popular in India, Bangladesh, Sri Lanka, Australia, and New Zealand. Like Pakistan, these countries were once British territories. In 1992, Pakistan's international cricket team won the Cricket World Cup.

Managing the Water Supply Pakistan's farmers use thousands of canals and ditches to move water from the Indus River and its tributaries to their fields. A **tributary** is a river that flows into a larger river. In this way, farmers maintain a steady flow of water, even during droughts. As more land is irrigated, more acres are farmed. This increases the amount of crops.

Irrigation solves many farming problems, but it creates others. For example, river water contains small amounts of salts. When water evaporates, the salts are left behind. Over time, salts build up in the soil, causing plant growth to slow. Pakistani scientists are trying to find a way to treat the salt-damaged soil. They are also working to develop a type of wheat that can grow in salty soil.

Pakistanis have another water problem, one that is the opposite of drought. During the monsoon season, damaging floods can occur. One solution is the large dams built by the government. The dams catch and hold monsoon rains. The waters are then released, as needed, into irrigation canals.

✓ **Reading Check** How has irrigation helped Pakistan develop an economy based on agriculture?

Industry in Pakistan

In addition to helping farmers, dams such as the Tarbela—on the Indus River in northern Pakistan—speed industrial growth. Dams capture the energy of rushing water to create hydroelectricity. In Pakistan, hydroelectric power plants produce electricity to run textile mills and other factories. Most industry is located near the sources of hydroelectric power, on the plains of the Indus River.

Making steel at a small factory near Lahore, Pakistan

Pakistan

As the map and graphs show, Pakistan has several different ethnic groups, whose members speak several different languages. However, Islam is very much the dominant religion. Islam is the majority religion for every major ethnic group in Pakistan. Only very small minorities practice religions other than Islam.

A Pashtun woman in Pakistan

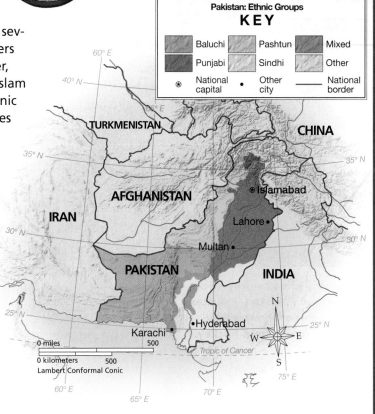

Pakistan: Ethnic Groups
KEY

- Baluchi
- Pashtun
- Mixed
- Punjabi
- Sindhi
- Other
- ⊛ National capital
- • Other city
- — National border

Religions*

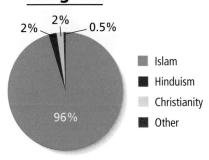

- 96% Islam
- 2% Hinduism
- 2% Christianity
- 0.5% Other

SOURCE: Pakistan Statistics Division
*Numbers may not equal 100% due to rounding.

Languages

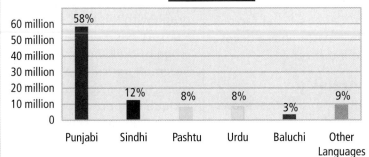

Punjabi	58%
Sindhi	12%
Pashtu	8%
Urdu	8%
Baluchi	3%
Other Languages	9%

SOURCE: *CIA World Factbook*

Map and Chart Skills

1. **Locate** Based on the map, which two languages are spoken across the largest areas of Pakistan?
2. **Identify** Based on the graph, which of these languages has the most speakers?
3. **Synthesize** What might explain why one language has so many more speakers, even though both are spoken across areas of similar size?

Use Web Code **nge-6802** for **DK World Desk Reference Online.**

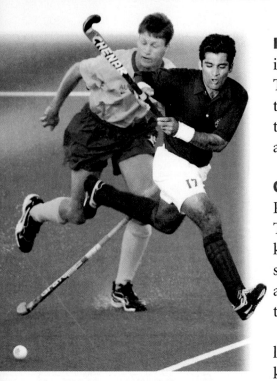

Top-quality field hockey sticks are made in Pakistan. Pakistan has won three Olympic gold medals in men's field hockey.

Industry Based on Agriculture Pakistan began its growth in industry by building on what its people knew best: agriculture. Today, Pakistan's economy depends largely on its textile industry. More than 60 percent of the country's exports come from the textile industry. Pakistan's textile products include yarn, cloth, and garments made from cotton grown by the country's farmers.

Other Industries in Pakistan Although most industries in Pakistan relate to farming, the nation has other industries as well. The chemical industry produces paint, soap, dye, and insect-killing sprays. Pakistan uses one of its natural resources, limestone, to make cement. Several steel mills allow Pakistan to make almost all the steel it needs. Producing steel can be less costly than buying it from other countries.

Millions of Pakistanis work in small workshops instead of in large factories. Workshops produce field hockey sticks, furniture, knives, saddles, and carpets. Pakistan is famous for its beautiful carpets. Some sell for as much as $25,000 in Pakistan—and $50,000 in New York or London.

✓ **Reading Check** Give an example of an industry in Pakistan based on agriculture.

Section 2 Assessment

Key Terms
Review the key terms at the beginning of this section. Use each term in a sentence that explains its meaning.

Target Reading Skill
Describe two or more effects of Pakistan's water supply on the economy. Use the information in your Taking Notes chart.

Comprehension and Critical Thinking
1. (a) Recall Where does most of the farming in Pakistan take place?

(b) Summarize How did the green revolution help Pakistan's farmers grow more wheat?
(c) Identify Effects What is one negative effect of heavy irrigation in Pakistan?
2. (a) Explain How does Pakistan's textile industry help the country's economy?
(b) Identify Causes What factor explains why Pakistan has a developed textile industry?

Writing Activity
Write a brief paragraph that shows your understanding of how the people of Pakistan have responded to conditions in their physical environment. Be sure to include ways Pakistan has developed an economy based mainly on agriculture even though it has a dry climate.

> **Writing Tip** Begin your paragraph with this topic sentence: *Pakistan has met the challenge of building an economy based on agriculture by developing a vast irrigation system.* Include supporting details about Pakistan's climate, the Indus River, Pakistan's irrigation system, and farming.

Prepare to Read

Objectives
In this section you will
1. Discover how Israel's economy has grown and changed over the years.
2. Learn about the different peoples living in Israel.

Taking Notes
As you read this section, look for the major ideas about the economy and cultures of Israel. Copy the diagram below, and record your findings in it.

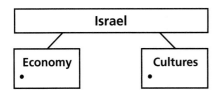

Target Reading Skill

Recognize Multiple Causes Sometimes multiple causes make one effect happen. As you read, look for three causes that have contributed to Israel's success in agriculture.

Key Terms
- **irrigation** (ihr uh GAY shun) *n.* the watering of crops using canals and other artificial waterways
- **kibbutz** (kih BOOTS) *n.* a cooperative settlement
- **West Bank** (west bank) *n.* a disputed region on the western bank of the Jordan River
- **Gaza Strip** (GAHZ uh strip) *n.* a disputed region on the Mediterranean coast

I t is spring in the country of Israel. The khamsin (kam SEEN) has come. The khamsin is a wind—a hot wind—that blows into the country from the south. *Khamsin* means "wind of 50 days."

For many days, the hot khamsin will blow over a harsh landscape. The southern half of Israel is the unforgiving Negev Desert, an arid land of plains and mountains. As the wind continues north, it raises waves on a huge salt-water lake with little life. The lake is called the Dead Sea. The shore of the Dead Sea is the lowest spot on Earth. Rocky highlands lie north of the lake.

Israel is a rugged land, as harsh as the khamsin is hot. Yet the peoples of Israel have turned this dry and rocky place into a country with a modern economy and vibrant cultures.

Harvesting hay on a kibbutz in Galilee, Israel

Israel's Economy

Fresh water and land suitable for farming are in especially short supply in Israel. Historically, people in the region made their living by herding animals across the desert, not by farming.

Agriculture The people of Israel have managed to make farms in their desert. They grow fruits, vegetables, cotton, and other crops. How can they farm in a land with little water?

As in Pakistan, the answer is irrigation. **Irrigation** is the watering of crops using canals and other artificial waterways. Water from the Sea of Galilee, a freshwater lake in northern Israel, is pumped through a vast network of canals and pipelines. Other technological achievements have contributed to Israel's success in agriculture. During the 1950s, the Israelis drained Lake Hula, in northern Israel, and nearby swamps. This created an additional 12,000 acres of farmland.

Another factor in the success of Israeli agriculture has been cooperation among farm workers. Most of them live in small farming villages called *moshavim* (moh shah VEEM). The workers cooperate by combining their money to buy equipment and sharing information about new methods of farming. They also pool their crops to get a better price.

Manufacturing Today, about one in four Israelis work in manufacturing. Major Israeli industries include textiles, processed foods, fertilizers, and plastics. Many companies manufacture goods for the Israeli military. But most Israeli industry is in high technology. Israeli electronic and scientific equipment is respected around the world.

This woman is making electronic cash registers at a factory in Dimona, a town in the Negev Desert.

Kibbutzim Some manufacturing is done on cooperative settlements called kibbutzim. People who live on a **kibbutz** (kih BOOTS) cooperate in all parts of life. They eat together, work together, and share profits equally. Originally, most kibbutzim were farming communities. Today, modern farming machinery has replaced the need for many farm workers. As a result, many kibbutzim have turned to manufacturing.

COUNTRY PROFILE

Focus on Government

Israel

Israel controls two types of land. The orange area on the map is Israel within its pre-1967 borders, which the United States and other countries consider part of Israel. Its people are mostly Israeli Jews. Since 1967, Israel has controlled the lands known by the Palestinians as the "occupied territories." The people who live there are mostly non-Israeli Arabs. However, in 2005 Israel withdrew from the Gaza Strip. Including the occupied territories, Israel controls an area slightly larger than New Jersey. Yet the population under Israeli control is larger than New Jersey's. Partly because there is so little land, there are sharp conflicts between Israelis and Arabs over control of this land.

Israel: Population, 2000

22% Arab and other
78% Jewish

- Jewish
- Arab and other

SOURCE: Encyclopedia Britannica

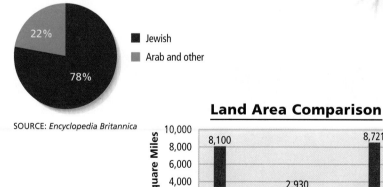

Land Area Comparison

	Square Miles	
Israel, 2006	8,100	
Golan Heights, West Bank, Gaza Strip	2,930	
New Jersey	8,721	

SOURCE: CIA World Factbook

Map and Chart Skills

1. **Identify** Of the two areas currently under Israeli control, which is larger?
2. **Locate** Which of these areas borders the Sea of Galilee?
3. **Synthesize** What percentage of the population of Israel is not Jewish?

Go Online
PHSchool.com

Use Web Code **nge-6803** for **DK World Desk Reference Online.**

Explore the city of Jerusalem in Israel.

Service Industries Today, service industries are the most important part of the Israeli economy. Service industries are industries that provide services instead of manufactured goods.

One type of service industry is trade. Israel borders the Mediterranean Sea. Its chief port city is Haifa, which has a deepwater harbor, excellent for docking ships. Many Israeli exports leave through Haifa. Many imports arrive there as well. Israel must import much of what it needs, since it has few natural resources. Imports include oil for energy and grain for food.

✓ **Reading Check** What industry is the most important part of the Israeli economy?

The People of Israel

Israel is home to about 6.5 million people. More than 90 percent of them live in cities. Israel's largest cities are Jerusalem, the manufacturing center of Tel Aviv, and the coastal city of Haifa.

Jews Today, about 80 percent of the people of Israel consider themselves to be Jews. Yet there is great diversity among Israeli Jews. When Israel was founded in 1948, most of the Jewish people who moved to Israel came from Europe and North America. They helped shape the culture and government of their new country. Because these people came from modern, developed countries, Israel became a modern, developed country, too.

Later, groups of Jews came from Middle Eastern countries. Beginning in the mid-1970s, tens of thousands of Ethiopian Jews from Africa have emigrated to Israel. More recently, many Jewish immigrants have come from Russia—nearly a million in the 1990s. Overall, nearly 3 million people have settled in Israel since the country was founded.

Children and teachers create crafts at a kibbutz daycare school in Israel.

Religious Diversity Most people in Israel practice Judaism. A small percentage of the country's population is Christian or follows other religions. The single largest religion after Judaism, however, is Islam. About 16 percent of Israel's population is Muslim.

Palestinian Arabs Most Muslims living under Israeli control are Palestinian Arabs. Israel was founded in 1948 on land that was known as Palestine. Both Jews and Palestinian Arabs have long claimed Palestine as their homeland. In a series of wars with its Arab neighbors, Israel won portions of Egypt, Jordan, and Syria. Arabs called these areas the "occupied territories." Today, the occupied territories include the West Bank and the Golan Heights. The **West Bank** is an area on the west bank, or edge, of the Jordan River. Israel gave up control of the Gaza Strip to the Palestinians in 2005. The **Gaza Strip** is a small area of land along the Mediterranean Sea.

For decades, relations between the Palestinians and the Israelis have been marked by violence despite efforts on both sides to achieve peace. Several issues have divided the two groups. For example, many Palestinians fled after the Arab-Israeli wars, and Israelis have opposed the return of large numbers of Palestinians. Many Israelis insisted that a peace agreement protect Israeli settlements in the occupied territories. Palestinians, however, have opposed this idea.

A Palestinian open-air market in Jerusalem, Israel

✓ **Reading Check** What is the single largest religion in Israel after Judaism?

Section 3 Assessment

Key Terms
Review the key terms at the beginning of this section. Use each term in a sentence that explains its meaning.

Target Reading Skill
What are three causes of Israel's success in agriculture?

Comprehension and Critical Thinking
1. (a) Explain How can Israeli farmers grow crops in a desert?

(b) Main Idea What type of industry is most important to the Israeli economy?
(c) Synthesize Information Why do you think high technology has become an important part of the Israeli economy?
2. (a) Recall About what percentage of Israel's population is Muslim?
(b) Identify the Main Idea Give an example of the diversity among Israeli Jews.

Writing Activity
Would you enjoy living on a kibbutz? Write a paragraph that explains why or why not.

Writing Tip Give specific reasons for your explanation. Your first sentence should answer the basic question—whether or not you would like to live on a kibbutz. The following sentences should give specific reasons for your answer.

Saudi Arabia
Oil and Islam

Prepare to Read

Objectives

In this section you will
1. Learn how oil has affected Saudi Arabia's development and economy.
2. Discover how Islam affects everyday life in Saudi Arabia.
3. Understand the main features of Saudi Arabia's government.

Taking Notes

As you read this section, look for ways in which oil and Islam have shaped Saudi Arabia. Copy the table below, and record your findings in it.

Oil	Islam
•	•
•	•

Target Reading Skill

Understand Effects
Sometimes one cause may produce several effects. As you read, note two effects of oil wealth on the development of Saudi Arabia. Write them in your Taking Notes chart.

Key Terms

- **hajj** (haj) *n.* a pilgrimage or journey to Mecca undertaken by Muslims during the month of the hajj
- **Quran** (koo RAHN) *n.* the holy book of Islam
- **monarchy** (MAHN ur kee) *n.* a state or a nation in which power is held by a monarch—a king, a queen, or an emperor

Kingdom Tower in Riyadh

For more than a thousand years, Muslims from all over the world have been making pilgrimages to Mecca, Saudi Arabia. By going to Mecca, they honor the memory of Abraham, who is said to have built the first house of worship there. The pilgrimage to Mecca is called the **hajj** (haj). Muslims must make the hajj at least once in their lifetime. The hajj used to be long, hard, and dangerous. Muslims traveled across mountains and deserts by foot, horse, or camel to reach Mecca. Today, many pilgrims travel there by airplane. Roads link Mecca with other Saudi Arabian cities. Modern hotels line the streets of Mecca. Mecca is the birthplace of Islam's founder, Muhammad, and considered the holiest city in Islam.

Oil Wealth and Saudi Arabia

In 1900, Mecca was a very poor town. Saudi Arabia was one of the poorest countries in the world. Many of its people made a living by herding livestock. Like most of the countries of Southwest Asia, Saudi Arabia is mostly desert.

An Economy Based on Oil But in the 1930s, everything changed. People discovered oil in Southwest Asia. Oil reserves changed the fortunes of Saudi Arabia and several other countries in the region. It made them rich. When night falls in Riyadh (ree YAHD), Saudi Arabia's capital, the skyline begins to glow. The lights of the many apartment and office buildings flicker on. Large buildings line the city streets. When oil prices are high, buildings go up at a rapid pace. Money pours in, allowing communities like Riyadh to modernize. But when oil prices are down, the economy of the entire country is affected. Many large building projects grind to a stop.

Saudi Arabia has the most important oil economy in the world. Under its deserts lie more than 260 billion barrels of oil. Saudi Arabia has about one fourth of the world's oil. No other country on Earth exports more petroleum.

Changes From Oil Wealth Projects paid for with oil money have changed the lives of all Saudi Arabians. Beginning in the late 1960s, the Saudi Arabian government spent billions of dollars from oil sales to modernize the country. The Saudis built modern highways, airports, seaports, and a telephone system. Villages that had always depended on oil lamps were hooked up to electric power grids.

The nation's oil wealth made it possible to build a large school system. Saudi Arabia built thousands of schools. The country has eight major universities. In 1900, many Saudi Arabians could not read or write. But today, Saudi students are becoming doctors, scientists, and teachers.

✔ **Reading Check** About how much of the world's oil is in Saudi Arabia?

Target Skill **Understand Effects** How does the blue heading signal information on the effects of oil on Saudi Arabia's economy?

Saudi and American men working at the Saudi American Bank in Riyadh

Saudi Arabia

Saudi Arabia has the world's largest known oil reserves. Its economy is heavily dependent on oil. As you can see on the map, much of Saudi Arabia's land area has little or no activity other than oil production. The rest of the land supports a thin population of nomadic herders. One result of Saudi Arabia's heavy dependence on oil is that its gross domestic product per capita, or the average value of goods and services per person, has not increased much over the years. This is because oil prices have been fairly steady in recent years. Although Saudi Arabia has increased oil production, its population has increased, too, so production per person has not changed much.

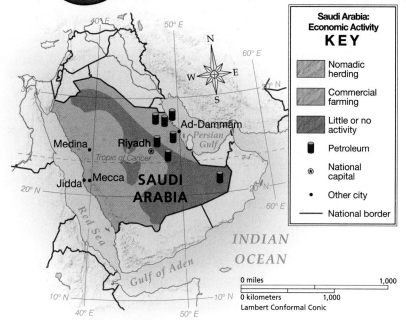

Saudi Arabia: Economic Activity
KEY

- Nomadic herding
- Commercial farming
- Little or no activity
- Petroleum
- National capital
- Other city
- National border

Exports

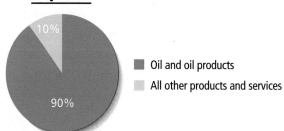

- Oil and oil products
- All other products and services

90%
10%

SOURCE: *CIA World Factbook*

Gross Domestic Product Per Capita, 1986–2005

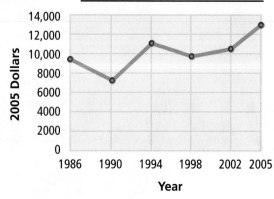

SOURCE: *CIA World Factbook*

Map and Chart Skills

1. **Identify** What percentage of Saudi Arabia's exports is made up of oil and oil products?
2. **Infer** How does the map help to explain Saudi Arabia's dependence on oil?
3. **Predict** How would Saudi Arabia's economy be affected if oil prices dropped sharply? If oil prices jumped?

 Use Web Code **nge-6804** for **DK World Desk Reference Online.**

Everyday Life in Saudi Arabia

Using their oil wealth, Saudis have imported computers, cellular phones, and televisions. But before a new product is used, the nation's religious leaders study it. They decide whether each import may be used by Muslims. Only imports that they believe do not undermine Muslim values may be used in daily life. In Saudi Arabia, Islam regulates most people's lives.

Islamic Traditions For example, cities like Riyadh have department stores, hotels, and universities. But they have no movie theaters or night clubs. The Wahhabi (wah HAH bee) branch of Islam, which most Saudi Arabians follow, forbids such entertainment.

Alcohol and pork are illegal in Saudi Arabia. All shops close five times a day when Muslims pray. Saudi Arabians use Western inventions to improve their lives, but they make sure these inventions do not interfere with Islamic traditions.

The Role of Women Many laws and traditions in Saudi Arabia deal with the role of women. Women are protected in certain ways, and they are also forbidden to do certain things. For example, when Saudi women go out in public, they must cover themselves with a full-length black cloak. They cannot vote.

However, women in Saudi Arabia today have more opportunities than in the past. Women can work as doctors, as journalists, and in other professions. They can own businesses. Today, more women than men are studying in Saudi universities.

Despite the changes, women and men usually remain separate. Boys and girls go to different schools. At the university level, women study separately from men. Female students watch male teachers over a video system.

Saudi Arabian Women
According to Islamic law, Saudi Arabian women appearing in public must wear a long, black cloak, a scarf, and a veil covering the face, (bottom photo). The small photo shows a female Saudi doctor examining a male patient.

Drilling for Oil

The modern world depends on oil. Oil affects people every day, in almost every way. It fuels cars, heats homes, and is used to create electricity. Oil is located deep within Earth's surface, on land and under the oceans. The rotary drill, shown here, is often used to extract oil from land. It works like a giant screwdriver. As the drill turns round and round, it forces itself deeper through the ground.

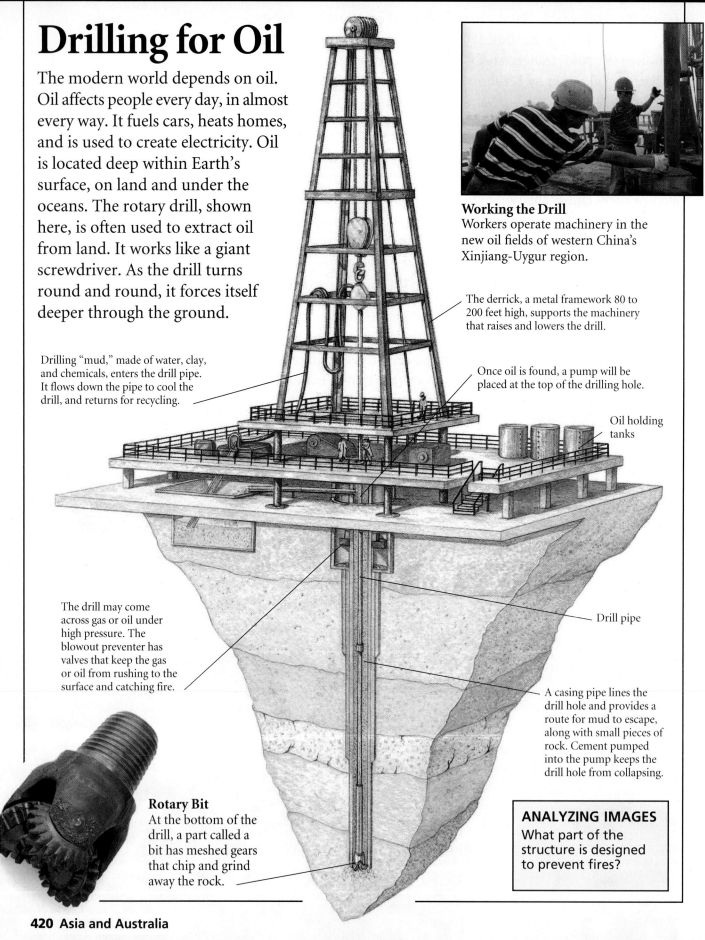

Working the Drill
Workers operate machinery in the new oil fields of western China's Xinjiang-Uygur region.

The derrick, a metal framework 80 to 200 feet high, supports the machinery that raises and lowers the drill.

Drilling "mud," made of water, clay, and chemicals, enters the drill pipe. It flows down the pipe to cool the drill, and returns for recycling.

Once oil is found, a pump will be placed at the top of the drilling hole.

Oil holding tanks

The drill may come across gas or oil under high pressure. The blowout preventer has valves that keep the gas or oil from rushing to the surface and catching fire.

Drill pipe

A casing pipe lines the drill hole and provides a route for mud to escape, along with small pieces of rock. Cement pumped into the pump keeps the drill hole from collapsing.

Rotary Bit
At the bottom of the drill, a part called a bit has meshed gears that chip and grind away the rock.

ANALYZING IMAGES
What part of the structure is designed to prevent fires?

The Influence of the Quran Most of the rules governing daily life in Saudi Arabia come from the Quran, the holy book of Islam. The word *Quran* means "the recitation" or "the reading." It consists of 114 chapters said to have been revealed by God to Muhammad. Muslims view the Quran as a guide for living. It provides guidelines on all aspects of life and religion.

✓ **Reading Check** How is Islam a part of daily life in Saudi Arabia?

The Government of Saudi Arabia

Islam guides more than daily life in Saudi Arabia. Saudi Arabia's government is based on the Quran and Islamic law. The country is an absolute monarchy ruled under Islamic law. A **monarchy** is a state or a nation in which power is held by a monarch. A monarch is a king, a queen, or an emperor.

The king serves as head of the Council of Ministers, which acts as the executive and legislative branches of the government. The king decides who will serve on the Council of Ministers. Traditionally, the Council includes the Crown Prince and members of the royal family. Political parties and elections are not allowed in Saudi Arabia.

✓ **Reading Check** What kind of government does Saudi Arabia have?

Links to
Science

Circles of Wheat In Saudi Arabia, some parts of the desert have what is called "sweet" sand. This sand is not too salty, so plants can grow in it. In a place with sweet sand, wells are dug and fields are planted. Often, the fields are circular, with the well at the center. A long pipe with sprinklers swings around the well, irrigating the field. Wheat, alfalfa, and even pumpkins are grown in such areas.

Discovery CHANNEL SCHOOL Video
Learn what brings millions of Muslims to Mecca each year.

Section 4 Assessment

Key Terms
Review the key terms at the beginning of this section. Use each term in a sentence that explains its meaning.

Target Reading Skill
What are two ways that oil wealth has affected the development of Saudi Arabia?

Comprehension and Critical Thinking
1. (a) Recall On what natural resource is Saudi Arabia's economy based?

(b) Apply Information How did wealth from oil change Saudi Arabia?
(c) Generalize How has the Saudi Arabian government used oil wealth to improve the lives of its citizens?
2. (a) Explain Give two examples of the ways Islam affects daily life in Saudi Arabia.
(b) Identify Point of View How do Muslims view the Quran?
3. (a) Describe Describe Saudi Arabia's system of government.
(b) Evaluate Information Why do you think political parties are not permitted in Saudi Arabia?

Writing Activity
Economists estimate that Saudi Arabia has enough oil to last for about 90 years of production at its present rate. In recent years, the Saudi Arabian government has used oil wealth to develop industries outside of petroleum. These include the iron and steel industries, construction, and chemicals. Write a paragraph that explains why Saudi Arabia might want to diversify its economy.

Writing Tip As you work on your paragraph, keep in mind that petroleum is a nonrenewable resource.

Look at the picture below. The man is pushing a standard-size oil barrel that holds 42 gallons. The barrel is about the size of a large trash can.

Imagine 20 of these barrels standing together in a corner of your classroom. Would they fill up your classroom? If you stacked them, how many could fit into the room? You could probably squeeze in a few hundred.

If just a few hundred barrels of oil would fill your classroom, imagine how much space 8 million barrels would fill! You probably can't even picture that many barrels. Yet it is important for people to visualize huge numbers like these because they often represent facts we need to understand.

 SS.3.02 Interpret graphs and charts

A bar graph is a useful tool for thinking about and comparing large numbers. It is a simple, easy-to-read way of showing a large amount of information.

Learn the Skill

Review the following steps to help you understand how to read bar graphs.

1 **Read the title to see what the bar graph is about.** The title identifies the topic of the bar graph.

2 **Read the labels to find out what each axis represents.** An axis is a line at the side or bottom of a graph. The horizontal axis is called the *x*-axis. Here you will find the categories of your data. The vertical axis is called the *y*-axis. The *y*-axis shows value or quantity.

3 **Look at the data to see if you can find similarities, differences, increases, or decreases.** What information does the horizontal axis show? What information does the vertical axis show?

4 **Make one or more general statements about what the graph shows.** You will have to compare and analyze the data in the bar graph in order to draw a conclusion or make a prediction about the topic of the bar graph.

Practice the Skill

Use the steps you have just learned to read the bar graph on the right.

1 Jot down the subject of the bar graph. What does the bar graph show?

2 Look at the labels. What does the *x*-axis represent? What does the *y*-axis represent?

3 Now compare the data. What information can you read from the *x*-axis and the *y*-axis? Use it to answer the following questions: About how much oil did Saudi Arabia produce in 1998? In 2003? In what year did Saudi Arabia produce 9.5 billion barrels of oil?

4 Analyze the data to make a prediction. From 2002 to 2003, Saudi Arabia increased its crude oil production by about half a billion barrels per year. Based on this rate of increase, how much crude oil would you expect Saudi Arabia to have produced in 2004?

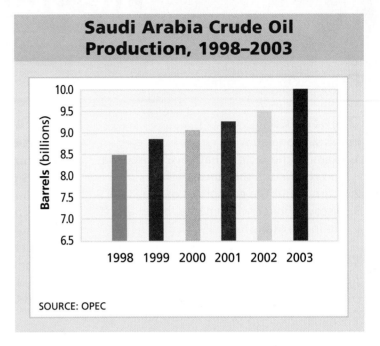

Saudi Arabia Crude Oil Production, 1998–2003

SOURCE: OPEC

Apply the Skill

Follow the steps in this skill lesson to read the bar graph below. What is the bar graph about? What does the *x*-axis represent? The *y*-axis? Which country has the greatest reserves?

Oil Reserves in Selected Southwest Asian Countries

SOURCE: *The NY Times Almanac*

Prepare to Read

Objectives

In this section you will

1. Examine the factors that have caused war and conflicts in the Stans.
2. Learn about the economies of the Stans.
3. Discover how environmental issues affect life in the Stans.

Taking Notes

As you read, look for details about the challenges facing Central Asian countries. Copy the chart below, and record your findings in it.

Challenges Facing Central Asian Countries		
Environmental damage		

🔄 Target Reading Skill

Recognize Cause-and-Effect Signal Words
Sometimes certain words, such as *because*, *affect*, or *as a result*, signal a cause or an effect. In this section, look for these words to better understand conditions in Central Asia.

Key Terms

- **refugee** (ref yoo JEE) *n.* a person who flees war or other disasters
- **dictatorship** (DIK tay tur ship) *n.* a form of government in which power is held by a leader who has absolute authority
- **landlocked** (LAND lahkt) *adj.* having no direct access to the sea

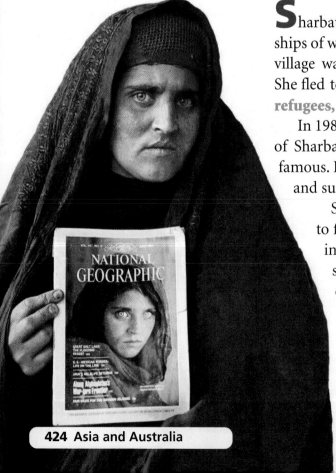

Sharbat Gula was a child when she first experienced the hardships of war. The Soviet Union invaded Afghanistan in 1979. Her village was destroyed in the fighting. Her parents were killed. She fled to neighboring Pakistan, where she lived in a camp for **refugees,** people who flee war or other disasters.

In 1985, a photographer named Steve McCurry took a picture of Sharbat at a refugee camp in Pakistan. The picture became famous. People around the world became more aware of the war and suffering in Afghanistan.

Seventeen years later, McCurry went back to the region to find Sharbat. He managed to trace her to a small village in Afghanistan. She was married and had children. She said she hoped that her children would have more opportunities than she had. She hoped they would get an education. Many people in Central Asia share Sharbat's hope for a better life. In addition to Afghanistan, this region includes Kazakhstan, Uzbekistan, Tajikistan, Turkmenistan, and Kyrgyzstan.

Sharbat Gula holds the magazine that made her picture famous.

Warfare and Unrest in Afghanistan

The war that caused Sharbat to flee Afghanistan lasted for ten years, until the Soviet troops withdrew in 1989. But that wasn't the end of the fighting in Afghanistan.

Conflict in Afghanistan A group of militant Islamic people called the Taliban gained power in Afghanistan in 1996. The Taliban established very strict Islamic rule. It limited freedoms and executed or severely punished those who violated their laws. Under the Taliban, girls were not allowed to attend school, and women were barred from working outside the home. Television, music, and the Internet were banned.

The Taliban had the support of radical Muslims from other countries. One of these supporters was Osama bin Laden, a wealthy Saudi Arabian who moved to Afghanistan. In 1996, the Taliban placed bin Laden under its protection.

A Campaign Against Terrorism Bin Laden was the leader of al Qaeda, a terrorist group. He was the leading suspect in the terrorist attacks of September 11, 2001 that destroyed the World Trade Center in New York City, damaged the Pentagon near Washington, D.C., and killed nearly 3,000 people. Because the Taliban refused to hand bin Laden over to the United States, American troops invaded Afghanistan in October 2001. Aided by Afghan rebels opposed to the Taliban, the United States quickly overthrew the Taliban government. Since 2001, Afghanistan has had a democratic government and, in 2004, Hamid Karzai became the country's first democratically elected president.

✓ **Reading Check** **What happened in Afghanistan after the terrorist attacks on September 11, 2001?**

An Afghan Classroom
This picture of a girl's school in Kabul was taken when schools reopened after the fall of the Taliban government. The Taliban shut down most schools when it took over in 1996. **Analyze** *Why was the reopening of schools in Afghanistan seen as a return to a stable life?*

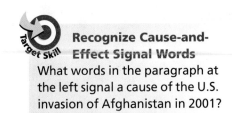

Recognize Cause-and-Effect Signal Words
What words in the paragraph at the left signal a cause of the U.S. invasion of Afghanistan in 2001?

Conflicts in Other Central Asian Countries

Afghanistan was not the only Central Asian country to experience conflict. Tensions among rival leaders, clans, and ethnic groups also affected other countries in the region.

Ethnic Disputes Central Asia is a mixture of various ethnic groups and cultures. For many years, strong Soviet rule kept ethnic and clan tensions under control. As Soviet rule came to an end, however, these tensions increased. In some countries, competing groups came into conflict. In Kazakhstan, for example, disputes arose between Kazakhs and Russians over issues of political and economic power under the new government.

Political Conflicts The situation in Tajikistan was worse. There, conflicts between rival groups erupted in violence. A bloody civil war raged through much of the 1990s and left the country in ruins. In Uzbekistan, conflict broke out in the Ferghana Valley. This fertile region, which borders Tajikistan and Kyrgyzstan, came under attack from radical Muslim groups. They wanted to overthrow the government of Uzbekistan and found an Islamic state.

Uzbekistan's government fought back against its opponents. It jailed critics of the government and outlawed radical groups. Other governments in the region also cracked down on opponents. They curbed political freedoms and violated human rights. Since independence, several countries of Central Asia have turned toward **dictatorship**—a form of government in which authority is held by an all-powerful ruler.

Children in Kyrgyzstan outside a yurt, a portable dwelling used by nomads in Central Asia

Help for Central Asia The United States and other Western countries expressed concern about the rise of dictators in the region. They called on the Stans to create democratic governments. The United States also took steps to help the region. It provided training, equipment, and money—$594 million in 2002—to build democracy and to improve economies. One program, for example, trained judges in Kyrgyzstan and Tajikistan.

✓ **Reading Check** What conflicts have disrupted life in the Stans?

COUNTRY PROFILE

Focus on History

The Stans

The Stans' ethnic and religious makeup reflects their history. Over the centuries, waves of invaders have swept across the Stans. People speaking Iranian languages came thousands of years ago. They adopted Islam more than 1,000 years ago. Iranian speakers today include the Tajiks, the Pashtuns, and the Hazaras. About a thousand years ago, invaders brought Turkic languages, such as Uzbek and Kazakh. Finally, during the 1800s, Russians conquered the region. The Russians brought a new religion, Orthodox Christianity. Still, most of the region's people practice Islam.

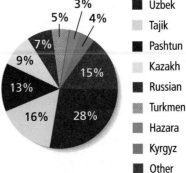

The Stans: Political

KEY

—— National border

⊛ National capital

• Other city

Religions*

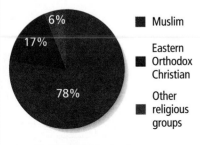

6%
17%
78%

■ Muslim

■ Eastern Orthodox Christian

■ Other religious groups

SOURCE: *CIA World Factbook*

*Numbers may not equal 100% due to rounding.

Ethnic Makeup

3%
5% 4%
7%
9%
13%
16% 28%
15%

■ Uzbek
■ Tajik
■ Pashtun
■ Kazakh
■ Russian
■ Turkmen
■ Hazara
■ Kyrgyz
■ Other

SOURCE: *CIA World Factbook*

Map and Chart Skills

1. **Name** What is the largest ethnic group in the Stans?
2. **Recall** What kind of language does this group speak?
3. **Synthesize** Based on the region's history, which ethnic group probably includes most of the region's Orthodox Christians?

Use Web Code **nge-6805** for **DK World Desk Reference Online.**

Economic Conditions in Central Asia

The Stans are generally poor countries. Agriculture is the main economic activity, although manufacturing, mining, and energy production are increasingly important. The growth of industry may offer better economic prospects in the future.

Agriculture Farming is the mainstay of Central Asian economies. During the Soviet era, large cotton farms produced huge amounts of cotton for export. Cotton farming is still important in the region—especially around the Ferghana Valley—but other types of farming have also increased. Production of grains, fruits, vegetables, and livestock has grown in recent years.

Some farms in Central Asia are large, like the cotton farms of Uzbekistan, but most are small. For most small farmers, life is a struggle. It is difficult to grow enough food or earn enough money to provide a decent living.

Sharbat Gula's life is typical for people who live in the country. Her village lies in the hills of eastern Afghanistan. Villagers plant small plots of corn, wheat, and rice on terraces built into the hillsides. They may also have a few walnut trees and maybe a sheep or two. To make money, Sharbat's husband works at a bakery in a nearby city. He makes less than one dollar a day. That's barely enough for Sharbat's family to buy the things they need to survive.

■ **Chart Skills**

The Stans are generally poor countries with developing economies. **Compare** What is one economic activity all the countries in the Stans have in common?

Economies of Central Asian Countries

Country	Economic Activities
Afghanistan	Farming and livestock raising. Small-scale production of textiles, furniture, cement.
Kazakhstan	Farming, oil and coal mining, steel production, textiles.
Kyrgyzstan	Farming and livestock raising. Cotton, tobacco, wool and meat.
Tajikistan	Mainly farming, mostly cotton. One large aluminum plant.
Turkmenistan	Major cotton-producing country. Production of natural gas, oil, and textiles.
Uzbekistan	Major cotton exporter. Large producer of gold and oil.

Working on a construction site in Turkmenistan

Industry Not all Central Asians live in rural areas, however. Many live in growing cities, like Almaty, Kazakhstan, and Tashkent, Uzbekistan. Many residents live in apartments and work in offices or factories. Many of the industries in the Stans date back to the Soviet era. They are generally old and unproductive. Gradually, however, some factories and mines are being modernized. Much of the focus is on the development of Central Asia's energy and mineral resources.

Several of the Stans are rich in oil, natural gas, and minerals such as coal, gold, iron ore, and uranium. Kazakhstan has major oil reserves, while Turkmenistan is rich in natural gas. Foreign oil and gas companies are exploring ways to develop and export these resources. One problem is that these countries are **landlocked, with no direct access to the sea.** Plans are underway to build pipelines to carry oil and gas out of the region.

✓ **Reading Check** **What are the main features of Central Asian economies?**

Environmental Issues

The new countries of Central Asia face the challenging task of restoring and protecting the environment. In the past, the Soviet Union caused great environmental damage in the region.

One major environmental challenge involves nuclear fallout. For years, the Soviet Union conducted nuclear tests in northern Kazakhstan. Nuclear explosions left the region with severe radiation pollution. Radiation has caused serious health problems, including cancer and birth defects. This pollution will take years, even decades, to clean up.

Links to **Art**

Saving Art Central Asia has a rich artistic tradition. Many works of art have been destroyed, however, as a result of war and other conflicts. In Kabul, Afghanistan, for example, the Taliban destroyed priceless art in the National Museum. They also destroyed two giant Buddha statues at Bamiyan. Efforts are now underway to restore or save the remaining art treasures. Foreign countries and international agencies, such as the United Nations, are working with the Afghan government to preserve the country's artistic heritage. An ancient bronze sculpture from the National Museum in Kabul is shown below.

The natural beauty of the Stans is an important asset for the future. Shown here are the Tian Shan mountains in Kyrgyzstan.

As you read in Chapter 9, another major challenge is the drying of the Aral Sea. For years, the Soviets diverted water from rivers feeding the sea to irrigate cotton fields. As a result, the sea is now drying up.

Still, vast areas of Central Asia remain undeveloped and undamaged. These environmentally healthy lands are a key resource for Central Asia. If the Stans can preserve their environment, it will be an important asset for their future.

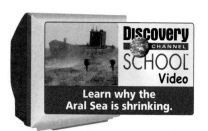

Learn why the Aral Sea is shrinking.

✓ **Reading Check** How have environmental problems affected the Stans?

Section 5 Assessment

Key Terms
Review the key terms at the beginning of this section. Use each term in a sentence that explains its meaning.

Target Reading Skill
Review the text about environmental issues. Find the words that signal effects on Central Asia's environment.

Comprehension and Critical Thinking
1. (a) Explain How did the Taliban come to power in Afghanistan?
(b) Summarize Why did the United States invade Afghanistan in 2001?

2. (a) Recall Name a Central Asian country other than Afghanistan that has experienced recent conflicts.
(b) Make Generalizations In general, how has the United States helped Central Asian countries?
3. (a) Identify What is the main economic activity in Central Asian countries?
(b) Apply Information How might mineral resources help Central Asian countries develop their economies?
4. (a) Recall How has nuclear testing affected Kazakhstan?
(b) Identify Causes What caused the Aral Sea to shrink?

Writing Activity
Suppose that you are a news reporter covering Central Asia. Write a brief news report about economic conditions and challenges in Central Asia.

For: An activity on the Stans
Visit: PHSchool.com
Web Code: ngd-6805

◆ Chapter Summary

Section 1: India

- India is the second-most-populated country in the world. India also has a rapidly growing population.
- India has a large middle class that provides a huge market for goods and services.
- Despite India's fast-growing economy, about one fourth of the population lives in poverty.

Israel

Section 3: Israel

- Service industries are the most important part of Israel's well-developed economy.
- About 80 percent of the people of Israel are Jewish. About 16 percent are Muslims.
- In 2005, Israel gave control of parts of the occupied territories to the Palestinians.

Section 4: Saudi Arabia

- Oil production is the main economic activity in Saudi Arabia. No other country in the world exports more petroleum.
- Saudi Arabia has used its wealth from oil to make the country more modern.
- Islam guides daily life in Saudi Arabia and is the basis for Saudi Arabia's laws.

India

Section 2: Pakistan

- Pakistan has been working hard to improve its economy.
- Pakistan's economy is based largely on agriculture.
- Pakistan's textile industry is an important part of the economy. Other industries include making chemicals and steel.

Section 5: The Stans

- The countries of Central Asia face many challenges in creating prosperous, stable nations.
- Agriculture is the main economic activity in Central Asia. Manufacturing, mining, and energy production are becoming important.

◆ Key Terms

Each of the statements below contains a key term from the chapter. If the statement is true, write *true*. If it is false, rewrite the statement to make it true.

1. Life expectancy measures the percentage of the population age 15 or over that can read and write.

2. Poor nutrition caused by a lack of food or an unbalanced diet is called malnutrition.

3. Drought, a long period of dry weather, is a major problem in Pakistan.

4. Irrigation is a worldwide effort to increase food production in developing countries.

5. Today, many Muslims make the hajj by airplane.

6. A refugee is a person who flees war or other disasters.

◆ Comprehension and Critical Thinking

7. (a) Recall What is the population of India?
(b) Summarize Why is India expected to have the world's largest population by 2050?

8. (a) Explain How does India's middle class help the nation's economy?
(b) Identify Effects What is one effect of India's efforts to improve health care?

9. (a) Explain Why is water shortage a major problem for Pakistan?
(b) Draw Inferences Why might a manufacturing company in Pakistan be located on the plains of the Indus River?
(c) Make Generalizations Why would education be considered important in making a nation more prosperous?

10. (a) Identify Give one example of how technology has helped Israel succeed in agriculture.
(b) Summarize How do the manufacturing and service industries improve Israel's economy?

11. (a) Identify What natural resource has helped Saudi Arabia build its economy and modernize the country?

(b) Identify Effects How has oil wealth affected the lives of Saudi Arabians?

12. (a) Describe What kind of government does Saudi Arabia have?
(b) Analyze What is the connection between Islam and the government of Saudi Arabia?

13. (a) Name Which Central Asian country was controlled by the Taliban?
(b) Summarize What factors have caused wars and conflicts in the Stans?

◆ Skills Practice

Interpreting Bar Graphs Name one Southwest Asian country that is not shown on the graph on the bottom of page 423. How would you find out whether it had any oil reserves?

◆ Writing Activity: Math

Use the Country Databank on pages 388–399 to look up the population of five countries discussed in this chapter. Make a bar graph that shows each country's population. Be sure to label the horizontal axis and the vertical axis of the graph. Include a title for your graph.

MAP MASTER™
Skills Activity

South, Southwest, and Central Asia

Place Location For each place listed below, write the letter from the map that shows its location.

1. Israel
2. India
3. Pakistan
4. Kazakhstan
5. Saudi Arabia
6. Aral Sea

Go Online
PHSchool.com Use Web Code **ngp-6820** for an interactive map.

Standardized Test Prep

Test-Taking Tips

Some questions on standardized tests ask you to analyze a reading selection. Read the passage below. Then follow the tips to answer the sample question at the right.

> The Negev Desert takes up two thirds of Israel's land. Only three or four inches of rain fall there each year. Yet Israeli farmers grow fruits and vegetables on the desert. They also plant trees there to prevent erosion. For water, Israeli farmers use an irrigation system that is controlled by computer. Plastic tubes carry underground water straight to the crops. This water is salty, so Israelis developed plants that can soak up the water but not the salt.

TIP Think about the author's purpose as you read. Is the author trying to give information, convince you about something, or explain how something works?

Pick the letter that best answers the question.

This paragraph answers which question?

A What is the Negev Desert in Israel like?

B What are Israeli farms like?

C How has Israel reclaimed the Negev Desert for farmland?

D How can an irrigation system bring water to desert land?

Think It Through Start with the author's purpose: to give you information about Israeli farms in the Negev Desert. What question is the passage answering about Israeli farms on the Negev Desert? You can eliminate D because it is not related specifically to Israeli farms. You can rule out A because it does not address the question of farms at all. That leaves B and C. Both ask questions about Israeli farms, but B does not include the Negev Desert. The correct answer is C.

Practice Questions

Use the tips above and other tips in this book to help you answer the following questions.

Use the passage below to answer Question 1.

> Landlocked Kazakhstan is the largest of the five former Soviet republics in Central Asia. It is about four times the size of Texas. Kazakhstan's most important natural resource is oil. In 2003, the country's oil reserves were estimated to be between 9 and 17.6 million barrels.

1. What information best supports the prediction that Kazakhstan could be a major oil exporter?

   A Kazakhstan is the largest of the former Soviet republics in Central Asia.

   B Kazakhstan is larger than Texas.

   C Kazakhstan's oil reserves are estimated to be as great as 17.6 million barrels.

   D Kazakhstan is landlocked.

2. What is one effect of India's efforts to improve health care?

   A India's literacy rate is increasing.

   B India's life expectancy is increasing.

   C Malnutrition is increasing.

   D India's film industry is growing.

Use Web Code **nga-6800** for **Chapter 15** self-test.

16

Southeast Asia and the Pacific Region

Chapter Preview

NC Standard Course of Study

7.5.01 How the location of natural resources affects economic development

7.5.02 Types of economic systems and their effectiveness in meeting needs

7.5.04 How specialization and interdependence influence trade patterns

7.6.01 Connection between economic development and standard of living

7.7.02 Causes and effects of historical events

7.9.01 Historical development of types of governments

7.9.03 Influence of values on how governments deal with issues of justices

Country Databank

Sections

1. Vietnam: A Nation Rebuilds
   7.5.02, 7.7.02, 7.9.01
2. Australia: A Pacific Rim Country
   7.5.01, 7.5.04, 7.6.01, 7.9.03

Target Reading Skill

Main Idea In this chapter you will focus on identifying main ideas and supporting details.

▶ **Hiking in the mountains of New Zealand**

Southeast Asia and the Pacific Region: Political

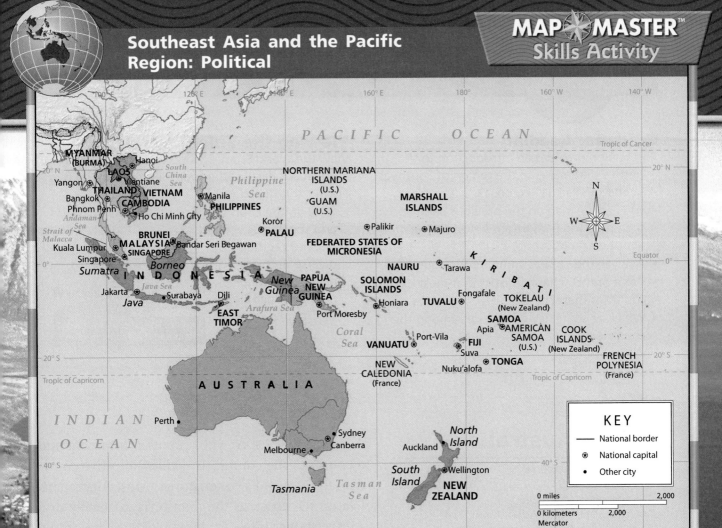

PACIFIC OCEAN

Tropic of Cancer

20° N

MYANMAR (BURMA)
Hanoi
LAOS
Yangon
THAILAND   Vientiane
Bangkok   VIETNAM
Phnom Penh   CAMBODIA
Andaman Sea
Ho Chi Minh City
Strait of Malacca
BRUNEI
MALAYSIA   Bandar Seri Begawan
Kuala Lumpur
SINGAPORE
Singapore
Sumatra
Borneo
INDONESIA
Jakarta
Java Sea
Surabaya
Java
Dili
New Guinea
EAST TIMOR

South China Sea
Philippine Sea
Manila
PHILIPPINES
Korór
PALAU

NORTHERN MARIANA ISLANDS (U.S.)
GUAM (U.S.)

Palikir
FEDERATED STATES OF MICRONESIA

MARSHALL ISLANDS
Majuro

NAURU   Tarawa
PAPUA NEW GUINEA
SOLOMON ISLANDS
Honiara
Port Moresby
Arafura Sea
Coral Sea
VANUATU   Port-Vila
NEW CALEDONIA (France)

KIRIBATI
Fongafale
TUVALU
TOKELAU (New Zealand)
SAMOA
Apia   AMERICAN SAMOA (U.S.)
FIJI
Suva
TONGA
Nuku'alofa

COOK ISLANDS (New Zealand)
FRENCH POLYNESIA (France)

Equator   0°

20° S
Tropic of Capricorn

AUSTRALIA

INDIAN OCEAN
Perth

Sydney
Canberra
Melbourne
Tasmania
Tasman Sea

Auckland
North Island
South Island
Wellington
NEW ZEALAND

40° S

KEY
— National border
⊛ National capital
• Other city

0 miles   2,000
0 kilometers   2,000
Mercator

Regions
Much of Southeast Asia and the Pacific Region is located between the Tropic of Cancer and the Tropic of Capricorn. **Identify** Which countries have land south of the Tropic of Capricorn? **Contrast** What climate would you expect most of these countries to have? Explain your answer.

Go Online
PHSchool.com Use Web Code ngp-6910 for step-by-step map skills practice.

Introducing Southeast Asia and the Pacific Region

Guide for Reading

This section provides an introduction to the countries that make up the region of Southeast Asia and the Pacific Region.

- Look at the map on the previous page and then read the paragraphs below to learn about each nation.
- Analyze the data to compare the countries.
- What are the characteristics that most of the countries share?
- What are some key differences among the countries?

Viewing the Video Overview

View the World Studies Video Overview to learn more about each of the countries. As you watch, answer this question:

- How do the countries in Southeast Asia and the Pacific depend on their diverse natural resources to support their people?

Discovery CHANNEL **SCHOOL** Video

Explore the land of Southeast Asia and the Pacific Region.

Australia

Capital	Canberra
Land Area	2,941,283 sq mi; 7,617,930 sq km
Population	19.6 million
Ethnic Group(s)	white, Asian, Aboriginal
Religion(s)	Protestant, Roman Catholic, traditional beliefs
Government	democratic, federal-state system recognizing the British monarch as sovereign
Currency	Australian dollar
Leading Exports	coal, gold, meat, wool, aluminum, iron ore, wheat, machinery and transport equipment
Language(s)	English (official), Italian, Cantonese, Greek, Arabic, Vietnamese, Aboriginal languages

Australia (aw STRAYL yuh) is both a continent and a country. The country is divided into five continental states and two territories. Most Australians live on the coast, as the interior is extremely dry. All the state capitals, including Sydney, are on the coast. The national capital, Canberra, is located inland. Australia is a country of great physical diversity, from deserts to snow-capped mountains. It also has the Great Barrier Reef, the largest coral reef in the world. Tourism is Australia's main industry, although it also has important farming and mining industries.

Wool is a leading Australian export.

Brunei

Capital	Bandar Seri Begawan
Land Area	2,035 sq mi; 5,270 sq km
Population	366,000
Ethnic Group(s)	Malay, Chinese, indigenous tribes
Religion(s)	Muslim, Buddhist, Christian, traditional beliefs
Government	constitutional sultanate
Currency	Brunei dollar
Leading Exports	crude oil, natural gas, refined products
Language(s)	Malay (official), English, Chinese

Brunei (broo NY) is a largely Muslim country in Southeast Asia. The same family, the Sultanate of Brunei, has been in power for more than six hundred years. At one point between the 1400s and 1600s, the nation controlled parts of Borneo and the Philippines. Later, the country experienced problems related to royal succession, colonization, and piracy. In the late 1800s, Brunei came under British rule for almost one hundred years, until it gained its independence in 1984. The nation is rich in oil and natural gas and has a relatively strong economy.

Cambodia

Capital	Phnom Penh
Land Area	68,154 sq mi; 176,520 sq km
Population	14.5 million
Ethnic Group(s)	Khmer, Vietnamese
Religion(s)	Buddhist
Government	multiparty democracy under a constitutional monarchy
Currency	riel
Leading Exports	clothing, timber, rubber, rice, fish
Language(s)	Khmer (official), French, English

Cambodia (kam BOH dee uh) is located on the Gulf of Thailand in Southeast Asia. It is bordered by Thailand, Vietnam, and Laos. Communist Khmer Rouge forces took over Cambodia in 1975. More than a million people died or were executed when the Khmer Rouge ordered the evacuation of all cities and towns. After decades of violent political conflict, the surrender of the Khmer Rouge in 1998 brought renewed political stability to Cambodia. Today, with massive international donations, Cambodia struggles to maintain a stable government and establish a working economy.

East Timor

Capital	Dili
Land Area	5,794 sq mi; 15,007 sq km
Population	820,000
Ethnic Group(s)	Austronesian (Malayo-Polynesian), Papuan, Chinese
Religion(s)	Roman Catholic, Muslim, Protestant, Hindu, Buddhist, traditional beliefs
Government	republic
Currency	U.S. dollar
Leading Exports	coffee, sandalwood, marble
Language(s)	Tetum (Portuguese-Austronesian) (official), Portuguese (official), Indonesian, English

East Timor (eest TEE mawr) is located in Southeast Asia, northwest of Australia. East Timor includes the eastern half and the Oecussi region of the island of Timor as well as two smaller islands. Once a Portuguese colony, East Timor declared its independence in 1975. Nine days after declaring independence, however, it was invaded and occupied by Indonesia. In 1999, the United Nations supervised an election in which the people of East Timor voted for independence from Indonesia. Though Indonesian militias protested with violence, East Timor was internationally recognized as an independent democratic nation in May 2002.

Introducing Southeast Asia and the Pacific Region

Federated States of Micronesia

Capital	Palikir
Land Area	271 sq mi; 702 sq km
Population	135,869
Ethnic Group(s)	Micronesian, Polynesian
Religion(s)	Roman Catholic, Protestant
Government	constitutional government
Currency	U.S. dollar
Leading Exports	fish, clothing, bananas, black pepper
Language(s)	English (official), Trukese, Pohnpeian, Mortlockese, Losrean

The Federated States of Micronesia (FED ur ayt id stayts uv my kruh NEE zhuh) is an island group in the North Pacific Ocean. It consists of all the Caroline Islands except Palau. Once under United States control, the Federated States of Micronesia (FSM) became independent in 1986. The United States still provides the country with financial aid and military protection. The FSM is working to overcome long-term concerns such as high unemployment, overfishing, and dependence on United States aid. Most Micronesians live without running water or electricity.

Fiji

Capital	Suva
Land Area	7,054 sq mi; 18,270 sq km
Population	856,346
Ethnic Group(s)	Fijian, South Asian, white, other Pacific Islander, East Asian
Religion(s)	Hindu, Protestant, Roman Catholic, Muslim
Government	republic
Currency	Fiji dollar
Leading Exports	sugar, clothing, gold, timber, fish, molasses, coconut oil
Language(s)	English (official), Fijian, Hindi, Urdu, Tamil, Telugu

Fiji (FEE jee) is an island group in the South Pacific Ocean. Fiji consists of two main islands and hundreds of smaller islands. After nearly one hundred years as a British colony, Fiji became an independent democracy in 1970. Fiji has a history of ethnic conflict between native Fijians and those of Indian ancestry. This conflict has caused great political instability over the past few decades and has weakened Fiji's economy.

Indonesia

Capital	Jakarta
Land Area	705,188 sq mi; 1,826,440 sq km
Population	231.3 million
Ethnic Group(s)	Javanese, Sundanese, Madurese, coastal Malay
Religion(s)	Muslim, Protestant, Roman Catholic, Hindu, Buddhist
Government	republic
Currency	rupiah
Leading Exports	oil and gas, electrical appliances
Language(s)	Bahasa Indonesia (official), Javanese, Sundanese, Madurese, Dutch

Indonesia (in duh NEE zhuh) is an island nation located between the Indian and Pacific Oceans. It is Southeast Asia's largest and most populous country, and the world's largest archipelago. It is also the world's most populous Muslim nation. Once known as the Dutch East Indies, Indonesia achieved independence from the Netherlands in 1949. When a giant tsunami struck in 2004, parts of Indonesia faced destruction, and about 129,000 people were killed. Although poverty and terrorism remain problems, the nation's government and economy have grown more stable.

Kiribati

Capital	Bairiki (Tarawa Atoll)
Land Area	313 sq mi; 811 sq km
Population	96,335
Ethnic Group(s)	Micronesian, Polynesian
Religion(s)	Roman Catholic, Protestant, Muslim, traditional beliefs
Government	republic
Currency	Australian dollar
Leading Exports	copra, coconuts, seaweed, fish
Language(s)	English (official), Micronesian dialect

Kiribati (kihr uh BAS) is a group of 33 coral atolls in the Pacific Ocean. It lies on the Equator about halfway between Hawaii and Australia. Once called the Gilbert Islands, part of a British colony, Kiribati became independent in 1979. Great Britain had mined the islands for their phosphate deposits for decades. Although the phosphate ran out in 1980, Kiribati succeeded in winning some payment from Britain for what it had taken. With very few natural resources, Kiribati has a limited economy. However, it grows enough food to support its citizens without imports.

Laos

Capital	Vientiane
Land Area	89,112 sq mi; 230,800 sq km
Population	5.8 million
Ethnic Group(s)	Lao Loum, Lao Theung, Lao Soung, Vietnamese, East Asian
Religion(s)	Buddhist, traditional beliefs
Government	communist state
Currency	new kip
Leading Exports	wood products, clothing, electricity, coffee, tin
Language(s)	Lao (official), Mon-Khmer, Yao, Vietnamese, Chinese, French

Laos (LAH ohs) is a landlocked Communist country in Southeast Asia bordered by Vietnam, Cambodia, Thailand, Myanmar, and China. After six hundred years as a monarchy, Laos became a communist nation in 1975. The country has many mineral resources and produces large amounts of coffee and timber. Still, it is one of the world's least developed countries and depends on foreign aid. Laotians are mostly Buddhists. The majority of the population lives in rural areas and works in farming.

Malaysia

Capital	Kuala Lumpur and Putrajaya
Land Area	126,853 sq mi; 328,550 sq km
Population	22.7 million
Ethnic Group(s)	Malay, East Asian, indigenous tribes, South Asian
Religion(s)	Muslim, Buddhist, traditional beliefs, Hindu, Christian
Government	constitutional monarchy
Currency	ringgit
Leading Exports	electronic equipment, petroleum and liquefied natural gas, wood
Language(s)	Bahasa Malaysia (official), Malay, Chinese, Tamil, English

Malaysia (muh LAY zhuh) consists of a peninsula and the northern third of the island of Borneo in the South China Sea. It shares borders with Thailand, Indonesia, Singapore, and Brunei. The country, made up of parts of former British colonies, was formed in 1963. Although Malaysia is considered a developing country, its economy was one of the fastest growing in the world from 1987 to 1997. The Asian financial crash of 1997 slowed but did not stop this growth. Malaysia exports large amounts of oil, natural gas, and palm oil.

Introducing Southeast Asia and the Pacific Region

Marshall Islands

Capital	Majuro
Land Area	70 sq mi; 181.3 sq km
Population	73,360
Ethnic Group(s)	Micronesian
Religion(s)	Christian
Government	constitutional government in free association with the United States
Currency	U.S. dollar
Leading Exports	copra (dried coconut), coconut oil, handicrafts
Language(s)	English (official), Marshallese (official), Japanese, German

The Marshall Islands (MAHR shul EYE lundz) is a group of 34 islands in the North Pacific Ocean. Once under United States control, the Marshall Islands became independent in 1986. The island nation maintains ties to the United States and heavily depends on it for economic support. The money the United States provides the islands makes up almost two thirds of its total income. The Marshall Islands faces ongoing problems of few natural resources, high unemployment, and poverty.

Myanmar

Capital	Rangoon
Land Area	253,953 sq mi; 657,740 sq km
Population	42.2 million
Ethnic Group(s)	Burman, Shan, Karen, Rakhine, East Asian, South Asian, Mon
Religion(s)	Buddhist, Christian, Muslim, traditional beliefs
Government	military regime
Currency	kyat
Leading Exports	clothing, food, wood products, precious stones
Language(s)	Burmese (Myanmar) (official), Karen, Shan, Chin, Kachin, Mon, Palaung, Wa

Myanmar (MYUN mahr), also known as Burma, is a Southeast Asian nation bordered by Thailand, China, India, the Andaman Sea, and the Bay of Bengal. There are mountains in the north, but the fertile Irrawaddy basin dominates the rest of the country. Myanmar is rich in natural resources, and its economy is mainly agricultural. Once a British colony, Myanmar gained its independence in 1948. Since that time, it has had a history of ethnic conflict and political instability. Today, its government is run by the military.

Nauru

Capital	Yaren District
Land Area	8 sq mi; 21 sq km
Population	12,329
Ethnic Group(s)	Nauruan, Pacific Islanders, East Asian, white
Religion(s)	Protestant, Roman Catholic
Government	republic
Currency	Australian dollar
Leading Exports	phosphate
Language(s)	Nauruan (official), Kiribati, Chinese, Tuvaluan, English

Nauru (nah OO roo) is an island in the South Pacific Ocean. The world's smallest independent republic, Nauru was once a German and then a British colony. It gained its independence in 1968. For decades, the United Kingdom, New Zealand, and Australia mined Nauru for its phosphate. The income from phosphate, Nauru's only export, has made its people very wealthy. However, mining activities caused great environmental damage. With phosphate mining expected to run out, Nauru faces the great challenge of keeping its economy from collapsing.

Sea kayaks in Milford Sound in Fiordland National Park, New Zealand

New Zealand

Capital	Wellington
Land Area	103,737 sq mi; 268,680 sq km
Population	3.8 million
Ethnic Group(s)	white, Maori, Pacific Islander, Asian
Religion(s)	Protestant, Roman Catholic
Government	parliamentary democracy
Currency	New Zealand dollar
Leading Exports	dairy products, meat, wood and wood products, fish, machinery
Language(s)	English (official), Maori (official)

New Zealand (noo ZEE lund) is made up of two large islands and a number of smaller islands in the South Pacific Ocean. It lies about 1,000 miles southeast of Australia. Settled by the Polynesian Maori in about A.D. 800, New Zealand became a British colony during the 1800s and an independent nation in 1907. New Zealand's economy is based on agricultural exports—particularly butter and wool—as well as manufacturing. New Zealand has some of the world's most varied scenery, and tourism is an important industry.

Palau

Capital	Koror
Land Area	177 sq mi; 458 sq km
Population	19,409
Ethnic Group(s)	Palauan, Asian, white
Religion(s)	Christian, traditional beliefs
Government	constitutional government in free association with the United States
Currency	U.S. dollar
Leading Exports	shellfish, tuna, copra, clothing
Language(s)	Palauan (official), English (official), Japanese, Angaur, Tobi, Sonsorolese

Palau (pah LOW) is an archipelago made up of several hundred islands in the North Pacific Ocean southeast of the Philippines. Palau, once governed by the United States and the United Nations, became independent in 1994. It is now a constitutional democracy but maintains close ties to the United States and relies on it for financial aid. Its economy is developing and is primarily agricultural, with a growing tourism industry.

Introducing Southeast Asia and the Pacific Region

Papua New Guinea

Capital	Port Moresby
Land Area	174,849 sq mi; 452,860 sq km
Population	5.2 million
Ethnic Group(s)	Melanesian, Papuan, Negrito, Micronesian, Polynesian
Religion(s)	Protestant, Roman Catholic, traditional beliefs
Government	constitutional monarchy with parliamentary democracy
Currency	kina
Leading Exports	oil, gold, copper ore, logs, palm oil, coffee, cocoa, crayfish, prawns
Language(s)	English (official), Pidgin English, Papuan, Motu, around 750 native languages

Papua New Guinea (pap YOO uh noo GIH nee) is a group of islands—including the eastern half of the island of New Guinea—located between the Coral Sea and the South Pacific Ocean. Papua New Guinea became independent from Australia in 1975. Since then, its political situation has been somewhat unstable due to conflicts between many political parties. Papua New Guinea's people are extraordinarily diverse, with around 750 different languages spoken there. Its economy is mainly agricultural, though it has significant mineral and oil resources as well. A gas pipeline between Papua New Guinea and Australia is expected to bring in almost $220 million per year.

Philippines

Capital	Manila
Land Area	115,123 sq mi; 298,170 sq km
Population	84.5 million
Ethnic Group(s)	Malay, East Asian
Religion(s)	Roman Catholic, Protestant, Muslim, Buddhist
Government	republic
Currency	Philippine peso
Leading Exports	electronic equipment, machinery and transport equipment
Language(s)	English (official), Filipino (official), Tagalog, Cebuano, Hiligaynon, Samaran, Ilocano, Bikol

The Philippines (FIL uh peenz) is an island nation in the western Pacific Ocean, between the Philippine Sea and the South China Sea. It consists of more than 7,000 islands, about 1,000 of which are inhabited. The Philippines became independent from the United States in 1946. Since that time, it has suffered a troubled political history, including dictatorships. The Philippines has more than 100 ethnic groups and is the only Christian nation in Southeast Asia. It has large mineral deposits that have not been fully developed.

Samoa

Capital	Apia
Land Area	1,133 sq mi; 2,934 sq km
Population	178,631
Ethnic Group(s)	Samoan, mixed white and Polynesian, white
Religion(s)	Protestant, Roman Catholic
Government	constitutional monarchy
Currency	tala
Leading Exports	fish, coconut oil and cream, copra
Language(s)	Samoan (official), English (official)

Samoa (suh MOH uh) is a group of nine volcanic islands located in the South Pacific Ocean. Only four of the nine islands are inhabited, and more than 70 percent of the population lives on one island. Samoa became independent from New Zealand in 1962, when it established a democratic government. Samoa is one of the world's least developed countries and is dependent on foreign aid. However, its expanding manufacturing and tourism industries and increasing agricultural exports are helping its economy to grow.

Singapore

Capital	Singapore
Land Area	264 sq mi; 683 sq km
Population	4.5 million
Ethnic Group(s)	East Asian, Malay, South Asian
Religion(s)	Buddhist, Muslim, Christian, Hindu, traditional beliefs
Government	parliamentary republic
Currency	Singapore dollar
Leading Exports	machinery and equipment (including electronics), consumer goods, chemicals, mineral fuels
Language(s)	Malay (official), English (official), Mandarin (official), Tamil (official)

Singapore (SING uh pawr) is a group of islands located in Southeast Asia between Malaysia and Indonesia. Singapore was established as a British trading colony in 1819. It became independent in 1965. Singapore is currently one of the most important trading ports in Asia and one of the world's most prosperous countries. Ethnic Chinese make up about 80 percent of its population.

Solomon Islands

Capital	Honiara
Land Area	10,633 sq mi; 27,540 sq km
Population	494,786
Ethnic Group(s)	Melanesian, Polynesian, Micronesian, white, East Asian
Religion(s)	Protestant, Roman Catholic, traditional beliefs
Government	parliamentary democracy
Currency	Solomon Islands dollar
Leading Exports	timber, fish, copra, palm oil, cocoa
Language(s)	English (official), Pidgin English, Melanesian Pidgin

The Solomon Islands (SAHL uh mun EYE lundz) is a group of islands in the South Pacific Ocean east of Papua New Guinea. The Solomons are an archipelago of several hundred islands spread over 250,000 square miles. Most are coral reefs, and the majority of the population lives on the six largest islands. The Solomon Islands have been settled for thousands of years. In 1978, the island nation achieved independence from the United Kingdom. However, ethnic conflict and a high crime rate have caused instability and weakened the economy in recent years.

Thailand

Capital	Bangkok
Land Area	197,594 sq mi; 511,770 sq km
Population	62.5 million
Ethnic Group(s)	Thai, East Asian
Religion(s)	Buddhist, Muslim, Christian, Hindu
Government	constitutional monarchy
Currency	baht
Leading Exports	computers, transistors, seafood, clothing, rice
Language(s)	Thai (official), Chinese, Malay, Khmer, Karen, Miao

Thailand (TY land) is located in Southeast Asia, between the Andaman Sea and the Gulf of Thailand. It is bordered by Laos, Cambodia, Myanmar, and Malaysia. Thailand's central plain is fertile and densely populated. The country has enjoyed rapid economic growth in recent decades. However, this growth has used up many of its natural resources and strained its water supplies. Thailand, once called Siam, is the only Southeast Asian country that has never been taken over by a European power. It is now a constitutional monarchy.

Introducing Southeast Asia and the Pacific Region

Tonga

Capital	Nuku'alofa
Land Area	277 sq mi; 718 sq km
Population	106,137
Ethnic Group(s)	Polynesian, white
Religion(s)	Christian
Government	hereditary constitutional monarchy
Currency	pa'anga (Tongan dollar)
Leading Exports	squash, fish, vanilla beans, root crops
Language(s)	Tongan (official), English (official)

Tonga (TAHNG guh) is an archipelago of 170 islands located in the South Pacific Ocean northeast of New Zealand. Tonga's economy is based on agriculture and tourism but depends heavily on foreign aid. The country also imports much of its food. Tonga remains the only monarchy in the Pacific region and its king controls the nation's politics, despite calls in recent years for greater democracy.

Tuvalu

Capital	Fongafale
Land Area	10 sq mi; 26 sq km
Population	10,800
Ethnic Group(s)	Polynesian, Micronesian
Religion(s)	Protestant, traditional beliefs
Government	constitutional monarchy with a parliamentary democracy
Currency	Australian dollar and Tuvaluan dollar
Leading Exports	copra, fish
Language(s)	English (official), Tuvaluan, Kiribati

Tuvalu (too vuh LOO) is a tiny island group located in the South Pacific Ocean. It lies about halfway between Hawaii and Australia, or about 650 miles north of Fiji. Tuvalu has a total land area of about 10 square miles (26 square kilometers). Tuvalu was part of a British colony until its independence in 1978. Tuvalu's economy is based mainly on subsistence farming and fishing. However, the tiny nation also gets about $50 million per year from leasing out its Internet domain name ".tv."

Vanuatu

Capital	Port-Vila
Land Area	4,710 sq mi; 12,200 sq km
Population	196,178
Ethnic Group(s)	Melanesian, white, Southeast Asian, East Asian, Pacific Islander
Religion(s)	Protestant, Roman Catholic, traditional beliefs
Government	parliamentary republic
Currency	vatu
Leading Exports	copra, kava, beef, cocoa, timber, coffee
Language(s)	Bislama (official), English (official), French (official)

Vanuatu (van wah TOO) is a small island nation located in the South Pacific Ocean. It lies about three quarters of the way from Hawaii to Australia, or about 500 miles west of Fiji. Vanuatu is an archipelago of 80 volcanic islands spread over about 450 miles. However, only about 12 of the islands are of any size. Vanuatu was once called the New Hebrides. The islands were settled in the 1800s and ruled jointly by Great Britain and France from 1906. In 1980, Vanuatu became an independent republic. The economy is based primarily on agriculture and fishing.

Vietnam

Capital	Hanoi
Land Area	125,621 sq mi; 325,360 sq km
Population	81.1 million
Ethnic Group(s)	Vietnamese, East Asian, Hmong, Thai, Khmer, Cham
Religion(s)	Buddhist, Christian, traditional beliefs, Muslim
Government	communist state
Currency	dông
Leading Exports	crude oil, marine products, rice, coffee, rubber, tea, clothing, shoes
Language(s)	Vietnamese (official), Chinese, Thai, Khmer, Muong, Nung, Miao, Yao, Jarai

SOURCES: DK World Desk Reference Online; CIA World Factbook Online; *World Almanac*, 2003

Vietnam (vee et NAHM) is located along the eastern coast of the Indochinese peninsula in the South China Sea. France occupied Vietnam during the late 1800s. France continued to rule until 1954, when Communist forces under leader Ho Chi Minh defeated the French and took over the northern part of the country. The United States then helped South Vietnam resist Communist rule by fighting the North Vietnamese in the Vietnam War. The United States withdrew its military forces in 1973, and all of Vietnam was united under Communist rule. Still recovering from years of war, the government has allowed some private enterprise to strengthen its weak economy.

A woman weaves in a village in Vietnam. Most people in Vietnam live in rural areas.

Assessment

Comprehension and Critical Thinking

1. Name Name two Southeast Asian countries that are island nations.

2. Draw Conclusions What are the characteristics that most of the countries share?

3. Contrast What are some key differences among the countries?

4. Categorize Which countries in the region have monarchies?

5. Contrast How are the governments of Laos and Vietnam different from those of the other countries in the region?

6. Make a Bar Graph Create a bar graph showing the land area of the five most populous countries in this region.

Keeping Current

Access the **DK World Desk Reference Online** at **PHSchool.com** for up-to-date information about all the countries in this chapter.

Go Online
PHSchool.com

Web Code: nge-6900

Prepare to Read

Objectives

In this section you will
1. Find out how Vietnam was divided by conflicts and war.
2. Learn how Vietnam has rebuilt its economy.

Taking Notes

As you read this section, look for details about how Vietnam has developed since the Vietnam War. Copy the diagram below and record your findings in it.

Target Reading Skill

Identify Main Idea The main idea of a paragraph tells what the whole paragraph is about. On page 450, the main idea of the paragraph with the heading Rebirth in Ho Chi Minh City is "Vietnam's greatest successes have been in rebuilding its cities." As you read this section, identify the main idea of each paragraph that follows a blue heading.

Key Terms

- **civil war** (SIV ul wawr) *n.* a war between political parties or regions within the same country
- **domino theory** (DAHM uh noh THEE uh ree) *n.* a belief that if one country fell to communism, neighboring nations would also fall, like a row of dominoes

New industries in Vietnam

It is summer in Vietnam, more than 25 years after the end of the Vietnam War. In countryside villages, people seed, harvest, and plow rice fields just as their parents and grandparents did. Unlike their parents and grandparents, however, many of these villagers are making money. In the cities, people are working in such growing industries as manufacturing and telecommunications. Private ownership of companies in Vietnam has been growing since the mid-1990s. Like China, communist Vietnam is taking steps toward an economy that allows some free enterprise.

Decades of Conflict and War

The people of Vietnam have survived a long period of conflict. First, an alliance of Communists and Nationalists in Vietnam fought against France from 1946 to 1954. Second, a civil war followed. A **civil war** is a war between political parties or regions within the same country. During the Vietnam War, North Vietnam fought South Vietnam and its ally, the United States.

Vietnam Divided After the French defeat in 1954, a treaty divided Vietnam into northern and southern parts. Communists controlled the northern half. A non-communist government supported by the United States ruled South Vietnam. The treaty said that, eventually, an election would be held to reunite the country under one government.

These elections were never held, largely because the United States and Ngo Dinh Diem (en GOH din dee EM), the leader of South Vietnam, feared that the Communists might win. At that time, U.S. leaders believed in the **domino theory**. They thought that a Communist victory would cause other countries in Southeast Asia to fall to communism, like a row of dominoes.

Meanwhile, the Communists were trying to take over the south by force. In 1959, they launched a war to achieve this goal. They were led by Communist leader Ho Chi Minh (hoh chee min). Ho Chi Minh's forces were called the Viet Cong.

Presidential Palace in Hanoi
The Presidential Palace is used as offices for Vietnam's government. The palace was built by the French and used as headquarters for the French government until 1954. Note the flag of Vietnam is displayed.
Analyze Images *How are change and continuity shown in this photo?*

U.S. troops taking part in a mission in South Vietnam in 1967

American Involvement in the Vietnam War Communist leader Ho Chi Minh wanted to unite Vietnam under northern rule. Operating from the north, he aided Communist forces in the south. As the Communists threatened South Vietnam, the United States took an active role. At first, the United States sent thousands of military advisors to help the South Vietnamese. Later, hundreds of thousands of American troops arrived. Through the 1960s, the United States sent more troops to Vietnam. By 1968, there were more than 500,000 U.S. troops in Vietnam.

By the early 1970s, Vietnam had been at war for more than 30 years. The fighting spread to neighboring Laos and Cambodia as well. North Vietnam sent supplies along the Ho Chi Minh Trail through Laos and Cambodia to its troops in South Vietnam. In 1970, the United States bombed the Ho Chi Minh Trail and then invaded Cambodia. In 1971, South Vietnamese troops attacked North Vietnamese bases in Laos.

As the fighting continued, American casualties increased. Millions of people in the United States were calling for an end to the war. In 1973, the United States finally ended its part in the war when the last American combat soldiers left South Vietnam. More than 3 million Americans had served in the Vietnam War. More than 58,000 American troops died in the war, and another 150,000 were seriously wounded.

√ Reading Check **Why did North Vietnam launch a war against South Vietnam?**

Links to Art

Water Puppets In Vietnam, a type of puppet theater uses a pond for a stage. Water puppet shows started centuries ago. In these shows, a puppeteer guides wooden figures so that they appear to wade through the water. The puppets are attached to rods and strings hidden underwater. Audiences sit at the water's edge. Stage settings of trees and clouds are also placed on the pond.

Vietnam

Most people in Vietnam are ethnic Vietnamese, but Vietnam has more than 90 ethnic minorities. Ethnic Vietnamese live mainly in the lowlands of the north, the south, and a thin coastal strip. Fertile soils in the lowlands support a dense population, as you can see on the map. The largest minority, the ethnic Chinese, live mainly in lowland cities. Other minorities inhabit the rugged highlands, where farming is difficult and population densities are low.

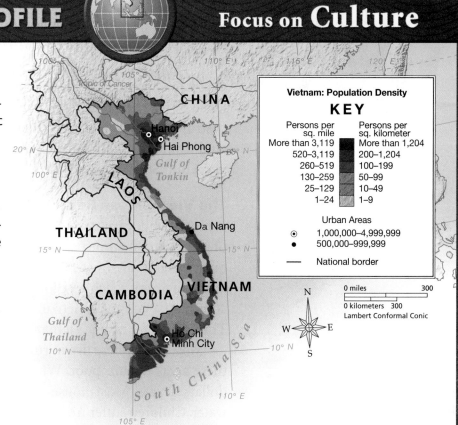

Vietnam: Population Density

KEY

Persons per sq. mile	Persons per sq. kilometer
More than 3,119	More than 1,204
520–3,119	200–1,204
260–519	100–199
130–259	50–99
25–129	10–49
1–24	1–9

Urban Areas
- ⊙ 1,000,000–4,999,999
- • 500,000–999,999
- — National border

0 miles 300
0 kilometers 300
Lambert Conformal Conic

Ethnic Groups

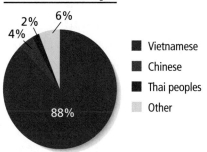

- 88%
- 6%
- 2%
- 4%

- ■ Vietnamese
- ■ Chinese
- ■ Thai peoples
- ■ Other

SOURCE: DK World Desk Reference

Peoples of Vietnam

Ethnic Group	Where They Live
Vietnamese	Coastal strip, lowlands, major cities
Chinese	Major cities, northern lowlands
Tai peoples	Northern highlands
Hmong peoples	Northern highlands
Other minorities	Northern and central highlands, border regions

SOURCE: Ethnologue

Map and Chart Skills

1. **Identify** What percentage of Vietnam's people are ethnically Vietnamese or Chinese?

2. **Describe** These groups live in the fertile lowlands, with more than 259 persons per square mile. Do these lowlands cover more than 50 percent of Vietnam's area?

3. **Analyze** How can you explain the difference between these percentages?

Use Web Code **nge-6901** for **DK World Desk Reference Online.**

After the Vietnam War

After the United States pulled out its troops, North Vietnam conquered South Vietnam in 1975. In 1976, the country was reunited under a communist government. Vietnam had been devastated by the war. More than a million Vietnamese had been killed or wounded. Homes, farms, factories, and forests had been destroyed. Bombs had torn cities apart. Fields were covered with land mines, or hidden explosives. The Vietnamese people were worn out. Still ahead was the huge effort of rebuilding.

The Vietnamese Rebuild In the years after the war, the communist government in Vietnam strictly controlled the lives of its citizens. As time passed, however, it was clear that the economy was not growing. Like the Chinese, the Vietnamese had to adapt their approach to economic growth. Although it is still a communist country, Vietnam now allows some free enterprise. This has helped many Vietnamese improve their lives.

Most Vietnamese live in rural areas. In spite of some progress, these areas remain poor. Whole families live on a few hundred dollars a year. Most houses have no indoor toilets or running water. Children suffer from a lack of healthy food. Vietnam is still among the poorest nations in Asia.

Contruction projects reflect the spirit of change in Vietnam. Here, workers lay a foundation for a new building in Ho Chi Minh City.

Rebirth in Ho Chi Minh City

Vietnam's greatest success has been in rebuilding its cities. Hanoi in the north is the capital. The city of Saigon (sy GAHN), in the south, was renamed Ho Chi Minh City after the Communist leader. It is the most prosperous city in Vietnam and is the center of trade. Americans who visit Ho Chi Minh City today find some of the same things they would find at home, such as American-style ice cream and cable news networks on television.

Some Vietnamese who live in the city enjoy greater prosperity. They buy designer clothing and watches, stereo systems, video recorders, and jewelry. Many of these people run restaurants or hotels, buy and sell land or buildings, or own factories, all of which help stimulate Vietnam's economy.

A girl from the Hmong ethnic group (left) and a city shopper (inset) show rural and urban life in Vietnam.

Economic Recovery In 1986, Vietnam's government began an economic recovery program aimed chiefly at attracting foreign investors. As a result, Vietnam became one of the fastest-growing economies in the world. From 1990 to 1997, the economy grew each year by an average of about 8 percent. Agricultural output doubled, turning Vietnam from a country once dependent on food imports to the world's second-largest exporter of rice. Government-led reforms have helped modernize the economy and promote economic growth in the 2000s. After committing to trade agreements with other countries, including the United States, Vietnam's exports have greatly increased.

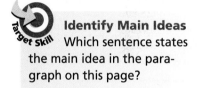 **Identify Main Ideas** Which sentence states the main idea in the paragraph on this page?

✓ **Reading Check** Which city in Vietnam is the most prosperous and the nation's center of trade?

Section 1 Assessment

Key Terms

Review the key terms at the beginning of this section. Use each term in a sentence that explains its meaning.

Target Reading Skill

Write the main idea of each paragraph that follows a blue heading in this section.

Comprehension and Critical Thinking

1. (a) Recall When did the United States withdraw from the Vietnam War?

(b) Summarize What conflicts have divided Vietnam since the end of World War II?

2. (a) Describe Describe conditions in Vietnam when the Vietnam War ended.

(b) Make Generalizations What successes has Vietnam had in rebuilding its economy?

(c) Identify Point of View Why do you think Saigon was renamed Ho Chi Minh City after the Vietnam War?

Writing Activity

Write a summary that describes Vietnam since the Vietnam War. Use this title for your summary: Vietnam: A Country, Not a War. Focus on the country's economic development.

Writing Tip Be sure to look closely at the pictures and the Country Profile in this section to help you as you write your description.

Using a Flowchart

Rice is one of the most important crops in Vietnam. It is grown on almost 75 percent of all cultivated land. Most Vietnamese farmers live in the lowland and delta area. This area's wetlands and heavy rains make it perfect for growing rice.

Most Southeast Asian farmers grow rice the same way that their ancestors did thousands of years ago. They build shallow fields called paddies. They flood the paddies with water. They plant rice in seedling beds. Farmers transplant the rice seedlings in the paddies by hand. They also harvest the rice by hand.

You've just read a description of how rice is grown. But sometimes it is easier to figure out how something works by following the steps in a flowchart.

Traditional Rice Farming

> Farmers build a rice paddy.

> The paddy is flooded with water.

> Farmers use water buffalo to plow and smooth out the paddy.

> Farmers prepare seedling beds alongside the paddy and plant rice seed in seedling beds.

> After seedlings are 4 to 6 inches tall, farmers transplant them into the paddy.

> Farmers weed, fertilize, and add water regularly to the paddy.

> When the rice turns from green to gold, it is harvested.

 SS.3.02 Interpret graphs and charts

A flowchart shows the sequence of steps used to complete an activity. It shows the steps in the order they happen. Sometimes the steps are illustrated. A flowchart usually uses arrows to show how steps follow one another.

Learn the Skill

Here are the steps you will need to follow when you read a flowchart.

1. **Read the title.** Read the title first to find out what the flowchart is about. The title of the flowchart at the left is Traditional Rice Farming.

2. **Find the arrows.** The arrows will tell you the order in which you should read the chart. Find the beginning and start there.

3. **Read the flowchart carefully.** If there are illustrations, study them, but be sure to read the text next to them. Think about how one step leads to the next step. What are the connections? If there are no illustrations, try imagining each step to help you understand the sequence.

Practice the Skill

Use the steps and the flowchart on the previous page to practice reading a flowchart.

1 Read the title of the flowchart first. Explain what the flowchart will tell you.

2 Find the beginning of the chart. Identify the first step of the chart. Start there and follow the arrows through each step.

3 Now read the flowchart carefully. Your reading of the flowchart should help you understand the steps in traditional rice farming. Now answer these questions: What is the first step in traditional rice farming? What happens after the paddy is flooded with water? Where do the farmers prepare seedling beds? How tall are the rice seedlings when the farmers transplant them into the paddy? How do the farmers know when it is time to harvest the rice?

Traditional Rice Processing

Thresh, or beat, the rice plants to separate the rice husks from the plant.

Dry the rice husks.

Thresh the rice husks to remove the rice grains from the husks.

Thresh the rice again to separate the husks from rice grains.

Store the rice in a dry place.

Apply the Skill

Use the steps in this skill to read the flowchart above. What is the chart about? How are the rice husks separated from the plant? Why is the rice threshed three times?

Section 2

Australia
A Pacific Rim Country

Prepare to Read

Objectives
In this section you will
1. Learn about the major economic activities in Australia.
2. Find out how Aboriginal people in Australia are working to improve their lives.

Taking Notes
Copy the diagram. As you read, record details about Australia's economy.

Trade / Australia

Target Reading Skill
Identify Supporting Details On page 456, look at the paragraph with the heading Ranching. The first sentence is the main idea. The rest of the sentences support the main idea. What details in this paragraph explain the part ranching plays in Australia's economy?

Key Terms
- **outback** (OWT bak) *n.* the dry land consisting of plains and plateaus that makes up much of central and western Australia
- **artesian well** (ahr TEE zhun wel) *n.* a well from which water flows under natural pressure without pumping

Michael Chang owns a successful trading company in Sydney, Australia's largest city. From his office in a modern glass skyscraper, he sometimes watches Sydney's busy harbor. What interests him most are the large cargo ships.

John Koeyers and his family own a huge cattle ranch in northwest Australia. He uses helicopters and trucks to round up the herds on his ranch. The Koeyers sell most of their cattle to companies in Asian nations.

Charlie Walkabout is director of Anangu Tours. Anangu Tours is owned and run by Aboriginal people. The company has won awards for its tours of Uluru, also known as Ayers Rock.

Sydney, Australia, has a beautiful and busy harbor.

Economic Activities

Michael Chang, the Koeyers, and Charlie Walkabout are all Australians. The meaning of *Australian* has changed since Australia achieved independence. It is no longer "British." It now reflects the diversity of Australia's people. Today, Australia has close ties with other nations of the Pacific Rim. These nations border the Pacific Ocean. They include Japan, South Korea, China, and Taiwan. The United States is another major Pacific Rim nation. It is one of Australia's key trading partners. Australia's economy depends on trade with Pacific Rim countries.

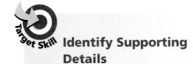
Identify Supporting Details
What details in this paragraph explain the meaning of the "Pacific Rim"?

Trade Michael Chang's trading company is just one of hundreds of companies that do business with Pacific Rim countries. He sends various products to many countries in Asia. Rancher John Koeyers is involved in trade, too. Large cargo ships transport his cattle to South Korea and Taiwan. Other cargo ships carry products such as Australian wool and meat to foreign markets. Cargo ships also carry Australia's minerals to Japan.

Farming It seems strange that farm products are an important export for Australia, because only about 7 percent of Australia's land is good for farming. Most of this land is in southeastern Australia and along the east coast. The country's few rivers are in those areas. Farmers use the river water to irrigate their crops. Australian farmers raise barley, oats, and sugar cane. However, their most valuable crop is wheat. Australia is one of the world's leading wheat growers and exporters.

Ranching Ranching is another major part of Australia's economy. Australian sheep and cattle provide lamb, mutton, and beef for export. Australia is the world's leading wool producer. Most cattle and sheep are raised on large ranches called stations. Some of the largest stations are in the outback. The **outback** is the name Australians use for the dry land that makes up much of the central and western part of the country. Few people live on its plains and plateaus.

COUNTRY PROFILE

Focus on Geography

Australia

Australia is a large but thinly populated country. It covers about the same area as the United States, not including Alaska and Hawaii. But it has only about 20 million people, a smaller population than Texas. As the graph shows, most of its people live in urban areas. Australia's largest urban areas lie along its southeast coast. On the map, they are the areas labeled "manufacturing and trade." They cover only a very small part of the country. Much of the country consists of huge ranches and farms—labeled "livestock raising" and "commercial farming" on the map—and large deserts—labeled "limited economic activity." There are also forests in the southeast and aboriginal land, used for hunting and gathering, mainly in the north.

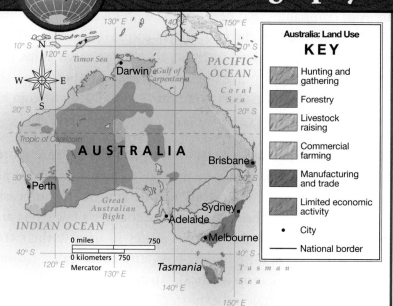

Australia: Land Use
KEY

- Hunting and gathering
- Forestry
- Livestock raising
- Commercial farming
- Manufacturing and trade
- Limited economic activity
- • City
- — National border

Urban and Rural Population

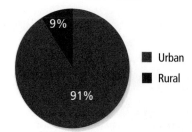

9%

91%

- ■ Urban
- ■ Rural

SOURCE: DK World Desk Reference

Map and Chart Skills

1. **Recall** Where do most Australians live?
2. **Infer** About how many people live in Australia's rural areas?
3. **Compare** How does Australia's population density compare with that of the United States?

Use Web Code **nge-6902** for **DK World Desk Reference Online.**

For example, the Koeyers' ranch is in a hot, dry area in northwest Australia. It covers 1 million acres (404,686 hectares) and has about 7,000 head of cattle. Another outback station, near Alice Springs in the center of Australia, is even larger. It covers nearly 12,000 square miles (31,080 square kilometers)—larger than the state of Maryland. Even with this much land, sometimes the cattle can barely find enough grass for grazing. Fresh water also is scarce. Rain falls rarely, and the region has only a few small streams. To supply water for their cattle, ranchers use underground **artesian wells**. These are wells from which water flows under natural pressure without pumping.

✓ Reading Check **How does ranching help Australia's economy?**

British Heritage in Australia
The majority of Australians have a British ancestry. Australia's British heritage is shown in Australia's national flag, which includes the flag of the United Kingdom. Australia's flag also includes the Southern Cross, a constellation visible in the Southern Hemisphere. **Conclude** *Why is the Southern Cross an appropriate symbol for Australia?*

Aborigines: Improving Lives

The people of Anangu Tours are proud of the awards they have won for their tours of Uluru. Aboriginal guides conduct the tours in their own language and an interpreter translates the words into English. Aboriginal people in Australia are working hard to preserve their culture. They are having a growing role in the economic life of the country.

Aboriginal leaders have worked to improve the lives of their people. Their schools now teach Aboriginal languages. Aborigines again celebrate important events with ancestral songs and dances. Artists have strengthened Aboriginal culture by creating traditional rock paintings and tree bark paintings.

Learn about the different regions of Australia.

Aboriginal leaders have helped their people in another important way, too. They have influenced the government of Australia. The government has begun to return Aboriginal land to them. The government has also built schools and hospitals on their land. It has begun to protect some of their sacred places as well.

Aborigines have gained more rights. But their main goal is to regain their ancestral lands. Though Australia's courts have helped, many ranchers and farmers now live on those lands. These people strongly oppose giving the land back. This issue may take many years to resolve.

✓ **Reading Check** **What is a main goal for Aboriginal people in Australia?**

Australian Aboriginal cave paintings date back thousands of years and are among the world's earliest art.

Section 2 Assessment

Key Terms
Review the key terms at the beginning of this section. Use each term in a sentence that explains its meaning.

 Target Reading Skill
Find the text on ranching on page 456. What details support the information about ranching in Australia?

Comprehension and Critical Thinking
1. (a) **Explain** What is the Pacific Rim?

(b) **Apply Information** Based on what you know about Australia's location, explain why Australia's economy depends on trade with Pacific Rim countries.
2. (a) **Recall** Give two examples showing how Aboriginal people are working to improve their lives.
(b) **Compare** As the United States grew, Native Americans were forced from their homelands and moved to reservations. For years, Native Americans have been fighting to regain their original homelands. How does this compare with the history and struggle of the Aborigines?

Writing Activity
Use the information in this section and in the Country Profile on page 436 to write an article about Australia for a news magazine. The article should describe the main types of work people do in Australia.

For: An activity about Australia
Visit: PHSchool.com
Web Code: ngd-6902

16 Review and Assessment

◆ Chapter Summary

Section 1: Vietnam

- After decades of conflict and war, Vietnam is now a communist country that allows some free enterprise.
- In recent years, Vietnam has made great strides toward modernizing and strengthening its economy.
- Vietnam has become a leading exporter of rice.

Section 2: Australia

- Australia is a Pacific Rim country with an economy based on trade.
- Farming and ranching are key parts of Australia's economy.
- Aboriginal people in Australia are working to preserve their culture and have a role in the economic life of the country.

Vietnamese water puppets

Sydney, Australia

◆ Key Terms

Match the definitions in Column I with the key terms in Column II.

Column I

1. a well from which water flows under natural pressure without pumping
2. a war between political parties or regions within the same country
3. a belief that if one country fell to communism, neighboring nations would also fall, like a row of dominoes
4. the dry land that makes up much of central and western Australia

Column II

A civil war

B outback

C artesian well

D domino theory

◆ Comprehension and Critical Thinking

5. **(a) Recall** Who was Vietnam in conflict with from 1946 to 1954?
(b) Explain What were the Viet Cong?
(c) Summarize Describe the involvement of the United States in the Vietnam War.

6. **(a) Recall** Why did the United States end its involvement in the Vietnam War?
(b) Identify Effects What was one result of the Vietnam War?

7. **(a) Note** Where do most people in Vietnam live?
(b) Contrast How are rural areas in Vietnam different from Ho Chi Minh City?

8. **(a) Name** What is the capital of Vietnam?
(b) Locate In what part of Vietnam is Hanoi located?
(c) Apply Information Why was Saigon renamed Ho Chi Minh City?

9. **(a) Recall** On what kinds of products does Australia depend for a prosperous foreign trade?
(b) Infer Why do few people make their home in Australia's outback?

10. **(a) Note** What are important goals for Australia's Aboriginal people?
(b) Conclude How is Anangu Tours helping to preserve Aboriginal culture?

◆ Skills Practice

Using a Flowchart In the Skills for Life activity in this chapter, you learned how to read a flowchart. Review the steps you learned to use this skill. Then use the flowchart on page 452 to tell what happens after farmers transplant rice seedlings into the rice paddy.

◆ Writing Activity: Language Arts

Storytelling is an important part of Aboriginal culture. Do library research to find and read an Aboriginal folk tale from Australia. Write a report that summarizes the folk tale.

MAP MASTER™
Skills Activity

Southeast Asia and the Pacific Region

Place Location For each place listed below, write the letter from the map that shows its location.

1. Pacific Ocean
2. Australia
3. Vietnam
4. Philippines
5. Sydney
6. New Zealand

Go Online
PHSchool.com Use Web Code **ngp-6920** for an **interactive map.**

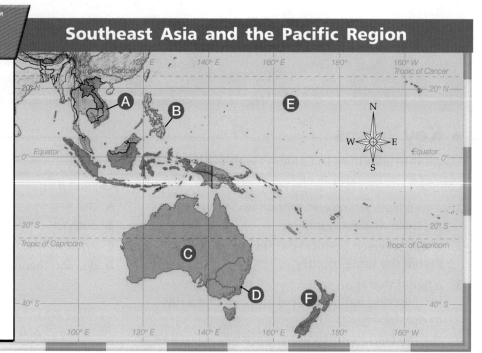

NC SS.4.02
Examine, understand, and
evaluate conflicting viewpoints

Standardized Test Prep

Test-Taking Tips

Some questions on standardized tests ask you to analyze point of view. Read the passage below. Then, follow the tips to answer the sample question.

> In 1973, the United States ended its part in the Vietnam War. American military advisers and troops were sent home. As American helicopters flew off from the capital, someone watching them said, "I had better hurry to the American embassy. Maybe one of my American friends there can help me escape from Vietnam and go to America."

Pick the letter that best answers the question.

Which onlooker might have made that statement?

A a North Vietnamese soldier who had been fighting for years

B an American soldier who got separated from his company

C a South Vietnamese woman who had worked for the Americans

D a protestor who had been supporting North Vietnam during the war

TIP Be sure you understand the question. Who said the words that begin, "I had better hurry to the American embassy . . ."?

Think It Through You can eliminate A and D because neither person would have friends at the American embassy. You can eliminate B because an American soldier would not have a reason to escape from Vietnam. The correct answer is C.

Practice Questions

Use the tips above and other tips in this book to help you answer the following questions.

1. What did the United States fear would happen if it did NOT help South Vietnam fight against North Vietnam?

   A The French would take control.

   B North Vietnam would invade China.

   C Communists would take over South Vietnam.

   D The United States would lose control of North Vietnam.

2. The Vietnam War finally ended in 1975 when

   A North Vietnam surrendered.

   B U.S. forces invaded Cambodia.

   C North Vietnam gained control over all of South Vietnam.

   D the United States signed a peace treaty with North Vietnam.

3. Some of Australia's trading partners in the Pacific Rim include the United States, China, Taiwan, and

   A India.

   B Italy.

   C Egypt.

   D Japan.

Use Web Code **nga-6900** for **Chapter 16 self-test.**

Projects

Create your own projects to learn more about Asia, Australia, and the Pacific Islands. At the beginning of this book, you were introduced to the **Guiding Questions** for studying the chapters and special features. But you can also find answers to these questions by doing projects on your own or with a group. Use the questions to find topics you want to explore further. Then try the projects described on this page or create your own.

1 **Geography** What are the main physical features of Asia, Australia, and the Pacific Islands?

2 **History** How have ancient civilizations of Asia, Australia, and the Pacific Islands influenced the world today?

3 **Culture** What are the main characteristics of the cultures of Asia, Australia, and the Islands?

4 **Government** What types of government exist in Asia, Australia, and the Pacific Islands?

5 **Economics** How do the people of this region make a living?

Project
RESEARCH EXPORTS AND TRADE

Asia and Australia Trade Fair

With your class, plan a trade fair for the countries of Asia, Australia, and the Pacific Islands. As you read this book, choose a country to research. Find out about its major products, factories, and trading partners. Set up a booth to show and tell visitors about trade in your country. Bring books about the country and make posters, pamphlets, and charts for your booth.

Project
CREATE A MAP AND POSTER DISPLAY

Agriculture in Asia, Australia, and the Pacific Islands

Draw a large map of Asia, Australia, and the Pacific Islands and hang it in your classroom. As you read about different kinds of farm products, mark them on the appropriate location on your map. Choose ten farm products and design a small poster for each one. On each poster, write the farm product and a country in Asia and Australia where this product comes from. Find or draw a picture for each poster.

Table of Contents

Atlas

SVALBARD
(Norway)

EUROPE AND SOUTHWEST ASIA
For detail, see maps Europe: Political
and Asia: Political.

RUSSIA

Moscow

ASIA

EUROPE

Astana
KAZAKHSTAN
UZBEKISTAN
Tashkent
Bishkek
Ulaanbaatar
MONGOLIA
Beijing
NORTH
KOREA
P'yŏngyang
JAPAN

Algiers Tunis
TUNISIA
Tripoli
Cairo
TURKMENISTAN
Ashgabat
Tehran
IRAN
Kabul
Islamabad
KYRGYZSTAN
Dushanbe
TAJIKISTAN
CHINA
Seoul
SOUTH
KOREA
Tokyo

DEIRA
tugal)
ARY
NDS
ain)
MOROCCO
Rabat
ALGERIA
LIBYA
EGYPT
Kuwait
KUWAIT
Manama BAHRAIN
Riyadh QATAR
Doha U.A.E.
Abu Dhabi Muscat
PAKISTAN
New Delhi
NEPAL
Kathmandu
Thimphu
BHUTAN
BANGLADESH
Taipei
TAIWAN
PACIFIC
OCEAN
Tropic of Cancer

STERN
HARA
rocco)
WEST AFRICA
r detail, see map
frica: Political.
NIGER
CHAD
Khartoum
SUDAN
ERITREA
Asmara
SAUDI
ARABIA
YEMEN
Sanaa
DJIBOUTI
Djibouti
SOCOTRA
(Yemen)
OMAN
INDIA
Dhaka
MYANMAR
Yangon
Hanoi
LAOS
Vientiane
THAILAND VIETNAM
Bangkok CAMBODIA
Phnom Penh
PHILIPPINES
Manila
NORTHERN
MARIANA
ISLANDS
(U.S.)

AFRICA
N'Djamena
NIGERIA
Abuja
CAMEROON
Yaoundé
CENTRAL
AFRICAN
REPUBLIC
Bangui
UGANDA
ETHIOPIA
Addis Ababa
SOMALIA
Colombo
SRI LANKA
Male
MALDIVES
Kuala Lumpur
BRUNEI
Bandar Seri Begawan
MALAYSIA
Singapore SINGAPORE
PALAU
Koror
GUAM
(U.S.)
Palikir
FEDERATED STATES
OF MICRONESIA
Equator

EQUATORIAL GUINEA
Malabo
São Tomé
O TOMÉ & PRÍNCIPE
GABON
Libreville
CONGO
Brazzaville
DEMOCRATIC
REPUBLIC
OF THE
CONGO
Kinshasa
Kampala
KENYA
Kigali
RWANDA
Nairobi
BURUNDI
Bujumbura
Mogadishu
Dodoma
Dar es Salaam
Victoria
SEYCHELLES
Jakarta
INDONESIA
Dili
EAST TIMOR
PAPUA
NEW
GUINEA
Port Moresby

CABINDA
(Angola)
Luanda
ANGOLA
Lilongwe
TANZANIA
MALAWI
COMOROS
Moroni
AUSTRALIA

Windhoek
NAMIBIA
Lusaka
ZAMBIA
Harare
ZIMBABWE
MOZAMBIQUE
MADAGASCAR
Antananarivo
MAURITIUS
Port Louis
RÉUNION
(France)
INDIAN
OCEAN
AUSTRALIA
Tropic of Capricorn

ATLANTIC
OCEAN
Windhoek
Gaborone
BOTSWANA
Pretoria
Mbabane
SWAZILAND
Maputo
Bloemfontein
Maseru
SOUTH
AFRICA
LESOTHO
Cape Town

SOUTHERN   OCEAN

Canberra

Antarctic Circle

ANTARCTICA

KEY

——	National border
- - -	Disputed border
⊛	National capital

The World: Physical

0 miles 2,000
0 kilometers 2,000
Robinson

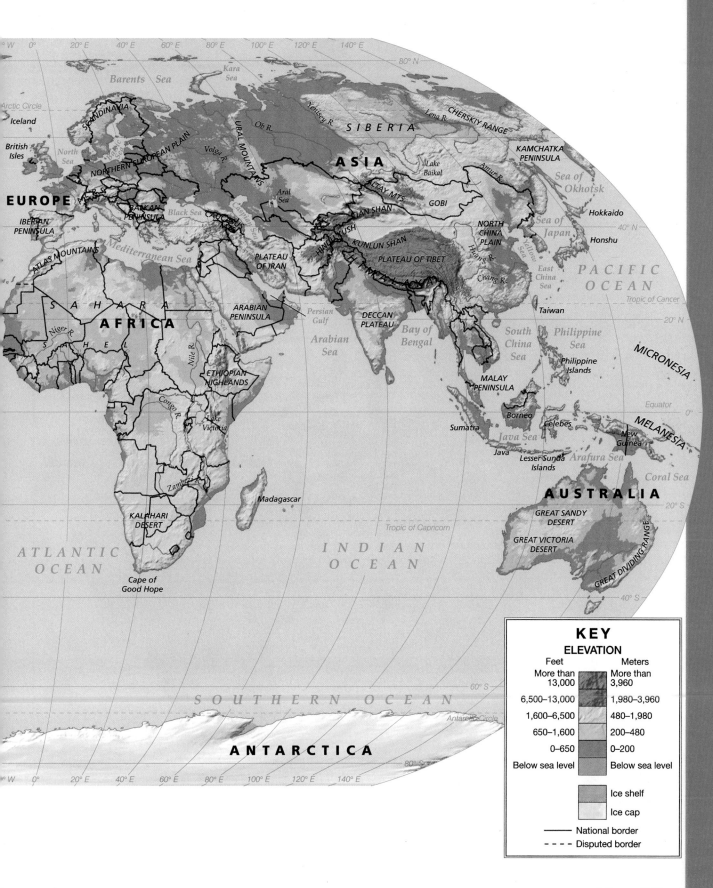

Barents Sea
Kara Sea
Arctic Circle
Iceland
British Isles
North Sea
SCANDINAVIA
NORTHERN EUROPEAN PLAIN
URAL MOUNTAINS
Ob R.
Yenisey R.
SIBERIA
Lena R.
CHERSKIY RANGE
KAMCHATKA PENINSULA
ASIA
Sea of Okhotsk
Volga R.
Aral Sea
ALTAY MTS.
Amur R.
EUROPE
ALPS
Black Sea
CAUCASUS MTS.
Caspian Sea
TIAN SHAN
GOBI
NORTH CHINA PLAIN
Lake Baikal
Sea of Japan
Hokkaido
Honshu
40° N
IBERIAN PENINSULA
BALKAN PENINSULA
HINDU KUSH
KUNLUN SHAN
PLATEAU OF TIBET
Huang R.
Yellow Sea
East China Sea
PACIFIC OCEAN
ATLAS MOUNTAINS
Mediterranean Sea
PLATEAU OF IRAN
HIMALAYA
Chang R.
Taiwan
Tropic of Cancer
SAHARA
ARABIAN PENINSULA
Persian Gulf
DECCAN PLATEAU
Bay of Bengal
South China Sea
Philippine Sea
20° N
AFRICA
Red Sea
Arabian Sea
Philippine Islands
MICRONESIA
SAHEL
Niger R.
Nile R.
ETHIOPIAN HIGHLANDS
MALAY PENINSULA
Equator
Congo R.
Lake Victoria
Sumatra
Borneo
Celebes
New Guinea
MELANESIA
Java Sea
Java
Lesser Sunda Islands
Arafura Sea
Coral Sea
Zambezi R.
Madagascar
AUSTRALIA
KALAHARI DESERT
GREAT SANDY DESERT
20° S
ATLANTIC OCEAN
INDIAN OCEAN
Tropic of Capricorn
GREAT VICTORIA DESERT
GREAT DIVIDING RANGE
Cape of Good Hope
40° S
SOUTHERN OCEAN
Antarctic Circle
ANTARCTICA
80° S

KEY

ELEVATION

Feet		Meters
More than 13,000		More than 3,960
6,500–13,000		1,980–3,960
1,600–6,500		480–1,980
650–1,600		200–480
0–650		0–200
Below sea level		Below sea level

Ice shelf

Ice cap

——— National border

- - - - Disputed border

North and South America: Political

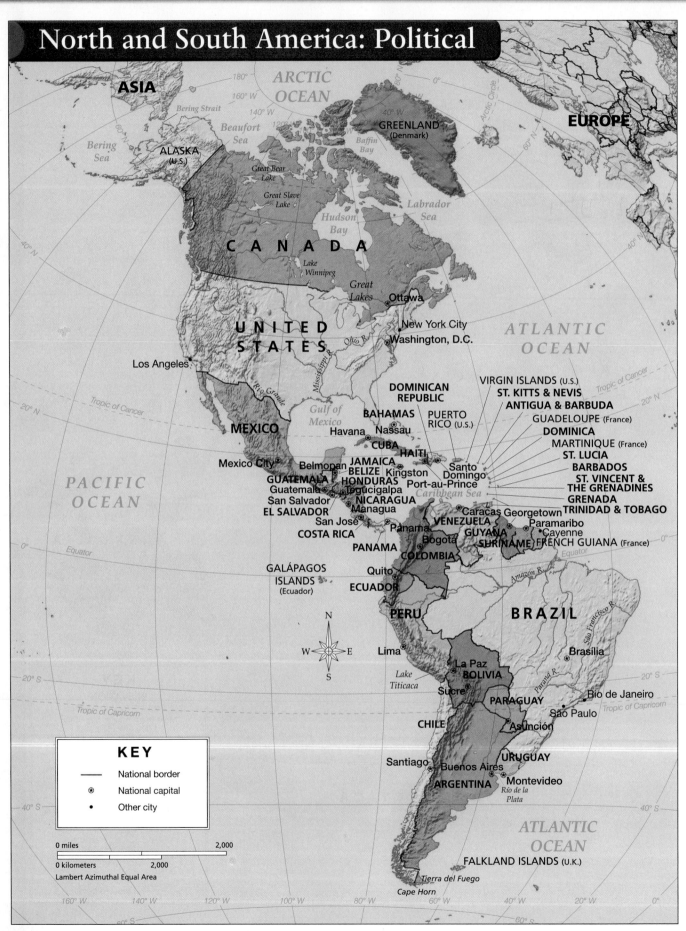

ASIA

ARCTIC OCEAN

EUROPE

Bering Strait

Bering Sea

Beaufort Sea

GREENLAND (Denmark)

ALASKA (U.S.)

Baffin Bay

Great Bear Lake

Great Slave Lake

Labrador Sea

Hudson Bay

C A N A D A

Lake Winnipeg

Great Lakes

Ottawa

New York City

Washington, D.C.

U N I T E D S T A T E S

Ohio R.

ATLANTIC OCEAN

Los Angeles

Mississippi R.

Rio Grande

Tropic of Cancer

Gulf of Mexico

MEXICO

VIRGIN ISLANDS (U.S.)
ST. KITTS & NEVIS
ANTIGUA & BARBUDA
GUADELOUPE (France)
DOMINICA
MARTINIQUE (France)
ST. LUCIA
BARBADOS
ST. VINCENT & THE GRENADINES
GRENADA
TRINIDAD & TOBAGO

DOMINICAN REPUBLIC

BAHAMAS

PUERTO RICO (U.S.)

Havana   Nassau

Mexico City

CUBA

HAITI

JAMAICA

BELIZE   Kingston

Santo Domingo

Belmopan

GUATEMALA   HONDURAS

Guatemala   Tegucigalpa   Port-au-Prince

San Salvador   NICARAGUA

EL SALVADOR   Managua

Caribbean Sea

San José

COSTA RICA

Panama

Caracas   Georgetown

VENEZUELA

GUYANA

Paramaribo

Cayenne

SURINAME   FRENCH GUIANA (France)

PANAMA

Bogotá

COLOMBIA

Equator

PACIFIC OCEAN

GALÁPAGOS ISLANDS (Ecuador)

Quito

ECUADOR

Amazon R.

PERU

B R A Z I L

São Francisco R.

Lima

Brasília

N
W   E
S

Lake Titicaca

La Paz

BOLIVIA

Rio de Janeiro

Sucre

Paraná R.

PARAGUAY

São Paulo

Tropic of Capricorn

Tropic of Capricorn

CHILE

Asunción

URUGUAY

Santiago   Buenos Aires   Montevideo

ARGENTINA

Río de la Plata

KEY

——— National border

⊛ National capital

• Other city

ATLANTIC OCEAN

FALKLAND ISLANDS (U.K.)

Tierra del Fuego

Cape Horn

0 miles   2,000

0 kilometers   2,000

Lambert Azimuthal Equal Area

North and South America: Physical

ASIA

ARCTIC OCEAN

EUROPE

Bering Strait

Beaufort Sea

Greenland

Bering Sea

Mt. McKinley
20,320 ft
(6,194 m)

Aleutian Islands

Alaska Range

Gulf of Alaska

Mackenzie R.

Great Bear Lake

Great Slave Lake

Baffin Bay

Baffin Island

Davis Strait

Labrador Sea

ROCKY MOUNTAINS

CANADIAN SHIELD

Hudson Bay

Newfoundland

Lake Winnipeg

GREAT PLAINS

Great Lakes

Missouri R.

Ohio R.

Appalachian Mts.

ATLANTIC OCEAN

Tropic of Cancer

Colorado R.

Mississippi R.

Tropic of Cancer

20° N

Baja California

Sierra Madre Occidental

Rio Grande

Sierra Madre Oriental

Gulf of Mexico

Gulf of California

PACIFIC OCEAN

Yucatán Peninsula

Cuba

Hispaniola

Greater Antilles

Lesser Antilles

Caribbean Sea

Isthmus of Panama

Orinoco R.

Guiana Highlands

Galápagos Islands

Equator

Amazon R.

AMAZON BASIN

São Francisco R.

ANDES

Brazilian Highlands

20° S

Lake Titicaca

Tropic of Capricorn

Paraguay R.

Paraná R.

Tropic of Capricorn

ANDES

Gran Chaco

Aconcagua
22,834 ft
(6,960 m)

Pampas

Río de la Plata

Patagonia

40° S

ATLANTIC OCEAN

Falkland Islands

Tierra del Fuego

Cape Horn

KEY
ELEVATION

Feet	Meters
More than 13,000	More than 3,960
6,500–13,000	1,980–3,960
1,600–6,500	480–1,980
650–1,600	200–480
0–650	0–200

Ice cap

—— National border

N
W E
S

0 miles 2,000
0 kilometers 2,000
Lambert Azimuthal Equal Area

United States: Political

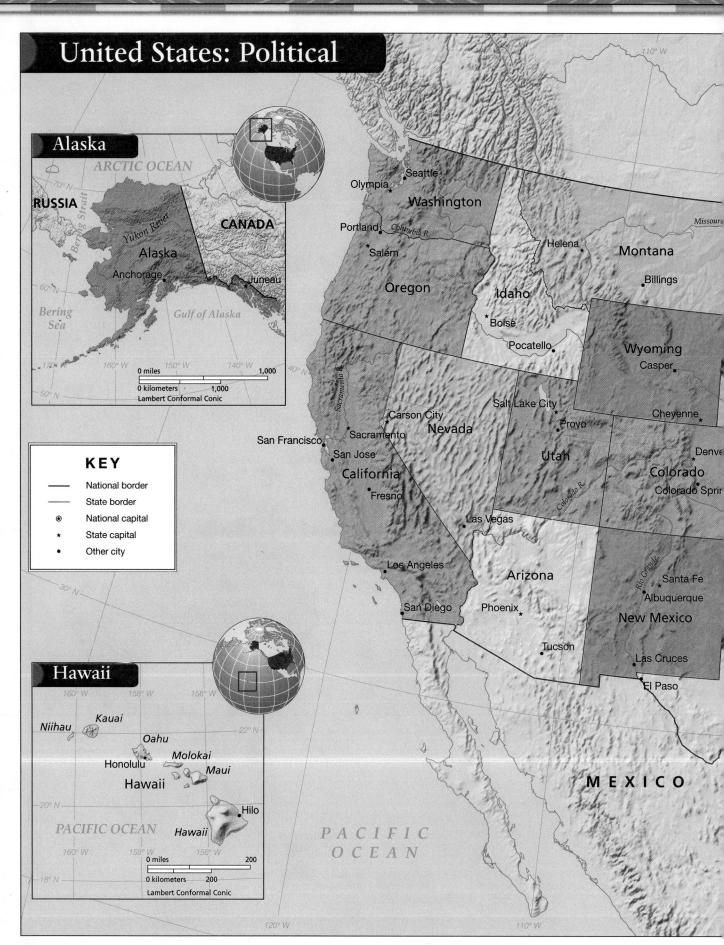

Alaska

ARCTIC OCEAN

RUSSIA

CANADA

Yukon River

Alaska

Anchorage

Juneau

Bering Strait

Bering Sea

Gulf of Alaska

0 miles 1,000
0 kilometers 1,000
Lambert Conformal Conic

KEY

— National border
— State border
⊛ National capital
★ State capital
• Other city

Hawaii

Niihau

Kauai

Oahu

Honolulu

Molokai

Maui

Hawaii

Hilo

Hawaii

PACIFIC OCEAN

0 miles 200
0 kilometers 200
Lambert Conformal Conic

Seattle
Olympia
Washington
Portland
Columbia R.
Salem
Oregon
Helena
Montana
Billings
Idaho
Boise
Pocatello
Wyoming
Casper
Cheyenne
Carson City
Salt Lake City
Nevada
Provo
Sacramento
San Francisco
San Jose
Utah
Colorado
Denver
California
Colorado Springs
Fresno
Colorado R.
Las Vegas
Los Angeles
Arizona
Santa Fe
Rio Grande
Albuquerque
San Diego
Phoenix
New Mexico
Tucson
Las Cruces
El Paso
Missouri
Sacramento R.

MEXICO

PACIFIC OCEAN

470 Reference

CANADA

North Dakota
Bismarck ★
Fargo •

Minnesota

South Dakota
Pierre ★
• Sioux Falls

Lake Superior

St. Paul ★
Minneapolis • Wisconsin
Mississippi R.
Milwaukee •
Madison ★

Michigan

Lake Michigan

Lake Huron

Grand Rapids •
Lansing ★
Detroit •

Lake Ontario

Lake Erie

Buffalo •

Maine
Augusta ★
Vermont   Portland •
Montpelier ★   New Hampshire
Concord ★
Boston ★
Albany ★   Massachusetts
New York   Providence ★ Rhode Island
Hartford ★   Connecticut
New York City •   40° N

Nebraska
Omaha •
Lincoln ★

Iowa
Des Moines ★
Cedar Rapids •

Missouri R.

Illinois

Chicago •

Fort Wayne •

Indiana

Ohio

Columbus ★

Pennsylvania
Harrisburg ★
Cleveland •
Pittsburgh •

New Jersey
Trenton ★
Philadelphia •
Delaware

Kansas
Topeka ★
Wichita •

Kansas City •
Jefferson City ★
St. Louis •

Missouri

Springfield ★

Indianapolis ★

Cincinnati •
Ohio R.

Louisville •

Frankfort ★

Kentucky

Charleston ★

West
Virginia

Baltimore •
Washington, D.C. •
Dover ★
Annapolis •
Maryland
District of Columbia
Richmond ★
Virginia
Norfolk •

Arkansas R.

Oklahoma
Oklahoma City ★

Tulsa •

Arkansas
Fort Smith •
Little Rock ★

Red R.

Memphis •

Mississippi R.

Nashville ★   Knoxville •

Tennessee

Tennessee R.

Raleigh ★

North Carolina
Charlotte •

South Carolina
Columbia ★
Charleston •

ATLANTIC
OCEAN

Texas

Dallas •
Fort Worth •

Austin ★
Houston •
San Antonio •

Mississippi
Jackson ★

Shreveport •
Louisiana

Baton Rouge •   Gulfport •
New Orleans •

Alabama
Montgomery ★

Birmingham •
Mobile •

Georgia
Columbus •

Atlanta ★

Savannah •

Jacksonville •

Tallahassee ★

Florida
Orlando •
Tampa •

Miami •

30° N

0 miles   250
0 kilometers   250
Lambert Azimuthal Equal Area

Gulf of Mexico

N
W   E
S

Europe: Political

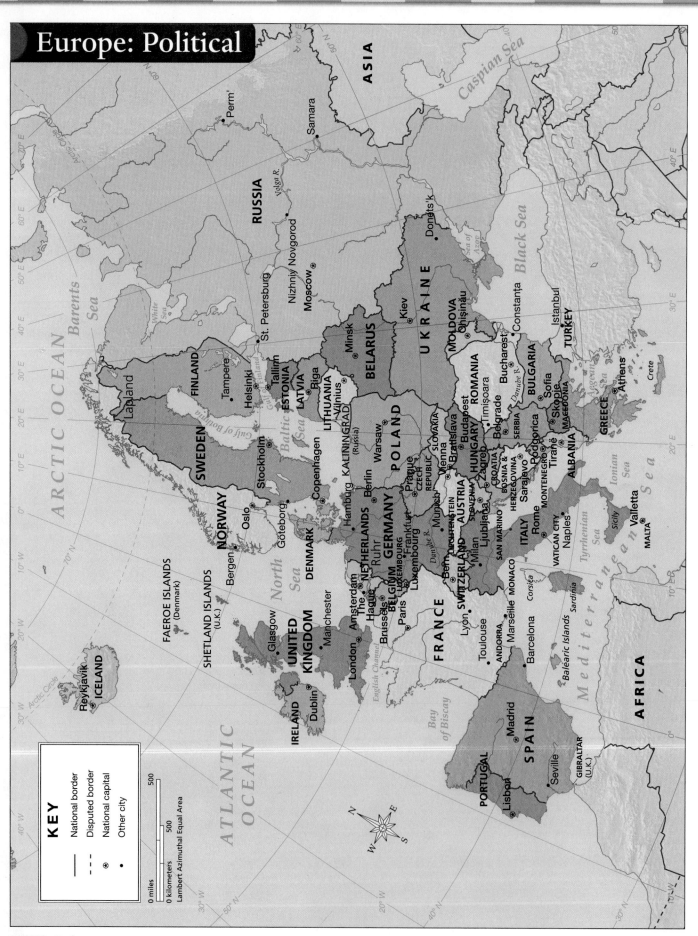

KEY

National border
Disputed border
⊛ National capital
• Other city

0 miles 500
0 kilometers 500
Lambert Azimuthal Equal Area

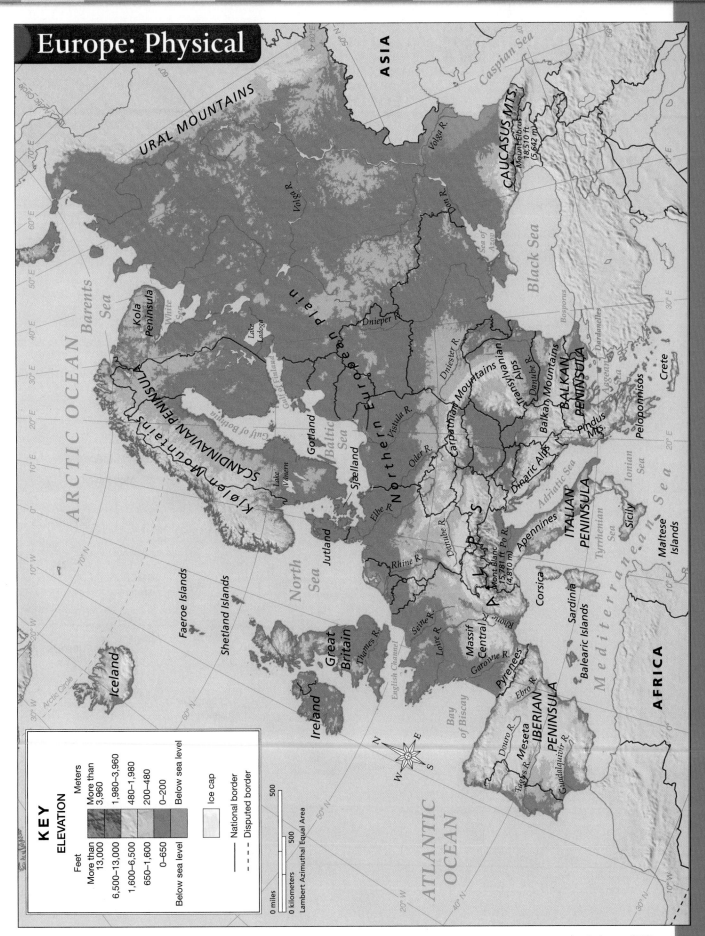

Europe: Physical

KEY

ELEVATION

Feet	Meters
More than 13,000	More than 3,960
6,500–13,000	1,980–3,960
1,600–6,500	480–1,980
650–1,600	200–480
0–650	0–200
Below sea level	Below sea level

ice cap

—— National border

– – – Disputed border

0 miles 500

0 kilometers 500

Lambert Azimuthal Equal Area

ASIA

URAL MOUNTAINS

Caspian Sea

CAUCASUS MTS.

Mount Elbrus
18,510 ft
(5,642 m)

Black Sea

Barents Sea

Kola Peninsula

White Sea

ARCTIC OCEAN

Volga R.

Volga R.

Don R.

Don R.

Sea of Azov

Lake Ladoga

Dnieper R.

Northern European Plain

Gulf of Finland

Dniester R.

Carpathian Mountains

Transylvanian Alps

Danube R.

Balkan Mountains

BALKAN PENINSULA

Bosporus

Dardanelles

Aegean Sea

Crete

Peloponnisos

Pindus Mts.

SCANDINAVIAN PENINSULA

Kjølen Mountains

Gotland

Baltic Sea

Vistula R.

Oder R.

Dinaric Alps

Adriatic Sea

Ionian Sea

Lake Vänern

Sjælland

Elbe R.

Danube R.

A L P S

Mont Blanc
15,781 ft
(4,810 m)

Po R.

Apennines

ITALIAN PENINSULA

Tyrrhenian Sea

Sicily

Maltese Islands

M e d i t e r r a n e a n   S e a

North Sea

Jutland

Rhine R.

Rhône R.

Corsica

Sardinia

Balearic Islands

Faeroe Islands

Shetland Islands

Great Britain

Thames R.

Seine R.

Loire R.

Massif Central

Garonne R.

AFRICA

English Channel

Bay of Biscay

Pyrenees

Ebro R.

IBERIAN PENINSULA

Meseta

Douro R.

Tagus R.

Guadalquivir R.

Iceland

Arctic Circle

Ireland

N

ATLANTIC OCEAN

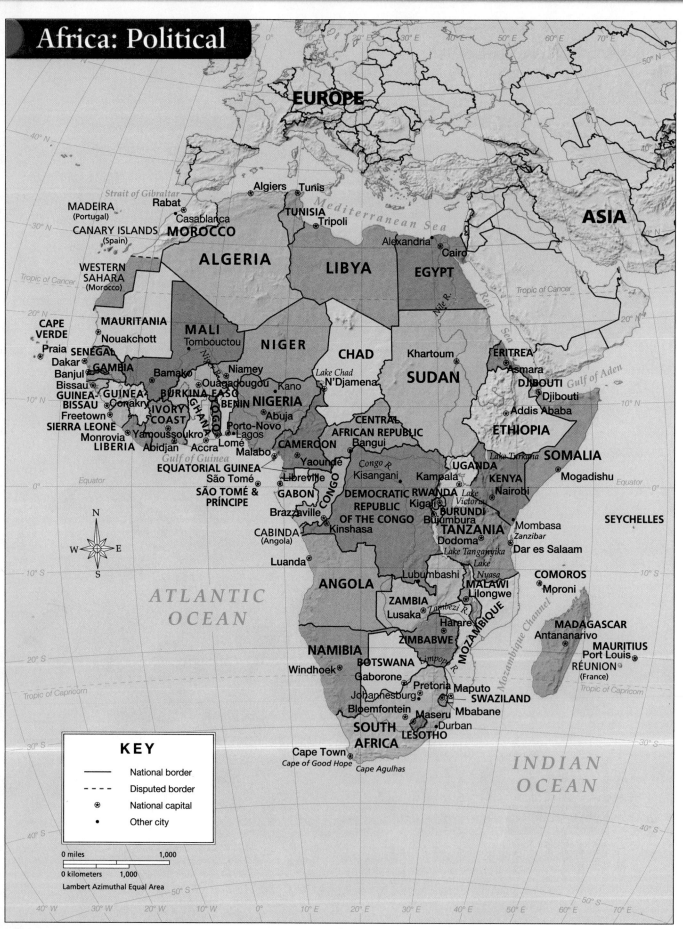

Africa: Political

EUROPE

ASIA

Strait of Gibraltar

MADEIRA (Portugal)

CANARY ISLANDS (Spain)

Mediterranean Sea

Algiers ⊛ ⊛ Tunis

Rabat ⊛

TUNISIA

Casablanca • Tripoli ⊛

MOROCCO

ALGERIA

LIBYA

EGYPT

Alexandria ⊛

Cairo ⊛

Tropic of Cancer

Tropic of Cancer

WESTERN SAHARA (Morocco)

CAPE VERDE

Praia ⊛

Nouakchott ⊛

MAURITANIA

MALI

Tombouctou •

NIGER

CHAD

Khartoum ⊛

ERITREA

Asmara ⊛

Red Sea

Dakar ⊛

SENEGAL

Bamako ⊛

Niamey ⊛

N'Djamena ⊛

SUDAN

DJIBOUTI

Gulf of Aden

Banjul ⊛

GAMBIA

Lake Chad

Djibouti •

Bissau ⊛

GUINEA BISSAU

Conakry ⊛

GUINEA

Ouagadougou ⊛

BURKINA FASO

Kano •

Addis Ababa •

Freetown ⊛

IVORY COAST

GHANA

BENIN

NIGERIA

Abuja ⊛

CENTRAL AFRICAN REPUBLIC

ETHIOPIA

SOMALIA

SIERRA LEONE

Yamoussoukro •

TOGO

Porto-Novo ⊛

Lagos •

Bangui ⊛

Lake Turkana

Monrovia ⊛

LIBERIA

Abidjan •

Accra ⊛

Lomé ⊛

CAMEROON

Yaoundé ⊛

UGANDA

KENYA

Mogadishu ⊛

Equator

Malabo ⊛

Congo R.

Kisangani •

Kampala ⊛

Equator

EQUATORIAL GUINEA

São Tomé ⊛

Libreville ⊛

DEMOCRATIC REPUBLIC OF THE CONGO

RWANDA

Kigali ⊛

Lake Victoria

Nairobi ⊛

SÃO TOMÉ & PRÍNCIPE

GABON

CONGO

BURUNDI

Bujumbura ⊛

SEYCHELLES

Brazzaville ⊛

TANZANIA

Mombasa •

Kinshasa ⊛

Dodoma ⊛

Zanzibar •

CABINDA (Angola)

Lake Tanganyika

Dar es Salaam •

ATLANTIC OCEAN

Luanda ⊛

Lubumbashi •

Lake Nyasa

COMOROS

Moroni •

ANGOLA

MALAWI

Lilongwe ⊛

ZAMBIA

Zambezi R.

MADAGASCAR

Lusaka ⊛

Antananarivo ⊛

Harare ⊛

MOZAMBIQUE

MAURITIUS

Port Louis ⊛

NAMIBIA

ZIMBABWE

RÉUNION (France)

Windhoek ⊛

BOTSWANA

Limpopo R.

Gaborone ⊛

Pretoria ⊛

Maputo ⊛

Johannesburg •

SWAZILAND

Mbabane ⊛

Bloemfontein •

Maseru ⊛

Durban •

SOUTH AFRICA

LESOTHO

Cape Town ⊛

Cape of Good Hope

Cape Agulhas

INDIAN OCEAN

KEY

——	National border
- - -	Disputed border
⊛	National capital
•	Other city

0 miles 1,000

0 kilometers 1,000

Lambert Azimuthal Equal Area

Africa: Physical

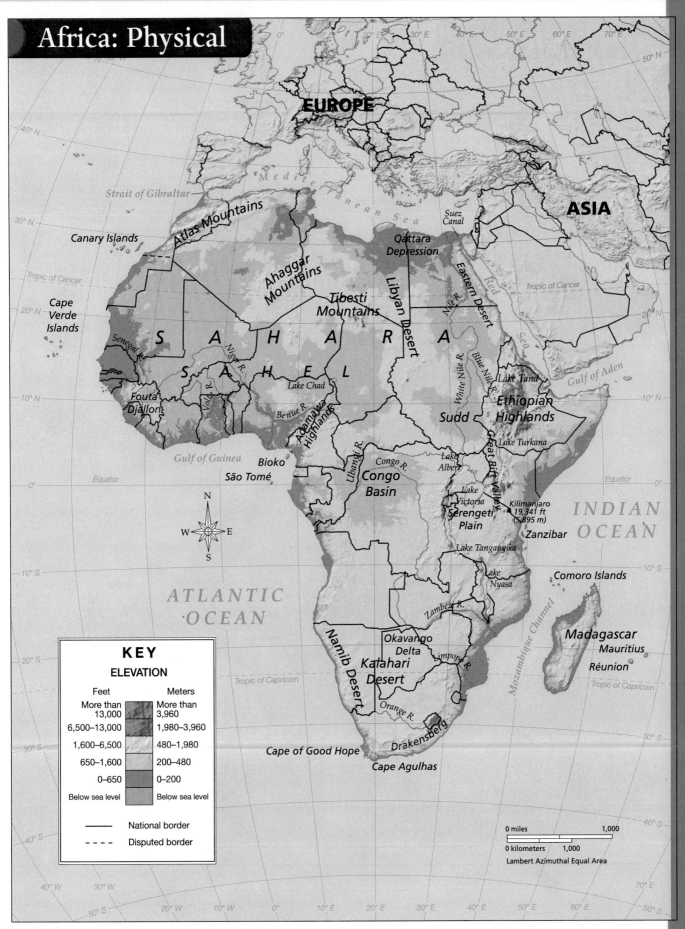

EUROPE

ASIA

Strait of Gibraltar

Canary Islands

Atlas Mountains

Mediterranean Sea

Qattara Depression

Suez Canal

Tropic of Cancer

Cape Verde Islands

Ahaggar Mountains

Tibesti Mountains

Libyan Desert

Eastern Desert

Nile R.

Red Sea

Tropic of Cancer

S A H A R A

Senegal R.

Niger R.

S A H E L

Lake Chad

White Nile R.

Blue Nile R.

Lake Tana

Gulf of Aden

Fouta Djallon

Volta R.

Benue R.

Adamawa Highlands

Sudd

Ethiopian Highlands

Gulf of Guinea

Bioko

São Tomé

Ubangi R.

Congo R.

Congo Basin

Lake Albert

Lake Turkana

Great Rift Valley

Equator

Lake Victoria

Serengeti Plain

Kilimanjaro 19,341 ft (5,895 m)

Zanzibar

INDIAN OCEAN

Equator

N
W   E
S

Lake Tanganyika

Lake Nyasa

Comoro Islands

ATLANTIC OCEAN

Zambezi R.

Madagascar

Mauritius

Réunion

Namib Desert

Okavango Delta

Kalahari Desert

Limpopo R.

Mozambique Channel

Tropic of Capricorn

Tropic of Capricorn

Orange R.

Drakensberg

Cape of Good Hope

Cape Agulhas

KEY

ELEVATION

Feet	Meters
More than 13,000	More than 3,960
6,500–13,000	1,980–3,960
1,600–6,500	480–1,980
650–1,600	200–480
0–650	0–200
Below sea level	Below sea level

————— National border

- - - - - Disputed border

0 miles   1,000

0 kilometers 1,000

Lambert Azimuthal Equal Area

Asia: Political

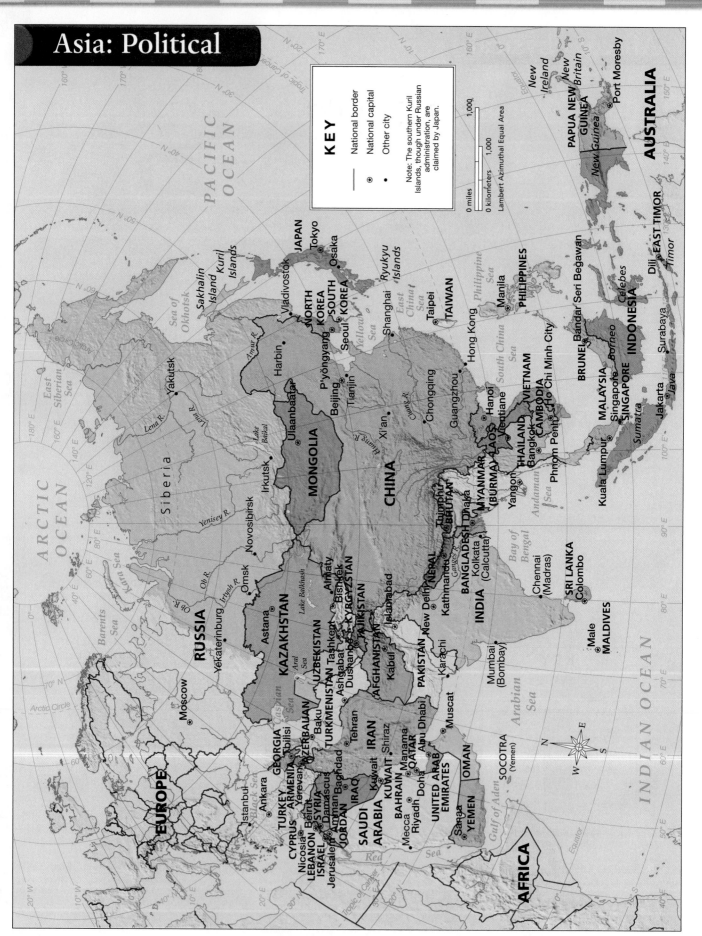

KEY

⊛ National border
⊛ National capital
• Other city

Note: The southern Kuril Islands, though under Russian administration, are claimed by Japan.

0 miles 1,000
0 kilometers 1,000
Lambert Azimuthal Equal Area

PACIFIC OCEAN

ARCTIC OCEAN

EUROPE

AFRICA

RUSSIA

Moscow

Yekaterinburg
Omsk
Novosibirsk
Irkutsk
Yakutsk

Siberia

Ob R.
Irtysh R.
Yenisey R.
Lena R.
Vilyui R.
Amur R.

Kara Sea
Barents Sea
Laptev Sea
East Siberian Sea
Sea of Okhotsk

Sakhalin Island
Kuril Islands

Vladivostok

JAPAN
Tokyo
Osaka

NORTH KOREA
P'yŏngyang
SOUTH KOREA
Seoul

Harbin
Beijing
Tianjin
Shanghai

Ryukyu Islands

TAIWAN
Taipei

Hong Kong

Guangzhou
Chongqing
Xi'an

CHINA

Huang R.
Chang R.

Yellow Sea
East China Sea
South China Sea
Philippine Sea

MONGOLIA
Ulaanbaatar

Lake Baikal

KAZAKHSTAN
Astana

Lake Balkhash
Aral Sea
Caspian Sea

Almaty
Bishkek
KYRGYZSTAN
Tashkent
UZBEKISTAN
TAJIKISTAN
Dushanbe
TURKMENISTAN
Ashgabat

AFGHANISTAN
Kabul
Islamabad
PAKISTAN
New Delhi
Kathmandu NEPAL
Thimphu BHUTAN
BANGLADESH
Dhaka
Kolkata (Calcutta)

INDIA

Karachi
Mumbai (Bombay)
Chennai (Madras)

Ganges R.

SRI LANKA
Colombo

Male
MALDIVES

MYANMAR (BURMA)
Yangon
LAOS
Vientiane
THAILAND
Bangkok
VIETNAM
Hanoi
CAMBODIA
Phnom Penh
Ho Chi Minh City

Bay of Bengal
Andaman Sea

Kuala Lumpur
MALAYSIA
SINGAPORE
Singapore
BRUNEI
Bandar Seri Begawan

Borneo
Sumatra
Java
Jakarta
Surabaya
Celebes
INDONESIA

EAST TIMOR
Dili
Timor

PHILIPPINES
Manila

PAPUA NEW GUINEA
New Guinea
Port Moresby

New Ireland
New Britain

AUSTRALIA

GEORGIA
Tbilisi
ARMENIA
Yerevan
AZERBAIJAN
Baku
TURKEY
Ankara
Istanbul
CYPRUS
Nicosia
LEBANON
Beirut
SYRIA
Damascus
ISRAEL
Jerusalem
JORDAN
Amman
IRAQ
Baghdad
IRAN
Tehran
Shiraz
KUWAIT
Kuwait
BAHRAIN
Manama
QATAR
Doha
UNITED ARAB EMIRATES
Abu Dhabi
OMAN
Muscat
SAUDI ARABIA
Mecca
Riyadh
YEMEN
Sanaa
SOCOTRA (Yemen)

Black Sea
Red Sea
Gulf of Aden
Arabian Sea

INDIAN OCEAN

N
W E
S

476 Reference

Asia: Physical

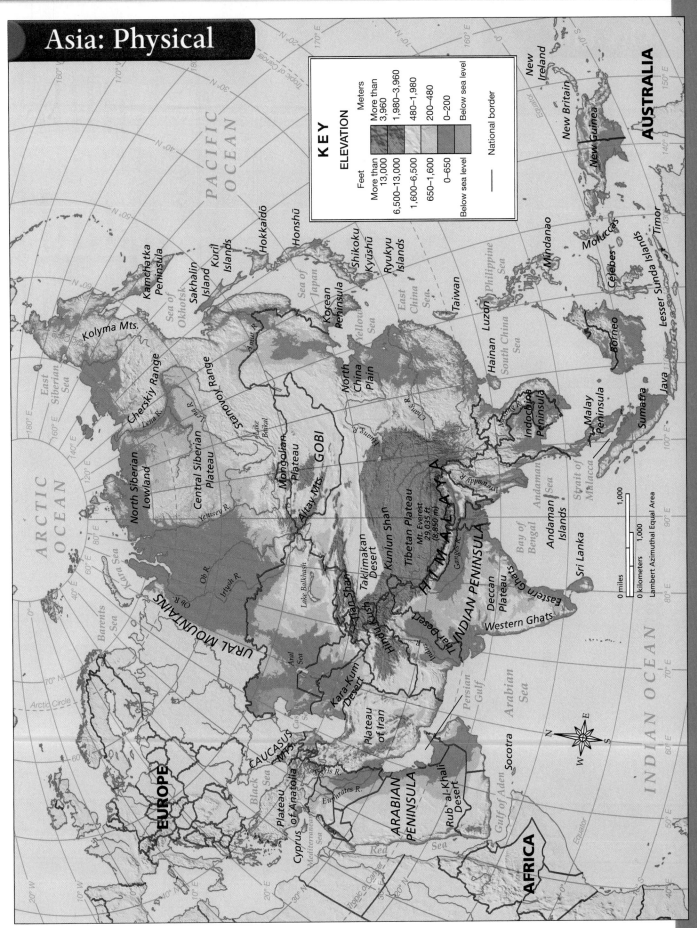

KEY

ELEVATION

Feet	Meters
More than 13,000	More than 3,960
6,500–13,000	1,980–3,960
1,600–6,500	480–1,980
650–1,600	200–480
0–650	0–200
Below sea level	Below sea level

— National border

ARCTIC OCEAN

PACIFIC OCEAN

INDIAN OCEAN

EUROPE

AFRICA

AUSTRALIA

Kolyma Mts.

Kamchatka Peninsula

Cherskiy Range

Stanovoy Range

Sakhalin Island

Kuril Islands

Hokkaidō

Honshū

Sea of Okhotsk

Sea of Japan

Shikoku

Kyūshū

Ryukyu Islands

Korean Peninsula

Yellow Sea

East China Sea

Taiwan

Luzon

Philippine Sea

Mindanao

Moluccas

Celebes

New Ireland

New Britain

New Guinea

Timor

Lesser Sunda Islands

Java

Sumatra

Borneo

Malay Peninsula

Hainan

South China Sea

Strait of Malacca

Indochina Peninsula

North China Plain

Mongolian Plateau

GOBI

Central Siberian Plateau

North Siberian Lowland

Lake Baikal

Altay Mts.

Tian Shan

Taklimakan Desert

Kunlun Shan

Tibetan Plateau

Mt. Everest 29,035 ft (8,850 m)

HIMALAYA

Hindu Kush

Thar Desert

INDIAN PENINSULA

Deccan Plateau

Eastern Ghats

Western Ghats

Sri Lanka

Bay of Bengal

Andaman Sea

Andaman Islands

Ganges R.

Brahmaputra R.

Irrawaddy R.

Mekong R.

Chang R.

Huang R.

Amur R.

Lena R.

Yenisey R.

Ob R.

Irtysh R.

Lake Balkhash

Aral Sea

Kara-Kum Desert

Plateau of Iran

Persian Gulf

Arabian Sea

ARABIAN PENINSULA

Rub' al-Khali Desert

Gulf of Aden

Socotra

Red Sea

Euphrates R.

Tigris R.

CAUCASUS MTS.

Plateau of Anatolia

Cyprus

Mediterranean Sea

Black Sea

Caspian Sea

Barents Sea

Kara Sea

East Siberian Sea

URAL MOUNTAINS

Arctic Circle

Tropic of Cancer

Equator

Tropic of Capricorn

1,000
0 miles

1,000
0 kilometers

Lambert Azimuthal Equal Area

Oceania

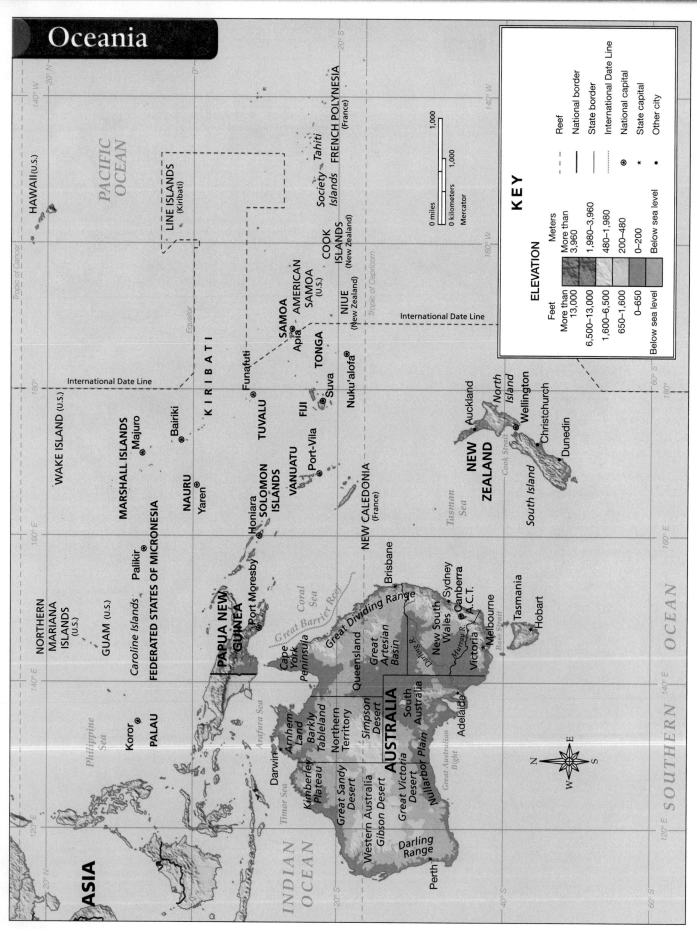

ASIA

INDIAN OCEAN

Philippine Sea

Koror ⊛
PALAU

NORTHERN MARIANA ISLANDS (U.S.)

GUAM (U.S.)

Caroline Islands

FEDERATED STATES OF MICRONESIA
Palikir ⊛

WAKE ISLAND (U.S.)

MARSHALL ISLANDS
Majuro ⊛

Bairiki ⊛

NAURU
Yaren ⊛

K I R I B A T I

PACIFIC OCEAN

HAWAII (U.S.)

Tropic of Cancer

Equator

LINE ISLANDS (Kiribati)

Funafuti ⊛

TUVALU

SAMOA
Apia ⊛

AMERICAN SAMOA (U.S.)

TONGA

Nuku'alofa ⊛

Suva ⊛

FIJI

NIUE (New Zealand)

COOK ISLANDS (New Zealand)

Tahiti

Society Islands **FRENCH POLYNESIA** (France)

Tropic of Capricorn

International Date Line

International Date Line

Honiara ⊛
SOLOMON ISLANDS

Port-Vila ⊛
VANUATU

NEW CALEDONIA (France)

PAPUA NEW GUINEA
Port Moresby ★

Coral Sea

Great Barrier Reef

Arafura Sea

Timor Sea

Darwin ★

Arnhem Land

Kimberley Plateau

Barkly Tableland

Northern Territory

Great Sandy Desert

Western Australia

Gibson Desert

Great Victoria Desert

South Australia

Nullarbor Plain

Great Australian Bight

Perth ★

Darling Range

Simpson Desert

AUSTRALIA

Great Artesian Basin

Great Dividing Range

Cape York Peninsula

Queensland

Brisbane ★

Murray R.

Darling R.

Adelaide ★

Victoria

Melbourne ★

New South Wales

Sydney ●
Canberra ⊛
A.C.T.

Bass Strait

Tasmania
Hobart ★

Tasman Sea

Auckland ●

North Island

Wellington ⊛

Christchurch ●

Cook Strait

South Island

Dunedin ●

NEW ZEALAND

SOUTHERN OCEAN

N E W S

KEY

	National border
— — — — Reef	
————	State border
··········	International Date Line
⊛	National capital
★	State capital
●	Other city

ELEVATION

Feet	Meters
More than 13,000	More than 3,960
6,500–13,000	1,980–3,960
1,600–6,500	480–1,980
650–1,600	200–480
0–650	0–200
Below sea level	Below sea level

0 miles 1,000
0 kilometers 1,000
Mercator

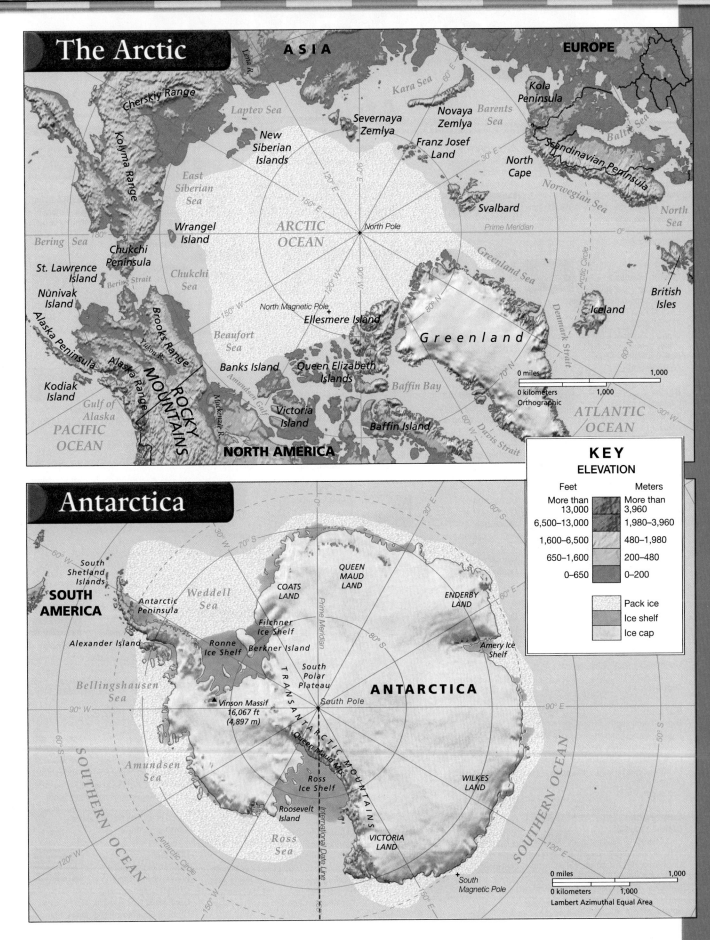

The Arctic

ASIA EUROPE

Cherskiy Range
Kolyma Range
Laptev Sea
Kara Sea
New Siberian Islands
Severnaya Zemlya
Novaya Zemlya
Franz Josef Land
Barents Sea
Kola Peninsula
Scandinavian Peninsula
Baltic Sea
North Cape
Norwegian Sea
East Siberian Sea
Svalbard
ARCTIC OCEAN
Prime Meridian
North Pole
Greenland Sea
North Sea
Bering Sea
Wrangel Island
Chukchi Peninsula
St. Lawrence Island
Chukchi Sea
North Magnetic Pole
Arctic Circle
Iceland
British Isles
Nunivak Island
Brooks Range
Ellesmere Island
Denmark Strait
Beaufort Sea
Greenland
Alaska Peninsula
Yukon R.
Alaska Range
ROCKY MOUNTAINS
Banks Island
Queen Elizabeth Islands
Baffin Bay
Kodiak Island
Amundsen Gulf
Gulf of Alaska
Mackenzie R.
Victoria Island
Baffin Island
Davis Strait
ATLANTIC OCEAN
PACIFIC OCEAN
NORTH AMERICA

0 miles 1,000
0 kilometers 1,000
Orthographic

Antarctica

SOUTH AMERICA
South Shetland Islands
Antarctic Peninsula
Weddell Sea
COATS LAND
QUEEN MAUD LAND
ENDERBY LAND
Alexander Island
Filchner Ice Shelf
Ronne Ice Shelf
Berkner Island
Prime Meridian
South Polar Plateau
Amery Ice Shelf
Bellingshausen Sea
Vinson Massif 16,067 ft (4,897 m)
TRANSANTARCTIC MOUNTAINS
South Pole
ANTARCTICA
SOUTHERN OCEAN
Amundsen Sea
Queen Maud Mts.
Ross Ice Shelf
WILKES LAND
Roosevelt Island
International Date Line
VICTORIA LAND
Ross Sea
Antarctic Circle
South Magnetic Pole
SOUTHERN OCEAN
Lambert Azimuthal Equal Area

0 miles 1,000
0 kilometers 1,000

KEY
ELEVATION

Feet		Meters
More than 13,000		More than 3,960
6,500–13,000		1,980–3,960
1,600–6,500		480–1,980
650–1,600		200–480
0–650		0–200

Pack ice
Ice shelf
Ice cap

Africa

Algeria
Capital: Algiers
Population: 32.3 million
Official Languages: Arabic and Tamazight
Land Area: 2,381,740 sq km; 919,590 sq mi
Leading Exports: petroleum, natural gas, petroleum products
Continent: Africa

Angola
Capital: Luanda
Population: 10.6 million
Official Language: Portuguese
Land Area: 1,246,700 sq km; 481,551 sq mi
Leading Exports: crude oil, diamonds, refined petroleum products, gas, coffee, sisal, fish and fish products, timber, cotton
Continent: Africa

Benin
Capital: Porto-Novo
Population: 6.9 million
Official Language: French
Land Area: 110,620 sq km; 42,710 sq mi
Leading Exports: cotton, crude oil, palm products, cocoa
Continent: Africa

Botswana
Capital: Gaborone
Population: 1.6 million
Official Language: English
Land Area: 585,370 sq km; 226,011 sq mi
Leading Exports: diamonds, copper, nickel, soda ash, meat, textiles
Continent: Africa

Burkina Faso
Capital: Ouagadougou
Population: 12.6 million
Official Language: French
Land Area: 273,800 sq km; 105,714 sq mi
Leading Exports: cotton, animal products, gold
Continent: Africa

Burundi
Capital: Bujumbura
Population: 6.4 million
Official Languages: Kirundi and French
Land Area: 25,650 sq km; 9,903 sq mi
Leading Exports: coffee, tea, sugar, cotton, hides
Continent: Africa

Cameroon
Capital: Yaoundé
Population: 16.1 million
Official Languages: English and French
Land Area: 469,440 sq km; 181,251 sqmi
Leading Exports: crude oil and petroleum products, lumber, cocoa, aluminum, coffee, cotton
Continent: Africa

Cape Verde
Capital: Praia
Population: 408,760
Official Language: Portuguese
Land Area: 4,033 sq km; 1,557 sq mi
Leading Exports: fuel, shoes, garments, fish, hides
Location: Atlantic Ocean

Central African Republic
Capital: Bangui
Population: 3.6 million
Official Language: French
Land Area: 622,984 sq km; 240,534 sq mi
Leading Exports: diamonds, timber, cotton, coffee, tobacco
Continent: Africa

Chad
Capital: N'Djamena
Population: 9 million
Official Languages: Arabic and French
Land Area: 1,259,200 sq km; 486,177 sq mi
Leading Exports: cotton, cattle, gum arabic
Continent: Africa

Comoros
Capital: Moroni
Population: 614,382
Official Languages: Arabic, Comoran, and French
Land Area: 2,170 sq km; 838 sq mi
Leading Exports: vanilla, ylang-ylang, cloves, perfume oil, copra
Location: Indian Ocean

Congo, Democratic Republic of the
Capital: Kinshasa
Population: 55.2 million
Official Language: French
Land Area: 2,267,600 sq km; 875,520 sq mi
Leading Exports: diamonds, copper, coffee, cobalt, crude oil
Continent: Africa

Congo, Republic of the
Capital: Brazzaville
Population: 3.3 million
Official Language: French
Land Area: 341,500 sq km; 131,853 sq mi
Leading Exports: petroleum, lumber, sugar, cocoa, coffee, diamonds
Continent: Africa

Djibouti
Capital: Djibouti
Population: 472,810
Official Languages: Arabic and French
Land Area: 22,980 sq km; 8,873 sq mi
Leading Exports: reexports, hides and skins, coffee (in transit)
Continent: Africa

Egypt
Capital: Cairo
Population: 70.7 million
Official Language: Arabic
Land Area: 995,450 sq km; 384,343 sq mi
Leading Exports: crude oil and petroleum products, cotton, textiles, metal products, chemicals
Continent: Africa

Equatorial Guinea
Capital: Malabo
Population: 498,144
Official Languages: Spanish and French
Land Area: 28,050 sq km; 10,830 sq mi
Leading Exports: petroleum, timber, cocoa
Continent: Africa

Eritrea
Capital: Asmara
Population: 4.5 million
Official Language: Tigrinya
Land Area: 121,320 sq km; 46,842 sq mi
Leading Exports: livestock, sorghum, textiles, food, small manufactured goods
Continent: Africa

Ethiopia
Capital: Addis Ababa
Population: 67.7 million
Official Language: Amharic
Land Area: 1,119,683 sq km; 432,310 sq mi
Leading Exports: coffee, qat, gold, leather products, oilseeds
Continent: Africa

Gabon
Capital: Libreville
Population: 1.2 million
Official Language: French
Land Area: 257,667 sq km; 99,489 sq mi
Leading Exports: crude oil, timber, manganese, uranium
Continent: Africa

Gambia
Capital: Banjul
Population: 1.5 million
Official Language: English
Land Area: 10,000 sq km; 3,861 sq mi
Leading Exports: peanuts and peanut products, fish, cotton lint, palm kernels
Continent: Africa

Ghana
Capital: Accra
Population: 20.2 million
Official Language: English
Land Area: 230,940 sq km; 89,166 sq mi
Leading Exports: gold, cocoa, timber, tuna, bauxite, aluminum, manganese ore, diamonds
Continent: Africa

Guinea
Capital: Conakry
Population: 7.8 million
Official Language: French
Land Area: 245,857 sq km; 94,925 sq mi
Leading Exports: bauxite, alumina, gold, diamonds, coffee, fish, agricultural products
Continent: Africa

Guinea-Bissau
Capital: Bissau
Population: 1.4 million
Official Language: Portuguese
Land Area: 28,000 sq km; 10,811 sq mi
Leading Exports: cashew nuts, shrimp, peanuts, palm kernels, lumber
Continent: Africa

Ivory Coast
Capital: Yamoussoukro
Population: 16.8 million
Official Language: French
Land Area: 318,000 sq km; 122,780 sq mi
Leading Exports: cocoa, coffee, timber, petroleum, cotton, bananas, pineapples, palm oil, cotton, fish
Continent: Africa

Kenya
Capital: Nairobi
Population: 31.3 million
Official Languages: Swahili and English
Land Area: 569,250 sq km; 219,787 sq mi
Leading Exports: tea, horticultural products, coffee, petroleum products, fish, cement
Continent: Africa

Lesotho
Capital: Maseru
Population: 2.2 million
Official Languages: Sesotho and English
Land Area: 30,355 sq km; 11,720 sq mi
Leading Exports: manufactured goods (clothing, footwear, road vehicles), wool and mohair, food and live animals
Continent: Africa

Liberia
Capital: Monrovia
Population: 3.3 million
Official Language: English
Land Area: 96,320 sq km; 37,189 sq mi
Leading Exports: rubber, timber, iron, diamonds, cocoa, coffee
Continent: Africa

Libya
Capital: Tripoli
Population: 5.4 million
Official Language: Arabic
Land Area: 1,759,540 sq km; 679,358 sq mi
Leading Exports: crude oil, refined petroleum products
Location: Indian

Madagascar
Capital: Antananarivo
Population: 16.5 million
Official Languages: French and Malagasy
Land Area: 581,540 sq km; 224,533 sq mi
Leading Exports: coffee, vanilla, shellfish, sugar, cotton cloth, chromite, petroleum products
Location: Indian Ocean

Malawi
Capital: Lilongwe
Population: 10.7 million
Official Languages: English and Chichewa
Land Area: 94,080 sq km; 36,324 sq mi
Leading Exports: tobacco, tea, sugar, cotton, coffee, peanuts, wood products, apparel
Continent: Africa

Mali
Capital: Bamako
Population: 11.3 million
Official Language: French
Land Area: 1,220,000 sq km; 471,042 sq mi
Leading Exports: cotton, gold, livestock
Continent: Africa

Mauritania
Capital: Nouakchott
Population: 2.8 million
Official Language: Arabic
Land Area: 1,030,400 sq km; 397,837 sq mi
Leading Exports: iron ore, fish and fish products, gold
Continent: Africa

Mauritius
Capital: Port Louis
Population: 1.2 million
Official Language: English
Land Area: 2,030 sq km; 784 sq mi
Leading Exports: clothing and textiles, sugar, cut flowers, molasses
Location: Indian Ocean

Morocco
Capital: Rabat
Population: 31.2 million
Official Language: Arabic
Land Area: 446,300 sq km; 172,316 sq mi
Leading Exports: phosphates and fertilizers, food and beverages, minerals
Continent: Africa

Mozambique
Capital: Maputo
Population: 19.6 million
Official Language: Portuguese
Land Area: 784,090 sq km; 302,737 sq mi
Leading Exports: prawns, cashews, cotton, sugar, citrus, timber, bulk electricity
Continent: Africa

Namibia
Capital: Windhoek
Population: 1.8 million
Official Language: English
Land Area: 825,418 sq km; 318,694 sq mi
Leading Exports: diamonds, copper, gold, zinc, lead, uranium, cattle, processed fish, karakul skins
Continent: Africa

Niger
Capital: Niamey
Population: 11.3 million
Official Language: French
Land Area: 1,226,700 sq km; 489,073 sq mi
Leading Exports: uranium ore, livestock products, cowpeas, onions
Continent: Africa

Nigeria
Capital: Abuja
Population: 129.9 million
Official Language: English
Land Area: 910,768 sq km; 351,648 sq mi
Leading Exports: petroleum and petroleum products, cocoa, rubber
Continent: Africa

Rwanda
Capital: Kigali
Population: 7.4 million
Official Languages: Kinyarwanda, French, and English
Land Area: 24,948 sq km; 9,632 sq mi
Leading Exports: coffee, tea, hides, tin ore
Continent: Africa

São Tomé and Príncipe
Capital: São Tomé
Population: 170,372
Official Language: Portuguese
Land Area: 1,001 sq km; 386 sq mi
Leading Exports: cocoa, copra, coffee, palm oil
Location: Atlantic Ocean

Senegal
Capital: Dakar
Population: 10.6 million
Official Language: French
Land Area: 192,000 sq km; 74,131 sq mi
Leading Exports: fish, groundnuts (peanuts), petroleum products, phosphates, cotton
Continent: Africa

Seychelles
Capital: Victoria
Population: 80,098
Official Languages: English and French
Land Area: 455 sq km; 176 sq mi
Leading Exports: canned tuna, cinnamon bark, copra, petroleum products (reexports)
Location: Indian Ocean

Sierra Leone
Capital: Freetown
Population: 5.6 million
Official Language: English
Land Area: 71,620 sq km; 27,652 sq mi
Leading Exports: diamonds, rutile, cocoa, coffee, fish
Continent: Africa

Somalia
Capital: Mogadishu
Population: 7.8 million
Official Languages: Somali and Arabic
Land Area: 627,337 sq km; 242,215 sq mi
Leading Exports: livestock, bananas, hides, fish, charcoal, scrap metal
Continent: Africa

South Africa
Capital: Cape Town, Pretoria, and Bloemfontein
Population: 43.6 million
Official Languages: Eleven official languages: Afrikaans, English, Ndebele, Pedi, Sotho, Swazi, Tsonga, Tswana, Venda, Xhosa, and Zulu
Land Area: 1,219,912 sq km; 471,008 sq mi
Leading Exports: gold, diamonds, platinum, other metals and minerals, machinery and equipment
Continent: Africa

Sudan
Capital: Khartoum
Population: 37.1 million
Official Language: Arabic
Land Area: 2,376,000 sq km; 917,374 sq mi
Leading Exports: oil and petroleum products, cotton, sesame, livestock, groundnuts, gum arabic, sugar
Continent: Africa

Swaziland
Capital: Mbabane
Population: 1.1 million
Official Languages: English and siSwati
Land Area: 17,20 sq km; 6,642 sq mi
Leading Exports: soft drink concentrates, sugar, wood pulp, cotton yarn, refrigerators, citrus and canned fruit
Continent: Africa

Tanzania
Capital: Dar es Salaam and Dodoma
Population: 37.2 million
Official Languages: Swahili and English
Land Area: 886,037 sq km; 342,099 sq mi
Leading Exports: gold, coffee, cashew nuts, manufactured goods, cotton
Continent: Africa

Togo
Capital: Lomé
Population: 5.2 million
Official Language: French
Land Area: 54,385 sq km; 20,998 sq mi
Leading Exports: cotton, phosphates, coffee, cocoa
Continent: Africa

Tunisia
Capital: Tunis
Population: 9.8 million
Official Language: Arabic
Land Area: 155,360 sq km; 59,984 sq mi
Leading Exports: textiles, mechanical goods, phosphates and chemicals, agricultural products, hydrocarbons
Continent: Africa

Uganda
Capital: Kampala
Population: 24.7 million
Official Language: English
Land Area: 199,710 sq km; 77,108 sq mi
Leading Exports: coffee, fish and fish products, tea, gold, cotton, flowers, horticultural products
Continent: Africa

Zambia
Capital: Lusaka
Population: 10.1 million
Official Language: English
Land Area: 740,724 sq km; 285,994 sq mi
Leading Exports: copper, cobalt, electricity, tobacco, flowers, cotton
Continent: Africa

Zimbabwe
Capital: Harare
Population: 11.3 million
Official Language: English
Land Area: 386,670 sq km; 149,293 sq mi
Leading Exports: tobacco, gold, iron alloys, textiles and clothing
Continent: Africa

Asia and the Pacific

Afghanistan
Capital: Kabul
Population: 27.8 million
Official Languages: Pashtu and Dari
Land Area: 647,500 sq km; 250,000 sq mi
Leading Exports: agricultural products, hand-woven carpets, wool, cotton, hides and pelts, precious and semiprecious gems
Continent: Asia

Armenia
Capital: Yerevan
Population: 3.3 million
Official Language: Armenian
Land Area: 29,400 sq km; 10,965 sq mi
Leading Exports: diamonds, scrap metal, machinery and equipment, brandy, copper ore
Continent: Asia

Australia
Capital: Canberra
Population: 19.6 million
Official Language: English
Land Area: 7,617,930 sq km; 2,941,283 sq mi
Leading Exports: coal, gold, meat, wool, alumina, iron ore, wheat, machinery and transport equipment
Continent: Australia

Azerbaijan
Capital: Baku
Population: 7.8 million
Official Language: Azerbaijani
Land Area: 86,100 sq km; 33,243 sq mi
Leading Exports: oil and gas, machinery, cotton, foodstuffs
Continent: Asia

Bahrain
Capital: Manama
Population: 656,397
Official Language: Arabic
Land Area: 665 sq km; 257 sq mi
Leading Exports: petroleum and petroleum products, aluminum, textiles
Continent: Asia

Bangladesh
Capital: Dhaka
Population: 133.4 million
Official Language: Bengali
Land Area: 133,910 sq km; 51,705 sq mi
Leading Exports: garments, jute and jute goods, leather, frozen fish and seafood
Continent: Asia

Bhutan
Capital: Thimphu
Population: 2.1 million
Official Language: Dzongkha
Land Area: 47,000 sq km; 18,147 sq mi
Leading Exports: electricity, cardamom, gypsum, timber, handicrafts, cement, fruit, precious stones, spices
Continent: Asia

Brunei
Capital: Bandar Seri Begawan
Population: 350,898
Official Language: Malay
Land Area: 5,270 sq km; 2,035 sq mi
Leading Exports: crude oil, natural gas, refined products
Continent: Asia

Cambodia
Capital: Phnom Penh
Population: 12.8 million
Official Language: Khmer
Land Area: 176,520 sq km; 68,154 sq mi
Leading Exports: timber, garments, rubber, rice, fish
Continent: Asia

China
Capital: Beijing
Population: 1.29 billion
Official Languages: Mandarin and Chinese
Land Area: 9,326,410 sq km; 3,600,927 sq mi
Leading Exports: machinery and equipment, textiles and clothing, footwear, toys and sports goods, mineral fuels
Continent: Asia

Cyprus
Capital: Nicosia
Population: 767,314
Official Languages: Greek and Turkish
Land Area: 9,240 sq km; 3,568 sq mi
Leading Exports: citrus, potatoes, grapes, wine, cement, clothing and shoes
Location: Mediterranean Sea

East Timor
Capital: Dili
Population: 952,618
Official Languages: Tetum and Portuguese
Land Area: 15,007 sq km; 5,794 sq mi
Leading Exports: coffee, sandalwood, marble
Continent: Asia

Fiji
Capital: Suva
Population: 856,346
Official Language: English
Land Area: 18,270 sq km; 7,054 sq mi
Leading Exports: sugar, garments, gold, timber, fish, molasses, coconut oil
Location: Pacific Ocean

Georgia
Capital: Tbilisi
Population: 5 million
Official Languages: Georgian and Abkhazian
Land Area: 69,700 sq km; 26,911 sq mi
Leading Exports: scrap metal, machinery, chemicals, fuel reexports, citrus fruits, tea, wine, other agricultural products
Continent: Asia

India
Capital: New Delhi
Population: 1.05 billion
Official Languages: Hindi and English
Land Area: 2,973,190 sq km; 1,147,949 sq mi
Leading Exports: textile goods, gems and jewelry, engineering goods, chemicals, leather manufactured goods
Continent: Asia

Indonesia
Capital: Jakarta
Population: 231.3 million
Official Language: Bahasa Indonesia
Land Area: 1,826,440 sq km; 705,188 sq mi
Leading Exports: oil and gas, electrical appliances, plywood, textiles, rubber
Continent: Asia

Iran
Capital: Tehran
Population: 66.6 million
Official Language: Farsi
Land Area: 1,636,000 sq km; 631,660 sq mi
Leading Exports: petroleum, carpets, fruits and nuts, iron and steel, chemicals
Continent: Asia

Iraq
Capital: Baghdad
Population: 24.7 million
Official Language: Arabic
Land Area: 432,162 sq km; 166,858 sq mi
Leading Exports: crude oil
Continent: Asia

Israel
Capital: Jerusalem
Population: 6.0 million
Official Language: Hebrew, Arabic
Land Area: 20,330 sq km; 7,849 sq mi
Leading Exports: machinery and equipment, software, cut diamonds, agricultural products, chemicals, textiles and apparel
Continent: Asia

Japan
Capital: Tokyo
Population: 127 million
Official Language: Japanese
Land Area: 374,744 sq km; 144,689 sq mi
Leading Exports: motor vehicles, semiconductors, office machinery, chemicals
Continent: Asia

Jordan
Capital: Amman
Population: 5.3 million
Official Language: Arabic
Land Area: 91,971 sq km; 35,510 sq mi
Leading Exports: phosphates, fertilizers, potash, agricultural products, manufactured goods, pharmaceuticals
Continent: Asia

Kazakhstan
Capital: Astana
Population: 16.7 million
Official Language: Kazakh
Land Area: 2,669,800 sq km; 1,030,810 sq mi
Leading Exports: oil and oil products, ferrous metals, machinery, chemicals, grain, wool, meat, coal
Continent: Asia

Kiribati
Capital: Bairiki (Tarawa Atoll)
Population: 96,335
Official Language: English
Land Area: 811 sq km; 313 sq mi
Leading Exports: copra, coconuts, seaweed, fish
Location: Pacific Ocean

Korea, North
Capital: Pyongyang
Population: 22.3 million
Official Language: Korean
Land Area: 120,410 sq km; 46,490 sq mi
Leading Exports: minerals, metallurgical products, manufactured goods (including armaments), agricultural and fishery products
Continent: Asia

Korea, South
Capital: Seoul
Population: 48.3 million
Official Language: Korean
Land Area: 98,190 sq km; 37,911 sq mi
Leading Exports: electronic products, machinery and equipment, motor vehicles, steel, ships, textiles, clothing, footwear, fish
Continent: Asia

Kuwait
Capital: Kuwait City
Population: 2.1 million
Official Language: Arabic
Land Area: 17,820 sq km; 6,880 sq mi
Leading Exports: oil and refined products, fertilizers
Continent: Asia

Kyrgyzstan
Capital: Bishkek
Population: 4.8 million
Official Languages: Kyrgyz and Russian
Land Area: 191,300 sq km; 73,861 sq mi
Leading Exports: cotton, wool, meat, tobacco, gold, mercury, uranium, hydropower, machinery, shoes
Continent: Asia

Laos
Capital: Vientiane
Population: 5.8 million
Official Language: Lao
Land Area: 230,800 sq km; 89,112 sq mi
Leading Exports: wood products, garments, electricity, coffee, tin
Continent: Asia

Lebanon

Capital: Beirut
Population: 3.7 million
Official Language: Arabic
Land Area: 10,230 sq km; 3,950 sq mi
Leading Exports: foodstuffs and tobacco, textile, chemicals, precious stones, metal and metal products, electrical equipment and products, jewelry, paper and paper products
Continent: Asia

Malaysia

Capital: Kuala Lumpur and Putrajaya
Population: 22.7 million
Official Language: Bahasa Malaysia
Land Area: 328,550 sq km; 126,853 sq mi
Leading Exports: electronic equipment, petroleum and liquefied natural gas, wood and wood products, palm oil, rubber, textiles, chemicals
Continent: Asia

Maldives

Capital: Malé
Population: 320,165
Official Language: Dhivehi (Maldivian)
Land Area: 300 sq km; 116 sq mi
Leading Exports: fish, clothing
Location: Indian Ocean

Marshall Islands

Capital: Majuro
Population: 73,360
Official Languages: Marshallese and English
Land Area: 181.3 sq km; 70 sq mi
Leading Exports: copra cake, coconut oil, handicrafts
Location: Pacific Ocean

Micronesia, Federated States of

Capital: Palikir (Pohnpei Island)
Population: 135,869
Official Language: English
Land Area: 702 sq km; 271 sq mi
Leading Exports: fish, garments, bananas, black pepper
Location: Pacific Ocean

Mongolia

Capital: Ulaanbaatar
Population: 2.6 million
Official Language: Khalkha Mongolian
Land Area: 1,555,400 sq km; 600,540 sq mi
Leading Exports: copper, livestock, animal products, cashmere, wool, hides, fluorspar, other nonferrous metals
Continent: Asia

Myanmar (Burma)

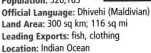

Capital: Rangoon (Yangon)
Population: 42.2 million
Official Language: Burmese (Myanmar)
Land Area: 657,740 sq km; 253,953 sq mi
Leading Exports: apparel, foodstuffs, wood products, precious stones
Continent: Asia

Nauru

Capital: Yaren District
Population: 12,329
Official Language: Nauruan
Land Area: 21 sq km; 8 sq mi
Leading Exports: phosphates
Location: Pacific Ocean

Nepal

Capital: Kathmandu
Population: 25.9 million
Official Language: Nepali
Land Area: 136,800 sq km; 52,818 sq mi
Leading Exports: carpets, clothing, leather goods, jute goods, grain
Continent: Asia

New Zealand

Capital: Wellington
Population: 3.8 million
Official Languages: English and Maori
Land Area: 268,680 sq km; 103,737 sq mi
Leading Exports: dairy products, meat, wood and wood products, fish, machinery
Location: Pacific Ocean

Oman

Capital: Muscat
Population: 2.7 million
Official Language: Arabic
Land Area: 212,460 sq km; 82,030 sq mi
Leading Exports: petroleum, reexports, fish, metals, textiles
Continent: Asia

Pakistan

Capital: Islamabad
Population: 147.7 million
Official Languages: Urdu and English
Land Area: 778,720 sq km; 300,664 sq mi
Leading Exports: textiles (garments, cotton cloth, and yarn), rice, other agricultural products
Continent: Asia

Palau

Capital: Koror
Population: 19,409
Official Languages: English and Palauan
Land Area: 458 sq km; 177 sq mi
Leading Exports: shellfish, tuna, copra, garments
Location: Pacific Ocean

Papua New Guinea

Capital: Port Moresby
Population: 5.2 million
Official Language: English
Land Area: 452,860 sq km; 174,849 sq mi
Leading Exports: oil, gold, copper ore, logs, palm oil, coffee, cocoa, crayfish, prawns
Location: Pacific Ocean

Philippines

Capital: Manila
Population: 84.5 million
Official Languages: Filipino and English
Land Area: 298,170 sq km; 115,123 sq mi
Leading Exports: electronic equipment, machinery and transport equipment, garments, coconut products
Continent: Asia

Qatar

Capital: Doha
Population: 793,341
Official Language: Arabic
Land Area: 11,437 sq km; 4,416 sq mi
Leading Exports: petroleum products, fertilizers, steel
Continent: Asia

Samoa

Capital: Apia
Population: 178,631
Official Languages: Samoan and English
Land Area: 2,934 sq km; 1,133 sq mi
Leading Exports: fish, coconut oil cream, copra, taro, garments, beer
Location: Pacific Ocean

Saudi Arabia

Capital: Riyadh and Jiddah
Population: 23.5 million
Official Language: Arabic
Land Area: 1,960,582 sq km; 756,981 sq mi
Leading Exports: petroleum and petroleum products
Continent: Asia

Singapore

Capital: Singapore
Population: 4.5 million
Official Languages: Malay, English, Mandarin, Chinese, and Tamil
Land Area: 683 sq km; 264 sq mi
Leading Exports: machinery and equipment (including electronics), consumer goods, chemicals, mineral fuels
Continent: Asia

Solomon Islands

Capital: Honiara
Population: 494,786
Official Language: English
Land Area: 27,540 sq km; 10,633 sq mi
Leading Exports: timber, fish, copra, palm oil, cocoa
Location: Pacific Ocean

Sri Lanka

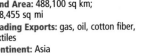

Capital: Colombo
Population: 19.6 million
Official Language: Sinhala, Tamil, and English
Land Area: 64,740 sq km; 24,996 sq mi
Leading Exports: textiles and apparel, tea, diamonds, coconut products, petroleum products
Continent: Asia

Syria

Capital: Damascus
Population: 17.2 million
Official Language: Arabic
Land Area: 184,050 sq km; 71,062 sq mi
Leading Exports: crude oil, textiles, fruits and vegetables, raw cotton
Continent: Asia

Taiwan

Capital: Taipei
Population: 22.5 million
Official Language: Mandarin Chinese
Land Area: 32,260 sq km; 12,456 sq mi
Leading Exports: machinery and electrical equipment, metals, textiles, plastics, chemicals
Continent: Asia

Tajikistan

Capital: Dushanbe
Population: 6.7 million
Official Language: Tajik
Land Area: 142,700 sq km; 55,096 sq mi
Leading Exports: aluminum, electricity, cotton, fruits, vegetables, oil, textiles
Continent: Asia

Thailand

Capital: Bangkok
Population: 62.5 million
Official Language: Thai
Land Area: 511,770 sq km; 197,564 sq mi
Leading Exports: computers, transistors, seafood, clothing, rice
Continent: Asia

Tonga

Capital: Nuku'alofa
Population: 106,137
Official Languages: Tongan and English
Land Area: 718 sq km; 277 sq mi
Leading Exports: squash, fish, vanilla beans, root crops
Location: Pacific Ocean

Turkey

Capital: Ankara
Population: 67.3 million
Official Language: Turkish
Land Area: 770,760 sq km; 297,590 sq mi
Leading Exports: apparel, foodstuffs, textiles, metal manufactured goods, transport equipment
Continent: Asia

Turkmenistan

Capital: Ashgabat
Population: 4.7 million
Official Language: Turkmen
Land Area: 488,100 sq km; 188,455 sq mi
Leading Exports: gas, oil, cotton fiber, textiles
Continent: Asia

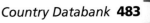

Asia and the Pacific (continued)

Tuvalu

Capital: Fongafale
Population: 10,800
Official Language: English
Land Area: 26 sq km; 10 sq mi
Leading Exports: copra, fish
Location: Pacific Ocean

United Arab Emirates
Capital: Abu Dhabi
Population: 2.4 million
Official Language: Arabic
Land Area: 82,880 sq km; 32,000 sq mi
Leading Exports: crude oil, natural gas, reexports, dried fish, dates
Continent: Asia

Uzbekistan
Capital: Tashkent
Population: 25.5 million
Official Language: Uzbek
Land Area: 425,400 sq km; 164,247 sq mi
Leading Exports: cotton, gold, energy products, mineral fertilizers, ferrous metals, textiles, food products, automobiles
Continent: Asia

Vanuatu
Capital: Port-Vila
Population: 196,178
Official Languages: English, French, and Bislama
Land Area: 12,200 sq km; 4,710 sq mi
Leading Exports: copra, kava, beef, cocoa, timber, coffee
Location: Pacific Ocean

Vietnam
Capital: Hanoi
Population: 81.1 million
Official Language: Vietnamese
Land Area: 325,320 sq km; 125,621 sq mi
Leading Exports: crude oil, marine products, rice, coffee, rubber, tea, garments, shoes
Continent: Asia

Yemen
Capital: Sanaa
Population: 18.7 million
Official Language: Arabic
Land Area: 527,970 sq km; 203,849 sq mi
Leading Exports: crude oil, coffee, dried and salted fish
Continent: Asia

Europe and Russia

Albania
Capital: Tiranë
Population: 3.5 million
Official Language: Albanian
Land Area: 27,398 sq km; 10,578 sq mi
Leading Exports: textiles and footwear, asphalt, metals and metallic ores, crude oil, vegetables, fruits, tobacco
Continent: Europe

Andorra
Capital: Andorra la Vella
Population: 68,403
Official Language: Catalan
Land Area: 468 sq km; 181 sq mi
Leading Exports: tobacco products, furniture
Continent: Europe

Austria
Capital: Vienna
Population: 8.2 million
Official Language: German
Land Area: 82,738 sq km; 31,945 sq mi
Leading Exports: machinery and equipment, motor vehicles and parts, paper and paperboard, metal goods, chemicals, iron and steel, textiles, foodstuffs
Continent: Europe

Belarus

Capital: Minsk
Population: 10.3 million
Official Languages: Belarussian and Russian
Land Area: 207,600 sq km; 80,154 sq mi
Leading Exports: machinery and equipment, mineral products, chemicals, textiles, food stuffs, metals
Continent: Europe

Belgium
Capital: Brussels
Population: 10.3 million
Official Languages: Dutch and French
Land Area: 30,230 sq km; 11,172 sq mi
Leading Exports: machinery and equipment, chemicals, metals and metal products
Continent: Europe

Bosnia and Herzegovina
Capital: Sarajevo
Population: 4.0 million
Official Language: Serbo-Croat
Land Area: 51,129 sq km; 19,741 sq mi
Leading Exports: miscellaneous manufactured goods, crude materials
Continent: Europe

Bulgaria
Capital: Sofía
Population: 7.6 million
Official Language: Bulgarian
Land Area: 110,550 sq km; 42,683 sq mi
Leading Exports: clothing, footwear, iron and steel, machinery and equipment, fuels
Continent: Europe

Croatia
Capital: Zagreb
Population: 4.4 million
Official Language: Croatian
Land Area: 56,414 km; 21,781 sq mi
Leading Exports: transport equipment, textiles, chemicals, foodstuffs, fuels
Continent: Europe

Czech Republic
Capital: Prague
Population: 10.3 million
Official Language: Czech
Land Area: 78,276 sq km; 29,836 sq mi
Leading Exports: machinery and transport equipment, intermediate manufactured goods, chemicals, raw materials and fuel
Continent: Europe

Denmark
Capital: Copenhagen
Population: 5.4 million
Official Language: Danish
Land Area: 42,394 sq km; 16,368 sq mi
Leading Exports: machinery and instruments, meat and meat products, dairy products, fish, chemicals, furniture, ships, windmills
Continent: Europe

Estonia
Capital: Tallinn
Population: 1.4 million
Official Language: Estonian
Land Area: 43,211 sq km; 16,684 sq mi
Leading Exports: machinery and equipment, wood products, textiles, food products, metals, chemical products
Continent: Europe

Finland
Capital: Helsinki
Population: 5.2 million
Official Languages: Finnish and Swedish
Land Area: 305,470 sq km; 117,942 sq mi
Leading Exports: machinery and equipment, chemicals, metals, timber, paper, pulp
Continent: Europe

France
Capital: Paris
Population: 59.8 million
Official Language: French
Land Area: 545,630 sq km; 310,668 sq mi
Leading Exports: machinery and transportation equipment, aircraft, plastics, chemicals, pharmaceutical products, iron and steel, beverages
Continent: Europe

Germany
Capital: Berlin
Population: 83 million
Official Language: German
Land Area: 349,223 sq km; 134,835 sq mi
Leading Exports: machinery, vehicles, chemicals, metals and manufactured goods, foodstuffs, textiles
Continent: Europe

Greece
Capital: Athens
Population: 10.6 million
Official Language: Greek
Land Area: 130,800 sq km; 50,502 sq mi
Leading Exports: food and beverages, manufactured goods, petroleum products, chemicals, textiles
Continent: Europe

Holy See (Vatican City)

Capital: Vatican City
Population: 900
Official Languages: Latin and Italian
Land Area: 0.44 sq km; 0.17 sq mi
Leading Exports: no information available
Continent: Europe

Hungary
Capital: Budapest
Population: 10.1 million
Official Language: Hungarian
Land Area: 92,340 sq km; 35,652 sq mi
Leading Exports: machinery and equipment, other manufactured goods, food products, raw materials, fuels and electricity
Continent: Europe

Iceland
Capital: Reykjavík
Population: 279,384
Official Language: Icelandic
Land Area: 100,250 sq km; 38,707 sq mi
Leading Exports: fish and fish products, animal products, aluminum, diatomite, ferrosilicon
Location: Atlantic Ocean

Ireland
Capital: Dublin
Population: 3.9 million
Official Languages: Irish Gaelic and English
Land Area: 68,890 sq km; 26,598 sq mi
Leading Exports: machinery and equipment, computers, chemicals, pharmaceuticals, live animals, animal products
Continent: Europe

Italy
Capital: Rome
Population: 57.7 million
Official Language: Italian
Land Area: 294,020 sq km; 113,521 sq mi
Leading Exports: fruits, vegetables, grapes, potatoes, sugar beets, soybeans, grain, olives, beef, diary products, fish
Continent: Europe

Latvia
Capital: Riga
Population: 2.4 million
Official Language: Latvian
Land Area: 63,589 sq km; 24,552 sq mi
Leading Exports: wood and wood products, machinery and equipment, metals, textiles, foodstuffs
Continent: Europe

Liechtenstein
Capital: Vaduz
Population: 32,842
Official Language: German
Land Area: 160 sq km; 62 sq mi
Leading Exports: small specialty machinery, dental products, stamps, hardware, pottery
Continent: Europe

Lithuania
Capital: Vilnius
Population: 3.6 million
Official Language: Lithuanian
Land Area: 65,200 sq km; 25,174 sq mi
Leading Exports: mineral products, textiles and clothing, machinery and equipment, chemicals, wood and wood products, foodstuffs
Continent: Europe

Luxembourg
Capital: Luxembourg
Population: 448,569
Official Languages: Luxembourgish, French, and German
Land Area: 2,586 sq km; 998 sq mi
Leading Exports: machinery and equipment, steel products, chemicals, rubber products, glass
Continent: Europe

Macedonia, The Former Yugoslav Republic of
Capital: Skopje
Population: 2.1 million
Official Languages: Macedonian and Albanian
Land Area: 24,856 sq km; 9,597 sq mi
Leading Exports: food, beverages, tobacco, miscellaneous manufactured goods, iron and steel
Continent: Europe

Malta
Capital: Valletta
Population: 397,499
Official Languages: Maltese and English
Land Area: 316 sq km; 122 sq mi
Leading Exports: machinery and transport equipment, manufactured goods
Location: Mediterranean Sea

Moldova
Capital: Chişinău
Population: 4.4 million
Official Language: Moldovan
Land Area: 33,371 sq km; 12,885 sq mi
Leading Exports: foodstuffs, textiles and footwear, machinery
Continent: Europe

Monaco
Capital: Monaco
Population: 31,987
Official Language: French
Land Area: 1.95 sq km; 0.75 sq mi
Leading Exports: no information available
Continent: Europe

Montenegro
Capital: Podgorica
Population: 620,145
Official Language: Serbian
Land Area: 13,812 sq km; 5,333 sq mi
Leading Exports: food products
Continent: Europe

Netherlands
Capital: Amsterdam and The Hague
Population: 16.1 million
Official Language: Dutch
Land Area: 33,883 sq km; 13,082 sq mi
Leading Exports: machinery and equipment, chemicals, fuels, foodstuffs
Continent: Europe

Norway
Capital: Oslo
Population: 4.5 million
Official Language: Norwegian
Land Area: 307,860 sq km; 118,865 sq mi
Leading Exports: petroleum and petroleum products, machinery and equipment, metals, chemicals, ships, fish
Continent: Europe

Poland
Capital: Warsaw
Population: 38.6 million
Official Language: Polish
Land Area: 304,465 sq km; 117,554 sq mi
Leading Exports: machinery and transport equipment, intermediate manufactured goods, miscellaneous manufactured goods, food and live animals
Continent: Europe

Portugal
Capital: Lisbon
Population: 10.1 million
Official Language: Portuguese
Land Area: 91,951 sq km; 35,502 sq mi
Leading Exports: clothing and footwear, machinery, chemicals, cork and paper products, hides
Continent: Europe

Romania
Capital: Bucharest
Population: 22.3 million
Official Language: Romanian
Land Area: 230,340 sq km; 88,934 sq mi
Leading Exports: textiles and footwear, metals and metal products, machinery and equipment, minerals and fuels
Continent: Europe

Russia
Capital: Moscow
Population: 145 million
Official Language: Russian
Land Area: 16,995,800 sq km; 6,592,100 sq mi
Leading Exports: petroleum and petroleum products, natural gas, wood and wood products, metals, chemicals, and a wide variety of civilian and military manufactured goods
Continents: Europe and Asia

San Marino
Capital: San Marino
Population: 27,730
Official Language: Italian
Land Area: 61 sq km; 24 sq mi
Leading Exports: building stone, lime, wood, chestnuts, wheat, wine, baked goods, hides, ceramics
Continent: Europe

Serbia
Capital: Belgrade
Population: 9.4 million
Official Language: Serbian
Land Area: 88,361 sq km; 34,116 sq mi
Leading Exports: food and live animals, manufactured goods, raw materials
Continent: Europe

Slovakia
Capital: Bratislava
Population: 5.4 million
Official Language: Slovak
Land Area: 48,800 sq km; 18,842 sq mi
Leading Exports: machinery and transport equipment, intermediate manufactured goods, miscellaneous manufactured goods, chemicals
Continent: Europe

Slovenia
Capital: Ljubljana
Population: 1.9 million
Official Language: Slovene
Land Area: 20,151 sq km; 7,780 sq mi
Leading Exports: manufactured goods, machinery and transport equipment, chemicals, food
Continent: Europe

Spain
Capital: Madrid
Population: 40.1 million
Official Languages: Spanish, Galician, Basque, and Catalan
Land Area: 499,542 sq km; 192,873 sq mi
Leading Exports: machinery, motor vehicles, foodstuffs, other consumer goods
Continent: Europe

Europe and Russia (continued)

Sweden
Capital: Stockholm
Population: 8.9 million
Official Language: Swedish
Land Area: 410,934 sq km; 158,662 sq mi
Leading Exports: machinery, motor vehicles, paper products, pulp and wood, iron and steel products, chemicals
Continent: Europe

Switzerland
Capital: Bern
Population: 7.3 million
Official Languages: German, French, and Italian
Land Area: 39,770 sq km; 15,355 sq mi
Leading Exports: machinery, chemicals, metals, watches, agricultural products
Continent: Europe

Ukraine
Capital: Kiev
Population: 48.4 million
Official Language: Ukrainian
Land Area: 603,700 sq km; 233,090 sq mi
Leading Exports: ferrous and nonferrous metals, fuel and petroleum products, machinery and transport equipment, food products
Continent: Europe

United Kingdom
Capital: London
Population: 59.8 million
Official Languages: English and Welsh
Land Area: 241,590 sq km; 93,278 sq mi
Leading Exports: manufactured goods, fuels, chemicals, food, beverages, tobacco
Continent: Europe

Latin America

Antigua and Barbuda
Capital: Saint John's
Population: 67,448
Official Language: English
Land Area: 442 sq km; 171 sq mi
Leading Exports: petroleum products, manufactured goods, machinery and transport equipment, food and live animals
Location: Caribbean Sea

Argentina
Capital: Buenos Aires
Population: 37.8 million
Official Language: Spanish
Land Area: 2,736,690 sq km; 1,056,636 sq mi
Leading Exports: edible oils, fuels and energy, cereals, feed, motor vehicles
Continent: South America

Bahamas
Capital: Nassau
Population: 300,529
Official Language: English
Land Area: 10,070 sq km; 3,888 sq mi
Leading Exports: fish and crawfish, rum, salt, chemicals, fruit and vegetables
Location: Caribbean Sea

Barbados
Capital: Bridgetown
Population: 276,607
Official Language: English
Land Area: 431 sq km; 166 sq mi
Leading Exports: sugar and molasses, rum, other foods and beverages, chemicals, electrical components, clothing
Location: Caribbean Sea

Belize
Capital: Belmopan
Population: 262,999
Official Language: English
Land Area: 22,806 sq km; 8,805 sq mi
Leading Exports: sugar, bananas, citrus, clothing, fish products, molasses, wood
Continent: North America

Bolivia
Capital: La Paz and Sucre
Population: 8.5 million
Official Language: Spanish, Quechua, and Aymara
Land Area: 1,084,390 sq km; 418,683 sq mi
Leading Exports: soybeans, natural gas, zinc, gold, wood
Continent: South America

Brazil
Capital: Brasília
Population: 176 million
Official Language: Portuguese
Land Area: 8,456,510 sq km; 3,265,059 sq mi
Leading Exports: manufactured goods, iron ore, soybeans, footwear, coffee, autos
Continent: South America

Chile
Capital: Santiago
Population: 15.5 million
Official Language: Spanish
Land Area: 748,800 sq km; 289,112 sq mi
Leading Exports: copper, fish, fruits, paper and pulp, chemicals
Continent: South America

Colombia
Capital: Bogotá
Population: 41 million
Official Language: Spanish
Land Area: 1,038,700 sq km; 401,042 sq mi
Leading Exports: petroleum, coffee, coal, apparel, bananas, cut flowers
Continent: South America

Costa Rica
Capital: San José
Population: 3.8 million
Official Language: Spanish
Land Area: 51,660 sq km; 19,560 sq mi
Leading Exports: coffee, bananas, sugar, pineapples, textiles, electronic components, medical equipment
Continent: North America

Cuba
Capital: Havana
Population: 11.2 million
Official Language: Spanish
Land Area: 110,860 sq km; 42,803 sq mi
Leading Exports: sugar, nickel, tobacco, fish, medical products, citrus, coffee
Location: Caribbean Sea

Dominica
Capital: Roseau
Population: 73,000
Official Language: English
Land Area: 754 sq km; 291 sq mi
Leading Exports: bananas, soap, bay oil, vegetables, grapefruit, oranges
Location: Caribbean Sea

Dominican Republic
Capital: Santo Domingo
Population: 8.7 million
Official Language: Spanish
Land Area: 48,380 sq km; 18,679 sq mi
Leading Exports: ferronickel, sugar, gold, silver, coffee, cocoa, tobacco, meats, consumer goods
Location: Caribbean Sea

Ecuador
Capital: Quito
Population: 13.5 million
Official Language: Spanish
Land Area: 276,840 sq km; 106,888 sq mi
Leading Exports: petroleum, bananas, shrimp, coffee, cocoa, cut flowers, fish
Continent: South America

El Salvador
Capital: San Salvador
Population: 6.4 million
Official Language: Spanish
Land Area: 20,720 sq km; 8,000 sq mi
Leading Exports: offshore assembly exports, coffee, sugar, shrimp, textiles, chemicals, electricity
Continent: North America

Grenada
Capital: Saint George's
Population: 89,211
Official Language: English
Land Area: 344 sq km; 133 sq mi
Leading Exports: bananas, cocoa, nutmeg, fruit and vegetables, clothing, mace
Location: Caribbean Sea

Guatemala
Capital: Guatemala City
Population: 13.3 million
Official Language: Spanish
Land Area: 108,430 sq km; 41,865 sq mi
Leading Exports: coffee, sugar, bananas, fruits and vegetables, cardamom, meat, apparel, petroleum, electricity
Continent: North America

Guyana
Capital: Georgetown
Population: 698,209
Official Language: English
Land Area: 196,850 sq km; 76,004 sq mi
Leading Exports: sugar, gold, bauxite/alumina, rice, shrimp, molasses, rum, timber
Continent: South America

Haiti
Capital: Port-au-Prince
Population: 7.1 million
Official Language: French and French Creole
Land Area: 27,560 sq km; 10,641 sq mi
Leading Exports: manufactured goods, coffee, oils, cocoa
Location: Caribbean Sea

Honduras
Capital: Tegucigalpa
Population: 6.6 million
Official Language: Spanish
Land Area: 111,890 sq km; 43,201 sq mi
Leading Exports: coffee, bananas, shrimp, lobster, meat, zinc, lumber
Continent: North America

Jamaica
Capital: Kingston
Population: 2.7 million
Official Language: English
Land Area: 10,831 sq km; 4,182 sq mi
Leading Exports: alumina, bauxite, sugar, bananas, rum
Location: Caribbean Sea

Mexico
Capital: Mexico City
Population: 103.4 million
Official Language: Spanish
Land Area: 1,923,040 sq km; 742,486 sq mi
Leading Exports: manufactured goods, oil and oil products, silver, fruits, vegetables, coffee, cotton
Continent: North America

Nicaragua
Capital: Managua
Population: 5 million
Official Language: Spanish
Land Area: 120,254 sq km; 46,430 sq mi
Leading Exports: coffee, shrimp and lobster, cotton, tobacco, beef, sugar, bananas, gold
Continent: North America

Panama
Capital: Panama City
Population: 2.9 million
Official Language: Spanish
Land Area: 75,990 sq km; 29,340 sq mi
Leading Exports: bananas, shrimp, sugar, coffee, clothing
Continent: North America

Paraguay
Capital: Asunción
Population: 5.9 million
Official Language: Spanish
Land Area: 397,300 sq km; 153,398 sq mi
Leading Exports: electricity, soybeans, feed, cotton, meat, edible oils
Continent: South America

Peru
Capital: Lima
Population: 28 million
Official Languages: Spanish and Quechua
Land Area: 1,280,000 sq km; 494,208 sq mi
Leading Exports: fish and fish products, gold, copper, zinc, crude petroleum and byproducts, lead, coffee, sugar, cotton
Continent: South America

Saint Kitts and Nevis
Capital: Basseterre
Population: 38,736
Official Language: English
Land Area: 261 sq km; 101 sq mi
Leading Exports: machinery, food, electronics, beverages, tobacco
Location: Caribbean Sea

Saint Lucia
Capital: Castries
Population: 160,145
Official Language: English
Land Area: 606 sq km; 234 sq mi
Leading Exports: bananas, clothing, cocoa, vegetables, fruits, coconut oil
Location: Caribbean Sea

Saint Vincent and the Grenadines
Capital: Kingstown
Population: 116,394
Official Language: English
Land Area: 389 sq km; 150 sq mi
Leading Exports: bananas, eddoes and dasheen, arrowroot starch, tennis racquets
Location: Caribbean Sea

Suriname
Capital: Paramaribo
Population: 436,494
Official Language: Dutch
Land Area: 161,470 sq km; 62,344 sq mi
Leading Exports: alumina, crude oil, lumber, shrimp and fish, rice, bananas
Continent: South America

Trinidad and Tobago
Capital: Port-of-Spain
Population: 1.2 million
Official Language: English
Land Area: 5,128 sq km; 1,980 sq mi
Leading Exports: petroleum and petroleum products, chemicals, steel products, fertilizer, sugar, cocoa, coffee, citrus, flowers
Location: Caribbean Sea

Uruguay
Capital: Montevideo
Population: 3.4 million
Official Language: Spanish
Land Area: 173,620 sq km; 67,100 sq mi
Leading Exports: meat, rice, leather products, wool, vehicles, dairy products
Continent: South America

Venezuela
Capital: Caracas
Population: 24.3 million
Official Language: Spanish
Land Area: 882,050 sq km; 340,560 sq mi
Leading Exports: petroleum, bauxite and aluminum, steel, chemicals, agricultural products, basic manufactured goods
Continent: South America

United States and Canada

Canada
Capital: Ottawa
Population: 31.9 million
Official Languages: English and French
Land Area: 9,220,970 sq km; 3,560,217 sq mi
Leading Exports: motor vehicles and parts, industrial machinery, aircraft, telecommunications equipment, chemicals, plastics, fertilizers, wood pulp, timber, crude petroleum, natural gas, electricity, aluminum
Continent: North America

United States
Capital: Washington, D.C.
Population: 281.4 million
Official Language: English
Land Area: 9,158,960 sq km; 3,536,274 sq mi
Leading Exports: capital goods, automobiles, industrial supplies and raw materials, consumer goods, agricultural products
Continent: North America

SOURCE: CIA World Factbook Online, 2002 and 2006

Glossary of Geographic Terms

basin
an area that is lower than surrounding land areas; some basins are filled with water

bay
a body of water that is partly surrounded by land and that is connected to a larger body of water

butte
a small, high, flat-topped landform with cliff-like sides

▲ **butte**

canyon
a deep, narrow valley with steep sides; often with a stream flowing through it

cataract
a large waterfall or steep rapids

◀ **cataract**

delta
a plain at the mouth of a river, often triangular in shape, formed where sediment is deposited by flowing water

flood plain
a broad plain on either side of a river, formed where sediment settles during floods

glacier
a huge, slow-moving mass of snow and ice

hill
an area that rises above surrounding land and has a rounded top; lower and usually less steep than a mountain

island
an area of land completely surrounded by water

isthmus
a narrow strip of land that connects two larger areas of land

mesa
a high, flat-topped landform with cliff-like sides; larger than a butte

mountain
a landform that rises steeply at least 2,000 feet (610 meters) above surrounding land; usually wide at the bottom and rising to a narrow peak or ridge

▶ **glacier**

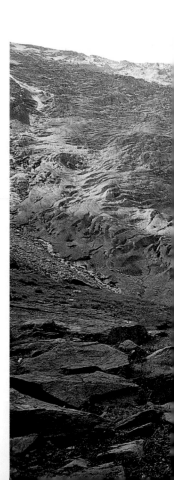

◀ **delta**

mountain pass

a gap between mountains

peninsula

an area of land almost completely surrounded by water but connected to the mainland

plain

a large area of flat or gently rolling land

plateau

a large, flat area that rises above the surrounding land; at least one side has a steep slope

river mouth

the point where a river enters a lake or sea

strait

a narrow stretch of water that connects two larger bodies of water

tributary

a river or stream that flows into a larger river

valley

a low stretch of land between mountains or hills; land that is drained by a river

volcano

an opening in Earth's surface through which molten rock, ashes, and gases escape from the interior

▶ **volcano**

Gazetteer

A

Abuja (9°12′ N, 7°11′ E) the capital of Nigeria, p. 140

Addis Ababa (9°2′ N, 38°42′ E) the capital of Ethiopia, p. 170

Aksum an ancient city in northern Ethiopia that was a powerful kingdom and trade center from about A.D. 200 to A.D. 600, p. 43

Algeria (28° N, 3° E) a country in North Africa, officially the Democratic and Popular Republic of Algeria, p. 118

Algiers (36°47′ N, 3°3′ E) the capital of Algeria, p. 119

Alice Springs (23°42′ S, 133°53′ E) a town in Northern Territory, Australia, p. 457

Almaty (43°15′ N, 76°57′ E) the largest city of Kazakhstan, a country in Central Asia, p. 429

Angkor Wat (13°26′ N, 103°52′ E) an archaeological site in present-day Angkor, in northwest Cambodia; the world's largest religious temple complex, p. 338

Aral Sea (45° N, 60° E), an inland saltwater sea in Kazakhstan and Uzbekistan, p. 262

Auckland (36°52′ S, 174°46′ E) the largest city in New Zealand, located on North Island, p. 280

B

Bangladesh (24° N, 90° E) a coastal country in South Asia, officially the People's Republic of Bangladesh, p. 390

Benin an ancient African kingdom in the forest region of West Africa, p. 49

C

Cairo (30°3′ N, 31°15′ E) the capital and most populous city of Egypt, p. 110

Canterbury Plain (44° S, 172° E) the lowland area of east-central South Island, New Zealand, p. 281

Cape of Good Hope (34°18′ S, 18°26′ E) the cape at the southern end of the Cape Peninsula in South Africa, p. 52

Cape Town (33°48′ S, 18°28′ E) one of the capitals and largest cities in South Africa, p. 98

Carthage an ancient city-state in present-day Tunisia that the Phoenicians established and that controlled Mediterranean trade from the late 500s B.C. through the 200s B.C., p. 46

Central Africa countries in the central region of Africa, p. 11

Central Asia a region in Asia including Kazakhstan, Kyrgystan, Tajikistan, Turkmenistan, Uzbekistan, and others, p. 260

Chang (32° N, 121° E) the longest river in Asia, flowing through China to the East China Sea, p. 227

Congo, Democratic Republic of the (4° S, 25° E) a country in Central Africa; formerly called Zaire, p. 200

Congo River a river in Central Africa that flows into the Atlantic Ocean, p. 14

D

Dar es Salaam (6°48′ S, 39°17′ E) one of two capitals of Tanzania, p. 96

E

East Africa countries in the eastern region of Africa, p. 11

East Asia a region of Asia including China, Japan, Mongolia, North Korea, South Korea, and Taiwan, p. 225

Eastern Ghats (14° N, 79° E) a mountain range forming the eastern edge of the Deccan Plateau in India, p. 248

Egypt (27° N, 30° E) a country in North Africa, officially the Arab Republic of Egypt, p. 110

Ethiopia (9° N, 39° E) a country in East Africa, p. 166

Euphrates River (31° N, 46° E) a river that flows south from Turkey through Syria and Iraq; the ancient civilizations of Babylon and Ur were situated near its banks, p. 253

G

Ganges River (23° N, 90° E) a river in India and Bangladesh flowing from the Himalaya Mountains to the Bay of Bengal; considered by Hindus to be the most holy river in India, p. 248

Ghana an early African empire located in parts of present-day Mauritania and Mali, p. 47

Ghana (8° N, 1° W) a country in West Africa, officially the Republic of Ghana, p. 142

Great Dividing Range (25° S, 147° E) a series of plateaus and mountain ranges in eastern Australia, p. 279

Great Rift Valley the major branch of the East African Rift System, p. 12

Great Wall of China (41° N, 117° E) a fortification wall which, with all its extensions, stretched 4,000 miles (6,400 km) through China; under construction from about 600 B.C. to A.D. 1600, p. 295

Great Zimbabwe an ancient city-state in southeastern Zimbabwe that was a powerful trade center from about A.D. 1100 to 1500, p. 45

H

Himalayas (28° N, 84° E) the Central Asian mountain range extending along the India-Tibet border, through Pakistan, Nepal, and Bhutan, and containing the world's highest peaks, p. 227

Hindu Kush (36° N, 72° E) a mountain range in Central Asia, p. 261

Ho Chi Minh City (10°45' N, 106°40' E) the largest city in Vietnam, named for a former President of North Vietnam; formerly Saigon, p. 450

Huang (38° N, 118° E) the second-longest river in China; it flows across northern China to the Yellow Sea; also known as the Yellow River, p. 227

I

Indus River (24° N, 68° E) a river rising in Tibet and flowing through India and Pakistan into the Arabian Sea, p. 248

Iraq (33° N, 44° E) a country in Southwest Asia, officially the Republic of Iraq, p. 252

J

Java (7° S, 110° E) the fourth-largest island in the Republic of Indonesia, an archipelago in the Indian and Pacific oceans, p. 271

K

Kalahari Desert a desert in Southern Africa, p. 11

Kashmir (34° N, 76° E) a disputed territory in northwest India, parts of which have been claimed by India, Pakistan, and China since 1947, p. 317

Kazakhstan (48° N, 68° E) the largest country in Central Asia, officially the Republic of Kazakhstan, p. 260

Kenya (1° N, 38° E) a country in East Africa, officially the Republic of Kenya, p. 178

Kilwa an Islamic city-state, located on an island off the coast of present-day Tanzania, that was powerful during the A.D. 1300s, p. 45

Kuwait (29° N, 48° E) a country in Southwest Asia, officially the Republic of Kuwait, p. 393

L

Lagos (6°27' N, 3°24' E) a city and main port of Nigeria, p. 140

Lalibela (12°2' N, 39°02' E) a town in Ethiopia that is famous for its stone churches carved in the 1100s, p. 168

M

Mali an ancient African empire located in present-day Mali, p. 48

Mali (17° N, 4° E) a country in West Africa, officially the Republic of Mali, p. 150

Mecca (21°27' N, 39°49' E) a city in western Saudi Arabia; birthplace of the prophet Muhammad and most holy city for Islamic people, p. 416

Mediterranean Sea (35° N, 20° E) the large sea that separates Europe and Africa, p. 253

Melanesia (13° S, 164° E) the most populous of the three groups of Pacific islands; includes Fiji, Papua New Guinea, and others, p. 284

Mesopotamia a historic region in western Asia between the Tigris and Euphrates rivers; one of the cradles of civilization, p. 253

Micronesia (11° N, 159° E) one of the three groups of Pacific islands; includes Guam, the Marshall Islands, and others, p. 284

Middle Kingdom the name given to China by its Chinese leaders, p. 295

Mount Everest (27°59' N, 86°56' E) the world's highest mountain peak, located in the Himalaya range in South Central Asia, p. 227

Mount Fuji (35°22' N, 138°44' E) the highest mountain in Japan; a dormant volcano and sacred symbol of Japan, p. 226

Mount Kenya (0°9' S, 37°19' E) a volcanic mountain in central Kenya, p. 179

Mount Kilimanjaro (3°04' S, 37°22' E) the tallest mountain in Africa, located in Tanzania, p. 11

N

Nairobi (1°17' S, 36°49' E) the capital of Kenya, p. 181

Namib Desert a desert extending along the Atlantic Coast of Southern Africa, p. 11

Negev Desert (30° N, 35° E) a triangular, arid region in southwest Israel, touching the Gulf of Aqaba, p. 411

Niger River a river in West Africa that flows from Guinea into the Gulf of Guinea, p. 15

Nigeria (10° N, 8° E) a country in West Africa, officially the Federal Republic of Nigeria, p. 136

Nile River the longest river in the world, flowing through northeastern Africa into the Mediterranean Sea, p. 13

North Africa countries in the northern region of Africa, p. 11

North China Plain a large, fertile plain in northeastern China, p. 227

North Island (39° S, 176° E) the smaller and more northern of the two islands composing New Zealand, p. 280

Nubia an ancient region in North Africa, p. 39

P

Palestine (32° N, 35° E) a historical region at the east end of the Mediterranean Sea, now divided between Israel and Jordan, p. 322

Pamir (38° N, 73° E) a mountain range in Central Asia, p. 261

Papua New Guinea (6° S, 150° E) an island country in the southwest Pacific; the eastern half of New Guinea, officially the Independent State of Papua New Guinea, p. 284

Philippines (13° N, 122° E) an island country in Southeast Asia, officially the Republic of the Philippines, p. 270

Polynesia (4° S, 156° W) largest of the three groups of Pacific islands, includes New Zealand, Hawaii, Easter, and Tahiti islands, p. 284

R

Riyadh (24°38' N, 46°43' E) the capital of Saudi Arabia, p. 417

Rub' al-Khali (20° N, 51° E) the largest all-sand desert in the world, located on the Arabian peninsula; the "Empty Quarter," p. 251

S

Sahara the largest tropical desert in the world, covering almost all of North Africa, p. 11

Sahel the region in West and Central Africa that forms an intermediate climate zone between the dry Sahara to the north and the humid savannas to the south, p. 21

Samarkand (39°40' N, 67°15' E) a city in Uzbekistan, p. 329

Seoul (37°33' N, 125°58' E) the capital of South Korea, p. 229

Silk Road a 4,000-mile-long ancient trade route linking China to the Mediterranean area in the west, p. 301

Songhai an ancient African empire located in present-day Mali, Niger, and Nigeria, p. 48

South Africa (30° S, 26° E) a country in Southern Africa, officially the Republic of South Africa, p. 208

South Asia a region of Asia that includes Afghanistan, Bangladesh, Bhutan, India, Maldives, Nepal, Pakistan, and Sri Lanka, p. 247

South Island (43° S, 171° E) the larger and more southern of the two islands composing New Zealand, p. 281

Southeast Asia a region of Asia including Brunei, Cambodia, Indonesia, Laos, Malaysia, Myanmar (Burma), Philippines, Singapore, Thailand, Timor, and Vietnam, p. 271

Southern Africa countries in the southern region of Africa, p. 11

Southwest Asia a region of Asia including Iran, Iraq, Israel, Jordan, Kuwait, Lebanon, Saudi Arabia, Syria, Turkey, and others, p. 252

Sydney (33°52' S, 151°13' E) the capital of New South Wales on the southeastern coast of Australia, and the largest city in Australia, p. 454

T

Taiwan (23° N, 121° E) a large island country off the southeast coast of mainland China, formerly Formosa; since 1949, the Nationalist Republic of China, p. 363

Tanzania (6° S, 35° E) a country in East Africa, officially the United Republic of Tanzania, p. 171

Thailand (15° N, 100° E) a country in Southeast Asia, officially the Kingdom of Thailand, p. 443

Tigris River (31° N, 47° E) a river that flows through Turkey, Iraq, and Iran to the Persian Gulf; the ancient civilizations of Nineveh and Ur were situated near its banks, p. 253

Tombouctou (16°46′ N, 3°1′ E) a city in Mali near the Niger River; in the past an important center of Islamic education and a stop along trans-Saharan trade routes (also spelled *Timbuktu*), p. 150

V

Vietnam (16° N, 108° E) a country in Southeast Asia, officially the Socialist Republic of Vietnam, p. 445

W

West Africa countries in the western region of Africa, p. 11

Western Ghats (14° N, 75° E) a mountain range forming the western edge of the Deccan Plateau in India, p. 248

Z

Zambezi River a river in Central and Southern Africa that flows into the Indian Ocean, p. 13

Glossary

Aborigine (ab uh RIJ uh nee) *n.* a member of the earliest people of Australia, who probably came from Asia, p. 347

alluvial (uh LOO vee ul) *adj.* made of soil deposited by rivers, p. 248

apartheid (uh PAHR tayt) *n.* the legal system of South Africa in which the rights of nonwhites were greatly restricted, p. 209

archipelago (ahr kuh PEL uh goh) *n.* a group of islands, p. 228

artesian well (ahr TEE zhun wel) *n.* a well from which water flows under natural pressure without pumping, p. 457

atoll (A tawl) *n.* a small coral island in the shape of a ring, p. 285

authoritarian government (uh thawr uh TEHR ee un GUV urn munt) *n.* a nondemocratic form of government in which a single leader or a small group of leaders has all the power, p. 203

B

bazaar (buh ZAHR) *n.* a traditional open-air market with shops or rows of stalls, p. 113

birthrate (BURTH rayt) *n.* the number of live births each year per 1,000 people, p. 374

boycott (BOY kaht) *n.* a refusal to buy or use goods and services to show disapproval or bring about change, p. 62, p. 317

C

Cairo (KY roh) *n.* the capital and the most populous city of Egypt, p. 110

Cape of Good Hope (kayp uv good hohp) *n.* a former province of the Republic of South Africa; the point of land at the southern end of the Cape Peninsula, South Africa, p. 52

casbah (KAHZ bah) *n.* an old, crowded section of a North African city, p. 121

cash crop (kash krahp) *n.* a crop that is raised for sale, p. 28, p. 250

caste (kast) *n.* in the Hindu religion, a social group into which people are born and which they cannot change; each group has assigned jobs, p. 313

city-state (SIH tee stayt) *n.* a city that is also an independent state, with its own traditions, government, and laws, p. 44

civil war (SIV ul wawr) *n.* a war between political parties or regions within the same country, p. 447

civilization (sih vuh luh ZAY shun) *n.* a society that has cities, a central government, and social classes and that usually has writing, art, and architecture, p. 39

clan (klan) *n.* a group of lineages, p. 86, p. 296

collective farm (kuh LEK tiv fahrm) *n.* in a Communist country, a large farm formed from many private farms collected into a single unit controlled by the government, p. 330

colonize (KAHL uh nyz) *v.* to settle in an area and take control of its government, p. 56

colony (KAHL uh nee) *n.* a territory ruled by another nation, p. 316

commercial farming (kuh MUR shul FAHR ming) *n.* the large-scale production of crops for sale, p. 67, p. 274

commune (KAHM yoon) *n.* a community in which people own land as a group and where they live and work together, p. 303

communist (KAHM yoo nist) *adj.* relating to a government that controls a country's large industries, businesses, and land, p. 299

compound (KAHM pownd) *n.* a fenced-in group of homes, p. 99

coral (KAWR ul) *n.* a rocklike material made up of the skeletons of tiny sea creatures, most plentiful in warm ocean water, p. 285

coup d'état (koo day TAH) *n.* the sudden overthrow of a government by force, p. 146

cultural diffusion (KUL chur ul dih FYOO zhun) *n.* the spread of customs and ideas from one culture to another, p. 82, p. 298

cultural diversity (KUL chur ul duh VUR suh tee) *n.* a wide variety of cultures, p. 84

culture (KUL chur) *n.* the way of life of people who share similar customs and beliefs, p. 79

D

deciduous (dee SIJ oo us) *adj.* falling off or shedding, as in leaves, seasonally or at a certain stage of development, p. 233

demilitarized zone (dee MIL uh tuh ryzd zohn) *n.* an area in which no weapons are allowed, p. 378

democracy (dih MAHK ruh see) *n.* a government over which citizens exercise power, p. 63

desertification (dih zurt uh fih KAY shun) *n.* the process by which fertile land becomes too dry or damaged to support life, p. 152

developed country (dih VEL upt KUN tree) *n.* a country with many industries and a well-developed economy, p. 237

developing country (dih VEL up ing KUN tree) *n.* a country that has low industrial production and little modern technology, p. 237

dialect (DY uh lekt) *n.* a variation of a language that is unique to a region or area, p. 305

dictatorship (DIK tay tur ship) *n.* a form of government in which power is held by a leader who has absolute authority, p. 426

discriminate (dih SKRIM ih nayt) *v.* to treat people differently, and often unfairly, based on race, religion, or sex, p. 209

diversify (duh VUR suh fy) *v.* to add variety; to expand a country's economy by increasing the variety of goods produced, p. 30, p. 379

domesticate (duh MES tih kayt) *v.* to adapt wild plants or animals and breed them for human use, p. 38

domino theory (DAHM uh noh THEE uh ree) *n.* a belief that if one country fell to communism, neighboring nations would also fall, like a row of dominoes, p. 447

double-cropping (DUB ul KRAHP ing) *v.* to grow two or more crops on the same land in the same season or at the same time, p. 240

drought (drowt) *n.* a long period of dry weather, p. 19, p. 406

dynasty (DY nus tee) *n.* a series of rulers from the same family, p. 295

E

economy (ih KAHN uh mee) *n.* a system for producing, distributing, consuming, and owning goods and services, p. 29

elevation (el uh VAY shun) *n.* the height of land above or below sea level, p. 11

emperor (EM pur ur) *n.* a male ruler of an empire, p. 295

Equiano, Olaudah (ek wee AHN oh, oh LOW duh) *n.* an antislavery activist who wrote an account of his enslavement, p. 54

ethnic group (ETH nik groop) *n.* a group of people that share such characteristics as language, religion, ancestry, and cultural traditions, p. 41, p. 306

extended family (ek STEN did FAM uh lee) *n.* the part of a family that includes parents, children, and other relatives, p. 86

F

famine (FAM in) *n.* a huge food shortage, p. 379

fellaheen (fel uh HEEN) *n.* peasants or agricultural workers in Egypt and other Arab countries, p. 115

fertile (FUR tul) *adj.* rich in the substances plants need to grow well, p. 14, p. 227

fiord (fyawrd) *n.* a long, narrow inlet or arm of the sea bordered by steep cliffs created by glaciers, p. 281

free enterprise system (free ENT ur pryz SIS tum) *n.* an economic system in which people can choose their own jobs, start private businesses, own property, and make a profit, p. 366

G

Gaza Strip (GAHZ uh strip) *n.* a disputed region on the Mediterranean coast, p. 415

Geez (gee EZ) *n.* an ancient Ethiopian language that was once used to write literature and religious texts but is no longer spoken, p. 167

geyser (GY zur) *n.* a hot spring that shoots a jet of water and steam into the air, p. 280

Green Revolution (green rev uh LOO shun) *n.* a worldwide effort to increase food production in developing countries, p. 407

gross domestic product (grohs duh MES tik PRAHD ukt) *n.* the total value of all goods and services produced in an economy, p. 368

H

hajj (haj) *n.* a pilgrimage or journey to Mecca undertaken by Muslims during the month of the hajj, p. 416

harambee (hah RAHM bay) *n.* a social policy started by Jomo Kenyatta and meaning "let's pull together" in Swahili, p. 180

Hausa-Fulani (HOW suh foo LAH nee) *n.* Nigeria's largest ethnic group, p. 137

heritage (HEHR uh tij) *n.* the values, traditions, and customs handed down from one's ancestors, p. 93

high island (hy EYE lund) *n.* an island formed from the mountainous tops of ancient volcanoes, p. 285

Holocaust (HAHL uh kawst) *n.* the systematic killing of more than six million European Jews and others by Nazi Germany before and during World War II, p. 324

homogeneous (hoh moh JEE nee us) *adj.* to be the same or similar, p. 306

hybrid (HY brid) *n.* a plant that is created by breeding different types of the same plant, p. 69

I

Igbo (IG boh) *n.* Nigeria's third-largest ethnic group, p. 137

irrigate (IHR uh gayt) *v.* to supply with water through a ditch, pipe, channel, or sprinkler, p. 19

irrigation (irh uh GAY shun) *n.* the artificial watering of crops using canals and other artificial waterways, p. 412

K

Khmer (kuh MEHR) *n.* an empire that included much of present-day Cambodia, Thailand, Malaysia, and part of Laos, p. 338

Khmer Rouge (kuh MEHR roozh) *n.* a Communist party that took over the government of Cambodia in 1975, p. 343

kibbutz (kih BOOTS) *n.* a cooperative settlement, p. 413

Kikuyu (kee KOO yoo) *n.* the largest ethnic group in Kenya, p. 179

kinship (KIN ship) *n.* a family relationship, p. 86

L

labor (LAY bur) *n.* the work people do for which they are paid, p. 375

landlocked (LAND lahkt) *adj.* having no direct access to the sea, p. 429

life expectancy (lyf ek SPEK tun see) *n.* the average length of time a person can expect to live, p. 71, p. 405

lineage (LIN ee ij) *n.* a group of families descended from a common ancestor, p. 86

lingua franca (LING gwuh FRANG kuh) *n.* a language used for communication among people who speak different first languages, p. 172

literacy rate (LIT ur uh see rayt) *n.* the percentage of a population age 15 and over that can read and write, p. 405

literate (LIT ur it) *adj.* able to read and write, p. 70

low island (loh EYE lund) *n.* an island formed from coral reefs or atolls, p. 285

M

Maasai (mah SY) *n.* a seminomadic ethnic group in Kenya, p. 179

malnutrition (mal noo TRISH un) *n.* poor nutrition caused by a lack of food or an unbalanced diet, p. 404

Mandela, Nelson (man DEL uh, NEL sun) *n.* black leader of the African National Congress and South Africa's first president after apartheid ended, p. 210

Maori (MAH oh ree) *n.* a native of New Zealand whose ancestors first traveled from Asia to Polynesia, and later to New Zealand, p. 347

marsupial (mahr SOO pea ul) *n.* an animal that carries its young in a body pouch, such as a kangaroo, p. 278

migrant worker (MY grunt WUR kur) *n.* a laborer who travels away from where he or she lives to find work, p. 99

migrate (MY grayt) *v.* to move from one place to settle in another, p. 40

monarchy (MAHN ur kee) *n.* a state or a nation in which power is held by a monarch—a king, queen, or emperor, p. 421

monastery (MAHN uh stehr ee) *n.* a place where people, especially men known as monks, live a religious life, p. 166

monotheism (MAHN oh thee iz um) *n.* a belief that there is only one god, p. 321

monsoon (mahn SOON) *n.* a wind that changes direction with the change of season, occurring especially in southern Asia and Africa, p. 231

muezzin (myoo EZ in) *n.* a person whose job is to call Muslims to pray, p. 321

multiethnic (mul tee ETH nik) *adj.* having many ethnic groups living within a society, p. 137

multiparty system (MUL tee pahr tee SIS tum) *n.* a political system in which two or more parties compete in elections, p. 175

N

nationalism (NASH uh nul iz um) *n.* a feeling of pride in one's homeland; a group's identity as members of a nation, p. 58

nationalist (NASH uh nul ist) *n.* person who is devoted to the interests of his or her country, p. 341

nationalize (NASH uh nuh lyz) *v.* to transfer ownership of something to a nation's government, p. 203

Nkrumah, Kwame (un KROO muh, KWAH mee) *n.* founder of Ghana's independence movement and Ghana's first president, p. 142

nomad (NOH mad) *n.* a person who has no settled home but moves from place to place, p. 22, p. 306

nonrenewable resource (nahn rih NOO uh bul REE sawrs) *n.* a natural resource that cannot be replaced once it is used, p. 255

nuclear family (NOO klee ur FAM uh lee) *n.* the part of a family that includes parents and children, p. 86

O

oasis (oh AY sis) *n.* a fertile place in a desert where there is water and vegetation, p. 19, p. 252

outback (OWT bak) *n.* the dry land consisting of plains and plateaus that makes up much of central and western Australia, p. 456

overgrazing (oh vur GRAYZ ing) *n.* allowing too much grazing by large herds of animals, p. 152

P

paddy (PAD ee) *n.* a level field that is flooded to grow rice, especially in Asia, p. 274

Pan-Africanism (pan AF rih kun iz um) *n.* the belief that all Africans should work together for their rights and freedoms, p. 59

partition (pahr TISH un) *n.* a division into parts or portions, p. 317

penal colony (PEEN ul KAHL uh nee) *n.* a place where people convicted of crimes are sent, p. 347

petroleum (puh TROH lee um) *n.* an oily liquid formed from the remains of ancient plants and animals; used as a fuel, p. 255

pilgrimage (PIL gruh mij) *n.* a religious journey, p. 48

plantation (plan TAY shun) *n.* a large farm where cash crops are grown, p. 53

plateau (pla TOH) *n.* a large, level area that rises above the surrounding land and has at least one side with a steep slope, p. 11, p. 226

population density (pahp yuh LAY shun DEN suh tee) *n.* the average number of people living in a square mile or square kilometer, p. 229

privatization (pry vuh tih ZAY shun) *n.* the sale of government-owned industries to private companies, p. 175

Q

Quran (koo RAHN) *n.* the sacred book of Islam; also spelled *Koran*, p. 80, p. 421

R

radical (RAD ih kul) *adj.* extreme, p. 365

recession (rih SESH un) *n.* a period during which an economy and the businesses that support it shrink, or make less money, p. 372

Red Guards (red gahrdz) *n.* groups of students who carried out Mao Zedong's policies during the Cultural Revolution, p. 365

refugee (ref yoo JEE) *n.* a person who flees war or other disasters, p. 424

rift (rift) *n.* a deep crack in Earth's surface, p. 12

S

savanna (suh VAN uh) *n.* a region of tall grasses with scattered trees, p. 20

self-sufficient (self suh FISH unt) *n.* able to supply one's own needs without outside assistance, p. 407

seminomadic (seh mee noh MAD ik) *adj.* combining nomadic wandering and farming in settlements, p. 179

Sharia (shah REE ah) *n.* Islamic law, based on the words and deeds of Muhammad and on comments written by Muslim scholars and lawmakers, p. 111

souq (sook) *n.* an open-air marketplace in an Arab city, p. 121

sovereignty (SAHV run tee) *n.* political control, p. 146

standard of living (STAN durd uv LIV ing) *n.* a measurement of a person's or a group's education, housing, health, and nutrition, p. 255

station (STAY shun) *n.* in Australia, a large ranch for raising livestock, p. 348

steppe (step) *n.* vast, mostly level treeless plains that are covered in grass, p. 261

subcontinent (SUB kahn tih nunt) *n.* a large land-mass that is a major part of a continent, p. 246

subsidy (SUB suh dee) *n.* money given by a government to assist a private company, p. 371

subsistence farming (sub SIS tuns FAHR ming) *n.* raising just enough crops to support one's family, p. 27, p. 274

Swahili (swah HEE lee) *n.* a Bantu language spoken in much of East Africa, p. 44; an ethnic group in East Africa that resulted from the mixing of African and Arab ways more than 1,000 years ago, p. 93

T

tectonic plate (tek TAHN ik playt) *n.* a huge slab of rock that moves very slowly over a softer layer beneath the surface of Earth, p. 278

terrace (TEHR us) *n.* a flat platform of earth cut into the side of a slope, used for growing crops in steep places, p. 121, p. 240

textiles (TEKS tylz) *n.* cloth made by weaving or knitting, p. 402

Tombouctou (tohm book TOO) *n.* a city in Mali near the Niger River; also spelled *Timbuktu*, p. 48

tributary (TRIB yoo tehr ee) *n.* a river or stream that flows into a larger river, p. 13, p. 408

truce (troos) *n.* a cease-fire agreement, p. 379

typhoon (ty FOON) *n.* a tropical storm in which winds reach speeds greater than 74 miles per hour and that occurs over the Pacific Ocean, p. 232

W

West Bank (west bank) *n.* a disputed region on the western bank of the Jordan River, p. 415

Y

Yoruba (YOH roo buh) *n.* Nigeria's second-largest ethnic group, p. 137

Index

The *m*, *g*, or *p* following some page numbers refers to maps (*m*), charts, diagrams, tables, timelines, or graphs (*g*), or pictures (*p*).

A

Aborigines, 346, 347, 348*p*, 457–458, 458*p*, 494
Abraham, 321, 322
absolute location, M
Abu Dhabi, United Arab Emirates, 398
Abu Kamil, 111
Abuja, Nigeria, 133, 140, 490
Accra, Ghana, 130
Adamawa Highlands, 4*m*, 475*m*
Addis Ababa, Ethiopia, 159*m*, 161, 169–170, 490
adobe, 79
Adulis, East Africa, 42
Afghanistan, 219*m*, 220*m*, 222–223*m*, 260, 427*m*, 476*m*
  art of, 429, 429*p*
  economic activity of, 428*g*
  ethnic groups in, 388
  government of, 388
  language of, 388
  location of, 247
  population of, 388
  religion in, 388
  war in, 328, 331, 425
Africa, M10*m*, M10*m*, M11*m*, M11*m*, 246, 465*m*, 467*m*, 474*m*, 475*m*
  cities of, 35*m*
  climate regions, 16, 17*m*, 18–19, 19*g*
  empires of, 35*m*
  kingdoms of, 35*m*, 47–49, 47*m*, 202
  land use in, 5, 5*m*, 27*m*
  landforms of, 11, 24–25
  languages of, 77*m*
  location of, 2, 2*m*
  natural resources, 29–30, 29*m*, 29*p*
  physical features of, 4*m*, 4*p*
  physical map, 475*m*

political map, 474*m*
  regions of, 9*m*, 11
  rivers of, 9*m*, 12*m*, 13–15, 14*p*, 15*p*
  size of, 2, 2*m*, 3, 3*m*
  vegetation of, 5, 5*m*, 16, 20–22
African Americans, 173
African National Congress (ANC), 58, 211
Afrikaans language, 98, 209
Afrikaners, 98
Afroasiatic languages, 77*m*
agriculture
  Bedouins and, 257
  in Central Asia, 428, 428*g*, 428*p*
  in Israel, 411*p*, 412
  in Pakistan, 407–408, 407*p*
  Projects, 462
  resources for, 27–28, 27*m*, 180, 180*g*
  See also farming
Ahaggar Mountains, 4*m*, 475*m*
AIDS (disease), 71, 193
Akan people, 143, 144, 144*p*
Akbar, 316
Aksum, 35*m*, 39, 42, 42*p*, 43–44, 490
Alexandria, Egypt, 167
Algeria, 3*m*, 4*m*, 5*m*, 6–7*m*, 105*m*, 474*m*, 490
  about, 80, 106, 118–122
  ancient, 46
  education in, 122
  ethnic groups of, 81, 106
  families in, 121, 122, 122*p*
  geography of, 121, 121*p*
  history of, 118–119, 120, 120*g*, 120*m*
  independence of, 60*m*, 61, 62, 119
  land use in, 120*g*
  languages of, 106, 119, 122
  natural resources of, 29
  population of, 106, 119
  religion in, 106, 119
  rural areas of, 121
  women of, 83*p*
Algiers, Algeria, 105*m*, 106, 119, 119*p*, 120*g*, 490

Alice Springs, 457, 490
alluvial soil, 248, 494
Almaty, Kazakhstan, 429, 490
al Qaeda, 425
Amazon Basin, 466*m*, 469*m*
American Samoa, 219*m*, 478*m*
Americas, migration to, M14, M14*m*, M15*m*
Americo-Liberians, 132
Amman, Jordan, 392
Amu Darya River, 264
Anatolia, Plateau of, 477*m*
ANC. *See* African National Congress
Angkor Wat, 338, 338*p*, 490
Angola, 3*m*, 4*m*, 5*m*, 6–7*m*, 191*m*, 192*p*, 474*m*
  about, 15, 192, 205
  cultures of, 100
  independence of, 60*m*, 192
  natural resources of, 29, 99
Ankara, Turkey, 398
Antananarivo, Madagascar, 191*m*, 196
apartheid, 198, 209–210, 209*p*, 215, 494
aquaculture, 239
Arabian Desert, 4*m*, 475*m*
Arabian Peninsula, 251, 252*m*, 477*m*
Arabic language, 80
Arabic numerals, 315
Arab-Israeli Wars, 397, 415
Aral Sea, 262, 262*m*, 264, 264*p*, 430, 490
archipelago, 228, 438
arid climate, 17*m*, 254, 254*m*, 262, 262*m*
Armenia, 219*m*, 220*m*, 222–223*m*, 389, 476*m*
art
  of Afghanistan, 429, 429*p*
  cave painting, 36*p*
  Islamic, 46*p*
  Maori canoes as, 347*p*
  of Mbuti people, 100
  rock painting, 457, 458*p*
  Swahili, 93*p*
  of Tanzania, 93*p*
  of Vietnam, 448, 448*p*, 459*p*
  of West Africa, 49*p*

R

Rabat, Morocco, 105*m*, 108
radiation, 429
radical, 365, 498
rain forests, 20, 132, 195, 201
rainfall, 19, 153*g*
Ramadan, 110, 110*p*
ranching, 456–457, 456*g*, 456*m*
Rawlings, Jerry, 147
reading skills
  analyze author's purpose, RW
  analyze word parts, 312, 318, 319, 325
  ask questions, 50, 236
  clarify meaning, 8, 244
  compare and contrast, 76, 78, 97, 358, 364, 370
  context clues, 292, 294, 299, 302, 306
  distinguish between facts and opinions, RW
  evaluate credibility, RW1
  identify cause and effect, 104, 110, 386, 400
  identify contrasts, 84
  identify evidence, RW1
  identify implied main ideas, 142
  identify main ideas, 126, 136, 268, 270, 284, 434, 446
  identify supporting details, 150, 277, 454
  informational texts, RW1
  interpret nonliteral meanings, 178
  paraphrase, 16, 251
  predict, 42, 66, 230
  read ahead, 246
  reading process, 34, 224
  recognize cause and effect signal words, 424
  recognize multiple causes, 411
  recognize root words, 332
  recognize signal words, 346, 350
  reread, 10, 246
  sequence, 190, 200, 208
  set a purpose, 36, 226
  summarize, 26, 260

  understand context, 158
  understand effects, 406, 416
  understand sequence, 336, 338, 343
  use context clues, 166, 171
  use prior knowledge, 57
  use signal words, 92, 118, 208
  word analysis, 310
  word origins, 328
recession, 372, 498
Red Guards, 365, 498
Red Sea, 159*m*, 252*m*, 253
refugee, 424, 498
regions, M1, 2, 2*m*, 218, 218*m*
relative location, M
relief, M11
religion. *See* Buddhism; Christianity; Hinduism; *individual African regions*; *individual countries*; Islam; Jainism; Judaism
Republic of China, 366. *See also* Taiwan
Republic of the Congo, 3*m*, 4*m*, 5*m*, 6–7*m*, 60*m*, 191*m*, 195, 474*m*
research papers, RW4–5
Rhodesia, 57
rice farming, M17*p*, 233, 240, 240*p*, 274, 274*p*, 452–453
rift, 12, 498
Ring of Fire, 221, 221*m*, 272
river mouth, 489
rivers, 9*m*, 12*m*, 13–15, 14*p*, 15*p*
Riyadh, Saudi Arabia, 396, 416*p*, 417, 492
Robinson maps, M7
rock paintings, 457, 458*p*
Rocky Mountains, 466*m*, 469*m*, 479*m*
Roha, 168
Roman Catholic Church, 337*m*
Roman Empire, 46
Roman Republic, 46
rotary drill, 420, 420*p*
rotation, M2
Rub' al-Khali Desert, 251, 251*p*, 252, 252*m*, 477*m*, 493
rubber, 274

rural areas
  of Algeria, 121
  of Egypt, 115
  of Ethiopia, 170
  of Kenya, 179–181
  of West Africa, 85
Rwanda, 3*m*, 4*m*, 5*m*, 6–7*m*, 159*m*, 474*m*
  about, 95, 162, 205
  independence of, 60*m*

S

Sahara, 4, 4*m*, 9*m*, 11, 19, 20*p*, 21–22, 21*m*, 22*p*, 36, 47*m*, 105*m*, 106, 118, 133, 151, 153*m*, 475*m*, 493
Sahel, 21*m*, 153*m*, 475*m*, 493
  about, 21, 133
  desertification in, 152, 152*g*
  resources of, 151
salt, 47, 47*m*, 249, 257
salt lakes, 249, 257, 262, 262*m*
Samarkand, Uzbekistan, 329, 329*p*, 335, 493
Sambhar Lake, 249
same-shape maps, M6
Samoa, 219*m*, 220*m*, 286, 442, 478*m*
samurai, 296
Sanskrit, 248
São Tiago, 129
São Tomè and Príncipe, 3*m*, 4*m*, 5*m*, 6–7*m*, 60*m*, 191*m*, 198, 474*m*
satellites, 260
Saudi Arabia, 219*m*, 220*m*, 222–223*m*, 387*m*, 476*m*
  economy of, 417
  ethnic groups of, 323, 396
  geography of, 245*m*
  government of, 396, 421
  language of, 396
  oil in, 255*p*, 256*m*, 259, 416–417, 418*g*, 418*m*, 423*g*
  population of, 396
  religion of, 396, 419
  water in, 256
  women in, 419, 419*p*
savanna, 20, 153*m*, 201, 498
scale bar, M8

Acknowledgments

Cover Design

Pronk & Associates

Staff Credits

The people who made up the *World Studies team*—representing design services, editorial, editorial services, educational technology, marketing, market research, photo research and art development, production services, project office, publishing processes, and rights & permissions—are listed below. Bold type denotes core team members.

Greg Abrom, Ernie Albanese, Rob Aleman, Susan Andariese, **Rachel Avenia-Prol**, Leann Davis Alspaugh, Penny Baker, Barbara Bertell, Megan Burnett, **Peter Brooks**, Rui Camarinha, John Carle, Lori-Anne Cohen, **Lisa Del Gatto**, Paul Delsignore, Kathy Dempsey, Anne Drowns, Deborah Dukeshire, Marlies Dwyer, **Frederick Fellows**, Paula C. Foye, Lara Fox, Julia Gecha, Annie Grear, Tom Greene, **Mary Hanisco**, Salena Hastings, Lance Hatch, Margaret Higgins, Kerri Hoar, **Beth Hyslip**, Katharine Ingram, Nancy Jones, Bret Kerr, Corrina Balash Kerr, John Kingston, Deborah Levheim, Constance J. McCarty, **Kathleen Mercandetti**, Art Mkrtchyan, Ken Myett, **Mark O'Malley**, Jen Paley, Ray Parenteau, **Gabriela Pérez Fiato**, Linda Punskovsky, Kirsten Richert, **Lynn Robbins**, Nancy Rogier, Bruce Rolff, Robin Samper, Mildred Schulte, Siri Schwartzman, **Malti Sharma**, Lisa Smith-Ruvalcaba, Roberta Warshaw, Sarah Yezzi

Additional Credits

Jonathan Ambar, Tom Benfatti, Lisa D. Ferrari, Paul Foster, Florrie Gadson, Phil Gagler, Ella Hanna, Jeffrey LaFountain, Karen Mancinelli, Michael McLaughlin, Lesley Pierson, Pronk&Associates, Debi Taffet

DK The DK Designs team who contributed to *World Studies* were as follows: Hilary Bird, Samantha Borland, Marian Broderick, Richard Czapnik, Nigel Duffield, Heather Dunleavy, Cynthia Frazer, James A. Hall, Lucy Heaver, Rose Horridge, Paul Jackson, Heather Jones, Ian Midson, Marie Ortu, Marie Osborn, Leyla Ostovar, Ralph Pitchford, Ilana Sallick, Pamela Shiels, Andrew Szudek, Amber Tokeley.

DK Maps and globes were created by **DK Cartography.** The team consisted of Tony Chambers, Damien Demaj, Julia Lunn, Ed Merritt, David Roberts, Ann Stephenson, Gail Townsley, and Iorwerth Watkins.

Illustrations

Kenneth Batelman: 24, 90; Richard Bonson/DK Images: 68, **297**; Richard Draper/DK Images: 114; Jen Paley: 10, 16, 19, 26, 36, 42, 50, 52–53, 57, 65, 66, 78, 80, 84, 87, 91, 92, 97, 103, 110, 112, 117, 118, 120; Jun Park: 152; **285**; Pronk & Associates: 136, 139, 142, 145, 149, 150, 151, 153, 169, 171, 174, 178, 180, 200, 203, 208, 211

Photos

Cover Photos

tl, Ted Meed/Getty Images, Inc.; **tm,** Mary Louise Macdonald/Masterfile Corporation; **tr,** Photodisc/Artbase Inc. **b,** Elinor Donohoe/Getty Images, Inc.

Title Page

Collage l–r © Carl Galie/Picturesque Stock; © Wayne Eastep/Getty Images; © JIM BRANDENBURG/Minden Pictures; **t,** © Bettmann/CORBIS; **b,** © Richard Parsley/Stock, Boston, Inc.; © Thinkstock LLC/Index Stock Imagery

Table of Contents

NC 5, © Will & Deni McIntyre/Corbis; NC 6–NC 7, Panoramic Images; NC 8, Damien Simonis/Lonely Planet Images; NC 9, F. Lemmens/Masterfile Corporation; NC 10, Boden-Ledingham/ Master-file; NC 11, Janet Wishnetsky/Corbis; NC 13, Tim Flach/Getty Images; NC 17, AFP/Corbis; NC 20, F. J. Jackson/Alamy Images

Student Guide to North Carolina Standard Course of Study and Testing

NC 21 © AGE FotoStock/SuperStock; NC 22 © Peter Horree/Alamy; NC 25 © Andre Jenny/Alamy; NC 26–27 © SuperStock/AGE FotoStock

Reading and Writing Handbook

RW, Michael Newman/PhotoEdit; RW1, Walter Hodges/Getty Images, Inc.; RW2, Digital Vision/Getty Images, Inc.; RW3, Will Hart/PhotoEdit; RW5, Jose Luis Pelaez, Inc./Corbis

MapMaster Skills Handbook

M, James Hall/Dorling Kindersley; M1, Mertin Harvey/Gallo Images/Corbis; M2–3 m, NASA; M2–3, (globes) Planetary Visions; M6 tr, Mike Dunning/Dorling Kindersley; M5 br, Barnabas Kindersley/Dorling Kindersley; M10 b, Bernard and Catherine Desjeux/Corbis; M11, Hutchison Library; M12 b, Pa Photos; M13 r, Panos Pictures; M14 l, Macduff Everton/Corbis; M14 t, MSCF/NASA; M15 b, Ariadne Van Zandbergen/Lonely Planet Images; M16 l, Bill Stormont/Corbis; M16 b, Pablo Corral/Corbis; M17 t, Les Stone/Sygma/Corbis; M17 b, W. Perry Conway/Corbis

Africa

Guiding Questions

1 t, Christies Images/SuperStock, Inc.; 1 b, Heini Schneebeli/Bridgeman Art Library

Regional Overview

2 l, G. Hind/Still Pictures; 3 t, Liba Taylor/Corbis; 4 t, Chris Lisle/Corbis; 4 b, Patrick Ward/Corbis; 5 t, Sharna Balfour/Gallo Images; 5 b, David Ball/Corbis; 6 ml, Liba Taylor/Corbis; 6 b, Leanne Logan/Lonely Planet Images; 7 t, Geert Cole/Lonely Planet Images; 7 mr, Harlmut Schwarzbach/Still Pictures; 7 br, Gallo Images/Corbis

Chapter One

8–9, Tim Davis/Corbis; 10, Richard Cummins/Corbis; 11 t, Discovery Channel School; 11 b, Martin Rogers/Getty Images, Inc.; 12–13, Jason Lauré/Lauré Communications; 14, Roger Wood/Corbis; 15, SuperStock, Inc.; 16, Jason Edwards/Lonely Planet Images; 18 t, Hal Beral/Corbis; 18–19 b, Panoramic Images; 20–21 b, SuperStock, Inc.; 21 t, F. Lemmens/Masterfile Corporation; 22, Lorne Resnick/Getty Images, Inc.; 23, Robert Patrick/Corbis Sygma; 25, Ariadne Van Zandbergen/Lonely Planet Images; 26, Victor Englebert/Victor Englebert Photography; 26 inset, Dave King/Dorling Kindersley; 28, Jason Lauré/Lauré Communications; 29 t, AFP/Corbis; 29 b, Tim Boyle/Getty Images, Inc.; 30, Eric Miller/iAfrika Photos; 31, Martin Rogers/Getty Images, Inc.

Chapter Two

34–35, J. D. Dallet/AGE Fotostock; 36, Juan Carlos Munoz/AGE Fotostock; 37 t, Lauros/Giraudon/The Bridgeman Art Library; 37 m, John Reader/Photo Researchers, Inc.; 37 b, Robert Sisson/National Geographic Image Collection; 38, Martin Harvey/Gallo Images/Corbis; 39 t, Erich Lessing/Art Resource, NY; 39 b, The Art Archive/Egyptian Museum Turin/Dagli Orti; 41, David Turnley/Corbis; 42 all, The British Museum; 44 t, Anthony Bannister/Gallo Images/Corbis; 44 b, Corbis; 45, David Reed/Corbis; 46 both, Pictor International/Agency ImageState/Alamy; 48 t, The Granger Collection, New York; 48 b, Saudi Arabia-Ramadan/AFP/Corbis; 49, Christie's Images/SuperStock, Inc.; 50, Yann Arthus Bertrand/Corbis; 51, Dorling Kindersley/The Science Museum London; 52 l, Ingrid Roddis/Lonely Planet Images; 52 r, 53 t, The Granger Collection, New York; 53 b, Discovery Channel School; 54 t, The Granger Collection, New York; 54 b, Wilberforce Museum, Hull/Dorling Kindersley; 56 l, The Art Archive/Private Collection; 56 r, The British Library, London, UK/Topham-HIP/The Image Works; 57, Chris Steele-Perkins/Magnum Photos; 58 both, Peter Turnley/Corbis; 59, UPI/Corbis-Bettman; 61 l, Hulton-Deutsch Collection/Corbis; 61 r, M. & E. Bernheim/Woodfin Camp & Associates; 62 t, Joao Silva/New York Times Pictures; 62–63 b, Peter Turnley/Corbis; 65, One Mile Up, Inc./Fotosearch Stock Photography; 66, Michael S. Lewis/Corbis; 67 t, A. Ramey/Woodfin Camp & Associates; 67 b, Charles O. Cecil/Words & Pictures/PictureQuest; 68 t, Michael S. Lewis/Corbis; 69 t, Yann Arthus-Bertrand/Corbis; 69 b, Sandro Vannini/Corbis; 70, Willem de Lange/PictureNET Africa; 71, Liba Taylor/Corbis; 72, Wolfgang Kaehler Photography; 73 l, Christie's Images/SuperStock, Inc.; 73 r, Peter Turnley/Corbis

Chapter Three

76–77, Kennan Ward/Corbis; 78, Getty Images, Inc.; 79, Glen Allison/Getty Images, Inc.; 80, Francois Perri/Cosmos/Woodfin Camp & Associates; 81, Jim Erickson/Corbis; 82, Jon Arnold Images/Alamy; 83, Francois Perri/Cosmos/Woodfin Camp & Associates; 84, Jason Lauré/Lauré Communications; 85, M. & E. Bernheim/Woodfin Camp & Associates; 86 t, Craig Pershouse/Lonely Planet Images; 86 b, Robert Frerck/Odyssey Productions, Inc.; 87, Yann Arthus-Bertrand/Corbis; 88 t, M. & E. Bernheim/Woodfin Camp & Associates; 88 b, Discovery Channel School; 89 l, Courtesy of Balla Tounkara; 89 r, Bob Burch/Index Stock Imagery/PictureQuest; 91 l, Gunter Ziesler/Peter Arnold, Inc.; 91 r, Rich Kirchner/NHPA; 92, Ariadne Van Zandbergen/Lonely Planet Images; 93, Yadid Levy/AGE Fotostock; 94–95 b, Wolfgang Kaehler Photography; 95 t, Peter Marlow/Magnum Photos; 96, Sipa Press; 97, Popperfoto/Alamy Images; 98, Chris Harvey/Stone Allstock/Getty Images Inc.; 99, Ian Murphy/Getty Images, Inc.; 100, Christie's Images, Inc.; 101 l, Jim Erickson/Corbis; 101 r, Ian Murphy/Getty Images

Chapter Four

104–105, Photolibrary.com; 106 t, Discovery Channel School; 106 b, Claudia Wiens/Peter Arnold, Inc.; 107 t, F. J. Jackson/Alamy Images; 107 b, Paul Hardy/Corbis; 108, Damien Simonis/Lonely Planet Images; 109, Patrick Ward/Corbis; 110, Harry Gruyaert/Magnum Photos; 111, Stock Image/SuperStock, Inc.; 112, Nik Wheeler/Corbis; 113, Nik Wheeler; 114 t, Lloyd Cluff/Corbis; 114 b, Dorling Kindersley; 115 t, Discovery Channel School; 115 b, Mark Henley/Panos Pictures; 116, David Young-Wolff/PhotoEdit; 117, Carmen Redondo/Corbis; 118, Robert Everts/Getty Images Inc.; 119, Francoise Perri/Woodfin Camp & Associates; 121 t, Abbas/Magnum Photos; 121 b, Discovery Channel School; 122, Tiziana and Gianni Baldizzone/Corbis; 123 l, Harry Gruyaert/Magnum Photos; 123 r, Robert Everts/Getty Images Inc.

Chapter Five

126–127, Yann Arthus-Bertrand/Corbis; 128 t, Discovery Channel School; 128 b, Art Directors/Jane Sweeney; 130 bl, Ancient Art&Architecture/DanitaDelimont.com; 130 br, Robert Burch/Bruce Coleman Inc.; 132 tr, Robert Burch; 132 b, AP/WideWorld Photos; 134 mr, AFP/Corbis; 134 b, Beryl Goldberg; 135 tr, Luis Marden/National Geographic/Getty Images, Inc.; 136 bl, Sally Mayman/Getty Images, Inc.; 137 br, Paul Almasy/Corbis; 137 bl, Werner Forman/Art Resource NY; 138 bl, McPherson Colin/Corbis/Sygma; 138 tr, Betty Press/Panos Pictures; 139 b, Hamill Gallery of African Art, Boston MA; 140 tl, Bruno Barbey/Magnum Photos; 141 tr, Campbell William/Corbis/Sygma; 142–143, Dave Starrett/Artbase Inc.; 142 bl, Bettman/Corbis; 143 tr, Hulton-Deutsch Collection/Corbis; 144 bl, Hamill Gallery of African Art, Boston MA; 146 t, Discovery Channel School; 146 b, AP/Wide World Photos; 147 tr, Robert Burch; 148 ml, Imagestate/firstlight.ca; 149 mr, Jonathan Nourok/PhotoEdit Inc.; 149 br, Dave Starrett/Artbase Inc.; 150–151, Ali Atay/Atlas; 150 bl, Wolfgang Kaehler/Corbis; 154 tl, Art Directors/Mary Jelliffe; 155 ml, Paul Almasy/Corbis; 155 mr, Art Directors/Mary Jelliffe

Chapter Six

158–159, Robert Bourgoing; 160, Discovery Channel School; 161 tr, Sheila McKinnon/Mira.com; 162 t, Edwards Roderick, Edward/MaXx Images; 163 m, © 2003 Norbert Wu/www.nobertwu.com; 163 mr, Wolfgang Kaehler Photography; 164 tr, AFP/Corbis; 165 m, Art Directors/Fiona Good; 166 b, Robert Patrick/Corbis/Sygma; 167 br, M. & E. Bernheim/Woodfin Camp & Associates; 167 tl, Dave Bartruff/Danita Delimont; 168 tr, Dave Bartruff/Danita Delimont; 168 tl, Kal Muller/Woodfin Camp & Associates; 170, Discovery Channel School; 170 ml, Robert Caputo/Aurora Photos; 170 br, Reuters; 173 t, Kwame Zikomo/SuperStock; 174, Discovery Channel School; 175 tr, Howard Davies/Corbis; 176 bl, Eric Draper/White House/Getty Images, Inc.; 177 tr, Art Directors/Andrew Gasson; 177 br, David Pluth/Fotografx; 178 b, Robert Burch; 179 tr, Michele Burgess/MaXx Images; 179 b, Discovery Channel School; 181 mr, Betty Press/Woodfin Camp & Associates; 182 tl, DigtalVision/Artbase Inc.; 183 tr, Dave Bartruff/Danita Delimont; 183 m, Robert Burch; 186 br, Paul Souders/Getty Images, Inc.; 187 tr, PhotodiscRed/Artbase Inc.; 188 bl, Jeremy Woodhouse/Masterfile Corporation; 189, Tololwa M. Mollel

Chapter Seven

190–191, Eric Nathan/Alamy Images; 192 t, Discovery Channel School; 192 b, Volkmar Wentzel/Getty Images, Inc.; 194 tr, AFP/Corbis; 194 tl, Max-Planck-Institut Seewiesen; 200 Jason Lauré/Lauré Communications; 201 b, Patrick Roberts/Corbis/Sygma; 202 bl, Bettmann/Corbis; 204 t, Discovery Channel School; 204 bl, Artbase Inc.; 205 tr, Reuters/Corbis; 206 tl, Photodisc/Artbase Inc.; 206 ml, Photodisc/Artbase Inc.; 206 bl, Photodisc/Artbase Inc.; 207 m, Paula Bronstein/Impact Visuals; 208 bl, Charles O'Rear/Corbis; 209 br, Time LifePictures/Getty Images, Inc.; 210 br, AP/WideWorld Photos; 211, Discovery Channel School; 212 tl, Owen Franken/Corbis; 213 ml, Artbase Inc.; 213 mr, AP/WideWorld Photos

Projects

216, Heini Schneebeli/Bridgeman Art Library

Asia and Australia

Regional Overview

218 l, David Ball/Corbis; 219 bl, Massimo Listri/Corbis; 220 t, José Fuste Raga/Corbis; 220 bl, Paul A. Souders/Corbis; 221 t, James A. Sugar/Corbis; 221 b, David Samuel Robbins/Corbis; 222 l, Richard T. Nowitz/Corbis; 222 br, Jeremy Horner/Corbis; 223 tr, Damien Simonis/Lonely Planet Images; 223 bl, Bohemian Nomad Picturemakers/Corbis

Chapter Eight

224f l, Royalty-Free/Corbis; 224f r, PhotoDisc/Getty Images, Inc.; 224–225, Boden-Ledingham/Masterfile; 226 bl, Dallas & John Heaton/Corbis; 227 tr, Karen Su/Getty Images; 228 bl, Michael S. Yamashita/Corbis; 229 tr, Catherine Karnow/Corbis; 230 b, Scott Markewitz/Getty Images; 230 ml, Private Collection/Ancient Art and Architecture Collection Ltd/Bridgeman Art Library; 233 tr, Heatons/Firstlight.ca; 235 tr, Mug Shots/Corbis; 235 tr(inset), Kevin Schafer/Corbis; 236 bl, AFP/Corbis; 238–239 b, Liu Liqun/Corbis; 239 tr, Keren Su/Corbis; 239 br, Keren Su/Corbis; 240 tl, B.S.P.I/Corbis; 241 ml, Karen Su/Getty Images; 241 mr, Scott Markewitz/Getty Images

Chapter Nine

244f l, Royalty-Free/Corbis; 244f r, PhotoDisc/Getty Images, Inc.; 244–245, Galen Rowell/Corbis; 246 b, Alan Kearney/Getty Images; 249 b, Will Curtis/Getty Images; 249 lr, Eisenhut & Mayer/Foodpix; 249 mr, Artbase Inc.; 250 tl, R. Ian Lloyd/Masterfile; 251 b, George Steinmetz; 253 b, George Gerster/Photo Researchers Inc.; 253 mr, H. Spichtinger/zefa; 255 r, George Steinmetz; 256 tl, Israel Talby; 257 tr, Hugh Sitton/Getty Images; 258 bl, Myrleen Ferguson/Photoedit Inc.; 259 tr, Business Essentials/Artbase Inc.; 259 br, Donovan Resse/Getty Images; 259 tr (inset), George Steinmetz; 260 bl, TASS/Sovfoto/Sergei Kazak; 261 tr, James Strachan/Getty Images; 263 tr, Reuters/Corbis; 264 tl, TASS-S-54679/Sovfoto/Eastfoto; 265 ml, James Strachan/Getty Images; 265 tr, Israel Talby

Chapter Ten

268f l, Royalty-Free/Corbis; 268f r, PhotoDisc/Getty Images, Inc.; 268–269, Paul A. Souders/Corbis; 270 bl, Photodisc/ArtBase Inc.; 271 br, Dorling Kindersley/DK Images; 272–273 bg, ACE; 273 in, AFP/Corbis; 274 ml, Martin Puddy/Getty Images; 274 b, R.Ian Lloyd/Masterfile; 276 tl, Frank Siteman/Maxximages.com; 277 br, Tui De Roy/Auscape; 277 mr, Artbase Inc.; 278 ml, Jeremy Woodhouse/Masterfile; 278 t, Tim Flach/Getty Images; 280 t, Mike Langford/Auscape; 281 tr, John Lamb/Getty Images; 282 b, William Gottlieb/Corbis; 283 bg, The Bridgeman Art Library/Getty Images; 284 bl, G.Bell/Zefa/Masterfile; 285 bm, Yann Arthurs-Bertrand/Corbis; 285 tr, Trip/Ask Images; 286 br, Photography.com.au; 286 bl, Photography.com.au; 286–287 bg, Macduff Everton/Getty Images; 287 mr, James Strachan/Getty Images; 288 tl, Trip/M.Jelliffe; 289 tr, AFP/Corbis; 289 bm, Jeremy Woodhouse/Masterfile; 289 bm, Tim Flach/Getty Images

Chapter Eleven

292e l, Royalty-Free/Corbis; **292e r,** PhotoDisc/Getty Images, Inc.; **292f l,** GeoStock/Getty Images, Inc.; **292f ml,** Comstock; **292f mr,** PhotoDisc/Getty Images, Inc.; **292f r,** SW Productions/Getty Images, Inc.; **292-293,** John Dakers: Eye Ubiquitous/Corbis; **294 bl,** Bridgeman Art Library; **295 tr,** Carl & Ann Purcell/ Corbis; **296 b,** © Lee Boltin/Boltin Picture Library; **297 t,** DK Images; Wolfgang Kaehler/Corbis; **297 b,** Macduff Everton/Corbis; **298 bl,** Haruyoshi Yamaguchi/ Corbis/Sygma; **299 tr,** AFP/Getty Images; **300 l,** Michael S. Yamashita/Corbis; **301 mr,** Werner Forman/Art Resource, NY; **302 bl,** Setboun/Corbis; **303 t,** Daryl Benson/Masterfile; **303 mr,** Dale Wilson/Masterfile; **304 t,** Paul Chesley/Getty Images; **306 tl,** James A.Sugar/Corbis; © Lee Boltin/Boltin Picture Library; **307 mr,** Dale Wilson/Masterfile

Chapter Twelve

310f l, Royalty-Free/Corbis; **310f r,** PhotoDisc/Getty Images, Inc.; **310-311,** Bob Krist/Corbis; **312 bl,** Archivo Iconografico S.A./Corbis; **314 tl,** Michael Freeman/Corbis; **314 tm,** Burstein collection/Corbis; **314 tr,** Burstein collection/Corbis; **315 tr,** Camermann International; **316 t,** Miles Ertman/Masterfile; **316 inset,** Archivo Iconografico S.A./Corbis; **317 tl,** Hulton Deutsch Collection/Corbis; **317 b,** Kapoor Baldev/Corbis; **318 tl,** Frans Lemmens/ZEFA/Masterfile; **319 br,** Gianni Dagli Orti/Corbis; **321 t,** Shai Ginott/Corbis; **322 tr,** Paul Chesley/Getty Images; **322 l,** Scala/Art Resource; **323 r,** Peter Turnley/Corbis; **324 tl,** Ricki Rosen/ Corbis; **324 tr,** Eddie Gerald/Alamy Images; **325 tr,** Pool/Reuters/Corbis; **326 l,** Ed Brock/Corbis; **327 r,** David W.Hamilton/Getty Images; **328 bl,** Dean Conger/Corbis; **329 t,** DanielSheehan/The Image Works; **329 br,** The Bridgeman Art Library/Getty Images; **330 t,** David Samuel Robbins/Corbis; **331 br,** David Samuel Robbins/Corbis; **332 tr,** Nevada Weir/Corbis; **333 tl,** Camermann International; **333 mr,** Daniel Sheehan/The Image Works

Chapter Thirteen

336e l, Royalty-Free/Corbis; **336e r,** PhotoDisc/Getty Images, Inc.; **336f l,** GeoStock/Getty Images, Inc.; **336f ml,** Conmstock; **336f mr,** PhotoDisc/Getty Images, Inc.; **336f r,** SW Productions/Getty Images, Inc.; **336-337,** David Noton/ Masterfile; **338 bl,** DK Images; **339 b,** Manfred Gottschalk/ agefotostock/firstlight.ca; **341 tl,** Miles Ertman/Masterfile; **342 t,** Paul Chesley/ Getty Images; **343 tr,** Howard Davies/Corbis; **344 bl,** Chad Elhers/Getty Images; **344 inset,** Foodphotography/MaxXimages.com; **345 b,** Leonard de Selva/Corbis; **346 bl,** Kevin Schafer/Getty Images; **347 b,** Graeme Matthews/Photo NewZealand.com; **348 br,** Reuters/Corbis; **348 bl,** Rob Walls; **349 t,** R. Ian Lloyd/Masterfile; **350 tl,** Nicolas DaVore/Getty Images; **351 bl,** Manfred Gottschalk/agefotostock/firstlight.ca; **351 tr,** Nicolas DaVore/Getty Images; **354 b,** Time-Life Pictures/Getty Images; **356 tl,** Jason Bleibtreu/Corbis/Sygma

Chapter Fourteen

358f l, Royalty-Free/Corbis; **358f r,** PhotoDisc/Getty Images, Inc.; **358-359,** John Elk/Getty Images; **360 b,** Grant Faint/Getty Images; **361 t,** Don Stevenson/MaxXImages.com; **362 b,** Nathan Benn/Corbis; **363 m,** Bill Lai/Index Stock/MaxX Images; **364 bl,** Chris Shinn/Getty Images; **365 t,** Bettmann/Corbis; **365 mr,** Collection: Stefan Landsberger; **366 ml,** Bettmann/Corbis; **366 br,** Reuters/Corbis; **368 t,** Walter Bibikow/Getty Images; **368 inset,** Walter Bibikow/Getty Images; **370 bl,** APWideWorld; **371 br,** Reuters/Corbis; **372 ml,** AFP/Corbis; **372 b,** Alan Levinson/Getty Images; **374-375 t,** Ettagale Blauer/Laure Communications; **376 ml,** Bob Daemmrich/StockBoston; **377 mr,** The Cover Story/Corbis; **378 b,** Janet Wishnetsky/Corbis; **379 b,** AP Wide World Photos; **380 t,** APWideWorld; **381 ml,** DigitalVision/Artbase Inc.; **382 ml,** Corbis/Artbase Inc.; **383 tr,** Chris Shinn/Getty Images; **383 mr,** Reuters/Corbis

Chapter Fifteen

386f l, Royalty-Free/Corbis; **386f r,** PhotoDisc/Getty Images, Inc.; **386-387,** Annie Griffiths Belt/Corbis; **388 r,** AFP/Corbis; **393 b,** Peter Turnley/Corbis; **397 t,** Alison Wright/Corbis; **400 bl,** Anna Clopet/Corbis; **401 t,** Kapoor Baldev/Corbis; **402 t,** Derimais Lionel/Corbis/Sygma; **402 in,** David H. Wells/Corbis; **404 tl,** Michael S. Yamashita/Corbis; **404 tr,** Sheldon Collins/Corbis; **405 tr,** David Katzenstein/Corbis; **406 bl,** Christine Osborne/Corbis; **407 t,** Johnathan Blair/Corbis; **407 in,** Johnathan Blair/Corbis; **408 br,** AFP/Corbis; **409 ml,** AntoineSerra/Corbis; **410 tl,** AFP/Corbis; **411 br,** RichardT. Nowitz/Corbis; **412 b,** Ricki Rosen/Saba/Corbis; **414 b,** Zev Radovan/PhotoEdit Inc.; **415 tr,** Izzet Keribar/Coral Planet; **416 bl,** James Sparshatt/Corbis;

417 b, John Moore/The Image Works; **419 in,** Jacques Langeuin/Corbis/Sygma; **419 b,** David Turnley/Corbis; **420 t,** DK Images; Still Pictures; **420 bl,** DK Images; **422 l,** Caroline Penn/Corbis; **423 b,** R. Ian Llloyd; **424 bl,** Steve McCurry/Magnum Photos Inc.; **425 t,** AFP/Corbis; **426 b,** Janet Wishnetsky/Corbis; **428 bl,** Zylberman Lauren/Corbis/Sygma; **429 br,** Volker Thewalt; **429 tl,** Zylberman Lauren/Corbis/Sygma; **430 tr,** James Strachan/Getty Images

Chapter Sixteen

434e l, Royalty-Free/Corbis; **434e r,** PhotoDisc/Getty Images, Inc.; **434f l,** GeoStock/Getty Images, Inc.; **434fml,** Comstock; **434f mr,** PhotoDisc/Getty Images, Inc.; **434f r,** SW Productions/Getty Images, Inc.; **434-435,** Philip & Karen Smith/Getty Images; **436 b,** J.Raga/Zefa/Masterfile; **437 t,** Paul A.Souders/Corbis; **445 m,** Alyx Kellington/MaxXimages.com; **446 ml,** Owen Franken/Corbis; **446 b,** Steve Raymer/Corbis; **447 t,** R. Ian Lloyd/Masterfile; **448 bl,** Dallas & John Heaton/Corbis; **448 tr,** Bettman/Corbis; **450 bl,** Tim Page/Corbis; **451 tl,** Charles Coates/Impact Photos; **451 tr,** AP WideWorld; **453 b,** Bohemian Nomad Picturemakers/Corbis; **454-455 b,** Ray Juno/Corbis; **457 t,** Corbis/Artbase Inc.; **458 mr,** John Van Hasselt/Corbis; **459 mc,** Ray Juno/Corbis; **459 tr,** Dallas & John Heaton/Corbis

Projects: 462 b, Robert Essel NYC/Corbis; **462 mr,** AFP/Corbis

Reference
463, PhotoEdit

Glossary of Geographic Terms
488 t, A. & L. Sinibaldi/Getty Images, Inc.; **488 b,** John Beatty/Getty Images, Inc.; **488-489 b,** Spencer Swanger/Tom Stack & Associates; **489 t,** Hans Strand/Getty Images, Inc; **489 m,** Paul Chesley/Getty Images, Inc.

Text

Africa

Chapter One

21, Excerpt from "Where Hospitality is an Oasis," by Christine Negroni, *The New York Times,* January 19, 2003. **26,** from *Cocoa Comes to Mampong,* by Dei Anang. Copyright © 1949. Reprinted with the permission of Methodist Book Depot. **93,** Excerpt from "Swahili Coast: East Africa's Ancient Crossroads," by Robert Caputo, *National Geographic,* October 2001.

Chapter Three

96, from "African Statesman Still Sowing Seeds for Future," by James C. McKinley, Jr., *The New York Times.*

Chapter Five

144, from *Ghana in Transition,* by David E. Apter. Copyright © 1955, 1963, and 1972 by Princeton University Press.

Chapter Six

172, 173, from "Three Leaders," by Andrew Meldrum, *Africa Report,* September–October 1994. Copyright © 1994 by *Africa Report.* **182,** from "Back to No Man's Land," by George Monbiot, *Geographical Magazine,* July 1994. Copyright © 1994 by *Geographical Magazine.* **186,** from *A Promise to the Sun* by Tololwa M. Mollel. Text Copyright © 1991 by Tololwa M. Mollel.

Chapter Seven

207, Excerpt from "Nelson Mandela's Statement After Voting in South Africa's First Democratic Election, Inanda, Kwazulu Natal, 27 April 1994," by Nelson Mandela, the African National Congress. **208,** Excerpt from "Preamble: Constitution of the Republic of South Africa by the Constitutional Assembly," Policy and Law Online News.

Asia and Australia

354, Excerpt from *The Clay Marble* by Minfong Ho. Copyright © 1991 by Minfong Ho.

Note: Every effort has been made to locate the copyright owner of material used in this textbook. Omissions brought to our attention will be corrected in subsequent editions.